CP-3	Work Sheet: Trial balance totals, $1,426,915; adjusted trial balance totals, $1,436,250	10-1	(c) Total cost, $96,870
		10-2	Total cost, $237,326
7-1	No key figure	10-3	Depreciation for 2001, (b) $61,500; (c) $64,800
7-2	No key figure	10-4	Depreciation for 2000, (b) $10,000; (c) $20,000
7-3	Adjusted cash balance, $47,556	10-5	Depreciation for 2002, (1) $18,000; (2) $32,000
7-4	(a) Adjusted cash balance, $31,142.30	10-6	Apr. 1, gain on sale, $275,000
7-5	(a) Adjusted cash balance, $21,142.30	10-7	(b) (1) Book value, $13,600
7-6	(a) Adjusted cash balance, $21,146.50	10-8	(b) (1) Book value, $25,500
7-7	(a) Adjusted cash balance, $21,007.29	10-9	No key figure
7-8	(a) Cash shortage, $8,150	10-10	No key figure
7-9	(a) Adjusted cash balance, $18,334	10-11	No key figure
7-10	(b) Adjusted cash balance, $8,552	10-12	(c) Accumulated depletion, $3,069,000
7-11	(b) Adjusted cash balance, $8,214.50		
7-12	No key figure	CP-4	(a) Revised total assets, Alpine, $499,900, Nordic, $486,300; (b) Revised cumulative net income, Alpine, $195,000, Nordic, $219,000
8-1	(a) Estimated uncollectible accounts, $18,120		
8-2	(a) Estimated uncollectible accounts, $12,960	11-1	No key figure
8-3	(a) Estimated uncollectible accounts, $23,080	11-2	(a) Current liabilities, $375,403
8-4	(b) Net accounts receivable, Jan. 31, $461,280	11-3	(b) Interest expense for National Bank note, $4,704
8-5	(a) Estimated uncollectible accounts, $6,740	11-4	(b) Interest Expense for Royal Bank note, $3,200
8-6	(b) Estimated uncollectible accounts, $52,500	11-5	(a) Monthly interest expense, $425
8-7	(a) (3) Debit uncollectible accounts expense, $726,000	11-6	(c) Total current liabilities, $337,186.50
8-8	(a) (2) Number of days' sales collected, Digital, 81 days	11-7	(c) Unpaid balance, Jan. 1, 2000, $539,370
8-9	(a) (1) Accounts receivable turnover, Molson, 12 times	11-8	(a) Unpaid balance, Dec. 31, 2001, $8,331
		11-9	No key figure
8-10	(a) Feb. 2, cash collected from note, $20,459	11-10	(b) Total payroll cost, $27,764
8-11	(a) Feb. 2, cash collected from note, $42,653	11-11	(b) (4) Total payroll cost, $250,058
8-12	(c) Total current assets, $373,179	11-12	(c) Total cost, $15,604
8-13	(c) Total current assets, $741,232		
8-14	(c) Sales revenue, $176,000	12-1	No key figure
8-15	(c) Sales revenue, $300,000	12-2	No key figure
		12-3	No key figure
		12-4	No key figure
9-1	No key figure	12-5	No key figure
9-2	(a) Inventory, May 31, $315	12-6	(a) 2001, Percentage of completion, $1 million; instalment method, $2 million
9-3	(a) Inventory, Sept. 30, $3,350		
9-4	(b) (3) Inventory (FIFO), Jan. 15, $4,750	12-7	(a) (1) Gross profit, $184,000
9-5	(a) (3) Ending inventory, LIFO, $18,550	12-8	No key figure
9-6	(a) (2) Ending inventory, FIFO, $18,700	12-9	No key figure
9-7	(b) (2) Write-down to market, $2,250		
9-8	(a) (2) Ending inventory, LIFO, $93,240	13-1	(b) Total assets, $187,400
9-9	(a) (2) Ending inventory, FIFO, $7,420	13-2	(b) Total assets, $220,800
9-10	(a) Gross profit, 2001, $318,400	13-3	(b) Glen's capital balance, Dec. 31, $65,000
9-11	(b) (3) Gross profit, $273,720	13-4	(a) Net income, $114,000; (c) total assets, $277,720
9-12	(b) (2) Current ratio, 4.5 to 1		

(continued on inside back cover)

ACCOUNTING
The Basis for Business Decisions

EIGHTH CANADIAN EDITION

Volume 2

ACCOUNTING
The Basis for Business Decisions

EIGHTH CANADIAN EDITION

Volume 2

ROBERT F. MEIGS
San Diego State University

MARY A. MEIGS
San Diego State University

MARK BETTNER
Bucknell University

RAY WHITTINGTON
San Diego State University

WAI P. LAM
University of Windsor

Toronto   Montréal   New York   Burr Ridge   Bangkok   Bogotá   Caracas
Lisbon   London   Madrid   Mexico City   Milan
New Delhi   Seoul   Singapore   Sydney   Taipei

*McGraw-Hill
Ryerson Limited*

A Subsidiary of The **McGraw·Hill** Companies

ACCOUNTING: THE BASIS FOR BUSINESS DECISIONS
Eighth Canadian Edition
Volume 2

Copyright © 1999, 1995, 1991, 1988, 1985, 1981, 1976, 1973, 1964 by McGraw-Hill Ryerson Limited, a Subsidiary of The McGraw-Hill Companies. Copyright © 1999, 1993, 1990, 1987, 1984, 1981, 1977, 1972, 1967, 1962 by McGraw-Hill, Inc. All rights reserved. No part of this publication may be reproduced or transmitted in any form or by any means, or stored in a data base or retrieval system, without the prior written permission of McGraw-Hill Ryerson Limited, or in the case of photocopying or other reprographic copying, a licence from CANCOPY (the Canadian Copyright Licensing Agency), 6 Adelaide Street East, Suite 900, Toronto, Ontario, M5C 1H6.

Any request for photocopying, recording, or taping of any part of this publication shall be directed in writing to CANCOPY.

ISBN: 0-07-560502-3

1 2 3 4 5 6 7 8 9 10   GTC   8 7 6 5 4 3 2 1 0 9

Printed and bound in Canada

Care has been taken to trace ownership of copyright material contained in this text. The publishers will gladly take any information that will enable them to rectify any reference or credit in subsequent editions.

Sponsoring Editor: Jennifer Dewey
Associate Editor: Janet Piper
Production Editor: Gail Marsden
Production Co-ordinator: Nicla Dattolico
Cover Designer: Dianna Little
Cover Illustration: Boris Lyubner/SIS©
Typesetter: Visutronx Services
Printer: Transcontinental Printing

Canadian Cataloguing in Publication Data

Main entry under title:

Accounting: the basis for business decisions

8th Canadian ed.
Includes index.
ISBN 0-07-560501-5 (v. 1)   ISBN 0-07-560502-3 (v.2)

1. Accounting.   I. Meigs, Robert F.

HF5635.M49 1999   657'.044   C99-930219-1

CONTENTS

Preface — xxi
Some Additional Information — xxvii

Volume 1 Part 1 An Introduction to Accounting — 1

CHAPTER 1 Accounting: The Language of Business — 2

WHAT IS ACCOUNTING? — 3

The Purpose of Accounting ■ Accounting from a User's Perspective ■ Types of Accounting Information

FINANCIAL REPORTING — 6

Financial Statements ■ The Functions of an Accounting System ■ Internal Control ■ Audits of Financial Statements ■ Annual Reports ■ *CASE IN POINT* ■ Financial Reporting: A Multimedia Process ■ *CASE IN POINT*

GENERALLY ACCEPTED ACCOUNTING PRINCIPLES (GAAP) — 12

The Nature of Accounting Principles ■ Organizations Influencing Accounting Practice

FINANCIAL STATEMENTS: THE STARTING POINT IN THE STUDY OF ACCOUNTING — 13

The Balance Sheet ■ Assets ■ Liabilities ■ Creditors' Claims Have Priority Over Those of Owners ■ Owner's Equity ■ The Accounting Equation

THE EFFECTS OF BUSINESS TRANSACTIONS: AN ILLUSTRATION — 19

Effects of These Business Transactions Upon the Accounting Equation

FORMS OF BUSINESS ORGANIZATIONS — 24

Sole Proprietorships ■ Partnerships ■ *CASE IN POINT* ■ Corporations ■ Summary Comparison of Forms of Business Organization ■ Reporting Ownership Equity in the Balance Sheet

THE USE OF FINANCIAL STATEMENTS BY OUTSIDERS — 27

The Need for Adequate Disclosure ■ *CASE IN POINT* ■ *CASE IN POINT* ■ The Reliability of Financial Statements ■ Management's Interest in Financial Statements ■ Competence, Integrity, and Professional Judgment ■ *CASE IN POINT* ■ Professional Accountants and Top Corporate Executives ■ *CASE IN POINT*

*Supplemental Topic: Careers in Accounting — 34

END-OF-CHAPTER REVIEW — 37

Key Terms Introduced or Emphasized in Chapter 1 ■ Demonstration Problem ■ Self-Test Questions

ASSIGNMENT MATERIAL — 41

Discussion Questions ■ Exercises ■ Problems ■ Analytical and Decision Problems and Cases ■ Answers to Self-Test Questions

vii

CHAPTER 2 Changes in Financial Position — 56

The Role of Accounting Records

THE LEDGER — 57
The Use of Ledger Accounts ■ Debit and Credit Entries ■ Double-Entry Accounting—The Equality of Debits and Credits ■ Recording Transactions in Ledger Accounts: An Illustration ■ Running Balance Form of Accounts

THE JOURNAL — 67
Why Use a Journal? ■ The General Journal: Illustration of Entries ■ Posting Journal Entries to the Ledger Accounts

THE TRIAL BALANCE — 73
Uses and Limitations of the Trial Balance

THE ACCOUNTING CYCLE: AN INTRODUCTION — 75
Manual and Computer-Based Systems: A Comparison

JOURNALS, LEDGERS, AND ACCOUNTING EDUCATION — 78
The Usefulness of Journals and Ledgers to Managers

*Supplemental Topic: Some Tips on Record-Keeping Procedures — 80

END-OF-CHAPTER REVIEW — 82
Key Terms Introduced or Emphasized in Chapter 2 ■ Demonstration Problem ■ Self-Test Questions

ASSIGNMENT MATERIAL — 86
Discussion Questions ■ Exercises ■ Problems ■ Analytical and Decision Problems and Cases ■ Answers to Self-Test Questions

COMPREHENSIVE PROBLEM 1: Little Bear Railroad, Inc. — 103

CHAPTER 3 Measuring Business Income and Completing the Accounting Cycle — 106

WHAT IS NET INCOME? — 107
The Income Statement: A Preview ■ CASE IN POINT ■ CASE IN POINT ■ Revenue ■ Expenses ■ Debit and Credit Rules for Revenue and Expense ■ Investments and Withdrawals by the Owner ■ Recording Revenue and Expense Transactions: An Illustration ■ The Journal ■ The Ledger ■ The Trial Balance

ADJUSTING ENTRIES: THE NEXT STEP IN THE ACCOUNTING CYCLE — 121
Shop Supplies: An Asset That Turns into an Expense ■ The Concept of Depreciation ■ CASE IN POINT ■ Recording Depreciation Expense: An Illustration ■ The Adjusted Trial Balance

PREPARING A "SET" OF FINANCIAL STATEMENTS — 127
The Income Statement ■ The Statement of Owner's Equity ■ The Balance Sheet ■ Relationship Among the Financial Statements

CLOSING THE "TEMPORARY" EQUITY ACCOUNTS — 130
Closing Entries for Revenue Accounts ■ Closing Entries for Expense Accounts ■ Closing the Income Summary Account ■ Closing the Owner's Drawing Account ■ Summary of the Closing Process ■ After-Closing Trial Balance

THE COMPLETE ACCOUNTING CYCLE 137

The Accrual Basis of Accounting ■ *CASE IN POINT* ■ The Usefulness of Revenue and Expense Data to Managers

SOME CONCLUDING REMARKS 139

The Accounting Cycle in Perspective ■ A Look Back at Overnight: Was December a "Good Month"?

END-OF-CHAPTER REVIEW 141

Key Terms Introduced or Emphasized in Chapter 3 ■ Demonstration Problem ■ Self-Test Questions

ASSIGNMENT MATERIAL 146

Discussion Questions ■ Exercises ■ Problems ■ Analytical and Decision Problems and Cases ■ Answers to Self-Test Questions

CHAPTER 4   Year End! 166

THE "BUSY SEASON" 167
ADJUSTING ENTRIES: A CLOSER LOOK 168

Types of Adjusting Entries ■ Characteristics of Adjusting Entries ■ Year-End at Overnight Auto Service ■ Apportioning Recorded Costs ■ Apportioning Unearned Revenue ■ *CASE IN POINT* ■ Recording Unrecorded Expenses ■ Recording Unrecorded Revenue ■ Adjusting Entries and Accounting Principles ■ The Concept of Materiality ■ *CASE IN POINT* ■ Effects of the Adjusting Entries

PREPARING THE STATEMENTS 183

Drafting the "Notes" That Accompany Financial Statements ■ What Types of Information Must Be Disclosed? ■ Closing the Accounts ■ A Last Look at Overnight: Was 2000 a "Good Year"? ■ Preparing Financial Statements Covering Different Periods of Time

*Supplemental Topic: The Work Sheet 191
END-OF-CHAPTER REVIEW 195

Key Terms Introduced or Emphasized in Chapter 4 ■ Demonstration Problem ■ Self-Test Questions

ASSIGNMENT MATERIAL 200

Discussion Questions ■ Exercises ■ Problems ■ Analytical and Decision Problems and Cases ■ Answers to Self-Test Questions

COMPREHENSIVE PROBLEM 2:   Friend with a Truck 222

Part 2 The Business World 225

CHAPTER 5   Accounting for Merchandising Activities; Classified Financial Statements 226

MERCHANDISING COMPANIES 227

The Operating Cycle of a Merchandising Company ■ Income Statement of a Merchandising Company ■ What Accounting Information Does a Merchandising Company Need? ■ General Ledger Accounts ■ Subsidiary Ledgers: A Source of More Detail ■ Two Approaches Used in Accounting for Merchandising Transactions

PERPETUAL INVENTORY SYSTEM 234

OTHER TRANSACTIONS RELATING TO PURCHASES — 237

Credit Terms and Cash Discounts ■ Returns of Unsatisfactory Merchandise ■ Transportation Costs on Purchases

OTHER TRANSACTIONS RELATING TO SALES — 240

Sales Returns and Allowances ■ Sales Discounts ■ Delivery Expenses ■ Accounting for Sales and Goods and Service Taxes ■ Taking a Physical Inventory ■ Closing Entries in a Perpetual Inventory System

PERIODIC INVENTORY SYSTEM — 245

Operation of a Periodic Inventory System ■ A Short-Cut System for Businesses with Little Inventory ■ Comparison of Perpetual and Periodic Inventory Systems ■ *CASE IN POINT* ■ Selecting an Inventory System

CLASSIFIED FINANCIAL STATEMENTS — 249

A Classified Balance Sheet ■ Using a Classified Balance Sheet in Evaluating Solvency ■ The Current Ratio ■ Working Capital ■ Evaluating Financial Ratios ■ *CASE IN POINT* ■ The Owner's Responsibility for Debts of the Business ■ *CASE IN POINT* ■ Classifications in an Income Statement ■ Multiple-Step Income Statements ■ Single-Step Income Statements ■ Evaluating the Adequacy of Net Income

END-OF-CHAPTER REVIEW — 260

Key Terms Introduced or Emphasized in Chapter 5 ■ Demonstration Problem ■ Self-Test Questions

ASSIGNMENT MATERIAL — 264

Discussion Questions ■ Exercises ■ Problems ■ Analytical and Decision Problems and Cases ■ Answers to Self-Test Questions

APPENDIX A: More about a Periodic Inventory System — 283

CHAPTER 6 Accounting Systems, Internal Control, and Audits — 296

ACCOUNTING SYSTEMS — 297

Determining Information Needs ■ The Cost of Producing Accounting Information ■ Basic Functions of an Accounting System ■ Who Designs and Installs Accounting Systems? ■ Recording Transactions: The Need for Special Journals ■ On-Line, Real-Time (OLRT) Systems ■ Recording Budgeted Amounts ■ Classifying and Storing the Recorded Data ■ Ledger Accounts ■ Database Systems ■ Comparison of Ledger Accounts to a Database ■ Summarizing and Communicating Accounting Information ■ Comparison of Manual and Computer-Based Systems

INTERNAL CONTROL — 307

Components of Internal Control ■ Guidelines for Achieving Strong Internal Control ■ The Role of Business Documents ■ Internal Control in Computer-Based Systems ■ *CASE IN POINT* ■ *CASE IN POINT* ■ Limitations of Internal Control ■ Prevention of Fraud ■ *CASE IN POINT* ■ Employee Fraud ■ Management Fraud ■ *CASE IN POINT* ■ *CASE IN POINT* ■ *CASE IN POINT*

AUDITS — 319
Audits of Financial Statements ■ *CASE IN POINT* ■ Operational Auditing ■ Compliance Auditing

END-OF-CHAPTER REVIEW — 325
Key Terms Introduced or Emphasized in Chapter 6 ■ Self-Test Questions

ASSIGNMENT MATERIAL — 327
Discussion Questions ■ Exercises ■ Problems ■ Analytical and Decision Problems and Cases ■ Answers to Self-Test Questions

APPENDIX B   Manual Special Journals — 337

COMPREHENSIVE PROBLEM 3: *The Next Dimension* — 359

Part 3 Accounting for Assets and Liabilities; Accounting Principles — 375

CHAPTER 7   The Control of Cash Transactions — 376
What Do Accountants Mean by "Cash"? ■ Reporting Cash in the Balance Sheet ■ *CASE IN POINT* ■ *CASE IN POINT* ■ The Cash Flow Statement ■ Cash Management ■ Cash Balances and Corporate Dividends ■ Internal Control over Cash ■ Cash Receipts ■ Cash Disbursements ■ The Voucher System ■ Recording Approved Vouchers ■ *CASE IN POINT* ■ Chequing Accounts ■ Bank Statements ■ Reconciling the Bank Statement ■ Electronic Funds Transfer Systems ■ Petty Cash Funds ■ The Cash Budget as a Control over Departmental Expenditures

END-OF-CHAPTER REVIEW — 396
Key Terms Introduced or Emphasized in Chapter 7 ■ Demonstration Problem ■ Self-Test Questions

ASSIGNMENT MATERIAL — 399
Discussion Questions ■ Exercises ■ Problems ■ Analytical and Decision Problems and Cases ■ Answers to Self-Test Questions

CHAPTER 8   Accounts Receivable and Notes Receivable — 422

ACCOUNTS RECEIVABLE — 423
CASE IN POINT ■ Uncollectible Accounts ■ The Allowance for Doubtful Accounts ■ Writing Off an Uncollectible Account Receivable ■ Recovery of an Account Receivable Previously Written Off ■ Monthly Estimates of Credit Losses ■ Direct Write-Off Method ■ Internal Controls for Receivables ■ Management of Accounts Receivable ■ Factoring Accounts Receivable ■ Credit Card Sales

NOTES RECEIVABLE — 434
Nature of Interest ■ Accounting for Notes Receivable ■ *CASE IN POINT* ■ Evaluating the Quality of Notes and Accounts Receivable ■ *CASE IN POINT* ■ *CASE IN POINT*

*Supplemental Topic: Notes Receivable with Interest Charges Included in the Face Amount — 441

END-OF-CHAPTER REVIEW — 448

Key Terms Introduced or Emphasized in Chapter 8 ■ Demonstration Problem ■ Self-Test Questions

ASSIGNMENT MATERIAL — 451

Discussion Questions ■ Exercises ■ Problems ■ Analytical and Decision Problems and Cases ■ Answers to Self-Test Questions

CHAPTER 9 Inventories and the Cost of Goods Sold — 468

Inventory Defined ■ *CASE IN POINT*

THE FLOW OF INVENTORY COSTS — 470

Which Unit Did We Sell? Does It Really Matter? ■ Data for an Illustration ■ Specific Identification ■ Cost Flow Assumptions ■ Average-Cost Method ■ First-In, First-Out Method ■ Last-In, First-Out Method ■ Evaluation of the Methods ■ *CASE IN POINT* ■ Do Inventory Methods Really Affect Performance? ■ The Principle of Consistency ■ Just-in-Time (JIT) Inventory Systems ■ *CASE IN POINT*

TAKING A PHYSICAL INVENTORY — 481

Recording Shrinkage Losses ■ Other Write-Downs of Inventory and LCM ■ *CASE IN POINT* ■ *CASE IN POINT* ■ The Year-End Cutoff of Transactions ■ Periodic Inventory Systems ■ Importance of an Accurate Valuation of Inventory ■ *CASE IN POINT* ■ Techniques for Estimating the Cost of Goods Sold and the Ending Inventory ■ The Gross Profit Method ■ The Retail Method ■ "Textbook" Inventory Systems Can Be Modified...and They Often Are ■ *CASE IN POINT*

EVALUATING THE LIQUIDITY OF INVENTORY — 492

Inventory Turnover Rate ■ *CASE IN POINT* ■ Accounting Methods Can Affect Analytical Ratios ■ Inventory Management

END-OF-CHAPTER REVIEW — 496

Key Terms Introduced or Emphasized in Chapter 9 ■ Demonstration Problem ■ Self-Test Questions

ASSIGNMENT MATERIAL — 499

Discussion Questions ■ Exercises ■ Problems ■ Analytical and Decision Problems and Cases ■ Answers to Self-Test Questions

CHAPTER 10 Capital Assets: Plant and Equipment, Intangible Assets, and Natural Resources — 516

CASE IN POINT ■ Plant and Equipment as a "Stream of Future Services" ■ Major Categories of Plant and Equipment ■ Accountable Events in the Lives of Plant Assets

ACQUISITIONS OF PLANT ASSETS — 518

Determining Cost: An Example ■ Some Special Considerations ■ Capital Expenditures and Revenue Expenditures

DEPRECIATION — 521

Allocating the Cost of Plant and Equipment over the Years of Use ■ Causes of Depreciation ■ Methods of Computing Depreciation ■ The Straight-Line Method ■ The Declining-Balance Method ■ Which Depreciation Methods Do Most Businesses Use? ■ *CASE IN POINT* ■ Financial Statement Disclosures ■ *CASE IN POINT*

CONTENTS **xiii**

DISPOSAL OF PLANT AND EQUIPMENT ... 531
Gains and Losses on Disposals of Plant and Equipment ■ Trading in Used Assets on New

INTANGIBLE ASSETS ... 533
Characteristics ■ Operating Expenses Versus Intangible Assets ■ Amortization ■ Goodwill ■ Patents ■ Trademarks and Trade Names ■ Franchises ■ Copyrights ■ Other Intangibles and Deferred Charges ■ Research and Development (R&D) Costs

NATURAL RESOURCES ... 539
Accounting for Natural Resources ■ *CASE IN POINT* ■ Depreciation, Amortization, and Depletion—A Common Goal ■ The Impairment of Plant Assets

END-OF-CHAPTER REVIEW ... 542
Key Terms Introduced or Emphasized in Chapter 10 ■ Demonstration Problem ■ Self-Test Questions

ASSIGNMENT MATERIAL ... 545
Discussion Questions ■ Exercises ■ Problems ■ Analytical and Decision Problems and Cases ■ Answers to Self-Test Questions

COMPREHENSIVE PROBLEM 4: Alpine Village and Nordic Sports ... 559

CHAPTER 11 Liabilities Common to Most Business Organizations ... 562
The Nature of Liabilities

CURRENT LIABILITIES ... 565
CASE IN POINT ■ Accounts Payable ■ Notes Payable ■ Comparison of the Two Forms of Notes Payable ■ The Current Portion of Long-Term Debt ■ Accrued Liabilities ■ Unearned Revenue

LONG-TERM LIABILITIES ... 572
Maturing Obligations Intended to Be Refinanced ■ Instalment Notes Payable ■ Disclosure Requirements for Long-Term Debt

ESTIMATED LIABILITIES, CONTINGENT LOSSES, AND COMMITMENTS ... 576
Estimated Liabilities ■ Contingent Losses ■ *CASE IN POINT* ■ *CASE IN POINT* ■ *CASE IN POINT* ■ Commitments ■ *CASE IN POINT*

EVALUATING THE SAFETY OF CREDITORS' CLAIMS ... 580
Analysis by Short-Term Creditors ■ Analysis by Long-Term Creditors ■ Summary ■ Less Formal Means of Determining Creditworthiness ■ Topics Deferred to Chapter 16

*Supplemental Topic: Accounting for Payrolls ... 584

END-OF-CHAPTER REVIEW ... 595
Key Terms Introduced or Emphasized in Chapter 11 ■ Demonstration Problem ■ Self-Test Questions

ASSIGNMENT MATERIAL ... 598
Discussion Questions ■ Exercises ■ Problems ■ Analytical and Decision Problems and Cases ■ Answers to Self-Test Questions

CHAPTER 12 Accounting Concepts, Professional Judgment, and Ethical Conduct — 614

The Need for Recognized Accounting Standards

GENERALLY ACCEPTED ACCOUNTING PRINCIPLES (GAAP) — 615

CASE IN POINT ■ Nature of Accounting Principles ■ Authoritative Support for Accounting Principles ■ The Accounting Entity Concept ■ The Going-Concern Assumption ■ The Time Period Principle ■ The Stable-Dollar Assumption ■ The Objectivity Principle ■ Asset Valuation: The Cost Principle ■ Revenue Recognition: The Realization (Recognition) Principle ■ Expense Recognition: The Matching Principle ■ *CASE IN POINT* ■ The Consistency Principle ■ The Disclosure Principle ■ *CASE IN POINT* ■ Materiality ■ *CASE IN POINT* ■ Conservatism as a Guide in Resolving Uncertainties

PROFESSIONAL JUDGMENT: AN ESSENTIAL ELEMENT IN FINANCIAL REPORTING — 628

International Accounting Standards

ETHICAL CONDUCT IN THE ACCOUNTING PROFESSION — 629

What Are "Ethics"? ■ Professional Codes of Ethics ■ A Closer Look at Some Key Principles ■ *CASE IN POINT* ■ The Challenge of Adhering to a Code of Ethics ■ *CASE IN POINT* ■ *CASE IN POINT* ■ *CASE IN POINT*

END-OF-CHAPTER REVIEW — 637

Key Terms Introduced or Emphasized in Chapter 12 ■ Demonstration Problem ■ Self-Test Questions

ASSIGNMENT MATERIAL — 640

Discussion Questions ■ Exercises ■ Problems ■ Analytical and Decision Problems and Cases ■ Answers to Self-Test Questions

Volume 2 Part 4 Partnerships and Corporations — 653

CHAPTER 13 Partnerships — 654

CASE IN POINT ■ Significant Features of a Partnership ■ *CASE IN POINT* ■ Advantages and Disadvantages of a Partnership ■ Limited Partnerships ■ The Partnership Agreement ■ Partnership Accounting ■ *CASE IN POINT* ■ Opening the Accounts of a New Partnership ■ Additional Investments ■ Drawing Accounts ■ Loans from Partners ■ Closing the Accounts of a Partnership at Year-End ■ Partnership Income and Income Taxes ■ The Nature of Partnership Net Income ■ Dividing Partnership Net Income among the Partners ■ Evaluating the Financial Statements of a Partnership ■ Admission of a New Partner ■ Withdrawal of a Partner ■ Death of a Partner ■ Liquidation of a Partnership

END-OF-CHAPTER REVIEW — 679

Key Terms Introduced or Emphasized in Chapter 13 ■ Demonstration Problem ■ Self-Test Questions

ASSIGNMENT MATERIAL — 683

Discussion Questions ■ Exercises ■ Problems ■ Analytical and Decision Problems and Cases ■ Answers to Self-Test Questions

CHAPTER 14 Corporations: Organization and Shareholders' Equity — 696

Why Businesses Incorporate ■ Publicly Owned and Closely Held Corporations ■ *CASE IN POINT* ■ *CASE IN POINT*

FORMATION OF A CORPORATION — 700

CASE IN POINT ■ Shareholders' Equity ■ Cash Dividends ■ Authorization and Issuance of Capital Stock ■ *CASE IN POINT* ■ No-par Value Capital Stock ■ Par Value Capital Stock ■ Preferred Stock and Common Stock ■ *CASE IN POINT* ■ Characteristics of Preferred Stock ■ *CASE IN POINT* ■ *CASE IN POINT* ■ *CASE IN POINT* ■ The Role of an Underwriter ■ Stocks Issued for Assets Other than Cash ■ Subscriptions to Capital Stock ■ Donated Capital ■ Shareholder Records in a Corporation ■ Illustration of a Corporate Balance Sheet ■ Book Value per Share of Common Stock ■ *CASE IN POINT*

MARKET VALUE — 721

CASE IN POINT ■ Market Price of Preferred Stock ■ Market Price of Common Stock ■ *CASE IN POINT* ■ "Following" the Market ■ Book Value and Market Price ■ *CASE IN POINT*

END-OF-CHAPTER REVIEW — 725

Key Terms Introduced or Emphasized in Chapter 14 ■ Demonstration Problem ■ Self-Test Questions

ASSIGNMENT MATERIAL — 728

Discussion Questions ■ Exercises ■ Problems ■ Analytical and Decision Problems and Cases ■ Answers to Self-Test Questions

CHAPTER 15 Reporting Special Events and Special Equity Transactions — 742

REPORTING THE RESULTS OF OPERATIONS — 743

Developing Predictive Information in the Income Statement ■ Reporting Special Events—An Illustration ■ Continuing Operations ■ Discontinued Operations ■ *CASE IN POINT* ■ *CASE IN POINT* ■ Extraordinary Items ■ Accounting Changes ■ Earnings per Share (EPS) ■ Basic and Fully Diluted Earnings per Share

OTHER SHAREHOLDERS' EQUITY TRANSACTIONS — 753

Cash Dividends ■ Dividend Dates ■ *CASE IN POINT* ■ Liquidating Dividends ■ Stock Dividends ■ *CASE IN POINT* ■ Stock Splits ■ Statement of Retained Earnings ■ *CASE IN POINT* ■ Treasury Stock ■ Recording Purchases of Treasury Stock ■ Reissuance of Treasury Stock ■ Stock "Buyback" Programs ■ *CASE IN POINT* ■ *CASE IN POINT* ■ Illustration of a Shareholders' Equity Section

END-OF-CHAPTER REVIEW — 765

Key Terms Introduced or Emphasized in Chapter 15 ■ Demonstration Problem ■ Self-Test Questions

ASSIGNMENT MATERIAL — 770

Discussion Questions ■ Exercises ■ Problems ■ Analytical and Decision Problems and Cases ■ Answers to Self-Test Questions

xvi CONTENTS

CHAPTER 16 Special Types of Liabilities — 786
BONDS PAYABLE — 787
What Are Bonds? ■ *CASE IN POINT* ■ *CASE IN POINT* ■ Tax Advantage of Bond Financing ■ Accounting for Bonds Payable ■ The Concept of Present Value ■ Bond Prices After Issuance ■ *CASE IN POINT* ■ *CASE IN POINT* ■ Early Retirement of Bonds Payable ■ Classification of Bonds Payable in a Balance Sheet ■ Commercial Paper

OTHER "CORPORATE" LIABILITIES — 798
Lease Obligations ■ Operating Leases ■ Capital Leases ■ Liabilities for Pensions and Postretirement Benefits ■ *CASE IN POINT* ■ Future (Deferred) Income Taxes ■ Disclosures About Financial Instruments ■ *CASE IN POINT* ■ Some Old Ratios Take On New Importance ■ Financing a Business with Debt

*Supplemental Topic A: Accounting for Bonds Issued at a Discount or a Premium — 812

**Supplemental Topic B: Convertible Bonds Payable — 816

END-OF-CHAPTER REVIEW — 818
Key Terms Introduced or Emphasized in Chapter 16 ■ Self-Test Questions

ASSIGNMENT MATERIAL — 820
Discussion Questions ■ Exercises ■ Problems ■ Analytical and Decision Problems and Cases ■ Answers to Self-Test Questions

APPENDIX C: The "Time-Value" of Money: Future Amounts and Present Values — 834

COMPREHENSIVE PROBLEM 5: Shadow Mountain Hotel — 856

CHAPTER 17 Investments in Corporate Securities — 862
INVESTMENT IN MARKETABLE SECURITIES — 863
CASE IN POINT ■ Accounting for Marketable Securities ■ Marketable Debt Securities (Bonds) ■ Marketable Equity Securities (Stocks) ■ Gains and Losses from Sales of Investments ■ Balance Sheet Valuation of Marketable Securities ■ Applying the Lower-of-Cost-and-Market Rule: An Illustration ■ Presentation of Marketable Securities in Financial Statements

INVESTMENTS FOR PURPOSES OF SIGNIFICANT INFLUENCE OR CONTROL — 869
The Equity Method ■ Parent and Subsidiary Companies ■ *CASE IN POINT* ■ Growth through the Acquisition of Subsidiaries ■ *CASE IN POINT* ■ Financial Statements for a Consolidated Economic Entity

CONSOLIDATED FINANCIAL STATEMENTS: CONCEPTS AND MECHANICS — 874
Methods of Consolidation ■ Consolidation at the Date of Acquisition ■ Intercompany Eliminations ■ Acquisition of Subsidiary's Stock at a Price above Book Value ■ Less than 100% Ownership in Subsidiary ■ Consolidated Income Statement ■ Accounting for Investments in Corporate Securities: A Summary

END-OF-CHAPTER REVIEW — 884
Key Terms Introduced or Emphasized in Chapter 17 ■ Self-Test Questions

ASSIGNMENT MATERIAL — 886
Discussion Questions ■ Exercises ■ Problems ■ Analytical and Decision Problems and Cases ■ Answers to Self-Test Questions

Part 5 Income Taxes, Cash Flows, Financial Statement Analysis, and Managerial Accounting — 899

CHAPTER 18 Income Taxes and Business Decisions — 900
The Federal Income Tax: History and Objectives ■ Provincial Income Tax ■ The Critical Importance of Income Taxes ■ Tax Planning versus Tax Evasion ■ *CASE IN POINT* ■ Classes of Taxpayers and Liability of Tax ■ Enforcement of Income Tax Laws

INCOME TAXES: INDIVIDUALS — 904
Accrual versus Cash Basis ■ Tax Rates for Individuals ■ Income Tax Formula for Individuals ■ Total Income ■ General Income Tax Formula for Individuals ■ Deductions ■ Net Income ■ Other Deductions ■ Taxable Income ■ Federal Income Tax Calculation ■ Tax Credits ■ Basic Federal Tax ■ Provincial Income Tax ■ Federal Dividend Tax Credit for Individuals ■ Instalment Payment of Estimated Tax for Individuals ■ Tax Returns, Tax Refunds, and Payment of the Tax ■ Computation of Individual Income Tax Illustrated

INCOME TAXES: CORPORATIONS — 912
Taxation and Tax Rates ■ Computation of Taxable Income of Corporations ■ Computation of Taxable Income and Federal Income Tax for Corporation Illustrated ■ Accounting Income versus Taxable Income ■ Capital Cost Allowance ■ Future (Deferred) Income Taxes ■ Accounting for Future (Deferred) Taxes: An Illustration ■ *CASE IN POINT*

TAX PLANNING OPPORTUNITIES — 919
Form of Business Organization ■ Planning Business Transactions to Minimize or Postpone Income Taxes ■ Tax Planning in the Choice of Financial Structure

END-OF-CHAPTER REVIEW — 922
Key Terms Introduced or Emphasized in Chapter 18 ■ Self-Test Questions

ASSIGNMENT MATERIAL — 923
Discussion Questions ■ Exercises ■ Problems ■ Analytical and Decision Problems and Cases ■ Answers to Self-Test Questions

CHAPTER 19 Measuring Cash Flows — 936
CASH FLOW STATEMENT — 937
Purpose of the Statement ■ Example of a Cash Flow Statement ■ Classification of Cash Flows ■ Critical Importance of Cash Flow from Operating Activities ■ The Approach to Preparing a Cash Flow Statement

PREPARING A CASH FLOW STATEMENT: AN ILLUSTRATION — 942

Operating Activities ■ Investing Activities ■ Financing Activities ■ Cash and Cash Equivalents ■ Cash Flows from Operating Activities ■ Cash Payments for Merchandise and for Operating Expenses ■ Differences Between Net Income and Net Cash Flow from Operating Activities ■ Reporting Operating Cash Flow: The Direct and Indirect Methods ■ Cash Flows from Investing Activities ■ Cash Flows from Financing Activities ■ Relationship Between the Cash Flow Statement and the Balance Sheet ■ Using the Cash Flow Statement

*Supplemental Topic A: The Indirect Method — 955

**Supplemental Topic B: A Work Sheet for Preparing a Cash Flow Statement — 960

END-OF-CHAPTER REVIEW — 965

Key Terms Introduced or Emphasized in Chapter 19 ■ Demonstration Problem ■ Self-Test Questions

ASSIGNMENT MATERIAL — 970

Discussion Questions ■ Exercises ■ Problems ■ Analytical and Decision Problems and Cases ■ Answers to Self-Test Questions

CHAPTER 20 Analysis and Interpretation of Financial Statements — 992

Essential Elements for Financial Statement Analysis and Interpretation ■ *CASE IN POINT* ■ Comparative Financial Statement ■ Tools of Analysis ■ Dollar and Percentage Changes ■ *CASE IN POINT* ■ Trend Percentages ■ Component Percentages ■ Ratios ■ Comparative Data in Annual Reports of Major Corporations ■ Standards of Comparison ■ Quality of Earnings ■ Quality of Assets and the Relative Amount of Debt ■ Impact of Inflation ■ Illustrative Analysis for Seacliff Corporation

ANALYSIS BY COMMON SHAREHOLDERS — 1003

CASE IN POINT ■ Return on Investment (ROI) ■ *CASE IN POINT* ■ *CASE IN POINT* ■ Measures of Profitability ■ *CASE IN POINT* ■ Leverage ■ *CASE IN POINT*

ANALYSIS BY LONG-TERM CREDITORS — 1011

ANALYSIS BY PREFERRED SHAREHOLDERS — 1013

ANALYSIS BY SHORT-TERM CREDITORS — 1013

CASE IN POINT ■ Cash Flow Analysis ■ Usefulness of Notes to Financial Statements

SUMMARY OF ANALYTICAL MEASUREMENTS

END-OF-CHAPTER REVIEW — 1019

Key Terms Introduced or Emphasized in Chapter 20 ■ Demonstration Problem ■ Self-Test Questions

ASSIGNMENT MATERIAL — 1026

Discussion Questions ■ Exercises ■ Problems ■ Real World Problems and Cases (RW) ■ Analytical and Decision Problems and Cases ■ Answers to Self-Test Questions

COMPREHENSIVE PROBLEM 6: Loblaw Companies Limited	1048
CHAPTER 21 Introduction to Managerial Accounting; Accounting for Manufacturing Operations	1052
INTRODUCTION TO MANAGERIAL ACCOUNTING	1053
Managerial Accounting ■ The Interdisciplinary Nature of Managerial Accounting ■ The Overlap of Managerial and Financial Accounting	
ACCOUNTING FOR MANUFACTURING OPERATIONS	1055
Classifications of Manufacturing Costs ■ Product Costs Versus Period Costs ■ Product Costs and the Matching Principle ■ Inventories of a Manufacturing Business ■ The Flow of Costs Parallels the Flow of Physical Goods ■ Accounting for Manufacturing Costs: An Illustration ■ Direct Materials ■ Direct Labour ■ Manufacturing Overhead ■ Direct and Indirect Manufacturing Costs ■ Overhead Application Rates ■ What "Drives" Overhead Costs? ■ *CASE IN POINT* ■ *CASE IN POINT* ■ Work in Process Inventory, Finished Goods Inventory, and the Cost of Goods Sold ■ The Need for Per-Unit Cost Data ■ Determining the Cost of Finished Goods Manufactured ■ Financial Statements of a Manufacturing Company	
END-OF CHAPTER REVIEW	1072
Key Terms Introduced or Emphasized in Chapter 21 ■ Demonstration Problem ■ Self-Test Questions	
ASSIGNMENT MATERIAL	1074
Discussion Questions ■ Exercises ■ Problems ■ Analytical and Decision Problems and Cases ■ Answers to Self-Test Questions	
APPENDIX D: The New Manufacturing Environment; Activity-Based Costing	1088
ANNUAL REPORT OF LOBLAW COMPANIES LIMITED, 1997	AR-1
INDEX	I-1
PHOTOGRAPH CREDITS	P-1

PREFACE

Welcome to the first financial accounting course. This course provides an introduction to the field of financial accounting and to the development and use of accounting information in the business world. It is intended for ***everyone,*** not just those students who may pursue careers in accounting. Today's students are tomorrow's business decision makers. And as we say in the title of this textbook, ***accounting is the basis for business decisions.***

There is more diversity today in the content of introductory financial accounting courses than at any time in the recent past. For example, the course may be structured to emphasize accounting techniques and procedures, accounting theory, or the interpretation and use of accounting information. There are many accounting textbooks available today, each with its own approach to the introductory course. Let us briefly explain ours.

OUR GOALS IN THIS EIGHTH CANADIAN EDITION

We have tried to improve this Eighth Canadian Edition in many ways. But three of our top priorities have been to:

1. Better develop the student's understanding of today's business environment.
2. Increase emphasis upon the ***interpretation*** and ***use*** of accounting information.
3. Retain a course structure that is familiar to faculty and meets the content requirements of most universities and colleges.

Providing Students with a Better "Business Background"

If students are to appreciate the nature of accounting, they first must understand the activities that accounting information describes. We find, however, that many introductory students lack this background. Often the introductory accounting course is also the students' first course in the business curriculum. In this edition, we give increased attention to explaining the nature of business activities before discussing the related accounting issues. Also, we add realism to the discussion and understanding of accounting issues by using real world events in the form of Case in Point boxes and in the assignment materials.

Our focus is upon the ***current and emerging*** business environment, not that of the past. We recognize the challenging reality that today's students will be ***just beginning*** their careers as we enter the twenty-first century.

Emphasizing the Interpretation and Use of Accounting Information

In today's business world, relatively few first-year accounting students will become professional preparers of accounting information. All, however, will become life-long ***users*** of this information. For this reason, we have reduced our emphasis on the techniques of preparing information, and increased our emphasis on its ***interpretation*** and ***use.***

This shift in perspective affects the text in several ways. For example, the assignment materials place greater emphasis on developing students' analytical, decision-making, and communication skills. Accordingly, these skills are required to solve the "Analytical and Decision Problems and Cases" in the final section of the assignment materials.

A more "user-oriented" approach also affects topical content and emphasis. Topics of crucial importance to decision makers are addressed, even if these topics traditionally have been deferred to later accounting courses. Examples include postretirement costs, income tax considerations, audits, and how different accounting methods affect key financial ratios.

The analysis and use of financial statement information, both by management and other users, are introduced in the early chapters and reinforced throughout the text. Thus, analytical ratios and other financial relationships are discussed throughout the text.

Some "traditional" accounting topics relate primarily to the preparation of accounting information and are of little significance to information users. Examples include the preparation of work sheets and alternative methods of recording accruals and deferrals. In our more user-oriented approach, such topics receive less emphasis.

Retaining a Familiar Course Structure

We regard our changes in this Eighth Canadian Edition as ***evolutionary,*** not revolutionary. Instructors who have used our past editions will find much that is familiar. They will also find that this edition supports—indeed encourages—evolutionary change from one semester to the next.

FOCUS AND ORGANIZATION OF THIS EIGHTH CANADIAN EDITION

This Eighth Canadian Edition, organized into two volumes, is focused on financial accounting. However, it also includes a brief introduction to managerial accounting.

Volume 1 covers the accounting cycle, merchandising operations and classified financial statements, accounting systems and internal control, assets, common liabilities, and accounting concepts, professional judgment, and ethical conduct.

Volume 2 covers partnerships, corporations, special types of liabilities, investments in corporate securities, income taxes, cash flows, analysis and interpretation of financial statements, and an introduction to managerial accounting.

ELEMENTS OF THE TEXTBOOK

This Eighth Canadian Edition is accompanied by a wide variety of in-the-text learning aids.

Chapter Introductions and Learning Objectives

Each chapter now starts with a "photo-opener." These photographs enable us to use non-technical images in describing each chapter's theme. Each chapter also includes a short set of ***learning objectives*** which are integrated with the text discussions and assignment materials.

Case in Point Boxes

A distinctive feature of our text is the use of short **Case in Point** boxes based upon real world events. This edition makes far greater use of this feature—it is part of our effort to more closely relate the study of accounting with today's business world. These Cases in Point are both informative and interesting. There are almost 100 of them in this edition.

Actual Annual Report and Financial Statements

The financial statements and other selected portions of the 1997 Annual Report of Loblaw Companies Limited are presented at the end of both *Volume 1* and *Volume 2*. The financial statements and other annual report information are referred to in these volumes to bring realism into classroom discussions. This represents another example of our efforts to more closely relate the study of accounting with today's business world.

*Supplemental Topics and Appendixes

Several chapters are accompanied by ***Supplemental Topic*** sections. These topics are not "optional" or unimportant. Rather, they relate closely to the chapter content. Students ***always*** should read the **Supplemental Topic* sections. However, instructors may decide whether these topics are of sufficient general interest for inclusion in class discussions, homework assignments, and examinations.

In contrast to the **Supplemental Topics,* our four **Appendixes** provide self-contained coverage of specialized topics. We consider these topics optional; students are ***not*** expected to read the appendixes unless they are assigned by the instructor.

End-of-Chapter Reviews

Each chapter is followed by a variety of learning aids. These include a **Glossary of Key Terms, Self-Test Questions,** and in most chapters, a **Demonstration Problem.** Solutions to the Self-Test Questions and Demonstration Problems are also provided.

Assignment Materials

A substantial number of new questions, exercises, problems, and cases have been incorporated into this Eighth Canadian Edition. Many of these new assignment materials are based on real world situations, such as the financial statements of internationally well-known corporations. In fact, there is a separate section of real world problems and cases in Chapter 20.

One of the distinctive features of this edition is the nature and variety of its assignment material. Increased emphasis is placed upon the development of students' analytical, decision-making, communication, and interpersonal skills.

There are five basic categories of assignments (1) *Discussion Questions,* (2) *Exercises,* (3) *Problems,* (4) *Analytical and Decision Problems and Cases* and (5) *Comprehensive Problems.*

Discussion Questions are short and usually call for expository answers. In addition to developing communication skills, these questions enhance students' conceptual understanding of accounting.

Exercises are short assignments, usually focusing upon a single concept. They are designed to illustrate basic concepts quickly, allowing more class time for discussing assignments such as the *Analytical and Decision Problems and Cases.*

Problems are longer than the *Exercises* and address several concepts at one time. Many problems require students to explain, interpret, or make use of the information they produce.

Users of prior editions will notice that we now have a single series of problems, rather than the traditional A and B sets. This single series enables us to offer ***greater variety*** in our assignment material.

Analytical and Decision Problems and Cases are intended to develop students' analytical, decision-making, and communication skills. These assignments readily lend themselves to group analysis and to class discussions.

Comprehensive Problems tie together concepts presented over a span of chapters. The text includes ***six*** of these problems, ranging in length from 50-minute assignments to term projects. These problems are described in detail in the prefaces to both the *Solutions Manual* and the *Instructor's Guide.*

A ***checklist of key figures*** for all *Problems* and *Comprehensive Problems* appears on the front and back inside covers of the text. The purpose of these figures is to aid students in verifying their solutions and discovering their own errors. Also, a supplemental package of ***partially completed work sheets*** supporting all *Problems* and *Comprehensive Problems* is available through campus bookstores.

NEW FEATURES AND SUPPLEMENTARY MATERIALS

Traditionally, we have included in our *Preface* brief descriptions of new and extensively revised chapters and of the many supplemental materials which accompany this text. As these discussions are of greater interest to faculty than to students, we have moved them to the several pages immediately following the *Preface.*

A NOTE TO STUDENTS: SOME GUIDELINES ON CONDUCTING INTERVIEWS

Several of our *Analytical and Decision Problems and Cases* call for you—or a member of your study group—to interview people in the business community. Please appreciate that business people granting these interviews are donating their time for your benefit. For this reason, we ask that you observe a few basic guidelines:

- Please make an appointment for the interview, don't just walk in expecting to talk to someone. And be on time—recognize that time is a very valuable commodity in the business world.
- Dress appropriately and conduct yourself in a business-like manner.

- Learn the name of the person you will be interviewing, including the correct spelling and pronunciation, and his or her position within the organization.
- Plan and write down *in advance* all of the questions you plan to ask.
- Take notes during the interview. You should never attempt to quote the person's statements from memory.
- Realize that business people may not want certain information about their business "spread around town." Tell them *in advance* that the general content of the interview will be discussed within your study group and, perhaps, in your classroom. Respect any requests that specific comments be kept "off-the-record."

ACKNOWLEDGMENTS

It is with great pleasure that I acknowledge the contributions of the instructors and students who used the preceding edition. Their helpful comments were much appreciated.

My sincere thanks go to those reviewers who provided perceptive and constructive suggestions and to those who bestowed on me valuable advice. Their suggestions and advice have greatly improved the text and assignment materials. Now, let me thank each of the following individuals:

> Cecile Ashman, Algonquin College
> Elizabeth Grasby, Richard Ivey School of Business, University of Western Ontario
> Elizabeth Hicks, Mount Saint Vincent University
> Ross Johnston, University of Windsor
> Loris Macor, PricewaterhouseCoopers
> Bob Madden, St. Francis Xavier University
> Jerry Mus, Assiniboine Community College
> Penny Parker, Fanshawe College
> Joe Pidutti, Durham College
> Brenda Warner, University of Windsor
> Betty Wong, Athabasca University

I appreciate the expert advice and assistance of the staff of McGraw-Hill Ryerson, especially Susan Calvert, Janet Piper, and Jennifer Dewey. Gail Marsden's professional and friendly approach to editing has made this project a more enjoyable experience. Also, I owe my thanks to Sandy Berlasty for her assistance in typing part of the manuscript.

Finally, let me express my gratitude to my family members—Jean, Gloria, Lambert, and Angela—for their support and understanding. I particularly want to thank Jean and Gloria for their excellent job in helping with various aspects of this project, especially in doing library research, and in typing, editing, and proofreading the manuscript of the text and solutions.

W.P. Lam

SOME ADDITIONAL INFORMATION

NEW OR EXTENSIVELY REVISED CHAPTERS

Many chapters in this Eighth Canadian Edition are either new or have been extensively revised. Among the changes which will be noticed most readily are:

The **first four** chapters utilize a new continuing example, are less procedural, and place more emphasis on the interpretation and use of accounting information. In **Chapter 1**, the coverage of the three forms of organizations has been revised and expanded. We now complete our coverage of the accounting cycle in **Chapter 3**, and our coverage of adjusting entries in that chapter has been expanded. **Chapter 4**, "Year-End!," provides a broader description of the many activities that make year-end the "busy season." Substantially less emphasis is given to the work sheet, which now appears in a *Supplemental Topic* section.

Chapter 5 continues to emphasize perpetual inventory systems, but the coverage of periodic systems has been expanded. Additional merchandising transactions have been moved from a supplemental topic to the main part of the chapter. Also "More About a Periodic Inventory System," is now an appendix, rather than a supplemental topic to this chapter.

Chapter 6, our accounting systems chapter, retains its focus on computer-based systems. However the chapter now is supplemented by Appendix B, illustrating the use of manual special journals, and by **THE NEXT DIMENSION**, which is our most challenging *Comprehensive Problem*. (NEXT makes an excellent group term project.)

Chapter 10, "Capital Assets: Plant and Equipment, Intangible Assets, and Natural Resources," emphasizes the depreciation methods that businesses use most—straight-line, declining balance, and units-of-production.

Chapter 12, "Accounting Concepts, Professional Judgment, and Ethical Conduct," is quite similar to that in our preceding edition. But we want to remind instructors that this chapter is at once a review of the first semester and an introduction to the second. It may well be worth repeating at the beginning of the second semester—particularly if students are returning from a long summer vacation.

Chapter 13, "Partnerships," has two significant changes. The first is the explanation of the distinction of the limited life of a partnership from the legal standpoint and the practical viewpoint, as many partnerships, such as accounting and law firms, continue to exist in spite of the changes of their partners. The second is the added discussion on the adequacy of partnership net income and the evaluation of partnership solvency.

Chapter 14, "Corporations: Organization and Shareholders' Equity," has been stream-lined. It also includes a new section on publicly owned and closely held corporations.

Chapter 15, "Reporting Special Events and Special Equity Transactions," has been updated by deleting the topic on prior period adjustments, as it is no longer a *CICA Handbook* recommendation.

Our coverage of bonds payable, in **Chapter 16**, differs substantially from past editions and from most accounting textbooks. For too long, coverage of long-term liabilities has focused upon the mechanics of amortizing bond discounts and premiums. But we find that bonds are almost never issued at a premium, and discounts generally are immaterial in dollar amount. Therefore, Chapter 16 now focuses upon topics of greater importance in today's business world, such as postretirement costs and the evaluation of credit risk. Bonds are addressed thoroughly in the chapter, but amortization of discount and premium is treated as a *Supplemental Topic*.

Chapter 19, "Measuring Cash Flows," is based on the most recent *CICA Handbook* recommendations, and consequently, this chapter is virtually new. The direct method for the preparation of the cash flow statement is covered in the main material of the chapter, while the indirect method is covered as a supplemental topic. The direct method is easier to understand and is preferred by the *CICA Handbook*.

Chapter 20, "Analysis and Interpretation of Financial Statements," has been revised and updated. The cash flow statement is now included and analyzed in this chapter. Also, the discussion on the measures of profitability has been revised and expanded.

One new feature to the assignment materials is a separate section of real world problems and cases, based on well-known corporations in North America.

Following this chapter is the new *Comprehensive Problem*. This problem requires the analysis and interpretation of the financial statements and other annual report information of Loblaw Companies Limited.

Chapter 21, "Introduction to Managerial Accounting; Accounting for Manufacturing Operations," is the final chapter of the text. While this chapter is essentially the same as it was in the previous edition, a new appendix on "The New Manufacturing Environment; Activity-Based Costing," has been added.

SUPPLEMENTARY MATERIALS

The text is accompanied by a large number of supplementary learning and teaching aids. These supplements are described below, with emphasis upon the features new to this eighth edition.

For the Student

1. *Study Guide.* The *Study Guide* enables students to measure their progress by providing immediate feedback. It includes a summary of the highlights of each chapter and an abundance of questions ranging from true/false to multiple choice to short problems and exercises. In fact, we have increased the number of short problems and exercises. The solutions are included at the end of each chapter with full explanations and worked-out solutions.
2. *Accounting Work Sheets.* Available in two volumes, (one for Chapters 1–12 and one for Chapters 13–21), students are provided with the appropriate type of working papers for each problem and comprehensive problem in the text.

3. ***Adders 'N Keyes,*** Fourth Edition, by Brenda Mallouk, *Adders 'N Keyes* is a sole proprietorship practice set that gives students exposure to a real life business setting.
4. ***Interactive Financial Accounting Lab*** by Ralph Smith, Rick Birney, and Alison Wiseman.
5. ***Student's Name CDs*** by Harvey Freedman. *Student's Name CDs* is an accounting practice set that requires students to analyze transactions using real life source documents.

U.S. Supplements For The Student

6. ***General Ledger Application Software***
7. ***Student SPATS for Accounting***
8. ***Tutorial Software—Windows***
9. ***Freewheel Practice Set***
10. ***Republic Practice Set***
11. ***Cogg Hill Practice Set***
12. ***Fast Mart Inc. Practice Set***

For the Instructor

The supplements listed here may accompany *Accounting: The Basis for Business Decisions*. Please contact your McGraw-Hill Ryerson representative for details concerning policies, prices, and availability as some restrictions may apply.

1. ***Solutions Manual.*** A comprehensive manual containing descriptions of each problem and case with the estimated time for completion and difficulty rating; suggested answers to the discussion questions; and solutions to the exercises, problems, cases, and comprehensive problems. All assignment material and solutions were developed by the authors of the text.
2. ***Instructor's Manual with PowerPoint Presentation.*** For each chapter, the *Instructor's Manual* contains a brief, topical outline, suggested assignment and topic coverage chart, teaching objectives, descriptions of new features, chapter outline, and teaching suggestions. In-class tests are a valuable new addition. These 3 to 4 question, 10 minute quizzes are a terrific new feature.
   A PowerPoint presentation and teaching transparencies are also included in the *Instructor's Manual*.
3. ***Computerized Test Bank.***

The *Study Guide, Instructor's Manual with PowerPoint Presentation,* and *Computerized Test Bank* were adapted by the following:
W.P. Doyle, Mt. Saint Vincent University
E.A.G. Hicks, Mt. Saint Vincent University
A.C. MacGillivary, Mt. Saint Vincent University
J.R. Tilley, Mt. Saint Vincent University

U.S. Instructor Supplements

4. ***Instructor Spreadsheet Application Templates***

PART 4

Partnerships and Corporations

13. Partnerships
14. Corporations: Organization and Shareholders' Equity
15. Reporting Special Events and Special Equity Transactions
16. Special Types of Liabilities
    Appendix C: The "Time-Value" of Money: Future Amounts and Present Values
    Comprehensive Problem 5: Shadow Mountain Hotel
17. Investments in Corporate Securities

Can you tell which is a partnership and which is a corporation? Why are some organized as partnerships and others as corporations? What are the unique accounting and business issues? To understand the business world, you should know the answer to these questions.

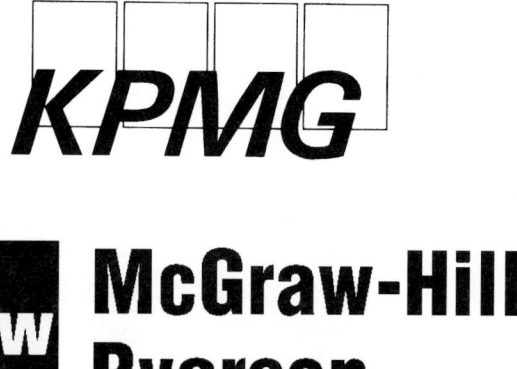

CHAPTER 13

Partnerships

PRICEWATERHOUSECOOPERS

Partnerships are a more common form of organization for the professionals—accountants, lawyers, and doctors. Many businesses, especially the smaller ones, are also organized as partnerships.

CHAPTER LEARNING OBJECTIVES

1. Describe the basic characteristics of a partnership.
2. Explain the advantages and disadvantages of the partnership as a form of business organization.
3. Distinguish between a regular partnership and a limited partnership.
4. Account for the formation of a partnership.
5. Divide the net income of a partnership among the partners.
6. Evaluate the adequacy of net income and solvency of a partnership.
7. Account for the admission of a new partner and the withdrawal of a partner.
8. Account for the liquidation of a partnership.

Three types of business organization are common to Canadian business: the sole proprietorship, the partnership, and the corporation. Partnerships are a popular form of organization because they provide a convenient, inexpensive means of combining the capital and the special abilities of two or more persons. The partnership form of organization is widely used in all types of small business and also in the professions. A partnership is often referred to as a ***firm***.

CASE IN POINT

The public accounting firm of Price Waterhouse, founded in 1865, began in England as a partnership between Samuel Price and Edwin Waterhouse. As the firm grew, qualified members of its professional staff were admitted to the partnership and it became an international public accounting firm with more than 3,000 partners. In 1998, it merged with Coopers & Lybrand, another international public accounting firm, to become PricewaterhouseCoopers.

In Canada, each province has its own partnership legislation. The provincial partnership legislation may consist of one or more acts. All provincial partnership legislation covers essentially the same ground and provides essentially the same fundamental rules on the nature, organization, and operation of partnerships.

What constitutes a partnership? The answer can be found in the partnerships act. The legal definition of a partnership is essentially the same in all provincial legislation, except for minor differences in wording. The Ontario Partnerships Act, for example, has the following definition:

> Partnership is the relation that subsists between persons carrying on a business in common with a view to profit, but the relation between the members of a company or association that is incorporated by or under the authority of any special or general Act in force in Ontario or elsewhere, or registered as a corporation under any such Act, is not a partnership within the meaning of this Act.

In this chapter, we shall concentrate on the significant features of and the accounting problems peculiar to a partnership.

Significant Features of a Partnership

LO 1: Describe the basic characteristics of a partnership.

Before taking up the accounting problems peculiar to partnerships, it will be helpful to consider briefly some of the distinctive characteristics of the partnership form of organization. These characteristics (such as limited life and unlimited liability) all stem from the concept that a partnership is not a separate legal entity in itself but merely a voluntary association of individuals.

Ease of Formation Generally, a partnership can be created with a minimum of formality. When two or more persons agree, orally or in writing, to carry on a business with a view to profit, such agreement constitutes a contract and a partnership is automatically created. The contract should be in writing in order to lessen the chances for misunderstanding and future disagreement. The voluntary aspect of a partnership agreement means that no one can be forced into a partnership or forced to continue as a partner.

CASE IN POINT

Richard and Mike were friends and employees of the same large corporation. They became interested in forming a partnership to acquire a nearby small business being offered for sale for a down payment of $50,000. They felt that they could manage the business (which had two employees) in their spare time. Richard and Mike agreed that each would deposit $25,000 in a partnership bank account. There was no written agreement of partnership. Richard made his deposit from his personal savings; Mike had only $10,000 of his own but was able to obtain the other $15,000 from his brother-in-law, Joe, to whom he described the business with great enthusiasm. Mike then deposited $25,000 in the partnership bank account and the business was purchased. Richard had never met Joe and was not aware of his $15,000 investment.

A few months later, Joe became annoyed because he had received no return on his investment. He appeared suddenly at the business while Richard was there, stating that he was a partner and demanding to see the accounting records and the bank statements. Richard refused, and after an angry argument, Joe was forcibly ejected. The question of whether Joe was a "silent partner" caused bitter disagreement among all three of the principals. During this dispute, the business was forced to shut down because of lack of working capital. Richard, Mike, and Joe each retained a lawyer to seek damages from the others.

Although a partnership may be at times a somewhat unstable form of organization, a written agreement of partnership might have avoided the problems encountered by Richard and Mike—and by Joe.

Limited Life From a legal standpoint, partnerships have limited lives. A partnership may be ended at any time by the admission, retirement, death, or withdrawal of a member of the firm. Other factors that may bring an end to a partnership include the bankruptcy or incapacity of a partner, the expiration of the period specified in the partnership contract, or the completion of the project for which the partnership was formed. However, many partnerships have continuity of existence extending beyond the participation of individual partners. Partnership agreements, such as those for major accounting and law firms, often have provisions that make the retirement and admission of partners a routine event that does not affect the continuity or the operations of the partnership.

Mutual Agency Each partner acts as an agent of the partnership, with authority to enter into contracts for the purchase and sale of goods and services. The partnership is bound by the acts of any partner as long as these acts are within the scope of normal operations. The factor of **mutual agency** suggests the need for exercising great caution in the selection of a partner. To be in partnership with an irresponsible person or one lacking in integrity is an intolerable situation.

Unlimited Liability Each partner is *personally* responsible for all the debts of the firm. The lack of any ceiling on the liability of a partner may deter a wealthy person from entering a partnership.

A new member joining an existing partnership may or may not assume liability for debts incurred by the firm prior to his or her admission. A partner withdrawing from membership must give adequate public notice of withdrawal; otherwise the former partner may be held liable for partnership debts incurred subsequent to his or her withdrawal. The retiring partner remains liable for partnership debts existing at the time of withdrawal unless the creditors agree to a release of this obligation.

Co-ownership of Partnership Property and Income When a partner invests a building, inventory, or other property in a partnership, he or she does not retain any personal right to the assets contributed. The property becomes jointly owned by all partners. Each member of a partnership also has an ownership right in the income of the partnership.

Advantages and Disadvantages of a Partnership

LO 2: Explain the advantages and disadvantages of the partnership as a form of business organization.

Perhaps the most important advantage of most partnerships is the opportunity to bring together sufficient capital to carry on a business. The opportunity to combine special skills, as, for example, the specialized talents of an engineer and an accountant, may also induce individuals to join forces in a partnership. To form a partnership is much easier and less expensive than to organize a corporation. Members of a partnership enjoy more freedom from government regulation and more flexibility of action than do the owners of a corporation. The partners may withdraw funds and make business decisions of all types without the necessity of formal meetings or legalistic procedures.

Operating as a partnership *may* in some cases produce income tax advantages as compared with doing business as a corporation. The partnership itself is neither a legal entity nor a taxable entity. A partnership does not pay income taxes. However, the individual partners must pay income taxes on their respective shares of the partnership's net income.

Offsetting these advantages of a partnership are such serious disadvantages as limited life, unlimited liability (except for a limited partner in a limited partnership, as discussed in the following section), and mutual agency. Furthermore, if a business is to require a large amount of capital, the partnership is a less effective device for raising funds than is a corporation. Many persons who invest freely in common stocks of corporations are unwilling to enter a partnership because of the unlimited liability imposed on partners.

Limited Partnerships

LO 3: Distinguish between a regular partnership and a limited partnership.

In past years a number of businesses have been organized as **limited partnerships**. This form of organization is widely used for businesses that provide tax-sheltered income to investors, such as real estate syndications and mining ventures. However, limited partnerships are *not* appropriate for businesses in which the owners intend to be active managers. Recent tax legislation has also reduced greatly the income tax advantages formerly available to investors in limited partnerships.

A limited partnership must have at least one **general partner** as well as one or more **limited partners**. The general partners are partners in the traditional sense, with unlimited liability for the debts of the business and the right to make managerial decisions. The limited partners, however, are basically *investors* rather than traditional partners. They have the right to participate in the income of the business, but their liability for losses is limited to the amount of their investment. Also, limited partners do not actively participate in management of the business. Thus, the concepts of unlimited liability and mutual agency apply only to the general partners in a limited partnership.

In this chapter, we emphasize the characteristics and accounting practices of conventional partnerships (also known as general partnerships) rather than limited partnerships. Limited partnerships are discussed in depth in courses on business law and income taxes.

The Partnership Agreement

Although a partnership can be formed by an oral agreement, it is highly desirable that a written **partnership agreement** (contract) be prepared, summarizing the partners' mutual understanding on such points as:

1. Names of the partners
2. The duties and rights of each partner, effective the specified date of formation of the partnership
3. Amount to be invested by each partner, including the procedure for valuing any noncash asset invested or withdrawn by partners
4. Methods of sharing net income and net losses
5. Withdrawals to be allowed each partner
6. Provision for the continuity of the partnership and for its liquidation, including the method for sharing a deficiency in a partner's capital account by other partners.

While a partnership agreement may not prevent disputes from arising among partners, it does provide a contractual foundation for their resolution.

Partnership Accounting

As mentioned earlier in this chapter, a partnership *does not* constitute a *legal* entity with an identity separate from its owners. However, from a record-keeping and reporting point of view, a partnership does constitute a *separate and distinct accounting entity*.

An adequate accounting system and an accurate measurement of income are needed by every business, but they are especially important in a partnership because the net income is divided among two or more owners. Each partner needs current, accurate information on operations so that he or she can make intelligent decisions on such questions as additional investments, expansion of the business, or sale of an interest in the partnership.

> **CASE IN POINT**
>
> Rowe and Davis were partners in an automobile dealership and auto repair shop. Rowe was the active manager of the business, but Davis had supplied nearly all the capital. Aware that the firm was quite profitable, Rowe devised a scheme to become the sole owner by buying out his partner. In order to persuade Davis to sell his interest at a bargain price, Rowe deliberately began falsifying the accounting records and financial statements in a manner to understate the earnings of the business. Much of the revenue from auto repair work was not recorded at all, depreciation expense was overstated, ending inventories were understated, and the cost of new items of plant and equipment were charged to expense. The result was a series of monthly income statements that showed the business operating at a larger loss each month. Faced with these discouraging financial statements, Davis became pessimistic over the prospects for the business and was on the verge of selling his interest to Rowe at a price far below the balance in his capital account.
>
> However, a friend suggested that before selling out, Davis should insist upon an audit of the business by a public accounting firm. An audit was performed and revealed that the business was in fact highly profitable. When confronted by Davis with the auditors' findings, Rowe withdrew from the partnership and Davis became the sole owner.

Opening the Accounts of a New Partnership

LO 4: Account for the formation of a partnership.

When a partner contributes assets other than cash, a question always arises as to the value of such assets. The valuations assigned to noncash assets should be their **current market values** rather than the **book values** (the balances in the accounting records) at the date of transfer to the partnership. The valuations assigned must be agreed to by all partners.

To illustrate the opening entries for a newly formed partnership, assume that on January 1, Joan Blair and Richard Cross, who operate competing retail stores, decide to form a partnership by consolidating their two businesses. A capital account will be opened for each partner and credited with the agreed valuation of the **net assets** (total assets less total liabilities) that the partner contributes. The journal entries to open the accounts of the partnership of Blair and Cross are as follows:

Entries for formation of partnership.

Cash	40,000	
Accounts Receivable	60,000	
Inventory	90,000	
Accounts Payable		30,000
Joan Blair, Capital		160,000

To record the investment by Joan Blair in the partnership of Blair and Cross.

Cash	10,000	
Inventory	60,000	
Land	60,000	
Building	100,000	
Accounts Payable		70,000
Richard Cross, Capital		160,000

To record the investment by Richard Cross in the partnership of Blair and Cross.

Partnership accounting is similar to that in a sole proprietorship, except that separate capital and drawing accounts are maintained for each partner. These capital and drawing accounts show for each partner the amounts invested, the amounts withdrawn, and the appropriate share of partnership net income. In brief, each partner is provided with a history of his or her equity in the firm.

The values assigned to assets in the accounts of the new partnership may be quite different from the book values (the amounts at which these assets were carried in the accounts) of their previous owners. For example, the land contributed by Cross and valued at $60,000 might have appeared in his accounting records at a cost of $20,000. The building that he contributed was valued at $100,000 by the partnership, but it might have cost Cross only $80,000 some years ago and might have been depreciated on his records to a net value of $60,000. Assuming that market values of land and building had risen sharply while Cross owned this property, it is only fair to recognize the **current market value** of these assets at the time he transfers them to the partnership and to credit his capital account accordingly. Depreciation of the building in the partnership accounts will be based on the assigned value of $100,000 at the date of acquisition by the partnership.

Additional Investments

Assume that after six months of operation the firm is in need of more cash, and the partners make an additional investment of $10,000 each on July 2. These additional investments are credited to the capital accounts as shown below:

Entry for additional investment

Cash	20,000	
Joan Blair, Capital		10,000
Richard Cross, Capital		10,000

To record additional investments.

Drawing Accounts

The drawing account maintained for each partner serves the same purpose as the drawing account of the owner of a sole proprietorship. The transactions calling for debits to the drawing accounts of partners may be summarized as follows:

1. Cash or other assets withdrawn by a partner
2. Payments from partnership funds of the personal debts of a partner
3. Partnership cash collected on behalf of the firm by a partner but retained by the partner personally

Loans from Partners

Ordinarily any funds furnished to the firm by a partner are recorded by crediting that partner's capital account. Occasionally, however, a partnership may be in need of funds but the partners do not wish to increase their capital investment in the business, or perhaps one partner is willing to advance funds when the others are not. Under these circumstances, the advance of funds may be designated as a loan from the partner and credited to a liability account. However, partnership liabilities to outsiders always take precedence over liabilities to partners.

Closing the Accounts of a Partnership at Year-End

At the end of the accounting period, the balance in the Income Summary account is closed into the partners' capital accounts. The net income or losses of a partnership may be divided among the partners in *any manner agreed upon* by the partners. However, this agreement should be carefully stipulated in the partnership contract. In the event that the partners *do not* have a formal income-and-loss sharing agreement, the law requires all net income or losses to be *divided equally* among the partners.

In our illustration, let us assume that Blair and Cross have agreed to share net income equally. (We will discuss other income-and-loss sharing arrangements later in this chapter.) Assuming that the partnership earns net income of $60,000 in the first year of operations, the entry to close the Income Summary account is as follows:

Closing income summary: net income shared equally

Income Summary	60,000	
Joan Blair, Capital		30,000
Richard Cross, Capital		30,000
To divide net income for the year in accordance with partnership agreement to share it equally.		

The next step in closing the accounts is to transfer the balance of each partner's drawing account to his or her capital account. Assuming that withdrawals during the year amounted to $24,000 for Blair and $16,000 for Cross, the entry at December 31 to close the drawing accounts is as follows:

Closing the drawing accounts to capital accounts

Joan Blair, Capital	24,000	
Richard Cross, Capital	16,000	
Joan Blair, Drawing		24,000
Richard Cross, Drawing		16,000
To transfer debit balances in partners' drawing accounts to their respective capital accounts.		

Income Statement for a Partnership The income statement for a partnership differs from that of a sole proprietorship in only one respect: a final section may be added to show the division of the net income between the partners, as illustrated below for the firm of Blair and Cross. The income statement of a partnership is consistent with that of a sole proprietorship in showing no income taxes expense and no salaries expense relating to services rendered by partners.

BLAIR AND CROSS
Income Statement
For the Year Ended December 31, 20__

Note division of net income

Sales			$600,000
Cost of goods sold			400,000
Gross profit			$200,000
Operating expenses:			
Selling expenses		$100,000	
General & administrative expenses		40,000	140,000
Net income			$ 60,000
Division of net income:			
To Joan Blair (50%)		$ 30,000	
To Richard Cross (50%)		30,000	$ 60,000

Statement of Partners' Equity The partners will usually want an explanation of the change in their capital accounts from one year-end to the next. A supplementary schedule called a **statement of partners' equity** is prepared to show this information. A statement of partners' equity for Blair and Cross follows:

BLAIR AND CROSS
Statement of Partners' Equity
for the Year Ended December 31, 20__

Changes in capital accounts during the year

	Blair	Cross	Total
Balances, Jan. 1, 20__	$160,000	$160,000	$320,000
Add: Additional Investments	10,000	10,000	20,000
Net income for the year	30,000	30,000	60,000
Subtotals	$200,000	$200,000	$400,000
Less: Drawings	24,000	16,000	40,000
Balances, Dec. 31, 20__	$176,000	$184,000	$360,000

The balance sheet of Blair and Cross would show the capital balance for each partner, as well as the total capital of $360,000.

Partnership Income and Income Taxes

Partnerships Are Not Required to Pay Income Taxes Partners must include their shares of the partnership net income (after certain technical adjustments) on their individual income tax returns. Partnership net income is thus taxable to the partners individually in the year in which it is earned. The income tax rules applicable to investment in a partnership are covered in advanced accounting courses.

Note that partners report and pay tax on their respective shares of the net income earned by the partnership during the year and **not** on the amounts that they have drawn out of the business during the year. ***The net income of the partnership is taxable to the partners each year***, even though there may have been no withdrawals. This treatment is consistent with that accorded a sole proprietorship.

The Nature of Partnership Net Income

The net income earned by partnerships, like those earned by sole proprietorships, compensate the owners for (1) personal services rendered to the business, (2) capital invested in the business, and (3) "entrepreneurial risk"—that is, taking the risk that the investments of personal services and of capital may be lost if the business is unsuccessful. Recognition of these three factors is helpful in developing an equitable plan for the division of partnership net income.

If one partner devotes full time to the business while another devotes little or no time, the difference in the partners' contributions of time and effort should be reflected in the income-sharing agreement. If one partner possesses special skills, the income-sharing agreement should reward this partner's talent. Also, partners may each provide different amounts of capital to the business entity. Again, the differences in the value of the partners' contributions to the business should be reflected in the income-and-loss sharing agreement.

To recognize the particular contributions of each partner to the business, partnership income-and-loss sharing agreements often include "salary allowances" to partners and "interest" on the balances of partners' capital accounts. These "salaries" and "interest" are **not expenses** of the business; rather, they are ***steps in the computation made to divide partnership net income among the partners***.

In the preceding illustrations of the partnership of Blair and Cross, we assumed that the partners invested equal amounts of capital, rendered equal services, and divided net income equally. We are now ready to consider cases in which the partners invest **unequal** amounts of capital and services.

Dividing Partnership Net Income among the Partners

LO 5: Divide the net income of a partnership among the partners.

Partners can share net income or loss in any manner they decide upon; however, most income-sharing agreements fall under one of the following types:

1. A fixed ratio. The fixed ratio method has already been illustrated in the example of the Blair and Cross partnership in which net

income was shared equally, that is, 50% and 50%. Partners may agree upon any fixed ratio such as 60% and 40%, or 70% and 30%.
2. Salary allowances to the partners, with remaining net income or loss divided in a fixed ratio.
3. Interest allowances on partners' capital balances, with remaining net income or loss divided in a fixed ratio.
4. Salary allowances to the partners, interest allowances on partners' capital balances, and remaining net income or loss divided in a fixed ratio.

All these methods of sharing partnership net income are intended to recognize differences in the personal services rendered by partners and in the amounts of capital invested in the firm.

In the illustrations that follow, it is assumed that beginning balances in the partners' capital accounts were Brooke Adams, $160,000, and Ben Barnes, $40,000. At year-end, the Income Summary account showed a credit balance of $96,000, representing the net income for the year before any allowances for partners' salaries or interest on capital account balances.

Salaries to Partners, with Remainder in a Fixed Ratio Because partners often contribute different amounts of personal services, partnership agreements often provide for partners' salaries as a factor in the division of net income.

For example, assume that Adams and Barnes agree to annual salary allowances of $24,000 for Adams and $48,000 for Barnes. These salaries, that total $72,000 per year, are agreed upon by the partners in advance. Of course, the net income of the business is not likely to be exactly $72,000 in a given year. Therefore, the income-and-loss sharing agreement should also specify a fixed ratio for dividing any income or loss remaining after giving consideration to the agreed-upon salary allowances. We will assume that Adams and Barnes agree to divide any remaining income or loss equally.

The division of the $96,000 in partnership net income between Adams and Barnes is illustrated in the following schedule. The first step is to allocate to each partner his or her agreed-upon salary allowance. This step allocates $72,000 of the partnership net income. The remaining $24,000 is then divided in the agreed-upon fixed ratio (50-50 in this example).

Division of Partnership Net Income

Income sharing; salary allowances and remainder in a fixed ratio

	Adams	Barnes	Net income
Net income to be divided			$96,000
Salary allowances to partners	$24,000	$48,000	(72,000)
Remaining income after salary allowances			$24,000
Allocated in a fixed ratio:			
Adams (50%)	12,000		
Barnes (50%)		12,000	(24,000)
Total share to each partner	$36,000	$60,000	$ –0–

Under this agreement, Adams's share of the $96,000 net income amounts to $36,000 and Barnes's share amounts to $60,000. The entry to close the Income Summary account would be:

Income Summary	96,000	
Brooke Adams, Capital		36,000
Ben Barnes, Capital		60,000
To close the Income Summary account by crediting each partner with agreed-upon salary allowances and dividing the remaining income equally.		

The "salary allowances" used in dividing partnership net income are sometimes misinterpreted, even by the partners. These salary allowances are merely an agreed-upon device for dividing net income; they are ***not expenses*** of the business and are ***not recorded in any ledger account***. A partner is considered an owner of the business, not an employee. Therefore, the services that a partner renders to the firm are assumed to be rendered in anticipation of earning a share of the net income, not a salary.

The amount of cash or other assets that a partner withdraws from the partnership may be greater than or less than the partner's salary allowance. Even if a partner decides to withdraw an amount of cash equal to his or her "salary allowance," the withdrawal should be recorded by debiting the partner's drawing account, ***not by debiting an expense account***. Let us repeat the main point: ***"salary allowances" to partners should not be recorded as expenses of the business***.[1]

Because of this treatment of salary allowances, the net income reported by a partnership will differ from the net income that would be reported if the business were organized as a corporation. Corporations do record as expenses any salaries paid to owners.[2]

Interest Allowances on Partners' Capital, with Remainder in a Fixed Ratio Next we shall assume a business situation in which the partners spend very little time in the business and net income depends primarily on the amount of money invested. The income-sharing plan then might emphasize invested capital as a basis for the first step in allocating income.

For example, assume that Adams and Barnes agree that both partners are to be allowed interest at ***15%*** on their beginning capital balances, with any remaining income or loss to be divided equally. Net income to be divided is $96,000 and the beginning capital balances are Adams, ***$160,000***, and Barnes, ***$40,000***.

---

[1] Some exceptions to this general rule will be discussed in advanced accounting courses.
[2] The net income reported by a corporation also differs from that reported by an unincorporated business because the corporation is subject to income taxes on its earnings. Accounting practices of corporations are discussed in later chapters.

Income sharing; interest on capital and remainder in a fixed ratio

Division of Partnership Net Income

	Adams	Barnes	Net income
Net income to be divided			$96,000
Interest allowances on beginning capital:			
Adams ($160,000 × 15%)	$24,000		
Barnes ($40,000 × 15%)		$ 6,000	
Total allocated as interest allowances			(30,000)
Remaining income after interest allowances			$66,000
Allocated in a fixed ratio:			
Adams (50%)	33,000		
Barnes (50%)		33,000	(66,000)
Total share to each partner	$57,000	$39,000	$ -0-

The entry to close the Income Summary account in this example would be:

Income Summary	96,000	
Brooke Adams, Capital		57,000
Ben Barnes, Capital		39,000

To close the Income Summary account by crediting each partner with interest at 15% on beginning capital and dividing the remaining income equally.

Interest allowances on partners' capital, like partners' salary allowances, are computational devices used in dividing partnership net income. This "interest" is not recorded as an expense of the business.

Salary Allowances, Interest Allowances on Capital, and Remainder in a Fixed Ratio The preceding example took into consideration the differences in amounts of capital provided by Adams and Barnes but ignored any difference in personal services performed. In the next example, we shall assume that the partners agree to an income-sharing plan providing for salaries and for interest on beginning capitals. Salary allowances, as before, are authorized at $24,000 for Adams, $48,000 for Barnes. Beginning capital balances are $160,000 for Adams, $40,000 for Barnes. Partners are to be allowed interest at 10% on their beginning capital balances, and any income or loss remaining after authorized salary and interest allowances is to be divided equally.

Income sharing; salaries, interest, and remainder in a fixed ratio

Division of Partnership Net Income

	Adams	Barnes	Net income
Net income to be divided			$96,000
Salary allowances to partners	$24,000	$48,000	(72,000)
Income after salary allowances			$24,000
Interest allowances on beginning capital:			
Adams ($160,000 × 10%)	16,000		
Barnes ($40,000 × 10%)		4,000	
Total allocated as interest allowances			(20,000)
Remaining income after salary and interest allowances			$ 4,000
Allocated in a fixed ratio:			
Adams (50%)	2,000		
Barnes (50%)		2,000	(4,000)
Total share to each partner	$42,000	$54,000	$ -0-

The journal entry to close the Income Summary account in this case will be:

Income Summary	96,000	
Brooke Adams, Capital		42,000
Ben Barnes, Capital		54,000
To close the Income Summary account by crediting each partner with authorized salary, interest at 10% on beginning capital, and dividing the remaining income equally.		

Authorized Salary and Interest Allowance in Excess of Net Income In the preceding example the total of the authorized salaries and interest was $92,000 and the net income to be divided was $96,000. Suppose that the net income had been only **$80,000**; how should the division have been made?

If the partnership agreement provides for salaries and interest on invested capital, these provisions are to be followed even though the net income for the year is *less* than the total of the authorized salaries and interest. If the net income of the firm of Adams and Barnes amounted to only $80,000, this amount would be allocated as follows:

Authorized salary and interest allowances in excess of net income

Division of Partnership Net Income

	Adams	Barnes	Net income
Net income to be divided			$ 80,000
Salary allowances to partners	$24,000	$48,000	(72,000)
Income after salary allowances			$ 8,000
Interest allowances on beginning capital:			
Adams ($160,000 × 10%)	16,000		
Barnes ($40,000 × 10%)		4,000	
Total allocated as interest allowances ..			(20,000)
Residual loss after salary and interest allowances			$(12,000)
Allocated in a fixed ratio:			
Adams (50%)	(6,000)		
Barnes (50%)		(6,000)	12,000
Total share to each partner	$34,000	$46,000	$ -0-

Notice that after deducting for the specified salary and interest allowances, there is a residual loss of $12,000 to be divided equally between Adams and Barnes. ***This does not mean that the partnership has generated a loss for the period.*** The partnership earned net income of $80,000. The residual loss allocation is simply a computational step in the process of dividing net income according to the partnership contract. The entry to close the Income Summary account will be as follows:

Income Summary	80,000	
Brooke Adams, Capital		34,000
Ben Barnes, Capital		46,000
To close the Income Summary account by crediting each partner with authorized salary and with interest on invested capital and by dividing the residual loss equally.		

Evaluating the Financial Statements of a Partnership

LO 6: Evaluate the adequacy of net income and solvency of a partnership.

The Adequacy of Net Income The net income in the income statement of a partnership is similar to that of a sole proprietorship. As mentioned earlier, it represents the partners' compensation for (1) personal services, (2) invested capital, and (3) entrepreneurial risk.

The services and capital provided by individual partners may vary, as may the degree of risk assumed. Therefore, it is quite difficult to evaluate the adequacy of the net income of a partnership "viewed as a whole." Rather, the individual partners must separately evaluate their *respective shares* of the partnership net income in light of their personal contributions to the firm and their personal assessment of the risk involved. This is similar to the evaluation of the adequacy of net income for a sole proprietorship discussed in Chapters 3 and 4.

Evaluating Solvency The balance sheet of a partnership is more meaningful than that of a sole proprietorship. This is because there are legal distinctions between partnership assets, which are jointly owned, and the personal assets of individual partners. Another reason is that personal responsibility for the partnership business debts may ***not*** extend to all of the partners.

Creditors should understand the distinctions among the types of partnerships. In a conventional or general partnership, all partners have unlimited personal liability for the debts of the business. This situation affords creditors the maximum degree of protection. In a limited partnership, only the ***general partners*** have personal liability for these obligations.

Admission of a New Partner

LO 7: Account for the admission of a new partner and the withdrawal of a partner.

An individual may gain admission to an existing partnership in either of two ways: (1) by buying an equity interest from one or more of the present partners or (2) by making an investment in the partnership. When an incoming partner purchases an equity interest from a present member of the firm, the payment goes personally to the old partner, and there is no change in the assets or liabilities of the partnership. On the other hand, if the incoming partner acquires an equity interest by making an investment in the partnership, the assets of the firm are increased by the amount paid in by the new partner.

By Purchase of an Interest When a new partner buys an equity interest from a present member of a partnership, the only change in the accounts will be a transfer from the capital account of the selling partner to the capital account of the incoming partner.

Assume, for example, that Pam Lee has an $80,000 equity interest in the partnership of Lee, Martin, and Nash. Lee arranges to sell her entire interest to Paul Trent for $100,000 cash. Partners Pat Martin and Tom Nash agree to the admission of Trent, and the transaction is recorded in the partnership accounts by the following entry:

Incoming partner buys interest from present partner

Pam Lee, Capital	80,000	
Paul Trent, Capital		80,000
To record the transfer of Pam Lee's equity interest to the incoming partner, Paul Trent.		

Note that the entry in the partnership accounts is for **$80,000**, the balance of Lee's capital account. The entry does **not** indicate the price paid by Trent to the retiring partner. The payment of $100,000 by Trent to Lee was a ***personal transaction*** between these two individuals; it does not affect the assets or liabilities of the partnership and, therefore, is **not** entered in the partnership accounting records.

As a separate but related example, assume that Trent is to gain admission to the firm of Lee, Martin, and Nash by purchasing one-fourth of the equity interest of each partner. The present capital accounts are as follows: Lee $80,000; Martin, $60,000; Nash, $100,000. Assume also that Trent makes payment directly to the old partners, **not to the partnership**. The amount paid to each existing partner for one-fourth of his or her equity interest is a privately negotiated matter, and the amounts of these payments are **not** recorded in the partnership records. The only entry required in the partnership accounting records is the following:

Pam Lee, Capital	20,000	
Pat Martin, Capital	15,000	
Tom Nash, Capital	25,000	
Paul Trent, Capital		60,000
To record purchase of 25% of each partner's equity by Paul Trent.		

This entry transfers to Paul Trent one-fourth of the balance formerly appearing in the capital accounts of each of the existing partners. The amounts actually paid to these partners by Trent are **not recorded** in the partnership accounts, because these payments did not flow into the partnership. Thus, the transfer of ownership equity among the partners does not affect the assets, liabilities, or ***total*** partners' equity in the business.

By Investing in the Firm Now let us assume that an incoming partner acquires his or her equity interest by making an investment directly into the firm. In this case the payment by the new partner goes to the partnership and not to the partners as individuals; the investment therefore increases the partnership assets and also the total partners' equity of the firm. The portion of total equity granted to a new partner is based upon the terms negotiated by both existing and incoming partners. This equity interest (credited to the new partner's capital account) may be equal to, less than, or greater than the amount invested in the partnership by the incoming partner.

Assume that Ann Phillips and Judy Ryan are partners, each having a capital account of $100,000. They agree to admit Bart Smith and negotiate to grant him a one-half equity interest in the business upon his investment of $200,000 in cash. The recording of Smith's admission to the partnership is based on the following calculations:

Net assets (partners' equity) of old partnership	$200,000
Cash investment by Bart Smith	200,000
Net assets (partners' equity) of new partnership	$400,000
Smith's one-half interest	$200,000

To acquire an interest of $200,000 in the net assets of $400,000, Smith invested $200,000. In this situation, the amount of equity interest acquired is equal to the amount of Smith's investment. The entry to record the admission of Smith would be as follows:

Investment in business by new partner

Cash	200,000	
Bart Smith, Capital		200,000
To record the admission of Bart Smith to a one-half interest in the firm.		

Although Smith has a one-half equity interest in the net assets of the new firm of Phillips, Ryan, and Smith, he is not necessarily entitled to receive one-half of the net income. Income sharing is a matter for agreement among the partners; if the new partnership contract contains no mention of income sharing, the assumption is that the three partners intended to share net income and losses equally.

Allowing a Bonus to Former Partners If an existing partnership has exceptionally high earnings year after year, the present partners may demand a ***bonus*** as a condition of admission of a new partner. In other words, to acquire an equity interest of, say, $80,000, the incoming partner may be required to invest $120,000 in the partnership. The excess investment of $40,000 may be regarded as a bonus to the old partners and credited to their capital accounts in the established ratio for income sharing.

To illustrate the recording of a bonus to the old partners, let us assume that Jane Rogers and Richard Steel are members of a highly successful partnership. Their partnership agreement calls for net income and losses to be divided 60% to Rogers and 40% to Steel. As a result of profitable operations, the partners' capital accounts have doubled within a few years and presently stand at $100,000 each. David Taylor desires to join the firm and offers to invest $100,000 for a one-third equity interest. Rogers and Steel refuse this offer but extend a counteroffer to Taylor of $120,000 for a one-fourth equity interest in the capital of the firm and a one-fourth interest in net income. Taylor accepts these terms because of his desire to share in the unusually large net income of the business. The recording of Taylor's admission to the partnership is based on the following calculations:

Calculation of bonus to old partners

Net assets (partners' equity) of old partnership	$200,000
Cash investment by David Taylor	120,000
Net assets (partners' equity) of new partnership	$320,000
Taylor's one-fourth equity interest	$ 80,000

To acquire an interest of $80,000 in the net assets of $320,000, Taylor has invested $120,000. His ***excess investment***, or ***bonus***, of $40,000 will be allocated 60% to Rogers ($24,000) and 40% to Steel ($16,000), in accordance with the income-sharing arrangement in effect prior to Taylor's admission.

The entry to record Taylor's admission to the partnership follows:

Recording bonus to old partners

Cash	*120,000*	
David Taylor, Capital		*80,000*
Jane Rogers, Capital		*24,000*
Richard Steel, Capital		*16,000*
To record admission of David Taylor as a partner with a one-fourth interest in capital and net income.		

The total capital of the new partnership is now $320,000, in which Taylor has a one-fourth equity interest ($80,000). Rogers' capital account is $124,000 and Steel's capital account is $116,000 after admission of Taylor. Although in this case Taylor was also granted a one-fourth share of future partnership net income, **the equity interest and the income-sharing ratio of a partner are not necessarily the same**. Old partners Rogers and Steel will set a new income-sharing arrangement for the remaining 75% of net income to be divided between themselves.

Allowing a Bonus to New Partner An existing partnership may sometimes be very anxious to bring in a new partner who can bring needed cash to the firm. In other instances the new partner may possess special talents or may have advantageous business contacts that will add to the profitability of the partnership. Under either of these sets of circumstances, the present partners may offer the new member a bonus in the form of a capital account larger than the amount of the incoming partner's investment.

Assume, for example, that John Bryan and Merle Davis are partners in an existing partnership. Their partnership agreement calls for partnership net income and losses to be divided 70% to Bryan and 30% to Davis. Capital account balances are presently $120,000 for Bryan and $100,000 for Davis. Since the firm is in desperate need of cash, they offer to admit Kay Grant to a one-third equity interest in the firm upon her investment of only $80,000 in cash. The recording of Grant's admission to the partnership is based on the following calculations:

Net assets (partners' equity) of old partnership	*$220,000*
Cash invested by Kay Grant	*80,000*
Net assets (partners' equity) of new partnership	*$300,000*
Grant's one-third interest	*$100,000*

To acquire an equity interest of $100,000 in the new partnership's net assets of $300,000, Grant has invested only $80,000. The $20,000 excess allocated to Grant's capital account is a bonus to Grant from the existing partners, Bryan and Davis. A bonus granted to a new partner is charged to the existing partners' capital accounts according to the income-sharing arrangement in effect **prior to** admission of the new partner.

The following journal entry records the admission of Grant to a one-third equity interest in the business, with allowance of the $20,000 bonus to Grant from the two old partners:

Entry for bonus to new partner

Cash	80,000	
John Bryan, Capital	14,000	
Merle Davis, Capital	6,000	
Kay Grant, Capital		100,000

To record admission of Grant to a one-third interest, and the allowance of a $20,000 bonus to Grant: 70% from Bryan and 30% from Davis.

Withdrawal of a Partner

To illustrate the withdrawal or retirement of a partner, assume the following data for the partnership of Acres, Bundy, and Coe:

	Capital Account	Share of Net Income
Chris Acres	$ 75,000	20%
Brit Bundy	125,000	30%
John Coe	100,000	50%
Total partners' capital	$300,000	

We will use this data to illustrate the retirement of Coe and the treatment accorded the partners' capital accounts under several different assumptions.

Coe Sells His Interest to Someone Else The simplest case is when Coe, with the consent of Acres and Bundy, sells his equity in the business to a new partner. In this case, the payment by the incoming partner goes directly to Coe, and there is **no change** in the assets or liabilities of the partnership. Regardless of the price received by Coe, the only entry required in the partnership accounts is to transfer the $100,000 balance in Coe's capital account into the capital account of the new partner. This transaction is virtually the same as the one described on page 669 for the admission of a new partner by purchase of an interest.

Now let us change this situation slightly and assume that Coe sells equal amounts of his equity in the business to his fellow partners, Acres and Bundy. If Acres and Bundy pay Coe from their **personal funds**, the assets and liabilities of the partnership are again unchanged. Regardless of the price Acres and Bundy pay to Coe, the transaction is recorded in the partnership accounting records merely by transferring the $100,000 in Coe's capital account into the capital accounts of the remaining two partners, as follows:

Notice there is no change in total capital

John Coe, Capital	100,000	
Chris Acres, Capital		50,000
Brit Bundy, Capital		50,000

To record the sale of Coe's interest to Acres and Bundy.

Coe's Interest Is Purchased by the Partnership Now let us assume that the partnership pays Coe in cash for his equity in the business. (The distribution of assets other than cash to a retiring partner will be discussed in advanced accounting courses.) If the partnership pays Coe exactly $100,000 cash for his equity—an amount equal to the balance in his capital account—the entry is simple: debit Coe's capital account $100,000 and credit Cash $100,000. However, the payment to Coe may be greater or less than the balance in his capital account.

Partnership Pays Coe More Than the Balance in His Capital Account A partner withdrawing from a partnership naturally expects to receive an amount for his or her equity that reflects the *current market value* of the partnership's net assets. Often, current market values exceed the book values appearing in the firm's balance sheet. For example, assets such as real estate may have appreciated greatly in value since they were acquired by the business. Also, if the business has been successful, it may have developed *unrecorded goodwill*.[3] Thus, the settlement paid to a retiring partner often is greater than the balance in the partner's capital account.

An amount paid to a retiring partner in excess of the balance in his or her capital account is treated as a *bonus to the withdrawing partner* and comes out of the capital accounts of the continuing partners. This bonus is charged against (debited to) the continuing partners' capital accounts in proportion to their *relative* income- and loss-sharing ratio.

The term *relative income-sharing ratio* describes the relationship between the income- and loss-sharing ratios of the continuing partners, excluding the share formerly received by the retiring partner. The relative income-and loss-sharing ratio of each continuing partner is computed by the following formula:

$$\frac{\text{Percentage Formerly Received by This Partner}}{\text{Total Percentage Formerly Received by All Continuing Partners}}$$

Based upon this formula, the relative income- and loss-sharing ratios of Acres and Bundy are as follows:

Acres (20% ÷ 50%) 40%
Bundy (30% ÷ 50%) 60%

Assume now that Coe receives **$140,000** in cash from the partnership in full settlement of his equity in the firm. As Coe's capital account has a balance of only $100,000, he is receiving a **$40,000 bonus** from Acres and Bundy. This bonus is charged against the capital accounts of Acres and Bundy in relation to their relative income- and loss-sharing ratios (Acres, 40%; Bundy, 60%). Thus, Coe's withdrawal from the firm is recorded as follows:

Bonus paid to withdrawing partner

John Coe, Capital (retiring partner)	*100,000*	
Chris Acres, Capital	*16,000*	
Brit Bundy, Capital	*24,000*	
Cash		*140,000*
To record the withdrawal of partner Coe, and payment of his capital account plus a bonus of $40,000. Bonus charged 40% to Acres, 60% to Bundy.		

---

[3] As discussed in Chapter 10, goodwill is recorded only when it is purchased.

Partnership Pays Coe Less Than the Balance in His Capital Account   Now assume that Coe is willing to accept a cash payment of **only $80,000** in full settlement of his $100,000 capital account. This situation might arise if, for example, Coe has a pressing need for cash or the future of the firm is jeopardized by contingent losses not yet recorded in its balance sheet accounts. In our example, the continuing partners' equity in the firm will *increase* by a total of $20,000 as a result of Coe's withdrawal. Acres and Bundy should divide this *"bonus to the continuing partners"* in their relative income- and loss-sharing ratios. The entry is:

Payment to withdrawing partner of less than book equity

John Coe, Capital	100,000	
Cash		80,000
Chris Acres		8,000
Brit Bundy		12,000

To record the withdrawal of Coe, and settlement in full for $20,000 less than the balance of his capital account. Bonus to continuing partners allocated 40% to Acres, 60% to Bundy.

Death of a Partner

A partnership is dissolved by the death of any member. To determine the amount owing to the estate of the deceased partner, it is usually necessary to close the accounts and prepare financial statements. This serves to credit all partners with their individual shares of the net income earned during the fractional accounting period ending with the date of **dissolution**.

The partnership agreement may prescribe procedures for making settlement with the estate of a deceased partner. Such procedures often include an audit by public accountants, appraisal of assets, and computation of goodwill. If payment to the estate must be delayed, the amount owed should be carried in a liability account replacing the deceased partner's capital account.

Insurance on Lives of Partners   Members of a partnership often obtain life insurance policies that name the partnership as the beneficiary. Upon the death of a partner, the cash collected from the insurance company is used to pay the estate of the deceased partner. In the absence of insurance on the lives of partners, there might be insufficient cash available to pay the deceased partner's estate without disrupting the operation of the business.

Liquidation of a Partnership

LO 8: Account for the liquidation of a partnership.

A partnership is terminated or dissolved whenever a new partner is added or an old partner withdraws. The termination or dissolution of a partnership, however, does not necessarily indicate that the business is to be discontinued. Often the business continues with scarcely any outward evidence of the change in membership of the firm. Termination of a partnership indicates a change in the membership of a firm, which may or may not be followed by liquidation.

The process of breaking up and discontinuing a partnership business is called **liquidation**. Liquidation of a partnership spells an end to the business. If the business is to be discontinued, the assets will be sold, the liabilities paid, and the remaining cash distributed to the partners.

Sale of the Business The partnership of Royal, Simms, and Tate sells its business to the North Corporation. The balance sheet appears as follows:

Partnership at time of sale

<table>
<tr><td colspan="4" align="center">**ROYAL, SIMMS, AND TATE**
Balance Sheet
December 31, 20__</td></tr>
<tr><td colspan="2" align="center">**Assets**</td><td colspan="2" align="center">**Liabilities & Partners' Equity**</td></tr>
<tr><td>Cash</td><td>$ 50,000</td><td>Accounts payable</td><td>$100,000</td></tr>
<tr><td>Inventory</td><td>200,000</td><td>Ann Royal, capital</td><td>140,000</td></tr>
<tr><td>Other assets</td><td>150,000</td><td>Ed Simms, capital</td><td>120,000</td></tr>
<tr><td></td><td></td><td>Jon Tate, capital</td><td>40,000</td></tr>
<tr><td>Total</td><td>$400,000</td><td>Total</td><td>$400,000</td></tr>
</table>

The terms of sale provide that the inventory and other assets will be sold to the North Corporation for a consideration of $230,000, a price resulting in a loss of $120,000. The liabilities will not be transferred to North Corporation, but will be paid by the partnership out of existing cash plus the proceeds of the sale, prior to any distribution of cash to the partners.

The entry to record the sale of the inventory and other assets to North Corporation is:

Entry to record the sale of the business

Cash	230,000	
Loss on Sale of Business	120,000	
Inventory		200,000
Other Assets		150,000

To record the sale of all assets other than cash to North Corporation

Division of the Gain or Loss from Sale of the Business The gain or loss from the sale of the business must be divided among the partners in the agreed income- and loss-sharing ratio **before** any cash is distributed to them. The amount of cash to which each partner is entitled in liquidation cannot be determined until each capital account has been increased or decreased by the proper share of the gain or loss on disposal of the assets. Assuming that Royal, Simms, and Tate share net income and losses equally, the entry to allocate the $120,000 loss on the sale of the business will be as follows:

Entry to divide loss on sale

Ann Royal, Capital	40,000	
Ed Simms, Capital	40,000	
Jon Tate, Capital	40,000	
Loss on Sale of Business		120,000

To divide the loss on the sale of the business among the partners in the established ratio for sharing net income and losses.

Distribution of Cash The balance sheet of Royal, Simms, and Tate appears as follows after the loss on the sale of the assets has been entered in the partners' capital accounts:

676 PARTNERSHIPS AND CORPORATIONS   PART 4

Balance sheet after sale of assets

ROYAL, SIMMS, AND TATE
Balance Sheet
(After the Sale of All Assets Except Cash)

Assets		Liabilities & Partners' Equity	
Cash	$280,000	Accounts payable	$100,000
		Ann Royal, capital	100,000
		Ed Simms, capital	80,000
		Jon Tate, capital	–0–
Total	$280,000	Total	$280,000

The creditors must be paid in full before cash is distributed to the partners. The sequence of entries will be as follows:

(1) Pay creditors

Accounts Payable	100,000	
Cash		100,000
To pay the creditors in full.		

(2) Pay partners

Ann Royal, Capital	100,000	
Ed Simms, Capital	80,000	
Cash		180,000
To complete liquidation of the business by distributing the remaining cash to the partners according to the balances in their capital accounts.		

Note that the equal division of the $120,000 loss on the sale of the business reduced the capital account of Jon Tate to zero; therefore, Tate received nothing when the cash was distributed to the partners. This action is consistent with the original agreement of the partners to share net income and losses equally. In working partnership liquidation problems, accounting students sometimes make the error of dividing the cash among the partners in the income- and loss-sharing ratio. An income- and loss-sharing ratio means just what the name indicates; it is a ratio for sharing net income and losses, *not a ratio for sharing cash or any other asset*. The amount of cash that a partner should receive in liquidation will be indicated by the balance in his or her capital account *after* the gain or loss from the disposal of assets has been divided among the partners in the agreed ratio for sharing net income and losses.

Treatment of Debit Balance in a Capital Account To illustrate this situation, let us change our assumptions concerning the sale of the assets by the firm of Royal, Simms, and Tate, and say that the partnership assets (except cash) are sold to North Corporation for $206,000. The amount of cash received by the partnership is $24,000 less than in the prior example, and the loss incurred on the sale of assets is *$144,000* rather than the *$120,000* previously illustrated. Tate's one-third share of a $144,000 loss would be $48,000, which would wipe out the $40,000 credit balance in his capital account and create an *$8,000 debit balance*. After the liabilities are paid, a balance sheet for the partnership would appear as follows:

ROYAL, SIMMS, AND TATE
Balance Sheet
(After the Sale of All Assets Except Cash)

Assets		Partners' Equity	
Cash	$156,000	Ann Royal, capital	$ 92,000
		Ed Simms, capital	72,000
		Jon Tate, capital (deficiency)	(8,000)
Total	$156,000	Total	$156,000

Tate now owes $8,000 to the partnership

To eliminate the debit balance in his capital account, Tate should pay $8,000 to the partnership. If Tate makes this payment, the balance in his capital account will become zero, and the cash on hand will be increased to $164,000, which is just enough to pay Royal and Simms the balances shown in their capital accounts.

If Tate is unable to pay the $8,000 due to the firm, how should the $156,000 of cash on hand be divided between Royal and Simms, whose capital accounts stand at $92,000 and $72,000, respectively? Failure of Tate to pay in the debit balance means an additional loss to Royal and Simms. According to the original partnership agreement, Royal and Simms have equal income- and loss-sharing ratios. Since partnership agreements generally specify that such a debit balance or deficiency be shared in the net income and loss ratio, let us assume that this was included in the liquidation provisions of the partnership agreement. Therefore, each must absorb $4,000 additional loss caused by Tate's inability to pay the $8,000 due to the partnership. The $156,000 of cash on hand should be divided between Royal and Simms in such a manner that the capital account of each will be paid down to $4,000, their respective shares of the additional loss. The journal entry to record this distribution of cash to Royal and Simms is as follows:

Entry to record distribution of cash on hand

Ann Royal, Capital	88,000	
Ed Simms, Capital	68,000	
Cash		156,000
To divide the remaining cash by paying down the capital accounts of Royal and Simms to a balance of $4,000 each, representing the division of Tate's loss between them.		

After this entry has been posted, the only accounts still open in the partnership records will be the capital accounts of the three partners. A trial balance of the ledger will appear as follows:

ROYAL, SIMMS, and TATE
Trial Balance
(After Distribution of Cash)

Trial balance after cash distribution

Ann Royal, capital		$4,000
Ed Simms, capital		4,000
Jon Tate, capital (deficiency)	$8,000	
	$8,000	$8,000

If Tate is able later to pay in the $8,000 debit balance, Royal and Simms will then receive the additional $4,000 each indicated by the credit balances in their accounts. However, if Tate is definitely unable to pay the $8,000, these accounts should be closed.

The sharing of a debit balance may become a rather difficult issue if the partnership agreement is silent or the partners fail to agree on how such a debit balance is to be shared. Even though there are provisions on this issue in the partnership legislation, they are potentially subject to different interpretations. One interpretation was provided in the English case *Garner v. Murray* (1904), where it was ruled that the debit balance was to be shared among the other partners in the ratio of their capital account balances as at the date of liquidation. The reason was that the debit balance was considered a personal debt of one partner to the other partners rather than a business or operating loss. As a practical matter, however, the issue of how the debit balance should be shared rarely arises, apparently because partnership agreements generally specify a method for such a situation.

In solving the problems on partnership liquidation in this text, it is assumed that the partnership agreement specifies the sharing of a debit balance of a partner's capital account by other partners in the net income and loss ratio.

End-of-Chapter Review

Key Terms Introduced or Emphasized in Chapter 13

Dissolution (of a partnership) *(p.674)* Termination of an existing partnership by any change in the personnel of the partners or by liquidating the business.

General partner *(p.658)* A partner in a limited partnership who has the traditional rights and responsibilities of a partner, including mutual agency and unlimited personal liability for the debts of the business.

Limited partner *(p.658)* A partner in a limited partnership who has the right to participate in income, but whose liability for losses is limited to the amount he or she has invested and who does not have the right to participate in management of the business. A limited partner's role is that of an investor rather than that of a traditional partner.

Limited partnership *(p.658)* A partnership that has one or more **limited partners** as well as one or more **general partners**. Limited partnerships are used primarily to attract investment capital from the limited partners for such ventures as mining and real estate development.

Liquidation of a partnership *(p.674)* The process of breaking up and discontinuing a partnership, including the sale of assets, payment of creditors, and distribution of remaining assets to the partners.

Mutual agency *(p.657)* Authority of each partner to act as agent for the partnership within its normal scope of operations and to enter into contracts that bind the partnership.

Partnership agreement *(p.658)* A contract among partners on the formation and operation of the partnership. Usually includes such points as a plan for sharing net income, amounts to be invested, and provision for dissolution and liquidation.

Statement of partners' equity *(p.662)* A financial statement that shows for each partner and for the firm the amounts of beginning capitals, additional investments, net income, drawings, and ending capitals.

DEMONSTRATION PROBLEM

The adjusted trial balance of Happy Times Party Store, a partnership, indicates the following account balances at the end of the current year:

	Debit	Credit
Cash	$ 18,800	
Accounts receivable	106,200	
Allowance for doubtful accounts		$ 3,000
Inventory	27,500	
Showroom fixtures	31,400	
Accumulated depreciation		6,400
Notes payable		8,000
Accounts payable		38,000
May Jones, capital		70,000
May Jones, drawing	32,000	
Al Lanid, capital		60,000
Al Lanid, drawing	24,000	
Sales		748,000
Cost of goods sold	491,000	
Selling expenses	110,000	
Administrative expenses	92,500	
Totals	$933,400	$933,400

There were no changes in partners' capital accounts during the year. Happy Times uses a perpetual inventory system. The partnership agreement provided that partners are to be allowed 15% interest on invested capital as of the beginning of the year and that the residual net income is to be divided equally.

INSTRUCTIONS

a. Prepare an income statement for the current year, using the appropriate accounts from the above list. At the bottom of the income statement, prepare a schedule showing the distribution of net income.

b. Prepare a statement of partners' equity for the current year.

c. Prepare a balance sheet at the end of the current year.

SOLUTION TO THE DEMONSTRATION PROBLEM

a.

HAPPY TIMES PARTY STORE
Income Statement
For Current Year

Sales			$748,000
Less: Cost of goods sold			491,000
Gross profit			$257,000
Operating expenses:			
Selling		$110,000	
Administrative		92,500	202,500
Net income			$ 54,500

	May Jones	Al Lanid	Total
Division of net income:			
Net income to be divided			$ 54,500
Interest allowances on beginning capital:			
May Jones ($70,000 × .15)	$10,500		
Al Lanid ($60,000 × .15)		$ 9,000	(19,500)
Remaining net income to be divided equally			$ 35,000
May Jones	17,500		
Al Lanid		17,500	(35,000)
Total share to each partner	$28,000	$ 26,500	$ -0-

b.

HAPPY TIMES PARTY STORE
Statement of Partners' Equity
For Current Year

	May Jones	Al Lanid	Total
Balance, beginning of year	$70,000	$60,000	$130,000
Add: Net income	28,000	26,500	54,500
Subtotal	$98,000	$86,500	$184,500
Less: Drawings	32,000	24,000	56,000
Balance, end of the year	$66,000	$62,500	$128,500

c.

HAPPY TIMES PARTY STORE
Balance Sheet
At End of Current Year

Assets

Current assets:
Cash		$ 18,800
Accounts receivable	$106,200	
Less: Allowance for doubtful accounts	3,000	103,200
Inventory		27,500
Total current assets		$149,500

Plant and equipment:
Showroom fixtures	$ 31,400	
Less: Accumulated depreciation	6,400	
Total plant and equipment		25,000
		$174,500

Liabilities & Partners' Equity

Current liabilities:
Notes payable		$ 8,000
Accounts payable		38,000
Total current liabilities		$ 46,000

Partners' equity:
May Jones, capital	$ 66,000	
Al Lanid, capital	62,500	
Total partners' equity		128,500
		$174,500

Self-Test Questions

The answers to these questions appear on page 694.

1. When a partnership is formed,
   a. A written partnership agreement, signed by all partners, must be filed in the jurisdiction in which the partnership is formed.
   b. Each partner may bind the business to contracts and may withdraw an unlimited amount of assets from the partnership, unless these rights are limited in the partnership agreement.
   c. Each member of the partnership is entitled to participate equally in the net income of and management of the partnership, unless the partnership is a limited partnership.
   d. The partnership must file an income tax return and pay income taxes on its net income.

2. Carter and Dixie have capital account balances of $80,000 and $100,000, respectively, at the beginning of 2000. Their partnership agreement provides for interest on beginning capital account balances, 10%; salaries to Carter, $30,000, and to Dixie, $24,000; residual income or loss divided 60% to Carter and 40% to Dixie. Partnership net income for 2000 is $62,000. Neither partner made any additional investment in the partnership during 2000, but Carter withdrew $1,500 monthly and Dixie withdrew $1,000 monthly throughout 2000. The partnership balance sheet at December 31, 2000, should include:
   a. Carter, Capital, $94,000
   b. Carter, Capital, $100,000

c. Dixie, Capital, $30,000
　　d. Total partners' equity, $242,000

3. Quinn and Ryan are partners who divide net income and losses 30% to Quinn and 70% to Ryan. At the present time, Quinn's capital account balance is $80,000 and Ryan's capital account balance is $160,000. Stone is admitted to a one-third equity interest in the partnership for an investment of $60,000. Each of the following statements relating to the admission of Stone is true with the exception of:
   a. Quinn has a capital account balance of $68,000 after recording Stone's admission.
   b. Stone has a capital account balance of $60,000 upon his admission to the partnership.
   c. Stone received a "bonus" of $40,000 from Quinn and Ryan.
   d. Total capital (equity) of the new partnership is $300,000 after Stone's admission is recorded.

4. Link, Martin, and Nolan are partners dividing net income and losses 30% to Link, 40% to Martin, and 30% to Nolan. Their capital accounts are as follows: Link, $500,000; Martin, $100,000; Nolan, $400,000. Nolan decides to retire and receives $393,000 from the partnership in exchange for his equity interest. Recording Nolan's withdrawal involves:
   a. A debit to Nolan's capital account for $393,000.
   b. Debits to Link's and to Martin's capital accounts for $3,500 each.
   c. A credit to Link's capital account for $3,000 and a credit to Martin's capital account for $4,000.
   d. Credits to Link's and to Martin's capital accounts for $200,000 each.

5. When a partnership is liquidated:
   a. Any cash distribution to partners is allocated according to the income- and loss-sharing ratios.
   b. Cash is distributed to each partner in an amount equal to his or her capital account balance prior to the sale of partnership assets.
   c. Any gain or loss on disposal of partnership assets is divided among the partners according to their relative capital account balances.
   d. A partner who maintained a credit balance in his or her capital account prior to liquidation may end up owing cash to the partnership if partnership assets are sold at a loss.

Assignment Material

Discussion Questions

1. Pauline David is the proprietor of a small manufacturing business. She is considering the possibility of joining in partnership with Sonia Lansing, whom she considers to be thoroughly competent and congenial. Prepare a brief statement outlining the advantages and disadvantages of the potential partnership to Pauline David.

2. Allen Bruce and Doug Cherry are considering forming a partnership. What do you think are the two most important factors for them to include in their partnership agreement?

3. What is meant by the term *mutual agency*?

4. A real estate development business is managed by two experienced developers and is financed by 50 investors from throughout the country. To allow maximum income tax benefits to the investors, the business is organized as a partnership. Explain why this type of business would probably be a limited partnership rather than a conventional (general) partnership.

5. What factors should be considered in drawing up an agreement as to the way in which net income shall be shared by two or more partners?

6. Scott has land having a book value of $50,000 and a current market value of $80,000 and a building having a book value of $70,000 and a current market value of $60,000. The land and building become Scott's sole capital contribution to a partnership. Assuming no bonus to any partner, what is Scott's capital balance in the new partnership? Why?

7. Is it possible that a partnership agreement containing interest and salary allowances as a step toward dividing net income could cause a partnership net loss to be distributed so that one partner's capital account would be decreased by *more* than the amount of the entire partnership net loss?

8. Partner John Young has a choice to make. His partners have offered him a choice between no salary allowance and a one-third share in the partnership net income or a salary of $16,000 per year and a one-quarter share of residual income. Explain the factors he should consider in reaching a decision.

9. Helen Lee withdraws $25,000 from a partnership during the year. When the financial statements are prepared at the end of the year, Lee's share of the partnership net income is $45,000. Which amount must Lee report on her income tax return?

10. What factors should be considered when comparing the net income figure of a partnership to that of a corporation of similar size?

11. How should the adequacy of the net income of a partnership be evaluated? Explain.

12. Explain the factors that are important in evaluating the solvency of a partnership.

13. Explain the difference between being admitted to a partnership by buying an equity interest from an existing partner and by making an investment in the partnership.

14. If C is going to be admitted to the partnership of A and B, why is it first necessary to determine the current market value of the assets of the partnership of A and B?

15. Shirley Bray and Carl Carter are partners who share net income and losses equally. The current balances in their capital accounts are: Bray, $50,000; Carter, $35,000. If Carter sells his equity interest in the firm to Jon Deacon for $70,000 and Bray consents to the sale, what entry should be made in the partnership accounting records?

16. Farley invests $80,000 cash in the partnership of Dale and Erskin, but is granted an equity interest of only $60,000 upon his admission to the partnership. What is the nature of the $20,000 difference between the amount invested by Farley and the equity interest he received? How is this $20,000 difference handled in the partnership accounting records?

17. Majors, who has a capital account balance of $90,000, received cash of $120,000 from the partnership of Linden, Majors, & Napp upon his retirement. Discuss the nature of the $30,000 paid to Majors in excess of his capital account balance and how this excess payment is handled in the partnership books upon Majors' withdrawal.

18. Describe how a *liquidation* of a partnership may differ from a *dissolution* of a partnership.

19. What measure can you suggest to prevent a partnership from having insufficient cash available to pay the estate of a deceased partner without disrupting the operation of the business?

20. Upon the death of Robert Bell, a partner in the firm of Bell, Cross, and Davis, Charles Bell, the son of Robert Bell, demanded that he replace his father as a member of the partnership. Can Charles Bell enforce this demand? Explain.

Exercises

EXERCISE 13-1
Accounting Terminology
(LO 1-8)

Listed below are nine technical terms introduced in this chapter:

Unlimited liability *Partnership agreement* *Dissolution of partnership*
Liquidation *Current market value* *Interest on partners' capital*
General partner *Limited partner* *Partnership net income*

Each of the following statements may (or may not) describe one of these technical terms. For each statement, indicate the accounting term described, or answer "None" if the statement does not correctly describe any of the terms.

a. Serves to identify partners, specify capital contributions, and establish income-sharing formula.
b. The process of breaking up and discontinuing a partnership business.
c. Amounts to be entered in asset accounts of a partnership to record the investment of noncash assets by partners.
d. A method of dividing partnership net income to ensure that no partner's share of net income will be less than the prime rate of interest applied to his or her capital account.
e. A characteristic of the partnership type of organization that causes many wealthy investors to choose investments in limited partnerships or corporations rather than in regular partnerships.
f. Results from the retirement of a partner from the firm or the admission of a new partner.
g. A partner whose financial responsibility does not exceed the amount of his or her investment and who does not actively participate in management.
h. An income-sharing provision designed to compensate for differences in dollar amounts invested by different partners.

EXERCISE 13-2
Formation of a Partnership
(LO 4)

A business owned by Ann Bowen was short of cash and Bowen therefore decided to form a partnership with Andy McKuen, who was able to contribute cash to the new partnership. The assets contributed by Bowen appeared as follows in the balance sheet of her business: cash, $800; accounts receivable, $32,700, with an allowance for doubtful accounts of $760; inventory, $47,800, and store equipment, $21,600. Bowen had recorded depreciation of $1,800 during her use of the store equipment in her sole proprietorship.

Bowen and McKuen agreed that the allowance for doubtful accounts was inadequate and should be $1,900. They also agreed that a current market value for the inventory was $56,000 and that the current market value of the store equipment was $19,100. You are to open the partnership accounts by making a general journal entry to record the investment by Bowen.

EXERCISE 13-3
Partners' Capital and Drawing Accounts
(LO 4)

Explain briefly the effect of each of the transactions given below on a partner's capital and drawing accounts:
a. Partner borrows funds from the business.
b. Partner collects a partnership account receivable while on vacation and uses the funds for personal purposes.
c. Partner receives in cash the salary allowance provided in the partnership agreement.
d. Partner takes home merchandise (cost $80, selling price $120; sales and goods and services taxes included) for personal use.
e. Partner has loaned money to the partnership. The principal together with interest at 15% is now repaid to the partner in cash.

EXERCISE 13-4
Dividing Partnership Income
(LO 5)

Guenther and Firmin, both of whom are public accountants, form a partnership, with Guenther investing $100,000 and Firmin, $80,000. They agree to share net income as follows:
1. Salary allowances of $80,000 to Guenther and $60,000 to Firmin.
2. Interest allowances at 15% of beginning capital account balances.
3. Any partnership net income in excess of the amount required to cover the interest and salary allowances to be divided 60% to Guenther and 40% to Firmin.

INSTRUCTIONS

The partnership net income for the first year of operations amounted to $267,000 before interest and salary allowances. Show how this $267,000 should be divided between the two partners. Use a three-column schedule of the type illustrated in this chapter. List on separate lines the amounts of interest, salaries, and the residual amount divided.

EXERCISE 13-5
Admission of a New Partner; Bonus to Old Partners
(LO 7)

Abrams and Boling are partners with capital account balances of $102,000 and $63,000. They divide net income and losses one-third to Abrams and two-thirds to Boling. The partnership has been quite profitable and has an excellent reputation. Abrams and Boling agree to admit Cato to a one-third equity interest in the partnership for an investment of $105,000. The assets of the business are *not* to be revalued. Explain how the bonus to the old partners is computed and prepare a general journal entry to record the admission of Cato.

EXERCISE 13-6
Admission of a New Partner; Bonus Computation
(LO 7)

Randall and Dirks are partners who divide net income and losses 60% to Randall and 40% to Dirks. At the present time, each partner's capital account balance is $140,000. Randall and Dirks agree to admit Foster to a one-fourth equity interest in the partnership for an investment of $75,000. Prepare a general journal entry to record the admission of Foster. Explain how any bonus (to existing partners *or* to the incoming partner) is computed.

EXERCISE 13-7
Withdrawal of a Partner
(LO 7)

The capital accounts of the Triple D partnership are as follows: Drake, $90,000; Dunlap, $210,000; Dyson, $180,000. Net income and losses are allocated 25% to Drake, 50% to Dunlap, and 25% to Dyson. Dyson is withdrawing from the partnership and it is agreed that he shall be paid $240,000 for his interest because the earnings of the business are high in relation to the assets of the firm. Assuming that the excess of the settlement over the amount of Dyson's capital account is to be recorded as a bonus to Dyson, prepare a general journal entry to record Dyson's retirement from the firm.

EXERCISE 13-8
Liquidation of a Partnership
(LO 8)

The CDE partnership is being liquidated. After all liabilities have been paid and all assets sold, the balances of the partners' capital accounts are as follows: Cooley, $42,000 credit balance; Dean, $16,000 ***debit*** balance; Emmett, $53,000 credit balance. The partners share net income and losses: Cooley, 10%; Dean, 60%; Emmet, 30%.

a. How should the available cash (the only remaining asset) be distributed if it is impossible to determine at this date whether Dean will be able to pay the $16,000 he owes the firm? Draft the journal entry to record payment of all available cash at this time.

b. Draft the journal entries to record a subsequent partial payment of $13,000 to the firm by Dean, and the distribution of this cash. Prepare a schedule (similar to the one prepared in part **a**) showing computation of amount to be distributed to each partner.

Problems

PROBLEM 13-1
Formation of a Partnership; Closing the Income Summary Account
(LO 4)

Ambrose Lee and Oliver French formed a partnership (Lee and French) on January 1 by investing assets from their respective businesses. The investment by the two partners is as follows:

	Ambrose Lee		Oliver French	
	Book value	Market value	Book value	Market value
Cash	$10,000	$10,000		
Accounts receivable	29,000	26,000	$81,680	$79,600
Inventory	48,000	50,000	11,400	13,200
Office equipment (net)			14,300	8,600

Also, it is agreed that French will transfer his business liabilities (accounts payable) of $15,400 to the partnership. Lee and French will share the partnership net income and losses equally.

INSTRUCTIONS

a. Draft entries (in general journal form) to record the investments of Lee and French in the new partnership.

b. Prepare the beginning balance sheet of the partnership (in report form) at the close of business January 1, reflecting the above transfers to the firm.

c. On December 31, after one year of operation, the Income Summary account showed a credit balance of $82,000 and the Drawing account for each partner showed a debit balance of $35,000. Prepare journal entries to close the Income Summary account and the Drawing accounts at December 31.

PROBLEM 13-2
Formation of a Partnership; Closing the Income Summary Account
(LO 4)

The partnership of Barton and Avery was formed on July 2, when Tina Barton and Sam Avery agreed to invest equal amounts and to share net income and losses equally. The investment by Barton consists of $30,000 cash and an inventory of merchandise valued at $66,000.

Avery also is to contribute a total of $96,000. However, it is agreed that his contribution will consist of the following assets of his business along with the transfer to the partnership of his business liabilities. The agreed values of the various items as well as their carrying values on Avery's records are listed below. Avery also contributes enough cash to bring his capital account to $96,000.

	Investment by Avery	
	Book value	Agreed value
Accounts receivable	$88,600	$88,600
Allowance for doubtful accounts	5,840	7,000
Inventory	9,800	13,800
Office equipment (net)	11,600	8,000
Accounts payable	28,800	28,800

INSTRUCTIONS

a. Draft entries (in general journal form) to record the investments of Barton and Avery in the new partnership.
b. Prepare the beginning balance sheet of the partnership (in report form) at the close of business July 2, reflecting the above transfers to the firm.
c. On the following June 30 after one year of operation, the Income Summary account showed a credit balance of $88,000 and the Drawing account for each partner showed a debit balance of $30,000. Prepare journal entries to close the Income Summary account and the Drawing accounts at June 30.

PROBLEM 13-3
Analysis of Partnership Accounts
(LO 4,6)

Lucky Burger is a fast food restaurant that is operated as a partnership of three individuals. The three partners share net income equally. Presented below are selected account balances for the current year before any closing entries are made.

	Debit	Credit
Glen, Capital		55,000
Chow, Capital		60,000
West, Capital		5,000
Glen, Drawing	15,000	
Chow, Drawing	15,000	
West, Drawing	30,000	
Income Summary		75,000

INSTRUCTIONS

On the basis of this information, answer the following questions and show any necessary computations.

a. How much must each of the three partners report on his individual income tax return related to this business?
b. Prepare a Statement of Partners' Equity for the current year ended December 31, 20__. Assume that no partner has made an additional investment during the year.
c. Assuming that each of the partners devote the same amount of time to the business, why might Glen and Chow consider the income-sharing agreement to be inequitable?
d. What factors should the partners consider when evaluating whether the net income from the partnership is adequate?

PROBLEM 13-4
Dividing Partnership Income; Financial Statements
(LO 4,5)

S&H Co-op's adjusted trial balance indicates the following account balances at the end of the current year:

	Debit	Credit
Cash	$ 22,620	
Accounts receivable (net)	71,000	
Inventory	28,200	
Prepaid expenses	3,900	
Equipment	190,000	
Accumulated depreciation		$ 38,000
Notes payable		9,600
Accounts payable		38,520
Accrued expenses		2,880
Bolton, capital (beginning of year)		70,000
Bolton, drawing	10,080	
Gorman, capital (beginning of year)		60,000
Gorman, drawing	7,200	
Sales		708,960
Cost of goods sold	390,960	
Selling expenses	112,380	
Administrative expenses	91,620	
Totals	$927,960	$927,960

A perpetual inventory system is used by the company. The partnership agreement provided that partners are to be allowed 10% interest on invested capital as of the beginning of the year and that the residual net income is to be divided equally.

INSTRUCTIONS

a. Prepare an income statement for the current year and, at the bottom of the income statement, prepare a schedule showing the division of net income.
b. Prepare a statement of partners' equity for the current year and a balance sheet at the end of the current year.

PROBLEM 13-5
Various Methods for Dividing Partnership Net Income
(LO 4,5)
INSTRUCTIONS

Alicia Dunn and Roberto Pascal, both real estate appraisers, formed a partnership, with Dunn investing $40,000 and Pascal investing $60,000. During the first year, the net income of the partnership amounted to $45,000.

a. Determine how the $45,000 net income would be divided under each of the following four independent assumptions as to the agreement for sharing net income and losses. Using schedules of the types illustrated in this chapter, show all steps in the division of net income between the partners.
   1. The partnership agreement does not mention income sharing.
   2. Interest at 15% to be allowed on beginning capital investments and balance to be divided equally.
   3. Salaries of $24,000 to Dunn and $20,000 to Pascal; balance to be divided equally.
   4. Salaries of $18,000 to Dunn and $26,000 to Pascal; interest at 15% to be allowed on beginning capital investments; balance to be divided equally.
b. Prepare the journal entry to close the Income Summary account, using the division of net income developed in part 4 above.

PROBLEM 13-6
Sharing Partnership Net Income: Various Methods
(LO 4,5)
INSTRUCTIONS

A small nightclub called Comedy Tonight was organized as a partnership with Lewis investing $90,000 and Martin investing $110,000. During the first year, net income amounted to $100,000.

a. Determine how the $100,000 net income would be divided under each of the following three independent assumptions as to the agreement for sharing net income and losses. Use schedules of the type illustrated in this chapter to show all steps in the division of net income between the partners.

1. Net income is to be divided in a fixed ratio: 40% to Lewis and 60% to Martin.
2. Interest at 15% to be allowed on beginning capital investments and balance to be divided equally.
3. Salaries of $36,000 to Lewis and $56,000 to Martin; interest at 15% to be allowed on beginning capital investments; balance to be divided equally.

b. Prepare the journal entry to close the Income Summary account, using the division of net income developed in part 3 above.

PROBLEM 13-7
Dividing Partnership Net Income and Loss
(LO 5)

Financial Planning consultants has three partners—Axle, Brandt, and Conrad. During the current year their capital balances were: Axle, $180,000; Brandt, $140,000; and Conrad, $80,000. The partnership agreement provides that partners shall receive salary allowances as follows: Axle, $10,000; Brandt, $50,000; Conrad, $28,000. The partners shall also be allowed 12% interest annually on their capital balances. Residual net income or loss is to be divided: Axle, one-half; Brandt, one-third; Conrad, one-sixth.

INSTRUCTIONS

Prepare separate schedules showing how net income will be divided among the three partners in each of the following cases.
a. Net income of $526,000
b. Net income of $67,000
c. Net loss of $32,000

PROBLEM 13-8
Dividing Partnership Net Income and Loss
(LO 5)

Executive Financial planners has three partners—Reed, Stein, and Trump. At the beginning their capital balances were: Reed, $120,000; Stein, $100,000; and Trump $80,000. The partnership agreement provides that partners shall receive salary allowances as follows: Reed, none; Stein, $60,000; and Trump, $38,000. The partners shall also be allowed 12% interest annually on their beginning capital balances. Residual income or loss is to be divided: Reed, 50%; Stein, 30%; Trump, 20%.

INSTRUCTIONS

Prepare separate schedules showing how net income or loss will be divided among the three partners in each of the following cases. The figure given in each case is the annual partnership net income or loss to be allocated among the partners.
a. Net income of $554,000
b. Net income of $83,000
c. Net loss of $19,000

PROBLEM 13-9
Admission of a New Partner
(LO 7)

Art of Asia is a partnership organized by Howell and So. On this date the two partners agreed to admit a new partner, Lee. Howell and So have been dividing net income in a ratio of 3:2 (that is, 60% and 40%). The new partnership will have an income- and loss-sharing ratio of Lee, 50%; Howell, 25%; and So, 25%. The following is the condensed balance sheet at September 30.

ART OF ASIA
Balance Sheet
September 30

Assets		Liabilities & Partners' Equity		
Current assets	$180,000	Liabilities		$160,000
Plant & equipment (net)	420,000	Partners' equity:		
		Howell, cap.	$280,000	
		So, cap.	160,000	440,000
Total	$600,000	Total		$600,000

INSTRUCTIONS

Described below are four different situations under which Lee might be admitted to partnership. Considering each independently, prepare the journal entries necessary to record the admission of Lee to the firm.

a. Lee purchases a one-half equity interest in the partnership from Howell for $280,000. Payment is made to Howell as an individual.
b. Lee purchases one-half of Howell's equity interest and one-half of So's equity interest, paying Howell $170,000 and So $100,000.
c. Lee invests $300,000 in the firm and receives a one-half interest in capital and net income. In addition to the journal entry to record Lee's admission, show computation of the equity interest received and bonus (if any) to either the old partners or to Lee.
d. Lee invests $560,000 in the firm and receives a one-half interest in the capital and net income of the business. In addition to the journal entry to record Lee's admission, show computation of the equity interest received and bonus (if any) to either the old partners or to Lee.

PROBLEM 13-10
Admission of a New Partner
(LO 7)

Algonquin Lodge is a partnership with a record of profitable operations. At the end of the current year the capital accounts of the three partners and the ratio for sharing net income and losses are as shown in the following schedule. At this date, it is agreed that a new partner, Wolfgang Ritter, is to be admitted to the firm.

	Capital	Income-Sharing Ratio
Olga Svenson	$300,000	60%
Jill Kidd	240,000	30%
Miles Kohl	180,000	10%

INSTRUCTIONS

For each of the following situations involving the admission of Ritter to the partnership, give the necessary journal entry to record his admission.

a. Ritter purchases one-half of Kidd's equity interest in the firm, paying Kidd personally $160,000.
b. Ritter buys a one-quarter equity interest in the firm for $210,000 by purchasing one-fourth of the present equity interest of each of the three partners. Ritter pays the three individuals directly.
c. Ritter invests $200,000 in the firm and receives a one-fourth interest in the equity and net income of the business. In addition to the journal entry to record Ritter's admission, show computation of the equity interest received and bonus (if any) to either the old partners or to Ritter.
d. Ritter invests $340,000 in the firm and receives a one-fourth interest in the equity and net income of the business. In addition to the journal entry to record Ritter's admission, show computation of the equity interest received and bonus (if any) to either the old partners or to Ritter.

PROBLEM 13-11
Withdrawal of a Partner
(LO 7)

Hull Management is a partnership of three individuals that specializes in the management of professional office buildings. The partnership owns and maintains offices in one such professional centre and provides management services for several other buildings owned by clients. At the end of the current year, the firm had the following balance sheet:

HULL MANAGEMENT
Balance Sheet
December 31, 20__

Assets		Liabilities & Partners' Equity		
Cash	$215,000	Liabilities		$268,000
Receivables	70,000	Partners' equity:		
Land	220,000	Spence, capital	$264,000	
Building (net of accumulated depreciation)	310,000	Carver, capital	180,000	
		Drake, capital	168,000	612,000
Furniture & fixtures (net of accumulated depreciation)	65,000			
Total	$880,000	Total		$880,000

The partners share net income and losses in the ratio of 50% to Spence, 30% to Carver, and 20% to Drake. It is agreed that Drake is to withdraw from the partnership on this date.

INSTRUCTIONS

Following are a number of different assumptions involving the withdrawal of Drake from the firm. Considering each case independently, prepare the general journal entry or entries needed to record Drake's withdrawal.

a. Drake, with the permission of the other partners, gives his equity to his brother-in-law, Holmes, who is accepted as a partner in the firm.

b. Drake sells one-fourth of his equity interest to Carver for $38,000 cash and sells the other three-fourths to Spence for $114,000 cash. The payments are made by Carver and Spence personally and not by the partnership.

c. Drake retires and agrees to accept as full settlement of his partnership interest $120,000 cash and accounts receivable having a book value of $36,000. These assets come from the firm. The partners agree that no revaluation of assets will be made.

d. The partners agree that land is worth $390,000 at present market prices. They do not wish to write up this asset in the accounts but believe that Drake is entitled to a settlement that includes his 20% interest in the increase in value. Drake is paid $96,000 in cash and given a 2-year, 12% note for $108,000.

PROBLEM 13-12
Retirement of a Partner
(LO 7)

In the partnership of Global Travel Agency, the partners' capital accounts at the end of the current year were as follows: Roy Kim, $220,000; Susan John, $148,000; and Mark Ray, $60,000. The partnership agreement provides that net income will be shared 40% to Kim, 50% to John, and 10% to Ray. At this time Kim decides to retire from the firm.

INSTRUCTIONS

Described below are a number of independent situations involving the retirement of Kim. In each case prepare the journal entries necessary to reflect the withdrawal of Kim from the firm.

a. Kim sells three-fourths of his equity interest to Ray for $204,000 and the other one-fourth to John for $68,000. The payments to Kim are made from the personal funds of Ray and John, not from the partnership.

b. Kim accepts $90,000 in cash and a patent having a book value of $100,000 in full payment for his equity interest in the firm. This payment consists of a transfer of partnership assets to the retiring partner. As the fair value of the patent is approximately $100,000, the continuing partners agree that a revaluation of assets is not needed.

c. Kim receives $100,000 in cash and a 10-year, 12% note for $180,000 in full payment for his equity interest. Assets are not to be revalued.

PROBLEM 13-13
Liquidation of a Partnership
(LO 8)

The partnership of MNP Talent Scouts has ended its operations and is in the process of liquidation. All assets except for cash and accounts receivable have already been sold. The task of collecting the accounts receivable is now to be carried out as rapidly as possible. The general ledger balances are as follows:

	Debit	Credit
Cash	$ 54,400	
Accounts receivable	233,600	
Allowance for doubtful accounts		$12,800
Liabilities		73,600
May, capital (income-loss share 30%)		86,400
Nix, capital (income-loss share 50%)		67,200
Peat, capital (income-loss share 20%)		48,000

INSTRUCTIONS

For each of the two independent situations shown below, prepare journal entries to record the collection or sale of the receivables, the payment of liabilities, and the distribution of all remaining cash to the partners. Support all entries with adequate explanation; the entries for distribution of cash to the partners should have explanations showing how the amounts were determined.

a. Collections of $132,800 are made on receivables, and the remainder are deemed uncollectible.

b. Receivables are sold to a collection agency; the partnership receives in cash as a final settlement 30% of the gross amount of its receivables. The personal financial status of the partners is uncertain, but all available cash is to be distributed at this time.

PROBLEM 13-14
Liquidation; Insolvent Partners
(LO 8)

The December 31 balance sheet of MRC Associates, a partnership specializing in market research and consulting, appears below. In order to focus attention on the principles involved in liquidating a partnership, the balance sheet has been shortened by combining all assets other than cash under the caption of "Other assets."

Merit, Rush, and Carroll share net income in a ratio of 3:2:1, respectively. At the date of the balance sheet the partners decided to liquidate the business.

MRC ASSOCIATES
Balance Sheet
December 31, 20__

Assets		Liabilities & Partners' Equity	
Cash	$ 90,000	Liabilities	$180,000
Other assets	450,000	Partners' equity:	
		Merit, cap. $135,000	
		Rush, cap. 120,000	
		Carroll, cap. 105,000	360,000
Total	$540,000	Total	$540,000

INSTRUCTIONS

For each of the three independent situations shown below, prepare journal entries to record the sale of the "other assets," payment of liabilities, division of the loss on the sale of "other assets" among the partners, and distribution of the available cash to the partners. Support all entries with adequate explanation;

the entries for distribution of cash to the partners should have explanations showing how the amounts were determined.

a. Other assets are sold for $378,000.
b. Other assets are sold for $144,000. Each partner has personal assets and will contribute the amount necessary to cover any debit balance in his or her capital account that may arise in the liquidation process.
c. Other assets are sold for $117,000. Rush has personal assets and will contribute any necessary amount. Merit and Carroll are both personally bankrupt; any deficiency in either capital account must be absorbed by remaining partners.

Analytical and Decision Problems and Cases

A&D 13-1
Reasons for and Problems of Partnership
(LO 1, 2, 3)

Interview the partners of a local small business. Focus on the flowing:
- Why was the business organized as a partnership?
- Have there been any unforeseen complications resulting from the partnership form of organization?
- Is the partnership form of organization likely to be changed to a corporation in the foreseeable future? And if so, why?

(*Note:* All interviews are to be conducted in accordance with the guidelines discussed in the Preface of this textbook.)

A&D 13-2
Developing an Equitable Plan for Dividing Partnership Income
(LO 4, 6)

Alan Bruce and Juan Foster are considering forming a partnership to engage in the business of aerial photography. Bruce is a licensed pilot, is currently earning $48,000 a year, and has $50,000 to invest in the partnership. Foster is a professional photographer who is currently earning $30,000 a year. He has recently inherited $70,000 that he plans to invest in the partnership.

Both partners will work full-time in the business. After careful study, they have estimated that expenses are likely to exceed revenue by $10,000 during the first year of operations. In the second year, however, they expect the business to become profitable, with revenue exceeding expenses by an estimated $90,000. (Bear in mind that these estimates of expenses do not include any salaries or interest to the partners.) Under present market conditions, a fair rate of return on capital invested in this type of business is 20%.

INSTRUCTIONS

a. On the basis of this information, prepare a brief description of the income-sharing agreement that you would recommend for Bruce and Foster. Explain the basis for your proposal.
b. Prepare a separate schedule for each of the next two years showing how the estimated amounts of net income would be divided between the two partners under your plan. (Assume that the original capital balances for both partners remain unchanged during the 2-year period. This simplifying assumption allows you to ignore the changes that would normally occur in capital accounts as a result of divisions of net income, or from drawings or additional investments.)
c. Write a brief statement explaining the differences in allocation of income to the two partners and defending the results indicated by your income-sharing proposal.

A&D 13-3
An Offer of Partnership
(LO 2, 4, 5, 6)

Upon graduation from university, Ray Bradshaw began work as a staff assistant for a national CA firm. During the next few years, Bradshaw received his CA certificate and was promoted to the level of senior on the firm's audit staff.

At this time, Bradshaw received an offer from a small local CA firm, Ames and Bolt, to join that firm as a third partner. Both Ames and Bolt have been working much overtime and they would expect a similar workload from Bradshaw. Ames and Bolt draw salaries of $60,000 each and share residual income equally. They offer Bradshaw a $60,000 salary plus one-third of residual income. The offer provides for Bradshaw to receive a one-third equity interest in the firm and requires him to make a cash investment of $120,000. Balance sheet data for the firm of Ames and Bolt are as follows:

Current assets	$ 72,000	Current liabilities	$ 36,000
Property & equipment	288,000	Long-term liabilities	174,000
		Ames, capital	75,000
		Bolt, capital	75,000
Total	$360,000	Total	$360,000

Projected net income of the local CA firm for the next four years is estimated below. These estimated earnings are before partners' salaries and are based on the assumption that Bradshaw joins the firm and makes possible an increased volume of business.

1st year	$192,000	3rd year	$228,000
2nd year	$204,000	4th year	$240,000

If Bradshaw decides to continue in his present position with the national CA firm rather than join the local firm, he estimates that his salary over the next four years will be as follows:

1st year	$62,000	3rd year	$73,000
2nd year	$66,000	4th year	$80,000

INSTRUCTIONS

a. Assuming that Bradshaw accepts the offer from Ames and Bolt, determine the amount of his beginning capital and prepare the entry in the partnership accounts to record Bradshaw's admission to the firm.
b. Compute the yearly amounts of Bradshaw's income from the partnership for the next four years. Compare these amounts with the salary that he will receive if he continues in his present employment and write a memo explaining the factors Bradshaw should consider in deciding whether to accept or decline the offer from Ames and Bolt.
c. Assuming that Bradshaw declines the offer, suggest some alternatives that he might propose if he decides to present a counteroffer to Ames and Bolt.

A&D 13-4
How Would Cash be Distributed?
(LO 8)

Iris, Jack, and Keith are partners and have the following balances in their capital accounts: Iris, $30,000; Jack, $90,000; and Keith, $60,000. The partnership has $8,000 cash and has other assets, and owes its creditors $220,000. The three partners share income or loss as follows: 3:2:1.

Assume that the other (non-cash) assets are sold for $152,000 cash and the partnership is liquidated. Keith is personally solvent and will contribute any amount for which he is liable. Iris and Jack both have personal debts in excess of their personal assets.

INSTRUCTIONS

Show how the cash should be distributed.

Answers to Self-Test Questions

1. b **2.** a **3.** b **4.** c **5.** d

CHAPTER 14

Corporations: Organization and Shareholders' Equity

"If a venture puts *my* capital at risk, it should be organized as a corporation." —Investor's proverb.

CHAPTER LEARNING OBJECTIVES

1. Discuss the advantages and disadvantages of organizing a business as a corporation.
2. Distinguish between publicly owned and closely held corporations.
3. Explain the rights of shareholders and the roles of corporate directors and officers.
4. Explain the nature of retained earnings; account for dividends and prepare closing entries.
5. Account for the issuance of capital stock; prepare the equity section of a corporate balance sheet.
6. Discuss the features of preferred stock and common stock.
7. Explain the significance of book value and market value of capital stock.
8. Discuss the factors affecting the market price of preferred stock and of common stock.

The corporate form is the "organization of choice" for many businesses—large and small. The owners of a corporation are called **shareholders**. In many small corporations, there are only one or two shareholders. But in large corporations, such as BCE, TransCanada Pipelines, and Canadian Pacific, there are literally thousands.

A **corporation** is the only form of business organization recognized under the law as a **legal entity**, with rights and responsibilities *separate from those of its owners*. The assets of a corporation belong to the corporation *itself*, not to the shareholders. The corporation is responsible for its own debts, and must pay income taxes on its earnings. As a "separate legal entity," a corporation has status in court; it may enter into contracts, and it may sue and be sued as if it were a person.

Why Businesses Incorporate

There are many reasons why businesses incorporate, but the two of greatest importance are (1) limited shareholder liability, and (2) transferability of ownership.

We have previously discussed the concept of **limited liability** *(limited personal liability)*. This simply means that shareholders have no *personal* liability for the debts of the corporation. Thus, if the corporation becomes insolvent, the most that a shareholder usually can lose is the amount of his or her equity investment. In this era of multi-million dollar lawsuits, limited personal liability appeals to the owners of large and small businesses alike.

Another special feature of the corporation is the ***transferability of ownership***—the idea that ownership is represented by transferable shares of **capital stock**. For a small, family-owned business, this provides a convenient means of gradually transferring ownership and control of the business from one generation to the next. For a large company, it makes ownership of the business a ***highly liquid investment***, which can be purchased and sold in organized securities exchanges.[1] This liquidity is essential to a large corporation's being able to raise equity capital from thousands—perhaps millions—of individual investors.

---

[1] These securities exchanges include, among others, the Toronto Stock Exchange, the Montreal Stock Exchange, the Vancouver Stock Exchange, Alberta Stock Exchange, Winnipeg Stock Exchange, the New York Stock Exchange, the National Association of Securities Dealers' Automated Quotations (NASDAQ), the Tokyo Stock Exchange, and Mexico's Bolsa. Collectively, stock exchanges often are described simply as ***"the stock market."***

LO 1: Discuss the advantages and disadvantages of organizing a business as a corporation.

Advantages of the Corporate Form	*Disadvantages* of the Corporate Form*
1. **Shareholders have no personal liability for the debts of the business** Shareholders are not *personally liable for the debts of a corporation.* Thus, the most that a shareholder can lose by investing in a corporation is the amount of his or her investment. This concept is called **limited liability**, and often is cited as the greatest advantage of the corporate form of organization.	1. **Greater regulation** *Corporations are affected by federal or provincial laws.* For example, the owners' ability to *remove business assets* from a corporation is restricted by law. A corporation must obtain authorization from government departments to issue capital stock. Also, these laws and provincial securities legislation require publicly owned corporations to make extensive public disclosure of their financial affairs.
2. **Transferability of ownership** *Ownership of a corporation is evidenced by transferable shares of capital stock*, which may be sold by one investor to another. Investment in these shares have the advantage of **liquidity**, because investors easily may convert their corporate ownership into cash by selling their shares.	2. **Cost of formation** An *unincorporated* business can be formed at little or no cost. Forming a corporation, however, normally requires the services of a lawyer.
3. **Professional management** *The shareholders own a corporation, but they do not manage it on a daily basis.* To administer the affairs of the corporation, the shareholders elect a **board of directors**. The directors, in turn, hire professional managers to run the business. An individual shareholder has *no right to participate in management unless he or she has been hired by the directors as a corporate manager.*	3. **Separation of ownership and management** *The separation of ownership and management is an advantage in many cases, but may be a disadvantage in others.* If shareholders do not approve of the manner in which management runs the business, they may find it difficult to take the united action necessary to remove that management group.
4. **Continuity of existence** *Changes in the names and identities of shareholders do not directly affect the corporation.* Therefore, the corporation may continue its operations **without disruption**, despite the retirement or death of individual shareholders. This characteristic is essential in the undertaking of most large-scale business ventures.	* *Taxation is generally neutral on the income of incorporated and unincorporated businesses.* This is because of the federal dividends tax credit for the shareholders, as discussed in Chapter 18.

Publicly Owned and Closely Held Corporations

LO 2: Distinguish between publicly owned and closely held corporations.

The capital stock of most large corporations can be bought and sold ("traded") through organized securities exchanges. As these shares are available for purchase by the general public, these large corporations are said to be **publicly owned**.

Far more people have a financial interest in the shares of publicly owned companies than one might expect. If you purchase the capital stock of such a corporation, you become a shareholder with a ***direct*** ownership interest—that is, ***you*** are a shareholder. But mutual funds and pension funds invest heavily in the capital stocks of many publicly owned corporations. Thus, if you invest in a mutual fund, or you are covered by a pension plan, you probably have an ***indirect*** financial interest in the capital stocks of many publicly owned corporations.

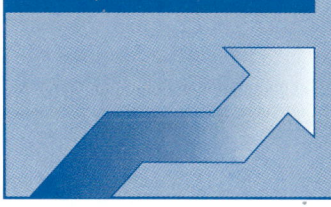

CASE IN POINT The shareholders in BCE Inc., TransCanada Pipelines, and Alcan Aluminium include thousands of men and women, and many pension funds, mutual investment funds, labour unions, universities, and other organizations. Almost every person covered by an employee pension plan has an indirect ownership interest in these and other large corporations.

Corporations whose shares are ***not*** traded on any organized stock exchanges are said to be **closely held**. Because there is no organized market for buying and selling their shares, these corporation usually have relatively few shareholders. Often, a closely held corporation is owned by one individual or by the members of one family. Seldom do closely held corporations have more than, say, 40 or 50 shareholders.

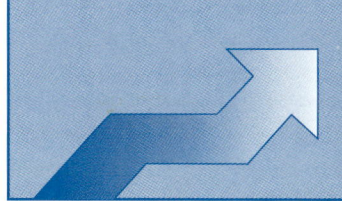

CASE IN POINT While most of the closely held corporations are small, some are among the largest companies in Canada, with revenues in the billions. McCain Foods, with revenue of more than $4 billion, is owned by the McCain family. Jim Pattison Group, with revenue of $4 billion, is owned by Jim Pattison. Charlwood Pacific Group, with revenue of about $3 billion, is owned by the Charlwood family. James Richardson & Sons, with revenue of more than $2 billion, is owned by the Richardson family.

Publicly Owned Corporations Face Different Rules Government seeks to protect the interests of the public. Therefore, publicly owned corporations are subject to far more regulation than those that are closely held. For example, publicly owned corporations are ***required by law*** to:

- Disclose much of their financial information to the public. (These disclosures are termed **public information**.)
- Prepare and issue quarterly and annual financial statements in conformity with generally accepted accounting principles. (These statements are public information.)
- Have their annual financial statements audited by an independent party (generally a firm of public accountants.)
- Comply with corporate and securities laws, which include both criminal penalties and civil liability for deliberately or carelessly distributing misleading information to the public.

- Submit much of their financial information to the provincial securities exchange commissions for review.

Closely held corporations normally are exempt from these requirements. But our discussions will focus upon the accounting and reporting issues confronting **publicly owned companies**. After all, these are the companies whose financial statements you are most likely to see—and the companies in which you are likely to invest.

FORMATION OF A CORPORATION

A corporation is created by obtaining **a certificate of incorporation** or **a corporate charter** from the federal or provincial government where the company is to be incorporated. To obtain a certificate of incorporation or a corporate charter, an application called the **articles of incorporation** is submitted to the federal or provincial government. Once the certificate or charter is obtained, the **shareholders** in the new corporation hold a meeting to elect **directors** and to pass **bylaws** as a guide to the company's affairs. The directors in turn hold a meeting at which officers of the corporation are appointed.

Organization Costs The formation of a corporation is a much more costly step than the organization of a partnership or a sole proprietorship. The necessary costs include the payment of an incorporation fee to the federal or provincial government, the payment of fees to lawyers for their services in drawing up the articles of incorporation, payments to promoters, and a variety of other outlays necessary to bring the corporation into existence. These costs are charged to an asset account called Organization Costs. In the balance sheet, organization costs appear under the "Other assets" caption, as illustrated on page 719.

The incurring of these organization costs leads to the existence of the corporate entity; consequently, the benefits derived from these costs may be regarded as extending over the entire life of the corporation. Since the life of a corporation may continue indefinitely, one might argue that organization costs are an asset with an unlimited life. However, such intangible assets as organization costs should be amortized over a maximum period of 40 years.[2] Income tax rules, on the other hand, permit three-quarters of the organization costs to be written off at an annual rate of 7% based on the declining balance method. Consequently, most companies have elected to write off organization costs in this manner. Because the amortization of organization costs usually is **immaterial** in dollar amount, this convenient treatment is justified by the accounting principle of **materiality**.

Thus, you will seldom see organization costs in the balance sheet of a publicly owned corporation. They have long since been amortized to expense.

LO 3: Explain the rights of shareholders and the roles of corporate directors and officers.

Rights of Shareholders A corporation is owned collectively by its shareholders. Each shareholder's ownership interest is determined by the number of **shares** that he or she owns.

---

[2] CICA, *CICA Handbook* (Toronto), section 3060.32

Assume that a corporation issues 10,000 shares of capital stock. If you own 1,000 of these shares, you own **10%** of the corporation. If you acquire another 500 shares from another shareholder, you will own **15%**.

Each shareholder receives from the corporation a **stock certificate** (or **share certificate**) indicating the number of shares he or she owns. (An illustration of a stock certificate appears below.)

The ownership of capital stock in a corporation usually carries the following basic rights:

1. To vote for directors and on certain other key issues. A shareholder has one vote for each share owned. (Some corporations have shares with more than one vote, such as Norcen's "multiple voting ordinary shares" with five votes each and its "subordinate voting ordinary shares" with one vote each.) The issues upon which shareholders may vote are specified in the corporation's bylaws.

   Any shareholder—or group of shareholders—that owns **more than 50%** of the capital stock has the power to elect the board of directors and to set basic corporate policies. Therefore, these shareholders "control" the corporation. Beyond their voting rights, shareholders have **no managerial authority** unless they have been appointed by the board to a management role.

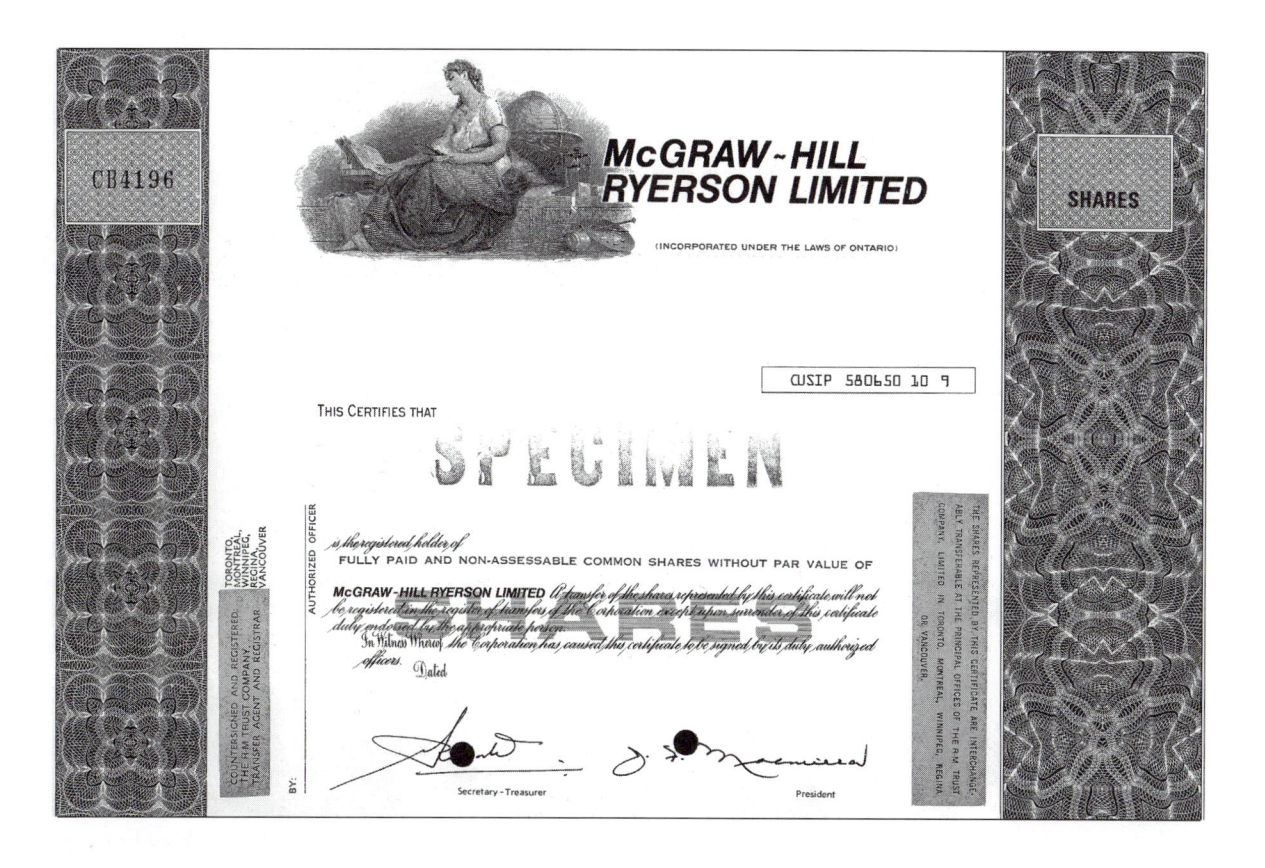

When a corporation issues two classes of capital stock such as *common* stock and *preferred* stock, voting rights generally are granted only to the holders of common stock. These two different types of capital stock will be discussed in detail later in this chapter.

2. To participate in any *dividends* declared by the board of directors. Shareholders in a corporation *may not* make withdrawals of company assets, as may the owners of unincorporated businesses. However, the directors may elect to distribute some or all of the earnings of a profitable corporation to its shareholders in the form of cash *dividends*.

   Dividends can be distributed only after they have been formally *declared* (authorized) by the board of directors. Also, the dividends are paid to all shareholders in proportion to the number of shares owned.

3. To share in the distribution of assets if the corporation is liquidated. When a corporation ends its existence, the creditors of the corporation must first be paid in full; any remaining assets are divided among shareholders in proportion to the number of shares owned.

4. To subscribe for additional shares in the event that the corporation decides to increase the amount of capital stock outstanding. This *pre-emptive right* entitles shareholders to maintain their percentages of ownership in the company by subscribing, in proportion to their present shareholdings, to any additional shares issued. Under the Canada Business Corporations Act, a corporation may provide such a pre-emptive right in its articles of incorporation if it so wishes.

Shareholders' meetings usually are held once each year. At these meetings, shareholders may ask questions of management and also vote upon certain issues. In large corporations, these meetings usually are attended by relatively few people—often less than 1% of the company's shareholders. Prior to these meetings, however, the management group requests that shareholders who do not plan to attend send in *proxy statements*, granting management the voting rights associated with their shares.

Through this proxy system, management usually can secure the voting rights to enough shares to ensure their control of the corporation. In a publicly owned corporation, dissatisfied shareholders seldom are able to muster the voting power to overrule management. Therefore, dissatisfied shareholders normally sell their shares and invest in a company more to their liking.

Functions of the Board of Directors The primary functions of the **board of directors** are to set corporate policies and to protect the interests of the shareholders. Specific duties of the directors include hiring corporate officers and setting these officers' salaries, declaring dividends, and reviewing the findings of both internal auditors and independent auditors.

A closely held corporation might have only one active director—who is also the principal shareholder. But publicly owned corporations have larger boards—usually a dozen people or more.

The board of a large corporation always includes several members of top management. In recent years, increasing importance has been attached to the inclusion of "outside" directors. The term **outside directors** refers to individuals who are **not** officers of the corporation and, therefore, bring an **independent perspective** to the board. The influence of outside directors on the corporation can be very significant. Also, the board of directors of large publicly owned corporations have recently become more aggressive and more responsive to the shareholders' interests.

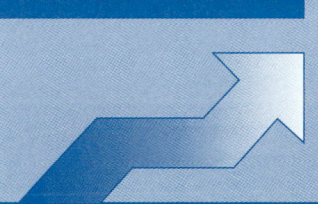

> **CASE IN POINT**
>
> In recent years, a number of chief executive officers of giant corporations have resigned or changed position or "retired" under the pressures of the corporations' boards of directors, especially the outside directors. These corporations include General Motors and IBM in the United States, and Petro-Canada in Canada.

Functions of the Corporate Officers The top management of a corporation is appointed (hired) by the board of directors. These individuals are called the **corporate officers**, or, more simply, "top management." Individual shareholders **do not** have the right to transact corporate business *unless they have been properly appointed to a managerial post*.

The top level of management usually includes a president or chief executive officer (CEO), a controller, a treasurer, and a secretary. In addition, a vice-president usually oversees each functional area, such as sales, human resources, and production.

The responsibilities of the controller, treasurer, and secretary are most directly related to the accounting phase of business operation. The **controller**, or chief accounting officer, is responsible for the maintenance of adequate internal control and for the preparation of accounting records and financial statements. Such specialized activities as budgeting, tax planning, and preparation of tax returns are usually placed under the controller's jurisdiction. The **treasurer** has custody of the company's funds and is generally responsible for planning and controlling the company's cash position. The treasurer's department also has responsibility for relations with the company's financial institutions and major creditors.

The **secretary** represents the corporation in many contractual and legal matters and maintains minutes of the meetings of directors and shareholders. Other responsibilities of the secretary are to coordinate the preparation of the annual report and to manage the "investor relations" department. In small corporations, one officer frequently acts as both secretary and treasurer.

The following organization chart indicates lines of authority extending from shareholders to the directors to the president and other officers.

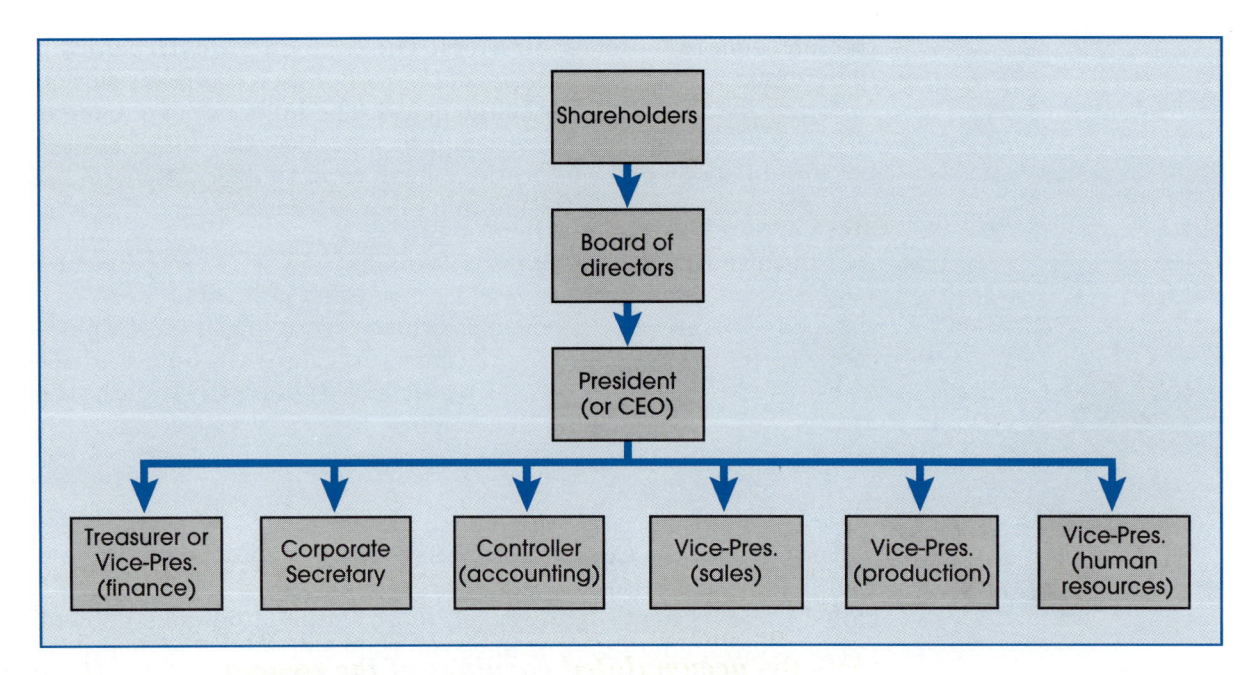

[Organizational chart: Shareholders → Board of directors → President (or CEO) → Treasurer or Vice-Pres. (finance), Corporate Secretary, Controller (accounting), Vice-Pres. (sales), Vice-Pres. (production), Vice-Pres. (human resources)]

Shareholders' Equity[3]

LO 4: Explain the nature of retained earnings; account for dividends and prepare closing entries.

The sections of the balance sheet showing assets and liabilities are much the same for a corporation as for a sole proprietorship. The owner's equity section is the principal point of contrast. In the balance sheet of a corporation, the term **shareholders' equity** is used instead of owner's equity.

The owner's equity in a corporation, as in other types of business organizations, is equal to the assets of the business minus the liabilities. However, corporate laws require that the shareholders' equity section of a corporate balance sheet clearly indicate the **source** of the owners' equity. The two basic sources of owners' equity are (1) investment by the shareholders (**contributed capital**), and (2) earnings from profitable operation of the business (**retained earnings**).

When shareholders invest cash or other assets in the business, the corporation issues to them in exchange shares of capital stock as evidence of their ownership. In the simplest case, capital invested by the shareholders is recorded in the corporation's accounting records by a credit to an account entitled **Capital Stock**. The capital paid in by shareholders is regarded as permanent capital, not ordinarily subject to withdrawal.

The increase in shareholders' equity arising from profitable operations is called **retained earnings**. At the end of the year the balance of the Income Summary account is closed into the Retained Earnings account. For example, if net income for the year is **$190,000**, the closing entry will be as follows:

---

[3] According to the CICA's *Financial Reporting in Canada,* Twenty-second Edition, 1997, pp. 249–250, the terms "shareholders' equity" and "capital stock" are most commonly used; thus, the first two terms are used in this book.

Entry to close the Income Summary in a *profitable* year...	*Income Summary* .... *Retained Earnings* .... *To close the Income Summary account by transferring the year's net income into the Retained Earnings account.*	190,000	190,000

If the company operates at a loss of, say **$105,000**, the Income Summary account will have a debit balance. The account must then be credited to close it. The closing entry will be:

...and in an *unprofitable* year.	*Retained Earnings* .... *Income Summary* .... *To close the Income Summary account by transferring the year's net loss into the Retained Earnings account.*	105,000	105,000

If a corporation has sufficient cash, a distribution of income or earnings may be made to shareholders. Distributions of this nature are termed **dividends** and decrease both total assets and total shareholders' equity. Because dividends are regarded as distributions of earnings, the decrease in shareholders' equity is reflected in the Retained Earnings account. Thus, the amount of retained earnings at any balance sheet date represents the **accumulated earnings of the company since the date of incorporation, minus any losses, and minus all dividends**.

Some people mistakenly believe that retained earnings represents a fund of cash available to a corporation. **Retained earnings is not an asset; it is an element of shareholders' equity.** Although the amount of retained earnings indicates the portion of total assets that are *financed* by earnings retained by the corporation, it does **not** indicate the *form* in which these resources are currently held. The resources generated by retaining earnings may have been invested in land, buildings, equipment, or any other kind of asset. The total amount of cash owned by a corporation is shown by the balance of the Cash account, which appears in the asset section of the balance sheet.

Shareholders' Equity in the Balance Sheet For a corporation with $1,000,000 of capital stock and $600,000 of retained earnings, the shareholders' equity section of the balance sheet (omitting certain details) will appear as follows:

Contributed capital plus the earnings retained ...	**Shareholders' equity:** Capital stock .... Retained earnings .... Total shareholders' equity	$1,000,000 600,000 $1,600,000

If this same company had been **unprofitable** and had incurred losses totalling, say, $300,000 since its organization, the shareholders' equity section of the balance sheet would be as follows:

... or less the accumulated deficit

Shareholders' equity:	
Capital stock	$1,000,000
Less: Deficit	300,000
Total shareholders' equity	$ 700,000

This second illustration tells us that $300,000 of the original $1,000,000 invested by shareholders has been lost as a result of unprofitable business operations. Note that the capital stock in both illustrations remains $1,000,000, representing the shareholders' original investment. The accumulated earnings or losses since the organization of the corporation are shown as *retained earnings* or as a *deficit* and are not intermingled with the contributed capital. The term *deficit* indicates a *negative amount* of retained earnings.

Cash Dividends

The term *dividend*, when used by itself, is generally understood to mean a distribution of cash by a corporation to its shareholders. Dividends are stated as a specific amount per share of capital stock, as, for example, a dividend of $1 per share. The amount received by each shareholder is in proportion to the number of shares owned. Thus, a shareholder who owns 100 shares will receive $100.

Dividends are paid only through action by the board of directors. The board has full discretion to declare a dividend or to refrain from doing so. Once the declaration of a dividend has been announced, the obligation to pay the dividend is a current liability of the corporation and cannot be rescinded.

Because a dividend is declared on one date by the board of directors and paid at a later date, two separate journal entries are necessary. To illustrate the entries for declaration and payment of a cash dividend, assume that Regal Corporation declares a dividend of $1 per share on 100,000 shares of outstanding capital stock. The dividend is declared on December 15 and is payable on January 25. The two entries would be as follows:

Dividends are first declared...

Dec. 15	Dividends	100,000	
	Dividends Payable		100,000
	To record declaration by the board of directors of a cash dividend of $1 per share on the 100,000 shares of capital stock outstanding.		

... and then paid

Jan. 25	Dividends Payable	100,000	
	Cash		100,000
	To record payment of the $1 per share dividend declared Dec. 15 on the 100,000 shares of capital stock outstanding.		

The account **Dividends Payable**, which was credited at the date of declaring the dividend, is a current liability. The **Dividends** account is a "temporary" owners' equity account, similar to the owner's drawing account in a sole proprietorship. A closing entry is required at the end of the year to transfer the debit balance in the Dividends account into the Retained Earnings account. Let us assume that Regal Corporation has declared *four* quarterly dividends during the current year, each in the amount of $100,000. The year-end entry to close the Dividends account would be:

Entry to close the Dividends account at year-end

Dec. 31	Retained Earnings	400,000	
	Dividends		400,000
	To close the Dividends account at year-end by transferring its debit balance into the Retained Earnings account.		

The effect of this entry is to reduce the balance in Retained Earnings account for the amount of all dividends declared during the entire year. If a company has more than one type of capital stock outstanding, a separate Dividends account is used for each issue. Each of these Dividends accounts is closed into the Retained Earnings account.

Closing Entries for a Corporation: A Summary The year-end closing entries for a corporation are quite similar to those required in a sole proprietorship. These entries, and the differences between those made in a proprietorship, are summarized below:

1. Close the revenue accounts into the Income Summary account.
2. Close the expense accounts into the Income Summary account.
3. Close the Income Summary account into the Retained Earnings account. (In a proprietorship, the Income Summary is closed into the Owner's Capital account.)
4. Close the Dividends account(s) into the Retained Earnings account. (A proprietorship uses an Owner's Drawing account, rather than a Dividend account—and this Drawing account is closed into the Owner's Capital account.)

Authorization and Issuance of Capital Stock

While the articles of incorporation *may* specify any maximum number of shares of capital stock that a corporation is authorized to issue, a corporation is **not required** to do so under the Canada Business Corporations Act. Thus, a corporation governed by the federal act does not have a limit on the maximum number of shares of capital stock it can issue unless it chooses to have one by stating such a limit in its articles of incorporation. The federal act does require, however, that the shares of capital stock of corporations be **without par or nominal value**. Provincial corporation legislation, such as the Ontario Business Corporations Act, parallels that of the federal act in these respects. On the other hand, certain provincial legislation (as well as legislation in the United States) still requires corporations to specify the maximum number of shares of capital stock they are authorized to issue and permits corporations to issue capital stock with a par value. Thus, some of the large corporations still have a maximum number of authorized capital stock and par value capital stock.

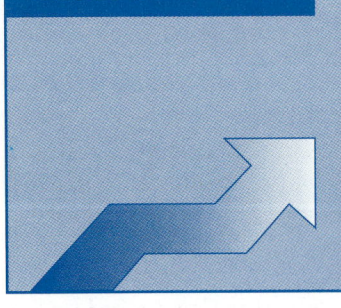

> **CASE IN POINT**
>
> In a recent CICA's *Financial Reporting in Canada*, 14 of the 186 public companies surveyed showed par value for one or more classes of their shares. For example, Maritime Telegraph and Telephone has maximum authorized preferred and common stock, the preferred shares have par value, and the premium on common stock (the excess of issue price over par value) is in excess of $38 million. In the United States, the common stock of Ford, AT&T, and Johnson & Johnson all have a par value of $1; in the United Kingdom, the ordinary share of Cadbury Schweppes has a par value of 25 pence.

It should be noted that mere authorization of a capital stock issue (with or without a maximum limit) does not bring an asset into existence, nor does it give the corporation any capital. The obtaining of authorization from the federal or provincial government for a capital stock issue merely affords a legal opportunity to obtain assets through the sale of capital stock.

No-par Value Capital Stock

Federal and provincial corporation legislation clearly indicates that **no-par value** capital stock will become increasingly common in Canada. The following are some of the important reasons for the concept of no-par value capital stock:

1. It avoids the assignment of an arbitrary amount as par value that is subject to misunderstanding by investors. For example, issued capital stock traded on stock exchanges at below its par value may sometimes be interpreted as a bargain even though the stock is at its fair market value. Thus, no-par stock eliminates such an opportunity for misunderstanding. Of course, the market value of any stock fluctuates according to the changes in the investors' perception about the value of the business, not according to the par value.
2. It provides a corporation with greater flexibility in the arrangement of its capital structure. For example, a corporation can split the existing no-par shares into a greater number of shares (as will be discussed in Chapter 15) without having to consider the effect on the par value. Also, no-par stock eliminates the problem of issuing stock at a discount, which generally is not allowed by law. Of course, since the par value is usually set at a very low amount, in reality the question of issuing stock at a discount seldom arises.
3. It eliminates the confusion and misunderstanding associated with the nature and meaning of such accounts as premium on capital stock, since no-par stock does not result in the establishment of these premium accounts.

CHAPTER 14   CORPORATIONS: ORGANIZATION AND SHAREHOLDERS' EQUITY   709

LO 5: Account for the issuance of capital stock; prepare the equity section of a corporate balance sheet.

Issuance of No-par Value Capital Stock   When no-par value capital stock is issued, the entire proceeds on the issue are credited to the Capital Stock account. Assuming that 60,000 shares of no-par value capital stock are issued at a price of $10 each, the entry to record the issue is as follows:

Entry for no-par capital stock

Cash	600,000	
Capital Stock		600,000
Issued 60,000 shares of no-par capital stock at a price of $10 a share.		

The amount credited to the Capital Stock account represents the **legal capital** or the **stated capital**[4]—the amount that cannot be reduced except by (1) losses from business operations or (2) legal action taken by a majority vote of shareholders or permitted by the legislation governing the corporation.

The shareholders' equity section of the balance sheet is illustrated as follows (assuming an unlimited number of authorized shares and the existence of $280,000 in retained earnings in order to have a complete illustration).

Shareholders' equity:
Capital stock, no-par value, authorized, an unlimited number of shares, issued and outstanding, 60,000 shares	$600,000
Retained earnings	280,000
Total shareholders' equity	$880,000

Par Value Capital Stock

The **par value** of capital stock represents the arbitrary amount assigned by a corporation as its legal capital per share. It merely indicates the amount per share to be entered in the Capital Stock account; it is *not* an indication of its market value. Par value may be $1, $2, $5, per share, or any amount decided upon by the corporation. Generally, the par values of most corporations are very small.

Issuance of Par Value Capital Stock   When par value capital stock is issued, the Capital Stock account is credited with the par value of the shares sold. Assuming that 80,000 shares of $2 par value capital stock are issued at a price of $2 each, the entry would be:

Entry for par value capital stock issued at par

Cash	160,000	
Capital Stock		160,000
Issued 80,000 shares of $2 par value capital stock at their par value.		

When capital stock is sold for more than its par value, the Capital Stock account is credited with the par value of the shares issued, and a separate account, **Premium on Capital Stock**, is credited for the excess of selling price over par. If, for example, the issuance price is $3 rather than $2, as in the previous illustration, the entry for the 80,000 shares would be:

---

[4] "Stated capital" is the term used in the Canada Business Corporations Act and certain provincial corporations acts.

Capital stock issued in excess of par value

```
Cash ..................................... 240,000
    Capital Stock ........................         160,000
    Premium on Capital Stock .............          80,000
Issued 80,000 shares of $2 par value capital stock at a
price of $3 a share.
```

The premium (the amount in excess of par value) does not represent an income to the corporation. It is part of the invested capital, and it will be added to the capital stock on the balance sheet to show the total contributed capital.[5] The shareholders' equity section of the balance sheet is illustrated as follows. (An authorization for 1,800,000 shares and the existence of $70,000 in retained earnings are assumed in order to have a complete illustration.)

Corporation's capital classified by source

Shareholders' equity:
Capital stock, $2 par value, authorized 1,800,000 shares, issued and outstanding, 80,000 shares	$160,000
Premium on capital stock	80,000
Total contributed capital	$240,000
Retained earnings	70,000
Total shareholders' equity	$310,000

Preferred Stock and Common Stock

LO 6: Discuss the features of preferred stock and common stock.

The account title **capital stock** is widely used when a corporation has issued one class of capital stock. In order to appeal to as many investors as possible, a corporation may issue more than one class of capital stock, each providing investors with different rights and opportunities. Under the Canada Business Corporations Act, a corporation may have more than one class of capital stock, provided that the rights, privileges, restrictions, and conditions of each class are set forth in the articles of incorporation and that at least one class of capital stock has the rights typically associated with what is traditionally known as "common stock." These rights are identical with the first three rights mentioned earlier, namely, (1) to vote at any meeting of shareholders of the corporation, (2) to receive any dividend declared by the corporation, and (3) to receive the remaining property of the corporation on dissolution. The federal act does not use the terms "common" and "preferred" to distinguish the different classes of capital stock. However, since the terms **"preferred stock"** and **"common stock"** are widely used in practice and have been proven useful in distinguishing classes of capital stock, they will be used throughout this book.

The basic type of capital stock issued by every corporation is generally called common stock. Common stock has the three basic rights previously mentioned. Whenever these rights are modified, the term preferred stock (or sometimes Class B Common) is used to describe this second type of capital stock. Some corporations issue two or more classes of preferred stock, each class having certain distinctive features designed to interest

---

[5] It is more appropriate to treat the premium on capital stock as part of the contributed capital than as part of contributed surplus, even though the latter is preferred by the *CICA Handbook*.

a particular type of investor. In summary, every business corporation has common stock; a good many corporations also issue preferred stock; and some companies have two or more types of preferred stock.

> **CASE IN POINT**
>
> The amount of preferred stock issued has been impressive. The annual dollar amount of preferred stock issued ranged from around $400 million to over $3 billion. Many of these issues were cumulative preferred stock and the amount ranged from $50 million (Consumers' Gas) to $300 million (Canutilities Holdings) per issue. Recently, BCE Inc. issued $250 million of fixed/floating rate cumulative preferred stock.

Common stock may be regarded as the basic, residual element of ownership. It carries voting rights and, therefore, is the means of exercising control over the business. Common stock has unlimited possibilities of increase in value; during periods of business expansion, the market prices of common stocks of some leading corporations may rise to many times their former values. On the other hand, common stocks lose value more rapidly than other types of securities when corporations encounter periods of unprofitable business.

The following shareholders' equity section illustrates the balance sheet presentation for a corporation having both preferred and common stock; note that the item of retained earnings is not apportioned between the two groups of shareholders.

Balance sheet presentation of shareholders' equity

Shareholders' equity:
$12 cumulative preferred stock, no-par value, authorized, an unlimited number of shares, issued and outstanding, 200,000 shares	$ 5,000,000
Common stock, no-par value, authorized, an unlimited number of shares, issued and outstanding, 2,000,000 shares	10,000,000
Total contributed capital	$15,000,000
Retained earnings	3,500,000
Total shareholders' equity	$18,500,000

Characteristics of Preferred Stock

The characteristics of preferred stocks vary from one issue to the next. The term ***preferred*** stems from the fact that these stocks almost always have "preference" —or priority—over the common stock in receiving dividends and in the event of liquidation. However, preferred shares usually ***lack*** significant advantages found in common stock. For example, the dividends paid to preferred shareholders normally ***do not increase*** if the company prospers. Also, preferred shareholders usually do ***not*** have voting rights and, therefore, have little say in management.

Among the features usually associated with preferred stock are the following:

1. Preferred as to dividends
2. Cumulative dividend rights

3. Preferred as to assets in event of the liquidation of the company
4. Callable or redeemable at the option of the corporation
5. No voting power

Another very important feature is a clause permitting the **conversion** of preferred stock into common at the option of the holder. Preferred stocks vary widely with respect to the special rights and privileges granted. Careful study of the terms of the individual preferred stock contract is a necessary step in the evaluation of any preferred stock.

Stock Preferred as to Dividends Stock preferred as to dividends is entitled to receive each year a dividend of specified amount before any dividend is paid on the common stock. The dividend is usually stated as a dollar amount per share. Some preferred stocks state the dividend preference as a *percentage of par value*. For example, a **9%** preferred stock with a par value of $100 per share would mean that $9 must be paid yearly on each share of preferred stock before any dividends are paid on the common. This dividend rate remains unchanged or fixed during the life of the preferred stock.

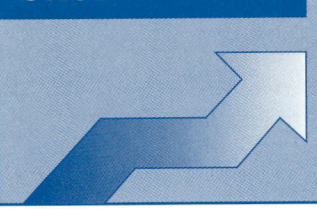

CASE IN POINT Bell Canada has a series of preferred stock at various dividend rates. For example, series 10 has a dividend rate of $1.86 per share, series 11 and 14, on the other hand, have dividend rates of 5.08%, and 4.68% respectively. (These rates may be reset from time to time.)

In recent years, corporations also issued preferred stock with a **floating rate** of dividend rather than a fixed rate as discussed above. The floating rate is tied to the bank prime rate (an interest rate given to the most credit-worthy customers). Thus, the amount of dividends the preferred shareholders receive changes as the bank prime rate changes. This means that these shareholders will receive and the corporations will pay a dividend rate that reflects the rate in the current market.

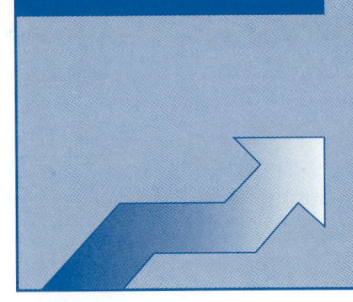

CASE IN POINT A number of large corporations have preferred stock with "floating rates," among them: Alcan Aluminium, Bombardier, Domtar, Gulf Canada Resources, National Bank, and Thomson. For example, Domtar's series B preferred shares carry a cumulative cash dividend equivalent to 72% of the bank prime rate; Bombardier's series 1, cumulative redeemable preferred shares have a quarterly dividend rate of "equal to the greater of (i) 1.875% and (ii) one-quarter of 75% of the average of the prime rates of three designated major Canadian banks for specified three-month periods."

The holders of preferred stock have no assurance that they will always receive the indicated dividend. A corporation is obligated to pay dividends to shareholders only when the board of directors declares a dividend. Dividends must be paid on preferred stock before anything is paid to the common shareholders, but if the corporation is not prospering, it may decide not to pay dividends on either preferred or common stock. For a corporation to pay dividends, income must be earned and cash must be available. However, preferred stocks in general offer *more assurance* of regular dividend payments than do common stocks.

Cumulative Preferred Stock The dividend preference carried by most preferred stocks is a *cumulative* one. If all or any part of the regular dividend on the preferred stock is omitted in a given year, the amount omitted is said to be *in arrears* and must be paid in a subsequent year before any dividend can be paid on the common stock. Assume that a corporation was organized January 1, 1999, with 10,000 shares of $8 cumulative preferred stock and 50,000 shares of common stock. Dividends paid in 1999 were at the rate of $8 per share of preferred stock and $2 per share of common. In 2000, earnings declined sharply and the only dividend paid was $2 per share on the preferred stock. No dividends were paid in 2001. What is the status of the preferred stock at December 31, 2001? Dividends are in arrears in the amount of $14 per share ($6 omitted during 2000 and $8 omitted in 2001). On the entire issue of 10,000 shares of preferred stock, the dividends in arrears amount to $140,000.

Dividends in arrears *are not listed among the liabilities of a corporation, because no liability exists until a dividend is declared by the board of directors*. Nevertheless, the amount of any dividends in arrears on preferred stock is an important factor to investors and should always be *disclosed*. This disclosure is usually made by a note accompanying the balance sheet such as the following:

Note disclosure of dividends in arrears

Note 6: Dividends in arrears
As of December 31, 2001, dividends on the $8 cumulative preferred stock were in arrears to the extent of $14 per share and amounted in total to $140,000.

In 2002, we shall assume that the company earned a large income and wished to pay dividends on both the preferred and common stocks. Before paying a dividend on the common, the corporation must pay the $140,000 in arrears on the cumulative preferred stock *plus* the regular $8 per share applicable to the current year. The preferred shareholders would, therefore, receive a total of $220,000 in dividends in 2002; the board of directors would then be free to declare dividends on the common stock.

For a *noncumulative* preferred stock, any omitted dividend is lost forever. Because of this factor, investors view the noncumulative feature as an unfavourable element, even though noncumulative preferred stocks are still issued.

> **CASE IN POINT**
>
> The investors' confidence that default on dividend obligations by large national financial institutions would be highly unlikely has enabled banks and trust companies to issue **noncumulative** preferred stocks. A number of banks and trust companies such as the Royal Bank, Toronto Dominion Bank, Bank of Montreal, Bank of Nova Scotia, and Royal Trustco issued over $1 billion of noncumulative preferred stock in one year. Recently, other companies also issued noncumulative preferred stock: Northern Telecom Limited, $350 million; Power Financial Corporation, $150 million.

Stock Preferred as to Assets Most preferred stocks carry a preference as to assets in the event of liquidation of the corporation. If the business is terminated, the preferred stock is entitled to payment in full of its par value or a higher stated liquidation value before any payment is made on the common stock. This priority also includes any dividends in arrears.

Callable or Redeemable Preferred Stock Most preferred stocks include a **call** or **redemption provision**. This provision grants the issuing corporation the right to repurchase the stock from the shareholders at a stipulated **call (redemption) price**. The call price is usually slightly higher than the issued price or par value of the stock. For example, $100 par value preferred stock may be callable at $105 or $110 per share. In addition to paying the call price, a corporation that redeems its preferred stock must pay any dividends in arrears. A call provision gives a corporation flexibility in adjusting its financial structure, for example, by eliminating a preferred stock and replacing it with other securities if future growth of the company makes such change advantageous.

Convertible Preferred Stock In order to add to the attractiveness of preferred stock as an investment, corporations sometimes offer a **conversion privilege** that entitles the preferred shareholders to exchange their shares for common stock in a stipulated ratio. If the corporation prospers, its common stock will probably rise in market value, and dividends on the common stock will probably increase. The investor who buys a convertible preferred stock rather than common stock has greater assurance of regular dividends. In addition, through the conversion privilege, the investor is assured of sharing in any substantial increase in value of the company's common stock.

As an example, assume that Remington Corporation issued a $9, no-par, convertible preferred stock on January 2, at a price of $100 per share. Each share was convertible into four shares of the company's no-par value common stock at any time. The common stock had a market price of $20 per share on January 2, and an annual dividend of $1 per share was being paid. During the next few years, Remington Corporation's earnings increased, the dividend on the common stock was raised to an annual rate of $3, and the market price of the common stock rose to $40 per share. At this point the preferred stock would have a market value of **at least $160**, since it could be converted at any time into four shares of common stock with a market value of $40 each. In other words, the market value of a convertible preferred stock will tend to move in accordance with the price of the common.

When the dividend rate is increased on the common stock, some holders of the preferred stock may convert their holdings into common stock in order to obtain a higher cash return on their investments. If the holder of 100 shares of the preferred stock presented these shares for conversion, Remington Corporation would make the following journal entry:

Conversion of preferred stock into common

$9 Convertible Preferred Stock	10,000	
Common Stock		10,000
To record the conversion of 100 shares of no-par preferred stock into 400 shares of no-par value common stock.		

Note that the issue price recorded for the 400 shares of common stock is based upon the *carrying value* of the preferred stock in the accounting records, not upon market prices at the date of conversion.

Participating Preferred Stock On rare occasions, a corporation may issue a participating preferred stock. A *participating* preferred stock is one that, in addition to the regular specified dividend, is entitled to participate (or share) in some manner in additional dividends declared by the board of directors.

For example, assume a corporation has outstanding both common stock and $8 *fully participating*, no-par value preferred stock issued at $100 each. Any dividends declared are first allocated (at $8 per share or 8%) to the preferred shareholders. After the common shareholders are allocated an equivalent dividend (8% of the amount of the common stock issued and outstanding), the preferred and common shareholder groups share proportionally the residual amount, if any. *Partially participating* preferred stock is subject to limits on amounts received in excess of the stated preferred dividend.

The Role of an Underwriter

When a large amount of capital stock is to be issued, most corporations use the services of an investment dealer, frequently referred to as an **underwriter**. The underwriter guarantees the issuing corporation a specific price for the capital stock and makes a profit by selling the shares to the investing public at a slightly higher price. The corporation records the issuance of the capital stock at the net amount received from the underwriter. The use of an underwriter assures the corporation that the entire capital stock issue will be sold without delay and that the entire amount of funds to be raised will be available on a specific date.

The price that a corporation will ask for a new issue of capital stock is based upon such factors as (1) expected future earnings and dividends, (2) the financial strength of the company, and (3) the current state of the investment markets. However, if the corporation asks too much, it simply will not find an underwriter or other buyers willing to purchase the shares.

Stock Issued for Assets Other Than Cash

Corporations generally sell their capital stock for cash and use the cash to buy the various types of assets needed in the business. Sometimes, however, a corporation may issue shares of its capital stock in a direct exchange for land, buildings, or other assets. Capital stock may also be issued in payment for services rendered by lawyers and promoters in the formation of the corporation.

When a corporation issues capital stock in exchange for services or for assets other than cash, the transaction should be recorded at the current *market value* of the goods or services received. For some types of assets such as land or buildings, the services of a firm of professional appraisers may be useful in establishing current market value.

Often, the best evidence as to the market value of these goods or services is the *market value of the shares* issued in exchange. For example, assume that a company issues 10,000 shares of its no-par value common stock in exchange for land. Competent appraisers may have differing opinions as to the market value of the land. But let us assume that the company's capital stock is currently selling on a stock exchange for $80 per share. It is logical to say that the cost of the land to the company is $800,000, the market value of the shares issued in exchange.

In summary, these transactions should be recorded either at the current market value of (1) the assets received, or (2) the shares issued in exchange—*whichever can be determined more objectively*. The responsibility for the determination of market value rests with the corporation's board of directors.

Once the valuation has been decided, the entry to record the issuance of the stock in exchange for the land is as follows:

Notice the use of current market values

Land	800,000	
Common Stock		800,000

To record the issuance of 10,000 shares of no-par value common stock in exchange for land. Current market value of stock ($80 per share) used as basis for valuing the land.

Subscriptions to Capital Stock

Small, newly formed corporations sometimes offer investors an opportunity to "subscribe" to shares of the company's capital stock. Under a subscription plan, the investors agree to purchase specified numbers of shares at a stated price *at a future date*, often by making a series of instalment payments. The stock is issued after the entire subscription price has been collected.

In summary, selling stock through subscriptions is similar to selling merchandise on a "layaway" plan. One reason for this procedure is to attract small investors. Another reason is to appeal to investors who prefer not to invest cash until the corporation is ready to start business operations. Accounting for subscriptions to capital stock is explained and illustrated in the intermediate accounting course.

Donated Capital

On occasion, a corporation may receive assets as a gift. To increase local employment, for example, some cities have given corporations the land upon which to build factories. When a corporation receives such a gift, both total assets and total shareholders' equity increase by the market value of the assets received. **No profit is recognized when a gift is received**; the increase in shareholders' equity is regarded as **contributed capital**. The receipt of a gift is recorded by debiting the appropriate asset accounts and crediting an account entitled **Donated Capital**.

The Donated Capital account appears in the shareholders' equity section of the balance sheet (as illustrated on page 719). In addition, the *notes* accompanying the financial statements normally explain the nature of the donation.

Shareholder Records in a Corporation

A large corporation with shares listed on the Toronto Stock Exchange and other exchanges usually has millions of shares outstanding and hundreds of thousands of shareholders. Each day many shareholders sell their shares; the buyers of these shares become new members of the company's family of shareholders.

We have mentioned that every shareholder in a corporation receives a **stock certificate** indicating the number of shares owned. If the shareholder later sells any of these shares, this certificate must be surrendered to the corporation for cancellation before a new certificate is issued to the new owner of the shares.

A corporation must have an up-to-date record of the names and addresses of this constantly changing army of shareholders so that it can send dividend cheques, financial statements, and voting forms to the right people. Also, the corporation must make sure that old stock certificates are cancelled as new ones are issued so that no excess certificates become outstanding.

Shareholders Subsidiary Ledger When there are numerous shareholders, it is not practical to include a separate account for each shareholder in the general ledger. Instead, a single controlling account entitled Capital Stock appears in the general ledger, and a **shareholders subsidiary ledger** is maintained. This ledger contains an account for each individual shareholder. Entries in the shareholders subsidiary ledger are made in **number of shares**, rather than in dollars. Thus, each shareholder's account shows the number of shares owned and the dates of acquisitions and sales. This record enables the corporation to send each shareholder a single dividend cheque, even though the shareholder may have acquired several stock certificates at different dates.

A corporation that has more than one type of capital stock will maintain a separate set of shareholders subsidiary records for each issue.

Stock Transfer Agent and Stock Registrar Large, publicly owned corporations use an independent **stock transfer agent** and a **stock registrar** to maintain their shareholder records and to establish strong internal control over the issuance of stock certificates. These transfer agents and registrars usually are large banks or trust companies. When stock certificates are to be transferred from one owner to another, the old certificates are sent to the transfer agent, who cancels them, makes the necessary entries in the shareholders subsidiary ledger, and prepares a new certificate for the new owner of the shares. This new certificate then must be registered with the stock registrar before it represents valid and transferable ownership of stock in the corporation.

Small, closely held corporations generally do not use the services of independent registrars and transfer agents. In these companies, the shareholder records usually are maintained by a corporate officer. To prevent the accidental or fraudulent issuance of an excessive number of stock certificates, the corporation should require that each certificate be signed by at least two designated corporate officers.

Illustration of a Corporate Balance Sheet

A fairly complete balance sheet for a corporation is illustrated on the following page. Note the inclusion in this balance sheet of liabilities for income taxes payable; this liability does not appear in the balance sheet of an unincorporated business. Note also that the caption for each capital stock account indicates the type of capital stock and the number of shares authorized and issued. The caption for preferred stock also indicates the dividend rate, call price, and other important features.

Bear in mind that current practice includes many alternatives in the choice of terminology and the arrangement of items in financial statements.

Book Value per Share of Common Stock

LO 7: Explain the significance of book value and market value of capital stock.

Because the equity of each shareholder in a corporation is determined by the number of shares he or she owns, an accounting measurement of interest to many shareholders is book value per share of common stock. **Book value per share** is equal to the ***net assets*** represented by one share of common stock. The term ***net assets*** means total assets minus total liabilities; in other words, net assets are equal to total shareholders' equity. Thus in a corporation that has issued common stock only, the book value per share is computed by dividing total shareholders' equity by the number of shares outstanding (or subscribed).

CHAPTER 14 CORPORATIONS: ORGANIZATION AND SHAREHOLDERS' EQUITY 719

Example of a corporate balance sheet

DEL MAR CORPORATION
Balance Sheet
December 31, 2000

Assets

Current assets:
Cash and cash equivalents		$ 155,200
Accounts receivable (net)		1,165,600
Inventories (lower of FIFO and net realizable value)		1,300,800
Short-term prepayments		125,900
Total current assets		$2,747,500

Plant and equipment:
Land—at cost		900,000
Buildings and equipment—at cost	$5,283,000	
Less: Accumulated depreciation	1,250,000	4,033,000
Other assets: Organization costs		14,000
Total assets		$7,694,500

Liabilities & Shareholders' Equity

Current liabilities:
Accounts payable		$1,097,800
Income taxes payable		124,300
Interest payable		30,000
Total current liabilities		$1,252,100
Long-term liabilities: Bonds payable, 12%, due Oct. 1, 2009		1,000,000
Total liabilities		$2,252,100

Shareholders' equity
Cumulative $8 preferred stock, no-par, callable at $104, authorized, an unlimited number of shares, issued and outstanding, 10,000 shares	$1,000,000	
Common stock, no-par, authorized, an unlimited number of shares, issued and outstanding, 600,000 shares	2,670,000	
Donated capital	230,000	
Total contributed capital	$3,900,000	
Retained earnings	1,542,400	
Total shareholders' equity		5,442,400
Total liabilities & shareholders' equity		$7,694,500

And remember to read the notes!

Note to financial statements:
As of December 31, 2000, dividends on the $8 cumulative preferred stock were in arrears to the extent of $8 per share and amounted in total to $80,000.

For example, assume that a corporation has 4,000 shares of capital stock outstanding and the shareholders' equity section of the balance sheet is as follows:

How much is book value per share?

Shareholders' Equity:
Capital stock, no-par value (4,000 shares outstanding)	$ 44,000
Retained earnings	76,000
Total shareholders' equity	$120,000

The *book value per share* is **$30**; it is computed by dividing the shareholders' equity of $120,000 by the 4,000 shares of outstanding stock. In computing book value, we are not concerned with the number of authorized shares but merely with the *outstanding* shares, because the total of the outstanding shares represents 100% of the shareholders' equity.

CASE IN POINT

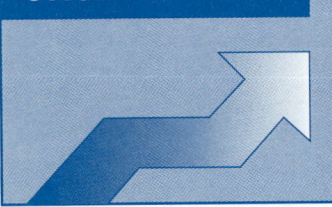

Book value per share (equity per share in some published financial statements) is regularly reported in such financial news media as *The Financial Post** and in the annual reports of such large corporations as Air Canada, Domtar, Bombardier, Hudson's Bay, Algoma Steel, and Maple Leaf Foods. For example, Domtar's book value in a recent year was $8.03.

*Now part of the *National Post*.

Book Value When a Company Has Both Preferred and Common Stock

Book value is usually computed only for common stock. If a company has both preferred and common stock outstanding, the computation of book value per share of common stock requires two steps. First, the *redemption value* or *call price* of the entire preferred stock issue and any *dividends in arrears* are deducted from total shareholders' equity. Second, the remaining amount of shareholders' equity is divided by the number of common shares outstanding to determine book value per common share. This procedure reflects the fact that the common shareholders are the residual owners of the corporate entity.

To illustrate, assume that the shareholders' equity of Carpetloy Corporation at December 31 is as follows:

Two classes of stock

$8 preferred stock, no-par, callable at $110, issued and outstanding, 10,000 shares	$1,000,000
Common stock, no-par, issued and outstanding, 50,000 shares	1,250,000
Retained earnings	130,000
Total shareholders' equity	$2,380,000

Because of a weak cash position, Carpetloy Corporation has paid no dividends during the current year. As of December 31, dividends in arrears on the cumulative preferred stock total **$80,000**.

All the equity belongs to the common shareholders, except the $1.1 million call price ($110 × 10,000 shares) applicable to the preferred stock and the $80,000 of dividends in arrears on preferred stock. The calculation of book value per share of common stock is as follows:

Total shareholders' equity		$2,380,000
Less: Equity of preferred shareholders:		
Call price of preferred stock	$1,100,000	
Dividends in arrears	80,000	1,180,000
Equity of common shareholders		$1,200,000
Number of common shares outstanding		50,000
Book value per share of common stock ($1,200,000 ÷ 50,000 shares)		$24

MARKET VALUE

After shares of capital stock have been issued, they often are sold by one investor to another. The prices at which these shares change hands represents the **current market price** of the stock. This market price may differ **substantially** from such amounts as par value, the original issue prices, and the current book value. Which is the *most relevant* amount? That depends upon your point of view.

After shares are issued, ***they belong to the shareholder***, not to the issuing corporation. Thus, changes in the market price of these shares affect the financial position *of the shareholder*, but ***not that of the issuing company***. This concept explains why the issuing company and shareholders apply very different accounting principles to the same outstanding shares.

Accounting by the Issuer From the viewpoint of the issuing company, outstanding stock represents **an amount invested in the company by its owners at a particular date.** While the market value of the shareholders' investment may change, the amount of resources that they originally invested **does not**.

Thus, the company issuing stock records ***the issue price***—that is, the proceeds received from issuing the stock—in its capital accounts. The balances in these accounts remain **unchanged** unless (1) more shares are issued, or (2) outstanding shares are permanently retired (*i.e.*, preferred stock is called).

CASE IN POINT

In a single day, the market price of IBM's capital dropped over $31 per share, falling from $135 to $103.25. Of course, this was not a "typical" day. The date, October 19, 1987, will long be remembered as "Black Monday." On this day, stock prices around the world suffered the greatest one-day decline in history.

Those stock listed on the New York Stock Exchange lost about 20% of their value in less than six hours. Given that the annual dividends on these stocks averaged about 2% of their market values, this one-day "market loss" was approximately equal to the loss by investors of all dividend revenue for about 10 years.

How did this disastrous decline in IBM's stock price affect the balance sheet of IBM?

Actually, it didn't.

Accounting by the Investor From the *investor's* point of view, shares in a publicly owned company are an *asset*, usually termed Marketable Securities.

To the investor, the *current market value* of securities owned is far more relevant than the original issue price—or than the securities' par values or book values. The *market value* indicates what the securities are "worth" today. Changes in market value *directly affect* the investor's solvency, financial position, and net worth. For these reasons, investors should show investments in marketable securities at *current market value* in their balance sheets.

Because market prices are of such importance to investors, we will briefly discuss the factors that most affect the market prices of preferred and common stocks.

Market Price of Preferred Stock

LO 8: Discuss the factors affecting the market price of preferred stock and of common stock.

Investors buy preferred stocks primarily to receive the dividends that these shares pay. Thus dividend rate is one important factor in determining the market price of a preferred stock. Another important factor is *risk*. In the long run, a company must be profitable to be able to pay dividends. If there is a distinct possibility that the company will not operate profitably and pay dividends, the price of its preferred stock will decline.

A third factor greatly affecting the value of preferred stocks is the level of *interest rates*. What happens to the market price of an 8% preferred stock, originally issued at $100, if government policies and other factors cause long-term interest rates to rise to, say, 15 or 16%. If investments offering a return of 16% with the same level of risk are readily available, investors will no longer pay $100 for a share of preferred stock that provides a dividend of only $8 per year. Thus, the market price of the preferred stock will fall to about half of its original issue price, or about $50 per share. At this market price, the stock offers a 16% return (called the *dividend yield*) to an investor purchasing the stock.

However, if the prevailing long-term interest rates should again decline to the 8% range, the market price of an 8% preferred stock should quickly rise to approximately the original issue price of $100.[6] In summary, the market price of preferred stock *varies inversely with interest rates*. As interest rates rise, preferred stock prices decline; as interest rates fall, preferred stock prices rise.

Market Price of Common Stock

Prevailing interest rates also affect the market price of common stock. However, dividends paid to common shareholders are not fixed in amount. Both the amount of the dividend and the market price of the stock may increase dramatically if the corporation is successful. Alternatively, if the company is unsuccessful, the common shareholders may not even recover their original investment. Therefore, the most important factors in the market price of common stock are *investors' expectations* as to the future profitability of the business, and the *risk* that this level of profitability may not be achieved.

---

[6]To simplify the discussion, the effect of dividend tax credit is ignored.

CASE IN POINT

In early 1982, things looked bad for Ford Motor. North America was in the midst of a recession and auto sales were down. In each of the two preceding years, Ford had lost over $1 billion, and the company recently had stopped paying dividends. Investors were pessimistic about the company's future, and Ford's common stock traded for less than $4 per share.*

Over the next five years, an improving economy, a weak dollar, and such popular new models as the Taurus helped to turn Ford around. Earnings and dividends increased steadily. By 1987, Ford was among the most profitable corporations in the world, earning net income of more than 4\frac{1}{2}$ billion and paying a substantial dividend. In mid-1987, the company's common stock was trading for more than $50 per share.*

*Per share prices have been adjusted for stock splits. Stock splits are discussed in Chapter 15.

We have mentioned that after shares have been issued they belong to the **shareholders**, not to the issuing corporation. Therefore, changes in the market price of the shares **do not affect the financial statements of the corporation**, and these changes are not recorded in the corporation's accounting records. The contributed capital shown in a corporate balance sheet represents the amount received **when the stock was issued**, not the current market value of shares.

"Following" the Market

As we have stated, the balance sheet of a corporation **does not** indicate the current market value of the shares outstanding. In their annual reports, however, companies **do** disclose the **range** of their stock's price—the high price and low—for each quarter within their fiscal year.

There are much easier ways to follow market prices. For example, the current market prices of publicly owned corporations appear daily in the financial pages of many newspapers.[7]

Shown on the following page is a typical newspaper summary of the daily trading in two issues of Domtar Inc. The date was late in April, 1998.

Domtar's stocks are listed on the Toronto Stock Exchange. Similar summaries are published daily for every stock listed on this exchange.

On this date, Domtar's stocks were trading near their 52-week highs. As indicated by the p/e ratio of **34.1,** the common stock is trading at 34.1 times Domtar's earnings per share.[8]

---

[7]For some investors, following market prices becomes virtually an obsession. Home computers can access up-to-the minute stock prices through database services. You can even carry a "beeper" which will signal you the moment that specific stocks trade above or below designated prices.

[8]The concepts **price/earnings** (p/e) **ratios** and of earnings per share will be discussed in Chapter 15. The p/e ratio is based on the earnings for the past twelve months.

Current stock prices appear in the daily newspaper

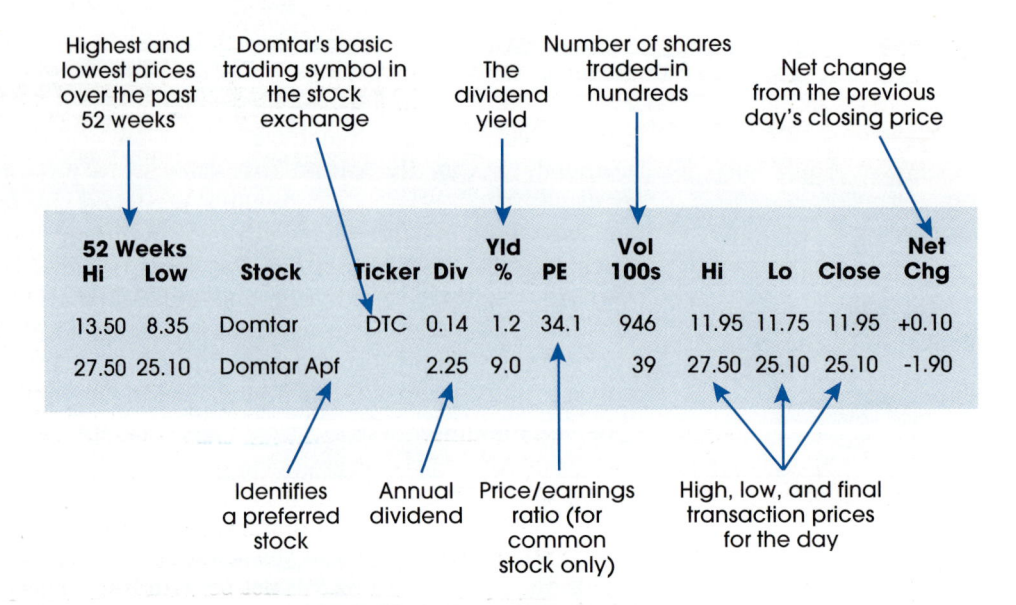

52 Weeks Hi	Low	Stock	Ticker	Div	Yld %	PE	Vol 100s	Hi	Lo	Close	Net Chg
13.50	8.35	Domtar	DTC	0.14	1.2	34.1	946	11.95	11.75	11.95	+0.10
27.50	25.10	Domtar Apf		2.25	9.0		39	27.50	25.10	25.10	−1.90

- Highest and lowest prices over the past 52 weeks
- Domtar's basic trading symbol in the stock exchange
- The dividend yield
- Number of shares traded—in hundreds
- Net change from the previous day's closing price
- Identifies a preferred stock
- Annual dividend
- Price/earnings ratio (for common stock only)
- High, low, and final transaction prices for the day

Book Value and Market Price

To some extent, **book value** may be used in evaluating the reasonableness of the market price of a stock. However, it must be used with great caution; the fact that a stock is selling at less than book value does not necessarily indicate a bargain.

Book value is a historical concept, representing the amounts invested by shareholders plus the amounts earned and retained by the corporation. If a stock is selling at a price well **above** book value, investors believe that management has created a business worth substantially more than the historical cost of the resources entrusted to its care. This, in essence, is the sign of a successful corporation. If the excess of market price over book value becomes very great, however, investors should consider whether the company's prospects really justify a market price so much above the underlying book value of the company's resources.

On the other hand, if the market price of a stock is **less than** book value, investors believe that the company's resources are worth less than their cost while under the control of current management. Thus, the relationship between book value and market price is one measure of investors' *confidence in a company's management*.

CASE IN POINT

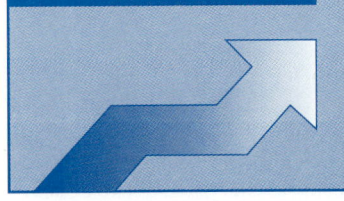

Shortly after the introduction of its **Windows** software, the common stock of Microsoft Corp. rose to a market value of more than $100 per share, although its book value per share was only about $6.50. Investors believed that Microsoft's products—and its management—made the business worth far more than the historical amounts of capital that had been invested.

End-of-Chapter Review

Key Terms Introduced or Emphasized in Chapter 14

Board of directors *(p.702)* Persons elected by common shareholders to direct the affairs of a corporation.

Book value per share *(p.718)* The shareholders' equity represented by each share of common stock, computed by dividing common shareholders' equity by the number of common shares outstanding.

Capital stock *(p.697)* Transferable units of ownership in a corporation. A broad term that may refer to common stock, preferred stock, or both.

Closely held corporation *(p.699)* A corporation owned by a small group of shareholders.

Common stock *(p.710)* A type of capital stock that possesses the basic rights of ownership including the right to vote. Represents the residual element of ownership in a corporation.

Contributed capital *(p.704)* The amounts invested in a corporation by its shareholders (also includes donated capital).

Corporation *(p.697)* A business organized as a legal entity separate from its owners, with ownership divided into shares of transferable stock. Shareholders are not liable for debts of the corporation.

Deficit *(p.706)* Accumulated losses incurred by a corporation. A negative amount of retained earnings.

Dividends *(p.702)* Distribution of assets (usually cash) by a **corporation** to its **shareholders**. Normally viewed as a distribution of income, it therefore cannot exceed the amount of **retained earnings**. Must be formally declared by the board of directors and distributed on a per-share basis. *Note:* Shareholders **cannot** simply "withdraw" assets from a corporation at will.

Dividend yield *(p.722)* The annual dividend paid to a share of stock, expressed as a percentage of the stock's market value. Indicates the "rate of return" represented by the dividend.

Donated capital *(p.717)* Capital given to a corporation, with no payment being made or capital stock being issued in exchange. Shown in the balance sheet as an element of contributed capital.

Floating rate *(p.712)* A dividend rate for preferred stock that is tied to the bank prime interest rate.

Legal capital *(p.709)* Equal to the proceeds of **no-par value** or the par value of capital stock issued. This amount represents a "permanent commitment" of capital by the owners of a corporation and cannot be removed without special legal action. Of course, it may be eroded by losses.

Limited liability *(p.697)* The concept that the owners of a corporation are not personally liable for the debts of the business. Thus, shareholders' potential financial losses are limited to the amount of their equity investment.

No-par value *(p.708)* Capital stock without nominal or par value.

Par value *(p.709)* The **legal capital** of a corporation. Represents the minimum amount per share to be invested in the corporation by its owners and cannot be withdrawn except by special legal action.

Preferred stock *(p.710)* A class of capital stock usually having preferences as to dividends and in the distribution of assets in event of liquidation.

Premium on capital stock *(p.709)* The amount paid by shareholders for the capital stock in excess of its par value.

Price/earnings (p/e) ratio *(p.723)* The ratio of a common stock's current market price to the underlying earnings per share. Viewed as an indicator of *investor's expectations* as to the levels of future earnings.

Public information *(p.699)* Information that, by law, must be made available to the general public. Includes the quarterly and annual financial statements—and other financial information—about **publicly owned corporations**.

Publicly owned corporation *(p.698)* Any corporation whose shares are offered for sale to the general public.

Retained earnings *(p.704)* That element of owners' equity in a corporation that has accumulated through profitable business operations. Net income increases retained earnings; net losses and **dividends** reduce retained earnings.

Shareholders *(p.697)* The owners of a corporation. The name reflects the fact that their ownership is evidenced by transferable shares of **capital stock**.

Shareholders subsidiary ledger *(p.717)* A record showing the number of shares owned by each shareholder.

Stock certificate *(p.701)* A document issued by a corporation (or its transfer agent) as evidence of the ownership of the number of shares stated on the certificate.

Stock registrar *(p.717)* An independent fiscal agent, usually a large trust company or bank, retained by a corporation to provide assurance against overissuance of stock certificates.

Stock transfer agent *(p.717)* A bank or trust company retained by a corporation to maintain its records of capital stock ownership and make transfers from one investor to another.

Underwriter *(p.715)* An investment dealer who handles the sale of a corporation's capital stock to the public.

DEMONSTRATION PROBLEM

The shareholders' equity section of Rockhurst Corporation's balance sheet appears below:

Shareholders' equity:

$6 preferred stock, no-par value, authorized, an unlimited number of shares, callable at $102 per share, issued and outstanding, 120,000 shares	$12,000,000
Common stock, no-par value, authorized, an unlimited number of shares, issued and outstanding, 2,800,000 shares	44,800,000
Donated capital	360,000
Retained earnings	2,680,000
Total shareholders' equity	$59,840,000

INSTRUCTIONS

On the basis of this information, answer the following questions and show any necessary support computations.

a. What is the total annual dividend requirement on the outstanding preferred stock?

b. What was the average price per share received by the corporation for its common stock?

c. What is the total amount of legal capital?

d. What is the total contributed capital?

e. What is the book value per share of common stock? (Assume no dividends in arrears.)

SOLUTION TO DEMONSTRATION PROBLEM

a. $720,000 (120,000 shares × $6 per share)

b.
Total issue price of common shares	$44,800,000
Shares issued (2,800,000)	2,800,000
Average issue price per share ($44,800,000 ÷ 2,800,000 shares)	$16

c. $57,160,000 ($12,000,000 preferred, $44,800,000 common, $360,000 donated capital)

d. Same as c above

e.
Total shareholders' equity	$59,840,000
Less: Claims of preferred shareholders (120,000 shares x $102 call price)	12,240,000
Equity of common shareholders	$47,600,000
Common shares outstanding	2,800,000
Book value per share ($47,600,000 ÷ 2,800,000 shares)	$17

Self-Test Questions

The answers to these questions appear on page 741.

1. When a business is organized as a corporation, which of the following is true?
   a. Shareholders are liable for the debts of the business only in proportion to their percentage ownership of capital stock.
   b. Shareholders have to pay personal income taxes on the corporation's income in proportion to their percentage ownership of capital stock.
   c. Fluctuations in the market value of outstanding shares of capital stock do *not* affect the amount of shareholders' equity shown in the balance sheet.
   d. Each shareholder has the right to bind the corporation to contracts and to make other managerial decisions.

2. Great Plains Corporation was organized with authorization to issue 100,000 shares of no-par value common stock. Forty thousand shares were issued to Helen Morgan, the company's founder, at a price of $5 per share. No other shares have yet been issued. Which of the following statements is true?
   a. Morgan owns *40%* of the shareholders' equity of the corporation.
   b. The corporation should recognize a $200,000 gain on the issuance of these shares.
   c. If the balance sheet includes retained earnings of $50,000, total *contributed* capital amounts to $550,000.
   d. In the balance sheet, the common stock account will have a $200,000 balance, regardless of the income earned or losses incurred since the corporation was organized.

3. Which of the following is *not* a characteristic of the *common stock* of a large, publicly owned corporation?
   a. The shares may be transferred from one investor to another without disrupting the continuity of business operations.
   b. Voting rights in the election of the board of directors.
   c. A cumulative right to receive dividends.
   d. After issuance, the market value of the stock is unrelated to its issued price or par value.

4. Leamington Electric is a profitable utility company that has increased its dividend to *common* shareholders every year for 42 consecutive years. Which of the following is *least* likely to affect the market price of the company's *preferred* stock by a significant amount?
   a. A decrease in long-term interest rates.
   b. An increase in long-term interest rates.
   c. The board of directors announces its intention to increase common stock dividends in the current year.
   d. Whether or not the preferred stock carries a conversion privilege.

5. The following information is taken from the balance sheet and related disclosures of Blue Oyster Corporation:

Total contributed capital	$5,400,000
Outstanding shares:	
Common stock, no-par value	100,000 shares
$6 preferred stock, no-par value, callable at	
$108 per share, issued at $100 per share	10,000 shares
Preferred dividends in arrears	2 years
Total shareholders' equity	$4,700,000

Which of the following statements is true? (For this question, more than one answer may be correct.)
   a. The preferred dividends in arrears amount to $120,000 and should appear as a liability in the corporate balance sheet.
   b. The book value per share of common stock is $35.
   c. The shareholders' equity section of the balance sheet should indicate a deficit of $700,000.
   d. The company has paid no dividend on its **common** stock during the past two years.

ASSIGNMENT MATERIAL

Discussion Questions

1. Why are large corporations often said to be **publicly owned**?
2. Distinguish between corporations and sole proprietorships in terms of the following characteristics:
   a. Owners' liability for debts of the business
   b. Transferability of ownership interest
   c. Continuity of existence
   d. Taxation on income
3. What are the basic rights of the owner of a share of corporate stock? In what way are these basic rights commonly modified with respect to the owner of a share of preferred stock?
4. Distinguish between **contributed capital** and **retained earnings** of a corporation. Why is such a distinction useful?
5. If the Retained Earnings account has a debit balance, how is it presented in the balance sheet and what is it called?
6. Explain the reasons for the concept of no-par value capital stock in federal and provincial corporation legislation.

7. Explain the significance of **par value**. Does par value indicate the reasonable market price for a share of capital stock? Explain.

8. Describe the usual nature of the following features as they apply to a share of preferred stock: (a) cumulative, (b) convertible, and (c) callable (redeemable).

9. Why is noncumulative preferred stock considered a very unattractive form of investment?

10. When capital stock is issued by a corporation in exchange for assets other than cash, accountants face the problem of determining the dollar amount at which to record the transaction. Discuss the factors to be considered and explain their significance.

11. State the classification (asset, liability, shareholders' equity, revenue, or expense) of each of the following accounts:
    a. Cash (received from the issuance of capital stock)
    b. Organization Costs
    c. Preferred Stock
    d. Retained Earnings
    e. Donated Capital
    f. Premium on Common Stock
    g. Income Taxes Payable

12. A professional baseball team received as a gift from the city the land upon which to build a stadium. What effect, if any, will the receipt of this gift have upon the baseball team's balance sheet and income statement? Explain.

13. Explain the following terms:
    a. Stock transfer agent
    b. Shareholders ledger
    c. Underwriter
    d. Stock registrar

14. What does **book value per share** of common stock represent? Does it represent the amount common shareholders would receive in the event of liquidation of the corporation? Explain briefly.

15. How is book value per share of common stock computed when a company has both preferred and common stock outstanding?

16. What would be the effect, if any, on book value per share of common stock as a result of each of the following independent events: (a) a corporation obtains a bank loan; (b) a dividend is declared (to be paid in the next accounting period).

17. In the great stock market crash of October 19, 1987, the market price of **IBM's** capital stock fell by over $31 per share. Explain the effects, if any, of this decline in share price on IBM's balance sheet.

18. Assume that you asked your stockbroker to purchase 100 shares of **Hudson's Bay** common stock. How would this transaction affect the financial statements of Hudson's Bay? Explain.

Exercises

EXERCISE 14-1
Accounting Terminology
(LO 1,2,3,4,6,7,8)

Listed below are twelve technical accounting terms discussed in this chapter.

No-par value	*Board of directors*	*Limited liability*
Book value	*Contributed capital*	*Dividends in arrears*
Market value	*Preferred stock*	*Closely held corporation*
Retained earnings	*Common stock*	*Publicly owned corporation*

Each of the following statements may (or may not) describe one of these technical terms. For each statement, indicate the term described, or answer "None" if the statement does not correctly describe any of the terms.
  a. A major **advantage** of the corporate form of organization.
  b. From investors' point of view, the most important "value" associated with capital stock.
  c. Cash available for distribution to the shareholders.
  d. The class of capital stock that normally has the most voting power.
  e. A distribution of assets that may be made in future years to the holders of common stock.
  f. The group of shareholders that controls more than 50% of a corporation's voting shares.
  g. A corporation whose shares are traded on an organized stock exchange.
  h. Equity arising either from investments by owners or from the donation of assets to a corporation.
  i. The element of shareholders' equity that is **reduced** by dividends.
  j. Total assets divided by the number of common shares outstanding.
  k. The class of stock whose market price normally rises as interest rates increase.

EXERCISE 14-2
Computing Retained Earnings
(LO 4)

Johnson Pump, Inc., began operations in 2000. In that year, the corporation earned net income of $195,000 and paid dividends of $2.25 per share on its 40,000 outstanding shares of capital stock. In 2001, the corporation incurred a net loss of $127,000 and paid no dividends.
  a. Prepare the journal entry to close the Income Summary account at December 31, 2001 (the year of the $127,000 net loss).
  b. Compute the amount of retained earnings or deficit that will appear in the company's balance sheet at December 31, 2001.
  c. Have Johnson Pump's operations been profitable for the two years since its formation? Is your answer consistent with your result in part **b**? Explain briefly.

EXERCISE 14-3
Shareholders' Equity Section of a Balance Sheet
(LO 5)

When Enviro Systems, Inc., was formed, the company was authorized to issue an unlimited number of shares of no-par value, $8 cumulative preferred stock, and an unlimited number of shares of no-par value common stock. The preferred stock is callable at $106.

Then, 2,500 shares of the preferred stock were issued at a price of $103 per share, and 70,000 shares of the common stock were sold for $13 per share. At the end of the current year, Enviro Systems, Inc., has retained earnings of $297,000.
  a. Prepare the shareholders' equity section of the company's balance sheet at the end of the current year.
  b. Assume Enviro Systems' common stock is trading at $22 per share and its preferred stock is trading at $105 per share at the end of the current year. Would the shareholders' equity section prepared in part **a** be affected by this additional information?

EXERCISE 14-4
Dividends: Preferred and Common
(LO 4,5,6)

A portion of the shareholders' equity section from the balance sheet of Palermo Corporation appears below:

> **Shareholders' equity:**
> Preferred stock, $4½ cumulative, no-par, 40,000 shares
>   issued and outstanding $2,000,000
> Preferred stock, $12 noncumulative, no-par, 8,000 shares
>   issued and outstanding 800,000
> Common stock, no-par, 400,000 shares issued
>   and outstanding 2,000,000
> Total contributed capital $4,800,000

Assume that all the stock was issued on January 1, 20__, and that no dividends were paid during the first two years of operations. During the third year, Palermo Corporation paid total cash dividends of $736,000.

a. Compute the amount of cash dividends paid during the third year to each of the three classes of stock.

b. Compute the dividends paid *per share* during the third year for each of the three classes of stock.

c. What was the average issue price of each type of preferred stock? Why would an investor buy noncumulative preferred stock, when cumulative stock is available from the same company at half the price per share?

EXERCISE 14-5
Analyzing Shareholders' Equity
(LO 4,5,6,7)

The year-end sheet of Maui Corporation includes the following shareholders' equity section (with certain details omitted):

> **Shareholders' equity:**
> 7% cumulative preferred stock, $100 par value,
>   callable at $105 .... $15,000,000
> Common stock, $5 par value, 5,000,000 shares
>   authorized, 4,000,000 shares issued 20,000,000
> Premium on preferred 300,000
> Premium on common 44,000,000
> Retained earnings 64,450,000
> Total shareholders' equity $143,750,000

From this information, compute answers to the following questions:

a. How many shares of preferred stock have been issued?

b. What is the total amount of the annual dividends paid to preferred shareholders?

c. What was the average issuance price per share of common stock?

d. What is the amount of contributed capital?

e. What is the book value per share of common stock?

f. Is it possible to determine the fair market value per share of common stock from the shareholders' equity section above? Explain.

EXERCISE 14-6
Issuing Stock for Assets Other than Cash
(LO 6)

Hudson Creek Development Limited issued 20,000 shares of its no-par value common stock in exchange for 300 hectares of land. The land recently had been appraised at $450,000.

a. Record this transaction under each of the following assumptions:
  1. Hudson is a closely held corporation. None of its shares have changed hands in several years.
  2. Hudson is a publicly owned corporation. Its stock currently is trading at $21.50 per share.

b. For each of your two journal entries, explain the reasoning behind the value that you assigned to the *land*.

EXERCISE 14-7
Reporting the Effects of Transactions
(LO 4,5,6,7)

Five events pertaining to Lowlands Manufacturing Inc. are described below.
a. Issued common stock for cash.
b. Issued common stock for equipment.
c. The market value of the corporation's common stock increased.
d. Declared and paid a cash dividend to shareholders.
e. Received a building site as a donation from the city.

Indicate the immediate effects of the events on the financial measurements in the four columnar headings listed below. Use the code letters, *I* for increase, *D* for decrease, and *NE* for no effect.

Event	Current Assets	Other Assets	Shareholders' Equity	Net Income
a				

EXERCISE 14-8
Computing Book Value
(LO 4,5,6,7)

Presented below is the information necessary to compute the net assets (shareholders' equity) and book value per share of common stock for Ringside Corporation:

$8 cumulative preferred stock, no-par (callable at $110), 2,000 shares issued	$200,000
Common stock, no-par, authorized unlimited shares, 60,000 shares issued and outstanding	752,800
Deficit	146,800
Dividends in arrears on preferred stock, 1 full year	16,000

a. Compute the amount of net assets (shareholders' equity).
b. Compute the book value per share of common stock.
c. Is book value per share (answer to part **b**) the amount common shareholders' should expect to receive if Ringside Corporation were to cease operations and liquidate? Explain.

EXERCISE 14-9
Nature of Market, Par, and Book Values
(LO 7,8)

SmithKline Beckman, the large pharmaceutical company that manufactures the cold remedy **Contac**, had a stated goal of increasing its net income by 10% each year. * As of mid-1988, the company's earnings growth had been "right on target" for several years, and most investors thought the company would again achieve its goal in 1988. In June 1988, however, the company surprised investors by announcing that earnings probably would not increase in 1988. In fact, management estimated that earnings for 1988 might be about 10% *below* the earn-

---

* SmithKline Beckman has since merged with **Beecham, Ltd.**, to form **SmithKline Beecham**.

ings of 1987. The reduced level of earnings, however, would not affect the company's ability to continue paying dividends at the current rate.

What would you expect the immediate effect of this announcement to be upon the following values of SmithKline's common stock? Explain.
a. Par value
b. Market value
c. Book value

EXERCISE 14-10
Reading the Financial Pages
(LO 7,8)

Presented below is an excerpt from a newspaper listing of stock transactions for a particular day. It presents the information about **Jannock Ltd.** stock for the day.

Stock	Ticker	Div	Vol 100s	Hi	Lo	Close	Net Chg
Jannock	JN	.50	242	22.00	21.80	21.80	-0.40
Jannock	JN	1.20	4	17.55	17.55	17.55	+0.25

From this information, answer the following questions:
a. How many shares of Jannock preferred stock were sold on this day?
b. If you had purchased 100 shares of Jannock common at the lowest price of the day, what would be the total purchase price of the stock?
c. What was the closing price of a share of Jannock preferred stock on the *previous* day?
d. Assume that you are assured of obtaining the $1.20 per share annual dividend on the preferred stock of Jannock, and you can buy and resell the stock at any time for $17.55 per share. Would it be better to invest in the stock, or to deposit your available funds in a savings account that pays interest at an annual rate of **5%**? Explain your answer.

Problems

PROBLEM 14-1
Journal Entries for Corporate Transactions
(LO 4,5,6)

Shown below are selected transactions of Harrow Vineyards Corporation for the year ended December 31, 2000:

Jan. 19 Issued capital stock to Martin DiBello in exchange for land. Two firms hired to appraise the land have differing opinions as to the fair market value of the real estate. DiBello, however, agrees to accept 10,000 shares of no-par value capital stock as a fair exchange. Harrow's stock is widely traded and is quoted at $19 per share on a stock exchange on this date.

June 10 At their June meeting, the board of directors declared a dividend of 20 cents per share, payable on July 15, to shareholders of the corporation's 200,000 outstanding shares of capital stock.

July 15 Paid the dividend declared on June 10.

Dec. 10 At their December meeting, the board of directors declared a dividend of 25 cents per share, payable on January 15 of the following year. No capital stock has been issued since the January 19 transaction.

Dec. 31 Recorded income tax expense for the three months ended December 31, 2000, $34,900. These taxes will be paid on January 15, 2001. (Income taxes for the first nine months of 2000 have already been recorded and paid.)

734 PARTNERSHIPS AND CORPORATIONS   PART 4

    Dec. 31   Closed the Income Summary account at the end of a profitable period. Net income, $365,000.

    Dec. 31   Closed the Dividends account.

INSTRUCTIONS

a. Prepare journal entries to record the above transactions.

b. Assume the balance sheet of Harrow Vineyards at December 31, 1999, reported retained earnings of $1,215,000. Compute the amount of retained earnings to be reported in the corporation's balance sheet at December 31, **2000**. Show computation.

PROBLEM 14-2
Shareholders' Equity in a Balance Sheet
(LO 4,5)

Early in 1996, Sinclair Press Ltd. was organized with authorization to issue an unlimited number of shares of no-par value preferred stock and no-par value common stock. Ten thousand shares of the preferred stock were issued at $100 each, and 170,000 shares of common stock were sold for $15 per share. The preferred stock pays an $8 cumulative dividend and is callable at $105.

During the first four years of operations (1996 through 1999), the corporation earned a total of $1,025,000 and paid dividends of 75 cents per share each year on the common stock. In 2000, however, the corporation reported a net loss of $340,000 and paid no dividends.

INSTRUCTIONS

a. Prepare the shareholders' equity section of the balance sheet at December 31, 2000. Include a supporting schedule showing your computation of the amount of retained earnings or deficit.

b. Draft a note to accompany the financial statements disclosing any dividends in arrears at the end of 2000.

c. In aggregate, have operations been profitable or unprofitable for the 5 years Sinclair Press has been in existence? Is your answer consistent with retained earnings or deficit determined in part **a**? Explain.

PROBLEM 14-3
Shareholders' Equity Section: an Alternate to Problem 14-2
(LO 4,5)

Banner Publications Inc. was organized early in 1996 with authorization to issue an unlimited number of shares of no-par value preferred stock and no-par value common stock. Twenty thousand preferred stock were issued at $100 each and 300,000 shares of common stock were sold for $20 per share. The preferred stock pays a $10 cumulative dividend and is callable at $105.

During the first five years of operations (1996 through 2000), the corporation earned a total of $4,460,000 and paid dividends of $1 per share each year on the common stock. In 2001, however, the corporation reported a net loss of $1,600,000 and paid no dividends.

INSTRUCTIONS

a. Prepare the shareholders' equity section of the balance sheet at December 31, 2001. Prepare a separate supporting schedule showing your computation of the amount of retained earnings or deficit.

b. Draft a note to accompany the financial statements disclosing any dividends in arrears at the end of 2001.

c. Do the dividends in arrears appear as a liability of the corporation as of the end of 2001? Explain.

PROBLEM 14-4
Shareholders' Equity Section—A More Challenging Problem
(LO 4,5,6)

Maria Martinez organized Manhattan Transport Limited in January 1998. The corporation immediately issued at $8 per share 100,000 of its unlimited authorized shares of no-par common stock. On January 2, **1999**, the corporation sold at $102 the entire 5,000 authorized shares of 8%, $100 par value, cumulative preferred stock. On January 2, **2000**, the company again needed money and issued 5,000 shares of its unlimited authorized shares of $9, no-par, cumulative preferred stock for a total of $502,000.

The company suffered losses in its first two years reporting a deficit of $170,000 at the end of 1999. During 2000 and 2001 combined, the company earned a total of $890,000. Dividends of 50 cents per share were paid on common stock in 2000 and $1.60 per share in 2001.

INSTRUCTIONS

a. Prepare the shareholders' equity section of the balance sheet at December 31, 2001. Include a supporting schedule showing your computation of retained earnings or deficit at the balance sheet date.

b. Assume that on January 2, 1999, the corporation could have borrowed $510,000 at 8% interest on a long-term basis instead of issuing the 5,000 shares of $100 par value cumulative preferred stock at $110. Identify two reasons why a corporation would issue cumulative preferred stock rather than finance operations with long-term debt.

PROBLEM 14-5
Reporting Shareholders' Equity: Two Short Cases
(LO 4,5,6,7)

The two cases described below are independent of each other. Each case provides the information necessary to prepare the shareholders' equity section of a corporate balance sheet.

1. Early in 1999, Bell Corporation was formed with authorization to issue an unlimited number of shares of no-par value common stock. Fifty thousand shares were issued at a price of $8 per share. The corporation reported a net loss of $82,000 for 1999 and a net loss of $25,000 in 2000. In 2001, net income was $70,000. No dividends were declared in any of the three years.

2. Parker Industries was organized early in 1997 and authorized to issue an unlimited number of shares of no-par value common and of $100 par value cumulative preferred stock. Thirty thousand shares of preferred stock were issued at $104 per share and 120,000 shares of common stock were sold for $15 per share.

   The preferred stock was callable at 105% of its $100 par value and was entitled to dividends of 10% before any dividends were paid to common stock. During the first five years of its existence, the corporation earned a total of $3,200,000 and paid dividends of 50 cents per share each year on the common stock.

INSTRUCTIONS

a. For each of the independent situations described, prepare in good form the shareholders' equity section of the balance sheet as of December 31, 2001. Include a supporting schedule for each case showing your determination of the balance of retained earnings that should appear in the balance sheet.

b. As of December 31, compute for each company the book value per share of common stock.

c. For each company, briefly explain why the book value is either higher or lower than the price at which the stock was originally issued.

PROBLEM 14-6
Dividends, Closing Entries, and Shareholders' Equity
(LO 4,5)

Hua Lai organized Pacific Rim Corporation early in 2000. On January 9, the corporation issued to Hua Lai and other investors 50,000 of its unlimited authorized shares of no-par value common stock at a price of $18 per share.

After the revenue and expense accounts (except income tax expense) were closed into the Income Summary account at the end of the year, that account showed a before-tax income of $144,000. Income taxes were determined to be $32,000. No dividends were paid during 2000.

On June 15, 2001, the board of directors declared a cash dividend of 90 cents per share, payable July 31.

INSTRUCTIONS

a. Prepare the journal entries for 2000 to (1) record the issuance of the common stock, (2) record the income tax liability at December 31, (3) close the

736 PARTNERSHIPS AND CORPORATIONS PART 4

Income Tax Expense account into the Income Summary account, and (4) close the Income Summary account.

b. Prepare the journal entries in 2001 for the declaration of the dividend on June 15 and payment of the dividend on July 31.

c. Operations in 2001 resulted in a $79,400 *net loss*. Prepare the journal entries to close the Income Summary account and the Dividends account at December 31, 2001.

d. Prepare the shareholders' equity section of the balance sheet at December 31, 2001. Include a separate supporting schedule showing your determination of retained earnings at that date.

PROBLEM 14-7
Shareholders' Equity: a Short, Comprehensive Problem
(LO 4,5)

Early in the year Roger Gordon and several friends organized a corporation called Mobile Communications Inc. The corporation was authorized to issue an unlimited number of shares of no-par value, $10 cumulative preferred stock and of no-par value common stock. The following transactions (among others) occurred during the year:

Jan. 6 Issued for cash 20,000 shares of common stock at $14 per share. The shares were issued to Gordon and 10 other investors.

Jan. 7 Issued an additional 500 shares of common stock to Gordon in exchange for his services in organizing the corporation. The shareholders agreed that these services were worth $7,000.

Jan. 12 Issued 2,500 shares of preferred stock for cash of $250,000.

June 4 Acquired land as a building site in exchange for 15,000 shares of common stock. In view of the appraised value of the land and the progress of the company, the directors agreed that the common stock was to be valued for purposes of this transaction at $15 per share.

Nov. 15 The first annual dividend of $10 per share was declared on the preferred stock to be paid December 20.

Dec. 20 Paid the cash dividend declared on November 15.

Dec. 31 After the revenue and expenses were closed into the Income Summary account, that account indicated a net income of $106,500.

INSTRUCTIONS

a. Prepare journal entries in general journal form to record the above transactions. Include entries at December 31 to close the Income Summary account and the Dividends account.

b. Prepare the shareholders' equity section of the Mobile Communications Inc., balance sheet at December 31.

PROBLEM 14-8
Incorporating a Going-concern
(LO 1,2,3,5,6)

Pancho's Cantina is the best Mexican restaurant in town—some customers say the best anywhere. For years, the restaurant was a sole proprietorship owned by Wayne Label. Many of Label's friends and customers had offered to invest in the business if he ever decided to open new locations. So, early this year, Label decided to expand the business. He formed a new corporation, called Pancho's Cantinas Inc., which planned to issue capital stock and use the money received to open new Pancho's restaurants in various locations.

The new corporation is authorized to issue an unlimited number of shares of no-par value capital stock. In April the corporation entered into the following transactions:

Apr. 1 Issued 25,000 shares of capital stock to Label in exchange for the assets of the original Pancho's Cantina. These assets and their current market value on this date are listed below.

Inventory	$ 20,000
Land	305,000
Building	280,000
Equipment and fixtures	145,000

Apr. 15 Issued for cash 25,000 shares of capital stock at a price of $30 per share. These shares were issued to Label's family, friends, several employees of the original Pancho's, and fourteen regular customers.

Apr. 20 Received an invoice from a lawyer for $6,200 for services relating to the formation of the new corporation. This invoice is due in 30 days.

Apr. 30 Issued 100 shares of capital stock to Label in exchange for $3,000 cash, thus assuring Label voting control of the corporation.

The new corporation will begin operation of the original Pancho's Cantina on May 1. Therefore, the corporation had no revenue or expenses relating to restaurant operations during April. No depreciation of plant assets or amortization of organization costs will be recognized until May when operations get under way.

INSTRUCTIONS

a. Prepare journal entries to record the April transactions in the accounting records of the new corporation.
b. Prepare a classified balance sheet for the corporation as of April 30, 20__.
c. Explain how the incorporation of Pancho's will affect Label's:
   1. Ability to withdraw assets from the business.
   2. Role in day-to-day operations.
   3. Liability for business debts.
   4. Personal income tax obligations.
d. Does Pancho's appear to be a closely held corporation, or publicly owned?
e. Did Label really need to increase his shareholdings on April 30 to have effective "voting control" of the corporation? Explain.

PROBLEM 14-9
Analysis of an Equity Section of a Balance Sheet
(LO 4,5,6,7)

The year-end balance sheet of DeskTop Products includes the following shareholders' equity section (with certain details omitted):

Shareholders' equity:	
$7.50 cumulative preferred stock, no-par value, callable at $105, authorized, unlimited shares, issued and outstanding, 24,000 shares	$ 2,400,000
Common stock, no-par value, authorized, unlimited shares, issued and outstanding, 450,000 shares	9,225,000
Donated capital	720,000
Retained earnings	2,595,000
Total shareholders' equity	$14,940,000

From this information, compute answers to the following questions:
a. What was the average issuance price per share of preferred stock?
b. What is the total amount of the annual dividends requirement on preferred stock?
c. What was the average issuance price per share of common stock?
d. What is the amount of contributed capital?
e. What is the book value per share of common stock? (There are no dividends in arrears.)
f. Assume that retained earnings at the beginning of the year amounted to $717,500, and that net income for the year was $3,970,000. What was the dividend declared during the year on *each share* of common stock?

PROBLEM 14-10
Analysis of Shareholder's Equity
(LO 4,5,6,7)

The year-end balance sheet of LaserTech, Inc., includes the following shareholders' equity section (with certain details omitted):

Shareholders' equity:
$8.80 cumulative preferred stock, $100 par value, callable at $110, authorized 30,000 shares	$ 1,200,000
Common stock, no-par value, authorized, unlimited shares, issued and outstanding, 310,000 shares	7,440,000
Premium on preferred stock	60,000
Donated capital	960,000
Retained earnings	4,680,000
Total shareholders' equity	$14,340,000

INSTRUCTIONS

On the basis of this information, answer the following questions and show any necessary supporting computations:
a. How many shares of preferred stock are outstanding?
b. What is the amount of the annual dividend requirement on preferred stock?
c. What was the average issuance price of a share of common stock?
d. What was the average issuance price of a share of preferred stock?
e. What is the current book value per share of common stock? (There are no dividends in arrears.)
f. What is the total contributed capital?
g. Assume that net income for the year was $2,100,000 and the balance of retained earnings at the beginning of the year was $3,302,000. What was the amount of dividends declared during the year for the preferred and common stock?

PROBLEM 14-11
Analysis of an Equity Section—More Comprehensive
(LO 1,2,5,6,7,8)

Quanex Corporation is a publicly owned company. The following information is excerpted from a recent balance sheet. Dollar amounts (except for per share amounts) are stated in thousands.

> **Shareholders' equity:**
> Convertible $17.20 preferred stock, no-par value, 1,000,000
>   shares authorized; 345,000 shares issued and outstanding;
> $250 per share liquidation preference (call price) .... $ 86,250
> Common stock, no-par value, unlimited number of shares
>   authorized, issued and outstanding, 13,638,000 shares 94,079
> Retained earnings 57,263
>   Total shareholders' equity $237,592

INSTRUCTIONS

From this information, answer the following questions:
a. What was the average issuance price per share of common stock?
b. What is the total amount of the annual dividends requirement on preferred stock?
c. What is the total amount of contributed capital?
d. What is the book value per share of common stock?
e. Briefly explain the advantages and disadvantages to Quanex of being publicly owned, rather than operating as a closely held corporation.
f. What is meant by the term "convertible" used in the caption of the preferred stock? Is there any more information that investors need to know in order to evaluate this conversion feature?
g. Assume that the preferred stock currently is selling at *$248* per share. Does this provide a higher or lower dividend yield than a $4, no-par value preferred with a market price of $57 per share? Show computations (round to the nearest tenth of one percent). Explain why one preferred stock might yield less than another.

Analytical and Decision Problems and Cases

A&D 14-1
Using a Corporate Balance Sheet
(LO 3,5,6,7,8)

Using the balance sheet of Del Mar Corporation on page 719, answer the following questions. Questions **a** and **b** require short computations. For the remaining questions, briefly ***explain your reasoning***. In some cases, the balance sheet may not provide sufficient information to answer the question. If this is the case, explain.
a. What was the average issue price of the common stock?
b. What is the book value per share of common stock at the balance sheet date?
c. What is the market price of the common stock at the balance sheet date?
d. What was the amount of cash dividends paid to holders of the ***common stock*** during 2000?
e. Can Del Mar quickly raise equity capital by issuing more shares of its $8 preferred stock?
f. Assume that on the balance sheet date, interest rates on high quality preferred stocks currently range between $7\frac{1}{2}\%$ and $7\frac{3}{4}\%$. Would you expect the market price of Del Mar's preferred stock to be above or below $100 per share?
g. Assume that at the end of ***2001***, the company has eliminated all dividends in arrears. How much cash will the holder of each share of preferred stock receive in that year?

740 PARTNERSHIPS AND CORPORATIONS PART 4

A&D 14-2
Par, Book, and Market Values.
An Open-Ended Discussion
(LO 7,8)

Microsoft Corp. is the producer of such software products as **Windows**, **Excel**, and **Word**. In mid-1990, an investment service published the following per-share amounts relating to Microsoft's only class of capital stock:

Par value	$ 0.001
Book value (estimated)	6.50
Market value	73.00

INSTRUCTIONS

a. Without reference to dollar amounts, explain the nature and significance of ***par value***, ***book value***, and ***market value***.

b. Comment upon the ***interrelationships***, if any, among the per-share amounts shown for Microsoft Corp. What do these amounts imply about the company and its operations? Also comment upon what these amounts imply about the security of ***creditors'*** claims against the company.

A&D 14-3
Factors Affecting the Market Prices of Preferred and Common Stocks
(LO 8)

ADM Labs is a publicly owned company with several issues of capital stock outstanding. Over the past decade, the company has consistently earned modest income and has increased its common stock dividend annually by 5 or 10 cents per share. Recently the company introduced several new products that you believe will cause future sales and income to increase dramatically. You also expect a gradual increase in long-term interest rates from their present level of about 11% to, perhaps, 12 or $12\frac{1}{2}$%. Based upon these forecasts, explain whether you would expect to see the market prices of the following issues of ADM capital stock increase or decrease. Explain your reasoning in each answer.

a. 10%, $100 par value, preferred stock (currently selling at $90 per share).

b. No-par value common stock (currently paying an annual dividend of $2.50 and selling at $40 per share).

c. $7, no-par value, convertible preferred stock (currently selling at $119 per share).

A&D 14-4
Whether or Not To Incorporate
(LO 1, 2)

Mario Valenti owns Valenti Ford, a successful automobile dealership. For 25 years, Valenti has operated the business as a sole proprietorship and has acted as both owner and manager. Now, he is 70 years old and is planning on retiring from active management. However, he wants the dealership to stay in the family; his long-term goal is to leave the business to his two children and five grandchildren.

Valenti is wondering whether or not he should incorporate his business. If he were to reorganize Valenti Ford as a corporation, he could then leave an appropriate number of shares of capital stock to each of his heirs. Otherwise, he could leave the entire business to his heirs to be operated as a partnership. In selecting the appropriate form of business entity, Valenti has formulated the following objectives:

1. **Ownership:** Valenti wants each of his two children to own 25% of the business and each of his five grandchildren to own 10%.

2. **Continuity of existence:** Valenti wants the business to continue indefinitely, even if one or more of the heirs should die or should no longer want to participate in ownership.

3. **Management:** When Valenti retires, he plans to give Joe Heinz, a long-time employee, responsibility for managing the business. Although Valenti wants to keep the ownership of the business in the family, he does not believe that any of his family members have the time or experience to manage the business on a daily basis. In fact, Valenti believes that two of his grandchildren simply have no "business sense," and he does not want them to participate in management.

4. **Income taxes:** Valenti wants to organize the business in a manner that will minimize the income taxes to be paid by his heirs. He expects that all the earnings of the business normally will be distributed to its owners on an annual basis.
5. **Owners' liability:** Valenti recognizes that an automobile dealership might become liable for vast amounts of money, if, for example, improper repairs caused a customer's car to be involved in an accident. Although the business carries insurance, he wants to be sure that his heirs' equity in the business does not place their personal assets at risk in the event of business losses.

INSTRUCTIONS

a. For each of the five numbered paragraphs above, explain how the choice of business organization (partnership or corporation) relates to Valenti's stated objective.
b. In light of your analysis in part **a**, above, would you recommend that Valenti reorganize Valenti Ford as a corporation, or leave the business unincorporated so that his heirs may operate it as a partnership?

A&D 14-5
Dividend Distribution and Policy
(LO 3,4,6)

Huron-Church Corporation has been in business for a number of years. Even though it has been profitable, the corporation's performance has been erratic: 2000, net loss of $182,000; 2001, net income of $212,000; and 2002, net income of $298,000. The shareholders' equity at December 31, 1999 showed, among other items, the following:

Capital stock issued and outstanding:
$8 noncumulative preferred, 5,000 shares	$ 500,000
$6 cumulative preferred, 6,000 shares	600,000
$5 cumulative fully-participating preferred, 10,000 shares	1,000,000
Common, 100,000 shares	2,000,000
Retained earnings	810,000

There were no capital stock transactions for the years 2000 to 2002.

INSTRUCTIONS

a. Compute the amount of dividends for each of the four classes of capital stock for the years 2000, 2001 and 2002, based on the following dividend policies:
   1. Distribute an amount that is the greater of the regular dividends or the net income for the year.
   2. Distribute an amount that is equal to the net income for the year.
b. Based on the answers in **a** above, which dividend policy is more beneficial to the common shareholders? Explain.

Answers to Self-Test Questions

1. c   2. d   3. c   4. c   5. b, c, d

CHAPTER 15

Reporting Special Events and Special Equity Transactions

The unexpected can happen—and the impact can be of great consequence. Such events deserve special consideration—by investors, management, and, in many cases, by government and the public. That's why these events are reported *separately* from the results of routine business operations.

CHAPTER LEARNING OBJECTIVES

1. Explain predictive information and its relation to the presentation of discontinued operations, extraordinary items, and accounting changes in the income and other financial statements.
2. Compute earnings per share.
3. Distinguish between basic and fully diluted earnings per share.
4. Account for stock dividends and stock splits, and explain the probable effect of these transactions upon market price.
5. Describe and prepare a statement of retained earnings.
6. Account for treasury stock transactions.

In this chapter we explore special topics relating primarily to the financial statements of large corporations. The chapter is divided into two major parts. In the first part, we show how an income statement is organized to present certain "unusual" items separately from the income or loss from normal business activities. Also, we illustrate and explain the presentation of earnings per share, with emphasis upon the interpretation of the different per-share amounts. In the second part, we look at various shareholders' equity transactions, including cash dividends, stock dividends, stock splits, and treasury stock transactions.

REPORTING THE RESULTS OF OPERATIONS

The most important aspect of corporate financial reporting, in the view of most investors, is the determination of periodic income. Both the market price of common stock and the amount of cash dividends per share depend on the current and future earnings of the corporation.

Developing Predictive Information in the Income Statement

LO 1: Explain predictive information and its relation to the presentation of discontinued operations, extraordinary items, and accounting changes in the income and other financial statements.

An income statement tells us a great deal about the performance of a company over the past year. For example, study of the income statement makes clear the types and amounts of revenue earned and expenses incurred as well as the amounts of gross profit and net income. But what can the current income statement tell us about the probable *future* earnings of the corporation? By analyzing the *trend* of earnings over time, we can often develop a reasonable estimate of future earnings, especially if we take into account significant changes in the corporation's business, its industry, and economic conditions.

If the transactions summarized in the income statement for the year just completed were of a normal recurring nature, such as selling merchandise, paying employees, and incurring other normal expenses, we can reasonably assume that the operating results were typical and that somewhat similar results can be expected in the following year. However, in any business, unusual and nonrecurring events may occur that cause the current year's net income to be quite different from the net income we should expect the company to earn in the future. For example, the company may have sustained large losses in the current year from an earthquake or some other event that is not likely to recur in the near future.

Ideally, the results of unusual and nonrecurring events should be shown in a separate section of the income statement *after* the income or loss from normal business activities has been determined. Income from *normal and recurring* activities presumably should be a more useful figure for *predicting future earnings* than is a net income figure that includes the results of nonrecurring events. The problem in creating such an income statement, however, is in determining which events are so unlikely to recur that they should be excluded from the results of "normal" operations. The categories of events that require special treatment in the income statement are (1) the results of *discontinued operations* and (2) *extraordinary items*. An income statement with such separate disclosures provides a better basis for evaluating past performance and for predicting future performance.

Reporting Special Events—An Illustration

To illustrate the presentation of these items, assume that Ross Corporation operates both a small chain of retail stores and two motels. Near the end of the current year, the company sells both motels to a national hotel chain. In addition, Ross Corporation reports two "extraordinary items." An income statement illustrating the format for reporting these events appears below.

Notice the order in which the "special events" are reported

ROSS CORPORATION
Income Statement
For the Year Ended December 31, 2000

Net sales		$8,000,000
Cost and expenses:		
Cost of goods sold	$4,580,000	
Selling expenses	1,500,000	
General and administrative expenses	920,000	
Income taxes (on continuing operations)	300,000	7,300,000
Income from continuing operations		$ 700,000
Discontinued operations:		
Operating loss on motels (net of $90,000 income tax benefit)	$ (210,000)	
Gain on sale of motels (net of $195,000 income taxes)	455,000	245,000
Income before extraordinary items		$ 945,000
Extraordinary items:		
Gain on expropriation of land for a highway (net of $45,000 income taxes)	$ 105,000	
Loss from tornado damage to a retail store (net of $75,000 income tax benefit)	(175,000)	(70,000)
Net income		$ 875,000

Note: This income statement is designed to illustrate the presentation of various "special events." Rarely, if ever, will all these types of events appear in the income statement of one company within a single year.

Continuing Operations

The first section of the income statement contains only the results of *continuing business activities*—that is, the retail stores. Notice that the income taxes expense shown in this section relates *only to continuing operations*. The income taxes relating to the "special events" are shown separately in the income statement as adjustments to the amounts of these items.

Income from Continuing Operations The subtotal *income from continuing operations* measures the profitability of the ongoing operations. This subtotal should be helpful in making predictions of the company's future earnings. For example, if we predict no significant change in the profitability of its retail stores, we would expect Ross Corporation to earn a net income of approximately $700,000 next year.

Discontinued Operations

The first category of events requiring disclosure in a separate section of the income statement is the result of discontinued operations. If management has sold or discontinued a *segment* of the business or enters into a formal plan to sell or discontinue a **segment of the business**, the results of that segment's operations are shown separately in the income statement. This enables users of the financial statements to better evaluate the performance of the company's ongoing (continuing) operations and to better predict the company's future performance.

Two items are included in the **discontinued operations** section of the income statement: (1) the income or loss from *operating* the segment prior to its disposal and (2) the gain or loss on *disposal* of the segment. Notice also that the income taxes relating to the discontinued operations are *shown separately* from the income taxes expense relating to continuing business operations.

Discontinued Operations Must Be a "Segment" of the Business To qualify for separate presentation in the income statement, the discontinued operations must represent an *entire segment* of the business. A "segment" of a business is a separate line of business activity or an operation that services a particular class of customers. For example, the sale of an oil and gas operation by a real estate company or the sale of the wholesale division selling food to retail stores by a company whose other operations consist of selling food through its restaurants would constitute a disposal of a segment of business.[1]

> **CASE IN POINT** Large corporations usually have many segments of business. Imasco has various segments, one of which is the Shoppers Drug Mart. If Imasco closes an individual Shoppers Drug Mart store, such a closure does not qualify as "discontinued operations" because Imasco remains in the drug store business. However, if Imasco were to sell the entire Shoppers Drug Mart operation, the drug store activities would be shown in Imasco's income statement as "discontinued operations."

---

[1] CICA, *CICA Handbook* (Toronto), section 3475.05.

Discontinued Operations Are Not Really "Unusual" In recent years, a characteristic of the Canadian economy has been the "restructuring" of many large corporations. As part of this restructuring, corporations often sell one or more segments of the business. Thus, the presence of "discontinued operations" is not uncommon in the income statements of large corporations.

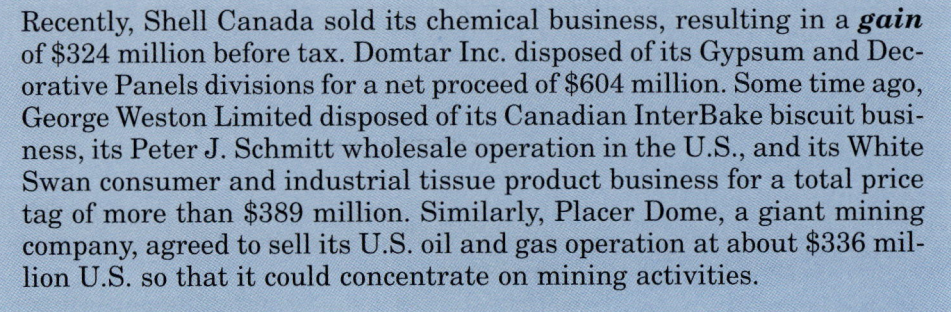

> **CASE IN POINT**
>
> Recently, Shell Canada sold its chemical business, resulting in a ***gain*** of $324 million before tax. Domtar Inc. disposed of its Gypsum and Decorative Panels divisions for a net proceed of $604 million. Some time ago, George Weston Limited disposed of its Canadian InterBake biscuit business, its Peter J. Schmitt wholesale operation in the U.S., and its White Swan consumer and industrial tissue product business for a total price tag of more than $389 million. Similarly, Placer Dome, a giant mining company, agreed to sell its U.S. oil and gas operation at about $336 million U.S. so that it could concentrate on mining activities.

Extraordinary Items

The second category of events requiring disclosure in a separate section of the income statement is **extraordinary items**. Extraordinary items are those items resulting from events or transactions that have met all of the following three characteristics or criteria:

1. not expected to occur frequently over several years
2. not typical of the normal business activities of the entity
3. not dependent primarily on decisions or determinations by management or owners[2]

To clarify the application of these characteristics, the Accounting Standards Board of the CICA has provided some explanations and examples. First, the determination of whether an event is expected to occur frequently over several years requires the determination of the frequency of the occurrence of such events in the recent past and in the foreseeable future. Accordingly, a farmer's crop loss from drought does not meet this first criterion if drought conditions in the area are normally experienced every three or four years.[3]

Second, the factors that determine whether a transaction or event typifies the normal business activities of the entity should include: "type and scope of operations, characteristics of the industry, operating policies, nature of products and services, and the environment in which the entity operates."[4] Thus, the following, regardless of size, do not qualify because they are from normal business activities: (1) losses and provisions for losses with respect to bad debts and inventories, (2) gains and losses from fluctuations in foreign exchange rates, (3) adjustments with respect to contract prices, (4) gains and losses from write-down or sale of property, plant, equipment or other investments, (5) income tax reductions on uti-

---
[2] CICA, *CICA Handbook* (Toronto), section 3480.02.
[3] Ibid., section 3480.03.
[4] Ibid., section 3480.04.

lization of prior period losses or reversal of previously recorded tax benefits, and adjustment resulting from changes in income tax rates or laws.[5]

Third, a transaction or event would not depend primarily on decisions or determinations by management or owners "if their decisions or determinations would not normally influence the transactions or events."[6] Therefore, sale of land originally intended for plant expansion, but later held for appreciation, would not meet this criterion.

Because the criteria for extraordinary items are very restrictive, extraordinary items are quite rare. The following are examples that are likely to meet the three criteria recommended in the *CICA Handbook*:

1. The expropriation of a corporation's land and buildings for a highway.
2. The destruction of a large portion of a wheat crop by a tornado.
3. An explosion in a nuclear reactor resulting in high-level radioactive emission.
4. The destruction of an airplane of a major airline by a terrorist attack.[7]

When a gain or loss resulting from a transaction or an event qualifies as an extraordinary item, it appears under a **separate heading** called **extraordinary items**, following the sub-heading "income before extraordinary items," net of applicable income taxes. The nature of the gain or loss should be adequately and clearly described. Such a separate and distinct presentation, as illustrated in the income statement of Ross Corporation, enables users of the financial statements to better evaluate and predict the performance of the company's on-going (continuing) operations.

Accounting Changes

Other matters having an effect on the evaluation and prediction of the trend of earnings include: (1) a change in an accounting policy, (2) a change in an accounting estimate, and (3) a correction of an error in prior period financial statements. These matters are covered by Section 1506, "Accounting Changes," of the *CICA Handbook*. The recommendations of the *CICA Handbook* are highlighted in the following paragraphs.

Changes in Accounting Policy encompass changes in accounting principles as well as accounting methods used in the preparation of financial statements. As stated in Chapter 12 and other chapters, the consistent application of accounting principles and methods from one accounting period to another enhances the usefulness of financial statements on a comparative basis. Also, management may justify a change to another acceptable accounting principle on the grounds that it is more appropriate. For example, a change in determining inventory cost from a weighted-average to a first-in first-out method or a change in recognizing depreciation expense from a straight-line to a declining-balance method

---

[5] Ibid.
[6] Ibid., section 3480.05.
[7] Ibid., section 3480.05 and .06.

constitutes a change in accounting policy, when such a change is **not** the result of changed circumstances, experience, or new information.[8]

Since a change in accounting policy affects two or more accounting periods, Section 1506 of the *CICA Handbook* recommends that the effect of an accounting policy change be reflected on a **retroactive** basis with a **restatement** of those prior period financial statements affected by the change. Thus, each of those prior period financial statements presented on a comparative basis is to be restated to reflect the new accounting policy. In addition, the cumulative effect of the change on the periods preceding the earliest period included in the **comparative financial statements** is treated as an adjustment to the beginning balance of retained earnings of the earliest period. If comparative statements are not prepared, an adjustment should be made to the current period's beginning retained earnings for the cumulative effect of the change on prior periods.

Changes in Accounting Estimates include such items as a revision of the estimate of the amount of allowance for doubtful accounts or a revision of the estimate of a nine-year useful life of a depreciable asset to a six-year life. A change in an estimate is a result of **changed circumstances**, **experience**, or **new information**. For example, a change in the method of depreciation of a plant asset that results from changed circumstances, experience, or new information would be treated as a change in accounting estimate, **not** a change of accounting policy. Section 1506 of the *CICA Handbook* recommends that the effect of such a change be accounted for in the period of change or in the period of change and the applicable future periods, depending on whether the change affects one or more periods. Thus, this differs from the treatment of a change in accounting policy in that a restatement of prior periods and a cumulative adjustment are **not** required.

Corrections of Errors are required when errors are discovered in prior period financial statements. Errors may result from a mistake in computation, a misinterpretation or misrepresentation of information, an oversight of available information, or a misappropriation of assets.[9] Examples of corrections of errors include the discovery that inventories were materially overstated and depreciation expenses were substantially understated in prior period financial statements. Section 1506 of the *CICA Handbook* recommends that a correction of an error be accounted for **retroactively** and that the prior period financial statements presented for comparative purposes be **restated**. In addition, it requires disclosure in the current period regarding: (1) a description of the error, (2) the effect of the correction of the error on the financial statements of the current and prior periods, and (3) the fact that the prior period financial statements presented for comparative purposes have been restated. The disclosure of the effect of the correction on such significant items as net income, earnings per share, and working capital also may be appropriate. These requirements for a correction of an error are logical because they make comparisons of performance of a business enterprise over a number of periods more meaningful and not misleading.

---

[8] Ibid., section 1506.03.
[9] Ibid., section 1506.26.

CHAPTER 15 REPORTING SPECIAL EVENTS AND SPECIAL EQUITY TRANSACTIONS   749

The following chart summarizes the accounting and reporting requirements of Section 1506 of the *CICA Handbook*.

Financial Statements Affected

Type of Accounting Change	Income	Retained Earnings	Accounting and Reporting Requirements
1. Change in accounting policy	Prior period	Current and prior periods	Retroactive application and restatement
2. Change in accounting estimate	Current or current and future periods	Not applicable	Current or current and prospective application
3. Correction of error in prior period	Prior period	Current and prior periods	Retroactive application and restatement

It is interesting to note that both a change in an accounting policy and a correction of an error in prior period financial statements receive the same treatment—retroactive application and restatement.

The in-depth coverage of the topic of accounting changes is more appropriately covered in the intermediate accounting course.

Earnings per Share (EPS)

LO 2: Compute earnings per share.

Perhaps the most widely used of all accounting statistics is **earnings per share** of common stock. Everyone who buys or sells stock in a corporation needs to know the annual earnings per share. Stock market prices are quoted on a per-share basis. If you are considering investing in BCE Inc. stock at a price of, say, $63 per share, you need to know the earnings per share and the annual dividend per share in order to decide whether this price is reasonable. In other words, how much earning power and how much dividend income would you be getting for each share you buy?

The relationship between earnings per share and stock price is expressed by the **price-earnings ratio** (p/e ratio). This ratio is simply the current stock price divided by the earnings per share for the year (the latest 12 months). (A p/e ratio is *not* computed if the company has sustained a net *loss* for this period.) The p/e ratios are of such interest to investors that they are published daily in the financial pages of major newspapers (an example appears in Chapter 14).

Stock prices actually reflect investors' expectations of *future* earnings. The p/e ratio, however, is based upon the earnings over the *past* year. Thus, if investors expect earnings to *increase* substantially from current levels, the p/e ratio will be quite high—perhaps 20, 30, or even more. But if investors expect earnings to *decline* from current levels, the p/e ratio will be quite low, say, 8 or less. A mature company with very stable earnings usually sells between 10 and 12 times earnings. Thus, the p/e ratio reflects *investors' expectations* of the company's future prospects.[10]

---

[10] A word of caution—if current earnings are *very low*, the p/e ratio tends to be quite high *regardless* of whether future earnings are expected to rise or fall. In such situations, the p/e ratio is not a meaningful measurement.

Let us now look more closely at the measurement that *underlies* the p/e ratio—*earnings per share*.

Computing Earnings Per Share To compute earnings per share, the common shareholders' share of the company's net income is divided by the average number of common shares outstanding. Notice that the concept of earnings per share applies only to **common stock**; preferred shareholders have no claim to earnings beyond the stipulated preferred stock dividends.

Computing earnings per share is easiest when the corporation has issued only common stock, and the number of outstanding shares has not changed during the year. In this case, earnings per share is equal to net income divided by the number of shares outstanding.

What Happens if More Shares Are Issued? In many companies, however, the number of shares of stock outstanding changes one or more times during the year. If additional shares are sold during the year, or if shares of common stock are retired (repurchased from the shareholders), the computation of earnings per share is based upon the **weighted-average number of shares outstanding**.[11]

The weighted-average number of shares for the year is determined by multiplying the number of shares outstanding by the fraction of the year that said number of shares outstanding remained unchanged. For example, assume that 100,000 shares of common stock were outstanding during the first nine months of 2000 and 140,000 shares during the last three months. Assume also that the increase in shares outstanding resulted from the sale of 40,000 shares for cash. The weighted-average number of shares outstanding during 2000 would be **110,000** determined as follows:

100,000 shares × 9/12 **of a year**	75,000
140,000 shares × 3/12 **of a year**	35,000
Weighted-average number of common shares outstanding	**110,000**

This procedure gives more meaningful earnings per share data than if the total number of shares outstanding at the end of the year were used in the calculations. By using the weighted-average number of shares, we recognize that the proceeds from the sale of the 40,000 shares were available to generate earnings only during the last three months of the year. Although the weighted-average number of shares outstanding must be used in earnings-per-share computations, this figure does not appear in the shareholders' equity section of the balance sheet. A balance sheet prepared at year-end reports the *actual* number of shares outstanding at that date, regardless of when the shares were issued during the year.

---

[11] When the number of shares outstanding changes as a result of a stock split or a stock dividend (discussed later in this chapter), the computation of the weighted-average number of shares outstanding should be adjusted **retroactively** rather than weighted for the period the new shares were outstanding. Earnings per share data for prior years thus will be consistently stated in terms of the current capital structure.

Preferred Dividends and Earnings per Share When a company has preferred stock outstanding, the preferred shareholders participate in net income to the extent of the preferred stock dividends. To determine the earnings *applicable to the common stock*, we first deduct from net income the amount of current year preferred stock dividends. The annual dividend on *cumulative* preferred stock is *always* deducted, even if not declared by the board of directors for the current year. Noncumulative preferred stock dividends are deducted only if declared.

To illustrate, let us assume that Tanner Corporation has 200,000 shares of common stock and 10,000 shares of $6 cumulative preferred stock outstanding throughout the year. Net income for the year 2000 totals $560,000. Earnings per share of common stock would be computed as follows:

Net income	$560,000
Less: Dividends on preferred stock (10,000 shares × $6)	60,000
Earnings applicable to common stock	$500,000
Weighted-average number of common shares outstanding	200,000
Earnings per share of common stock ($500,000 ÷ 200,000 shares)	$ 2.50

Even when there are dividends in arrears, only the **current year's** cumulative preferred stock dividend is deducted in the earnings per share computation. Dividends in arrears from previous years have already been deducted in the prior years' earnings per share computations.

Presentation of Earnings per Share in the Income Statement All publicly owned corporations are *required* to present earnings per share data in their income statements.[12] If an income statement includes subtotals for Income from Continuing Operations, or for Income before Extraordinary Items, per-share figures are shown for income before discontinued operations and extraordinary items as well as for net income. These additional per-share amounts are computed by substituting the amount of the appropriate subtotal for the net income figure in the preceding calculation. Also, it is desirable to show the earnings per share for discontinued operations and extraordinary items to stress their effect on the final earnings per share.[13]

To illustrate all of the potential per-share computations, we will expand our Tanner Corporation example to include income from continuing operations and income before extraordinary items. We should point out, however, that all of these figures seldom appear in the same income statement. Very few companies have discontinued operations and an extraordinary item to report in the same year. The condensed income statement shown below is intended to illustrate the proper format for presenting earnings per share figures and to provide a review of the calculations.

---

[12] CICA, *CICA Handbook* (Toronto), section 3500.06.
[13] Ibid., section 3500.12.

Earnings per share figures are required in the income statement

TANNER CORPORATION
Condensed Income Statement
For the Year Ended December 31, 2000

Net sales	$9,000,000
Costs and expenses (including income taxes on continuing operations)	8,310,000
Income from continuing operations	$ 690,000
Loss from discontinued operations (net of income tax benefits)	(90,000)
Income before extraordinary items	$ 600,000
Extraordinary loss (net of income tax benefit)	(40,000)
Net income	$ 560,000
Earnings per share of common stock:	
Earnings from continuing operations	$3.15[a]
Loss from discontinued operations	(.45)
Earnings before extraordinary items	$2.70[b]
Extraordinary loss	(.20)
Net earnings	$2.50[c]

[a] ($690,000 − $60,000 preferred dividends) ÷ 200,000 shares
[b] ($600,000 − $60,000) ÷ 200,000 shares
[c] ($560,000 − $60,000) ÷ 200,000 shares

Interpreting the Different Per-Share Amounts To knowledgeable users of financial statements, each of these figures has a different significance. Earnings per share from continuing operations represents the results of continuing and ordinary business activity. This figure is the most useful one for predicting future operating results. **Net earnings** per share, on the other hand, shows the overall operating results of the current year, including any discontinued operations or extraordinary items.

Unfortunately, the term *earnings per share* often is used without qualification in referring to various types of per-share data. When using per-share information, it is important to know exactly *which* per-share statistic is being presented. For example, the price-earnings ratios (market price divided by earnings per share) for common stocks listed on major stock exchanges are reported daily in *The Globe and Mail* and many other newspapers. Which earnings per share figures are used in computing these ratios? If a company reports discontinued operations and an extraordinary item, the price-earnings ratio is computed using the per-share *earnings before the discontinued operations and extraordinary item*. Otherwise, the ratio is based upon *net earnings* (net income) per share.

Basic and Fully Diluted Earnings per Share

LO 3: Distinguish between basic and fully diluted earnings per share.

Let us assume that a company has an outstanding issue of preferred stock that is convertible into shares of common stock at a rate of, say, two shares of common for each share of preferred. The conversion of this preferred stock would increase the number of common shares outstanding and might *dilute* (reduce) earnings per share. Any common shareholder interested in the trend of earnings per share will want to know what effect the conversion of the preferred stock would have upon this statistic.

To inform investors of the potential dilution that might occur, two figures are presented for each earnings per share statistic. The first figure, called **basic earnings per share**, is based upon the weighted-average number of common shares **actually outstanding** during the year. Thus, this figure ignores the potential dilution represented by the convertible preferred stock.[14] The second figure, called **fully diluted earnings per share**, shows the **impact that conversion** of the preferred stock would have upon basic earnings per share.

Basic earnings per share are computed in the same manner illustrated in our preceding example of Tanner Corporation. Fully diluted earnings per share, on the other hand, are computed on the assumption that all the preferred stock **had been converted into common stock at the beginning of the current year**.[15] (The mechanics of computing fully diluted earnings per share are covered in the intermediate accounting course.)

It is important to remember that fully diluted earnings per share represent a **hypothetical case**. This statistic is computed even though the preferred stock actually was **not** converted during the year. The purpose of showing fully diluted earnings per share is to warn common shareholders what **could** have happened. When the difference between basic and fully diluted earnings per share becomes significant, investors should recognize the **risk** that future earnings per share may be reduced by conversions of other securities into common stock.

When a company reports both basic and fully diluted earnings per share, the price-earnings ratio shown in newspapers is based upon the **basic** figure (that is, before discontinued operations and extraordinary items).

OTHER SHAREHOLDERS' EQUITY TRANSACTIONS

Cash Dividends

The prospect of receiving cash dividends is a principal reason for investing in the capital stocks of corporations. An increase or a decrease in the established rate of dividends will usually cause an immediate rise or fall in the market price of the company's capital stock. Shareholders are keenly interested in prospects for future dividends and as a group are strongly in favour of more generous dividend payments. The board of directors, on the other hand, is primarily concerned with the long-run growth and financial strength of the corporation; it may prefer to restrict dividends to a minimum in order to conserve cash for the purchase of plant and equipment or for other needs of the company. Many of the so-called "growth companies" plow back into the business most of their earnings and pay little or no cash dividends.

The preceding discussion suggests three requirements for the payment of a cash dividend. These are:

---

[14] If certain criteria are met, preferred shares are treated, for example, as "**common stock**" and are entered into the computation of basic earnings per share. This and other complex issues relating to earnings per share are discussed in section 3500 of the *CICA Handbook* and in intermediate accounting texts.

[15] If the preferred stock had been issued during the current year, we would assume that it was converted into common stock on the date it was issued.

1. **Retained earnings.** Since dividends represent a distribution of earnings to shareholders, the theoretical maximum for dividends is the total undistributed net income of the company, represented by the credit balance of the Retained Earnings account. As a practical matter, many corporations limit dividends to somewhere near 40% of annual net income, in the belief that a major portion of the net income must be retained in the business if the company is to grow and to keep pace with its competitors.
2. **An adequate cash position.** The fact that the company reports large earnings does not mean that it has a large amount of cash on hand. Cash generated from earnings may have been invested in such assets as inventory or new plant and equipment, or used in paying off debts. There is no necessary relationship between the balance in the Retained Earnings account and the balance in the Cash account. The traditional expression of "paying dividends out of retained earnings" is misleading. Cash dividends can be paid only "out of" cash.
3. **Dividend action by the board of directors.** Even though a company's net income is substantial and its cash position seemingly satisfactory, dividends are not paid automatically. A formal action by the board of directors is necessary to declare a dividend.

Dividend Dates

Four significant dates are involved in the distribution of a dividend. These dates are:

1. **Date of declaration.** On the day on which the dividend is declared by the board of directors, a liability to make the payment comes into existence.
2. **Date of record.** The date of record always follows the date of declaration, usually by a period of two to four weeks, and is always stated in the dividend declaration. In order to be eligible to receive the dividend, a person must be listed as the owner of the capital stock on the date of record.
3. **Ex-dividend date.** The ex-dividend date is significant for investors in companies with capital stocks traded on the stock exchanges. To permit the compilation of the list of shareholders as of the record date, it is customary for the capital stock to go *ex-dividend* two business days before the date of record. A stock is said to be selling ex-dividend on the day that it *loses* the right to receive the latest declared dividend. A person who buys the stock before the ex-dividend date is entitled to receive the dividend; conversely, a shareholder who sells shares before the ex-dividend date does not receive the dividend.
4. **Date of payment.** The declaration of a dividend always includes announcement of the date of payment as well as the date of record. Usually the date of payment comes from two to four weeks after the date of record.

Journal entries are required only on the dates of declaration and of payment, as these are the only "transactions" affecting the corporation declaring the dividend. These entries were illustrated in the preceding chapter. For your convenience, similar entries are illustrated below, this time indicating the official date of record.

Entries made on declaration date and...	Dec. 15	Dividends	100,000	
		Dividends Payable		100,000
		To record declaration of a cash dividend of $1 per share on the 100,000 shares of common stock outstanding. Payable Jan. 25 to shareholders of record on Jan. 10.		
... on payment date	Jan. 25	Dividends Payable	100,000	
		Cash		100,000
		To record payment of $1 per share dividend declared Dec. 15 to shareholders of record on Jan. 10.		

Notice that no entries are made on either the date of record (January 10), or on the ex-dividend date. These dates are of importance only in determining **to whom** the dividend cheques should be sent. From the shareholders' point of view, it is the **ex-dividend date** that determines who receives the dividend. The date of record is of significance primarily to the stock transfer agent and the stock register.

Just when is the ex-dividend date in our example? It falls two **business days** before the date of record. Weekends and holidays are not counted as "business days." Thus, if January 10 is a Friday, the ex-dividend date is **January 8**. But if January 10 falls on a Monday, the ex-dividend date would be **January 6**. In this case, investors would need to purchase their shares on or before **January 5** if they are to receive this dividend.

At the end of the accounting period, a closing entry is required to transfer the debit balance of the Dividends account into the Retained Earnings account.(Some companies follow the alternative practice of debiting Retained Earnings when the dividend is declared instead of using a Dividends account. Under either method, the balance of the Retained Earnings account ultimately is reduced by all dividends declared during the period.)

Most dividends are paid in cash, but occasionally a dividend declaration calls for payment in assets **other than** cash. A large distillery once paid a dividend consisting of a bottle of whiskey for each share of capital stock. When a corporation goes out of existence (particularly a small corporation with only a few shareholders), it may choose to distribute non-cash assets to its owners rather than to convert all its assets into cash.

In some cases, a cash dividend may be "paid" in common stock through an "automatic dividend reinvestment plan" whereby the cash dividends may be **automatically** reinvested. Thus, those shareholders who have chosen this plan will receive the cash dividends in common stock and the entry would debit dividends and credit common stock. To make such a plan attractive to the shareholders, the price for these new shares is usually below the current market price. Such a plan is beneficial to the company as it can conserve the cash needed for operations and expansion.

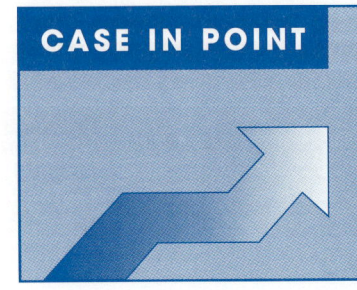

> **CASE IN POINT**
>
> Hudson's Bay Company's dividend reinvestment plan allows its common shareholders to reinvest their dividends in common shares at the weighted average market price during the three business days immediately preceding the dividend payment date; prior to this date, dividends would be reinvested in common shares at 95% of their weighted average market price. Other companies such as Dofasco Inc. and Bank of Montreal also have dividend reinvestment plans.

Liquidating Dividends

A *liquidating dividend* occurs when a corporation pays a dividend that *exceeds the balance in the Retained Earnings account*. Thus, the dividend returns to shareholders all or part of their capital investment. Liquidating dividends usually are paid only when a corporation is going out of existence or is making a permanent reduction in the size of its operations. Normally dividends are paid as a result of profitable operations; shareholders may assume that a dividend represents a distribution of profits unless they are notified by the corporation that the dividend is a return of invested capital.

Stock Dividends

LO 4: Account for stock dividends and stock splits, and explain the probable effect of these transactions upon market price.

Stock dividend is a term used to describe a distribution of *additional shares of capital stock* to a company's shareholders in proportion to their present holdings. In brief, the dividend is payable in *additional shares of capital stock* rather than in cash. Most stock dividends consist of additional shares of common stock distributed to holders of common stock, and our discussion will be limited to this type of stock dividend.

An important distinction must be drawn between a cash dividend and a stock dividend. In a *cash dividend*, assets are distributed by the corporation to the shareholders. Thus, a cash dividend reduces both assets and shareholders' equity. In a *stock dividend*, however, *no assets are distributed*. Thus, a stock dividend causes no change in assets or in total shareholders' equity. Each shareholder receives additional shares, but his or her percentage ownership in the corporation is *no larger than before*.

To illustrate this point, assume that a corporation with 2,000 shares of common stock is owned equally by James Davis and Susan Miller, each owning 1,000 shares of common stock. The corporation declares a stock dividend of 10% and distributes 200 additional shares (10% of 2,000 shares), with 100 shares going to each of the two shareholders. Davis and Miller now hold 1,100 shares apiece, but each *still owns one-half of the business*. Furthermore, the corporation has not changed in size; its assets and liabilities and its total shareholders' equity are exactly the same as before the stock dividend.

Now let us consider the logical effect of this stock dividend upon the *market price* of the company's common stock. Assume that before the stock dividend, the outstanding 2,000 shares in our example had a market price of $110 per share. This price indicates a total market value for the corporation of $220,000 (2,000 shares × $110 per share). As the stock dividend does not change total assets or total shareholders' equity, the total market value of the corporation ***should remain $220,000*** after the stock dividend. As 2,200 shares are now outstanding, the market price of each share ***should fall*** to $100 ($220,000 ÷ 2,200 shares). In short, the market value of the stock ***should fall in proportion*** to the number of new shares issued. Whether the market price per share ***will*** fall in proportion to a small increase in number of outstanding shares is another matter. The market prices of common stocks are influenced by many different factors.

Large stock dividends (for example, those in excess of 20 to 25%), on the other hand, generally have the effect of **proportionately** reducing the market price of the stock. For example, a 100% stock dividend would reduce the market price by about 50%, because twice as many shares would be outstanding. A 100% stock dividend is very similar to the 2-for-1 ***stock split*** discussed in the following section of this chapter.

Entries to Record a Stock Dividend In accounting for ***small*** stock dividends (say, less than 20%), the ***market value*** of the new shares is transferred from the Retained Earnings account to the capital account. This process sometimes is called ***capitalizing*** retained earnings. The overall effect is the same as if the dividend had been paid in cash, and the shareholders had immediately reinvested the cash in the business in exchange for additional shares of common stock. Of course, no cash actually changes hands—the new shares of common stock are sent directly to the shareholders.

To illustrate, assume that on June 1, Aspen Corporation has outstanding 100,000 shares of no-par value common stock with a market value of $25 per share. On this date, the company declares a 10% stock dividend, distributable on July 15 to shareholders of record on June 20. The entry at June 1 to record the ***declaration*** of this dividend is:

Stock dividend declared; note use of market price of stock

Retained Earnings (or Stock Dividends)	250,000	
Stock Dividend to Be Distributed		250,000
Declared a 10% stock dividend consisting of 10,000 shares (100,000 shares × 10%) of no-par value common stock, market price $25 per share. Distributable July 15 to shareholders of record on June 20.		

The Stock Dividend to Be Distributed account is ***not a liability***, because there is no obligation to distribute cash or any other asset. If a balance sheet is prepared between the date of declaration of a stock dividend and the date of distribution of the shares, this account should be presented in the shareholders' equity section of the balance sheet. If the debit is to the Stock Dividends account, it is closed to retained earnings at year end.

Notice that the Retained Earnings account was debited for the ***market value*** of the shares to be issued (10,000 shares × $25 per share = $250,000). Notice also that ***no change*** occurs in the total amount of shareholders' equity. The amount removed from the Retained Earnings account was simply transferred into another shareholders' equity account.

On July 15, the entry to record the **distribution** of the dividend shares is:

Stock dividend distributed

Stock Dividend to Be Distributed	250,000	
Common Stock		250,000
Distributed 10,000 share stock dividend declared June 1.		

Reasons for Stock Dividends Although stock dividends cause **no change** in total assets, liabilities, or shareholders' equity, they are popular both with management and with shareholders. Management likes stock dividends because they do not cost anything (other than administrative costs)—the corporation does not distribute any assets.

Shareholders like stock dividends because **large** stock dividends tend to keep the stock price down in a "trading range" that appeals to most investors.

CASE IN POINT

An investor who purchased 100 shares of Home Depot, Inc., early in 1985 would have paid about $1,700. By 1997, twelve years later, that stock was worth over **$92,000**!

Does this mean that each share increased in value from $17 to more than $920? No—in fact, this probably couldn't happen. Investors like to buy stock in "lots" of 100 shares. At $920 per share, who could afford 100 shares? Certainly not the average "small investor."

Home Depot's board of directors **wanted** to attract small investors. These investors help create more demand for the company's stock—and in many cases, they also become loyal customers.

So as the price of Home Depot's stock rose, the board declared numerous large stock dividends. By 1997, the investor who had purchased 100 shares in 1985 owned over **1,300** shares. But, most importantly, each of these shares was trading at a price affordable to the average investor.

As Home Depot's board knows well, investors don't buy stocks at prices that they can't afford.

Stock Splits

A corporation may **split** its stock by increasing the number of outstanding shares of common stock. As with a large stock dividend, the purpose of a stock split is to reduce substantially the market price of the common stock, with the intent of making the stock more affordable to investors.

For example, assume that Pelican Corporation has outstanding 1 million shares of no-par value common stock. The market price is $90 per share. The corporation now increases the number of shares from 1 million to 2 million. This action would be called a 2-for-1 stock split. A shareholder who owned 100 shares of the common stock before the split would own 200 shares after the split. Since the number of outstanding shares has been doubled without any change in total assets or total shareholders' equity, the market price of the common stock should drop from $90 to approximately $45 a share.

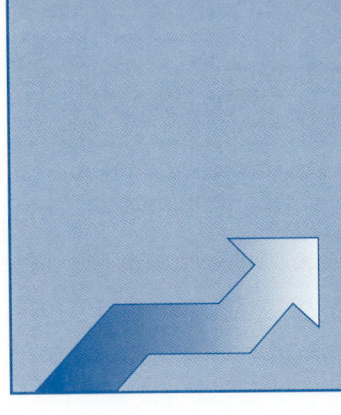

A stock split does not change the balance of any ledger account; consequently, the transaction may be recorded merely by **a memorandum** entry in the general journal and in the Common Stock account. For Pelican Corporation, this memorandum entry might read:

Memorandum entry to record a stock split

Sept. 30 Memorandum: Issued additional 1 million shares of common stock in a 2-for-1 stock split.

The description of common stock also is changed in the balance sheet to reflect the greater number of shares outstanding.

Stock may be split in any desired ratio. Among the more common ratios are 2 for 1, 3 for 2, and 3 for 1. The determining factor is the number of shares needed to bring the price of the stock into the desired trading range. For example, assume that the common stock is selling at a price of $150 per share and that management wants to reduce the price to approximately $30 per share. This objective may be accomplished with a **5-for-1** stock split ($150 ÷ 5 = $30).

Distinction Between Stock Splits and Large Stock Dividends What is the difference between a 2-for-1 stock split and a 100% stock dividend? There is very little difference; both will double the number of outstanding shares without changing total shareholders' equity, and both should serve to cut the market price of the stock approximately in half. The stock dividend, however, will cause a transfer from the Retained Earnings account to the Common Stock account equal to the declared dollar amount for no-par value or to the par value of the dividend shares. A 2-for-1 stock split will reduce the par value per share by one-half, but it will not change the dollar balance of any account.

After an increase in the number of shares as a result of a stock split or stock dividend, earnings per share are computed in terms of the increased number of shares. In presenting 5- or 10-year summaries, the earnings per share for earlier years are retroactively restated to reflect the increased number of shares currently outstanding and thus make the trend of earnings per share from year to year a more valid comparison.

Statement of Retained Earnings

LO 5: Describe and prepare a statement of retained earnings.

The term **retained earnings** refers to the portion of shareholders' equity derived from profitable operations. Retained earnings is increased by earning net income and is reduced by incurring net losses and by the declaration of dividends.

In addition to a balance sheet, an income statement, and a cash flow statement, a complete set of financial statements includes a **statement of retained earnings**, as illustrated below:

SHORE LINE CORPORATION
Statement of Retained Earnings
For the Year Ended December 31, 2000

Retained earnings, December 31, 1999		$600,000
Net income for 2000		180,000
Subtotal		$780,000
Less: Cash dividends:		
Preferred stock ($5 per share)	$ 17,500	
Common stock ($2 per share)	55,300	
10% stock dividend	140,000	212,800
Retained earnings, December 31, 2000		$567,200

Appropriations and Restrictions of Retained Earnings A few corporations transfer a portion of their retained earnings into separate accounts called *appropriations* or *reserves*. The purpose of such appropriations or reserves is to indicate to users of financial statements that a portion of retained earnings is not available for the declaration of cash dividends. The limitation on cash dividends may be established voluntarily by the board of directors or it may be required by law or contract.

Most corporations disclose restrictions on the declaration of cash dividends in notes accompanying the financial statements. For example, a company with total retained earnings of $10,000,000 might include the following note in its financial statements:

Note disclosure of restrictions placed on retained earnings

Note 7: Restriction of retained earnings
As of December 31, 2000 certain long-term debt agreements prohibited the declaration of cash dividends that would reduce the amount of retained earnings below $5,200,000. Retained earnings not so restricted amounted to $4,800,000.

CASE IN POINT   A note of the financial statements of Canadian Utilities Limited states: The debenture trust indenture places certain limitations on Canadian Utilities which include restrictions on the payment of dividends on Class A non-voting and Class B common shares. Consolidated retained earnings in the amount of $218.4 million are free from such restrictions.

Treasury Stock

Corporations sometimes acquire shares of their own capital stock by purchase in the open market. Paying out cash to acquire shares will reduce the assets of the corporation and reduce the shareholders' equity by the same amount. One reason for such purchases is to have stock available to reissue to officers and employees under stock option or bonus plans. Other reasons may include a desire to increase the reported earnings per share or to support the current market price of the stock.

Treasury stock may be defined as shares of a corporation's own capital stock that have been issued and later *acquired by the issuing company*, but that have not been cancelled or permanently retired. Treasury shares may be held indefinitely or may be issued again at any time. Shares of capital stock held in the treasury are not entitled to receive dividends, to vote, or to share in assets upon dissolution of the company. In the computation of earnings per share, shares held in the treasury are not regarded as outstanding shares.

A corporation may, under certain provincial legislation, acquire its own capital stock for the purpose of reissuing or cancelling it in the future. However, other legislation such as the Canada Business Corporations Act and the Ontario Business Corporations Act require that such acquired capital stock be cancelled or restored to the authorized but unissued status. Thus, corporations under such legislation are prohibited from having treasury stock. Also, corporation legislation does not permit a corporation to acquire its own capital stock when it is insolvent or if such an acquisition would render it insolvent.

Recording Purchases of Treasury Stock

LO 6: Account for treasury stock transactions.

Purchases of treasury stock should be recorded by debiting the Treasury Stock account with the cost of the stock. For example, if Torrey Corporation acquires 1,500 shares of its own no-par common stock at a price of $100 per share, the entry is as follows:

Treasury Stock	150,000	
Cash		150,000
Purchased 1,500 shares of no-par treasury stock at $100 per share.		

Treasury Stock Is Not an Asset When treasury stock is purchased, the corporation is eliminating part of its shareholders' equity by a payment to one or more shareholders. The purchase of treasury stock should be regarded as a ***reduction of shareholders' equity***, not as the acquisition of an asset. For this reason, the Treasury Stock account should appear in the balance sheet ***as a deduction in the shareholders' equity section***. The presentation of treasury stock in a corporate balance sheet is illustrated on page 764.

Reissuance of Treasury Stock

When treasury shares are reissued, the Treasury Stock account is credited for the cost of the shares reissued and Contributed Capital from Treasury Stock Transactions is debited or credited for any ***difference*** between cost and the reissue price. To illustrate, assume that 1,000 of the treasury shares acquired by Torrey Corporation at a cost of $100 per share are now reissued at a price of $115 per share. The entry to record the reissuance of these shares at a price above cost would be:

Treasury stock reissued at a price above cost

Cash	115,000	
Treasury Stock		100,000
Contributed Capital from Treasury Stock Transactions		15,000
Sold 1,000 shares of treasury Stock, which cost $100,000 at a price of $115 per share.		

If treasury stock is reissued at a price below cost, contributed capital from previous treasury stock transactions is reduced (debited) by the excess of cost over the reissue price.[16] To illustrate, assume the Torrey Corporation reissues its remaining 500 shares of treasury stock (cost $100 per share) at a price of $90 per share. The entry would be:

Reissued at a price below cost

Cash	45,000	
Contributed Capital from Treasury Stock Transactions	5,000	
Treasury Stock		50,000

Sold 500 shares of treasury stock, which cost $50,000, at a price of $90 each.

If there is insufficient or no contributed capital from previous treasury stock transactions to cover the excess, the balance or the entire excess of the cost of the treasury shares over the reissue price may be recorded as a debit to Retained Earnings.[17]

No Income or Loss on Treasury Stock Transactions Notice that **no income or loss is recognized on treasury stock transactions**, even when the shares are reissued at a price above or below cost. A corporation earns income by selling goods and services to outsiders, not by issuing or reissuing shares of its own capital stock. When treasury shares are reissued at a price above cost the corporation receives from the new shareholder an amount of capital larger than the reduction in shareholders' equity when the corporation acquired the treasury shares. Conversely, if treasury shares are reissued at a price below cost, the corporation ends up with less contributed capital as a result of the purchase and reissuance of the shares. Thus, any changes in shareholders' equity resulting from treasury stock transactions are regarded as changed in **contributed capital** and are **not** included in the measurement of net income.

Restriction of Retained Earnings for Treasury Stock Owned Purchases of treasury stock, like cash dividends, are distributions of assets to the shareholders in the corporation. Corporate laws generally require that distributions to shareholders (including purchases of treasury stock) cannot exceed the balance in the Retained Earnings account. Therefore, retained earnings usually are restricted by an amount equal to the cost of any shares held in the treasury.

Stock "Buyback" Programs

In past years, most treasury stock transactions involved relatively small dollar amounts. Hence, the topic was not of much importance to investors or other users of financial statements. Late in 1987, however, many corporations initiated large "buyback" programs, in which they purchased

---

[16] CICA, *CICA Handbook* (Toronto), section 3240.20.
[17] Ibid.

huge amounts of their own common stock.[18] As a result of these programs, stock buybacks and treasury stock have become very material transactions for many corporations.

CASE IN POINT Recently, Shell Canada "purchased 15,999,784 of its class "A" Common Shares (14% of the total) at a price of $61 a share for a total of $976 million." Similarly, Northern Telecom purchased more than 10 million (about 2%) of its common shares, and Bank of Montreal purchased 5 million common shares at an average price of $32.41 for $162 million.

CASE IN POINT Shown below is the cost of the treasury stock listed in the balance sheets of several publicly owned corporations in the United States at the end of a recent year.

Company	Treasury Stock At Cost (in Thousands)	As a % of Other Elements of Shareholders' Equity*
Coca-Cola	$ 5,201,194	57
Exxon	16,887,000	33
Lotus	287,655	41
KingWorld	162,054	32

*To place these holdings in perspective, we have shown the cost of the treasury stock as a percentage of total shareholders' equity before deducting the cost of the purchased shares.

These large buyback programs serve several purposes. First, by creating demand for the company's capital stock in the marketplace, these programs tend to increase the market value of the shares. Also, reducing the number of shares outstanding usually increases earnings per share. When stock prices are low, some companies find that they can increase earnings per share by a greater amount through purchasing shares than through expanding business operations.

Illustration of a Shareholders' Equity Section

The following shareholders' equity section of a balance sheet illustrates the various items discussed in this chapter. You should be able to explain the nature and origin of each account and disclosure.

The published financial statements of leading corporations indicate that there is no one standard arrangement for the various items making

---

[18] On October 19, 1987, a date known as **Black Monday**, stocks around the world suffered the largest one-day decline in history. Within hours of the market's close on Black Monday, many large corporations announced their intention to enter the market and spend hundreds of millions of dollars purchasing their own shares. In the opinion of these authors, these announcements helped stabilize the investment markets and avoid a possible stock market "collapse."

up the shareholders' equity section. Variations occur in the selection of titles, in the sequence of items, and in the extent of detailed classification. Many companies will combine several related ledger accounts into a single balance sheet item and explain the details in the notes to the financial statements.

Shareholders' equity:
  Capital stock:
    $9 preferred stock, no-par value, unlimited authorized
      shares, 1,000 shares issued and outstanding .... $ 260,000
    Common stock, no-par value, unlimited authorized
      shares, issued 60,000 shares, of which 1,000 are
      held in treasury 573,000
    Contributed capital from treasury stock transactions 5,000
      Total contributed capital .... $ 838,000
  Retained earnings (of which $12,000, an amount equal
    to the cost of treasury stock purchased, is unavailable
    for dividends) 162,000
                                                      $1,000,000
  Less: Treasury stock, common, 1,000 shares at cost 12,000
  Total shareholders' equity .... $ 988,000

End-of-Chapter Review

Key Terms Introduced or Emphasized in Chapter 15

Basic earnings per share *(p.753)* Net income applicable to the common stock divided by weighted-average number of common shares outstanding during the year.

Changes in accounting estimates *(p.748)* Include such items as a revision of the estimate of the amount of allowance for doubtful accounts or a revision of the estimate of a nine-year useful life of a depreciable asset to a six-year life.

Changes in accounting policy *(p.747)* Encompass changes in accounting principles as well as accounting methods used in the preparation of financial statements.

Comparative financial statements *(p.748)* Financial statements of the current year and the preceding year or years that are presented together to facilitate comparison.

Corrections of errors *(p.748)* Required when errors are discovered in prior period financial statements. Such errors may result from a mistake in computation, a misinterpretation or misrepresentation of information, an oversight of available information, and a misappropriation of assets.

Date of record *(p.754)* The date on which a person must be listed as a shareholder in order to be eligible to receive a dividend. Follows the date of declaration of a dividend by two to four weeks.

Discontinued operations *(p.745)* The net operating results (revenue and expenses) of a segment of a company that has been or is being sold, as well as the gain or loss on disposal.

Earnings per share *(p.749)* Net income applicable to the common stock divided by the weighted-average number of common shares outstanding during the year.

Ex-dividend date *(p.754)* A date two days prior to the date of record specified in a dividend declaration. A person buying a stock prior to the ex-dividend date also acquires the right to receive the dividend. The two-day interval permits the compilation of a list of shareholders as of the date of record.

Extraordinary items *(p.746)* Transactions and events that are not dependent on decisions by management or owners, unusual in nature, and occur infrequently—for example, a large earthquake loss. Such items are shown separately in the income statement after the determination of Income before Extraordinary Items.

Fully diluted earnings per share *(p.753)* Earnings per share computed under the assumption that all convertible securities had been converted into additional common shares at the beginning of the current year. The purpose of this hypothetical computation is to warn common shareholders of the risk that future earnings per share might be diluted by the conversion of other securities into common stock.

Price-earnings (p/e) ratio *(p.749)* Market price of a share of common stock divided by annual earnings per share.

Segment of a business *(p.745)* Those elements of a business that represent a separate and distinct line of business activity or that service a particular class of customers.

Statement of retained earnings *(p.759)* A basic financial statement explaining the change during the year in the amount of retained earnings.

Stock dividend *(p.756)* A distribution of additional shares to common shareholders in proportion to their holdings.

Stock split *(p.758)* An increase in the number of shares outstanding. The additional shares are distributed proportionately to all common shareholders. Purpose is to reduce market price per share and encourage wider public ownership of the company's stock. A 2-for-1 stock split will give each shareholder twice as many shares as previously owned.

Treasury stock *(p.760)* Shares of a corporation's stock that have been issued and then acquired, but not cancelled by the corporation.

Demonstration Problem

The shareholders' equity of Sutton Corporation at December 31, 2000, is shown below:

Shareholders' equity:
Common stock, no-par, unlimited shares authorized, 40,000 shares issued and outstanding	$ 600,000
Retained earnings	1,500,000
Total shareholders' equity	$2,100,000

Transactions affecting shareholders' equity during 2001 are as follows:

Mar. 31 A 5-for-4 stock split proposed by the board of directors was approved by vote of the shareholders. The 10,000 new shares were distributed to shareholders.

Apr. 1 The company purchased 2,000 shares of its common stock on the open market at $37 per share.

July 1 The company reissued 1,000 shares of treasury stock at $45 per share.

July 1 Issued for cash 20,000 shares of previously unissued no-par value common stock at a price of $45 per share.

Dec. 1 A cash dividend of $1 per share was declared, payable on December 30, to shareholders of record at December 14.

Dec. 22 A 10% stock dividend was declared; the dividend shares are to be distributed on January 15 of the following year. The market price of the stock on December 22 was $48 per share.

The net income for the year ended December 31, 2001, amounted to $177,000, after an extraordinary loss of $35,400 (net of $17,600 income tax benefits).

INSTRUCTIONS

a. Prepare journal entries (in general journal form) to record the transactions relating to shareholders' equity that took place during the year.

b. Prepare the lower section of the income statement for 2001, beginning with the *income before extraordinary items* and showing the extraordinary loss and the net income. Also illustrate the presentation of earnings per share in the income statement, assuming that earnings per share is determined on the basis of the *weighted-average* number of shares outstanding during the year.

c. Prepare a statement of retained earnings for the year ending December 31, 2001.

SOLUTION TO DEMONSTRATION PROBLEM

a.

GENERAL JOURNAL — Page 1

Date	Account Titles and Explanations	LP	Debit	Credit
Mar. 31	Memorandum: Shareholders approved a 5-for-4 stock split. This action increased the number of shares of common stock outstanding from 40,000 to 50,000. The 10,000 new shares were distributed.			
Apr. 1	Treasury Stock		74,000	
	Cash			74,000
	Acquired 2,000 shares of treasury stock at $37 per share.			
July 1	Cash		45,000	
	Treasury Stock			37,000
	Contributed Capital from Treasury Stock Transactions			8,000
	Sold 1,000 shares of treasury stock at $45 per share.			
1	Cash		900,000	
	Common Stock			900,000
	Issued 20,000 shares.			
Dec. 1	Dividends		69,000	
	Dividends Payable			69,000
	To record declaration of cash dividend of $1 per share on 69,000 shares of common stock outstanding (1,000 shares in treasury are not entitled to receive dividends).			
	Note: Entry to record the payment of the cash dividend is not shown here since the action does not affect the shareholders' equity.			
22	Retained Earnings		331,200	
	Stock Dividends to Be Distributed			331,200
	To record declaration of 10% stock dividend consisting of 6,900 shares of common stock to be distributed on Jan. 15 of next year.			
31	Income Summary		177,000	
	Retained Earnings			177,000
	To close Income Summary account.			
31	Retained Earnings		69,000	
	Dividends			69,000
	To close Dividends account.			

b.

SUTTON CORPORATION
Partial Income Statement
For Year Ended December 31, 2001

Income before extraordinary items	$212,400
Extraordinary loss (net of $17,600 income tax benefits)	(35,400)
Net income	$177,000
Earnings per share:*	
Income before extraordinary items	$ 3.60
Extraordinary loss	(0.60)
Net income	$ 3.00

* On 59,000 weighted-average number of shares of common stock outstanding during 2001, determined as follows:

Jan. 1 – Mar. 31: (40,000 + 10,000 shares issued pursuant to a 5-for-4 split) × ¼ of year	12,500
Apr. 1 – June 30: (50,000 – 2,000 shares of treasury stock) × ¼ of year	12,000
July 1 – Dec. 31: (50,000 + 20,000 shares of new stock – 1,000 shares of treasury stock) × ½ of year	34,500
Weighted-average number of shares outstanding	59,000

c.

SUTTON CORPORATION
Statement of Retained Earnings
For Year Ended December 31, 2001

Retained earnings, December 31, 2000		$1,500,000
Add: Net income for 2001		177,000
Subtotal		$1,677,000
Less: Cash dividends ($1 per share)	$ 69,000	
10% stock dividend	331,200	400,200
Retained earnings, December 31, 2001		$1,276,800

Self-Test Questions

The answers to these questions appear on page 785.

1. The primary purpose of showing special types of events separately in the income statement is to:
   a. Increase earnings per share.
   b. Assist users of the income statement in evaluating and predicting the profitability of normal, ongoing operations.
   c. Minimize the income taxes paid on the results of ongoing operations.
   d. Prevent unusual losses from recurring.
2. Which of the following situations would be presented in a separate section of the current year's income statement of Marlow Corporation? During the current year (more than one answer may be correct):
   a. Marlow's Winnipeg headquarters are destroyed by a tornado.

b. Marlow sells its entire juvenile furniture operations and concentrates upon its remaining children's clothing segment.
   c. Marlow changes from the straight-line method of depreciation to the declining-balance method.
   d. Marlow's accountant discovers that the entire price paid several years ago to purchase company offices in Ottawa had been charged to a Land account; consequently, no depreciation has ever been taken on these buildings.

3. When a corporation has outstanding both common and preferred stock:
   a. Basic and fully diluted earnings per share are reported only if the preferred stock is cumulative.
   b. Earnings per share are reported for each type of stock outstanding.
   c. Earnings per share may be computed without regard to the amount of dividends declared on common stock.
   d. Earnings per share may be computed without regard to the amount of the annual preferred dividends.

4. The statement of retained earnings:
   a. Is a basic financial statement that shows the changes in retained earning during a year.
   b. Indicates the amount of cash available for the payment of dividends.
   c. Includes cash dividends but not stock dividends.
   d. Shows revenue, expenses, and dividends for the accounting period.

5. On December 10, 2000, Totem Corporation acquired 2,000 shares of its own no-par stock at a price of $60 per share. In 2001, 500 of the treasury shares are reissued at a price of $70 per share. Which of the following statements is correct?
   a. The treasury stock purchased is recorded at cost and is shown in Totem's December 31, 2000, balance sheet as an asset.
   b. The two treasury stock transactions result in an overall reduction in Totem's shareholders' equity of $85,000.
   c. Totem recognizes a gain of $10 per share on the reissuance of the 500 treasury shares in 2001.
   d. Totem's shareholders' equity was increased by $110,000 when the treasury stock was acquired.

ASSIGNMENT MATERIAL

Discussion Questions

1. What is the purpose of arranging an income statement to show subtotals for *Income from Continuing Operations* and for *Income before Extraordinary Items*?

2. Pappa Joe's owns 30 pizza parlors and a minor league baseball team. During the current year, the company sold three of its pizza parlors and closed another when the lease on the building expired. Should any of these events be classified as "discontinued operations" in the company's income statement? Explain.

3. Define *extraordinary items*. Give three examples of losses that qualify as extraordinary items and three examples of losses that would *not* be classified as extraordinary.

4. Briefly describe the nature and accounting treatment of a change in an accounting policy.

5. Briefly explain the nature and accounting treatment of a change in an accounting estimate.

6. Briefly explain the nature and accounting treatment of a correction of an error in prior period financial statements.

7. In past years, the management of Dundas Leisure Equipment had consistently estimated the allowance for doubtful accounts at 2% of total accounts receivable. At the end of the current year, management estimated that uncollectible accounts would equal 4% of accounts receivable. Should the uncollectible accounts expense of prior years be recomputed in order to show in the comparative income statements of previous years the effect of this change in accounting estimate?

8. In the current year, Garden Products decided to switch from use of an accelerated method of depreciation to the straight-line method. Will the cumulative effect of this change in accounting principle increase or decrease the amount of retained earnings reported at the beginning of the preceding year (assume a two-year comparative statement is presented)? Explain.

9. *Earnings per share* and *book value per share* are statistics that relate to common stock. When both preferred and common stock are outstanding, explain the computation involved in determining the following:
    a. Earnings allocable to the common shareholders
    b. Aggregate book value allocable to the common shareholders

10. Assume a corporation has only common stock outstanding. Is the number of common shares used in the computation of earnings per share *always* the same as the number of common shares used in computing book value per share for this corporation? Is the number of common shares used in computing these two statistics *ever* the same? Explain.

11. Explain how each of the following is computed:
    a. Price-earnings ratio
    b. Basic earnings per share
    c. Fully diluted earnings per share

12. Throughout the year, Park Plaza Limited had 4 million shares of common stock and 120,000 shares of convertible preferred stock outstanding. Each share of preferred is convertible into four shares of common. What number of shares should be used in the computation of (a) basic earnings per share and (b) fully diluted earnings per share?

13. A financial analyst notes that Baxter Corporation's earnings per share have been rising steadily for the last five years. The analyst expects the company's net income to continue to increase at the same rate as in the past. In forecasting future basic earnings per share, what special risk should the analyst consider if Baxter's basic earnings are significantly larger than its fully diluted earnings?

14. Explain the significance of the following dates relating to dividends: date of declaration, date of record, date of payment, ex-dividend date.

15. What is the purpose of a *stock split*?

16. Distinguish between a *stock split* and a *stock dividend*. Is there any reason for the difference in accounting treatment of these two events?

17. Identify two items that usually appear in a statement of retained earnings as changes in the amount of retained earnings.

18. What is *treasury stock*? Why do corporations purchase their own shares? Is treasury stock an asset? How should it be reported in the balance sheet?

19. Corporation laws generally require that retained earnings be restricted for dividend purposes to the extent of the cost of treasury shares. What is the reason for this legal rule?

Exercises

EXERCISE 15-1
Accounting Terminology
(LO 1,2,3,4,6)

Listed below are nine technical accounting terms introduced or emphasized in this chapter:

P/e ratio	Treasury stock	Discontinued operations
Stock dividend	Extraordinary item	Change in accounting estimate
Basic earnings per share	Change in accounting policy	Fully diluted earnings per share

Each of the following statements may (or may not) describe one of these technical terms. For each statement, indicate the term described, or answer "None" if the statement does not correctly describe any of the terms.

a. A gain or loss that is unusual in nature, not expected to recur in the foreseeable future, and beyond management's control.

b. The asset represented by shares of capital stock that have not yet been issued.

c. A distribution of additional shares of capital stock that reduces retained earnings but causes no change in total shareholders' equity.

d. The inventory method has been changed from weighted average to first-in, first-out.

e. The useful life of a computer system has been shortened by two years.

f. A statistic expressing a relationship between the current market value of a share of common stock and the underlying earnings per share.

g. A separate section sometimes included in an income statement as a step in helping investors to evaluate and predict the profitability of ongoing business activities.

h. A hypothetical figure indicating what earnings per share would have been if all securities convertible into common stock had been converted at the beginning of the current year.

EXERCISE 15-2
Discontinued Operations
(LO 1,2)

During the current year, SunSports, Inc., operated two business segments: a chain of surf and dive shops and a small chain of tennis shops. The tennis shops were not profitable and were sold near year-end to another corporation. SunSports' operations for the current year are summarized below. The first two captions, "Net sales" and "Costs and expenses," relate only to the company's continuing operations.

Net sales	$9,800,000
Costs and expenses (including applicable income taxes)	8,600,000
Operating loss from tennis shops (net of $76,800 income tax benefit) .	192,000
Loss on sale of tennis shops (net of $129,200 income tax benefit) . .	348,000

The company had 150,000 shares of a single class of capital stock outstanding throughout the year.

a. Prepare a condensed income statement for the year. At the bottom of the statement, show any appropriate earnings-per-share figures.

b. Which earnings-per-share figure in part **a** do you consider most useful in predicting future operating results for SunSports, Inc.? Why?

EXERCISE 15-3
Reporting an Extraordinary Item
(LO 1,2)

For the year ended December 31, Union Chemical had net sales of $8,000,000, costs and other expenses (including income taxes) of $7,060,000, and an extraordinary gain (net of $200,000 income taxes) of $400,000.

a. Prepare a condensed income statement (including earnings per share), assuming that 500,000 shares of common stock were outstanding throughout the year.

b. Which earnings-per-share figure is used in computing the price-earnings ratio for Union Chemical reported in newspapers such as *The Globe and Mail*? Explain briefly.

EXERCISE 15-4
Extraordinary Items and Accounting Changes
(LO 1)

Select the ***best*** answer for each of the following multiple-choice questions:
1. Accounting changes include
   a. A change in accounting policy and in accounting estimate
   b. A correction of error in a prior period
   c. Extraordinary items
   d. **a** and **b**
   e. **a**, **b**, and **c**
2. An extraordinary item reflects an event that is
   a. Unusual, material, and beyond management's control
   b. Not reasonably estimated, not related to economic events, but within management's control
   c. Not typical, infrequent, and beyond management's control
   d. Not typical, irregular, but a recurring factor for ordinary operation evaluation
   e. An element of an accounting change
3. Changes in accounting policy encompass
   a. Changes in the financial position
   b. Changes in accounting principles and methods
   c. Changes in accounting estimates

        d. Corrections of errors in prior period financial statements
        e. Extraordinary items
    4. Changes in accounting estimates include
        a. Revision of the amount of allowance for doubtful accounts
        b. Revision of the useful life of a depreciable asset
        c. Revision of the residual value of a depreciable asset
        d. A change of depreciation method
        e. **a**, **b**, and **c**
    5. Retroactive application and restatement are required by
        a. A change in accounting policy
        b. A change in accounting estimate
        c. A correction of an error in a prior period
        d. **a** and **c**
        e. **a** and **c** and extraordinary items
    6. An accounting change requiring a current or current and prospective application is
        a. A change in accounting estimate
        b. A change in accounting policy and accounting estimate
        c. A change in accounting policy and accounting estimate as well as a correction of a prior period error
        d. An extraordinary item
        e. **c** and **d**

EXERCISE 15-5
Computing Earnings Per Share: Changes in Number of Shares Outstanding
(LO 2)

In the year just ended, Sunshine Citrus earned net income of $6,300,000. The company has issued only one class of no-par value capital stock, of which 1 million shares were outstanding at January 1.

a. Compute the company's earnings per share under each of the following *independent* assumptions:
   1. No change occurred during the year in the number of shares outstanding.
   2. On October 1, the company issued an additional 200,000 shares of capital stock in exchange for cash of $1,500,000.
   3. On July 1, the company distributed an additional 200,000 shares of capital stock as a 20% stock dividend. On July 1, Sunshine's stock had a market value of $7.25 per share.

b. In computing *earnings per share*, we must determine the *weighted-average* number of common shares outstanding during the period. In computing *book value per share*, however, we simply divide by the *actual number* of shares outstanding on a specific date. Explain briefly the concept behind the difference in approach.

EXERCISE 15-6
Computing Earnings Per Share: Effect of Preferred Stock
(LO 2)

The net income of Carriage Trade Clothiers amounted to $2,550,000 for the current year.

a. Compute the amount of earnings per share assuming that the shares of capital stock outstanding throughout the year consisted of:
   1. 300,000 shares of no-par value common stock and no preferred stock.
   2. 200,000 shares of $9 preferred stock and 300,000 shares of no-par value common stock. The preferred stock has a call price of $105 per share.

b. Is the earnings-per-share figure computed in part **a(2)** considered to be basic or fully diluted? Explain.

774 PARTNERSHIPS AND CORPORATIONS PART 4

EXERCISE 15-7
Restating Earnings per Share After a Stock Dividend
(LO 2,4)

The 1993 annual report of **Microsoft Corp.** included the following comparative summary of earnings per share over the previous three years:

	1993	1992	1991
Earnings per share	$3.15	$2.41	$1.64

In 1994, Microsoft Corp. declared and distributed a 100% stock dividend. Following this stock dividend, the company reported earnings per share of $1.88 for 1994.

a. Prepare a three-year schedule similar to the one above, but compare earnings per share during the years 1994, 1993, and 1992.

b. In preparing your schedule, which figure (or figures) did you have to restate? Why? Explain the logic behind your computation.

EXERCISE 15-8
Restating Earnings per Share After a Stock Split
(LO 2,4)

The 1996 annual report of **Shell Canada Limited** included the following comparative summary of earnings per share for its class "A" common shares over the previous three years:

	1996	1995	1994
Earnings per share	5.30	4.66	2.85

During 1997, Shell Canada split its class "A" common shares 3 for 1. Following this stock split, the company reported earnings per share of 1.69 in 1997.

a. Prepare a three-year schedule similar to the one above, but compare earnings per share during the years 1997, 1996, and 1995.

b. In preparing your schedule, which figure (or figures) did you have to restate? Why? Explain the logic behind your computation.

EXERCISE 15-9
Cash Dividends, Stock Dividends and Stock Splits
(LO 4)

Global Technology Corporation has 500,000 shares of no-par value capital stock outstanding on January 1. The following equity transactions occurred during the current year:

Apr. 30 Distributed additional shares of capital stock in a 2-for-1 stock split. Market price of stock was $35 per share.

June 1 Declared a cash dividend of 60 cents per share.

July 1 Paid the 60-cent cash dividend to shareholders.

Aug. 1 Declared a 5% stock dividend. Market price of stock was $19 per share.

Sept. 10 Issued shares pursuant to the 5% stock dividend declared on August 1.

a. Prepare journal entries to record the above transactions.

b. Compute the number of shares of capital stock outstanding at year-end.

c. Determine the effect of each of the following on *total* shareholders' equity: stock split, declaration and payment of a cash dividend, declaration and distribution of a small stock dividend. (Your answers should be *increase*, *decrease*, or *no effect*.)

EXERCISE 15-10
Effect of Stock Dividends on Stock Price
(LO 4)

Tarreytown Corporation has a total of 80,000 shares of common stock outstanding and no preferred stock. Total shareholders' equity at the end of the current year amounts to $5 million and the market value of the stock is $66 per share. At year-end, the company declares a 10% stock dividend—one share for each ten shares held. If all parties concerned clearly recognize the nature of the stock dividend, what should you expect the market price per share of the common stock to be on the ex-dividend date?

EXERCISE 15-11
Recording Treasury Stock Transactions
(LO 6)

Cachet Inc., engaged in the following transactions involving treasury stock:

Feb. 10 Purchased for cash 14,500 shares of treasury stock at a price of $30 per share.

June 4 Reissued 6,000 shares of treasury stock at a price of $33 per share.

Dec. 22 Reissued 4,000 shares of treasury stock at a price of $28 per share.

a. Prepare general journal entries to record these transactions.
b. Compute the amount of retained earnings that should be restricted because of the treasury stock still owned at December 31.
c. Does a restriction on retained earnings affect the dollar amount of retained earnings reported in the balance sheet? Explain briefly.

EXERCISE 15-12
Reporting the Effects of Transactions
(LO 4, 6)

Five events pertaining to Lowlands Manufacturing Limited are described below.
a. Declared and paid a cash dividend.
b. Issued a 10% stock dividend.
c. Issued a 2-for-1 stock split.
d. Purchased treasury stock.
e. Reissued the treasury stock at a price greater than the purchase price.

Indicate the immediate effects of the events on the financial measurements in the three columnar headings listed below. Use the code letters, *I* for increase, *D* for decrease, and *NE* for no effect.

Event	Current Assets	Shareholders' Equity	Net Income

EXERCISE 15-13
Effects of Various Transactions upon Earnings per Share
(LO 2,4, 6)

Explain the immediate effects, if any, of each of the following transactions upon a company's net earnings per share:
a. Split the common stock 3 for 1.
b. Realized a gain from the sale of a discontinued operation.
c. Switched from an accelerated method of depreciation to the straight-line method, resulting in a large debit to the Accumulated Depreciation account.
d. Declared and paid a cash dividend on common stock.
e. Declared and distributed a stock dividend on common stock.
f. Acquired several thousand shares of treasury stock.

EXERCISE 15-14
Where to Find Financial Information
(LO 1,2, 6)

You have now been exposed to the following financial statements issued by corporations: balance sheet, income statement, and statement of retained earnings. Listed below are various items frequently of interest to a corporation's owners, potential investors, and creditors, among others. You are to specify which of the above corporate financial statements, if any, reports the desired information. If the listed item is not reported in any formal financial statement issued by a corporation, indicate an appropriate source for the desired information.
a. Number of shares of stock outstanding as of year-end
b. Total dollar amount of cash dividends declared during the current year
c. Market value per share at balance sheet date
d. Dollar effect of an accounting error made in a previous year
e. Disposal of a business segment
f. Loss from an earthquake
g. Earnings per share of common stock
h. Book value per share
i. Price/earnings (p/e) ratio
j. The total amount the corporation paid to buy back shares of its own stock that it now holds

Problems

PROBLEM 15-1
Reporting Special Events; Using Predictive Subtotals
(LO 1, 2)

Gulf Coast Airlines operated both an airline and several motels located near airports. During the year just ended, all motel operations were discontinued and the following operating results were reported:

Continuing operations (airlines):	
Net sales	$51,120,000
Costs and expenses (including income taxes on continuing operations)	43,320,000
Other data:	
Operating income from motels (net of $388,000 income taxes)	864,000
Gain on sale of motels (net of $2,230,000 income taxes)	4,956,000
Extraordinary loss (net of $1,512,000 income tax benefit)	3,360,000

The extraordinary loss resulted from the destruction of an airliner by terrorists. Gulf Coast Airlines had 1,200,000 shares of capital stock outstanding throughout the year.

INSTRUCTIONS

a. Prepare a condensed income statement including proper presentation of the discontinued motel operations and the extraordinary loss. Include all appropriate earnings per share figures.
b. Assume that you expect the profitability of Gulf Coast's airlines operations to *decline by* 6% next year, and the profitability of the motels to decline by 10%. What is your estimate of the company's net earnings per share next year?

PROBLEM 15-2
Accounting Changes
(LO 1)

The following comparative statement of retained earnings relates to Garden Corporation, which began operations in 1999.

	December 31	
	2001	**2000**
Retained earnings at beginning of year	$ 900,000	$680,000
Net income	260,000	220,000
Retained earnings at end of year	$1,160,000	$900,000

Garden decided on January 1, 2002, to change its depreciation method from declining-balance to straight-line. The information for the depreciation expense is as follows:

Year	Declining-Balance	Straight-Line
1999	$100,000	$42,000
2000	75,000	42,000
2001	56,250	42,000

INSTRUCTIONS

a. Compute the amount of cumulative effect on the beginning balance of retained earnings for 2001, as a result of the change in depreciation method and indicate whether the effect is an increase or a decrease. (Disregard income tax considerations.)
b. How would the income statements for 2000 and 2001 be affected by the change in depreciation method? (Disregard income tax considerations.)
c. Assuming that after the 2002 net income of $188,000 was recorded, the company discovered that it should have changed the useful life of the assets

in 2002. This change would have increased the depreciation expense by $12,000 for each of 2001, 2002, and 2003. Explain how this change would affect the net income and retained earnings for these three years. (Disregard income tax considerations.)

PROBLEM 15-3
Accounting Changes
(LO 1)

The following is a comparative statement of retained earnings for Seaview Resort Limited for the last two years.

	December 31 2001	2000
Retained earnings at beginning of year	$480,000	$300,000
Net income	200,000	180,000
Retained earnings at end of year	$680,000	$480,000

Seaview Resort was incorporated on January 2, 1999, and used a straight-line method of depreciation for its depreciable assets until January 1, 2002. At that time, Seaview changed its depreciation method from straight-line to double-declining. The net income for 2002, based on the new depreciation method, is $286,000. The information for depreciation expense is as follows:

Year	Straight-Line	Declining-Balance
1999	$54,000	$120,000
2000	54,000	72,000
2001	54,000	43,200

INSTRUCTIONS

a. Prepare a comparative statement of retained earnings for 2001 and 2002. (Disregard income tax considerations.)
b. How would the income statement for 2000 be affected by the change in depreciation method? Explain. (Disregard income tax considerations.)
c. Assuming that after the net income of $286,000 for 2002 was recorded, an engineering report showed that the company should have changed the useful life of its depreciable assets in 2002. Such a change would have decreased the depreciation expense by $14,600 for 2001 and by $8,620 for 2002. Explain how this change would affect the net income and retained earnings for 2001, 2002, and 2003. (Disregard income tax considerations.)

PROBLEM 15-4
Format of an Income Statement and a Statement of Retained Earnings
(LO 1, 2, 5)

The following are data relating to the operations of Academic Testing Services Inc, during 2000:

Continuing operations
Net sales $15,750,000
Costs and expenses (including applicable income taxes) 12,800,000
Other data:
Operating income during 2000 on segment of the business
  discontinued near year-end (net of $112,500 income taxes) 225,000
Loss on disposal of discontinued segment (net of $337,500
  income tax benefit) 675,000
Extraordinary loss (net of $390,000 income tax benefit) 780,000
Cumulative effect of change in accounting principle for a
  three-year period to December 31, 1999, resulted in an
  increase in total net income 135,000
Correction of an error understated the 1998 net income 150,000
Cash dividends declared 925,000

778 PARTNERSHIPS AND CORPORATIONS PART 4

INSTRUCTIONS

a. Prepare a condensed income statement for 2000, including earnings per share statistics. Academic Testing Services Inc. had 300,000 shares of no-par value common stock and 40,000 shares of $6.25, no-par value preferred stock outstanding throughout the year.

b. Prepare a statement of retained earnings for the year ended December 31, 2000. As originally reported, retained earnings at December 31, 1999 amounted to $6,450,000.

c. Compute the amount of cash dividend *per share* of *common stock* declared by the board of directors for 2000. Assume no dividends in arrears on the preferred stock.

d. Assume that 2001 earnings per share is a single figure and amounts to $8.00. Assume also that there are no changes in outstanding common or preferred stock in 2001. Do you consider the $8.00 earnings-per-share figure in 2001 to be a favourable or unfavourable statistic in comparison with 2000 performance? Explain.

PROBLEM 15-5
Reporting Special Events: A Comprehensive Problem
(LO 1, 2, 6)

The following income statement was prepared by a new and inexperienced employee in the accounting department of Keller Interiors, a business organized as a corporation.

KELLER INTERIORS
Income Statement
For the Year Ended December 31, 2001

Net sales		$10,800,000
Gain on sale of treasury stock		564,000
Correction of an error in a prior period		60,000
Extraordinary gain (net of $18,000 income taxes)		36,000
Total revenue		$11,460,000
Less:		
Cost of goods sold	$6,000,000	
Selling expenses	1,128,000	
General and administrative expenses	1,896,000	
Income taxes (on continuing operations)	720,000	
Operating loss on discontinued operations (net of $126,000 income tax benefit)	252,000	
Loss on disposal of discontinued operations (net of $210,000 income tax benefit)	420,000	
Cumulative effect of change in accounting principle	84,000	
Dividends declared on capital stock	350,000	
Total costs and expenses		10,850,000
Net income		$ 610,000

INSTRUCTIONS

a. Prepare a corrected income statement for the year ended December 31, 2001. Include at the bottom of your income statement all appropriate earnings per share figures. Assume that throughout the year, the company had outstanding a weighted average of 200,000 shares of a single class of capital stock.

b. Prepare a statement of retained earnings for 2001. (As originally reported, retained earnings at December 31, 2000 amounted to $1,400,000.)

c. What does the $564,000 "gain on sale of treasury stock" represent? How did you report this "gain" in Keller's financial statements at December 31, 2001?

CHAPTER 15 REPORTING SPECIAL EVENTS AND SPECIAL EQUITY TRANSACTIONS   779

PROBLEM 15-6
Effects of Stock Dividends, Stock Splits, and Treasury Stock Transactions
(LO 4, 6)

At the beginning of the year, Recovery Sciences Inc., has total shareholders' equity of $660,000 and 20,000 outstanding shares of a single class of capital stock. During the year, the corporation completes the following transactions affecting its shareholders' equity accounts;

Jan. 10   A 10% stock dividend is declared and distributed. (Market price, $40 per share.)

Mar. 15   The corporation acquires 1,000 shares of its own capital stock at a cost of $40.50 per share.

May 30   All 1,000 shares of the treasury stock are reissued at a price of $44.90 per share.

July 31   The capital stock is split 2 for 1.

Dec. 15   The board of directors declares a cash dividend of $1.10 per share, payable on January 15.

Dec. 31   Net income of $127,600 (equal to $2.90 per share) is reported for the year ended December 31.

INSTRUCTIONS

Compute the amount of total shareholders' equity, the number of shares of capital stock outstanding, and the book value per share following each successive transaction. Organize your solution as a three-column schedule with these separate column headings: (1) Total Shareholders' Equity, (2) Number of Shares Outstanding, and (3) Book Value per Share.

PROBLEM 15-7
Recording Stock Dividends and Treasury Stock Transactions
(LO 4, 6)

At the beginning of 2001, OverNight Letter showed the following amounts in the shareholders' equity section of its balance sheet:

Shareholders' equity:
Capital stock, no-par value, unlimited shares authorized,
issued and outstanding, 382,000 shares $4,584,000
Retained earnings 2,704,600
Total shareholders' equity $7,288,600

The transactions relating to shareholders' equity during the year are as follows:

Jan. 3   Declared a dividend of $1 per share to shareholders of record on January 31, payable on February 15.

Feb. 15   Paid the cash dividend declared on January 3.

Apr. 12   The corporation purchased 6,000 shares of its own capital stock at a price of $40 per share.

May 9   Reissued 4,000 shares of the treasury stock at a price of $44 per share.

June 1   Declared a 5% stock dividend to shareholders of record at June 15, to be distributed on June 30. The market price of the stock at June 1 was $42 per share.

June 30   Distributed the stock dividend declared on June 1.

Aug. 4   Reissued 600 of the 2,000 remaining shares of treasury stock at a price of $37 per share.

Dec. 31   The Income Summary account, showing net income for the year of $1,928,000 was closed into the Retained Earnings account.

Dec. 31   The $382,000 balance in the Dividends account was closed into the Retained Earnings account.

INSTRUCTIONS

a. Prepare in general journal form the entries to record the above transactions.
b. Prepare the shareholders' equity section of the balance sheet at December 31, 2001. Include a supporting schedule showing your computation of retained earnings at that date.
c. Compute the maximum cash dividend per share that legally could be declared at December 31, 2001 without impairing the contributed capital of OverNight Letter.

PROBLEM 15-8
Recording Stock Dividends and Treasury Stock Transactions
(LO 4, 6)

The shareholders' equity of Cornish Productions Inc. at January 1, 2002 is as follows:

Shareholders' equity:
Common stock, no-par value, authorized, unlimited shares,
  issued and outstanding, 260,000 shares $5,365,000
Retained earnings 2,810,000
Total shareholders' equity $8,175,000

During the year the following transactions relating to shareholders' equity occurred:

Jan. 15 Paid a $1.50 per share cash dividend declared in December of the preceding year. This dividend was properly recorded at the declaration date and was the only dividend declared during the preceding year.

June 10 Declared a 10% stock dividend to shareholders of record on June 30, to be distributed on July 15. At June 10, the market price of the stock was $35 per share.

July 15 Distributed the stock dividend declared on June 10.

Aug. 4 Purchased 10,000 shares of treasury stock at a price of $30 per share.

Oct. 15 Reissued 6,000 shares of treasury stock at a price of $32 per share.

Dec. 10 Reissued 2,000 shares of treasury stock at a price of $28.50 per share.

Dec. 15 Declared a cash dividend of $1.50 per share to be paid on January 15 to shareholders of record on December 31.

Dec. 31 The Income Summary account, showing net income of $1,620,000, was closed into the Retained Earnings account.

INSTRUCTIONS

a. Prepare in general journal form the entries necessary to record these transactions.
b. Prepare the shareholders' equity section of the balance sheet at December 31, 2002 following the format illustrated in this chapter. Include a note following your shareholders' equity section indicating any portion of retained earnings that is not available for dividends. Also include a supporting schedule showing your computation of the balance of retained earnings at year-end.
c. Comment on whether Cornish Productions Inc. increased or decreased the total amount of cash dividends declared during the year in comparison with dividends declared in the preceding year.

PROBLEM 15-9
Effects of Transactions
(LO 4, 6)

Tobin Inc., manufactures a variety of computer peripherals, such as disk drives and printers. Listed below are five events that occurred during the current year.

1. Declared a $1.00 per share cash dividend.
2. Paid the cash dividend.
3. Purchased 1,000 shares of treasury stock for $20.00 per share.
4. Reissued 500 shares of the treasury stock at a price of $18.00 per share.
5. Declared a 15 percent stock dividend.

INSTRUCTIONS

a. Indicate the effects of each of these events upon the financial measurements in the three columnar headings listed below. Use the following code letters: *I* for increase, *D* for decrease, and *NE* for no effect.

Event	Current Assets	Shareholders' Equity	Net Income

b. For each event, ***explain fully*** the reasoning behind your answers. Also be prepared to explain this reasoning in class.

PROBLEM 15-10
Preparing the Shareholders' Equity Section: A Challenging Case
(LO 4, 6)

The Mandella family decided early in 2000 to incorporate their family-owned vineyards under the name Mandella Corporation. The corporation was authorized to issue unlimited shares of a single class of no-par value capital stock. Presented below is the information necessary to prepare the shareholders' equity section of the company's balance sheet at the end of 2000 and at the end of 2001.

2000. In January the corporation issued to members of the Mandella family 150,000 shares of capital stock in exchange for cash and other assets used in the operations of the vineyards. The fair market value of these assets indicated an issue price of $30 per share. In December, Joe Mandella died, and the corporation purchased 10,000 shares of its own capital stock from his estate at $34 per share. Because of the large cash outlay to acquire this treasury stock, the directors decided not to declare cash dividends in 2000 and instead declared a 10% stock dividend to be distributed in January of 2001. The stock price at the declaration was $35 per share. Net income for 2000 was $940,000.

2001. In January the corporation distributed the stock dividend declared in 2000, and in February, the 10,000 treasury shares were sold to Maria Mandella at $39 per share. In June, the capital stock was split 2 for 1. On December 15, the directors declared a cash dividend of $2 per share, payable in January of 2002. Net income for 2001 was $1,080,000.

INSTRUCTIONS

Using the format illustrated in the chapter, prepare the shareholders' equity section of the balance sheet at:
a. December 31, 2000
b. December 31, 2001

Show any necessary computations in supporting schedules.

PROBLEM 15-11
Format of an Income Statement; EPS
(LO 1)

The following information is selected from **Shell Canada Limited's** recent consolidated statement of earnings and a note thereto.

Revenues	($ millions)
Sales and other operating revenues	$5,140
Dividends, interest and other income	47
Expenses	
Purchased crude oil, petroleum products, and other merchandise	2,961
Operating, selling, and general	1,144
Exploration	84
Depreciation, depletion, amortization, and retirements	393
Interest on long-term debt	80
Income taxes (on continuing operations)	199

Note 2
The Corporation sold its Chemicals business ... to Shell Chemicals Ltd. The sale of the Chemicals business resulted in a gain of $324 million before tax, or $226 million after tax.

	($ millions)
Revenues from (Chemical business) operations	$606
Earnings from (Chemical business) operations before income taxes	$ 66
Income taxes	23
Earnings from (Chemical Business) operations after income taxes	$ 43
Gain on disposals (of the Chemical business) before income taxes	$324
Income taxes	98
Gain on disposals (of the Chemical business) after income taxes	$226
Total	$269

INSTRUCTIONS

a. Prepare an income statement for the year ended December 31 for Shell Canada Limited in the format illustrated in the chapter.
b. Compute all appropriate earnings per share figure for Shell Canada's 112 million Class A common shares.

Analytical and Decision Problems and Cases

**A&D 15-1
Reporting Issues
(LO 1)**

The following information is selected from a note to the recent financial statements of **Hudson's Bay Company**.

During the current year ended January 31, ... the Company recorded ... charges totalling $243,000,000 ($144,000,000 after deducting related income tax credits of $99,000,000). Of this total amount, $159,500,000 represented inventory valuation adjustments resulting from strategic changes in merchandising policies, $31,200,000 was provided for the closure of a distribution centre and stores that no longer meet the criteria for long-term investment, $45,000,000 was provided for the reorganizing and restructuring of the Company's operating and sourcing structures and $7,300,000 comprised other nonrecurring items.

During the preceding year ended January 31, ... the Company incurred ... charges amounting to $64,000,000 ($36,400,000 after deducting income tax credits of $27,600,000). Included in these costs were lease termination costs, severance payments, moving expenses, asset write-downs and other related expenses incurred as a result of the consolidation of the operations of Zellers, formerly located in Montreal, with the Bay's offices and the Company's corporate offices in Toronto.

CHAPTER 15 REPORTING SPECIAL EVENTS AND SPECIAL EQUITY TRANSACTIONS

INSTRUCTIONS

Indicate how the above charges should be reported in the financial statements. Explain the reasoning behind your answers.

**A&D 15-2
Reporting Issues
(LO 1)**

The following events have been reported in the financial statements of large corporations.
  a. **TransCanada PipeLines** sold all of its United States oil and gas properties held by its wholly owned subsidiary for approximately $150 million. In the year of disposal, the U.S. operation had an operating income of $2.4 million. Also, the loss on disposal of the U.S. operation amounted to $52.7 million.
  b. **Banister Continental Ltd.** reduced the remaining useful lives of certain older pieces of construction equipment. This change increased depreciation expense and decreased net income for the year by $1,030,000.
  c. **Union Carbide Corp.** sustained a large loss as a result of the explosion of a chemical plant.
  d. **Derlan Industries Limited** changed its policy of accounting for capital stock issue costs by charging these costs to retained earnings rather than capitalizing them as an asset. The cumulative effect of this change affecting the beginning balance of retained earnings for the preceding year was $2,370,000. Also, the effect of this change for the preceding year was $2,734,000.

INSTRUCTIONS

Indicate how each of these items should be accounted for or presented in the financial statements. Briefly explain the reasons for your answers.

**A&D 15-3
The Case of the
Extraordinarily Ordinary Loss
(LO 1, 2)**

In 1999, a large corporation recognized a $68 million loss from the write-off of certain foreign-based assets due to "escalating war, social upheaval, the weakening economies of oil-producing nations, and growing political instability." (The operations in these foreign countries were not discontinued.) The company originally classified this loss as an extraordinary item. Upon reviewing the company's financial statements, however, the securities commission requested that the company reclassify this item as a normal operating loss. In 2000, the company revised its 1999 income statement to comply with the commission's request.

INSTRUCTIONS

Indicate the effect of the reclassification of this loss upon the company's:
  a. Net income for 1999.
  b. Income before extraordinary items for 1999.
  c. Income from continuing operations in 1999.
  d. Price-earnings ratio as shown in newspapers such as *The Globe and Mail*.
  e. 2000 financial statements.
  f. Ability to pay cash dividends.

Explain the reasoning behind your answers.

**A&D 15-4
Is There Life without Baseball?
(LO 1)**

Midwestern Publishing Inc. publishes two newspapers and until recently owned a professional baseball team. The baseball team had been losing money for several years and was sold at the end of 2000 to a group of investors who plan to move it to a larger city. Also in 2000, Midwestern suffered an extraordinary loss when its Raytown printing plant was damaged by a tornado. The damage has since been repaired. A condensed income statement follows:

MIDWESTERN PUBLISHING INC.
Income Statement
For the Year Ended December 31, 2000

Net revenue		$41,000,000
Costs and expenses		36,500,000
Income from continuing operations		$ 4,500,000
Discontinued operations:		
Operating loss on baseball team	$(1,300,000)	
Gain on sale of baseball team	4,700,000	3,400,000
Income before extraordinary items		$ 7,900,000
Extraordinary loss:		
Tornado damage to Raytown printing plant		(600,000)
Net income		$ 7,300,000

INSTRUCTIONS

On the basis of this information, answer the following questions. Show any necessary computations and explain your reasoning.

a. What would Midwestern's net income have been for 2000 if it **had not** sold the baseball team?

b. Assume that for 2001, you expect a 7% increase in the profitability of Midwestern's newspaper business but had projected a $2,000,000 operating loss for the baseball team if Midwestern had continued to operate the team in 2001. What amount would you forecast as Midwestern's 2001 net income *if the company had continued to own and operate the baseball team*?

c. Given your assumptions in part **b**, but given that Midwestern **did** sell the baseball team in 2000, what would you forecast as the company's estimated net income for 2001?

d. Assume that the expenses of operating the baseball team in 2000 amounted to $32,200,000, net of any related income tax effects. What was the team's **net revenue** for the year?

A&D 15-5
Using Earnings per Share Statistics
(LO 1, 2, 3)

For many years Canadian Studios has produced television shows and operated several FM radio stations. Late in the current year, the radio stations were sold to Times Publishing Inc. Also during the current year, Canadian Studios sustained an extraordinary loss. Throughout the current year, the company had 3 million shares of common stock and a large quantity of convertible preferred stock outstanding. Earnings per share reported for the current year were as follows:

	Basic	Fully Diluted
Earnings from continuing operations	$8.20	$6.80
Earnings before extraordinary items	$6.90	$5.50
Net earnings	$3.80	$2.40

INSTRUCTIONS

a. Briefly explain why Canadian Studios reports fully diluted earnings per share amounts as well as earnings per share computed on a basic basis. What is the purpose of showing investors the fully diluted figures?

b. What was the total dollar amount of the extraordinary loss sustained by Canadian Studios during the current year?

c. Assume that the price-earnings ratio shown in the daily newspaper for Canadian Studios' common stock indicated that the stock is selling at a price equal to 10 times the reported earnings per share. What is the approximate market price of the stock?

d. Assume that you expect both the revenue and expenses involved in producing television shows to increase by 10% during the coming year. What would you forecast as the company's net earnings per share (basic basis) for the coming year under each of the following independent assumptions? (Show your computations and explain your reasoning.)
   1. *None* of the convertible preferred stock is converted into common stock during the coming year.
   2. *All* of the convertible preferred stock is converted into common stock at the beginning of the coming year.

A&D 15-6
Classification of Unusual Items—and the Potential Financial Impact
(LO 1, 2)

Elliot-Cole is a publicly owned international corporation, with operations in over 90 countries. Net income has been growing at approximately 15% per year, and the stock consistently trades at about 20 times earnings.

As part of their compensation packages, members of the corporation's top management have been granted **stock options**, entitling them to buy large quantities of the company's stock at a stipulated price. At the time these options were granted, this stipulated price was equal to the stock's market price. Due to the company's success, however, today's market price is well above the stipulated "option price." Thus, managers can realize substantial gains by exercising their options and reselling the shares at the market price.

During the current year, political unrest and economic upheaval threatened Elliot-Cole's business operations in several foreign countries. At year-end, the company's independent auditors insisted that management write-off the company's assets in these countries, stating that these assets were "severely impaired." Said one corporate official, "We can't argue with that. Each of these countries is a real trouble spot. We might be pulling out of these places at any time, and any assets probably would just be left behind."

Management agreed that the carrying value of Elliot-Cole's assets in these three countries should be reduced to "scrap value"—which was nothing. These write-downs amounted to approximately 18% of the company's income **prior** to recognition of these losses. (These write-offs are for financial reporting purposes only; they have **no effect** upon the company's income tax obligations.)

At the meeting with the independent auditors, one of Elliot-Cole's officers states, "There's no doubt we should write these assets off. But of course, this is an extraordinary loss. A loss of this size can't be considered a routine matter."

INSTRUCTIONS

a. Explain the logic behind writing down the book values of assets that are still in operation.
b. Evaluate the officer's statement concerning the classification of these losses. Do you agree that they should be classified as an extraordinary item? Explain.
c. Explain the effect that the classification of these losses—that is, as ordinary or extraordinary—will have in the current period upon Elliot-Cole's:
   1. Net income.
   2. Income before extraordinary items.
   3. Income from continuing operations.
d. Explain how the classification of these losses will affect the p/e ratio reported in newspapers such as *The Globe and Mail*.
e. Does management appear to have any "self-interest" in the classification of these losses? Explain.
f. Explain how (if at all) these write-offs are likely to affect the earnings of *future* periods.
g. What "ethical dilemma" confronts management in this case?

Answers to Self-Test Questions

1. b   2. a, b   3. c   4. a   5. b

CHAPTER 16

Special Types of Liabilities

Think of debt the way a hiker thinks of a backpack full of supplies. It's essential, but it's also a burden. Every business needs "enough," but too much can doom the venture.

CHAPTER LEARNING OBJECTIVES

1. Describe the typical characteristics of corporate bonds.
2. Explain the tax advantage of raising capital by issuing bonds instead of stock.
3. Account for the issuance of bonds, accrual and payment of interest, and retirement of bonds.
4. Explain the concept of present value.
5. Describe the relationship between interest rates and bond prices.
6. Explain the accounting treatment of operating leases and of capital leases.
7. Account for the costs of pensions and other postretirement benefits.
8. Explain the nature of future (deferred) income taxes.
*9. Explain the effects of amortizing bond discount and premium upon bond interest expense.
**10. Explain the accounting treatment of convertible bonds payable.

"Routine" types of business liabilities were discussed in Chapter 11. In this second chapter about liabilities we explore certain special types of liabilities. We will consider such questions as: How can a corporation borrow a huge amount of money on a long-term basis from many small, short-term investors? Why are some long-term lease agreements viewed as liabilities, whereas others are not? How can the balance sheet of a large corporation that has promised millions of dollars of retirement benefits to its employees include no liability for this obligation? And just what are future (deferred) taxes, anyway?

The liabilities discussed in this chapter appear primarily in the financial statements of large, publicly owned corporations. Some, however, also affect the financial statements of smaller organizations.

BONDS PAYABLE

Long-term financing by issuing notes payable to banks or to insurance companies can provide corporations with only a limited amount of funds. To finance a large project, such as developing an oil field or purchasing a controlling interest in the capital stock of another company, a corporation may need more capital than any single lender can supply. When a corporation needs to raise large amounts of long-term capital—perhaps 50, 100, or 500 million dollars (or more)—it generally sells additional shares of capital stock or issues **bonds payable**.

What Are Bonds?

LO 1: Describe the typical characteristics of corporate bonds.

The issuance of bonds payable is a technique for splitting a very large loan into a great many transferable units, called bonds. Each bond represents a ***long-term, interest-bearing note payable***, usually in the face amount (or par value) of $1,000. The bonds are sold to the investing public, enabling many different investors (bondholders) to participate in the loan.

Bonds usually are very long-term notes, maturing in perhaps 20 or 30 years. The bonds are ***transferable***, however, so individual bondholders may sell their bonds to other investors at any time. Most bonds call for semiannual interest payments to the bondholders, with interest computed

---
* *Supplemental Topic A,* "Accounting for Bonds Issued at a Discount or a Premium."
** *Supplemental Topic B,* "Convertible Bonds Payable."

at a specified **contract rate** throughout the life of the bond. Thus, investors often describe bonds as "fixed income" investments. An example of a corporate bond issue is the 1990 Series 11.70% bonds of Canadian Utilities Limited, due November, 2020. With this bond issue, Canadian Utilities borrowed $100 million in 1990, at an annual contract interest rate of 11.70%. Each bondholder is issued a single **bond certificate** indicating the number of bonds purchased. An illustration of a bond certificate appears on the following page. Investors such as mutual funds, banks, and insurance companies often buy thousands of bonds at one time.

Bonds payable differ from capital stock in several ways. First, bonds payable are a liability; thus, bondholders are **creditors** of the corporation, not owners. Bondholders generally do not have voting rights and do not participate in the earnings of the corporation beyond receiving contractual interest payments. Next, bond interest payments are **contractual obligations** of the corporation. Dividends, on the other hand, do not become legal obligations of the corporation until they have been formally declared by the board of directors. Third, bonds generally have a specified **maturity date**, upon which the corporation must redeem the bonds at their face amount. Capital stock, on the other hand, does not have a maturity date and may remain outstanding indefinitely. Finally, bond contracts, called bond indentures, often place restriction on corporate management, such as a restriction on the declaration of dividends.

Authorization of Bond Issue Formal approval of the board of directors usually is required before bonds can be issued. If the bonds are to be sold to the general public, certain requirements of the provincial securities commissions must be met, just as for an issue of capital stock to be offered to the public.

When bonds are issued, the corporation usually utilizes the services of an investment dealer, called an **underwriter**. The underwriter guarantees the issuing corporation a specific price for the entire bond issue and makes a profit by selling the bonds to the investing public at a higher price. The corporation records the issuance of the bonds at the net amount received from the underwriter. The use of an underwriter assures the corporation that the entire bond issue will be sold without delay, and the entire amount of the proceeds will be available at a specific date.

Transferability of Bonds Corporate bonds, like capital stocks, are traded daily on organized securities markets. The holders of a 20-year bond issue need not wait 20 years to convert their investments into cash. By placing a telephone call to a broker, an investor may sell bonds within a matter of minutes at the going market price. This quality of **liquidity** is one of the most attractive features of an investment in corporate bonds.

Quoted Market Prices Bond prices are quoted as a **percentage** of their face value or **maturity value**, which is usually $1,000. The maturity value is the amount the issuing company must pay to redeem the bond at the date it matures (becomes due). A $1,000 bond quoted at **102** would therefore have a market price of $1,020 (102% of $1,000). The following

CHAPTER 16 SPECIAL TYPES OF LIABILITIES 789

line from *The Financial Post* (now the *National Post*) summarizes certain information on one of Bell Canada's bonds:

What is the market value of this bond?

Bonds	Interest Rate	Maturity date	Bid	Yield
Bell Canada	8.875%	Apr. 17/26	$131.48	6.43%

This line of condensed information indicates that Bell Canada's 8.875% (contract interest rate) bonds will be matured on April 17, 2026, the buyers were willing to pay $131.48 or $1,314.80 for a bond of $1,000 face value, and the yield rate (the effective interest rate) on the bid price is 6.43%.

The primary factors that determine the market value of a bond are (1) the relationship of the bond's contract interest rate to the market interest rate for similar investments, (2) the length of time until the bond matures, and (3) investors' confidence that the issuing company has the financial strength to make all future interest and principal payments promptly. Thus, a bond with a 10% interest rate will command a higher market price than an 8% bond with the same maturity date if the two companies issuing the bonds are of equal financial strength.

CASE IN POINT

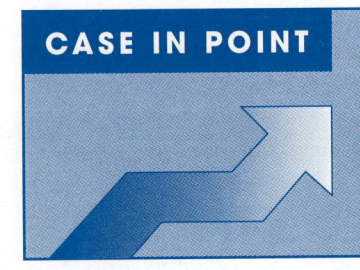

Bank of Nova Scotia has two bond issues maturing on March 24 and April 1, 2003 respectively. The one, with a higher contract interest rate of 8.10%, has a higher bid price of 110.48 (that is $1,104.80 for a $1,000 bond); while the other, which matures almost at the same time, with a lower contract interest rate of 5.40%, has a bid price of only 99.15 (that is $991.50 for a $1,000 bond). However, both bonds provide a 5.6% yield.

When a bond sells at a market price greater than its maturity value, it is said to be selling at a **premium**; a bond selling at a price below its maturity value is selling at a **discount**. Bonds sell at a premium when the contract interest rate on the bond exceeds the market rate for similar bonds. When the contract rate is less than the market rate, they sell at a discount. As a bond nears its maturity date, the market price of the bond moves toward the maturity value. At the maturity date the market value of the bond will be exactly equal to its maturity value, because the issuing corporation will redeem the bond for that amount.

Types of Bonds Bonds secured by the pledge of specific assets are called ***mortgage bonds***. An unsecured bond is called a ***debenture*** or ***debenture bond***; its value rests upon the general credit of the corporation. A debenture bond issued by a very large and strong corporation may have a higher investment rating than a secured bond issued by a corporation in less satisfactory financial condition.

Bond interest is usually paid semiannually by mailing to each bondholder a cheque for six months' interest on the bonds he or she owns.[1] Almost all bonds are ***callable (redeemable)***, which means that the corporation has the right to redeem the bonds ***in advance*** of the maturity date by paying a specified ***call (redemption) price***. To compensate bondholders for being forced to give up their investments, the call price usually is somewhat higher than the face value of the bonds.

Traditionally, bonds have appealed to conservative investors, interested primarily in a reliable income stream and in the safety of the principal that they have invested. To make a bond issue more attractive to these investors, some corporations create a bond **sinking fund**, designated for repaying the bonds at maturity. At regular intervals, the corporation deposits cash into this sinking fund. A bond sinking fund is not classified as a current asset, because it is not available for the payment of current liabilities. Such funds are shown in the balance sheet under the caption "Long-term Investments," which appears just below the current asset section.

As an additional attraction to investors, corporations sometimes include a conversion privilege in the bond indenture. A **convertible bond**

---

[1] In recent years, corporations have issued only ***registered*** bonds, for which interest is paid by mailing a cheque to the registered owners of the bonds. In past decades, some companies issued ***coupon bonds*** or ***bearer bonds***, which had a series of redeemable coupons attached. At each interest date, the bondholder was to "clip" the coupon and present it to the bank to collect the interest. These bonds posed a considerable hazard to investors—if the investor lost the coupon, or forgot about an interest date, he or she received no interest.

is one that may be exchanged at the option of the bondholder for a specified number of shares of common stock. Thus, the market value of a convertible bond tends to fluctuate with the market value of an equivalent number of shares of common stock. As an example, assume that a corporation has issued $1,000 face value bonds that are convertible into 50 shares of common stock. If the market value of the stock is $30 per share, the **stock value** of the bond is $1,500 (50 x $30). With this underlying stock value, the bonds will sell for about $1,500, regardless of the contract interest rate. (Accounting for convertible bonds is illustrated in *Supplemental Topic B* at the end of this chapter.)

"Junk Bonds" In recent years, some corporations have issued securities that have come to be known as **junk bonds**. This term describes a bond issue that involves a substantially greater risk of default than normal. A company issuing junk bonds usually has so much long-term debt that its ability to meet interest and principal repayment obligations has become questionable. To compensate bondholders for this unusual level of risk, junk bonds provide for a substantially higher rate of interest than do more "highly rated" bonds.

CASE IN POINT Junk Bonds became popular during the 1980s as a financing technique to acquire publicly owned corporations. Some of the biggest **corporate takeovers** in the history of North American business were financed with junk bonds, including Federated Stores (acquired by a Canadian corporation), RJR Nabisco, Beatrice Companies, and Storer Communications. Most of the bonds were sold through the junk bond department of Drexel Burnham Lambert, which was managed by Michael Milken. Milken, who has been referred to as the "junk bond king," was instrumental in creating a junk bond market of over $200 billion. Much of the corporate restructuring and downsizing of North American business in the 1990s has been attributed to the heavy burden of the debt that was taken on in the 1980s.

Tax Advantage of Bond Financing

LO 2: Explain the tax advantage of raising capital by issuing bonds instead of stock.

A principal advantage of raising money by issuing bonds instead of stock is that interest payments are **deductible** in determining income subject to corporate income taxes. Dividends paid to the shareholders are not tax deductible.

To illustrate, assume that a corporation pays income taxes at a rate of **30%** on its taxable income. If this corporation issues $10 million of 10% bonds payable, it will incur interest expense of $1 million per year. This interest expense, however, will reduce taxable income by $1 million, thus reducing the corporation's annual income taxes by $300,000. As a result, the annual after-tax cost of borrowing the $10 million is only **$700,000**, as shown below:

Interest expense ($10,000,000 × 10%)	$1,000,000
Less: Income tax savings ($1,000,000 deduction × 30%)	300,000
After-tax cost of borrowing	$ 700,000

A short-cut approach to computing the after-tax cost of borrowing is simply multiplying the interest expense by *1 minus the company's tax rate*, as follows: $1,000,000 \times (1 - .30) = $700,000$.

Accounting for Bonds Payable

LO 3: Account for the issuance of bonds, accrual and payment of interest, and retirement of bonds.

Accounting for bonds payable closely parallels accounting for notes payable. The "accountable events" in the life of a bond issue usually are (1) issuance of the bonds, (2) semiannual interest payments, (3) accrual of interest payable at the end of each accounting period,[2] and (4) retirement of the bonds at maturity.

To illustrate these events, assume that on March 1, 2000, Wells Corporation issues $1 million of 12%, 20-year bonds payable.[3] These bonds are dated March 1, 2000, and interest is computed from this date. Interest on the bonds is payable semiannually, each September 1 and March 1. If all of the bonds are sold at par value (face amount), the issuance of the bonds on March 1 will be recorded by the following entry:

Entry at the issuance date

Cash	1,000,000	
Bonds Payable		1,000,000
Issued 12%, 20-year bonds payable at a price of 100.		

Every September 1 during the life of the bond issue, Wells Corporation must pay $60,000 to the bondholders ($1,000,000 \times .12 \times \frac{1}{2} = $60,000$). This semiannual interest payment will be recorded as shown below:

Entry to record semiannual interest payments

Bond Interest Expense	60,000	
Cash		60,000
Semiannual payment of bond interest.		

Every December 31 (the year-end date), Wells Corporation must make an adjusting entry to record the four months interest that has accrued since September 1:

Adjusting entry at year-end—if necessary

Bond Interest Expense	40,000	
Bond Interest Payable		40,000
To accrue bond interest payable for four months ended Dec. 31 ($1,000,000 \times .12 \times \frac{4}{12} = $40,000$).		

The accrued liability for bond interest payable will be paid within a few months and, therefore, is classified as a current liability.

Two months later, on March 1, a semiannual interest payment is made to bondholders. This transaction represents payment of the four months' interest accrued at December 31, and of two months' interest that has accrued since year-end. The entry to record the semiannual payments every March 1 will be:

---

[2] To simplify our illustrations, we assume in all of our examples and assignment material that adjusting entries for accrued bond interest payable are made **only at year-end**. In practice, these adjustments usually are made on a monthly basis.

[3] The amount of $1 million is used only for purposes of illustration. As explained earlier, actual bond issues are for many millions of dollars.

Interest payment following the year-end adjusting entry	Bond Interest Expense	20,000	
	Bond Interest Payable	40,000	
	Cash		60,000
	To record semiannual interest payment to bondholders, and to recognize two months' interest expense accrued since year-end ($1,000,000 × .12 × 2/12 = $20,000).		

When the bonds mature 20 years later on March 1, 2020, two entries are required: one entry to record the regular semiannual interest payment (on March 1, which is the same as the above entry) and a second entry to record the retirement of the bonds. The entry to record retirement of the bond issue is:

Redeeming the bonds at the maturity date	Bonds Payable	1,000,000	
	Cash		1,000,000
	Paid face amount of bonds at maturity.		

Bonds Issued Between Interest Dates The semiannual interest dates (such as January 1 and July 1, or April 1 and October 1) are printed on the bond certificates. However, bonds are often issued between the specified interest dates. The ***investor*** is then required to pay the interest accrued to the date of issuance ***in addition*** to the stated price of the bond. This practice enables the corporation to pay a full six months' interest on all bonds outstanding at the semiannual interest payment date. The accrued interest collected from investors purchasing bonds between interest payment dates is thus returned to them on the next interest payment date.

To illustrate, let us modify our illustration to assume that Wells Corporation issued $1 million of 12% bonds at a price of 100 on ***May 1***—two months ***after*** the date printed on the bonds. The amount received from the bond purchasers now will include two months' accrued interest, as follows:

Bonds issued between interest dates	Cash	1,020,000	
	Bonds Payable		1,000,000
	Bond Interest Payable		20,000
	Issued $1,000,000 face value of 12%, 20-year bonds at 100 plus accrued interest for two months ($1,000,000 × 12% × 2/12 = $20,000).		

Four months later on the regular semiannual interest payment date, a full six months' interest ($60 per each $1,000 bond) will be paid to all bondholders, ***regardless of when they purchased their bonds***. The entry for the semiannual interest payment is illustrated below:

Notice only part of the interest payment is charged to expense	Bond Interest Payable	20,000	
	Bond Interest Expense	40,000	
	Cash		60,000
	Paid semiannual interest on $1,000,000 face value of 12% bonds.		

Now consider these interest transactions from the standpoint of the *investors*. They paid for two months' accrued interest at the time of purchasing the bonds, and then received cheques for six months' interest after holding the bonds for only four months. They have, therefore, been compensated properly for the use of their money for four months.

When bonds are subsequently sold by one investor to another, they sell at the quoted market price **plus accrued interest** since the last interest payment date. This practice enables the issuing corporation to pay all the interest for an interest period to the investor owning the bond at the interest date. Otherwise, the corporation would have to make partial payments to every investor who bought or sold the bond during the interest period. This would be costly and impractical.

The amount that investors will pay for bonds is the **present value** of the principal and interest payments they will receive. Before going further in our discussion of bonds payable, it will be helpful to review the concepts of present value and effective interest rate.

The Concept of Present Value

LO 4: Explain the concept of present value.

The concept of present value is based upon the "time value" of money—the idea that receiving money today is preferable to receiving money at some later date. Assume, for example, that a bond will have a maturity value of $1,000 five years from today but will pay no interest in the meantime. Investors would not pay $1,000 for this bond today, because they would receive no return on their investment over the next five years. There are prices less than $1,000, however, at which investors would buy the bond. For example, if the bond could be purchased for $600, the investor could expect a return (interest) of $400 from the investment over the five-year period.

The **present value** of a future cash receipt is the amount that a knowledgeable investor will pay **today** for the right to receive that future payment. The exact amount of the present value depends upon (1) the amount of the future payment, (2) the length of time until the payment will be received, and (3) the rate of return required by the investor. However, the present value will always be *less* than the future amount. This is because money received today can be invested to earn interest and thereby becomes equivalent to a larger amount in the future.

The rate of interest that will cause a given present value to grow to a given future amount is called the **discount rate** or **effective interest rate**. The effective interest rate required by investors at any given time is regarded as the going market rate of interest. (The procedures for computing the present value of a future amount are illustrated in Appendix C at the end of this Chapter.)

LO 5: Describe the relationship between interest rates and bond prices.

The Present Value Concept and Bond Prices The price at which bonds will sell is the present value to investors of the future principal and interest payments. If the bonds sell at par, the market interest rate is equal to the **contract interest rate** (or nominal rate) printed on the bonds. The **higher** the effective interest rate that investors require, the less they will pay for bonds with a given contract rate of interest. For example, if investors insist upon a 10% return, they will pay *less* than $1,000 for a 9%, $1,000 bond. Thus, if investors require an effective interest rate *greater* than the contract rate of interest for the bonds, the bonds will sell at a ***discount*** (price less than face value). On the other hand, if investors require an effective interest rate of *less* than the contract interest rate, the bonds will sell at a ***premium*** (price above face value).

A corporation wishing to borrow money by issuing bonds must pay the going market rate of interest. Since market rates of interest are fluctuating constantly, it must be expected that the contract rate of interest may vary somewhat from the market interest rate at the date the bonds are issued. Thus, bonds may be issued at either a discount or a premium. (Accounting for bonds payable issued at a discount or a premium is illustrated in *Supplemental Topic A* at the end of this chapter.)

Bond Prices After Issuance

As stated earlier, many corporate bonds are traded daily on organized securities markets at quoted market prices. After bonds are issued, their market prices vary ***inversely*** with changes in market interest rates. As interest rates rise, investors will be willing to pay less money to own a bond that pays a given contract rate of interest. Conversely, as interest rates decline, the market prices of bonds rise.

CASE IN POINT

A large corporation sold to underwriters $500 million of 9 3/8%, 25-year debenture bonds. The underwriters planned to sell the bonds to the public at a price of 99 5/8. Just as the bonds were offered for sale, however, a change in general business conditions and government policy started an upward surge in interest rates. The underwriters encountered great difficulty selling the bonds. Within one week, the market price of the bonds had fallen to 94 1/2. The underwriters dumped their unsold inventory at this price and sustained one of the largest underwriting losses in the history of the underwriting business.

During the months subsequent to the issuance, interest rates soared to record levels. Within five months, the price of the bonds had fallen to 76 3/8. Thus, nearly one-fourth of the market value of these bonds evaporated in less than half a year. At this time, the financial strength of the issuing corporation was never in question; this dramatic loss in market value was caused entirely by rising interest rates.

Changes in the current level of interest rates are not the only factors influencing the market prices of bonds. The length of time remaining until the bonds mature is another major force. As a bond nears its maturity date, its market price normally moves closer and closer to the maturity value. This trend is dependable because the bonds are redeemed at par value on the maturity date.

> **CASE IN POINT**
>
> Ontario Hydro has outstanding two issues of 10% bonds, one issue maturing in 5 years and the other in 12 years. When the going market rate of interest was much greater than 10%, both bonds were selling at a discount. The bonds maturing in 5 years, however, were selling at a market price of $91.10, whereas the bonds maturing in 12 years were selling at a price of only $86.20. Both bonds pay the same amount of interest, were issued by the same company, and have the same credit ratings. Thus, the difference in the market prices is caused mainly by the difference in the bonds' maturity dates.[4]

Volatility of Short-Term and Long-Term Bond Prices When interest rates fluctuate, the market prices of long-term bonds are affected to a far greater extent than are the market prices of bonds due to mature in the near future. To illustrate, assume that market interest rates suddenly soar from 9% to 12%. A 9% bond scheduled to mature in but a few days will still have a market value of approximately $1,000—the amount to be collected in a few days from the issuing corporation. However, the market price of a 9% bond maturing in 10 years will drop significantly. Investors who must accept these "below market" interest payments for many years will buy the bonds only at a discounted price.

In summary, fluctuations in interest rates have a far greater effect upon the market prices of long-term bonds than upon the prices of short-term bonds.

Remember that after bonds have been issued, they belong to the bondholder, *not to the issuing corporation*. Therefore, changes in the market price of bonds subsequent to their issuance *do not* affect the amounts shown in the financial statements of the issuing corporation, and these changes are not recorded in the corporation's accounting records.

Early Retirement of Bonds Payable

Bonds are sometimes retired before the maturity date. The principal reason for retiring bonds early is to relieve the issuing corporation of the obligation to make future interest payments. If interest rates decline to the point that a corporation can borrow at an interest rate below that being paid on a particular bond issue, the corporation may benefit from retiring those bonds and issuing new bonds at a lower interest rate.

Most bond issues contain a call (redemption) provision, permitting the corporation to redeem the bonds by paying a specified price, usually a few points above par. Even without a call provision, the corporation may retire its bonds before maturity by purchasing them in the open market. If the bonds can be purchased by the issuing corporation at less than their carrying value, a *gain* is realized on the retirement of the debt. If the bonds are acquired by the issuing corporation at a price in excess of their carrying value, a *loss* must be recognized.

---

[4] The expected future interest rate is also a factor. The yield rates for these two bonds are 12.60% and 12.32% respectively, suggesting an expected decline in future long-term interest rates.

For example, assume that Briggs Corporation has outstanding a 13%, $10 million bond issue, callable on any interest date at a price of 104. Assume also that the bonds were issued at par and will not mature for nine years. Recently, however, market interest rates have declined to far below 13%, and the market price of Briggs' bonds has increased to 105.[5]

Regardless of the market price, Briggs can call these bonds at 104. If the company exercises this call provision for 10% of the bonds ($1,000,000 face value), the entry will be:

Bonds called at a price above carrying value

Bonds Payable	1,000,000	
Loss on Early Retirement of Bonds	40,000	
Cash		1,040,000
To record the call of $1 million in bonds payable at a call price of 104.		

Notice that Briggs **called** these bonds, rather than purchasing them at market prices. Therefore, Briggs is able to retire these bonds at their call price of 104. (Had the market price of the bonds been **below** 104, Briggs might have been able to retire the bonds at less cost by purchasing them in the open market.)

Classification of Bonds Payable in a Balance Sheet

Bonds payable generally are classified as **long-term** liabilities, even when the bonds are within one year of maturity. This is because the obligation for maturing bonds usually is paid either (1) by issuing new bonds and using the proceeds to retire the maturing bond issue or (2) from a bond **sinking fund.**

If new bonds are issued, the maturing bond liability has been **refinanced**. As explained in Chapter 11, maturing obligations that will be refinanced on a long-term basis are classified as long-term liabilities rather than current liabilities. Now consider maturing bonds that will be repaid from a sinking fund accumulated over the years specifically for this purpose. A sinking fund is not regarded as a current asset, because its contents **cannot be used** for paying operating expenses or the claims of short-term creditors. The bonds payable, therefore, do not become a current liability, as they will be paid from the sinking fund **rather than from current assets**.

Accrued interest payable on long-term bonds is regarded as a current liability, because accrued interest normally is paid in cash within six months or less.

Commercial Paper

The term **commercial paper** describes **very short-term** notes payable issued by financially strong corporations. These notes mature generally in 30 days to 270 days and are issued in denominations of $25,000 or more.

---

[5] Falling interest rates cause bond prices to rise. On the other hand, falling interest rates also provide the issuing company with an incentive to call the bonds and, perhaps, replace them with bonds bearing a lower rate of interest. For this reason, call prices often serve as an approximate "ceiling" on market prices.

Commercial paper is similar to bonds payable in that it splits a large loan into small units, enabling many different investors to act as the lender. Also, an organized marketplace exists in which the holders of commercial paper may sell their investment immediately at a quoted market price.

No interest payments are made to holders of commercial paper. Instead, the notes are issued at a discount—that is, a price below their maturity value. (This also means that interest charges are included in the face amount, similar to the short-term notes payable with interest included in the face amount discussed in Chapter 11.) Because commercial paper matures so quickly, it is regarded as a safer and more liquid investment than are stocks or bonds. The market price of commercial paper does not fluctuate significantly as a result of changes in interest rates. Rather, the market price tends to increase day by day toward maturity value.

Many investors purchase commercial paper as a means of earning interest revenue on idle cash balances for very short periods of time—perhaps over a weekend. For this reason, investors usually regard commercial paper as a cash equivalent. The issuing corporation, of course, views these notes as a current liability.

OTHER "CORPORATE" LIABILITIES

Bonds payable and commercial paper are issued only by large corporations. These debt instruments are attractive to investors only if the continued existence and solvency of the business enterprise can be reasonably assumed.

We now will discuss the liabilities arising from lease agreements, pension plans, and the deferral of income taxes. These liabilities appear primarily in the financial statements of large corporations, but they may also affect smaller business organizations. Many small businesses, however, do not have financial reporting obligations to investors and creditors. Therefore, these businesses sometimes use income tax rules, rather than accounting principles, in recording the liabilities and expenses relating to leases and pensions. Our discussion of these topics emphasizes generally accepted accounting principles—the accounting standards used in the financial statements of publicly owned companies.

Lease Obligations

LO 6: Explain the accounting treatment of operating leases and of capital leases.

A company may purchase the assets needed in its business operations or, as an alternative, it may lease them. A **lease** is a contract in which the **lessor** gives the **lessee** the right to use an asset for a specified period of time in exchange for periodic rental payments. The lessor is the owner of the property; the lessee is a tenant or renter. Examples of assets frequently acquired by lease include automobiles, building space, computers, and equipment. Depending upon their terms, leases generally are classified as being either operating leases or capital leases.

Operating Leases

When the lessor gives the lessee the right to use leased property for a limited period of time but retains the usual risks and benefits (rewards) of ownership, the contract is known as an **operating lease**. This is the type of arrangement that most people think of when they hear the term "lease." An example of an operating lease is a contract leasing office space in an office building. If the building increases in value, the *lessor* can receive the benefits of this increase by either selling the building or increasing the rental rate once the lease term has expired. On the other hand, if the building declines in value, it is the lessor who bears the loss.

In accounting for an operating lease, the lessor views the monthly lease payments received as *rental revenue*, and the lessee regards these payments as *rental expense*. No asset or liability (other than a short-term liability for accrued rent payable) relating to the lease appears in the lessee's balance sheet. Thus, operating leases are sometimes termed **off-balance-sheet financing**.

Capital Leases

Some lease contracts are intended to provide financing to the lessee for the eventual purchase of the property or to provide the lessee with use of the property over most of its useful life. These lease contracts are called **capital leases** (direct financing or sales-type leases). In contrast to an operating lease, a capital lease transfers most of the risks and benefits of ownership from the lessor to the *lessee*. Assume, for example, that City Realty leases a new automobile from a car dealer for a period of three years. Also assume that at the end of the lease, title to the automobile transfers to City Realty at no additional cost. Clearly, City Realty is not merely "renting" the use of the automobile; rather, it is using the lease agreement as a means of *buying* the car. Also, the dealer is using the lease as a means of *selling* the car.

From an accounting viewpoint, capital leases are regarded as ***essentially equivalent*** to a sale of the property by the lessor to the lessee, even though title to the leased property has not been transferred. Thus, a capital lease should be recorded by the *lessor as a sale* of property and by the *lessee as a purchase*. In such lease agreements, an appropriate interest charge usually is added to the regular sales price of the property in determining the amount of the lease payments.

Some companies use capital lease agreements as a means of selling or financing the sale of their products to customers. In accounting for merchandise "sold" through a capital lease, the lessor debits **Lease Payments Receivable** and credits **Sales** for an amount equal to the *present value* of the future lease payments. In most cases, the present value of these future payments is equal to the regular sales price of the merchandise. In addition, the lessor transfers the cost of the leased merchandise from the Inventory account to the Cost of Goods Sold account. When lease payments are received, the lessor should recognize an appropriate portion of the payment as representing interest revenue and the remainder as a reduction in Lease Payments Receivable.

When equipment is acquired through a capital lease, the lessee should **debit an asset account**, Leased Equipment, and **credit a liability account**, Lease Payment Obligation, for the present value of the future lease payments. Lease payments made by the lessee are allocated between Interest Expense and a reduction in the liability, Lease Payment Obligation. The portion of the lease payment obligation that will be repaid within the next year is classified as a current liability, and the remainder is classified as long-term.

No rent expense is involved in a capital lease. The asset account, Leased Equipment, is depreciated by the lessee over the life of the equipment rather than the life of the lease. (The journal entries used in accounting for a capital lease are illustrated in Appendix C at the end of this chapter.)

Distinguishing Between Capital Leases and Operating Leases The CICA requires that a lease that meets any one of the following criteria be accounted for as a capital lease:

1. The lease transfers ownership of the property to the lessee at the end of the lease term.
2. The lease contains a "bargain purchase option."
3. The lease term is equal to 75% or more of the estimated economic life of the leased property.
4. The present value of the minimum lease payments amounts to 90% or more of the fair value of the lease property.[6]

Only those leases that meet **none** of the above criteria may be accounted for as operating leases.

Liabilities for Pensions and Postretirement Benefits

LO 7: Account for the costs of pensions and other postretirement benefits.

Many employers agree to pay their employees a pension; that is, monthly cash payments for life, beginning after they retire. Pensions are not an expense of the years in which cash payments are made to retired workers. Employees earn the right to receive the pension **while they are working for their employer**. Therefore, the employer's cost of future pension payments **accrues** over the years that each employee is "on the payroll."

Employers do not usually pay retirement pensions directly to retired employees. Most employers meet their pension obligations by making periodic deposits in a **pension fund** (or pension plan) throughout the years of each worker's employment.

A pension fund is **not an asset** of the employer. Rather, it is an **independent entity** managed by a trustee (usually a bank or an insurance company). As the employer makes deposits in the pension fund, the trustee invests the money in securities such as stocks and bonds. Over time, the pension fund earns investment income and normally accumulates to a balance far in excess of the employer's deposits. It is the **pension fund**—not the employer—that disburses monthly pension benefits to retired workers.

---

[6] CICA, *CICA Handbook* (Toronto), section 3065.06.

If the employer meets *all* of its estimated pension obligations by promptly depositing cash in a pension fund, the pension fund is said to be *fully funded*. The operation of a fully funded pension plan is summarized in the following illustration:

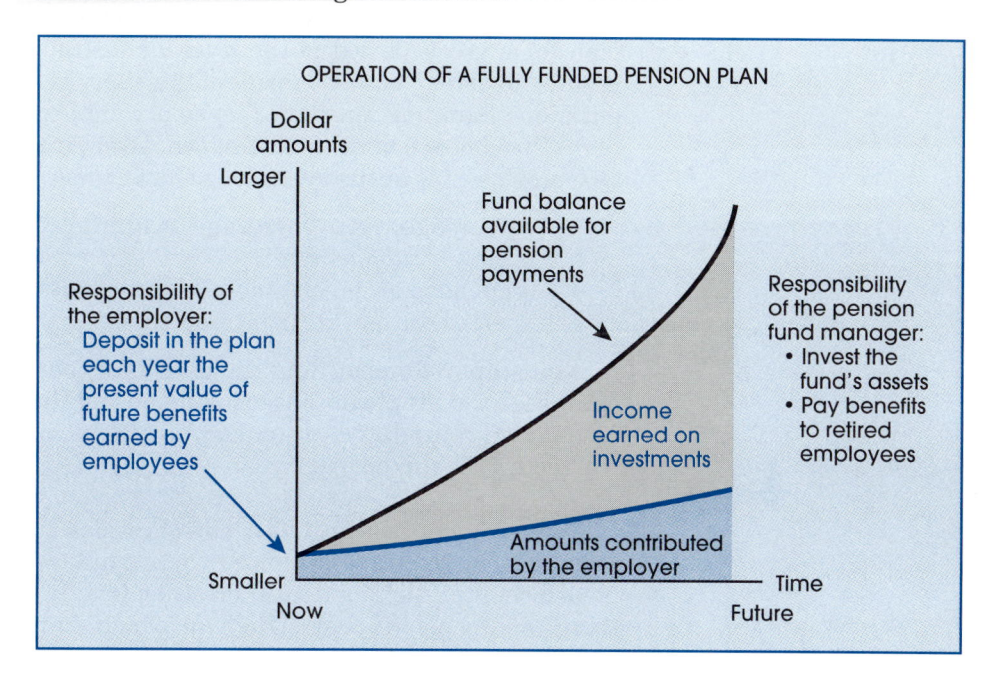

OPERATION OF A FULLY FUNDED PENSION PLAN

Responsibility of the employer: Deposit in the plan each year the present value of future benefits earned by employees

Responsibility of the pension fund manager:
- Invest the fund's assets
- Pay benefits to retired employees

If a pension plan is fully funded, *no liability* for pension payments appears in the employer's balance sheet. The employer's obligation is discharged in the *current period* through the payments made to the pension fund. The employer records each payment to this fund by debiting Pension Expense and crediting Cash.

Most pension plans are fully funded; therefore, most corporations do not report any pension liability. However, an employer must credit a liability account, Unfunded Pension Liability, for any portion of its periodic pension expense that *is not* paid immediately to the pension fund.

Determining Pension Expense The amount of the pension expense for a period depends upon the type of pension plan. There are two basic types: the defined contribution plan and the defined benefit plan.

An employer that establishes a **defined contribution plan** agrees to deposit a certain amount with the trustee each year to pay for future retirement benefits. When employees retire, they receive their share of the funds that have accumulated in the plan. From the employer's perspective there is no uncertainty in offering this type of plan. Pension expense is simply equal to the required deposit (contribution) for each period. Therefore, the remainder of our discussion will focus on defined benefit plans.

In a **defined benefit plan**, the employer generally agrees to pay all employees a percentage of their highest annual salary for life after they retire. The amounts of these *defined* benefits that must be paid to today's workers after they retire is not known with certainty. Among other things, the amounts depend upon how much the employees are making when they retire and how long they will live. Therefore, the employer's obligation for future pension payments arising during the current year *can only be estimated*.

From a conceptual point of view, the pension expense of a defined benefit plan for a given period is the *present value* of the future pension rights granted to employees as a result of their services during the period. The computation of annual pension expense is complex and involves many assumptions. The amount of this expense is not computed by accountants, but rather by a professional **actuary**. Among the factors considered by the actuary are:

- Average age, retirement age, and life expectancy of employees.
- Employee turnover rates.
- Compensation levels and estimated rate of pay increases.
- Expected rate of return to be earned on pension fund assets.

As a step in determining the pension expense for the year, the actuary estimates the employer's total pension liability as of year-end. Thus, the estimates are updated annually, and estimating errors in prior years are "corrected" in the current year.

Postretirement Benefits Other Than Pensions In addition to pension plans, many companies have promised their employees other types of postretirement benefits, such as dental or other health insurance. In most respects, these "non-pension" postretirement benefits are accounted for in the same manner as are pension benefits. Most companies, however, have not fully funded their obligations for nonpension postretirement benefits. Thus, recognition of the annual expense often involves a credit to an unfunded liability.

To illustrate, assume that at the end of 2000 Cable Corporation receives the following report from its actuaries:

CABLE CORPORATION
Summary of Postretirement Benefits Expenses and Unfunded Liabilities
For the Year Ended December 31, 2000
Prepared by Gibson & Holt, Professional Actuaries

Defined Benefit Pension Plan (fully funded):
Estimated present value of benefits accruing to employees during 2000 (expense for the year)	$400,000
Less: Payments during the year to National Trust (trustee)	400,000
Increase during the year in the present value of unfunded benefits	$ -0-
Add: Unfunded liability at Dec. 31, 1999	-0-
Unfunded liability at Dec. 31, 2000	$ -0-

Nonpension Postretirement Benefits Plan (partially funded):
Estimated present value of benefits accruing to employees during 2000 (expense for the year)	$250,000
Less: Payments during the year to National Trust (trustee)	140,000
Increase during the year in the present value of unfunded benefits	$110,000
Add: Unfunded liability at Dec. 31, 1999	860,000
Unfunded liability at Dec. 31, 2000	$970,000

As the pension plan is fully funded, an entry summarizing Cable's pension expense for 2000 is shown below:

When the expense is fully funded, there is no liability ...

Pension Expense	400,000	
Cash		400,000
Pension expense for the year as determined by actuarial firm of Gibson & Holt. Fully funded by payments to National Trust.		

The company's "nonpension" postretirement benefits expense was only partially paid in cash. The entry to summarize this expense for the year is:

... but when it is only partially funded, there is.

Nonpension Postretirement Benefits Expense	250,000	
Cash		140,000
Unfunded Liability for Nonpension Postretirement Benefits		110,000
To record nonpension postretirement benefits expense per report of Gibson & Holt, actuaries. Expense funded to the extent of $140,000.		

Any portion of the unfunded liability that the company intends to fund during the next year is classified as a current liability; the remainder is classified as a long-term liability.

Unfunded Postretirement Costs Are "Noncash" Expenses Postretirement costs are recognized as expense as workers earn the right to receive these benefits. If these costs are fully funded, the company makes cash payments within the current period equal to this expense. But if these benefits are *not* funded, the cash payments are not made until after the employees retire. Thus, an unfunded retirement plan involves a long "lag" between the recognition of expense and the related cash payments.

Unfunded retirement benefits often are called a "noncash" expense. That is, the expense is charged against current earnings. But there are no corresponding cash payments in the period. In the journal entry above, notice that expense exceeds the cash outlays by $110,000 ($250,000 - $140,000 = $110,000). This corresponds to the growth in the unfunded liability.

Unfunded Liabilities for Postretirement Costs: Can They Really Be Paid? Many of North America's largest and best-known corporations have obligations for unfunded postretirement benefits that can only be described as enormous.

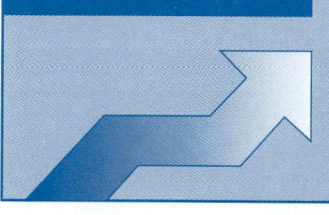

CASE IN POINT In a recent balance sheet, General Motors reports an unfunded liability for postretirement costs of more than ***$35 billion***. This compares with total shareholders' equity of a little more than $6 billion. One might say that GM's employees have a far greater "financial stake" in the company's long-term prospects than do its shareholders.

Until recently, companies in the United States were not required to show their unfunded liability for postretirement costs in their balance sheets. Instead, they charged benefit payments for retired workers directly to expense. This "pay-as-you-go" treatment, however, fails to achieve the *matching principle*. It is the cost of benefits earned by *today's* workers that are helping the company produce revenue, not the cost of benefits now being paid to workers who have already retired.

While there is no official pronouncement in Canada on how this issue should be addressed, the FASB in the United States recently changed the rules for measuring postretirement costs.[7] Companies now must estimate the present value of the retirement benefits earned each year by their employees. This estimated amount is recognized as expense, and any unfunded portion is recorded as a liability.

Now that these liabilities are "on the books," many people are stunned by their size. They wonder—with just cause—whether General Motors and other large corporations can really pay liabilities this large. Interesting question.

Let us suggest some things to consider in evaluating a company's ability to pay its unfunded liability for postretirement costs. First, remember that this liability represents only the *present value* of the estimated future payments. Thus, the future payments are expected to be *substantially more* than the amount shown in the balance sheet. Next, this liability may *continue to grow*, especially if the company has more employees today than in the past. On the other hand, this liability does *not* have to be paid all at once. It will be paid over a *great many years*—the life spans of today's workforce.

In evaluating a company's ability to meet its postretirement obligations, we suggest looking to the *cash flow statement*, rather than the balance sheet. In the cash flow statement, payments of postretirement costs are classified as operating activities. Thus, if a company has a steadily increasing net cash flow from operating activities, it apparently is able to handle these costs—at least at present.

But if the net cash flow from operating activities starts to decline, the company may have no choice but to reduce the benefits it provides to retired employees. Often these benefits are *not* contractual and can be reduced at management's discretion.

Future (Deferred) Income Taxes[8]

LO: 8 Explain the nature of future (deferred) income taxes.

We have seen in earlier chapters that differences sometimes exist between the dates certain types of revenue or expense are recognized in financial statements and the dates these items are reported in income tax returns. For example, sales revenue usually is recognized in an income statement in the period in which the sale occurs. Income tax rules, however, may permit use of the instalment method, which delays recognition of the revenue

---

[7] The CICA's Emerging Issues Committee simply identified the alternative treatments and the need to disclose the treatment used.
[8] Section 3465 of the *CICA Handbook* recommends that the term "future income taxes" replace "deferred income taxes" for financial statements after January 1, 2000 and it encourages earlier adoption of the new term.

in income tax returns until cash is collected from the customer. Moreover, the amount of depreciation reported for financial statement purposes may be different from income tax purposes.

Because of such *timing differences* between accounting principles and tax rules, income or expenses may be reported in the income statement of one year but in the income tax return of a *different* year. Most timing differences result in *postponing* (deferring) the recognition of income or early recognition of expenses for tax purposes.[9] The recognition of income in income tax returns is postponed by those tax rules that enable taxpayers either to (1) delay the recognition of revenue (such as the instalment method) or (2) accelerate the recognition of expense (such as accelerated depreciation methods).

In summary, income appearing in the income statement today may not be subject to income taxes until future years. However, the *matching principle* requires that the income shown in an income statement be offset by all related income taxes expense, regardless of when these taxes will be paid. Thus, the entry to record a corporation's income taxes expense often appears as follows:

Payment of some taxes expense often can be deferred

Income Taxes Expense	1,000,000	
Income Taxes Payable		800,000
Future Income Taxes		200,000
To record corporate income taxes applicable to the income of the current year.		

Income Taxes Payable is a current liability representing the portion of the income taxes expense that must be paid when the company files its income tax return for the current year. That portion of the income taxes expense which is deferred to future tax returns is credited to a liability account entitled **Future Income Taxes**.

Future Income Taxes in Financial Statements Whether future income taxes are classified as current or long-term liabilities depends upon the classification of the assets and liabilities that *caused* the tax deferrals. For example, instalment receivables are classified as current assets. Therefore, if the methods used in accounting for instalment receivables result in deferred taxes, the future (deferred) taxes are classified as a current liability. Depreciable assets, however, are not viewed as current assets. Therefore, if future (deferred) taxes result from the use of accelerated depreciation methods in income tax returns, the future (deferred) tax liability is classified as long-term.

The amount of income taxes deferred during the current period is recognized as expense, but does *not* require an immediate cash outlay. Bear in mind, however, that future (deferred) income taxes are tax obligations

---

[9] In some situations, income may be subject to income taxes *prior* to recognition of the income for financial reporting purposes. In these instances, the taxpayer *prepays* its income taxes expense. Prepaid income taxes is an asset, similar to prepaid rent. In this chapter, we limit our discussion to the more common situation in which the payment of income taxes is *deferred* to later periods.

that have been **postponed** to future periods. The company has **not eliminated** its obligation to pay these taxes.

Growing businesses often are able to defer part of their income taxes expense every year. Of course, some of the income taxes deferred in prior years constantly are coming due. Nonetheless, the liability for future (deferred) taxes usually continues to grow as the company grows—just as does the overall liability for accounts payable.

Accounting for future (deferred) taxes involves a number of complex issues that will be addressed in the intermediate accounting course.

Disclosures About Financial Instruments

Except for future (deferred) income taxes, all the liabilities discussed in this chapter are among the contracts often regarded as financial instruments. The term **financial instruments** describes cash, equity investments in another business, and any contracts calling for the receipt or payment of cash. Notice that this term applies to certain assets, as well as to most liabilities.

Section 3860 of the *CICA Handbook* recommends that companies **disclose** the **fair value** of their financial instruments, either in the balance sheet or a note thereto. When such a disclosure is impracticable, this fact should be disclosed together with information on the financial instrument's principal characteristics that are pertinent to its fair value. Fair value generally means **current market value**.

The disclosure of fair value enables users to make meaningful comparison of similar financial instruments. It also provides a neutral basis for evaluating the results of management decision on financial instruments, e.g. the decision to incur, maintain, or discharge financial liabilities.

Measuring Fair Value Bonds payable usually have quoted market prices. Thus, the fair value of an issue of bonds payable is determined by multiplying the quoted price by the number of bonds outstanding. Investments in stocks and bonds also are financial instruments that usually have readily determinable market values. For financial instruments that **do not** have quoted market prices, fair value often is considered to be the **present value** of the future cash flows, computed under current market conditions. (Computation of the present value of future cash flows is explained and illustrated in Appendix C, at the end of this chapter.)

Cash, accounts receivables, accounts payable, and commercial paper, for example, normally have carrying values that **closely approximate** their fair values. Bonds payable, long-term notes payable or receivable, and investments in stocks and bonds, however, often **do** have fair values differing from their carrying values. Thus, the requirement for disclosure of fair value applies primarily to these types of financial instruments.

CASE IN POINT

Bombardier Inc. shows the following note disclosure:

Fair value of financial instruments

The carrying amounts and fair values of financial instruments, other than those disclosed elsewhere in these consolidated financial statements, are as follows (in millions of dollars):

	1998 Carrying amount $	1998 Fair value $	1997 Carrying amount $	1997 Fair value $
Bombardier Inc. consolidated				
Financial assets				
Cash and term deposits	1,227.7	1,227.7	895.7	895.7
Accounts receivable	693.2	693.2	358.4	358.4
Finance receivables and other	2,683.0	2,693.0	1,461.0	1,463.1
Investment in Eurotunnel share units	50.0	42.1	50.0	50.5
Financial liabilities				
Short-term borrowings	2,265.6	2,265.6	1,402.4	1,402.4
Accounts payable and accrued liabilities	2,663.0	2,663.0	2,124.6	2,124.6
Income taxes payable	56.6	56.6	65.9	65.9
Long-term debt	1,548.7	1,632.7	1,354.9	1,367.4
Off-balance-sheet				
Foreign exchange contracts				
—favourable	—	17.5	—	100.0
—unfavourable	—	(387.1)	—	(39.5)
Interest-rate swap agreements				
—favourable	—	2.0	—	0.2
—unfavourable	—	(10.4)	—	(1.4)

The following methods and assumptions were used in estimating the fair value of financial instruments:

Cash and term deposits, accounts receivable, short-term borrowings, accounts payable and accrued liabilities and income taxes payable: The carrying amounts reported in the balance sheet approximate the fair values of these items due to their short-term nature.

Finance receivables and other: The carrying amounts of finance receivables and other exclude assets under operating leases. The fair values of floating rate finance receivables and other that reprice frequently and have no significant change in credit risk approximate the carrying values. The fair values of fixed rate finance receivables and other are estimated using discounted cash flow analyses, using interest rates offered for loans with similar terms to borrowers of similar credit quality.

Investment in Eurotunnel share units: The fair value of the investment in Eurotunnel share units is estimated using the quoted market price.

Long-term debt: The fair values of long-term debt are estimated using public quotations or discounted cash flow analyses, based on current corresponding borrowing rates for similar types of borrowing arrangements.

Foreign exchange contracts and interest-rate swap agreements: The fair values generally reflect the estimated amounts that the Corporation would receive on settlement of favourable contracts or be required to pay to terminate unfavourable contracts at the reporting dates, thereby taking into account the current unrealized gains or losses on open contracts. Investment dealers' quotes or quotes from the Corporation's bankers are available for substantially all of the Corporation's foreign exchange contracts and interest-rate swap agreements.

Credit support and guarantees: The determination of the fair values of bank guarantees and other forms of guarantees related to long-term contracts is not practicable within constraints of timeliness and cost but such guarantees usually decrease in value in relation to the percentage of completion of the related contracts and usually expire without being exercised. The fair values of credit support and guarantees provided to purchasers of manufactured products are not determinable due to a lack of reliable evidence.

Liability and Equity Financial Instrument Traditionally, all preferred stocks have been treated as equity and all convertible bonds payable treated as liabilities. Now, section 3860 of the *CICA Handbook* treats certain redeemable preferred stock as *liability* and convertible bonds payable as a combination of *liability and equity*. The critical criterion of distinguishing a financial liability from an equity instrument is whether there exists a contractual obligation on the part of the issuer to deliver cash or another financial asset or to exchange another financial instrument under conditions that are potentially unfavourable to the issuer.[10] When such an obligation exists, it is a liability. On the other hand, when such an obligation does not exist, it is an equity instrument. Thus, a preferred stock is a financial liability if it has a mandatory redemption for a fixed or determinable amount at a fixed or determinable future date or it gives the holder the right to require the issuer to redeem the shares at or after a particular date for a fixed or determinable amount.[11]

Accordingly, *retractible preferred stock* must be presented in the balance sheet as a *liability* because it is redeemable at the option of the preferred shareholders. Also, its *dividends* must be reported as an *expense* in the income statement. On the other hand, *convertible bonds payable* must be separated into the *liability* component and the *equity* component and presented as such in the balance sheet. The interest expense related to the liability component is charged to income while the interest expense related to the equity component is charged to retained earnings, net of income taxes.

---

[10] CICA, *CICA Handbook* (Toronto), Section 3860.20 and .21
[11] Ibid., Section 3860.22.

Disclosure of Off-Balance-Sheet Risk Some financial instruments do not create assets or liabilities that appear in financial statements but still create a risk of *future losses*. When a financial instrument does not appear in the balance sheet, the risk of loss created by the instrument is called an **off-balance-sheet risk**.

The possibility of *future losses* ordinarily is *not* disclosed in financial statements, because all of the situations that may cause future losses cannot be identified. However, if the risk of a future loss *is created by an existing contract* (financial instrument), current practices require disclosure of the potential for loss.

As an example, large and financially strong corporations sometimes guarantee bank loans or other specific liabilities of less financially sound corporations. In these situations, the guarantor promises to repay the loan if the original borrower is unable to do so. The basic purpose of a loan guarantee is to enable the weaker company to borrow money at more favourable terms than its own credit rating would justify.

Why would one company guarantee the debts of another? Often the borrower pays the guarantor a fee for this service. In other cases, the borrower may be an important customer or supplier of the guarantor.

A loan guarantee (also called an **accommodation endorsement**) creates a contingent loss for the guarantor.[12] Unless a loss is considered *likely* and *reasonably determinable*, however, no liability appears in the guarantor's financial statements. Therefore, the guarantor's risk of loss—that is, the possibility of having to assume responsibility for the guaranteed loan—is an **off-balance-sheet risk**.

Current practices require companies to disclose any material off-balance-sheet risk created by financial instruments. The required disclosure is to include a written explanation of the nature and terms of the financial instrument, and the maximum amount of loss that might be sustained. (See Bombardier Inc., in the preceding Case In Point.)

Some Old Ratios Take On New Importance

Two ratios that we discussed in Chapter 11 are widely used by long-term creditors in evaluating the safety of their investments: the *debt ratio* and the *interest coverage ratio*.

The **debt ratio**, which is total liabilities divided by total assets, indicates the percentage of total assets financed with borrowed money. Creditors prefer a *low* debt ratio, as this indicates that their claims amount to only a small percentage of the company's total assets. The **interest coverage ratio**, which equals operating income divided by interest expense, indicates how many times the company's earnings for the period "covered" its interest obligations. Creditors prefer a high interest coverage ratio.

The ability of large corporations to meet their interest obligations has taken on new importance in recent years. During the 1980s, a number of well-known corporations borrowed startling amounts of money by issuing "junk bonds" bearing interest rates of 12, 14, and 16%—and sometimes even higher. As a result, the very existence of some of these corporations

---

[12] Accounting for contingent losses is discussed in Chapter 11.

now is threatened by the size of the companies' annual interest obligations. A long-established company such as Federated Department Stores owned by Campeau Corporation (a Canadian company) already has declared bankruptcy.

Bankruptcy affects much more than the claims of long-term creditors. Shareholders have only a residual claim to assets; therefore, capital stocks are the first securities to lose value. Top management often is replaced, and many employees usually lose their jobs. Perhaps most devastating in human terms, bankrupt companies may be unable to meet unfunded postretirement obligations.

In conclusion, debt ratios and interest coverage ratios have become measurements of importance to **everyone** concerned with the long-run survival and health of a business organization.

Financing a Business with Debt

All businesses incur some debt as a result of normal business operations. These include, for example, accounts payable and accrued liabilities. But many businesses aggressively use long-term debt, such as mortgages and bonds payable, to finance growth and expansion. These businesses regard long-term debt as an alternative to issuing capital stock as a way of financing the business. However, there are distinct differences. The following table summarizes the principle advantages and disadvantages of financing a business with debt rather than equity.

Advantages	Disadvantages
• Interest on debt is tax deductible by the corporation; dividends are not.	• Interest and principle on debt must be paid when due; dividends are payable only when declared by the board of directors, and capital stock does not have a maturity date.
• Control of the corporation is not given up by incurring liabilities, because creditors do not have voting rights.	• Creditors often place restrictions on corporate management, such as restrictions on the declaration of dividends.
• Incurring debt does not dilute earnings-per-share as does the issuance of common stock.	

How Much Debt Should a Business Have? Determining whether to incur additional debt is not simply a matter of considering its advantages and disadvantages. Businesses strive to achieve an optimal mix of debt and equity, considering the nature of the business. In general, a business should continue to borrow funds *as long as the funds can be invested to earn a rate of return higher than the rate of interest paid to creditors*. The rate of return earned on invested capital usually is viewed as the overall *return on assets*—that is, operating income divided by average total assets.

Using borrowed money to finance business operations is called "applying **leverage**." Extensive use of leverage—that is, a great deal of debt—may benefit a business dramatically. But if things don't work out, it can also "wipe out" the borrower.

If borrowed money can be invested to earn a rate of return **higher** than the interest paid to the lenders, net income and the return on shareholders' equity will **increase**. **Return on equity** is net income expressed as a percentage of average shareholders' equity. For example, if you borrow money at an interest rate of 9% and invest it to earn 15%, you will benefit by doing so.

But leverage is a "double-edged sword"—that is, the effects may be favourable or unfavourable. If the rate of return earned on the borrowed money falls **below** the rate of interest being paid, the use of borrowed money **reduces** net income and the return on equity. Companies with large amounts of debt sometimes become "victims" of their own **debt-service requirements**.

The effects of leverage may be summarized below:

Relationship of Return on Assets to Interest Rate on Borrowed Funds	Effect Upon Net Income and Return on Equity
Return on Assets > Interest Rates being Paid	Increase
Return on Assets < Interest Rates being Paid	Decrease

Bear in mind that over time, both the return on assets and interest rates that the company must pay may change.

The more leverage a company applies, the greater the effects upon net income and the return on equity become. Using more leverage simply means having more debt. Therefore, the **debt ratio** is a basic measure of the amount of leverage being applied.

*Supplemental Topic A

ACCOUNTING FOR BONDS ISSUED AT A DISCOUNT OR A PREMIUM

LO 9: Explain the effects of amortizing bond discount and premium upon bond interest expense.

Underwriters normally sell corporate bonds to investors either at par or at a price very close to par. Therefore, the underwriter usually purchases these bonds from the issuing corporation at a discount—that is, at a price below par. The discount generally is quite small—perhaps 1 or 2% of the face amount of the bonds.

When bonds are issued, the borrower records a liability equal to the *amount received*. If the bonds are issued at a small discount—which is the normal case—this liability is slightly smaller than the face value of the bond issue. At the maturity date, of course, the issuing corporation must redeem the bonds at full face value. Thus, over the life of the bond issue, the borrower's liability gradually *increases* from the original issue price to the maturity value.

Bond Discount: Part of the Cost of Borrowing When bonds are issued at a discount, the borrower must repay more than the amount originally borrowed. Thus, any discount in the issuance price becomes an "extra cost" in the overall borrowing transaction.

In terms of cash outlays, the "extra cost" represented by the discount is not paid until the bonds mature. But the *matching principle* may require the borrower to recognize this cost gradually over the life of the bond issue.[1] After all, the borrower does benefit from the use of the borrowed funds throughout this entire period.

Accounting for Bond Discount: An Illustration

To illustrate, assume that on January 1, 2000, SCUBA TECH sells $1 million of 9%, 20-year bonds to an underwriter at a price of **98** ($980 for each bond). On January 1, 2000, SCUBA TECH receives $980,000 cash from the underwriter and records a liability in this amount. But when these bonds mature in 20 years, SCUBA TECH will owe its bondholders $1,000,000. Thus, the company's liability to bondholders will *increase by $20,000* over the life of the bond issue. The gradual "growth" in this liability is illustrated below:

---

[1] If the amount of the discount is immaterial, it may be charged directly to expense as a matter of convenience.

CHAPTER 16 SPECIAL TYPES OF LIABILITIES **813**

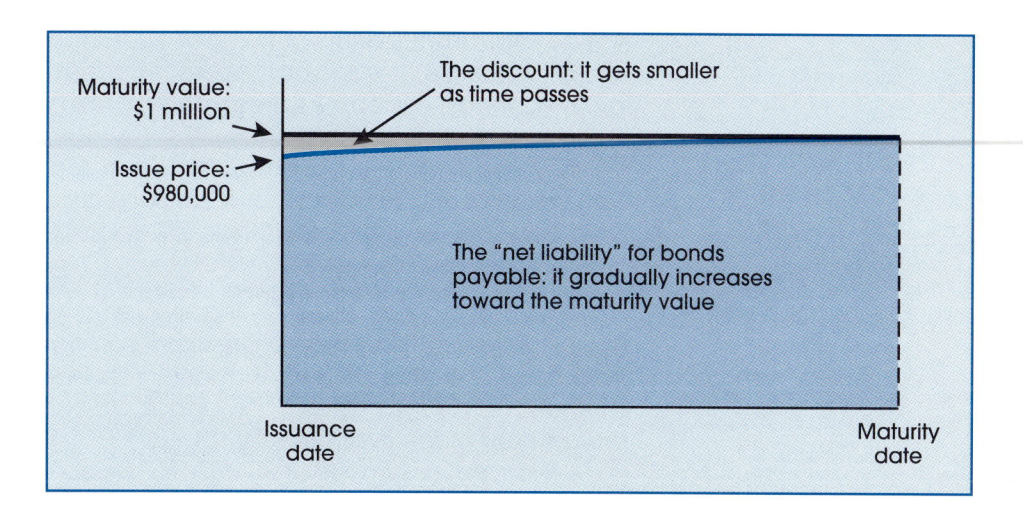

Figure: Bond liability over time showing Maturity value $1 million, Issue price $980,000, with the discount getting smaller as time passes. The "net liability" for bonds payable gradually increases toward the maturity value from Issuance date to Maturity date.

Notice that the long-term liability is increasing very **gradually**—at an average rate of $1,000 per year ($20,000 increase ÷ 20-year life of the bond issue).

When bonds are issued, the amount of any discount is debited to an account entitled **Discount on Bonds Payable**. Thus, SCUBA TECH will record the issuance of these bonds as follows:

Cash	*980,000*	
Discount on Bonds Payable	*20,000*	
Bonds Payable		*1,000,000*
Issued $1,000,000 face value, 9%, 20-year bonds to an underwriter at a price of 98.		

SCUBA TECH's liability at the date of issuance will appear as follows:

The "net" liability for bonds payable

Long-term liabilities:		
Bonds payable	$1,000,000	
Less: Discount on Bonds Payable	20,000	$980,000

The debit balance account, Discount on Bonds Payable, is a **contra-liability account**. In the balance sheet, it is shown as a **reduction** in the amount of the long-term liability. Thus, the net liability originally is equal to the **amount borrowed**.

Amortization of the Discount Over the 20-year life of the bond issue, adjusting entries are made to gradually transfer the balance in the Discount account into interest expense. Thus, the balance in the Discount account gradually declines, and the carrying value of the bonds—face value *less* the unamortized discount—rises toward the bonds' maturity value.

At the end of each year, SCUBA TECH will make the following **adjusting entry** to amortize the bond discount:

Amortization of bond discount **increases** interest expense

Interest Expense	*1,000*	
Discount on Bonds Payable		*1,000*
Recognized one year's amortization of discount on 20-year bonds payable ($20,000 original discount × 1/20).		

Notice that amortization of the discount *increases* SCUBA TECH's annual interest expense. It does not, however, require any immediate cash outlay. The interest expense represented by the discount will not be paid until the bonds mature.

Also, bond discount is amortized from the date of issue. If the bonds were issued on March 1 rather than January 1, the discount will be amortized over 238 months rather than 240 months (20 years).

Accounting for Bond Premium

When bonds are issued at a **premium** (a price above par), the borrower pays back less than the amount originally borrowed. As a result, the total interest cost over the life of the bonds is equal to the interest paid *minus the amount of the premium*.

To illustrate, assume that SCUBA TECH issued the $1 million, 9%, 20-year bonds at a price of *102* ($1,020 for each $1000 bond). The entry to record the issuance of the bonds is shown below:

Issuance of bonds at the premium

Cash	1,020,000	
Bonds Payable		1,000,000
Premium on Bonds Payable		20,000
Issued $1,000,000 face value 9%, 20-year bonds at a price of 102.		

If a balance sheet is prepared immediately following the issuance of the bonds, the liability will be shown as follows:

A premium is part of the overall liability

Long-term liabilities:
Bond Payable	$1,000,000	
Add: Premium on Bonds Payable	20,000	$1,020,000

The amount of any unamortized premium is *added* to the maturity value of the bonds payable to show the current carrying value of the liability. Over the life of the bond issue, this carrying value will be *reduced* toward the maturity value of $1 million, as the premium is amortized.

Amortization of the Premium Premium is amortized over the 20-year life of the bonds in a manner similar to the amortization of discount. However, instead of increasing interest expense, amortization of premium *decreases* interest expense. The **adjusting entry** to amortize bond premium for one year is illustrated below:

Amortization of bond premium *reduces* interest expense

Premium on Bonds Payable	1,000	
Interest Expense		1,000
Recognized one year's amortization of premium on 20-year bonds payable ($20,000 original premium × 1/20).		

As with bond discount, bond premium is amortized from the date of issue. If the bonds were issued on March 1 rather that January 1, the premium will be amortized not over 240 months (20 years), but only over 238 months.

Bond Discount and Premium in Perspective

From a conceptual point of view, investors might pay a premium price to purchase bonds that pay an *above market* rate of interest. If the bonds pay a *below* market rate, investors will buy them only at a discount.

But these concepts seldom "come into play" when bonds are issued. Most bonds are issued *at* the market rate of interest. Corporate bonds *almost never* are issued at a premium. Bonds often are issued at a small discount, but this discount represents only the underwriter's profit margin, not investors' response to a below market interest rate.[2] The annual effects of amortizing bond discount or premium are diluted further because these amounts are amortized over the entire life of the bond issue—usually 20 years or more.

In summary, bond discounts and premiums *seldom have a material effect* upon a company's annual interest expense or its financial position.[3] For this reason, we defer further discussion of this topic to the intermediate accounting course.

---

[2] Professor Bill Schartz of Virginia Commonwealth University conducted a study of the 685 American corporate bond issues in one recent year. *None* of these bonds was issued at a premium, and *over 95%* were issued either at par or at a discount of less than 2% of face value.

[3] Some companies issue *zero-coupon* bonds that pay *no* interest, but are issued at huge discounts. In these situations, amortization of the discount *is* material and may comprise much of the company's total interest expense. Zero-coupon bonds are a specialized form of financing that will be discussed in later accounting courses and courses in corporate finance.

**Supplemental Topic B

CONVERTIBLE BONDS PAYABLE

LO 10: Explain the accounting treatment of convertible bonds payable.

Convertible bonds represent a popular form of financing, particularly during periods when common stock prices are rising. The conversion feature gives bondholders an opportunity to profit from a rise in the market price of the issuing company's common stock while still maintaining their status as creditors rather than shareholders.[1] Because of this potential gain, convertible bonds generally carry **lower interest rates** than nonconvertible bonds.

The number of shares of common stock into which each bond may be converted is termed the **conversion ratio**. The market value of this number of shares represents the **stock value** of the bond. When the bond is originally issued, a conversion ratio is selected that sets the stock value well below the face value of the bond. In future periods, however, both the price of the stock and the stock value of the bond may increase without limit.

For example, assume that the current market rate of interest on long-term bonds with a face value of $1,000 each is 9%, and that the common stock of Ling Corporation has a current market price of **$27** per share. Instead of issuing 9% bonds payable, the company might issue **7% convertible bonds**, with a conversion ratio of 20 to 1 or a **conversion price** of $50 ($1,000 face value ÷ 20 shares). At the issuance date, the stock value of each convertible bond would be only $540 (20 shares × $27). If the value of the common stock rises above **$50** per share, however, the stock value will rise above the $1,000 face value of the bond.

When the price of the common stock rises above the conversion price, the stock value of the bond becomes far more important than the current level of interest rates in establishing the market price of a convertible bond. (See, for example, the Case in Point on the following page.)

Ling Corporation benefits from issuing these convertible bonds because it is able to pay less than the going market rate of interest. The bondholders also may benefit from the conversion feature, **but only if the price of the common stock rises above the conversion price** ($50 per share) during the life of the bonds.

Let us assume that Ling Corporation issues $5 million of these convertible bonds at par. Some years later, when the price of the common stock has risen to $90 per share, holders of 100 bonds decide to convert their bonds into common stock. Ling Corporation will record this conversion as follows:

Conversion of bonds into common stock

Convertible Bonds Payable	100,000	
Common Stock		100,000
To record the conversion of 100 bonds payable into 2,000 shares of common stock.		

---

[1] Because of this unique feature, convertible bonds payable are considered to have two components—liability and equity, as discussed earlier in the chapter.

Notice that the current market price of the stock ($90 per share) *does not* affect this entry. The carrying value of the bonds is simply assigned to the common stock issued in exchange. Thus, the effect of the entry is to transfer the carrying value of the bonds from the liability section to the shareholders' equity section of the balance sheet. (If the bonds had been issued at a price above or below the face amount, any unamortized premium or discount relating to the converted bonds would be written off at the time of conversion in order to assign the *net* carrying value of the bonds to the common stock.)

CONVERSION OF BONDS FROM THE INVESTOR'S VIEWPOINT

Investors do not always convert their investment in convertible bonds into capital stock as soon as the market value of the capital stock they would receive rises above the $1,000 maturity value of their bonds. As the bonds easily can be converted into capital stock, their market value *rises right along* with that of the capital stock.

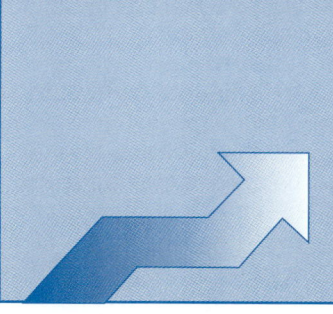

> **CASE IN POINT**
>
> Norcen had an outstanding issue of more than $149 million of 6% bonds payable (maturing December 15, 2006) in which each bond was convertible into 64.52 shares of the company's capital stock. The company's capital stock was selling at $24 per share, indicating a market value for 64.52 shares of $1,548. The market value of the convertible bonds was quoted at 154 (that is, $1,540 for a $1,000 bond), even though the bonds would mature at a price of only 100 (that is, at $1,000 for a $1,000 bond) in the near future. Also, the going market interest rate of about 13% was more than twice the 6% for the bonds, indicating that the stock value of the bonds was more important than the market interest rate in establishing the market price of a convertible bond.

When are the owners of convertible bonds likely to exchange their bonds for shares of capital stock? The exchange point is reached when the dividends (net of the income tax effect) that would be received from the capital stock **exceed the interest payments** (net of the income tax effect) currently being received from the investment in bonds.[2] When the capital stock dividends increase to this level, the bondholders **can increase their cash receipts** by converting their bonds into shares of capital stock. Regardless of the relationship between interest and dividends, convertible bonds should be converted prior to their maturity date if the market price of the common stock exceeds the conversion price.

---

[2] Dividends, because of the dividend tax credit, are taxed at a lower rate than interest income. Thus, it takes a larger interest income to yield the same amount of dividend income. Dividend tax credit is discussed in Chapter 18.

End-of-Chapter Review

Key Terms Introduced or Emphasized in Chapter 16

Actuary *(p.802)* A professional statistician who performs computations involving assumptions as to human life spans. One function is computing companies' liabilities for pension and postretirement benefits.

Bonds payable *(p.787)* Long-term debt securities that subdivide a very large and long-term corporate debt into transferable increments of $1,000 or multiples thereof.

Capital lease *(p.799)* A lease contract that, in essence, finances the eventual purchase by the lessee of leased property. The lessor accounts for a capital lease as a sale of property; the lessee records an asset and a liability equal to the present value of the future lease payments. Also called a ***sale-type*** or ***direct financing lease***.

Commercial paper *(p.797)* Very short-term notes payable issued by financially strong corporations. Highly liquid from the investors' point of view.

Convertible bond *(p.790)* A bond that may be exchanged (at the bondholders' option) for a specified number of shares of the company's capital stock.

Debt ratio *(p.809)* Total liabilities divided by total assets. Indicates the percentage of total assets financed with creditors' capital.

Debt-service requirement *(p.811)* The combined cash outlays required for repayment of principal amounts borrowed and for payments of interest expense during the period.

Defined benefit plan *(p.801)* A pension plan in which the employer agrees to pay each employee a defined benefit based on the employee's highest salary. Pension expense is equal to the increase in the present value of the benefit each period.

Defined contribution plan *(p.801)* A pension plan in which the employer agrees to make a specified contribution each year. Pension expense each year is the amount of the required contribution.

Discount on bonds payable *(p.790)* Amount by which the face amount of the bond exceeds the price received by the corporation on the date of issuance. Indicates that the contractual rate of interest is lower than the market rate of interest.

Financial instrument *(p.806)* Cash, equity investments in another business, and contracts involving the receipt or payment of cash.

Future (deferred) income taxes *(p.805)* Income taxes upon income that already has been reported for financial reporting purposes but that will not be reported in income tax returns until future periods.

Interest coverage ratio *(p.809)* Operating income divided by interest expense. Indicates the number of times that the company was able to earn the amount of its interest charges.

Junk bonds *(p.791)* Bonds payable that, when issued, were abnormally risky but also offered an abnormally high contract rate of interest.

Lessee *(p.798)* The tenant, user, or renter of leased property.

Lessor *(p.798)* The owner of property leased to a lessee.

Leverage *(p.810)* The use of borrowed money to finance business operations.

Off-balance-sheet financing *(p.799)* An arrangement in which the use of resources is financed without the obligation for future payments appearing as a liability in the balance sheet. An operating lease is a common example of off-balance-sheet financing.

Off-balance-sheet risk *(p.809)* The risk of future losses resulting from an existing financial instrument that does not currently appear on the balance sheet. An example is the risk of loss from a loan guarantee.

Operating lease *(p.799)* A lease contract that is in essence a rental agreement. The lessee has the use of the leased property, but the lessor retains the usual risks and benefits of ownership. The periodic lease payments are accounted for as rent expense by the lessee and as rental revenue by the lessor.

Premium on bonds payable *(p.790)* Amount by which the issuance price of a bond exceeds the face value. Indicates that the contractual rate of interest is higher than the market rate.

Present value (of a future amount) *(p.794)* The amount of money that an informed investor would pay today for the right to receive the future amount, based upon a specific rate of return required by the investor.

Sinking fund *(p.790)* Cash set aside by a corporation at regular intervals (usually with a trustee) for the purpose of repaying a bond issue at its maturity date.

Self-Test Questions

Answers to these questions appear on page 833.

1. Which of the following statements are correct? (More than one statement may be correct.)
   a. A bond issue is a technique for subdividing a very large loan into a great many small, transferable units.
   b. Bond interest payments are contractual obligations, whereas the board of directors determines whether or not dividends will be paid.
   c. As interest rates rise, the market prices of bonds fall; as interest rates fall, bond prices tend to rise.
   d. Bond interest payments are deductible in determining income subject to income taxes, whereas dividends paid to shareholders are not deductible.

2. A few years ago, Glasco issued 30-year, 9% bonds payable, callable at 105. At the issuance date, the market interest rate for such bonds was about $8^{1}/_{2}$%; today, it is about 11%. Indicate statement(s) with which you agree. (More than one answer may be correct.)
   a. The bonds probably were issued at a discount.
   b. Glasco's disclosure of current fair value probably shows these bonds trading at a discount.
   c. The market price of these bonds probably has increased since the issuance date.
   d. Glasco is unlikely to call these bonds in the near future even if it has the resources to do so.

3. Lawton International leases its manufacturing equipment from Atlas under an arrangement that qualifies as a capital lease. Lawton's financial statements should include which of the following? (More than one answer may be correct.)
   a. Depreciation expense on the leased equipment.
   b. Rent expense each period for the amount of the lease payment made.
   c. A liability for the present value of all future lease payments.
   d. A liability for the total amount of all future lease payments.

4. Silverado maintains a fully funded defined benefit pension plan. During 2000, $1 million was paid to retired workers, and workers currently employed by the company earned the right to receive pension payments expected to total $3 million *over their lifetimes*. Silverado's pension *expense* for 2000 amounts to:
   a. $1
   b. $3 million
   c. $4 million
   d. Some other amount

5. Future (deferred) income taxes result from:
   a. The fact that bond interest is deductible in the computation of taxable income.
   b. Depositing income taxes due in future years in a special fund managed by an independent trustee.
   c. Timing differences between when income is recognized in financial statements and in income tax returns.
   d. The inability of a bankrupt company to pay its income tax liability on schedule.

6. Identify those trends that are *unfavourable* from the viewpoint of a bondholder. (More than one answer may be correct.)
   a. Market interest rates are steadily rising.
   b. The issuing company's interest coverage ratio is steadily rising.
   c. The issuing company's net cash flow from operation is steadily declining.
   d. The issuing company's debt ratio is steadily declining.

Assignment Material

Discussion Questions

1. Distinguish between the two terms in each of the following pairs:
   a. Bonds payable; commercial paper
   b. Mortgage bond; debenture
   c. Callable (redeemable) bond; convertible bond
   d. Junk bond; zero coupon bond

2. The financial section of a newspaper recently quoted a market price of *102* for an issue of 8% bonds of a large corporation. What would be the market price for $25,000 face value of these bonds (ignoring accrued interest)? Is the market rate of interest for bonds of this quality higher or lower than 8%? Explain.

3. Briefly explain the income tax advantage of raising capital by issuing bonds rather than by capital stock.

4. Tampa Boat Limited pays income taxes at a rate of 30% on taxable income. Compute the company's annual *after-tax* cost of borrowing on a 10%, $5 million bond issue. Express this after-tax cost as a percentage of the borrowed $5 million.

5. Why is the *present value* of a future amount always less than the future amount?

6. Why do bond prices *vary inversely* with interest rates?

7. Some bonds now being bought and sold by investors on organized securities markets were issued when interest rates were much higher than they are today. Would you expect these bonds to be trading at prices above or below their face values? Explain.

8. The 6% bonds of Central Gas & Electric Limited are selling at a market price of 72, whereas the 6% bonds of Power Corporation are selling at a price of 97. Does this mean that Power has a better credit rating than Central Gas & Electric? Explain. (Assume current long-term interest rates are in the 11% to 13% range.)

9. Discuss the advantages and disadvantages of a *call (redemption) provision* in a bond contract from the viewpoint of (a) the bondholder and (b) the issuing corporation.

10. Explain how the lessee accounts for an operating lease and a capital lease. Why is an operating lease sometimes called *off-balance-sheet financing*?

11. Distinguish between a defined contribution and a defined benefit pension plan. For which type of plan is the accounting most difficult?

12. Ortega Industries has a fully funded defined benefit pension plan. Each year, pension expense runs in excess of $10 million. At the present time, employees are entitled to receive pension benefits with a present value of $125 million. Explain what liability, if any, Ortega Industries should include in its balance sheet as a result of this pension plan.

13. Why do large corporations often show no liability for pensions owed to retired employees, but may show huge liabilities for "nonpension postretirement benefits"?

14. When are the costs of postretirement benefits recognized as expense? When are the related cash payments made?

15. What is meant by the term *future (deferred) income taxes*? Identify two measurement techniques often used in income tax returns that result in the deferral of income taxes.

16. Define *financial instruments*. What are the basic reasons for disclosing the fair value of these instruments when this value differs significantly from the carrying values shown in the balance sheet?

17. Why does the requirement for disclosure of fair value often apply to financial instruments such as bonds payable, long-term notes payable and receivable, and investments in stocks and bonds, but usually *not* to cash, accounts payable or receivable, or commercial paper?

18. What is meant by a financial instrument creating *off-balance-sheet risk*? Provide an example.

19. As a result of issuing 20-year bonds payable, Low-Cal Foods now has an interest coverage ratio of *.75 to 1*. Should this ratio be of greater concern to short-term creditors or to shareholders? Explain.

20. A $200 million bond issue of Gerrard Corporation (a solvent company) recently matured. The entire maturity value was paid from a bond sinking fund. What effect did this transaction have upon the company's current ratio? Upon its debt ratio? Explain.

21. There is an old business saying that "You shouldn't *be* in business if your company doesn't earn a return higher than bank rates." This means that if a company is to succeed, its return on assets should be *significantly higher* than its cost of borrowing. Why is this so important?

* 22. Does issuing bonds at a discount increase or decrease the issuing company's cost of borrowing? Explain.

* 23. Explain why the effective rate of interest expense differs from the contract rate when bonds are issued (a) at a discount and (b) at a premium.

** 24. What is a *convertible bond*? Discuss the advantages and disadvantages of convertible bonds from the standpoint of (a) the investor and (b) the issuing corporation.

** 25. What situation or condition is most likely to cause the holders of convertible bonds to convert their bonds into shares of common stock? (Do not assume that the bonds have been called or that they are about to mature.)

---

* *Supplemental Topic A*, "Accounting for Bonds Issued at a Discount or a Premium."
** *Supplemental Topic B*, "Convertible Bonds Payable."

Exercises

EXERCISE 16-1
Accounting Terminology
(LO 4–8)

Listed below are nine technical accounting terms introduced or emphasized in this chapter.

Unfunded pension liability *Future (deferred) income taxes* *Present value of future amounts*
Off-balance-sheet risk *Defined benefit plan* *Defined contribution plan*
Operating lease *Financial instruments* *Capital lease*

Each of the following statements may (or may not) describe one of these technical terms. For each statement, indicate the term described, or answer "None" if the statement does not correctly describe any of the terms.

a. The measurement concept applied to the liabilities for capital lease obligations and to unfunded pension liabilities.
b. Income taxes applicable to earnings that have already been included in the income statement but that appear in the income tax returns of a future year.
c. Cash, equity investments in another business organization, or contracts calling for receipts or payments of cash.
d. A pension plan in which the benefits paid to the employees depends on the amount accumulated in the pension fund.
e. The current market value of a long-term debt.
f. A long-term liability appearing in the balance sheet of any company that offers a pension to retired workers.
g. A lease agreement that results in the lessee recording ownership of an asset and a long-term liability to the lessor.
h. Potential future losses that could result from existing financial instruments that are not listed either as assets or as liabilities.

EXERCISES 16-2
Effects of Bond Transactions upon the Accounting Equation
(LO 1, 3, 4, 5)

Listed below are seven events relating to debt instruments issued by Wizard Computer Inc.:

a. Issued 30-year bonds payable at face value.
b. Issued 90-day commercial paper at a discount.
c. Made a semiannual interest payment on the bond issue described in part **a**, above.
d. Made a semiannual interest payment on a 20-year bond issue that has been outstanding for nine years.
e. Due to a decline in interest rates, the market value of the bond issues described in both parts **a** and **d** have increased in market value.
f. Called bonds payable described in part **d**, above, at a price above carrying value but below current market value. (Assume all interest expense already has been properly recorded.)
g. Redeemed at face value the commercial paper described in part **b**, above.

Indicate the effects of each of these transactions upon the following financial statement categories. Organize your answer in tabular form, using the illustrated column headings. Use the following code letters to indicate the effects of each transaction upon the accounting element listed in the column heading:

I = Increase D = Decrease NE = No Effect

	Income Statement			Balance Sheet		
Trans-action	Revenue −	Expenses and Losses =	Net Income	Assets =	Current Liab. +	Long-Term Liab. + Share-holders' Equity
a						

EXERCISE 16–3
Effects upon the Accounting Equation—Transactions Other Than Bonds
(LO 6-8)

The following seven items are among the transactions of Commuter Train Corporation during the current year:

a. Leased equipment, signing a five-year capital lease payable in monthly instalments.
b. Leased land to be used as a storage yard, signing a one-year lease payable in monthly instalments.
c. Paid a monthly instalment on a capital lease (assume all remaining payments on this particular lease are due within one year).
d. Made a monthly payment on an operating lease (assume all remaining payments on this particular lease are due within one year).
e. Recorded pension expense on a fully funded pension plan and remitted in cash the amount owed to the trustee.
f. Recorded expense relating to postretirement benefits other than pensions earned by employees during the current period. This liability is *partially* funded; no payments are made now, but 50% of the obligation arising this period will be funded within the next 12 months.
g. Made an adjusting entry recording income taxes expense for the period, including a considerable amount of future (deferred) taxes (classified as long-term).

Indicate the effects of each of these transactions upon the financial statement categories shown below. Organize your answer in tabular form, using the illustrated column headings. Use the following code letters to indicate the effects of each transaction upon the accounting element listed in the column heading:

I = Increase   *D* = Decrease   *N* = No Effect

Transaction	Income Statement			Balance Sheet			
	Revenue	− Expenses	= Net Income	Assets =	Current Liab. +	Long-Term Liab. +	Shareholders' Equity

EXERCISE 16-4
After-Tax Cost of Borrowing
(LO 2)

Metro Inc. issued $20 million of 12% bonds payable at face value. The company pays income taxes at an average rate of 35% of its taxable income.

Compute the company's annual *after-tax* cost of borrowing on this bond issue, stated as (a) a total dollar amount and (b) a percentage of the amount borrowed.

EXERCISE 16-5
Bond Interest (Bonds Issued at Par)
(LO 3)

On March 31, Bancor Corporation received authorization to issue $30 million of 12%, 30-year debenture bonds. Interest payment dates were March 31 and September 30. The bonds were all issued at par on April 30, one month after the interest date printed on the bonds.

a. Prepare the journal entry at April 30, to record the sale of the bonds.
b. Prepare the journal entry at September 30, to record the semiannual bond interest payment.
c. Prepare the adjusting entry at December 31, to record bond interest accrued since September 30.
d. Explain *why* the issuing corporation charges the initial purchasers of the bonds for interest accrued prior to the issuance date.
e. Why was Bancor Corporation able to issue the bonds at par value?

EXERCISE 16-6
Reading Bond Prices
(LO 1, 4)

Presented below is an excerpt from a newspaper listing of bond transactions for a particular day. It presents information about two bond issues:

Bonds	Interest Rate	Maturity Date	Bid	Yield
Cdn Imp. Bank	7.400	Jan 31/06	110.13	?
Bank of N.S.	7.400	Feb 8/06	110.15	?

From the above information, answer:
a. Why do these bonds sell at a premium?
b. Would the yield rate for the two bonds be the same or different?

EXERCISE 16-7
Account for Leases
(LO 6)

On July 1, City Hospital leased equipment from MedTech Instruments for a period of five years. The lease calls for monthly payments of $2,000, payable in advance on the first day of each month, beginning July 1.

Prepare the journal entry needed to record this lease in the accounting records of City Hospital on July 1 under each of the following independent assumptions:
a. The lease represents a simple rental arrangement (an operating lease).
b. At the end of five years, title to this equipment will be transferred to City Hospital at no additional cost. The present value of the 60 monthly lease payments is $90,809, of which $2,000 is paid in cash on July 1.
c. Why is an operating lease sometimes called *off-balance-sheet financing*?

EXERCISE 16-8
Pension Plans
(LO 7)

During the current year, Deltron Corporation paid $5 million into a fully funded defined benefit pension plan for the company's employees. At year-end, the plan has total assets of $40 million, equal to the present value of all future pension payments earned by employees to date. During the current year, the plan paid $3 million in pension benefits to retired Deltron employees.
a. What is Deltron's pension expense for the year?
b. Identify any assets or liabilities relating to this pension plan that will appear in Deltron's balance sheet, and indicate the appropriate dollar amount.
c. If Deltron becomes insolvent in future years, what prospects, if any, do today's employees have of receiving the pension benefits that they have earned to date?

EXERCISE 16-9
Account for Retirement Benefits
(LO 7)

At the end of the current year, Krepshaw Power Tools Inc. received the following information from its actuary:

Pension expense	$1,790,000
Nonpension postretirement benefits expense	316,000

The pension plan is fully funded. Krepshaw has funded only $23,000 of the nonpension postretirement benefits this year.

Prepare a separate journal entry to summarize for the entire year (a) the pension expense and (b) the nonpension postretirement benefits expense.

EXERCISE 16-10
Future (Deferred) Income Taxes
(LO 8)

The following journal entry summarizes for the current year the income taxes expense of Scotian Coachworks:

Income Taxes Expense	14,000,000	
Cash		9,000,000
Income Taxes Payable		2,900,000
Future Income Taxes		2,100,000
To record income taxes expense for the current year.		

Of the future income taxes, only $240,000 is classified as a current liability.

a. Define *future income taxes*.
b. What is the amount of income taxes that the company has paid or expects to pay in conjunction with its income tax return for the current year?
c. Illustrate the allocation of the liabilities shown in the above journal entry between the classifications of *current liabilities* and *long-term liabilities*.

*EXERCISE 16-11
Basic Entries for a Bond Issue at a Discount: Issuance, Interest Payment, and Retirement
(LO 3, *9)

La Paloma Corporation issued $10 million of 15-year, 10½% bonds on July 1, 2000, at 98½. Interest is due on June 30 and December 31 of each year, and the bonds mature on June 30, 2015. The fiscal year ends on December 31; bond discount is amortized by the straight-line method. Prepare the following journal entries:

a. July 1, 2000, to record the issuance of the bonds
b. December 31, 2000, to pay interest and amortize the bond discount (make two entries)
c. June 30, 2015, to pay interest, amortize the bond discount, and retire the bonds at maturity (make three entries)
d. Briefly explain the effect of amortizing the bond discount upon annual net income.

*EXERCISE 16-12
Bond Prices and Accrued Interest
(LO 3, *9)

On August 1, 2001, Cellular Industries issued $10 million face value, 9%, 20-year bonds payable to an underwriter for total cash proceeds of $10,064,000. The bonds were dated April 1, 2001, and pay interest semiannually at October 1 and April 1.

a. State the issue price of these bonds as a *percentage* of the face amount. (Round to the nearest ¹⁄₁₀ of 1%.)
b. Compute the amount of cash paid to bondholders at each semiannual interest date.
c. Compute the company's semiannual bond interest expense (for a full six-month period), assuming that any discount or premium is amortized by the straight-line method.

**EXERCISE 16-13
Convertible Bonds
(LO 10)

Several years ago an annual report of a large corporation showed that 406 of the company's 3⅞%, $1,000 face amount, convertible bonds were still outstanding. These bonds were to mature in less than three years and had a conversion ratio of 32 to 1. The company's common stock had a current market price of $60 per share, and paid dividends of $1.68 per share.

a. Prepare the journal entry to record the conversion of these outstanding convertible bonds into shares of common stock. (Assume the bonds originally were issued at par.)
b. Under the circumstances described above, would it be advantageous for the bondholders to exchange the bonds for common stock? Explain.

---

* *Supplemental Topic A*, "Accounting for Bonds Issued at a Discount or a Premium."
** *Supplemental Topic B*, "Convertible Bonds Payable."

Problems

PROBLEM 16-1
Bond Interest (Bonds Issued at Par)
(LO 1, 2, 3)

Bar Harbor Gas & Electric obtained authorization to issue $90 million face value of 10%, 20-year bonds, dated May 1, 2000. Interest payment dates were November 1 and May 1. Issuance of the bonds did not take place until August 1, 2000. On this date all the bonds were sold at a price of 100 plus three months' accrued interest.

INSTRUCTIONS

Prepare the necessary entries in general journal form on:
a. August 1, 2000, to record the issuance of the bonds
b. November 1, 2000, to record the first semiannual interest payment on the bond issue
c. December 31, 2000, to accrue bond interest expense through year-end
d. May 1, 2001, to record the second semiannual interest payment
e. Describe the factors that Bar Harbor should have considered in deciding whether to issue bonds rather than more capital stock.

PROBLEM 16-2
An Alternate to Problem 16-1
(LO 1, 3)

Park Plaza Hotels obtained all necessary approvals to issue $20,000,000 face value of 9%, 20-year bonds dated April 1, 2001. Interest payment dates were October 1 and April 1. The bonds were not issued, however, until two months later, June 1, 2001. On this date the entire bond issue was sold to an underwriter at a price of 100 plus accrued interest.

INSTRUCTIONS

Prepare the required entries in general journal form on:
a. June 1, to record the issuance of the bonds
b. October 1, to record the first semiannual interest payment on the bonds
c. December 31, to accrue bond interest expense through year-end
d. April 1, 2002, to record the second semiannual interest payment
e. Describe what probably will happen to the market value of the bonds if the market rate of interest for bonds with similar risk: (1) drops to 8%, or (2) rises to 10%.

PROBLEM 16-3
Factors Affecting Bond Prices
(LO 1, 4, 5, **10)

Shown below are three independent cases, each involving two bond issues of a large corporation. In each case, both bond issues have identical credit ratings.

a. **Ontario Hydro** has two bond issues maturing in the year 2010; one has a contract interest rate of 10.5%, and the other, a contract rate of 13.25%.
b. **National Bank of Canada** has outstanding two issues of 7½% bonds—one issue maturing in 2003 and the other in 2006.
c. **Canadian Western Bank has two convertible bonds: (1) 6¾% bonds maturing in 2006, with a conversion price of $12.50 per share of common stock, and (2) 5½% bonds maturing in 2006, with a conversion price of $30.50 per share of common stock. In May, 1998, the market price of Canadian Western Bank's common stock was $24 per share.

INSTRUCTIONS

For each case, explain which of the two bonds you would expect to have been selling at a higher market price in May, *1998*. Also indicate whether each bond should have been selling at a premium or a discount at that time. Explain the reasoning behind your answers. Assume that in May, 1998, market interest rates for bonds of this quality were as follows:

Maturity	Market Interest Rate
Years 1998–2000	5¼%
Years 2001–2003	6%
Year 2004 and beyond	7%

**Supplemental Topic B, "Convertible Bonds Payable."

CHAPTER 16 SPECIAL TYPES OF LIABILITIES 827

PROBLEM 16-4
Factors Affecting Bond Prices
(LO 1, 4, 5, **10)

Shown below are three independent cases, each involving two bond issues of a large corporation or provincial government. In each cash, both bond issues have identical credit ratings.

  a. **Quebec** has two outstanding issues of 10% bond—one issue maturing in 2002 and the other in 2010.
  b. **Ontario Hydro** has two bond issues maturing in the year 2025—one has a contract interest rate of 9%, and the other, a contract rate of 8.5%.
 c. **Cambridge Shopping Centres Ltd. has two convertible bonds maturing in the year 2004: (1) 6% bonds with a conversion price of $22.50 per share of common stock, and (2) 7.50% bonds with a conversion price of $35.51 per share of common stock. In May, 1998, the market price of Cambridge's common stock was $13.30 per share.

INSTRUCTIONS

For each case, explain which of the two bonds you would expect to have been selling at the higher market price in May, 1998. Also indicate whether each bond should have been selling at a premium or a discount at that time. Explain the reasoning behind your answers. Assume that in May, 1998, market interest rates for bonds were as follows:

Maturity	Market Interest Rate
Years 1998–2000	5½%
Years 2001–2003	6%
Year 2004 and beyond	7%

PROBLEM 16-5
Accounting for Leases
(LO 6)

Ardmar Inc. leased four different assets on June 30, 2000. The terms of the leases are presented below:

Lessor	Dunn Real Estate	Warren Limited	Gilbert Ford	R & J Leasing
Asset	Building	Machinery	Truck	Computer
Fair market value of asset	$1,000,000	$250,000	$35,000	$74,000
Estimated useful (economic) life of the asset	50 years	9 years	6 years	6 years
Term of the lease	5 years	6 years	4 years	5 years
Present value of minimum payments	$150,000	$250,000	$23,500	$65,000
Ardmar retains title to asset at end of the lease term	No	Yes	No	No
Lease has bargain purchase option	No	No	No	No

INSTRUCTIONS

  a. Identify those leases that would be classified as capital leases. Explain your reasoning.
  b. Prepare the general journal entry that is necessary to record on Ardmar's books the signing of the lease with R & J Leasing, assuming that the lease required no initial cash payment.
  c. Prepare the general journal entries in **Warren Limited's** accounts to record the signing of the lease with Ardmar. Assume that Warren manufactured the machinery at a cost of $200,000 and frequently uses capital leases to finance the sale of machinery to customers.
  d. Calculate the total amount of **off-balance-sheet financing** relating to Ardmar's lease arrangements as of June 30, 2000.

**Supplemental Topic B, "Convertible Bonds Payable."

PROBLEM 16-6
Capital Leases: A Comprehensive Problem
(LO 6)

Beach Equipment frequently used long-term contracts as a means of financing the sale of its products. On November 1, 2000, Beach Equipment leased to Star Industries a machine carried in the perpetual inventory records at a cost of $18,120. The terms of the lease called for 48 monthly payments of $650 each, beginning November 30, 2000. The present value of these payments, after considering a built-in interest charge of 1% per month, is equal to $24,680, the regular sales price of the machine. At the end of the 48-month lease, title to the machine will transfer to Star Industries at no additional cost.

INSTRUCTIONS

a. Prepare journal entries for 2000 in the accounts of Beach Equipment on:
   1. November 1, to record the sale financed by the lease and the related cost of goods sold.
   2. November 30, to record receipt of the first $650 monthly payment.
   3. December 31, to record receipt of the second monthly payment.
b. Prepare journal entries for 2000 in the accounts of Star Industries on:
   1. November 1, to record acquisition of the leased machine.
   2. November 30, to record the first monthly lease payment.
   3. December 31, to record the second monthly lease payment.
   4. December 31, to recognize depreciation on the leased machine through year-end. Compute the depreciation expense by the straight-line method, using a 10-year service life and an estimated salvage value of $6,680.
c. Compute the net carrying value of the leased machine in the balance sheet of Star Industries at December 31, 2000.
d. Compute the amount of Star Industries' lease payment obligation at December 31, 2000.

PROBLEM 16-7
Pension and Postretirement Benefits
(LO 7)

Shown below is the report of the actuaries on the pension plan and nonpension post-retirement benefits plan of Georgian Corporation.

GEORGIAN CORPORATION
Summary of Postretirement Benefits Expenses and Unfunded Liabilities
For the Year Ended December 31, 2000
Prepared by Yeager & Yeager, Professional Actuaries

Defined Benefit Pension Plan (fully funded):
Estimated present value of benefits accruing to employees during 2000 (expense for the year)	$800,000
Less: Payments during the year to Bankers' Trust (trustee)	800,000
Increase during the year in the present value of unfunded benefits	$ -0-
Add: Unfunded liability at Dec. 31, 1999	-0-
Unfunded liability at Dec. 31, 2000	$ -0-

Nonpension Postretirement Benefit Plan (partially funded):
Estimated present value of benefits accruing to employees during 2000 (expense for the year)	$700,000
Less: Payments during the year to Bankers' Trust (trustee)	300,000
Increase during the year in the present value of unfunded benefits	$400,000
Add: Unfunded liability at December 31, 1999	520,000
Unfunded liability at Dec. 31, 2000	$920,000

INSTRUCTIONS

a. Prepare a summary general journal entry to record:
   1. Pension expense and the deposit of funds into that plan.
   2. Nonpension postretirement benefits expense and the deposit of funds into that plan.
b. Identify several factors considered by the actuaries in determining the present value of pension benefits accruing during 2000.
c. What does the unfunded liability for nonpension postretirement benefits of $920,000 represent?
d. Why would it be *inappropriate* to wait until employees retire before recognizing the expense of postretirement benefits?

PROBLEM 16-8
Reporting Liabilities in a Balance Sheet
(LO 1, 6, 7, 8, *9)

Listed below are selected items from the accounting records of Gulf Telephone Corporation (GulfTel) for the year ended December 31, **2000** (dollar amounts in thousands):

Accounts payable	$ 65,600
Accrued expenses payable (other than interest)	11,347
6¾% Bonds payable, due Feb. 1, 2001	100,000
8½% Bonds payable, due June 1, 2001	250,000
Unamortized bond discount (8½% bonds of '01)	260
11% Bonds payable, due June 1, 2008	300,000
Unamortized bond premium (11% bonds of '08)	1,700
Accrued interest payable	7,333
Bond interest expense	61,000
Other interest expense	17,000
Commercial paper (net of unamortized discount)	110,000
Lease payment obligations—capital leases	23,600
Pensions obligation	410,000
Unfunded obligation for postretirement benefits other than pensions	72,000
Future income taxes	130,000
Income taxes expense	66,900
Income taxes payable	17,300
Accommodation endorsement (loan guarantees)	28,600
Operating income	280,800
Net income	134,700
Total assets	2,093,500

OTHER INFORMATION
(dollar amounts in thousands)

1. The 6¾% bonds due in February, 2001 will be refinanced in January 2001 through the issuance of $150,000 in 9%, 20-year general debentures.
2. The 8½% bonds due June 1, 2001, will be repaid entirely from a bond sinking fund.
3. GulfTel is committed to total lease payments of $14,400 in 2001. Of this amount, $7,479 is applicable to operating leases, and $6,921 to capital leases. Payments on capital leases will be applied as follows: $2,300 to interest expense and $4,621 to reduction in the capitalized lease payment obligation.
4. GulfTel's pension plan is fully funded with an independent trustee.
5. The obligation for postretirement benefits other than pensions consists of a commitment to maintain dental and other health insurance for retired workers. During 2001, GulfTel will fund $18,000 of this obligation.

---

*Supplemental Topic A, "Accounting for Bonds Issued at a Discount or a Premium."

830 PARTNERSHIPS AND CORPORATIONS PART 4

6. The $17,300 in income taxes payable relates to income taxes levied in 2000 and must be paid on or before March 15, 2001. No portion of the future income tax liability is regarded as a current liability.
7. The accommodation endorsements are guarantees of bank loans and other indebtedness of various suppliers of specialized telecommunications equipment. In the opinion of management, the risk of material losses arising from these loan guarantees is not likely.

INSTRUCTIONS

a. Using this information, prepare the current liabilities and long-term liabilities sections of a classified balance sheet as of December 31, 2000. (Within each classification, items may be listed in any order.)
b. Explain briefly how the information in each of the seven numbered paragraphs affected your presentation of the company's liabilities.
c. Compute as of December 31, 2000, the company's (1) debt ratio and (2) interest coverage ratio.
d. Based solely upon information stated in this problem, indicate whether this company appears to be an outstanding, medium, or poor long-term credit risk. State specific reasons for your conclusion.

*PROBLEM 16-9
Amortization of Bond Discount: Straight-line Method
(LO 3, *9)

On May 1, 2000, Festival Cruise Ships Inc. sold a $60 million face value, 11%, 10-year bond issue to an underwriter at a price of 98. Interest is payable semiannually on May 1 and November 1. Company policy is to amortize bond discount by the straight-line method at each interest payment date and at year-end. The company's fiscal year ends at December 31.

INSTRUCTIONS

a. Prepare journal entries to record the issuance of these bonds, the payment of interest at November 1, 2000, and the bond interest expense through year-end.
b. Show the proper balance sheet presentation of all liabilities relating to this bond issue at December 31, 2000. Include captions indicating whether the liabilities are classified as current or long-term.
c. Why do you think that Festival was able to receive a price of only 98 for these bonds, rather than being able to issue them at par? What will issuing these bonds at a discount mean about the relationship between Festival's annual bond interest expense and the amount of cash paid annually to bondholders? Explain.

*PROBLEM 16-10
Amortizing Bond Discount and Premium: Straight-line Method
(LO 3, *9)

On September 1, 2001, North American Farm Equipment issued $60 million in 10% debenture bonds. Interest is payable semiannually on March 1 and September 1, and the bonds mature in 20 years. Company policy is to amortize bond discount or premium by the straight-line method at each interest payment date and at year-end. The company's fiscal year ends at December 31.

INSTRUCTIONS

a. Make the necessary adjusting entries at December 31, 2001, and the journal entry to record the payment of bond interest on March 1, 2002, under each of the following assumptions:
   1. The bonds were issued at 98.
   2. The bonds were issued at 101.
b. Compute the bond liability at December 31, 2002, under assumptions **1** and **2** above.

*PROBLEM 16-11
Comprehensive Problem: Straight-line Amortization
(LO3, *9)

Country Recording Studios obtained the necessary approvals to issue $30 million of 12%, 10-year bonds, dated March 1, 2001. Interest payment dates were September 1 and March 1. Issuance of the bond did not occur until June 1, 2001.

---
*Supplemental Topic A, "Accounting for Bonds Issued at a Discount or a Premium."

On this date, the entire bond issue was sold to an underwriter at a price that included three months' accrued interest. Country Recording Studios follows the policy of amortizing bond discount or premium by the straight-line method at each interest date as well as for year-end adjusting entries at December 31.

INSTRUCTIONS

a. Prepare all journal entries necessary to record the issuance of the bonds and bond interest expense during 2001, assuming that the total proceeds from issuance of the bonds on June 1 amounted to **$30,315,000** including accrued interest.

b. Assume that the proceeds received from the underwriter on June 1 had amounted to **$31,180,800** including accrued interest. Prepare journal entries for 2001 parallel to those in part **a** above.

c. Show the proper balance sheet presentation of the liability for bonds payable (including accrued interest) in the balance sheet prepared at December 31, **2006**; assuming that the total proceeds from issuance of the bonds (including accrued interest) had been:
  1. $30,315,000, as described in part **a**
  2. $31,180,800, as described in part **b**

Analytical and Decision Problems and Cases

A&D 16-1
Factors Affecting Bond Prices
(LO 1, 4, 5)

The following cases are related to large corporations, a partnership, and a provincial government and their bond issues.

a. Two of **Bell Canada's** bond issues are: 9.65% bond maturing in 2009; 9.70% bond maturing in 2032.

b. **Royal Bank** has two bond issues maturing in 2002; one at 10.50% and the other at 5.40%.

c. **Molson Breweries** (a partnership) has an 8.2% bond issue maturing on March 11, 2003 and **Bank of Nova Scotia** has an 8.1% bond issue maturing on March 24, 2003.

d. Four bond issues mature at about the same time:

Name	Rate (%)	Maturity Date
MacMillan Bloedel	10.125	January 23, 2002
Imasco	9.850	April 22, 2002
Bell Canada	9.500	June 15, 2002
Ontario Hydro	9.000	April 16, 2002

INSTRUCTIONS

For each case, explain which bond would sell at a higher market price and whether the bonds would be selling at a premium or a discount in May, 1998. Also, rank the bonds in each case by the yield rate that you would expect the bonds would earn. Assume that in May, 1998, market interest rates for bonds were:

Maturity	Market Interest Rate
Years 1998–2002	5.5%
Years 2003–2007	6.5%
Years 2008 and beyond	7.0%

A&D 16-2
Don't Call us...We'll Call You
(LO 1, 4, 5)

On December 31 of the current year, Synex Corporation has outstanding $200 million of 14½% bonds payable that mature in 20 years. These bonds were issued at par and are callable at a price of 106. Because of a recent decline in market interest rates, the company today can issue, at par, $200 million of 20-year bonds with an interest rate of only 11% and use the proceeds to call the 14½% bonds; the issuing cost is $3 million.

INSTRUCTIONS

a. Would you recommend that Synex replace the 14½% bond issue, or leave it outstanding? Justify your recommendation.

b. Assume that you are an investor willing to earn the current market rate of return of 11%. If you were to purchase the Synex 14½% bonds at a price of 113 and hold these bonds until their maturity date, you would earn a return slightly greater than 11%. Does this investment sound attractive? Explain.

A&D 16-3
Accounting for Leases
(LO 6)

At the beginning of the current year, Cable TV entered into the two long-term lease agreements described below:

Building Lease. Leased from Lamden Properties the use of an office building for a period of 5 years. The monthly payments are based upon the square metres of the building and increase by 5% each year. The estimated useful life of the building is 40 years.

Satellite Lease. Leased from SpaceNet Inc. the use of a communications satellite for a period of 5 years. The monthly payments are intended to pay SpaceNet the current sales price of the satellite, plus a reasonable charge for interest. At the end of the lease, ownership of the satellite will transfer to Cable TV at no additional cost. The estimated useful life of the satellite is 15 years.

INSTRUCTIONS

Answer each of the following questions as they relate to the building lease. After answering all four questions, answer them again as they relate to the satellite lease.

a. Is this agreement an operating lease or a capital lease? Why?

b. Will this lease result in any assets or liabilities being included in Cable TV's future balance sheets? If so, identify these assets and liabilities.

c. Indicate the nature of any expenses that will appear in Cable TV's future income statements as a result of the lease, and indicate the number of years for which the expense will be incurred.

d. Briefly explain how the ***lessor*** should account for this lease agreement, including the receipt of future lease payments. Indicate whether the lessor should recognize depreciation on the leased asset.

*A&D 16-4
Accrual and Payment of Interest, Amortization of Bond Discount, and Bond Redemption
(LO 9)

Chelsea Duchess has the following items in its year-end adjusted trial balance at December 31, 2000:

Bond interest payable (for three months from October 1 to Dec. 31)	$ 300,000
Bonds payable, 12%, due Mar. 31, 2011	10,000,000
Discount on bonds payable	196,800

The bonds are redeemable on any interest date. On September 30, 2001, Chelsea Duchess redeemed $2,000,000 of the bonds at 102.

INSTRUCTIONS

a. Prepare a journal entry to record the semiannual payment on March 31, 2001. Discount is amortized by the straight-line method at each interest payment date and at year-end date.

b. Prepare journal entries to record the amortization of bond discount and payment of bond interest at September 30, 2001, and also to record the redemption of $2,000,000 of the bonds at this date.

c. Prepare a journal entry to record the accrual of interest at December 31, 2001.

---

* *Supplemental Topic A*, "Accounting for Bonds Issued at a Discount or a Premium."

**A&D 16-5
Convertible Bonds
(LO 1,5, **10)**

Dreyer's Grand Ice Cream Inc. has outstanding $50 million face value of 6½% convertible bonds payable, callable at 106½, maturing in 2011. Each $1,000 bond is convertible into 31.25 shares of the company's common stock. Today's newspaper indicates a market price for the company's common stock, which pays a dividend of 20 cents per share, of $36. On this date, the market rate of interest for bonds of similar quality and maturity date but *without* a conversion feature is approximately 10%.

INSTRUCTIONS

a. Compute the conversion price and the stock value for one of these bonds.
b. Prepare journal entries in the company's accounting records to record the following alternative possibilities:
  1. Dreyer's calls the bonds (assume the bonds were originally issued at par).
  2. Bondholders convert the entire bond issue into common stock.
c. Given the circumstances described above, would you expect:
  1. The bonds to be selling at a discount or a premium?
  2. Dreyer's to call the bonds in the immediate future?
  3. Bondholders to convert the bonds into common stock in the immediate future?

Explain the reasons for your answers to each question in part **c**.

Answers to Self-Test Questions

1. a, b, c, d   **2.** b, d   **3.** a, c   **4.** d (The pension expense is equal to the *present value* of the $3 million in estimated future payments; this amount will be considerably less than $3 million.)   **5.** c   **6.** a, c

---

** *Supplemental Topic B*, "Convertible Bonds Payable."

APPENDIX C

THE "TIME-VALUE" OF MONEY: FUTURE AMOUNTS AND PRESENT VALUES

LEARNING OBJECTIVES

1. Explain what is meant by the "*time-value*" of money.
2. Describe the relationships between *present values* and *future amounts*.
3. Explain three basic ways in which decision makers apply the time-value of money.
4. Compute future amounts and the investments necessary to accumulate future amounts.
5. Compute the present values of future cash flows.
6. Discuss accounting applications of the concept of present value.

THE CONCEPT

LO 1: Explain what is meant by the "time-value" of money.

One of the most basic—and important—concepts of investing is the ***time-value of money***. This concept is based upon the idea that an amount of money available today can be safely invested to accumulate to a larger amount in the future. As a result, an amount of money available today is considered to be "equivalent in value" to a ***larger sum*** available at a future date.

In our discussions, we will refer to an amount of money available today as a ***present value***. In contrast, an amount receivable or payable at a future date will be described as a ***future amount***.

To illustrate, assume that you place $500 in a savings account in a bank that earns interest at the rate of 8% per year. The balance of your account at the end of each of the next four years is illustrated on the following page.

These balances represent different "time values" of your $500 investment. When you first open the account, your investment has a ***present value*** of only $500. As time passes, the value of your investment increases to the ***future amounts*** illustrated in the graph.

Relationships Between Present Values and Future Amounts

LO 2: Describe the relationships between *present values and* future amounts.

The difference between a present value and any future amount is the ***interest*** that is included in the future amount. We have seen that interest accrues over time. Therefore, the difference between the present value and a future amount depends upon **two factors**: (1) the **rate of interest** at which the present value increases, and (2) the **length of time** over which interest accumulates. (Notice in our graph, the further away the future date, the larger the future amount.)

Future values are "bigger," but are they "worth more"? This is the real issue.

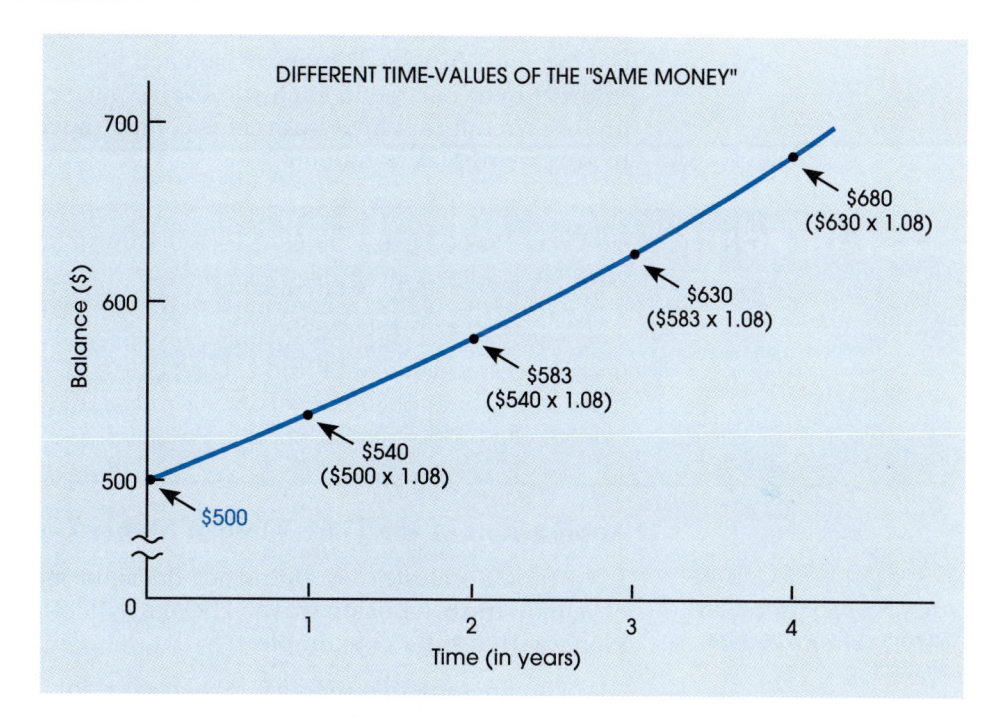

DIFFERENT TIME-VALUES OF THE "SAME MONEY"

- $500
- $540 ($500 × 1.08)
- $583 ($540 × 1.08)
- $630 ($583 × 1.08)
- $680 ($630 × 1.08)

Balance ($) vs. Time (in years)

Present Values Change Over Time The present value of an investment gradually increases toward the future amount. In fact, when a future date **arrives**, what once was a future amount becomes the present value of the investment. For example, at the end of the first year, $540 will no longer be a future amount—it will be the present value of your savings account.

The Basic Concept (Stated Several Different Ways) Notice that the present value of our savings account is **always less than its future amounts**. This is the basic idea underlying the time-value of money. But this idea often is expressed in different ways, including:

- A present value is always **less than** a future amount.
- A future amount is always **greater than** a present value.
- A dollar available today is always worth **more** than a dollar that does not become available until a future date.
- A dollar available at a future date is always worth **less** than a dollar that is available today.

Read these statements carefully. All four reflect the idea that a present value is the "equivalent" of a larger number of dollars at a future date. This is what is meant by the "time-value" of money.

Compound Interest

The relationships between present values and future amounts assume that the interest earned on the investment is *reinvested*, rather than withdrawn. This concept often is called **compounding the interest**. Compounding has an interesting effect. Reinvesting the interest causes the "amount invested" to increase each period. This, in turn, causes more interest to be earned in each successive period. Over a long period of time, an investment in which interest is compounded continuously will increase to surprisingly large amounts.

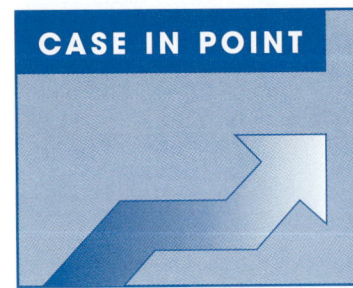

> **CASE IN POINT**
>
> In 1626, Peter Minuit is said to have purchased Manhattan Island in New York City from a group of Indians for $24 worth of "beads, cloth, and trinkets." This episode often is portrayed as an incredible bargain—even a "steal." But if the Indians could have invested this $24 to earn interest at a compound interest rate of, say, 8%, they would have more than enough money today to buy the island back—along with everything on it.

Applications of the Time-Value of Money Concept

LO 3: Explain three basic ways in which decision makers apply the time-value of money.

Investors, accountants, and other decision makers apply the time-value of money in three basic ways. These applications are summarized below, along with a typical example:

1. The amount to which an investment will accumulate over time.
   Example: If we invest $5,000 each year and earn an annual rate of return of 10%, how much will be accumulated after 10 years?
2. The amount that must be invested every period to accumulate a required future amount.
   Example: We must accumulate a $200 million bond sinking fund over the next 20 years. How much must we invest into this fund each year, assuming that the fund's assets will be invested to earn an annual rate of return of 8%?
3. The present value of cash flows expected to occur in the future.
   Example: Assuming that we require a 15% return on our investments, how much can we afford to pay for new machinery that is expected to reduce production costs by $20,000 per year for the next 10 years?

We will now introduce a framework for answering such questions.

FUTURE AMOUNTS

A future amount is simply the dollar amount to which a present value ***will accumulate*** over time. As we have stated, the difference between a present value and a related future amount depends upon (1) the interest rate, and (2) the period of time over which the present value accumulates.

Starting with the present value, we may compute future amounts through a series of multiplications, as illustrated in our graph on the preceding page. But there are faster and easier ways. For example, many financial calculators are programmed to compute future amounts; you merely enter the present value, the interest rate, and the number of periods. Or, you may use a *table of future amounts*, such as *Table FA-1* illustrated below.

The "Tables Approach"

LO 4: Compute future amounts and the investments necessary to accumulate future amounts.

A table of future amounts shows the future amount to which *$1* will accumulate over a given number of periods, assuming that it has been invested to earn any of the illustrated interest rates. We will refer to the amounts shown in the body of this table as *factors*, rather than as dollar amounts.

To find the future amount of a present value *greater* than $1, simply multiply the present value by the factor obtained from the table. The formula for using the table in this manner is:

Approach to computing future amount

Future amount = Present value × Factor (from Table FA-1)

TABLE FA-1
Future Value of $1 After *n* Periods

Number of Periods (n)	1%	1½%	5%	6%	8%	10%	12%	15%	20%
1	1.010	1.015	1.050	1.060	1.080	1.100	1.120	1.150	1.200
2	1.020	1.030	1.103	1.124	1.166	1.210	1.254	1.323	1.440
3	1.030	1.046	1.158	1.191	1.260	1.331	1.405	1.521	1.728
4	1.041	1.061	1.216	1.262	1.360	1.464	1.574	1.749	2.074
5	1.051	1.077	1.276	1.338	1.469	1.611	1.762	2.011	2.488
6	1.062	1.093	1.340	1.419	1.587	1.772	1.974	2.313	2.986
7	1.072	1.110	1.407	1.504	1.714	1.949	2.211	2.660	3.583
8	1.083	1.127	1.477	1.594	1.851	2.144	2.476	3.059	4.300
9	1.094	1.143	1.551	1.689	1.999	2.358	2.773	3.518	5.160
10	1.105	1.161	1.629	1.791	2.159	2.594	3.106	4.046	6.192
20	1.220	1.347	2.653	3.207	4.661	6.728	9.646	16.367	38.338
24	1.270	1.430	3.225	4.049	6.341	9.850	15.179	28.625	79.497
36	1.431	1.709	5.792	8.147	15.968	30.913	59.136	153.152	708.802

Let us demonstrate this approach using the data for our savings account, illustrated on page 835. The account started with a present value of $500, invested at an annual interest rate of 8%. Thus, the future values of the account in each of the next four years can be computed as follows (rounded to the nearest dollar):

Using the table to compute the amounts in our graph

Year	Future Amount	Computation (Using Table FA-1)
1:	$540	$500 × 1.080 = $540
2:	$583	$500 × 1.166 = $583
3:	$630	$500 × 1.260 = $630
4:	$680	$500 × 1.360 = $680

Computing a future amount is relatively easy. The more interesting question is: How much must we *invest today* to accumulate a required future amount?

Computing the Required Investment At the end of 2000, Metro Recycling agrees to create a fully funded pension plan for its employees by December 31, 2005 (in five years). It is estimated that $5 million dollars will be required to fully fund the pension plan at December 31, 2005. How much must Metro invest in this plan *today* (December 31, 2000) to accumulate the promised $5 million by the end of 2005, assuming that payments to the fund will be invested to earn an annual return of 8%?

Let us repeat our original formula for computing future amounts using *Table FA-1*:

Our original formula...

Future amount = Present value × Factor (from Table FA-1)

In this situation, we *know* the future amount—$5 million. We are looking for the *present value* that, when invested at an interest rate of 8%, will accumulate to $5 million in five years. To determine the *present value*, the formula shown above may be restated as follows:

... restated to find the present value

$$\text{Present value} = \frac{\text{Future amount}}{\text{Factor (from Table FA-1)}}$$

Referring to *Table FA-1*, we get a factor of *1.469* at the intersection of five periods and 8% interest. Thus, the amount of the required investment at the end of 2000 is $3,403,676 ($5 million ÷ 1.469). Invested at 8%, this amount will accumulate to the required $5 million at the end of five years as illustrated below:

The future amount of a single investment

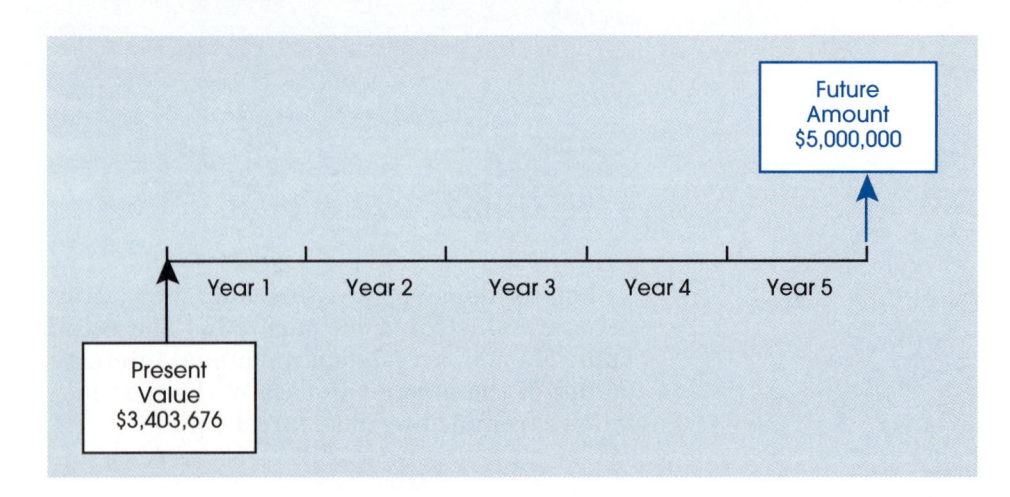

[Timeline diagram: Present Value $3,403,676 at start, progressing through Year 1, Year 2, Year 3, Year 4, Year 5 to Future Amount $5,000,000]

The Future Amount of an Annuity

In many situations, an investor is to make a *series* of investment payments rather than just one. As an example, assume that you plan to invest $500 into your savings account at the *end* of each of the next five years. If the account pays annual interest of 8%, what will be the balance in your savings account at the end of the fifth year? Tables, such as **Table FA-2** below, may be used to answer this question. **Table FA-2** presents the future amount of an ***ordinary annuity of $1***, which is a series of payments of $1 made at the end of each of a specified number of periods.

To find the future amount of an ordinary annuity of payments greater than $1, we simply multiply the amount of the periodic payment by the factor appearing in the table, as follows:

Approach to computing the future amount of an annuity

Future amount of an annuity = **Periodic payment × Factor (from Table FA-2)**

In our example, a factor of 5.867 is obtained from the table at the intersection of five periods and 8% interest. If this factor is multiplied by the periodic payment of $500, we find that your savings account will accumulate to a balance of $2,934 ($500 × 5.867) at the end of five years. Therefore, if you invest $500 at the end of each of the next 5 years in the savings account, you will accumulate $2,934 at the end of the 5-year period.

TABLE FA-2
Future Values of $1 Paid Periodically for n Periods

Number of Periods (n)	1%	1½%	5%	6%	8%	10%	12%	15%	20%
1	1.000	1.000	1.000	1.000	1.000	1.000	1.000	1.000	1.000
2	2.010	2.015	2.050	2.060	2.080	2.100	2.120	2.150	2.200
3	3.030	3.045	3.152	3.184	3.246	3.310	3.374	3.473	3.640
4	4.060	4.091	4.310	4.375	4.506	4.641	4.779	4.993	5.368
5	5.101	5.152	5.526	5.637	5.867	6.105	6.353	6.742	7.442
6	6.152	6.230	6.802	6.975	7.336	7.716	8.115	8.754	9.930
7	7.214	7.323	8.142	8.394	8.923	9.487	10.089	11.067	12.916
8	8.286	8.433	9.549	9.898	10.637	11.436	12.300	13.727	16.499
9	9.369	9.559	11.027	11.491	12.488	13.580	14.776	16.786	20.799
10	10.462	10.703	12.578	13.181	14.487	15.937	17.549	20.304	25.959
20	22.019	23.124	33.066	36.786	45.762	57.275	72.052	102.444	186.688
24	26.974	28.634	44.502	50.816	66.765	88.497	118.155	184.168	392.484
36	43.079	47.276	95.836	119.121	187.102	299.127	484.463	1014.346	3539.009

While computing the future amount of an investment is sometimes necessary, many business and accounting problems require us to determine the *amount of the periodic payments* that must be made to accumulate the required future amount.

Computing the Required Periodic Payments Assume that Ultra Tech Company is required to accumulate $10 million in a **bond sinking fund** to retire bonds payable 5 years from now. The **bond indenture** requires Ultra Tech to make equal payment to the fund at the *end* of each of the next 5 years. What is the amount of required periodic payment, assuming that the fund will earn 10% annual interest? To answer this question, we simply rearrange the formula shown below for computing the future amount of an annuity:

Our original formula ...

$$\text{Future amount of an annuity} = \text{Periodic payment} \times \text{Factor (from Table FA-2)}$$

In our example, we know that Ultra Tech is required to accumulate a future amount of $10 million. However, we need to know the amount of the periodic payments that, when invested at 10% annual interest, will accumulate to that future amount. To make this calculation, the formula shown above may be restated as follows:

... restated to find the amount of the periodic payments

$$\text{Periodic payment} = \frac{\text{Future amount of an annuity}}{\text{Factor (from Table FA-2)}}$$

The amount of each required payment, therefore, is $1,638,000 ($10 million ÷ 6.105). If payments of $1,638,000 are made at the end of each of the next five years to a bond sinking fund that earns 10% annual interest, the fund will accumulate to $10 million:

Future amount of a series of investments

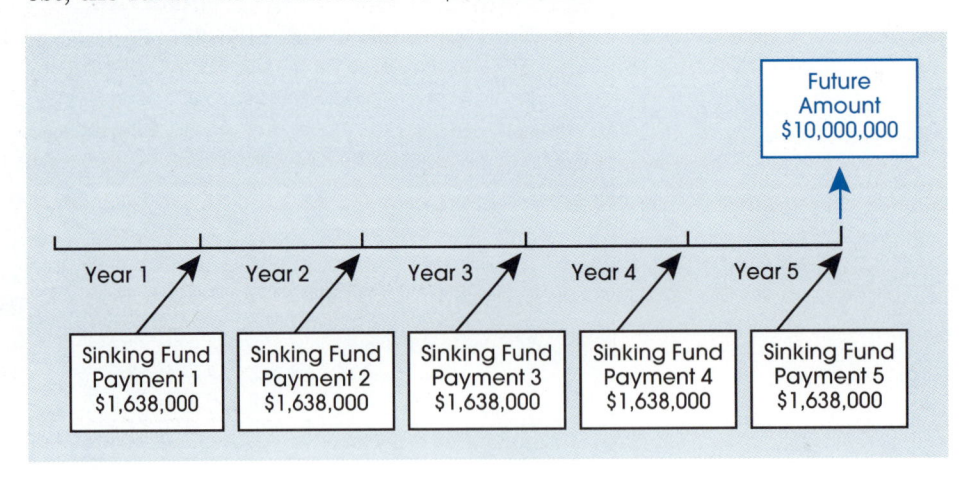

Year 1	Year 2	Year 3	Year 4	Year 5	Future Amount $10,000,000
Sinking Fund Payment 1 $1,638,000	Sinking Fund Payment 2 $1,638,000	Sinking Fund Payment 3 $1,638,000	Sinking Fund Payment 4 $1,638,000	Sinking Fund Payment 5 $1,638,000	

Interest Periods of Less Than One Year

In our computations of future amounts, we have assumed that interest is paid (compounded) or payments are made annually. Therefore, in using the tables, we used **annual** periods and an **annual** interest rate. Investment payments or interest payments may be made on a more frequent basis, such as monthly, quarterly, or semiannually. **Tables FA-1 and FA-2** may be used with any of these payment periods, *but the rate of interest must represent the interest rate for that period*.

As an example, assume that 24 monthly payments are to be made to an investment fund that pays 12% annual interest rate. To determine the future amount of this investment, we would multiply the amount of the monthly payments by the factor from *Table FA-2* for 24 periods, using a *monthly* interest rate of 1%—the 12% annual rate divided by 12 months.

PRESENT VALUES

LO 5: Compute the present values of future cash flows.

As indicated previously, the present value is *today's* value of funds to be received in the future. While present value has many applications in business and accounting, it is most easily explained in the context of evaluating investment opportunities. In this context, the present value is the amount that a knowledgeable investor would pay *today* for the right to receive an expected future amount of cash. The present value is always *less* than the future amount, because the investor will expect to earn a return on the investment. The amount by which the future cash receipt exceeds its present value represents the investor's profit.

The amount of the profit on a particular investment depends upon two factors: (1) the rate of return (called the *discount rate*) required by the investor, and (2) the length of time until the future amount will be received. The process of determining the present value of a future cash receipt is called *discounting* the future amount.

To illustrate the computation of present value, assume that an investment is expected to result in a $1,000 cash receipt at the end of one year, and that an investor requires a 10% return on this investment. We know from our discussion of present and future values that the difference between a present value and a future amount is the return (interest) on the investment. In our example, the future amount would be equal to 110% of the original investment, because the investor expects 100% of the investment back plus a 10% return on the investment. Thus, the investor would be willing to pay **$909** ($1,000 ÷ 1.10) for this investment. This computation may be verified as follows (amounts rounded to the nearest dollar):

Amount to be invested (present value)	$ 909
Required return on investment ($909 x 10%)	91
Amount to be received in one year (future value)	$1,000

If the $1,000 is to be received *two years* in the future, the investor would pay only **$826** for the investment today [($1,000 ÷ 1.10) ÷ 1.10]. This computation may be verified as follows (amounts rounded to the nearest dollar):

Amount to be invested (present value)	$ 826
Required return on investment in first year ($826 x 10%)	83
Amount invested after one year	$ 909
Required return on investment in second year ($909 x 10%)	91
Amount to be received in two years (future value)	$1,000

The amount that our investor would pay today, $826, is the present value of $1,000 to be received two years later, discounted at an annual rate of 10%. The $174 difference between the $826 present value and the $1,000 future amount is the return (interest revenue) to be earned by the investor over the two-year period.

Present value of a single future cash flow

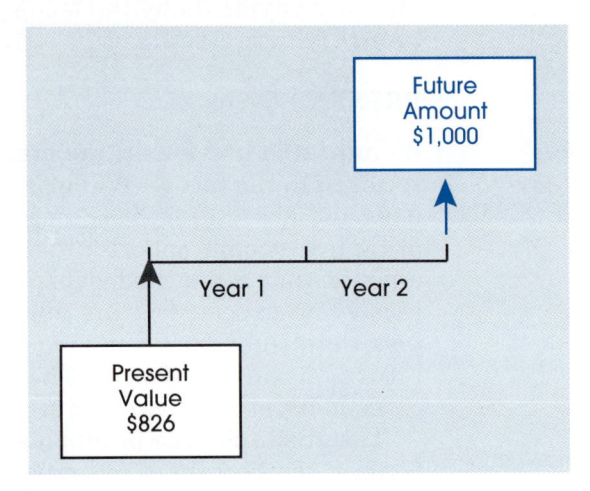

```
                                        ┌──────────┐
                                        │  Future  │
                                        │  Amount  │
                                        │  $1,000  │
                                        └──────────┘
                                             ▲
                                             │
                          ───────────────────┘
                          ▲
                          │     Year 1      Year 2
             ┌──────────┐
             │ Present  │
             │  Value   │
             │   $826   │
             └──────────┘
```

Using Present Value Tables

Although we can compute the present value of future amounts by a series of divisions as illustrated on page 841, tables are available that simplify the calculations. We can use a table of present values to find the present value of $1 at a specified discount rate and then multiply that value by the future amount as illustrated in the formula below:

Formula for finding present value

Present value = Future amount × Factor (from Table PV-1)

Referring to **Table PV-1** on the next page, we find a factor of **0.826** at the intersection of two periods and 10% interest. If we multiply this factor by the expected future cash receipt of $1,000, we get a present value of **$826** ($1,000 × 0.826), the same amount produced by the series of divisions in our previous illustration.

TABLE PV-1
Present Values of $1 Due in *n* Periods

Number of Periods (n)	1%	1½%	5%	6%	8%	10%	12%	15%	20%
1	.990	.985	.952	.943	.926	.909	.893	.870	.833
2	.980	.971	.907	.890	.857	.826	.797	.756	.694
3	.971	.956	.864	.840	.794	.751	.712	.658	.579
4	.961	.942	.823	.792	.735	.683	.636	.572	.482
5	.951	.928	.784	.747	.681	.621	.567	.497	.402
6	.942	.915	.746	.705	.630	.564	.507	.432	.335
7	.933	.901	.711	.665	.583	.513	.452	.376	.279
8	.923	.888	.677	.627	.540	.467	.404	.327	.233
9	.914	.875	.645	.592	.510	.424	.361	.284	.194
10	.905	.862	.614	.558	.463	.386	.322	.247	.162
20	.820	.742	.377	.312	.215	.149	.104	.061	.026
24	.788	.700	.310	.247	.158	.102	.066	.035	.013
36	.699	.585	.173	.123	.063	.032	.017	.007	.001

What Is the Appropriate Discount Rate?

As explained above, the ***discount rate*** may be viewed as the investor's required rate of return. All investments involve some degree of risk that actual future cash flows may turn out to be less than expected. Investors will require a rate of return that justifies taking this risk. In today's market conditions, investors require annual returns of between 5% and 8% on low-risk investments, such as government bonds and certificates of deposit. For relatively high-risk investments, such as the introduction of a new product line, investors may expect to earn an annual return of perhaps 15% or more. When a higher discount rate is used, the present value of the investment will be lower. In other words, as the risk of an investment increases, its value to investors decreases.

The Present Value of an Annuity

Many investment opportunities are expected to produce annual cash flows for a number of years, instead of one single future cash flow. Let us assume that Camino Limited is evaluating an investment that is expected to produce an ***annual net cash flow*** of $10,000 in ***each of the next three years***.[1] If Camino Limited expects a 12% return on this type of investment, it may compute the present value of these cash flows as follows:

---

[1] An "annual net cash flow" normally is the net result of a series of cash receipts and cash payments occurring throughout the year. For convenience, we follow the common practice of assuming that the entire net cash flow for each year occurs at ***year-end***. This assumption causes relatively little distortion and greatly simplifies computations.

Year	Expected Net Cash Flow	×	Present Value of $1 Discounted at 12%	=	Present Value of Net Flows
1	$10,000		.893		$ 8,930
2	10,000		.797		7,970
3	10,000		.712		7,120
Total present value of the investment					$24,020

This analysis indicates that the present value of the expected net cash flows from the investment, discounted at an annual rate of 12%, amounts to $24,020. This is the maximum amount that Camino Limited could afford to pay for this investment and still expect to earn the 12% required rate of return, as shown below:

Present value of a series of cash flows

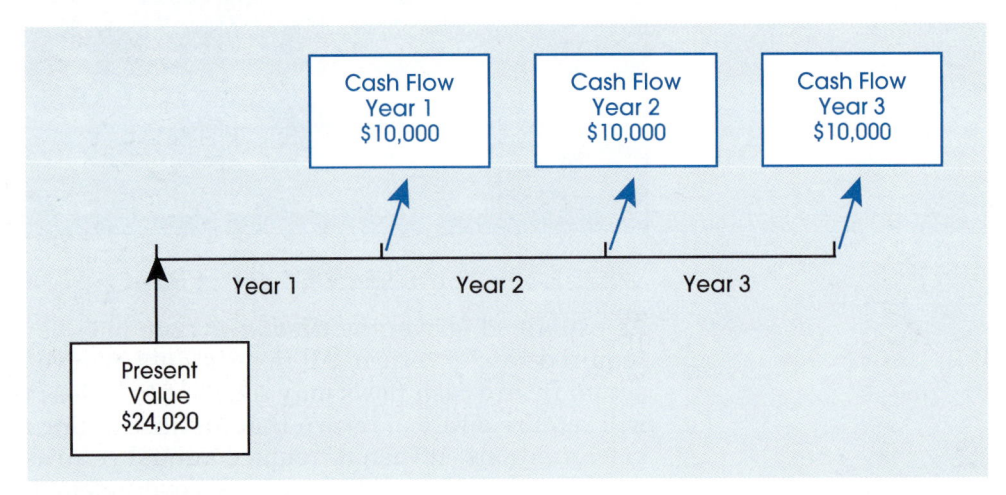

[Diagram: Cash Flow Year 1 $10,000, Cash Flow Year 2 $10,000, Cash Flow Year 3 $10,000, discounted back to Present Value $24,020]

In the preceding schedule, we computed the present value of the investment by separately discounting each period's cash flow, using the appropriate factors from **Table PV-1**. Separately discounting each period's cash flow is necessary only when the cash flows vary in amount from period to period. Since the annual cash flows in our example are **uniform in amount**, there are easier ways to compute the total present value.

Many financial calculators are programmed to compute the present value of an investment, after the interest rate, the future cash flows, and the number of periods have been entered. Another approach is to refer to a *present value annuity table*, which shows the present value of *$1 to be received each period for a specified number of periods*. An annuity table appears on the next page and is labeled as **Table PV-2**.[2]

To illustrate the use of **Table PV-2**, let's return to the example of the investment by Camino Limited. That investment was expected to return $10,000 per year for the next three years, and the company's required rate of return was 12% per year. Using **Table PV-2**, we can compute the present value of the investment with the formula illustrated below:

Formula to find the present value of a series of cash flows

Present value of an annuity = **Periodic cash flow × Factor (from Table PV-2)**

---
[2] This table assumes that the periodic cash flows occur at the *end* of each period.

TABLE PV-2
Present Values of $1 to Be Received Periodically for *n* Periods

Number of Periods (n)	1%	1½%	5%	6%	8%	10%	12%	15%	20%
1	0.990	0.985	0.952	0.943	0.926	0.909	0.893	0.870	0.833
2	1.970	1.956	1.859	1.833	1.783	1.736	1.690	1.626	1.528
3	2.941	2.912	2.723	2.673	2.577	2.487	2.402	2.283	2.106
4	3.902	3.854	3.546	3.465	3.312	3.170	3.037	2.855	2.589
5	4.853	4.783	4.329	4.212	3.993	3.791	3.605	3.352	2.991
6	5.795	5.697	5.076	4.917	4.623	4.355	4.111	3.784	3.326
7	6.728	6.598	5.786	5.582	5.206	4.868	4.564	4.160	3.605
8	7.652	7.486	6.463	6.210	5.747	5.335	4.968	4.487	3.837
9	8.566	8.361	7.108	6.802	6.247	5.759	5.328	4.772	4.031
10	9.471	9.222	7.722	7.360	6.710	6.145	5.650	5.019	4.192
20	18.046	17.169	12.462	11.470	9.818	8.514	7.469	6.259	4.870
24	21.243	20.030	13.799	12.550	10.529	8.985	7.784	6.434	4.937
36	30.108	27.661	16.547	14.621	11.717	9.677	8.192	6.623	4.993

As illustrated in **Table PV-2**, the present value of $1 to be received at the end of the next three years, discounted at an annual rate of 12% is **$2.402**. If we multiply 2.402 by the expected future annual cash receipt of $10,000, we get a present value of $24,020, which is the same amount produced by the series of calculations made earlier.

Discount Periods of Less Than One Year

The interval between regular periodic cash flows is called the **discount period**. In our preceding examples, we have assumed cash flows once a year. Often cash flows occur on a more frequent basis, such as monthly, quarterly, or semiannually. The present value tables can be used with discount periods of any length, **but the discount rate must be for that length of time**. For example, if we use **Table PV-2** to find the present value of a series of **quarterly** cash payments, the discount rate must be the **quarterly** rate.

There are a great many applications of the present value concept in accounting. In the next several pages, we will discuss some of the most important of these applications.

VALUATION OF FINANCIAL INSTRUMENTS

LO 6: Discuss accounting applications of the concept of present value.

Accountants use the term **financial instruments** to describe cash, equity investments in another business, and any contracts that call for receipts or payments of cash. (Notice that this term applies to all financial assets, as well as most liabilities. In fact, the only common liabilities **not** considered financial instruments are unearned revenue and future (deferred) income taxes.)

Whenever the present value of a financial instrument **differs significantly** from the sum of the expected future cash flows, the instrument is recorded in the accounting records at its *present value*—not at the expected amount of the future cash receipts or payments.

Let us illustrate with a few common examples. Cash appears in the balance sheet at its face amount. This face value *is* a present value—that is, the value of the cash today.

Marketable securities appear or are disclosed in the balance sheet at their *current market values*. These too are present values—representing the amount of cash into which the security can be converted *today*.

Accounts receivable and accounts payable normally appear in the balance sheet at the amounts expected to be collected or paid in the near future. Technically, these are *future amounts*, not present values. But they usually are received or paid within 30 or 60 days. Considering the short periods of time involved, the differences between these future amounts and their present values simply are *not material*.

Interest-Bearing Receivables and Payables

When a financial instrument calls for the receipt or payment of interest, the difference between present value and the future amounts *does* become material. Thus, interest-bearing receivables and payables initially are recorded in accounting records at the *present value* of the future cash flows—also called the "principal amount" of the obligation. This present value often is *substantially less* than the sum of the expected future amounts.

Consider, for example, $100 million in 30-year, 9% bonds payable issued at par. At the issuance date, the present value of this bond issue is $100 million—the amount of cash received. But the future payments to bondholders are expected to total *$370* million, computed as follows:

Future interest payments ($100 million × 9% × 30 years)	$270,000,000
Maturity value of the bonds (due in 30 years)	100,000,000
Sum of the future cash payments	$370,000,000

Thus, the $100 million issuance price represents the present value of $370 million in future cash payments to be made over a period of 30 years.

In essence, interest-bearing financial instruments are "automatically" recorded at their present values simply because we do not include future interest charges in the original valuation of the receivable or the liability.

"Non-Interest-Bearing" Notes

On occasion, companies may issue or accept notes that make no mention of interest, or in which the stated interest rates are unreasonably low. If the difference between the present value of such a note and its face amount is *material*, the note initially is recorded at its present value.

To illustrate, assume that on January 1, 2000, Elron Corporation purchases land from Sungan Development Limited. As full payment for this land, Elron issues a $300,000 instalment note payable, due in 3 annual instalments of $100,000, beginning on December 31, 2000. This note makes *no mention* of interest charges.

Clearly, three annual instalments of $100,000 are not the equivalent of $300,000 available today. Elron should use the **present value** of this note—not the face amount—in determining the cost of the land and reporting its liability.

Assume that a realistic interest rate for financing land over a 3-year period currently is 10% per annum. The present value of Elron's instalment note, discounted at 10%, is **$248,700** [$100,000 3-year annuity × **2.487** (from **Table PV-2**)]. Elron should view this $248,700 as the "principal amount" of this instalment note payable. The remaining $51,300 ($300,000 - $248,700) represents "interest charges" included in the instalment payments.

Elron should record the purchase of the land and this issuance of this note as follows:[3]

Land	248,700	
Notes Payable		248,700

Purchased land, issuing a 3-year instalment note payable with a present value of $248,700

(Sungan Development Limited should make similar computations in determining the sales price of the land and the valuation of its note receivable.)

Elron also should prepare an **amortization table** to allocate the amount of each instalment payment between interest expense and reduction in the principal amount of this obligation. This table, based upon an original "unpaid balance" of $248,700, three annual payments of $100,000, and an annual interest rate of 10% is illustrated below:

AMORTIZATION TABLE
(3-Year, $300,000 Instalment Note Payable, Discounted at 10% per annum)

Interest Period	Payment Date	Annual Payment	Interest Expense (10% of the Last Unpaid Balance)	Reduction in Unpaid Balance	Unpaid Balance
Issue date	Jan. 1, 2000				$248,700
1	Dec. 31, 2000	$100,000	$24,870	$75,130	173,570
2	Dec. 31, 2001	100,000	17,357	82,643	90,927
3	Dec. 31, 2002	100,000	9,073*	90,927	-0-

*In the last period, interest expense is equal to the amount of the final payment minus the remaining unpaid balance. This compensates for the use of a present value table with factors carried to only three decimal places.

---

[3] There is an alternative recording technique that makes use of an account entitled Discount on Notes Payable. This alternative approach produces the same results.

The entry at December 31, 2000 to record the first instalment payment will be:

Interest Expense	24,870	
Notes Payable	75,130	
Cash		100,000
Made annual payment on instalment note payable to Sungan Development Limited		

Market Prices of Bonds

The market price of bonds may be regarded as the ***present value*** to bondholders of the future principal and interest payments. To illustrate, assume that a corporation issues $1,000,000 face value of 10-year, 9% bonds when the going market rate of interest is 10%. Assume that bond interest is paid semiannually, we use 20 ***semiannual*** periods as the life of the bond issue and a 5% ***semiannual*** market rate of interest in our present value calculations. The expected issuance price of this bond issue may be computed as follows:

Present value of future principal payments:
   $1,000,000 due after 20 semiannual periods, discounted at 5%:
   $1,000,000 × .377 (from **Table PV-1**) **$377,000**
Present value of future interest payments:
   $45,000 per period ($1,000,000 × 9% × ½) for 20 semiannual
   periods, discounted at 5%: $45,000 × 12.462 (from **Table PV-2**) **560,790**
Expected issuance price of bond issue **$937,790**

Capital Leases

We briefly discussed capital leases in Chapter 16, but did not illustrate the accounting for these instruments. We will use this appendix as an opportunity to explore this topic in greater detail.

A capital lease is regarded as a sale of the leased asset by the lessor to the lessee. At the date of this sale, the lessor recognizes sales revenue equal to the ***present value*** of the future lease payments receivable, discounted at a realistic rate of interest. The lessee also uses the present value of the future payments to determine the cost of the leased asset and the valuation of the related liability.

To illustrate, assume that on December 1, Pace Tractor uses a ***capital lease*** to finance the sale of a tractor to Kelly Grading Limited. The tractor was carried in Pace Tractor's perpetual inventory records at a cost of $15,000. Terms of the lease call for Kelly Grading to make **24** monthly payments of **$1,000** each, beginning on December 31. These lease payments include an interest charge of **1%** per month. At the end of the 24-month lease, title to the tractor will pass to Kelly Grading at no additional cost.

Accounting by the Lessor (Pace Tractor) *Table PV-2* shows that the present value of $1 to be received monthly for 24 months, discounted at 1% per month, is **21.243**. Therefore, the present value of the 24 future lease payments is $1,000 × 21.243, or **$21,243**. Pace Tractor should record this capital lease as a sale of the tractor at a price equal to the present value of the lease payments, as follows:

Lease Payment Receivable (net)	21,243	
Sales		21,243
Financed sale of a tractor to Kelly Grading Limited, using a capital lease requiring 24 monthly payments of $1,000. Payments include a 1% monthly interest charge.		
Cost of Goods Sold	15,000	
Inventory		15,000
To record cost of tractor sold under capital lease.		

Notice that the sales price of the tractor is only $21,243, even though the gross amount to be collected from Kelly Grading amounts to $24,000 ($1,000 × 24 payments). The difference between these two amounts, $2,757, will be recognized by Pace Tractor as interest revenue over the life of the lease.

To illustrate the recognition of interest revenue, the entry on December 31 to record collection of the first monthly lease payment (rounded to the nearest dollar) is:

Cash	1,000	
Interest Revenue		212
Lease Payments Receivable (net)		788
Received first lease payment from Kelly Grading Limited:		
Lease payment received	*$1,000*	
Interest revenue ($21,243 × 1%)	*(212)*	
Reduction in lease payments receivable	*$ 788*	

After this first monthly payment is collected, the present value of the lease payments receivable is reduced to $20,455 ($21,243 original balance, less $788). Therefore, the interest revenue earned during the **second** month of the lease (rounded to the nearest dollar) will be **$205** ($20,455 × 1%).[4]

Accounting by the Lessee (Kelly Grading Limited) Kelly Grading Limited also should use the present value of the lease payments to determine the cost of the tractor and the amount of the related liability, as follows:

Leased Equipment	21,243	
Lease Payment Obligation		21,243
To record acquisition of a tractor through a capital lease from Pace Tractor. Terms call for 24 monthly payments of $1,000, which include a 1% monthly interest charge.		

The entry on December 31 to record the first monthly lease payment (rounded to the nearest dollar) will be:

---

[4] Both Pace Tractor and Kelly Grading Limited would prepare **amortization tables** showing the allocation of each lease payment between interest and the principal amount due.

Interest Expense	212	
Lease Payment Obligation	788	
Cash		1,000

To record first monthly lease payment to Pace Tractor:
Amount of payment	$1,000
Interest expense ($21,243 × 1%)	(212)
Reduction in lease payment obligation	$ 788

Obligations for Postretirement Benefits

As explained in Chapter 16, any unfunded obligation for postretirement benefits appears in the balance sheet at the ***present value*** of the expected future cash outlays to retired employees. The computation of this present value is so complex that it is performed by a professional actuary. But the present value of this obligation normally is far less than the expected future payments, as the cash payments will take place many years in the future.

Each year, the present value of an unfunded obligation for postretirement benefits will increase—as the future payment dates become closer. This steady "growth" in the present value of the unfunded obligation is recognized annually as part of the company's current postretirement benefits expense. (One might argue that the growth in this liability actually represents "interest expense." Nonetheless, the present value of the liability increases as the payment dates draw closer.)

Disclosure of Up-to-Date Present Value Information

Financial instruments originally are recorded in accounting records at (or near) their present values. But present values represent future cash flows discounted at ***current market*** interest rates. Thus, as market interest rates change, so do the present values of many financial instruments.

Cash, investments in marketable securities, and postretirement obligations appear in the financial statements at current values. For most short-term instruments, current values remain quite close to the original carrying values. But for long-term financial instruments, such as bonds payable, current values may differ substantially from the amounts originally recorded.

Companies should disclose the fair (current) values of financial instruments whenever these values ***differ significantly*** from the recorded amounts. These disclosures are most likely to affect long-term notes receivable and payable (including bonds payable), and long-term lease obligations.

In computing fair value, current market interest rates serve as the discount rate. Thus, as interest rates ***rise***, fair values ***fall***; as interest rates ***fall***, fair values ***rise***. The amount of change is greatest on long-term financial instruments for which the future cash flows are "fixed"—that is, not adjustable to reflect changes in interest rates.

The disclosure of fair values can shed light upon a company's past investing and financing activities. Assume, for example, that a company's long-term debt has a fair value well ***below*** its carrying value in the company's balance sheet. This means that interest rates have ***increased*** since the company arranged this debt. Thus, the company apparently arranged its long-term financing in a period of low interest rates—a good move.

Future (Deferred) Income Taxes

The only long-term liability **not** shown at the present value of the expected future payments is the obligation for future (deferred) income taxes. Future taxes are treated differently because they do not involve a "contract" for future payments. Future payments of these taxes, if any, depend upon the company's taxable income in future periods and also the corporate income tax laws in future years.

Many accountants believe that future income taxes **should** be shown at the estimated present value of the future outlays. This is not likely to happen, however, as the computations would be overwhelmingly complex.

In conclusion, the obligation for future (deferred) income taxes is the only long-term liability that is **not** reported at its present value. Hence, one might argue that these obligations are "overstated" in terms of an equivalent number of "today's dollars."

CAPITAL BUDGETING: ANOTHER APPLICATION OF PRESENT VALUE

Capital budgeting is the process of planning and evaluating proposals for capital expenditures, such as the acquisition of plant assets or the introduction of a new product line. Perhaps the most widely used approach in the evaluation of proposed capital expenditures is *discounting* the expected future cash flows to their *present value*.

Assume that Globe Mfg. Ltd. is considering a proposal to purchase new equipment in order to produce a new product. The equipment costs $400,000, has an estimated 10-year service life, and has an estimated salvage value of $50,000. Globe estimates that production and sale of the new product will increase the company's annual net cash flow by $100,000 per year for the next 10 years. If Globe requires a 15% annual rate of return on investments of this nature, the present value of these cash flows may be computed as shown below:

Is this project worth a $400,000 investment?

Present value of expected annual net cash inflows of $100,000 for 10 years, discounted at 15% per year: $100,000 × 5.019 (from Table PV-2)	$501,900
Present value of estimated salvage value to be received at the end of the tenth year: $50,000 × .247 (from Table PV-1)	12,350
Present value of estimated future cash inflows	$514,250
Less: Amount to be invested (already a present value)	400,000
Net present value of proposal	$114,250

This analysis indicates that the present value of the expected net cash flows from this investment, discounted at an annual rate of 15%, amounts to $514,250. This is the maximum amount that Globe could afford to invest in this project and still expect to earn the required 15% annual rate of return. As the cost of this investment is only $400,000, Globe can expect to earn more than its required 15% return.

The ***net present value*** of a proposal is the ***difference*** between the total present value of the future net cash flows and the cost of the investment. When the net present value is equal to zero, the investment provides a rate of return exactly equal to the rate used in discounting the cash flows. A ***positive*** net present value means that the investment provides a rate of return ***greater*** than the discount rate; a ***negative*** net present value means that the investment yields a return of ***less*** than the discount rate.

Since the discount rate usually is the minimum rate of return required by the investor, proposals with a positive net present value are considered acceptable, and those with a negative net present value are viewed as unacceptable.

Capital budgeting techniques are discussed further in courses in management accounting, cost accounting, and finance.

Assignment Material

Discussion Questions

1. Explain what is meant by the phrase the "***time-value*** of money."
2. Explain why the present value of a future amount is always ***less*** than the future amount.
3. Identify the two factors that determine the difference between the present value and the future amount of an investment.
4. Describe three basic investment applications of the concept of the time-value of money.
5. Briefly explain the relationships between present value and (a) the length of time until the future cash flow occurs, and (b) the discount rate used in determining present value.
6. Define ***financial instruments***. Explain the valuation concept used in initially recording financial instruments in financial statements.
7. Are normal accounts receivable and accounts payable "financial instruments"? Are these items shown in the balance sheet at their present values? Explain.
8. Identify three financial instruments shown in financial statements at present values that may ***differ significantly*** from the sum of the expected future payments or receipts.
9. What is the only long-term liability that is ***not*** recorded at its present value? What are the implications in terms of "today's dollars"?
10. Assuming no change in the expected amount of future cash flows, what factors may cause the present value of a financial instrument to change? Explain fully.
11. Define ***capital budgeting***. Explain briefly how the present-value concept relates to capital budgeting decisions.

Problems

PROBLEM C-1
Using Future Amount Tables
(LO 1, 2, 4)

Use the tables on pages 837 and 839 to determine the future amounts of the following investments:
a. $20,000 is invested for ten years, at 6% interest, compounded annually.
b. $100,000 to be received five years from today, at 10% annual interest.
c. $10,000 is invested in a fund at the end of each of the next ten years, at 8% interest, compounded annually.
d. $50,000 initial investment plus $5,000 invested annually at the end of each of the next three years, at 12% interest, compounded annually.

PROBLEM C-2
Bond Sinking Fund
(LO 3, 4)

Tilman Corporation is required by a bond indenture to make equal annual payments to a bond sinking fund at the end of each of the next 20 years. The sinking fund will earn 8% interest, and must accumulate to a total of $500,000 at the end of the 20-year period.
a. Calculate the amount of the annual payments.
b. Calculate the total amount of interest that will be earned by the fund over the 20-year period.
c. Make the general journal entry to record redemption of the bond issue at the end of the 20-year period, assuming that the sinking fund is recorded on Tilman's accounting records at $500,000 and bonds payable are recorded at the same amount.
d. What would be the effect of an increase in the rate of return on the required annual payment? Explain.

PROBLEM C-3
Using Present Value Tables
(LO 1, 2, 5)

Use the tables on pages 843 and 845 to determine the present value of the following cash flows:
a. $15,000 to be paid annually for ten years, discounted at an annual rate of 6%. Payments are to occur at the end of each year.
b. $9,200 to be received today, assuming that money will be invested in a 2-year certificate of deposit earning 8% annually.
c. $300 to be paid monthly for 36 months, with an additional "balloon payment" of $12,000 due at the end of the thirty-sixth month, discounted at a monthly interest rate of 1½%. The first payment is to be one month from today.
d. $25,000 to be received annually for the first three years, followed by $15,000 to be received annually for the next two years (total of five years in which collections are received), discounted at an annual rate of 8%. Assume collections occur at year-end.

PROBLEM C-4
Present Value and Bond Prices
(LO 3, 5, 6)
INSTRUCTIONS

On June 30 of the current year, Rural Gas & Electric Ltd. issued $50,000,000 face value, 9%, 10-year bonds payable, with interest dates of December 31 and June 30. The bonds were issued at a discount, resulting in an effective **semi-annual** interest rate of 5%.
a. Compute the issuance price for the bond issue that results in an effective semi-annual interest rate of 5%.
b. Prepare a journal entry to record the issuance of the bonds at the sales price you computed in part **a**.
c. Explain why the bonds were issued at a discount.

PROBLEM C-5
Valuation of a Note Payable
(LO 3, 5, 6)

On December 1, Showcase Interiors purchased a shipment of furniture from Colonial House by paying $10,500 cash and issuing an instalment note payable in the face amount of $28,800. The note is to be paid in 24 monthly instalments of $1,200 each. Although the note makes no mention of an interest charge, the rate of interest usually charged to Showcase Interiors in such transactions is 1½% per month.

INSTRUCTIONS

a. Compute the present value of the note payable, using a discount rate of 1½% per month.
b. Prepare the journal entries in the accounts of Showcase Interiors on:
   1. December 1, to record the purchase of the furniture (debit Inventory).
   2. December 31, to record the first $1,200 monthly payment on the note and to recognize interest expense for one month by the effective interest method. (Round interest expense to the nearest dollar.)
c. Show how the liability for this note would appear in the balance sheet at December 31. (Assume that the note is classified as a current liability.)

PROBLEM C-6
Capital Leases: A Comprehensive Problem
(LO 3, 5, 6)

Custom Truck Builders frequently uses long-term lease contracts to finance the sale of its trucks. On November 1, 2000, Custom Truck Builders leased to Interpro Van Lines a truck carried in the perpetual inventory records at $33,520. The terms of the lease call for Interpro Van Lines to make 36 monthly payments of $1,400 each, beginning on November 30, 2000. The present value of these payments, after considering a built-in interest charge of 1% per month, is equal to the regular $42,150 sales price of the truck. At the end of the 36-month lease, title to the truck will transfer to Interpro Van Lines.

INSTRUCTIONS

a. Prepare journal entries for 2000 in the accounts of Custom Truck Builders on:
   1. November 1, to record the sale financed by the lease and the related cost of goods sold. (Debit Lease Payments Receivable for the $42,150 present value of the future lease payments.)
   2. November 30, to record receipt of the first $1,400 monthly payment. (Prepare a compound journal entry that allocates the cash receipt between interest revenue and reduction of Lease Payments Receivable. The portion of each monthly payment recognized as interest revenue is equal to 1% of the balance of the account Lease Payments Receivable, at the beginning of that month. Round all interest computations to the nearest dollar.)
   3. December 31, to record receipt of the second monthly payment.
b. Prepare journal entries for 2000 in the accounts of Interpro Van Lines on:
   1. November 1, to record acquisition of the leased truck.
   2. November 30, to record the first monthly lease payment. (Determine the portion of the payment representing interest expense in a manner parallel to that described in part **a**.)
   3. December 31, to record the second monthly lease payment.
   4. December 31, to recognize depreciation on the leased truck through year-end. Compute depreciation expense by the straight-line method, using a 10-year service life and an estimated salvage value of $6,150.
c. Compute the net carrying value of the leased truck in the balance sheet of Interpro Van Lines at December 31, 2000.
d. Compute the amount of Interpro Van Lines' lease payment obligation at December 31, 2000.

PROBLEM C-7
Capital Budgeting—Evaluating Capital Lease Proposals
(LO 3, 5, 6)

Metropolitan Transit District (MTD) plans to acquire a large computer system by entering into a long-term lease agreement with the computer manufacturer. The manufacturer will provide the computer system under either of the following lease agreements:

Five-year lease. MTD is to pay $2,500,000 at the beginning of the lease (delivery date) and $1,000,000 annually at the end of each of the next 5 years. At the end of the fifth year, MTD may take title to the system for an additional payment of $3,000,000.

Ten-year lease. MTD is to pay $2,000,000 at the beginning of the lease and $900,000 annually at the end of each of the next 10 years. At the end of the tenth year, MTD may take title for an additional payment of $1,300,000.

Under either proposal, MTD will buy the computer at the end of the lease. MTD is a governmental agency that does not seek to earn a profit and is not evaluating alternative investment opportunities. However, MTD does attempt to minimize its costs and it must borrow the money to finance either lease agreement at an annual interest rate of 10%.

INSTRUCTIONS

a. Determine which lease proposal results in the lower cost for the computer system when the future cash outlays are discounted at an annual interest rate of 10%.
b. Prepare a journal entry to record the acquisition of the computer system under the lowest cost lease agreement as determined in part **a**. (This journal entry will include the initial cash payment to the computer manufacturer required at the beginning of the lease.)

PROBLEM C-8
Valuation of a Note Receivable with an Unrealistic Interest Rate
(LO 5, 6)

On December 31, Richland Farms sold a tract of land, which had cost $930,000, to Skyline Developers in exchange for $150,000 cash and a five-year, 4%, note receivable for $900,000. Interest on the note is payable annually, and the principal amount is due in five years. The accountant for Richland Farms did not notice the unrealistically low interest rate on the note and made the following entry on December 31 to record this sale:

Cash	150,000	
Notes Receivable	900,000	
Land		930,000
Gain on Sale of Land		120,000
Sold land to Skyline Developers in exchange for cash and a five-year note with interest due annually.		

INSTRUCTIONS

a. Compute the present value of the note receivable from Skyline Developers at the date of sale, assuming that a realistic rate of interest for this transaction is 12%.
b. Prepare the journal entry on December 31 to record the sale of the land correctly. Show supporting computations for the gain or loss on the sale.
c. Explain what effects the error made by Richland Farms' accountant will have upon (1) the net income in the year of the sale and (2) the combined net income of the next five years. Ignore income taxes.

Analytical and Decision Problems and Cases

A&D C-1
Implications of Present Value
(LO 6)

Sylmar Industries buys a substantial amount of equipment having an estimated service life of five years by issuing a two-year note payable. The note includes no mention of an interest charge. Explain the errors that will result in the future financial statements of Sylmar Industries if the equipment and related liability are recorded at the face value, rather than the present value, of the note.

A&D C-2
Changes in Current Value
(LO 2, 6)

Indicate how an increase in interest rates is likely to affect the fair or *current value* (present value determined under current market conditions) of the following items. Explain your reasoning.
a. Accounts payable
b. Long-term receivables with "fixed" interest rates.
c. An "adjustable rate" mortgage payable. (The interest rate is adjusted monthly to reflect current market rates.)
d. Outstanding bonds payable.
e. Unfunded pension obligations.

COMPREHENSIVE PROBLEM 5

SHADOW MOUNTAIN HOTEL

A corporate "practice set."

Note to Students and Instructors: This problem ***requires*** use of the partially completed working papers that accompany this textbook.

Shadow Mountain Hotel is a profitable resort hotel and convention centre that has been in operation for several years. Max Griffith, a motion picture producer, organized a new corporation called Shadow Mountain Corporation to purchase and operate the Shadow Mountain Hotel. The new corporation raised capital by issuing both capital stock and bonds payable, and on July 1, 2000 purchased the Shadow Mountain Hotel from the previous owners.

You have been hired as the corporation's controller. The hotel's accounting staff records and posts all the routine transactions, but you have instructed them ***not*** to record any transaction that they do not understand. Rather, they are to prepare a written description of these items for your review, and you will handle the recording of these transactions. You also perform the end-of-period procedures, including the preparation of a work sheet, adjusting and closing entries, and financial statements. The corporation adjusts and closes its accounting records at the end of each ***calendar quarter*** (three-month period).

It is now September 30, 2000, the end of the first calendar quarter after Shadow Mountain Corporation acquired the Shadow Mountain Hotel. Management has asked you to provide an income statement and statement of retained earnings for this three-month period, and also a balance sheet as of September 30. Almost all of the routine transactions have ***already been recorded*** in the accounting records and posted to ledger accounts by your staff. Per your instructions, they have prepared the following written description of each transaction or event ***not yet recorded***, as well as information necessary for end-of-period adjustments.

Transactions or Events Not Recorded by Staff

Date 2000	Transaction or Event
June 2	Max Griffith organized Shadow Mountain Corporation with an unlimited number of authorized no-par common stock, and $100 par value, 6% convertible preferred stock (each convertible into 6 shares of common stock).

June 3   Griffith and other investors purchased 480,000 shares of the corporation's common stock at a price of $16 per share, paying cash. Griffith states that he expects to line up investors to purchase another 70,000 shares by the end of the month.

June 4   Issued to Dianna Trump 25,000 shares of the convertible preferred stock at par, receiving $2,500,000 cash.

June 6   Underwriters Dunstone & Reed agreed to purchase $10 million of 15%, 20-year bonds payable to be issued by the corporation on July 1, 2000. The bonds will pay interest every December 31 and June 30. The exact issue price will be determined at the date of issuance, based upon an index of interest rates and bond prices.

June 29   Issued an additional 2,000 shares of common stock to Griffith for his services in organizing the corporation. The board of directors agree that these services were worth the $32,000 market value of these shares.

July 1   Issued the $10 million of 15%, 20-year bonds payable, dated today, to underwriters Dunstone & Reed. The issue price was 98, and the corporation received $9,800,000 in cash from the underwriters.

July 1   Purchased Shadow Mountain Hotel by assuming the liabilities of the hotel and paying an additional $19 million cash to National Resorts Inc. Exhibit 1 indicates the current values of the specific assets purchased, and also the amounts of the liabilities assumed. The excess of the $19 million purchase price over the current value of the net *identifiable* assets is regarded as a purchase of unrecorded goodwill.

EXHIBIT 1
Shadow Mountain Hotel
Valuation of Assets Purchased and Liabilities Assumed
July 1, 2000

Assets acquired:

Accounts receivable	$ 50,800	
Allowance for doubtful accounts	(1,000)	(credit)
Inventory	36,200	
Supplies	44,000	
Land	10,570,000	
Buildings	14,000,000	
Furnishings & equipment	1,200,000	
Total identifiable assets	$25,900,000	

Liabilities assumed:

Accounts payable	$ 99,000	
Interest payable	41,000	
Unearned deposits	615,000	
Income taxes payable	305,000	
Mortgage note payable (10%)	9,840,000	
Total liabilities	$10,900,000	
Current value of net identifiable assets purchased	$15,000,000	
Purchase price	$19,000,000	

July 4   Isadora Duncan, a shareholder who owned 12,000 shares of common stock in Shadow Mountain Corporation, was killed in an automobile accident. Duncan was a personal friend of Max Griffith.

July 10   Shadow Mountain Corporation purchased 12,000 shares of its common stock from the estate of Isadora Duncan at a price of $18 per share. These shares temporarily will be held as treasury stock, and will be reissued in the near future.

July 11   Dunstone & Reed, the underwriters of the bond issue, reported that they had resold all the bonds to investors at an average price of 101.

July 12   As part of the normal refurbishing of hotel rooms, older furniture was sold to Freight Liquidators for $119,900 cash. In the acquisition transaction on July 1, these furnishings had been assigned a cost of $200,000. (As these assets were sold less than one-half month after acquisition, there is no related accumulated depreciation, and no depreciation need be computed through the date of sale.)

July 14   Purchased new furnishings for $500,000 cash to replace those sold on July 12.

Aug. 10   Dianna Trump converted 10,000 shares of her $100 par value convertible preferred stock into 60,000 shares of common stock. In light of her increased voting rights, Trump was given a seat on the corporation's board of directors.

Aug. 18   The City of Shadow Mountain gave to Shadow Mountain Corporation several hectares of land including the riverbed along the western boundary of the hotel parking lot. The land was given to the corporation at no cost, but with the understanding that the corporation would build a flood control channel in this riverbed to prevent land erosion. The corporation intends to build the channel underground, and then to expand the parking lot on top of the riverbed and the donated land.

     The donated land currently is estimated to be worth $320,000 in its present condition.

Sept. 2   Received a $48,000 advance deposit from the Canadian Academic Accounting Association to reserve a block of 300 rooms for its national convention next May.

Sept. 10   The board of directors declared the regular quarterly dividend of $1.50 per share on the shares of 6% convertible preferred stock still outstanding. The dividend is payable on October 10 to shareholders of record on September 20.

Sept. 10   The board of directors declared a 2% stock dividend on currently outstanding shares of common stock. The current market price of the common stock is $20 per share. The dividend will be distributed on September 30 to shareholders of record on September 20.

Sept. 20 Date of record for the stock dividend declared on September 10. The market value of the stock today is $21 per share.

Sept. 24 Reissued 10,400 shares of the common stock held in the treasury at a price of $21; receiving $218,400 in cash.

Sept. 26 The provincial government paid Shadow Mountain Corporation cash of $310,000 in compensation for land that was expropriated by the province to permit widening of a highway. The cost of this land to the corporation, based upon the July 1 purchase transaction, was $200,000. In this case, the transaction also is *material in dollar amount*.

Sept. 27 Max Griffith sold 100,000 shares of his common stock in Shadow Mountain Corporation to Dianna Trump at a price of $20 per share. On this date, Griffith resigned as the corporation's chief executive officer, and the board named Trump as his replacement.

You remain the company's controller.

Sept. 30 Distributed the 10,600 share stock dividend declared on September 10. The market price of the common stock today is $22 per share.

Sept. 30 Paid all of the liabilities for income taxes withheld from employees (account no. 221) and for payroll taxes payable (account nos. 222, 223, 224, and 225). Payroll taxes consist of employment insurance and Canada Pension Plan. Although the staff had properly recorded routine payroll expense and payroll taxes, the required amounts had not been remitted to taxing authorities. (Make one journal entry to record payment of these liabilities.)

Information for End-of-Period Adjustments

a. Hotel guests normally are billed for their room rental when they check out. As of September 30, guests currently registered at the hotel owe $44,100 in room rental charges that have not yet been recorded or billed.
b. The hotel's accounts receivable consist primarily of amounts owed by current guests who have not yet checked out. Based upon experience, the company's policy is to provide an allowance for uncollectible accounts equal to 2% of these receivables. The amount of the allowance determined in this matter is rounded to the nearest one hundred dollars.
c. The Unearned Deposits account represents advance deposits made by conventions and other groups to reserve large blocks of rooms for future dates. As of September 30, $402,300 of the amount credited to this account has been earned, and $642,000 remains unearned.
d. Supplies on hand at September 30 amount to $40,000.
e. The insurance policies were purchased on July 1 for $300,000 and cover a period of twelve months.

f. Depreciation on the hotel building and other structures is computed by the ***straight-line*** method, assuming a 25-year life and no salvage value.

g. Depreciation on furniture and equipment is computed by the ***double-declining-balance*** method, assuming a 5-year life. (Depreciation for fractional periods is rounded to the nearest full month. In this case, you are to take three full months' depreciation on all assets included in the Furniture & Equipment account at September 30.)

h. Goodwill is amortized by the straight-line method over a 40-year amortization period.

i Organization costs are amortized by the straight-line method over a five-year period.

j. Property taxes payable accrue at the rate of $30,000 per month, beginning on July 1. These taxes are payable within one year.

k. Interest accrues on the mortgage note payable at the annual rate of 10%, and accrued interest is payable on the 15th of each month. Thus, at September 30, one-half month's interest expense has accrued. (The principal amount of this note is not due until April 30, 2003.)

l. In recognizing interest expense on the 15% bonds payable, bond discount is amortized by the straight-line method.

m. A public accountant has determined that the company's income taxes applicable to the quarter ended September 30 amount to $256,000, including $212,000 in taxes applicable to normal operations, and $44,000 in taxes resulting from the gain from the expropriation of land by the provincial government. The $44,000 in taxes relating to this gain should be debited to ***account no. 600***, Gains on Disposals of Plant Assets, rather than to the Income Taxes Expense account.

All income tax obligations will be paid within 90 days.

INSTRUCTIONS

a. Prepare general journal entries to record any of the transactions and events listed above that should be recorded in the accounting records of Shadow Mountain Corporation.

Next, post your journal entries to the general ledger accounts in the partially completed accounting work sheets booklet (a supplement to the text). You will find the company's chart of accounts in the work sheets booklet.

Remember, your accounting staff ***already*** has recorded and posted the routine transactions occurring during the quarter ended September 30. Entries summarizing the transactions recorded by your staff ***already appear*** in the general ledger accounts, and are identified by the caption "Summary of entries posted by staff." After ***you*** post an entry to the ledger, enter the new balance of the ledger account.

b. Prepare a 10-column work sheet for the ***three months*** ended September 30, 2000, using the information for end-of-period adjustments provided. (We have included in this work sheet a ***correct and complete unadjusted trial balance*** as of September 30, 2000. By comparing your September 30 account balances to the

amounts shown, you may determine whether or not you have correctly completed the earlier portions of this problem.)
c. Prepare the following financial statements:
1. An income statement for the three months ended September 30, 2000, using single-step format.
    Your income statement is to include the **earnings per share figures** normally found in the income statement of a publicly owned corporation. (Assume the weighted average number of common shares outstanding during the period to have been **515,350**. Round per-share amounts to the nearest cent. Fully diluted amounts are not required.)
2. A statement of retained earnings for the three months ended September 30, 2000.
3. A classified balance sheet as of September 30, 2000. Include a separate classification in your balance sheet for Intangible assets, immediately following the Plant and Equipment section. For retained earnings, show only the ending balance as of September 30.
d. Journalize and post the adjusting and closing entries.
e. Prepare an after-closing trial balance as of September 30, 2000.

CHAPTER 17

Investments in Corporate Securities

Who invests in these companies? How are these investments measured and reported? To understand corporate financial statements, you should know the answers to these and other questions.

CHAPTER LEARNING OBJECTIVES

1. Account for short-term investments in stocks and bonds.
2. Account for an investment in common stock by the equity method.
3. Explain how a parent company "controls" its subsidiaries.
4. Describe the distinctive feature of consolidated financial statements.
5. Explain why intercompany transactions must be eliminated as a step in preparing consolidated financial statements.
6. Prepare a consolidated balance sheet.

Capital stocks, bonds, commercial papers, and similar financial instruments issued by corporations are called *corporate securities*. These securities, as mentioned in previous chapters, are owned by individual investors, mutual funds, and pension funds. Also, corporations often own securities of other corporations. The reasons that corporations invest in corporate securities of others range from generating income from temporary excess cash to significantly influencing or controlling other corporations. Thus, most investments in corporate securities fall into two broad categories: (1) investments in *marketable securities* and (2) investments for purposes of *significant influence or control*.

INVESTMENT IN MARKETABLE SECURITIES

Marketable securities consist primarily of the bonds and stocks of large corporations and government bonds. These securities are traded on organized securities markets. Thus, they are easily purchased or sold at quoted market prices. Investments in marketable securities earn a return for the investor, in the form of interest, dividends, and perhaps an increase in market value. Meanwhile these investments are *almost as liquid as cash itself*. For this reason, marketable securities, which also are called short-term investments, are listed in the balance sheet as current assets, either together with cash or immediately after cash. The investments can be quite large.

CASE IN POINT

Recently, Air Canada showed its $611 million marketable securities as part of "Cash and short-term investments" under current assets. Domtar Inc., on the other hand, listed its marketable securities of $274 million as short-term investments under current assets, immediately after cash.

To qualify as a current asset, an investment in marketable securities must be readily marketable. *Readily marketable* means immediately salable at a quoted market price. In addition, management must be *willing* to use the invested funds to pay current liabilities or to use in current operations. Investments that are not readily marketable, or that management intends to hold on a long-term basis, are *not* current assets. Such investments should be shown in the balance sheet just below the current asset section under the caption Long-Term Investments.

Quoted Market Prices The current market prices of most marketable securities are quoted daily by securities exchanges, by brokerage houses, and in the financial pages of major newspapers. The market prices of stocks are quoted in terms of dollars per share. As illustrated in Chapter 16, bond prices are stated as a percentage of the bond's maturity value, which usually is $1,000. Thus, a bond with a quoted price of **87** has a market value of **$870** ($1,000 × 87%).

Accounting for Marketable Securities

LO 1: Account for short-term investments in stocks and bonds.

Accounting differs somewhat between investments in marketable equity securities (stocks) and in marketable debt securities (bonds). The principal distinction in accounting for investments in stocks and bonds is that *interest on bonds accrues* from day to day. An investor in bonds must account for this accrued interest when the bonds are purchased, at the end of each accounting period, and when the bonds are sold. Dividends on stock, however, *do not accrue*. For this reason, separate controlling accounts are used in the general ledger for each type of investment. For each controlling account, a subsidiary ledger is maintained, which shows for each security owned the acquisition date, total cost, number of shares (or bonds) owned, and the cost per share (or bond). This subsidiary ledger provides the information necessary to determine the amount of gain or loss when an investment in a particular stock or bond is sold.

Marketable Debt Securities (Bonds)

The amount of interest paid annually to bondholders is equal to a stated percentage of the bond's face or maturity value. Thus, the owner of a 10% bond received $100 interest ($1,000 × 10%) every year. Since bond interest usually is paid semiannually, the bondholder receives two semiannual interest payments of $50 each.

When bonds are purchased between interest dates, the purchaser pays the quoted market price for the bond *plus* the interest accrued since the last interest payment date. By this arrangement the new owner becomes entitled to receive in full the next semiannual interest payment. An account called Bond Interest Receivable should be debited for the amount of accrued interest purchased.

To illustrate the accounting entries for an investment in bonds, assume that on August 1 an investor purchases ten 6%, $1,000 bonds of Rider Corporation that pay interest on June 1 and December 1. The investor buys the bonds on August 1 at a price of 101 (or $10,100), plus a brokerage commission of $50 and two months' accrued interest of $100 ($10,000 × 6% × 2/12 = $100). The brokerage commission is viewed as part of the cost of the bonds. However, the accrued interest receivable at the time of purchase must be accounted for separately. Therefore, the journal entry made by the investor on August 1 is:

Marketable Debt Securities	10,150	
Bond Interest Receivable	100	
Cash		10,250
Purchased ten 6% bonds of Rider Corporation for $10,100 plus a brokerage commission of $50 and two months' accrued interest.		

Separate account for accrued bond interest purchased

On December 1, the semiannual interest payment date, the investor will receive an interest cheque for $300, which will be recorded as follows:

Cash	300	
Bond Interest Receivable		100
Bond Interest Revenue		200
Received semiannual interest on Rider Corporation bonds.		

Note portion of interest cheque earned

The $200 credit to Bond Interest Revenue represents the amount actually earned during the four months the bonds were owned by the investor ($6\% \times \$10,000 \times {}^4\!/_{12} = \$200$).

If the investor's accounting records are maintained on a calendar-year basis, the following adjusting entry is required at December 31 to record bond interest earned since December 1:

Bond Interest Receivable	50	
Bond Interest Revenue		50
To accrue one month's interest earned (Dec. 1–Dec. 31) on Rider Corporation bonds ($\$10,000 \times 6\% \times {}^1\!/_{12} = \$50$).		

Amortization of Bond Discount or Premium from the Investor's Viewpoint
Should an investor in bonds amortize any difference between the cost of the investment and its future maturity value in order to measure investment income correctly? The answer to this question depends upon whether the investor considers the bonds to be a current asset (short-term investment) or a long-term investment.

When an investment in bonds is classified as a current asset, the investor usually ***does not*** amortize discount or premium. The justification for this practice is the accounting principle of ***materiality***. Given that the investment may be held for but a short period of time, amortization of bond discount or premium probably will not have a material effect upon reported net income. When an investment in bonds will be held for the long term, however, the investor should amortize discount or premium. Amortization of a discount will increase the amount of interest revenue recognized by the investor; amortization of a premium will reduce the amount of interest revenue recognized.

Marketable Equity Securities (Stocks)

Since dividends on stock do not accrue, the ***entire cost*** of purchasing stock (including brokerage commissions) is debited to the Marketable Equity Securities account. Dividend revenue usually is recognized when the dividend cheque arrives; the entry consists of a debit to Cash and a credit to Dividend Revenue. No adjusting entries are needed to recognize dividend revenue at the end of an accounting period.

Additional shares of stock received in stock splits or stock dividends *are not income* to the shareholder, and only a *memorandum entry* is used to record the increase in the number of shares owned. The *cost basis per share* is decreased, however, because of the larger number of shares comprising the investment after receiving additional "free" shares from a stock split or a stock dividend.

As an example, assume that an investor purchases 100 shares of Delta Limited common stock at a total cost of $7,200, including commission. The investor's original cost basis is $72 per share ($7,200 ÷ 100 shares). Later the investor receives an additional 20 shares as the result of a 20% stock dividend. The investor's cost basis per share is thereby reduced to *$60* per share, computed by dividing the total cost of $7,200 by the *120* shares owned after the stock dividend. The memorandum entry to be made in the investor's general journal would be:

July 10 Memorandum: Received 20 additional shares of Delta Limited common stock as a result of 20% stock dividend. Now own 120 shares with a cost basis of $7,200, or $60 per share.

Gains and Losses from Sales of Investments

The sale of an investment in *stocks* is recorded by debiting Cash for the amount received and crediting the Marketable Equity Securities account for the cost of the securities sold. Any difference between the proceeds of the sale and the cost of the investment is recorded by a debit to Loss on Sale of Marketable Securities or by a credit to Gain on Sale of Marketable Securities.

At the day of sale of an investment in *bonds*, any interest that has accrued since the last interest payment date (or year-end) should be recognized as interest revenue. For example, assume that 10 bonds of the Elk Corporation carried in the accounts of an investor at $9,600 are sold at a price of *94*, plus accrued interest of *$90*, and less a brokerage commission of *$50*. The gain or loss may be computed as follows:

Proceeds from sale ($9,400 + $90 − $50)	$9,440
Less: Proceeds representing interest revenue	90
Sales price of investment in bonds	$9,350
Cost of investment in bonds	9,600
Loss on sale	$ 250

This sale should be recorded by the following journal entry:

Investment in bonds sold at a loss

Cash	9,440	
Loss on Sale of Marketable Securities	250	
Marketable Debt Securities		9,600
Bond Interest Revenue		90
Sold 10 bonds of Elk Corporation at 94 and accrued interest of $90, less broker's commission of $50.		

Balance Sheet Valuation of Marketable Securities

The market values of securities such as bonds and stocks fluctuate from day to day. An investor who sells an investment in marketable securities at a price above or below cost will recognize a gain or loss on the sale. But what if the investor continues to hold securities after a significant change in their market value? In this case, should any gain or loss be recognized in the financial statements? The answer depends on whether the securities are short-term or long-term investments and whether the change in market value is temporary in nature.

Short-term marketable securities should be shown as a current asset in the balance sheet at the *lower* of their aggregate cost and market value. The effect of the **lower-of-cost-and-market (LCM)** rule is to recognize losses from drops in market value without recognizing gains from rising prices.

Marketable securities classified as long-term investments are accounted for in the balance sheet by either the cost method or the equity method. The *cost method* is used for long-term *portfolio investments* where the investor is not able to exercise significant influence over the investee. The account title for this type of investment is commonly called Marketable Securities—Long-Term. The *equity method* is used for those long-term investments where *the investor is able to exercise significant influence over the investee*. The common account title for this type of investment is Investment in X Corporation. When there is a decline in the market value of these long-term investments that is other than a temporary decline, these investments should be shown in the balance sheet at their lower market value. Consequently, a lower market value is also used for long-term investments if the decline in market value is not temporary in nature.

The lower-of-cost-and-market rule produces *conservative results* in both the balance sheet and the income statement. In the balance sheet, the investment in marketable securities is shown at the lowest justifiable amount—that is, the lower of its cost and market value. In the income statement, declines in market value below cost immediately are recognized as losses. Increases in market value above cost or the carrying value (if lower), however, are not recognized until the securities are sold.

Accountants traditionally have applied different criteria in recognizing gains and losses. One of the basic principles in accounting is that gains shall not be recognized until they are *realized*, and the usual test of realization is the sale of the asset in question. Losses, on the other hand, are recognized as soon as *objective evidence* indicates that a loss has been incurred.

Applying the Lower-of-Cost-and-Market Rule: An Illustration

In applying the lower-of-cost-and-market rule, the total cost of the marketable securities is compared with their current market value, and the *lower* of these two amounts is used as the balance sheet valuation. If the market value is below cost, an entry is made to reduce the carrying value of the marketable securities to current market value and to recognize a *loss* for the amount of the market decline. The write-down of an investment in marketable securities to a market value below cost is an end-of-period adjusting entry and should be based upon market prices at the balance sheet date.

To illustrate the lower-of-cost-and-market adjustment, assume the following facts for the investment of Eagle Corporation at December 31, 2000:

	Cost	Market Value
Common stock of Adams Corporation	$100,000	$106,000
Common stock of Barnes Limited	60,000	52,000
Preferred stock of Parker Industries	200,000	182,000
Other marketable securities	25,000	25,000
Totals	$385,000	$365,000

Since the total market value of the securities in our example is less than their cost to Eagle Corporation, the balance sheet valuation would be the lower amount of $365,000. This downward adjustment of $20,000 means that a loss of $20,000 will be included in the determination of the year's net income. Also the $365,000 market value becomes the ***carrying value*** for these securities and is used as the "new cost" for future applications of the lower-of-cost-and-market rule. The balance sheet presentation would be:

Current assets:
Marketable securities (as the lower of cost and market,
cost —$385,000) $365,000

The significance of the carrying value deserves an explanation. Since the carrying value is considered to be the "new cost" for the marketable securities, if there is a further decline in market value, this carrying value will be adjusted to the lower market value.[1] However, if there is a recovery in market value, the recovery is not recognized because the market value is higher than the carrying value even though it is still lower than the original cost. For example, if the marketable securities of Eagle Corporation were held until December 31, 2001, and the market value were $380,000 (still $5,000 below the original cost of $385,000), these securities would be stated in the balance sheet at the carrying value of $365,000 because it is lower than the current market value of $380,000. Consequently, the recovery in market value of $15,000 was not recognized. This current practice of not recognizing the recovery in the decline of market value below cost lacks logical support.

Moreover, it is conceptually superior to report marketable securities at current market value, regardless of whether it is higher or lower than cost. Such reporting enhances comparison of marketable securities valuation among companies and provides a meaningful basis for evaluating the effects of management decision on acquiring, holding, or selling these securities. The gain and loss from changing market value can be labelled as "unrealized gain" and "unrealized loss." This will distinguish them from the "realized gain" and "realized loss" from sale of marketable securities. The "unrealized gains" and "unrealized losses" should be reported in the income statement.

---

[1] CICA, *CICA Handbook* (Toronto), section 3010.06

Presentation of Marketable Securities in Financial Statements

Gains and losses from the decline in market value of marketable securities or on the sale of marketable securities, as well as interest and dividend revenue, are types of nonoperating income. These items should be specifically identified in the income statement and shown after the determination of operating income.

Those marketable securities classified as current assets should be presented in the balance sheet at the lower of cost and market; those classified as long-term investments should be presented in the balance sheet at cost, unless the decline in market value is not temporary, in which case the lower of cost and market should be used.

We mentioned earlier that separate controlling accounts are usually used in the general ledger for marketable equity securities and marketable debt securities. In the balance sheet, however, these two types of investments are combined and shown under a single caption, such as **Marketable Securities**, or **Short-term Investments**.

Presentation of Investments That Are Not Readily Marketable Securities issued by small businesses may not be traded on securities exchanges and, therefore, may not have quoted market prices. These securities are not "readily marketable"; an investor owning such securities should classify the investment as long-term, rather than as a current asset. Also, such investments should be identified as "Other Long-Term Investments," rather than as marketable securities. As these securities do not have quoted market prices, the lower-of-cost-and-market rule is not applied. These investments normally are shown in the investor's balance sheet at **cost**.[2]

INVESTMENTS FOR PURPOSES OF SIGNIFICANT INFLUENCE OR CONTROL

An investor may acquire enough of a company's common stock to ***significantly influence or control*** that company's strategic operating, investing, and financing policies through the voting rights of the shares owned. Such large holdings of common stock create an important business relationship between the investor and the issuing company (called the ***investee***). Since investments of this type cannot be sold without disrupting this relationship, they are not included in the portfolio of marketable securities. Such investments are shown in the investor's balance sheet under the caption Long-Term Investments and are accounted for quite differently from an investment in marketable securities.

If an investor is able to exercise ***significant influence*** over the investee's management, dividends paid by the investee may no longer be a good measure of the investor's income from the investment. This is because the investor may influence the investee's dividend policy. In such cases, dividends paid by the investee are likely to reflect the ***investor's*** cash needs and income tax considerations, rather than the profitability of the investment.

---

[2] As with any asset valued at cost, the asset should be written down to an estimated recoverable amount if it becomes apparent that the original cost cannot be recovered.

For example, assume that Sigma Corporation owns 49% of the common stock of Davis Limited. For three years Davis is very profitable but pays no dividends, because Sigma has no need for additional cash. In the fourth year, Davis pays a large cash dividend to Sigma despite operating at a loss for that year. Clearly, it would be misleading for Sigma to report no investment income while the company it owns is operating profitably, and then to show large investment income in a year when Davis incurred a net loss.

The investor does not have to own 49% of the common stock of the investee to exercise a significant degree of influence. An investor with much less than 49% of the voting stock may have significant influence, since the remaining shares are not likely to vote as an organized block. In the absence of other evidence (such as another large shareholder), ownership of **20% or more** (but below 50%) of the investee's common stock is viewed as giving the investor significant influence over the investee's policies and operations. In such cases, the investor should account for the investment by using the ***equity method***.[3]

The Equity Method

LO 2: Account for an investment in common stock by the equity method.

When the **equity method** is used, an investment in common stock is first recorded at cost but later is adjusted each year for changes in the shareholders' equity in the investee. As the investee earns net income, the shareholders' equity in the company increases. An investor using the equity method recognizes its ***proportionate share of the investee's net income*** as an increase in the carrying value of its investment. A proportionate share of a net loss reported by the investee is recognized as a decrease in the investment.

When the investee pays dividends, the shareholders' equity in the company is reduced. The investor, therefore, treats dividends received from the investee as a conversion of part of the investment into cash, thus reducing the carrying value of the investment. In effect, the equity method causes the carrying value of the investment (the amount reported in the balance sheet) to rise and fall with changes in the book value of the shares. As mentioned earlier, if the market value is lower than cost (or carrying value) and the decline is not temporary, the lower market value should be used.[4]

Illustration of the Equity Method Assume that Cove Corporation purchases 10,000 shares (25%) of the common stock of Bay Limited for $200,000, which corresponds to 25% of the underlying book value of Bay. During the following year, Bay earns net income of $120,000 and pays dividends of $80,000. Cove Corporation would account for its investment as follows:

---

[3] CICA, *CICA Handbook* (Toronto), section 3050.06.
[4] Ibid., section 3050.25.

Investment in Bay Limited	200,000	
Cash		200,000
To record acquisition of 25% of the common stock of Bay Limited		

Investment in Bay Limited	30,000	
Investment Income		30,000
To increase the investment for 25% share of net income earned by Bay Limited (25% × $120,000).		

Cash	20,000	
Investment in Bay Limited		20,000
To reduce investment for dividends received from Bay Limited (25% × $80,000).		

The net result of these entries by Cove Corporation is to increase the carrying value of the Investment in Bay Limited account by $10,000, to $210,000. This corresponds to 25% of the increase reported in Bay Limited's retained earnings during the period [25% × ($120,000 - $80,000) = $10,000]. Cove Corporation **reports in its balance sheet** the investment in Bay Limited at $210,000 under the caption Long-Term Investments.

In this illustration of the equity method, we have made several simplifying assumptions: (1) Cove Corporation purchased the stock of Bay Limited at a price equal to the underlying book value; (2) Bay Limited had issued common stock only and the number of shares outstanding did not change during the year; and (3) there were no intercompany transactions between Cove Corporation and Bay Limited. If we were to change any of these assumptions, the computations in applying the equity method would become more complicated. Application of the equity method in more complex situations is discussed in advanced accounting courses.

Parent and Subsidiary Companies

LO 3: Explain how a parent company "controls" its subsidiaries.

A corporation that owns **all or a majority** of another corporation's outstanding voting stock is called a **parent company**, and the corporation that is wholly owned or majority-held is called a **subsidiary**.[5] Through the voting rights of the owned shares, the parent company can elect the board of directors of the subsidiary company and thereby **control** the subsidiary's resources and policies.[6] In effect, the **affiliated companies** (the parent and its subsidiaries) function as a **single economic unit** controlled by the directors of the parent company. This relationship is illustrated in the following diagram.

---

[5] Ownership of a majority of a company's voting stock means holding at least 50% plus one share.

[6] Control may exist even when ownership of voting stock is less than 50%, as discussed in *CICA Handbook*, section 1590. These exceptional cases are topics for advanced accounting courses.

PARENT COMPANY AND TWO SUBSIDIARIES

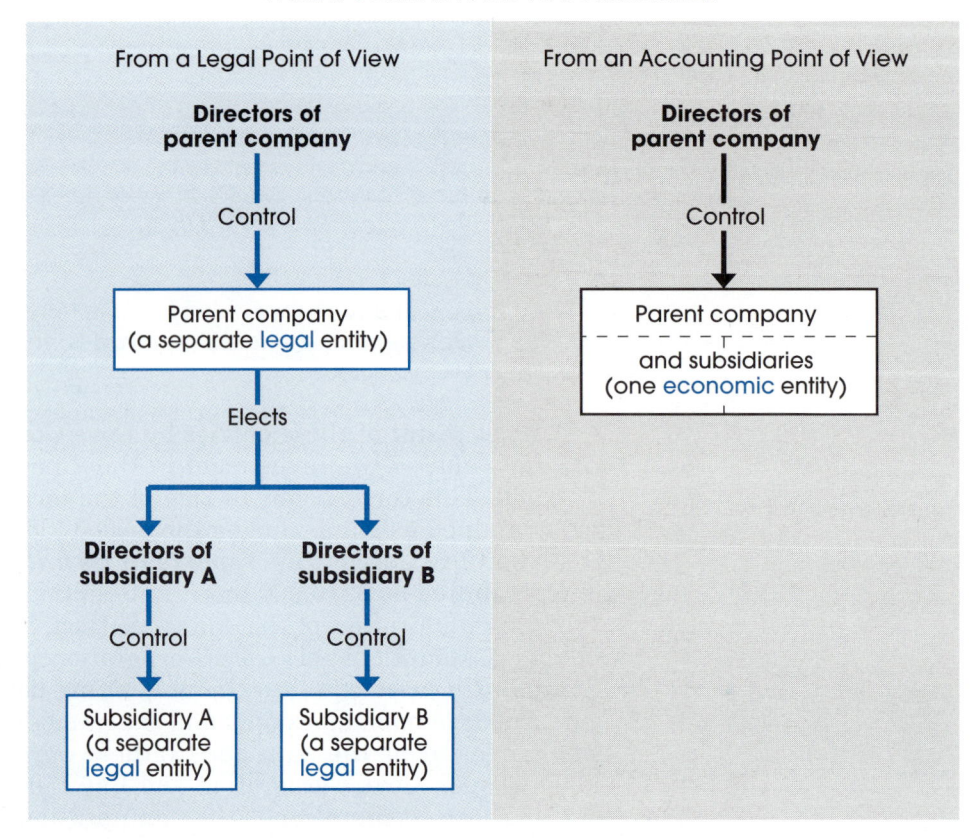

From a Legal Point of View

Directors of parent company
↓ Control
Parent company (a separate *legal* entity)
↓ Elects
Directors of subsidiary A / Directors of subsidiary B
↓ Control / ↓ Control
Subsidiary A (a separate *legal* entity) / Subsidiary B (a separate *legal* entity)

From an Accounting Point of View

Directors of parent company
↓ Control
Parent company and subsidiaries (one *economic* entity)

For simplicity, our illustration shows a parent company with only two subsidiaries. It is not unusual, however, for a parent company to own and control a dozen or more subsidiaries.

There are a number of economic, legal, and income tax advantages that encourage large business organizations to operate through subsidiaries rather than through a single legal entity. Although we think of BCE Inc. and Noranda Inc. as single companies, each of these organizations is really a parent company with many subsidiaries. Since the parent company in each case controls the resources and policies of its subsidiaries, it is logical for us to consider an organization such as BCE as one *economic* entity.

CASE IN POINT

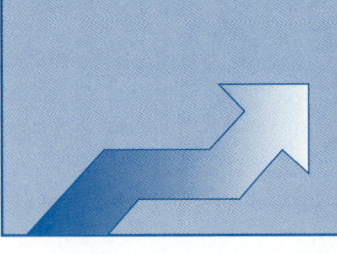

The subsidiaries of BCE Inc. include: Bell Canada (which owns 100% of Bell Sygma Inc.), BCE Mobile Communications Inc., New Tel Enterprises Ltd., Northern Telecom Ltd., Northern Telephone Ltd., Northwestel Inc., and Télébec Ltée. Noranda Inc.'s subsidiaries include: Canadian Hunter Explorations Ltd., Noranda Aluminium Inc., Noranda Forest Inc., Noranda Metallurgy Inc., Noranda Mining and Explorations Inc., and Novicourt Inc. These subsidiaries are among the top 100 subsidiaries in Canada, with revenues ranging from $66 million to $17.5 billion, and assets from $132 million to $15 billion.

Growth through the Acquisition of Subsidiaries

A parent company may acquire another corporation as a subsidiary by purchasing more than 50% of the other corporation's voting stock. The purchase of one corporation by another may be termed a **merger**, a **business combination**, an *acquisition*, or a *takeover*. The acquisition of new subsidiaries is a fast and effective way for a company to grow, to diversify into new product lines, and to acquire new technology. In recent years, the price tag for these acquisitions and mergers has run into billions of dollars.

> **CASE IN POINT**
>
> Just a few well-known billion-dollar acquisitions or mergers: Campeau Corporation greatly increased its size and diversified its operations by two takeovers of two large American companies—Allied Stores Corporation for $5 billion ($3.6 billion U.S.) and Federated Department Stores Incorporated at $8.2 billion ($6.6 billion U.S.). Imasco Limited entered the financial institution business by acquiring Genstar Corporation for the control of Canada Trust for $2.6 billion. Noranda Inc. teamed up with Trelleborg AB of Sweden to acquire Falconbridge for a total price tag of $2.2 billion, thereby adding nickel as another core business and increasing substantially the copper and zinc production and reserves. Stone Container Corporation (U.S.) extended its operation to Canada by its takeover of Consolidated Bathurst Inc. for $2.6 billion. Nova Corporation expanded and diversified its operations by the acquisition of Polysar Energy and Chemical Corporation for $1.4 billion, and later Nova's merger with TransCanada Pipelines, a $15.6 billion deal. The $1.6 billion merger of Molson and Carling O'Keefe Breweries propelled the merged company to the top position in its industry. Interprovincial Pipe Line expanded its scope of operation by acquiring Home Oil Limited for $1.1 billion. The acquisition of London Insurance by Great-West Life for $2.8 billion gave it the dominant position in the life insurance industry. Cambridge Shopping Centres Ltd.'s acquisition of Markborough Properties Inc. for $1.2 billion greatly expanded its operations. Finally, the $92 billion (U.S.) merger of Daimler-Benz and Chrysler is the largest industrial merger.

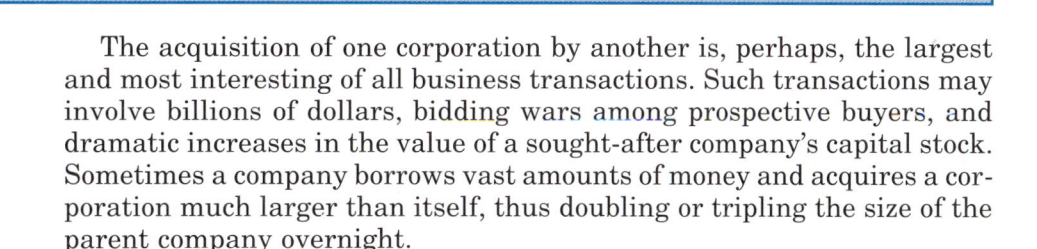

The acquisition of one corporation by another is, perhaps, the largest and most interesting of all business transactions. Such transactions may involve billions of dollars, bidding wars among prospective buyers, and dramatic increases in the value of a sought-after company's capital stock. Sometimes a company borrows vast amounts of money and acquires a corporation much larger than itself, thus doubling or tripling the size of the parent company overnight.

Financial Statements for a Consolidated Economic Entity

LO 4: Describe the distinctive feature of consolidated financial statements.

Because the parent company and its subsidiaries are separate legal entities, separate financial statements are prepared for each company. In the *separate* financial statements of the parent company, the subsidiaries appear only as assets classified as long-term investments. Since the affiliated companies function as a single economic unit, the parent company also prepares **consolidated financial statements** that show the financial position and operating results of the *entire group of companies*.[7] It is these consolidated financial statements that are of greatest interest to the investing public and that are included in the parent company's annual report to its shareholders.

In consolidated financial statements, the parent company and its subsidiaries are viewed as *one economic* or *business entity*. The distinctive feature of these statements is that the assets, liabilities, revenue, and expenses of *two or more separate legal entities* are combined in a single set of financial statements. For example, the amount shown as cash in a consolidated balance sheet is the total of the cash owned by all of the affiliated companies. Liabilities of the parent and subsidiary companies also are combined. Similarly, in a consolidated income statement, the revenue and expenses of the affiliated companies are combined to show the operating results of the consolidated economic entity.

Shareholders and creditors of the parent company have a vital interest in the financial results of all operations under the parent company's control, including those conducted by subsidiaries. Therefore, it is the consolidated financial statements that are included in the parent company's annual and quarterly reports to shareholders.

There are many interesting accounting issues involved in the preparation of consolidated financial statements. A brief introduction to some of these issues is provided in the following section of this chapter. However, *no special problems are posed in reading a set of consolidated financial statements*. The number of separate legal entities within the consolidated organization is an unimportant detail. For most purposes, consolidated financial statements may be interpreted as if the parent company and its subsidiaries *were just one organization*.

CONSOLIDATED FINANCIAL STATEMENTS: CONCEPTS AND MECHANICS

Methods of Consolidation

The purchase of an entire corporation usually is a very big investment. To accumulate the money necessary to buy another corporation, the parent company often needs to issue capital stock or bonds payable. If the parent company pays cash or issues debt securities to purchase the other corporation's capital stock, the business combination is accounted for by the **purchase method**.

A second method of accounting for a business combination is called a *pooling of interests*. The pooling method may be appropriate if the stock

---

[7] In the past, some subsidiaries were omitted from the consolidated financial statements for such reasons as the subsidiaries being engaged in business activities substantially different from those of the parent company. New rules, however, require every subsidiary controlled by the parent company to be included in the consolidated statements unless this control will be temporary. In this case, the investment in the subsidiary is shown in the balance sheet at cost and is classified as a long-term investment; dividends received are recorded as revenue.

of a subsidiary is obtained in direct exchange for shares of the parent company's capital stock and neither company can be identified as the acquirer.[8] A key aspect of such a transaction is that the former shareholders of the subsidiary *become shareholders in the parent corporation*.

The vast majority of business combinations are viewed as purchases, rather than poolings. In this textbook, we shall illustrate only the purchase method of accounting for business combinations. The special case of a pooling of interests will be covered in more advanced accounting courses.

Consolidated financial statements are prepared by combining the amounts that appear in the separate financial statements of the parent and subsidiary companies. In the combining process, however, certain adjustments are made to *eliminate the effects of intercompany transactions* and thus to reflect the assets, liabilities, and shareholders' equity as those of a single economic entity.

LO 5: Explain why intercompany transactions must be eliminated as a step in preparing consolidated financial statements.

Intercompany Transactions The term **intercompany transactions** refers to transactions between affiliated companies. These transactions may include, for example, the sale of merchandise, the leasing of property, and the making of loans. When the affiliated companies are viewed separately, these transactions may create assets and liabilities for the individual companies. However, when the affiliated companies are viewed as a single business entity, these assets and liabilities are merely the result of internal transfers within the business organization and should *not appear* in the consolidated financial statements.

For example, if a subsidiary borrows money from the parent company, a note payable will appear as a liability in the balance sheet of the subsidiary company and a note receivable will appear as an asset in the separate balance sheet of the parent. When the two companies are viewed as a single consolidated entity, however, this "loan" is nothing more than a transfer of cash from one part of the business to another. Transferring assets between two parts of a single business entity does not create either a receivable or a payable for that entity. Therefore, the parent company's note receivable and the subsidiary's note payable should not appear in the consolidated financial statements.

Preparing Consolidated Financial Statements Separate accounting records are maintained for each company in an affiliated group, but no accounting records are maintained for the consolidated entity. The amounts shown in consolidated financial statements *do not come from a ledger;* they are determined on a *working paper* by combining the amounts of like items on the financial statements of the affiliated companies. For example, the inventories of all the affiliated companies are combined into one amount for inventories. Entries to eliminate the effects of intercompany transactions are made *only* on this working paper. These elimination entries are *not recorded in the accounting records* of either the parent company or its subsidiaries.

---

[8] CICA, *CICA Handbook* (Toronto), section 1580.08.

Consolidation at the Date of Acquisition

LO 6: Prepare a consolidated balance sheet.

To illustrate the basic principles of consolidation, we will now prepare a consolidated balance sheet. Assume that on January 1 Post Corporation purchases for cash 100% of the capital stock of Sun Limited at its book value of $3,000,000. (The shares are purchased from Sun's former shareholders.) Also on this date, Post Corporation lends $200,000 cash to Sun, receiving a note as evidence of the loan. Immediately after these two transactions, the separate balance sheet accounts of Post Corporation and Sun Limited are as shown in the first two columns of the following working paper:

POST CORPORATION AND SUBSIDIARY
Working Paper—Consolidated Balance Sheet
January 1, 19__ (Date of Acquisition)

	Post Corporation	Sun Limited	Intercompany Eliminations Debit	Intercompany Eliminations Credit	Consolidated Balance Sheet
Cash & cash equivalents	500,000	350,000			850,000
Notes receivable	200,000			(b)200,000	—
Accounts receivable (net)	300,000	400,000			700,000
Inventories	1,100,000	950,000			2,050,000
Investment In Sun Limited	3,000,000			(a) 3,000,000	—
Plant & equipment (net)	2,800,000	1,800,000			4,600,000
Totals	7,900,000	3,500,000			8,200,000
Notes payable		200,000	(b)200,000		—
Accounts payable	425,000	300,000			725,000
Capital Stock—					
Post Corporation	4,000,000				4,000,000
Sun Limited		2,000,000	(a)2,000,000		—
Retained earnings—					
Post Corporation	3,475,000				3,475,000
Sun Limited		1,000,000	(a)1,000,000		—
Totals	7,900,000	3,500,000	3,200,000	3,200,000	8,200,000

Explanation of elimination:
(a) To eliminate the Investment in Sun Limited against Sun Limited's shareholders' equity.
(b) To eliminate intercompany note receivable against related note payable.

Intercompany Eliminations

Before the balance sheet amounts of Post Corporation and Sun Limited are combined, entries are made in the working paper to eliminate the effects of intercompany transactions. Intercompany eliminations may be classified into three basic types:

1. Elimination of intercompany stock ownership
2. Elimination of intercompany debt
3. Elimination of intercompany revenue and expenses

The first two types of eliminations are illustrated in our example of Post Corporation and Sun Limited. The elimination of intercompany revenue and expenses will be discussed later in this chapter.

To understand the need for elimination entries, we must adopt the viewpoint of the consolidated entity, in which Post Corporation and Sun Limited are regarded as two business operations within a single company.

Entry (a): Elimination of Intercompany Stock Ownership The purpose of entry (a) in the working paper on page 876 is to eliminate from the consolidated balance sheet both the asset account and the shareholders' equity accounts representing the parent company's ownership of the subsidiary.

Post Corporation's ownership interest in Sun Limited appears in the *separate* balance sheets of both corporations. In the parent's balance sheet, this ownership interest is shown as the asset Investment in Sun Limited. In the separate balance sheet of the subsidiary, the parent company's ownership interest is represented by the shareholders' equity accounts Capital Stock and Retained Earnings. In the *consolidated* balance sheet, however, this "ownership interest" is neither an asset nor a part of shareholders' equity.

From the viewpoint of the single consolidated entity, *there are no shareholders in Sun Limited*. "Shareholders" are outside investors who have an ownership interest in the business. All of Sun's capital stock is "internally owned" by another part of the consolidated entity. A company's "ownership" of its own stock does not create either an asset or shareholders' equity. Therefore the asset account Investment in Sun Limited and Sun Limited's related shareholders' equity accounts must be eliminated from the consolidated balance sheet.

Entry (b): Elimination of Intercompany Debt When Post Corporation loaned $200,000 to Sun Limited, the parent company recorded a note receivable and the subsidiary recorded a note payable. This "receivable" and "payable" exist only when Post Corporation and Sun Limited are viewed as two separate entities. When both corporations are viewed as a single company, this "loan" is merely a transfer of cash from one part of the business to another. Such internal transfers of assets do not create either a receivable or a payable for the consolidated entity. Therefore, entry (b) is made to eliminate Post Corporation's note receivable and Sun Limited's note payable from the consolidated balance sheet.

After the necessary eliminations have been entered in the working paper, the remaining balance sheet amounts of Post Corporation and Sun Limited are combined to determine the assets, liabilities, and shareholders' equity of the consolidated entity. The following consolidated balance sheet is then prepared from the last column of the working paper.

POST CORPORATION AND SUBSIDIARY
Consolidated Balance Sheet
January 1, 19__

Assets

Current assets:	
Cash & cash equivalents	$ 850,000
Accounts receivable (net)	700,000
Inventories	2,050,000
Total current assets	$3,600,000
Plant & equipment (net)	4,600,000
Total assets	$8,200,000

Liabilities & Shareholders' Equity

Current liabilities:		
Accounts Payable		$ 725,000
Shareholders' equity:		
Capital stock	$4,000,000	
Retained earnings	3,475,000	
Total shareholders' equity		7,475,000
Total liabilities & shareholders' equity		$8,200,000

Notice the shareholders' equity is that of the parent company

Acquisition of Subsidiary's Stock at a Price above Book Value

When a parent company purchases a controlling interest in a subsidiary, it usually pays a price for the shares *in excess of* their book value.[9] We cannot ignore a difference between the cost of the parent company's investment and the underlying book value of these shares. In consolidation, the parent's investment is offset against the shareholders' equity accounts of the subsidiary, and if the two amounts are not equal, we must determine what the difference between them represents.

To illustrate, let's use the preceding example with one significant change. Assume that on January 1 Post Corporation purchases all of the outstanding shares of Sun Limited for $3,400,000 instead of $3,000,000. On this date, Sun Limited's balance sheet shows total shareholders' equity of $3,000,000, consisting of capital stock of $2,000,000 and retained earnings of $1,000,000. In preparing the elimination entry on the working papers for consolidated balance sheet, we must determine what to do with the $400,000 difference between the price paid, $3,400,000, and the shareholders' equity (book value) of Sun Limited, $3,000,000.

Why would Post Corporation pay a price in excess of book value for Sun Limited's stock? Post's management must believe that either (1) the fair market value of certain specific assets of Sun (such as land or buildings) is in excess of book value or (2) Sun's future earnings prospects are so favourable as to justify paying $400,000 for Sun's unrecorded **goodwill**.

If we assume that the $400,000 represents unrecorded goodwill, entry (*a*) in the working papers to eliminate Post Corporation's investment account against the shareholders' equity accounts of Sun Limited would be:

---

[9] The parent company also might acquire the shares of the subsidiary at a price below book value. This situation will be discussed in an advanced accounting course.

Capital Stock—Sun Limited			2,000,000	
Retained Earnings—Sun Limited			1,000,000	
Goodwill			400,000	
Investment in Sun Limited (Post Corporation's asset account)				3,400,000
To eliminate the cost of Post Corporation's 100% interest in Sun Limited against Sun's shareholders' equity accounts and to recognize Sun Limited's unrecorded goodwill.				

Note: This entry is made only in the working papers, not in the accounting records of either company

Although we have shown this entry in general journal form, it actually would be made ***only*** in the Intercompany Eliminations columns of the working paper for a consolidated balance sheet, as illustrated below:

POST CORPORATION AND SUBSIDIARY
Working Paper—Consolidated Balance Sheet
January 1, 19__ (Date of Acquisition)

	Post Corporation	Sun Limited	Intercompany Eliminations Debit	Intercompany Eliminations Credit	Consolidated Balance Sheet
Cash & cash equivalents	100,000	350,000			450,000
Notes receivable	200,000			(b)200,000	—
Accounts receivable (net)	300,000	400,000			700,000
Inventories	1,100,000	950,000			2,050,000
Investment in Sun Limited	3,400,000			(a)3,400,000	
Plant & equipment (net)	2,800,000	1,800,000			4,600,000
Goodwill			(a) 400,000		400,000
Totals	7,900,000	3,500,000			8,200,000
Notes payable		200,000	(b) 200,000		—
Accounts payable	425,000	300,000			725,000
Capital stock—					
Post Corporation	4,000,000				4,000,000
Sun Limited		2,000,000	(a) 2,000,000		
Retained earnings—					
Post Corporation	3,475,000				3,475,000
Sun Limited		1,000,000	(a) 1,000,000		
Totals	7,900,000	3,500,000	3,600,000	3,600,000	8,200,000

Explanation of elimination:

(a) To eliminate the Investment in Sun Limited against Sun Limited's shareholders' equity, and to recognize goodwill.

(b) To eliminate intercompany note receivable against related note payable.

The following consolidated balance sheet is then prepared from the last column of the working paper. It is important to note that the $400,000 of goodwill will appear as an asset only in the ***consolidated*** balance sheet, ***not*** in the accounting records of Sun Limited or Post Corporation.[10] This asset will be amortized to expense over its useful life.

---

[10] If specific assets of Sun Limited had been undervalued, the $400,000 would be allocated to increase the valuation of those assets in the consolidated working papers. The revaluation of specific assets is beyond the scope of our introductory discussion.

Notice that goodwill appears only in the consolidated balance sheet

POST CORPORATION AND SUBSIDIARY
Consolidated Balance Sheet
January 1, 19__

Assets

Current assets:	
Cash & cash equivalents	$ 450,000
Accounts receivable (net)	700,000
Inventories	2,050,000
Total current assets	$3,200,000
Plant & equipment (net)	4,600,000
Goodwill	400,000
Total assets	$8,200,000

Liabilities & Shareholders' Equity

Current liabilities:		
Accounts payable		$ 725,000
Shareholders' equity:		
Capital stock	$4,000,000	
Retained earnings	3,475,000	
Total shareholders' equity		7,475,000
Total liabilities & shareholders' equity		$8,200,000

Less Than 100% Ownership in Subsidiary

If a parent company owns a majority interest in a subsidiary but less than 100% of the outstanding shares, a new kind of ownership equity known as the **non-controlling (minority) interest** will appear in the consolidated balance sheet. This non-controlling interest represents the ownership interest in the subsidiary held by shareholders other than the parent company.

When there are non-controlling (minority) shareholders, only the portion of the subsidiary's shareholders' equity owned by the parent company is eliminated. The remainder of the shareholders' equity of the subsidiary is included in the consolidated balance sheet under the caption Non-controlling Interest.

To illustrate, assume that on January 1 Park Limited purchases 75% of the outstanding capital stock of Sims Corporation for $150,000 cash, an amount equal to 75% of the book value (shareholders' equity) of Sims. The working paper to prepare a consolidated balance sheet on the date that control of Sims Corporation is acquired appears as follows:

PARK LIMITED AND SUBSIDIARY
Working Paper—Consolidated Balance Sheet
January 1, 20__ (Date of Acquisition)

	Park Limited	Sims Corporation	Intercompany Eliminations Debit	Intercompany Eliminations Credit	Consolidated Balance Sheet
Cash	200,000	50,000			250,000
Other assets	500,000	210,000			710,000
Investment in Sims Corporation	150,000			(a) 150,000	
Totals	850,000	260,000			960,000
Liabilities	250,000	60,000			310,000
Capital stock—					
Park Limited	500,000				500,000
Sims Corporation		120,000	(a) 90,000 (b) 30,000		
Retained earnings—					
Park Limited	100,000				100,000
Sims Corporation		80,000	(a) 60,000 (b) 20,000		
Non-controlling interest (25% of $200,000)				(b) 50,000	50,000
Totals	850,000	260,000	200,000	200,000	960,000

Explanation of elimination:

(a) To eliminate Park Limited's investment in 75% of Sims Corporation's shareholders' equity.

(b) To classify the remaining 25% of Sims Corporation's shareholders' equity as a non-controlling interest.

Entry (a) in this working paper offsets Park's asset, Investment in Sims Corporation, against 75% of Sims Corporation's capital stock and retained earnings. The purpose of this entry is to eliminate intercompany stock ownership from the assets and shareholders' equity shown in the consolidated balance sheet. Entry (b) reclassifies the remaining 25% of Sims Corporation's capital stock and retained earnings into a special account entitled Non-controlling Interest. The CICA recommends that the non-controlling interest appear separately from the shareholders' equity section of the consolidated balance sheet usually between total liabilities and shareholders' equity.[11]

Non-Controlling Interest Why is the non-controlling interest shown separately in the consolidated balance sheet instead of being included in the amounts shown for capital stock and retained earnings? The reason for this separate presentation is to distinguish between the ownership equity of the controlling shareholders and the equity of the non-controlling shareholders.

The shareholders in the parent company own the controlling interest in the consolidated entity. Because these shareholders elect the directors of the parent company, they control the entire group of affiliated companies.

---

[11] CICA, *CICA Handbook* (Toronto), section 1600.69.

The non-controlling interest, however, has **no control** over any of the affiliated companies. Because they own shares only in a subsidiary, they cannot vote for the directors of the parent company. Also, they can never outvote the parent shareholder (the parent company) in electing the directors or establishing the policies of the subsidiary.

The non-controlling shareholders receive 25% of the dividends declared by Sims but do not participate in dividends declared by the parent company. The controlling shareholders, on the other hand, receive all the dividends declared by Park but do not receive directly dividends declared by the subsidiary.

Consolidated Income Statement

At date of acquisition of a controlling interest, the consolidated balance sheet is the only appropriate financial statement, as no revenue or expenses have yet occurred. Once operations begin, however, a complete set of four corporate financial statements is required: consolidated income statement, consolidated statement of retained earnings, consolidated balance sheet, and consolidated cash flow statement. We shall discuss briefly some of the basic concepts involved in the preparation of a consolidated income statement.

A *consolidated income statement* is prepared simply by combining the revenue and expense accounts of the parent and subsidiary. Revenue or expenses that are the result of *intercompany transactions* are eliminated because they do not change the net assets from a consolidated viewpoint—they merely reflect transfers of assets from one affiliated company to another. Assume a subsidiary pays $12,000 to its parent company for rent of warehouse facilities during the year. The subsidiary's $12,000 rent expense as well as the parent's $12,000 rental income should be disregarded (eliminated) in reporting the results of operations for the consolidated entity. This rental transaction neither increased nor decreased the net assets *of the consolidated entity*.

Elimination of Intercompany Revenue and Expenses Some of the more common examples of intercompany items that should be eliminated in preparing a consolidated income statement are:

- Sales to affiliated companies
- Cost of goods sold resulting from sales to affiliated companies
- Interest expense on loans from affiliated companies
- Interest revenue on loans made to affiliated companies
- Rent or other revenue received for services rendered to affiliated companies
- Rent or other expenses paid for services received from affiliated companies

Because of the complexity of the intercompany eliminations, the preparation of a consolidated income statement, a consolidated statement of retained earnings, and a consolidated cash flow statement are topics appropriately deferred to an advanced accounting course.

CHAPTER 17 INVESTMENTS IN CORPORATE SECURITIES

Accounting for Investments in Corporate Securities: A Summary

In this chapter, we have discussed the accounting principles applied to investments in corporate securities under various circumstances. The accounting treatment accorded to investments in **bonds** depends upon whether the investment is viewed as a current asset or a long-term investment. The accounting treatment of an investment in **stocks** depends primarily upon the ***degree of influence*** or ***control*** that the investor is able to exercise over the issuing corporation. These relationships are summarized as follows:

Situation	Accounting Practice
Investments in bonds:	
Classified as current asset	Combined with current asset portfolio of stocks and shown as marketable securities. Interest revenue accrues each period. Difference between cost and maturity value (discount or premium) generally is not amortized.
Classified as a long-term investment	Combined with long-term portfolio of stocks and shown as marketable securities, under the classification Long-Term Investments. Interest revenue accrues each period. Difference between cost and maturity value is amortized.
Investment in stocks:	
Noninfluential interest (ownership of less than 20% of the voting stock)	(Readily marketable) Shown as a marketable security (may be classified as a current asset or a long-term investment). For those classified as current assets, each portfolio is valued at lower-of-cost-and-market. For those classified as long-term investments, each portfolio is valued at cost; when the decline in the lower market value is not temporary in nature, the lower market value is used. Dividends recorded as revenue when received. (Not readily marketable) Shown as a long-term investment and carried at cost or estimated recoverable amount. Dividends recorded as revenue when received.
Influential but noncontrolling interest (ownership from 20% to 49% of the voting stock)	Shown as a long-term investment, accounted for by the equity method. A lower market value is used if the decline in market value is not temporary in nature.
Controlling interest (ownership of more than 50% of voting stock)	The assets, liabilities, revenue, and expenses of controlled subsidiary are combined with those of the parent corporation in consolidated financial statements.

End-of-Chapter Review

Key Terms Introduced or Emphasized in Chapter 17

Business combination *(p.873)* The combining of two or more companies into a single economic or business entity. Also called a ***merger***, an ***acquisition***, or a ***takeover***.

Consolidated financial statements *(p.874)* A set of statements presenting the combined financial position and operating results of a consolidated entity consisting of a parent company and one or more subsidiaries.

Equity method *(p.870)* The method of accounting used when the investment by one corporation in another is large enough to significantly influence the policies of the ***investee***. The investor recognizes as investment income its proportionate share of the investee's net income, rather than considering dividends received as income.

Intercompany transactions *(p.875)* Transactions between two affiliated companies. The effects of intercompany transactions, such as intercompany loans, are eliminated as a step in preparing consolidated financial statements.

Lower-of-cost-and-market (LCM) *(p.867)* The conservative practice of valuing marketable securities in the balance sheet at the lower of total cost and current market value.

Marketable securities *(p.863)* Investments in stocks (equity securities) and bonds (debt securities). These are highly liquid investments that may be sold at any time. Classified as a current asset, second only to cash in liquidity.

Non-controlling (minority) interest *(p.880)* Shares of a subsidiary owned by investors other than the parent.

Parent company *(p.871)* A corporation that owns a controlling interest in another company.

Purchase method *(p.874)* The method used in preparing consolidated financial statements when the parent company has purchased the shares of its subsidiary by paying cash or issuing debt securities. The purchase method is not used for those special transactions that qualify as a ***pooling of interests***.

Subsidiary *(p.871)* A corporation in which a controlling stock interest is held by another corporation (the parent).

Self-Test Questions

The answers to these questions appear on page 898.

1. During, 2000, Bonner Company bought and sold a short-term investment in $200,000 face value, 9% bonds that pay interest each April 1 and October 1. Bonner purchased the bonds at 98 plus accrued interest on February 1, 2000, and held the bonds until December 1, 2000, when the entire investment was sold for $200,000, including accrued interest. Each of the following is true, *except*:
   a. Bonner recognizes bond interest revenue of $15,000 for 2000.
   b. Bonner paid a total of $202,000 to acquire the investment on February 1, 2000.
   c. Bonner recognizes a gain of $1,000 on the sale of these marketable securities on December 1, 2000.
   d. Bonner received semiannual interest cheques in the amounts of $3,000 on April 1 and $9,000 on October 1.

2. Early in 2000, Rodgers Corp. purchased for $1,000,000 several marketable equity securities as a short-term investment. The market value of this investment was $900,000 at the end of 2000, $990,000 at the end of 2001, and $1,180,000 at the end of 2002. Based on these facts:
   a. Rodgers will recognize in its income statement a loss of $100,000 in 2000, and a gain of $90,000 in both 2001 and 2002.

b. At the end of 2001, Rodgers will recognize a gain of $90,000.
   c. In 2002, Rodgers will report the investment in the balance sheet at $1,000,000.
   d. Rodgers will recognize in its 2000 income statement a loss of $100,000.

3. Which of the following is *true* with regard to investments in corporate securities:
   a. When an investor acquires more than 20% of the common stock of a company, the investment is no longer classified as a marketable security even if it is traded on the stock exchanges.
   b. An investor who owns more than 20% of the outstanding bonds of a company should account for this investment by using the equity method.
   c. Whenever an investor owns less than 50% of the common stock of a corporation, the investment is valued at the lower-of-cost-and-market value.
   d. Regardless of percentage ownership, an investor in the common stock of another corporation records dividends as revenue when they are received.

4. On January 1, 2001, Stockdale Limited purchased 30% (30,000 shares) of the common stock of Equus Inc. for $600,000. At December 31, 2001, Equus reported net income of $200,000 and paid cash dividends of $80,000. At December 31, 2001, Equus' stock is trading at $19 per share. With regard to this investment, Stockdale's financial statements for 2001 should report:
   a. Dividend revenue of $24,000.
   b. Investment in Equus, Inc., of $636,000.
   c. Investment income of $36,000.
   d. A loss on marketable securities of $30,000.

5. When consolidated financial statements are issued by a parent and a subsidiary:
   a. The consolidated balance sheet includes the shareholders' equity accounts of both the parent and the subsidiary.
   b. Intercompany transactions are reported in separate sections of the income statement and the balance sheet.
   c. There is no need for the parent and the subsidiary to maintain separate accounting records or prepare separate financial statements.
   d. Non-controlling interest appears in the consolidated balance sheet whenever the parent does not own 100% of the outstanding shares of the subsidiary.

Assignment Material

Discussion Questions

1. Why do corporations invest in the securities issued by others?
2. Why are investments in marketable securities usually regarded as current assets?
3. Why must an investor who owns numerous marketable securities maintain a marketable securities subsidiary ledger?
4. If an investor buys a bond between interest dates, he or she pays as a part of the purchase price the accrued interest since the last interest date. On the other hand, if the investor buys a share of common or preferred stock, no "accrued dividend" is added to the quoted price. Explain why this difference exists.
5. Should stock dividends received be considered revenue to an investor? Explain.
6. In the current asset section of its balance sheet at December 31, 2000, Soho Industries shows marketable securities at a market value of $3,000,000, which is $190,000 below cost. If the market value of these securities rises by $250,000 during 2001, how should Soho Industries account for such an increase in its 2001 income statement under current practice? Is it conceptually acceptable?
7. Ancaster Corporation has a large investment in stocks and bonds. The market value of this investment is significantly below cost at December 31, 2001, but is slightly above cost at April 30, 2002. Explain how Ancaster should value this investment in the balance sheet if it is (a) a short-term investment (b) a long-term portfolio investment.
8. When should investors use the equity method to account for an investment in common stock?
9. Dividends on stock owned are usually recognized as income when they are received. Does an investor using the *equity method* to account for an investment in common stock follow this policy? Explain fully.
10. When the equity method is used to account for an investment in common stock that is traded on organized exchanges, is the investment adjusted to the lower-of-cost-and-market at the end of each accounting period? Explain your answer.
11. Alexander Corporation owns 80% of the outstanding stock of Benton Limited. Explain the basis for the assumption that these two companies constitute a single economic entity operating under unified control.
12. What are consolidated financial statements? Explain briefly how these statements are prepared.
13. List the three basic types of intercompany eliminations that should be made as a step in the preparation of consolidated financial statements.
14. Explain why the price paid to acquire a controlling interest in a subsidiary company may be different from the book value of the equity acquired.

15. The following items appear on the consolidated balance sheet: "Non-controlling interest in subsidiary... $620,000." Explain the nature of this item, and where you would expect to find it on the consolidated balance sheet.

16. Briefly explain when a business combination is viewed as a **purchase** and when it might be viewed as a **pooling of interests**.

17. As a general rule, when are consolidated financial statements appropriate?

18. What groups of investors are likely to be primarily interested in consolidated financial statements? Why?

Exercises

EXERCISE 17-1
Accounting Terminology
(LO 1–6)

Listed below are nine technical accounting terms emphasized in this chapter:

Consolidated financial statements
Lower-of-cost-and-market
Elimination of inter-company transactions
Parent company
Non-controlling interest
Equity method
Goodwill
Subsidiary
Marketable securities

Each of the following statements may (or may not) describe one of these technical terms. For each statement, indicate the accounting term described, or answer "None" if the statement does not correctly describe any of the terms.

a. A separate legal entity owned and controlled by another corporation.
b. An accounting procedure that is a necessary step in preparing consolidated financial statements, but that does not involve making entries in the ledger accounts.
c. A single set of financial statements showing the assets, liabilities, revenue, and expenses of all companies in a given industry.
d. An investment in voting stock of a large corporation that is too small to give the investor significant influence within the issuing company and that is almost as liquid an asset as cash.
e. Procedures used to account for an investment in which a corporate investor has significant influence over the policies of another corporation.
f. An unrecorded asset that often explains why a parent company pays far more than book value to acquire the capital stock of a subsidiary.
g. The equity in a subsidiary held by shareholders other than the parent company.
h. Method used in the balance sheet valuation of an investment in marketable securities.

EXERCISE 17-2
Investment in Bonds
(LO 1)

Bay Limited purchased as a short-term investment $300,000 face value of the 7% bonds of Lorenzo Inc. on May 31 of the current year, at a total cost of $305,750, including interest accrued since January 1. Interest is paid by Lorenzo Inc. on June 30 and December 31. On October 31, five months after the purchase, Bay sold the bonds and interest accrued since July 1 for a total price of $304,900.

INSTRUCTIONS

Prepare in general journal form all entries required in the accounting records of Bay relating to the investment in Lorenzo Inc. bonds. (Commissions are to be ignored.)

EXERCISE 17-3
Investment in Stocks
(LO 1)

During the current year, the following events occurred with respect to the Deutz Corporation's investments in stocks:

Jan. 17 Purchased as a short-term investment 5,000 shares of Cooper Industries common stock at a price of $83.50 pre share, plus a brokerage commission of $2,500.

Mar. 10 Received a cash dividend of $1.25 per share on the investment in Cooper Industries stock.

July 9 Received an additional 250 shares of Cooper Industries common stock as a result of a 5% stock dividend.

Sept. 11 Sold 2,500 shares of Cooper Industries common stock at a price of $85 per share, less a brokerage commission of $1,450.

INSTRUCTIONS

a. Prepare the journal entries in the accounting records of the Deutz Corporation to record the above transactions. Include a memorandum entry on July 9 to show the change in the cost basis per share.

b. Assume the stock of Cooper Industries is widely traded and has a quoted market price of $87 per share at the end of the current year. What is the amount reported in Deutz company's year-end *balance sheet* for this investment?

EXERCISE 17-4
Valuation at Lower-of-Cost-and-Market
(LO 1)

The cost and market value of Escobar Corporation's marketable securities at the end of 2000 and 2001 are shown below. The marketable securities are viewed as a current asset.

	Cost	Market Value
2000	$395,000	$334,000
2001 (carrying value $334,000)	395,000	415,000

INSTRUCTIONS

Show how the investment would appear *in the balance sheet* at the end of 2000 and at the end of 2001, based on current practice. Briefly explain why this practice is not conceptually sound.

EXERCISE 17-5
The Equity Method
(LO 2)

On January 1, 2000, Southern Transport purchases 40% of the common stock of Delta Shipping Inc. for $900,000, which corresponds to the underlying book value. Delta Shipping Inc. has issued common stock only. At December 31, 2000, Delta Shipping reported net income for the year of $400,000 and paid cash dividends of $180,000. Southern Transport uses the equity method to account for this investment.

INSTRUCTIONS

a. Prepare all journal entries in the accounting records of Southern Transport relating to the investment during 2000.

b. During 2001, Delta Shipping Inc. reports a net loss of $300,000 and pays no dividends. Compute the carrying value of Southern Transport's investment in Delta Shipping Inc. at the end of 2000 (refer to your answer to part **a**) and at the end of 2001.

c. Based upon quoted market prices, the fair market value of Southern Transport's investment in Delta Shipping Inc. was $995,000 at the end of 2000 but has temporarily fallen to $850,000 at the end of 2001. Do these market values affect amounts reported *in the balance sheet* for this investment? Are these market values reflected *in any way* in the financial statements?

EXERCISE 17-6
Eliminating Intercompany Stock Ownership; Recording Goodwill
(LO 4, 6)

Merit Brands Inc. has purchased all the outstanding shares of Eduardo Foods for $670,000. At the date of acquisition, Eduardo Foods' balance sheet showed total shareholders' equity of $600,000, consisting of $250,000 capital stock and $350,000 retained earnings. The excess of this purchase price over the book value of Eduardo Foods' shares is regarded as payment for Eduardo Foods' unrecorded goodwill.

In general journal entry form, prepare the eliminating entry necessary on the working paper to consolidate the balance sheets of these two companies.

EXERCISE 17-7
Computing Consolidated Amounts
(LO 4, 5, 6)

Selected account balances from the separate balance sheets of Primis Corporation and its wholly owned subsidiary, Syntech Inc., immediately after acquisition, are as follows:

	Primis Corporation	Syntech Inc.	Consolidated
Accounts receivable	$ 300,000	$ 140,000	$
Rent receivable—Primis Corporation		7,000	
Investment in Syntech, Inc.	1,475,000		
Accounts payable	390,000	120,000	
Accrued expenses payable	29,000		
Bonds payable	1,400,000	900,000	
Capital stock	4,000,000	1,000,000	
Retained earnings	2,934,000	475,000	

Primis Corporation owes Syntech Inc. $7,000 in accrued rent payable and Syntech Inc. owes Primis Corporation $24,000 on account for services rendered prior to acquisition.

INSTRUCTIONS

Indicate the amount that should appear in the consolidated balance sheet for each of these selected accounts. If the account would not appear in the consolidated balance sheet, enter -0- as the consolidated account balance. Show supporting computations.

EXERCISE 17-8
Preparing a Consolidated Balance Sheet; Noncontrolling Interest
(LO 4, 5, 6)

On June 30 Peabody Inc. **purchased** 80% of the stock of Stern Ltd. for $1,200,000 in cash. The separate condensed balance sheets immediately after the purchase are as follows:

	Peabody Inc.	Stern Ltd.
Cash	$ 350,000	$ 225,000
Investments in Stern Ltd.	1,200,000	
Other assets	5,450,000	1,775,000
	$7,000,000	$2,000,000
Liabilities	$1,500,000	$ 500,000
Capital stock	3,000,000	1,000,000
Retained earnings	2,500,000	500,000
	$7,000,000	$2,000,000

INSTRUCTIONS

Prepare a consolidated balance sheet immediately after Peabody Inc. acquired control of Stern Ltd.

Problems

PROBLEM 17-1
Investments in Marketable Debt Securities
(LO 1)

On June 1, 2000, Allied Chemical purchased $400,000 face value of the 9% bonds of Tiger Trucking at a price of 102 plus accrued interest. The bonds pay interest semiannually on April 1 and October 1. Allied Chemical regards these bonds as a short-term investment.

INSTRUCTIONS

a. In general journal form, prepare the entries required in 2000 to record:
  1. Purchase of the bonds on June 1.
  2. Receipt of the semiannual interest payment on October 1.
  3. Adjustment of the accounts at December 31 for bond interest earned since October 1. (Allied Chemical adjusts and closes its accounts annually, using the calendar year.)

b. Assume that on February 28, 2001, Allied Chemical sells the entire investment in Tiger Trucking bonds for total proceeds of $416,800, which includes accrued interest. Prepare the entries to:
  1. Accrue bond interest earned from December 31, 2000, through the date of sale.
  2. Record the sale of the bonds on February 28, 2001.

PROBLEM 17-2
Investments in Marketable Debt Securities
(LO 1)

On April 1, 2000, Imperial Motors purchased $450,000 face value of the 8% bonds of AMC Theatres Inc. at a price of 98 plus accrued interest. The bonds pay interest semiannually on March 1 and September 1. Imperial sold these bonds on January 31, 2001 for $444,700 plus accrued interest.

INSTRUCTIONS

In general journal form, prepare the entries required to record:
1. Purchase of the bonds on April 1, 2000.
2. Receipt of the semiannual interest payment on September 1, 2000.
3. Adjustment of the accounts at December 31, 2000 for bond interest earned. (Imperial Motors adjusts and closes its accounts annually, using the calendar year.)
4. Accrue bond interest earned from December 31, 2000 through the date of sale on January 31, 2001.
5. Record the sale of the bonds on January 31, 2001.

PROBLEM 17-3
Investments in Marketable Equity Securities
(LO 1)

During the current year, Overnight Express Limited (OEL) engaged in the following transactions relating to marketable securities in stock:

Feb. 28 Purchased 5,000 shares of National Products common stock for $88.50 per share plus a broker's commission of $1,500.

Mar 15 National Products paid a cash dividend of 75 cents per share that had been declared on February 20, payable on March 15 to shareholders of record on March 6.

May 31 National Products distributed a 20% stock dividend.

Nov. 15 National Products distributed additional shares as the result of a 2-for-1 stock split.

Dec. 5 OEL sold 3,500 shares of its National Products stock at $39 per share, less a broker's commission of $450.

Dec. 10 National Products paid a cash dividend of 30 cents per share. Dividend was declared November 20, payable December 10 to shareholders of record on November 30.

As of December 31, National Products common stock had a market value of $35 per share. OEL classifies its National Produces stock as a current asset and owns no other marketable securities.

INSTRUCTIONS

Prepare journal entries to account for this investment in OEL's accounting records. Include memorandum entries when appropriate. For journal entries involving computations, the explanation portion of the entry should include the computation. Also show how the investment should appear in the balance sheet at December 31.

PROBLEM 17-4
Accounting for Marketable Securities: A Comprehensive Problem
(LO 1)

The marketable securities owned by Bar Harbour Corporation at January 1 consisted of the three securities listed below. All marketable securities are classified as current assets. The company adjusts and closes its books at December 31.

$200,000 maturity value Copper Products Ltd. 9% bonds due Apr. 30, 2008. Interest is payable on Apr. 30 and Oct. 31 of each year. Cost basis $990 per bond	$198,000
3,000 shares of Aztec Corporation common stock. Cost basis $38.50 per share.	115,500
1,500 shares of Donner-Pass Inc. $7.00 cumulative preferred stock. Cost basis $55 per share	82,500

Jan. 10 Acquired 1,000 shares of Rhodes Ltd. common stock at $65.50 per share. Brokerage commissions paid amounted to $500.

Jan. 21 Received quarterly dividend on $1.75 per share on 1,500 shares of Donner-Pass Inc. preferred stock.

Mar. 5 Sold all 1,500 shares of Donner-Pass Inc. preferred stock at $58 per share less a brokerage commission of $375.

Apr. 1 Received additional 2,000 shares of Rhodes Ltd. common stock as a result of a 3-for-1 split.

Apr. 30 Received semiannual interest on Copper Products Ltd. 9% bonds.

June 30 Sold $100,000 face value of Copper Products Ltd. 9% bonds at 93, plus two months' accrued interest, less a commission of $125.

July 10 Received additional 300 shares of Aztec Corporation common stock as a result of 10% stock dividend.

Sept. 24 Sold 1,300 shares of Aztec Corporation common stock at $40 per share, less a brokerage commission of $250.

Oct. 31 Received semiannual interest payment on remaining $100,000 face value of Copper Products Ltd. 9% bonds.

At December 31, 19__, the quoted market prices of the marketable securities owned by Bar Harbour Corporation were as follows: Aztec Corporation common stock, $37; and Rhodes common stock, $18. Copper Products 9% bonds, $960 per bond.

INSTRUCTIONS

a. Prepare journal entries to record the transactions listed above. Include an adjusting entry to record accrued interest on the remaining Copper Products bonds through December 31.

b. Prepare a schedule showing the cost and market value of the marketable securities owned by Bar Harbour Corporation at December 31.

c. Show how the marketable securities should be presented in the balance sheet at December 31.

PROBLEM 17-5
Accounting for Marketable Securities: Another Comprehensive Problem
(LO 1)

The marketable securities owned by Keele Development at the beginning of the current year are listed below. Management considers all investments in marketable securities to be current assets. The company adjusts and closes its books at year-end, December 31.

$300,000 maturity value of Micro Computer 8% bonds due Apr. 30, 2006. Interest payable on Apr. 30 and Oct. 31 of each year. Cost basis $990 per bond	$297,000
4,000 shares of Ryan Corporation common stock. Cost basis $52.50 per share	210,000

Transactions relating to marketable securities during the current year were as follows:

Jan. 21 Received semiannual cash dividend of 90 cents per share on the 4,000 shares of Ryan Corporation common stock.

Feb. 8 Purchased 1,500 shares of Gramm Ltd. common stock at $39 3/4 per share. Brokerage commissions amounted to $375.

Mar. 15 Received an additional 1,500 shares of Gramm Ltd. common stock as a result of a 2-for-1 split.

Apr. 30 Received semiannual interest on Micro Computer 8% bonds.

May 31 Sold $200,000 face value of Micro Computer 8% bonds at a price of 103, plus one month's accrued interest, less a brokerage commission of $575.

July 21 Received cash dividend on 4,000 shares of Ryan Corporation common stock. Amount of dividend has increased to $1.05 per share.

Oct. 18 Received an additional 200 shares of Ryan Corporation common stock as a result of a 5% stock dividend.

Oct. 19 Sold 1,200 shares of Ryan Corporation common stock at $47 per share, less a brokerage commission of $250.

Oct. 31 Received semiannual interest payment on remaining $100,000 face value of Micro Computer 8% bonds.

At December 31 of the current year, the quoted market prices of the marketable securities owned by Keele Development were as follows: Ryan Corporation, $46 per share; Gramm Ltd. $21.50 per share; Micro Computer 8% bonds, $1,025 per bond.

INSTRUCTIONS

a. Prepare journal entries to record the transactions listed above and any adjusting entry at year-end.
b. Prepare a schedule showing the cost and market value of the marketable securities owned by Keele Development at December 31.
c. Show how the marketable securities should appear in the balance sheet at December 31.

CHAPTER 17 INVESTMENTS IN CORPORATE SECURITIES

PROBLEM 17-6
Equity Method—Financial Statement Effects
(LO 2)

On January 1, 2000, Minelli Foods purchased 30% (300,000 shares) of the widely traded common stock of Kansas Grain Products Inc. for $5,100,000. (This price was equal to 30% of Kansas Products' book value at that date.) The following data is available regarding Kansas Grain Products Inc. for 2000 and 2001:

	2000	2001
Net income (loss)	$2,500,000	$(900,000)
Dividends declared & paid	$1,300,000	$ 650,000
Quoted market price per share at December 31	$ 19	$ 14

INSTRUCTIONS

a. Briefly describe how Minelli Foods should account for this investment. Identify the principal factors that determine the accounting treatment.
b. Compute each of the following amounts relating only to Minelli's investment in Kansas Grain Products Inc.
  1. Cash dividends received by Minelli in 2000 and in 2001.
  2. Amounts (if any) reported in Minelli's *income statement* in 2000 and in 2001 for each of the following: Dividend Revenue; Investment Income (or Loss).
  3. Carrying value of this investment reported in Minelli's *balance sheet* at December 31, 2000 and at December 31, 2001.
c. Compute the *market value* of Minelli Foods' investment in Kansas Grain Products Inc. at the end of 2000 and 2001. How are these market values reflected in Minelli Foods' financial statements, if at all? Assume that the market value of Kansas' stock went up to $17.50 per share in early 2002.

PROBLEM 17-7
Equity Method—Financial Statement Effects
(LO 2)

On January 1, 2000, Bishop Industries purchased 60,000 shares of the widely traded common stock of Franklin-Parker Corporation for $1,500,000. On this date, Franklin-Parker had 150,000 shares of a single class of stock outstanding and total shareholders' equity of $3,750,000. The following data is available regarding Franklin-Parker Corporation for 2000 and 2001:

	2000	2001
Net income (loss)	$(300,000)	$1,500,000
Dividends declared & paid	$ 75,000	$ 600,000
Quoted market price per share at December 31	$ 22	$ 30

INSTRUCTIONS

a. Briefly describe how Bishop Industries should account for this investment. Identify the principal factors that determine the accounting treatment.
b. Compute each of the following amounts relating only to Bishop's investment in Franklin-Parker Corporation.
  1. Cash dividends received by Bishop in 2000 and 2001.
  2. Amounts (if any) reported in Bishop's *income statement* in 2000 and in 2001 for each of the following: Dividend Revenue; Investment Income (or Loss).
  3. Carrying value of this investment reported on Bishop's *balance sheet* at December 31, 2000, and at December 31, 2001.
c. Compute the *market value* of Bishop Industries' investment in Franklin-Parker at December 31, 2000, and December 31, 2001. How are these market values reflected in Bishop's financial statements, if at all?

894 PARTNERSHIPS AND CORPORATIONS   PART 4

PROBLEM 17-8
Investments in Marketable Equity Securities
(LO 1, 2)

During the current year, the following transactions occurred relating to Talley Manufacturing Limited's investments in marketable equity securities:

Jan. 2 Purchased as a short-term investment 4,000 shares of Raleigh Corporation common stock at $64.75 per share, plus broker's commission of $1,400.

Mar. 31 Received a cash dividend of 50 cents per share from Raleigh Corporation. Raleigh declared the dividend on February 15, payable on March 31 to shareholders of record on March 15.

June 30 Raleigh Corporation distributed a 5% stock dividend.

July 31 Raleigh Corporation shares were split 2 for 1; Talley Manufacturing received additional shares pursuant to this stock split.

Sept. 30 Raleigh Corporation paid a cash dividend of 70 cents per share. Dividend was declared on August 25 payable on September 30 to shareholders of record on September 15.

Dec. 21 Talley Manufacturing sold 3,000 shares of Raleigh Corporation stock at $29 per share. Commission charges on the sale amounted to $600.

Raleigh Corporation had a net income of $100,000 for the year; its common stock had a market value of $28.50 per share at December 31 but went up to $30 per share a month later. Talley Manufacturing classifies its Raleigh Corporation stock as a current asset and owns no other marketable equity securities.

INSTRUCTIONS

a. Prepare journal entries to account for this investment in Talley manufacturing's accounting records. Include memorandum entries when appropriate. For journal entries involving computations, the explanation portion of the entry should include the computation. Also show how the investment should appear in the balance sheet at December 31.

b. Explain how your answer in **a** would change *if* these marketable securities were 25% of Raleigh Corporation's common stock and none of the securities were sold during the year.

PROBLEM 17-9
Consolidated Balance Sheet—Basic Elements
(LO 4, 5, 6)

On December 31, 2000, Delta Building Materials purchased for cash 80% of the capital stock of Olds Electrical Supply. The separate year-end balance sheets of the two companies include the following items:

	Delta Building Materials	Olds Electrical Supply
Accounts receivable—Olds Electrical Supply	130,000	-0-
Investment in Olds Electrical Supply	1,600,000	-0-
Total assets	9,800,000	2,200,000
Accounts payable—Delta Building Materials	-0-	130,000
Total liabilities	3,600,000	700,000
Total shareholders' equity	6,200,000	1,500,000

The excess of the $1,600,000 purchase price over the book value of the acquired shares in Olds is regarded as a purchase of Olds' unrecorded goodwill.

INSTRUCTIONS

Compute the amounts to appear in the year-end consolidated balance sheet for each of the following (show supporting computations):
a. Goodwill
b. Non-controlling interest
c. Total assets
d. Total liabilities
e. Total shareholders' equity

PROBLEM 17-10
Basic Elements of a Consolidated Balance Sheet
(LO 4, 5, 6)

On December 31, 2001, Camry Home Improvement Inc. purchased for cash 70% of the capital stock of Cadillac Paint Ltd. The separate year-end balance sheets of the two companies include the following items:

	Camry Home Improvement Inc.	Cadillac Paint Ltd.
Accounts receivable—Camry Home Improvement Inc.	-0-	315,000
Investments in Cadillac Paint Ltd.	1,050,000	-0-
Total assets	6,500,000	2,180,000
Accounts payable—Cadillac Paint Ltd.	315,000	-0-
Total liabilities	3,900,000	980,000
Total shareholders' equity	2,600,000	1,200,000

The excess of the $1,050,000 purchase price over the book value of the acquired shares in Cadillac Paint Ltd. is regarded as a purchase of Cadillac Paint's unrecorded goodwill.

INSTRUCTIONS

Compute the amounts to appear in the year-end consolidated balance sheet for each of the following (show supporting computations):
a. Goodwill
b. Non-controlling interest
c. Total assets
d. Total liabilities
e. Total shareholders' equity.

PROBLEM 17-11
Preparation of a Consolidated Balance Sheet
(LO 4, 5, 6)

On June 30, 19__, Pokfulam Sportswear paid $1,800,000 cash to acquire all the outstanding capital stock of Jeans by Jorge. Immediately **before** this acquisition, the condensed separate balance sheets of the two companies were as shown below. (As these balance sheets were prepared immediately **before** the acquisition, the current assets of Pokfulam Sportswear still include the $1,800,000 in cash that will be paid to acquire Jeans by Jorge.)

Assets	Pokfulam Sportswear	Jeans by Jorge
Current assets	$ 3,760,000	$ 640,000
Plant and equipment	3,040,000	1,800,000
Total assets	$ 6,800,000	$2,440,000

Liabilities & Shareholders' Equity		
Current liabilities	$ 1,080,000	$ 560,000
Long-term debt	2,400,000	400,000
Capital stock	1,200,000	600,000
Retained earnings	2,120,000	880,000
Total liabilities & shareholders' equity	$ 6,800,000	$2,440,000

INSTRUCTIONS

The excess, if any, of the purchase price over the book value of Jeans by Jorge shares acquired is regarded as payment for unrecorded goodwill.

Prepare a consolidated balance sheet for Pokfulam Sportswear and its newly acquired subsidiary (Jeans by Jorge) on June 30, 19__, the date of acquisition.

PROBLEM 17-12
Preparing a Consolidated Balance Sheet
(LO 4, 5, 6)

On January 1, 2001, Cavomy Entertainment purchased all the outstanding common stock of Video Scene Inc. for $800,000. Immediately *before* the acquisition, the condensed separate balance sheets of the two companies were as shown below.

Assets	Cavomy Entertainment	Video Scene Inc.
Current assets	$1,630,000	$240,000
Other assets	1,970,000	660,000
Total assets	$3,600,000	$900,000

Liabilities & Shareholders' Equity		
Current liabilities	$ 580,000	$120,000
Long-term debt	900,000	208,000
Capital stock	1,000,000	200,000
Retained earnings	1,120,000	372,000
Total liabilities & shareholders' equity	$3,600,000	$900,000

The excess, if any, of the purchase price over the book value of Video Scene's acquired shares is regarded as payment for Video Scene's unrecorded goodwill.

INSTRUCTIONS

Prepare a consolidated balance sheet for Cavomy Entertainment and its newly acquired subsidiary (Video Scene Inc.) on January 1, 2001, the date of acquisition.

PROBLEM 17-13
Working Paper for a Consolidated Balance Sheet
(LO 4, 5, 6)

On September 30, 2000, Morse Communications purchased 80% of the stock of Graham Cable for cash. The separate balance sheets of the two companies immediately after this purchase are as follows:

Assets	Morse Communications	Graham Cable
Cash	$ 52,000	$ 45,000
Note receivable from Graham Cable	50,000	
Accounts receivable	108,000	60,000
Inventories	120,000	174,000
Investment in Graham Cable	570,000	
Plant and equipment (net)	252,000	440,000
Total assets	$1,152,000	$719,000

Liabilities & Shareholders' Equity		
Notes payable	$ 120,000	$ 50,000
Accounts payable	144,000	45,000
Accrued liabilities	36,000	24,000
Common stock	500,000	350,000
Retained earnings	352,000	250,000
Total liabilities & shareholders' equity	$1,152,000	$719,000

CHAPTER 17 INVESTMENTS IN CORPORATE SECURITIES 897

ADDITIONAL INFORMATION

1. Morse Communications' asset account Investment in Graham Cable represents ownership of 80% of Graham Cable's shareholders' equity. Any excess of the investment account balance over Graham Cable's book value represents unrecorded goodwill.
2. Graham Cable's $50,000 note payable is owed to Morse Communications. (All interest has been paid through September 30.)
3. The accounts payable of Morse Communications include $15,000 owed to Graham Cable. This amount also is included in the accounts receivable of Graham Cable.

INSTRUCTIONS

Prepare a working paper for a consolidated balance sheet at September 30, 2000 immediately after the purchase of Graham Cable. Include at the bottom of the working paper explanations of the elimination entries.

Analytical and Decision Problems and Cases

A&D 17-1
Marketable Securities—Lower-of-Cost-and-Market vs. Market
(LO 1)

The following information relates to the two investments (acquired during the year) in publicly owned companies by Charles Software Limited at December 31, 2001, the year-end date:

	Cost	Market Value
Quality Computers Inc. (5,000 shares; cost, $50 per share; market value, $65)	$250,000	$325,000
Global Network Limited (8,000 shares; cost, $40 per share; market value, $37.50)	320,000	300,000
Total	$570,000	$625,000

As the two stocks were declining in value in early 2002, Charles Software sold all the Quality Computers stock at $63 per share and all of the Global Network stock at $37 per share, in two separate transactions (disregard brokerage commissions).

INSTRUCTIONS

a. Prepare journal entries to record the disposal of the two investments according to the
   1. Lower-of-cost-and-market basis (the current practice)
   2. Market value basis (the conceptual basis)
b. Compute the gain or loss that should be reported in the income statements in 2001 and 2002 under the
   1. Lower-of-cost-and-market basis
   2. Market value basis
c. Explain which basis—the lower-of-cost-and-market or the market value—provides better information to evaluate management's performance on the investment in marketable securities.

A&D 17-2
Apples and Oranges
(LO 1, 2, 3)

Dane Electronics has the following investments in the securities of other corporations:

a. 2,000 shares of the common stock of Apple Computer. Apple is a large publicly owned corporation and sells at a quoted market price in excess of Dane's cost. Dane's management stands ready to sell these shares at any time.
b. $100,000 face amount of Central Telephone's 4.60% bonds maturing in 10 years. The bonds were acquired at a discount. These bonds are readily marketable, and Dane's management stands ready to sell them to meet any current cash requirements.

c. 5 million of the 15 million voting shares in Micro-Desk Inc. Micro-Desk is a publicly owned corporation, and its quoted stock price recently has declined to a level below Dane's cost.

d. $300,000 face value of Carver Stores 11.20% bonds maturing in 10 years. These bonds are readily marketable at a quoted price. However, Dane intends to hold these bonds until their maturity date. The bonds were acquired at a substantial premium.

e. 51% of the voting stock in Consumer Corp. Consumer is a profitable company, but it is not publicly owned. There is no quoted market price for Consumer's capital stock.

f. 50,000 of the 1 million outstanding shares of SIMCO Products, a publicly owned corporation. The market price of SIMCO's shares has declined steadily since Dane purchased its shares. Dane's management, however, believes in the long-run prospects of SIMCO and intends to hold this investment for at least 10 years.

g. 5,000 shares of voting stock of Orange Express. Orange Express operates profitably, but it is not publicly owned and has no quoted market value. This investment does not give Dane an influential interest in Orange Express. Dane's management stands ready to sell these shares at any time that an attractive offer is received.

INSTRUCTIONS

Explain how Dane Electronics should account for each of these investments. Your explanations should include discussion of the three topics listed below.

1. Whether the investment qualifies for consolidation and, if not, the appropriate balance sheet classification of the investment account.
2. The basis for balance sheet valuation (e.g., consolidation, equity method, cost, cost adjusted for amortization of bond discount or premium, or lower-of-cost-and-market).
3. The factors involved in the recognition of income (or loss) from the investment (e.g., Does the lower-of-cost-and-market rule enter into the determination of net income? Is bond discount or premium amortized? Are dividends recorded as income when received? Is the equity method in use?).

A&D 17-3
Success or Failure and Why?
(LO 3)

There have been many well-known, well-publicized business acquisitions and mergers in recent years. The results of these acquisitions and mergers have been mixed—some successes, some failures, and a few disasters. In addition, the fate of the more recent acquisitions and mergers is still pending.

INSTRUCTIONS

Select one of the acquisitions or mergers cited in the "CASE IN POINT" in this chapter and determine why it has been a success or a failure.

Answers to Self-Test Questions

1. d　2. d　3. a　4. b　5. d

PART 5

Income Taxes, Cash Flows, Financial Statement Analysis, and Managerial Accounting

18. Income Taxes and Business Decisions
19. Measuring Cash Flows
20. Analysis and Interpretation of Financial Statements
    Comprehensive Problem 6: Loblaw Companies Limited
21. Introduction to Managerial Accounting: Accounting for Manufacturing Operations
    Appendix D: The New Manufacturing Environment; Activity-Based Costing

Investors and managers have at their fingertips a wealth of information about every publicly owned company in the world. But that information is only useful if you know what it means.

CHAPTER 18

Income Taxes and Business Decisions

We said earlier that an understanding of accounting is not just useful—it's a survival skill. Income taxes prove our point.

CHAPTER LEARNING OBJECTIVES

1. Describe the history and objectives of the federal income tax, the highlights of the 1988 tax reform measures, and the basic structure of the tax system.
2. Explain the formula for determining the taxable income and tax liability of an individual taxpayer.
3. Explain the income tax treatment of dividends received by individuals.
4. Determine the tax liability of an individual.
5. Determine the taxable income and income tax of a corporation.
6. Determine the amount of capital cost allowance.
7. Describe the circumstances that create a liability for future (deferred) income taxes.
8. Explain how tax planning is used in choosing the form of business organization, timing and nature of transactions, and the capital structure.

The Federal Income Tax: History and Objectives

LO 1: Describe the history and objectives of the federal income tax, the highlights of the 1988 tax reform measures, and the basic structure of the tax system.

The federal income tax legislation, the **Income Tax Act**, has undergone many changes since its inception as the **Income War Tax Act** in 1917. The more significant changes occurred in the years 1948, 1952, and 1972. In 1988, the federal government enacted new income tax legislation that brought sweeping changes in income tax rules and rates. These changes represented some of the most drastic in the history of the federal income tax. The five most striking characteristics of this major tax legislation are the broadening of the tax base, the lowering of tax rates, the reduction of the number of tax brackets, the replacement of various exemptions and deductions with tax credits, and a shifting of the tax burden from individuals to corporations and to sales tax.

The objectives of income tax legislation also have been changed and expanded over the years. Originally, the objective of the federal income tax was simply to obtain revenue to help meet Canada's growing war expenditures. It was intended as a temporary measure and the tax rates were quite low. Today, the objectives are many and the tax rates are significantly higher.

The objectives of federal income tax today include a number of broad ones in addition to raising revenue. Among these broad objectives are to combat inflation, to influence the rate of economic growth, to encourage full employment, to provide incentive for small businesses, and to redistribute national income on a more equal basis.

The administration and enforcement of the Income Tax Act rest with the Department of National Revenue for Taxation, commonly known as Revenue Canada, Taxation.

Provincial Income Tax

All ten provinces as well as the Northwest Territories and Yukon levy income tax. The federal government collects the income tax of individuals and corporations except for the Provinces of Ontario, Alberta, and Quebec; Ontario and Alberta collect their corporate income tax and Quebec collects its income tax on both individuals and corporations. The rate of income tax varies among the jurisdictions. The tax rate for individuals is expressed as a percentage of the individual's basic federal tax. The tax rate for corporations, on the other hand, applies to the corporation's taxable income. The computations of provincial income tax will be illustrated later.

The Critical Importance of Income Taxes

Taxes levied by federal and provincial governments are a significant part of the cost of operating a typical household, as well as a business enterprise. Every manager who makes business decisions, and every individual who makes personal investments, urgently needs some knowledge of income taxes. A general knowledge of income taxes will help any business manager or owner to benefit more fully from the advice of the professional tax accountant.

Some understanding of income taxes will also aid the individual citizen in voting intelligently, because a great many of the issues decided in every election have tax implications. Such issues as pollution, inflation, foreign policy, and employment are quite closely linked with income taxes. For example, the offering of special tax incentives to encourage businesses to launch massive programs to reduce pollution is one approach to protection of the environment.

In terms of revenue generated, income taxes constitute one of the most important sources of revenue in Canada. Income taxes also exert a pervasive influence on all types of business decisions and affect millions of individuals. For example, tax returns filed annually in a recent year were over 20 million for individuals and 1 million for corporations. The annual income tax revenue from individuals and corporations in a recent year was over $118 billion. For this reason we shall limit our discussion to the basic federal and provincial income tax rules applicable to individuals and corporations.

Income tax returns are based on accounting information. In many respects this information is consistent with the accounting concepts we have discussed in earlier chapters. However, the measurement of ***taxable income*** includes some unique principles and computations that differ from those used for published financial statements. An understanding of the unique aspects of taxable income can assist an individual or a business in minimizing the amount of income taxes owed.

Tax Planning versus Tax Evasion

Tax Planning Taxpayers who manage their affairs in ways that *legally* minimize their income tax obligations are engaging in a practice called **tax planning**. Tax planning is both legal and ethical.

The goals of tax planning usually are either to minimize the total amount of taxes owed or to postpone into future years the dates at which the taxes become due. Tax planning may take many forms; for example: Should business automobiles be leased or purchased? Should needed capital be financed by issuing bonds or preferred stock? Should a business be incorporated? Some of these choices may significantly affect the amount and timing of the taxpayer's income tax obligations.

If tax planning is to be efficient, it should be undertaken ***before*** the taxpayer engages in the related transactions. Once a transaction is complete, it usually is ***too late*** to change its tax consequences. Every taxpayer, whether an individual or a corporation, can benefit from thoughtful tax planning. Tax planning is one of the major services that public accounting firms offer their clients.

Tax Evasion In contrast to tax planning, ***tax evasion*** refers to ***illegal*** efforts by taxpayers to avoid their tax obligations. Examples include failure to file an income tax return or fraudulently understating the amount of taxable income reported in the return. By definition, tax evasion is a crime, punishable by fines, imprisonment, or both.

> **CASE IN POINT**
>
> Al Capone, one of the most infamous gangsters in American history, was believed to have committed many crimes, including bootlegging, extortion, and murder. Capone was the subject of an intense criminal investigation conducted by the American federal law enforcement agents—including the legendary Elliot Ness and "The Untouchables."
>
> The only crime for which the American government was able to convict Capone was income tax evasion. The result, however, was the same as if he had been convicted of murder and given a life sentence. He died in prison while serving his term.

Classes of Taxpayers and Liability of Tax

In the eyes of the income tax law, the classes of taxpayers are: individuals (people and trusts) and corporations.

Proprietorships and partnerships are not taxed as business units; their income is taxed directly to the individual proprietor or partners (partners include corporations), ***whether or not actually withdrawn from the business***. A proprietor reports his or her business income on an individual tax return; the members of a partnership include on their individual tax returns their respective shares of the partnership net income. An individual taxpayer's income tax return must include not only any business income from a proprietorship or partnership, but also any salary or income from other sources and any deductions affecting the tax liability.

A corporation is a separate taxable entity; it must file an income tax return and pay a tax on its annual taxable income. In addition, individual shareholders must report dividends received as part of their personal taxable income. This is sometimes called "double taxation" of corporate income—once to the corporation and again when it is distributed as dividends to shareholders. However, this double taxation is minimized or neutralized by the "dividend tax credit" claimed by the shareholders.

The income tax law stipulates that income tax is payable on the taxable income for each taxation year of every person resident in Canada. Moreover, income tax is payable on the taxable income earned in Canada by a nonresident person. The word "person" includes an individual or a corporation.

Enforcement of Income Tax Laws

Our system of income taxes relies upon taxpayers measuring their own taxable income, computing the taxes that they owe, and filing an income tax return in which these amounts are reported to governmental income tax authorities. For this reason, our system of collecting income taxes often is described as a system of ***self-assessment***.

However, income tax authorities have several means of enforcing this "self-assessment" system. To begin with, much of the taxable income earned by taxpayers is reported to the tax authorities by a third party. For example, employers must send **T4** forms to the government indicating the total salary or wages paid to each employee during the year. Corporations and banks are required to send **T5** forms reporting to the government the dividends and interest earned by each investor and creditor. Through the use of its computers, Revenue Canada traces many of these reported amounts directly into the recipient's income tax return.

Next, each year income tax authorities ***audit*** selected tax returns filed by taxpayers. Only a small percentage of the returns filed each year are audited; however, Revenue Canada has considerable experience in identifying those returns in which taxable income may be understated. Many of the returns selected for audit are those that appear "suspicious" in some way, or in which taxpayers have claimed deductions to which they might not be entitled. Thus, by claiming certain deductions (such as expenses relating to a "home office" or a large business loss), a taxpayer may increase the chances that his or her return will be audited.

An interesting quirk in the tax law is that when a tax return is audited, ***the burden of proof rests with the taxpayer***. Thus, taxpayers who do not maintain adequate records may lose deductions to which they otherwise would be entitled.

Finally, tax authorities may impose financial penalties upon taxpayers who have understated their taxable incomes. First, the taxpayer must pay interest on any additional taxes owed. In addition, substantial fines and penalties may be levied if the taxpayer has been grossly negligent or fraudulent. As previously stated, fraudulent tax evasion is a criminal offense and may be punishable by imprisonment, as well as by financial penalties.

INCOME TAXES: INDIVIDUALS

Accrual versus Cash Basis

Business income of individuals is reported on an accrual basis except for farmers and fishermen. Interest income may be reported on the modified accrual or cash basis at the taxpayer's choice, unless it is less frequent than once a year, in which case, the accrual basis or modified accrual basis is used.[1] Salaries, wages, and dividends are reported on a cash basis.

The cash basis is advantageous for the individual taxpayer for several reasons. It is simple and requires a minimum of record keeping. At the end of each year, employers are required to inform each employee (and Revenue Canada, Taxation) of the salary earned and the income tax withheld during the year. The report (a T4 form) must be prepared on the cash basis without any accrual of unpaid salaries. Companies paying interest and dividends also use the cash basis in reporting the amounts paid during the year. Thus, most individuals are provided with reports prepared on a cash basis for use in preparing their individual tax returns.

---

[1] The modified accrual basis requires interest to be reported no later than the anniversary date of the debt.

Tax Rates for Individuals

All taxes may be characterized as progressive, proportional, or regressive with respect to any given base. A ***progressive*** tax becomes a larger portion of the base as that base increases. A ***proportional*** tax remains a constant percentage of the base no matter how that base changes. For example, an 8% sales tax remains a constant percentage of sales regardless of changes in the dollar amount of sales. A ***regressive*** tax becomes a smaller percentage of the base as the base increases. Regressive taxes, however, are extremely rare.

Federal income tax is ***progressive*** with respect to income, since a higher tax ***rate*** applies as the amount of taxable income increases. Since provincial income tax is expressed as a percentage of "basic federal tax," it is also progressive with respect to income. The 1997 federal and provincial tax rates for individuals are as follows:

Federal Tax Rates for Individuals—1997

Taxable Income	Marginal Tax Rate
$0—29,590	17%
$29,591–59,180	26%
Over $59,180	29%

Provincial Tax Rates for Individuals*—1997

Alberta	45.5%
British Columbia	51%
Manitoba	52%
New Brunswick	63%
Newfoundland	69%
Nova Scotia	58.5%
Ontario	48%
Prince Edward Island	59.5%
Saskatchewan	50%

*There was a surtax or flat tax or both for all provinces.

(The province of Quebec collects its own individual income tax. The 1997 rate ranges from 16% to 24%, and the rate applies to taxable income as computed under the Quebec Taxation Act.)

As mentioned earlier, two of the most striking characteristics of the 1988 tax reform legislation are the reduction of the number of tax brackets and the lowering of tax rates. In contrast to the 10 tax brackets and **marginal tax rates** ranging from 6% to 34% prior to the tax reform, the current tax legislation provides for only 3 tax brackets and 3 marginal tax rates ranging from 17% to 29%.

Income Tax Formula for Individuals

LO 2: Explain the formula for determining the taxable income and tax liability of an individual taxpayer.

The federal government supplies several standard income tax forms on which individual taxpayers are guided to a proper computation of their taxable income and the amount of the tax. It is helpful to visualize the computation in terms of an income tax formula. Moreover, it is easier to understand the structure and logic of income tax and to analyze tax rules and their effect by referring to a tax formula. The general income tax formula, based on one of the standard income tax forms for individuals, is outlined below. The items in the formula are explained in more detail in the following paragraphs.

Total Income

The **total income** of an individual taxpayer is his or her world income from all sources except those explicitly excluded by the income tax law. If an amount received by an individual is income and not a return of capital and it is not explicitly excluded by the tax law, then it should be included as income. To identify whether an amount is excluded as income for tax purposes, it is necessary to refer to the income tax law, regulations, and court decisions.

The major categories of income for tax purposes are on the next page.

General Income Tax Formula for Individuals

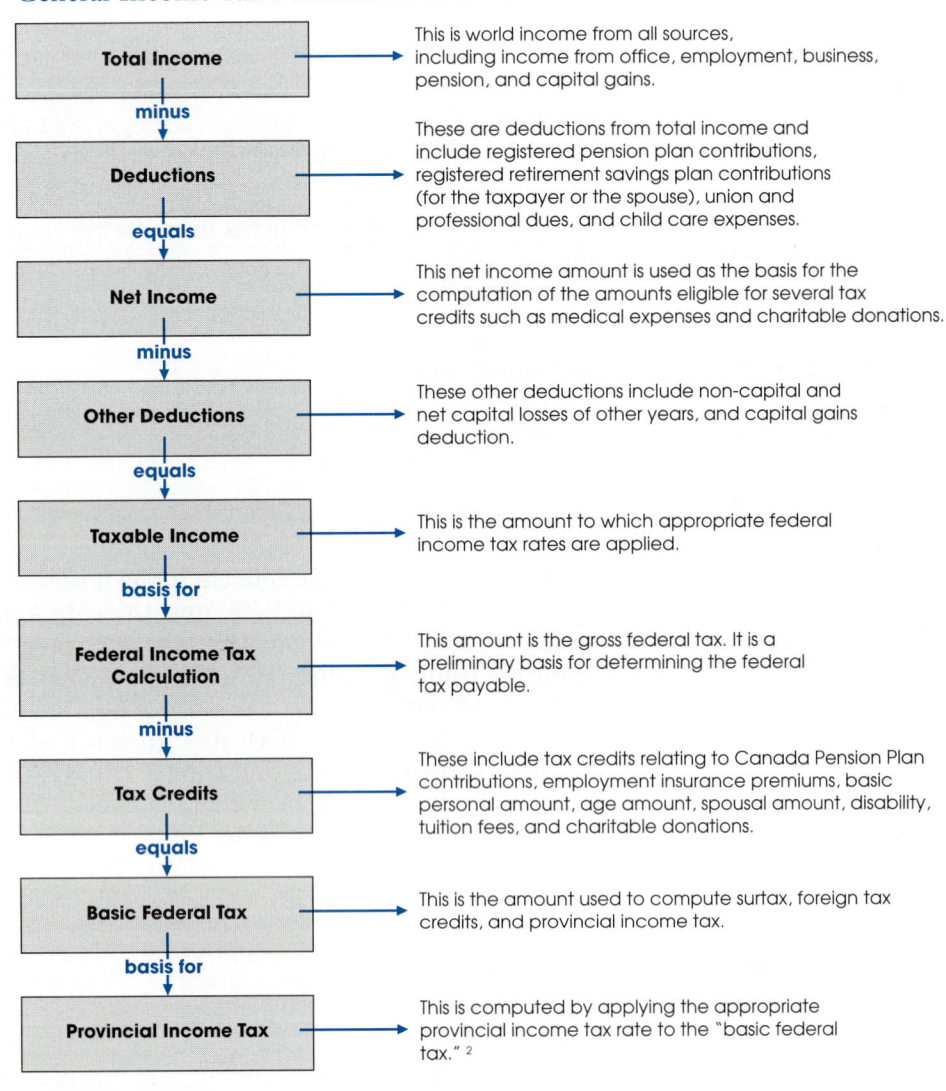

Total Income — This is world income from all sources, including income from office, employment, business, pension, and capital gains.

minus

Deductions — These are deductions from total income and include registered pension plan contributions, registered retirement savings plan contributions (for the taxpayer or the spouse), union and professional dues, and child care expenses.

equals

Net Income — This net income amount is used as the basis for the computation of the amounts eligible for several tax credits such as medical expenses and charitable donations.

minus

Other Deductions — These other deductions include non-capital and net capital losses of other years, and capital gains deduction.

equals

Taxable Income — This is the amount to which appropriate federal income tax rates are applied.

basis for

Federal Income Tax Calculation — This amount is the gross federal tax. It is a preliminary basis for determining the federal tax payable.

minus

Tax Credits — These include tax credits relating to Canada Pension Plan contributions, employment insurance premiums, basic personal amount, age amount, spousal amount, disability, tuition fees, and charitable donations.

equals

Basic Federal Tax — This is the amount used to compute surtax, foreign tax credits, and provincial income tax.

basis for

Provincial Income Tax — This is computed by applying the appropriate provincial income tax rate to the "basic federal tax." [2]

---

[2] As mentioned earlier, the province of Quebec applies its tax rate to taxable income under the Quebec Taxation Act.

1. ***Income from an office or employment*** This category includes salaries, wages, directors' fees, and other remuneration and taxable fringe benefits such as bonuses, tips, honoraria, certain allowances for personal or living expenses, and group term life insurance.
2. ***Income from a business or property*** This category includes net income from a proprietorship, partnership, or a professional business, as well as rental, royalty, interest, and dividend (at 125%) income. Also, income from a business of an illegal nature is to be included in income for tax purposes.
3. ***Capital gains*** This category includes gains from selling capital assets such as stocks, bonds, land, and depreciable properties used in the business at prices higher than their costs or adjusted costs. For 1997, ***three-quarters*** of **capital gains** (known as "taxable capital gains") were to be included as income for tax purposes. These gains may be offset by the same proportion of **capital losses** (known as "allowable capital losses") for a given year. Any remaining allowable capital losses may be carried back against taxable capital gains of the three preceding years and may be carried forward indefinitely against taxable capital gains in future years.
4. ***Other sources of income*** This category includes all income items not covered by the preceding three categories. The more common items are: benefits from Old Age Security Pension, Canada or Quebec Pension Plan, other pensions or superannuation, employment insurance benefits, and spousal and child support payments received.[3]

As mentioned earlier, certain items are explicitly excluded as income for tax purposes; the more common items include lottery winnings, war disability pensions, inheritance, and income from personal injury awards.[4]

Deductions

There are a number of deductions from total income. The more common ones include: registered pension plan contributions, registered retirement savings plan contributions, annual union and professional dues, child care expenses, moving expenses, spousal and child support payments[5] (alimony or separation allowance), carrying charges such as interest expense on money borrowed to earn investment income, safety deposit box charges for storing investment documents, and social benefits repayment for employment insurance and old age security when the amount of net income before the repayment, called "net income before adjustments," is over a certain limit. (The amount of repayment is first deducted from "net income before adjustments" and then added back to the federal and provincial taxes to arrive at the total amount of taxes payable to the government.)

---

[3] Generally, child support payment that becomes legally payable after April 30, 1997 cannot be included.
[4] Workers' compensation payments are first included in total income and then deducted, as "other deductions," from net income.
[5] See footnote 3.

Net Income

The net income of an individual taxpayer is his or her total income minus the deductions. This amount is important because it is the basis for computing the amounts eligible for medical expense and charitable donation tax credits.

Other Deductions

There are very few items in this category. The deductions for 1997 include: workers' compensation payments, social assistance payments, non-capital and net capital losses of other years, and capital gain deductions (i.e., taxable capital gain). For many taxpayers, their net income would be the same as taxable income unless they had business and net capital losses in other years to be carried over to the current year.

Taxable Income

This is the amount subject to federal income tax. It is computed by deducting from total income the allowable deductions to arrive at net income and then deducting from net income the allowable other deductions. The concept of **taxable income** is most important because it is the amount to which the appropriate tax rate is applied to determine the amount of **"gross" federal income tax**

Federal Income Tax Calculation

This is the amount of "gross" federal income tax. It is not the amount of tax payable because there are a number of tax credits to be deducted from it to determine the basic federal tax and the federal tax payable.

Tax Credits

As mentioned earlier, one of the most striking characteristics of the tax reform legislation was the replacement of various deductions and exemptions with **tax credits**. Deductions such as Canada Pension Plan contributions, employment insurance premiums, tuition fees, education amount, medical expenses in excess of 3% of net income, and charitable donations were substituted by tax credits. Similarly, all the personal exemptions—basic, married, equivalent to married, disability, and age—were replaced by tax credits. While some of the tax credits may be transferred to a spouse or a parent, any unused tax credits are not refundable. Since the tax credits are set at the lowest rate of 17%, (except for total donations in excess of $200) this is an example of the broadening of the tax base as taxpayers with taxable income above the 17% bracket will be paying more income tax. The more common tax credits and the amounts for 1997 are:

1. Personal tax credits
    (a) basic, for the taxpayer ($6,456 × 17%) $1,098
    (b) married, for the taxpayer's spouse ($5,380 × 17%)*   915

---

* A spouse can earn a net income of $538 without reduction in the amount of tax credits. The tax credit will be reduced by 17% of net income in excess of this limit.

(c) age, 65 and over ($3,482[6] × 17%)	592
(d) disability ($4,233 × 17%)	720

2. **Deduction tax credits** based on 17% of the amount of the allowable deductions.
    (a) Canada Pension Plan contributions
    (b) Employment insurance premiums
    (c) Tuition fees
    (d) Education amount of $150 ($200 for 1998 and subsequent years) for each month in full-time attendance at a designated educational institution and enrolled in a qualifying educational program.
    (e) Medical expenses in excess of $1,614 or 3% of net income (this excess is commonly called "allowable medical expenses"), *whichever is less*
    (f) Charitable donations (the 17% is for the first $200 in donations and 29% for the amount in excess of $200, up to a maximum of 75% of net income.)
3. **Dividend tax credit** ($13\frac{1}{3}$% of the grossed-up dividend.)

Basic Federal Tax

The amount of **basic federal tax** is "gross" federal income tax (federal income tax calculation) minus tax credits. It is the basis for computing the provincial income tax. This amount plus the federal surtax** (3% on basic federal tax and 5% of basic federal tax of $12,500) and minus any foreign tax credit becomes the amount of federal tax payable.

Provincial Income Tax

The amount of provincial income tax is determined by applying the appropriate provincial tax rate to the amount of basic federal tax. Since the tax rate varies among provinces, an average rate of 55% (surtax included) will be used as a provincial tax rate for illustration purposes and for the assignment materials, unless it is indicated otherwise.

LO 3: Explain the income tax treatment of dividends received by individuals.

Federal Dividend Tax Credit for Individuals

To minimize or neutralize the impact of double taxation on corporate income upon its subsequent distribution as dividends to individual shareholders, income tax law allows a special deduction from tax called "federal **dividend tax credit**." However, an individual taxpayer must first include in his or her income the dividends from taxable Canadian corporations at 125% for 1997 (known as the "gross-up" or "taxable" amount of dividends). This "grossed-up" amount is taxed at the normal rate of the taxpayer. The federal income tax is then reduced by the dividend tax credit at $13\frac{1}{3}$% of the "grossed-up" amount of dividends. Since income tax is progressive, the dividend tax credit provides more tax benefit to tax-

---

[6] This amount is reduced by the amount of net income exceeding $25,921 times 15%. If a senior's net income is $49,134 or more, he or she is not entitled to the age tax credit.
** In 1998, the surtax will be reduced for lower income taxpayers and increased for higher income taxpayers.

payers with lower income. To illustrate, let us assume that the federal tax rates for three individuals are 17%, 26%, and 29% and each has $8,000 of dividends from taxable Canadian corporations.

		17%	26%	29%
Tax Rate		17%	26%	29%
Dividends	(a)	$8,000	$8,000	$8,000
Add: "gross-up" of 25%		2,000	2,000	2,000
Taxable (grossed-up) amount of dividends (125% of dividends received)		$10,000	$10,000	$10,000
Federal income tax on taxable amount of dividends		$1,700	$2,600	$2,900
Less: dividend tax credit of 13⅓% on taxable (grossed-up) amount of dividends (13⅓% x $10,000)		1,333	1,333	1,333
Federal tax on dividends	(b)	$ 367	$ 1,267	$ 1,567
Effective rate of federal tax on dividends (b) ÷ (a)		4.6%	15.8%	19.6%

It is clear from the preceding illustration that the difference in the effective tax rate on the dividend income between the lowest and the highest tax brackets is very substantial—a 15% difference. The 15% difference is greater than the 12% (29% − 17%) difference between the tax rates for these two tax brackets. This is, of course, in keeping with the progressive nature or the "ability to pay" philosophy of our current income tax system.

Instalment Payment of Estimated Tax for Individuals

For self-employed persons such as public accountants, doctors, dentists, and owners of unincorporated businesses, there is, of course, no salary and no tax withholding. Other examples of income on which no withholding occurs are rental income, dividends, and interest income. In these cases, tax instalments are required if the taxpayer's tax in the year or in either of the two preceding years is $2,000 ($1,200 in Quebec) or more. The amount of instalment payments, due on or before March 15, June 15, September 15, and December 15, is based either on a reasonable estimate or on the tax applicable to the taxable income of the preceding year, whichever is lower. Any additional tax is due on or before April 30 of the following year.

Tax Returns, Tax Refunds, and Payment of the Tax

All individuals with tax owing must file an income tax return on or before April 30 for the preceding calendar year; otherwise, late filing penalties and interest will be charged. The payment of income taxes is on a "pay as you go" basis. The procedure by which employers withhold income taxes from the salaries of employees has been discussed previously in Chapter 11. The amounts withheld from an employee's salary for income taxes can be considered as payment on account. If the amount of income taxes as computed by preparing a tax return is less than the amount withheld during the year, the taxpayer is entitled to a refund. On the other hand, if the tax computed is more than the amount withheld, the balance should be paid with the filing of the tax return. Individuals who are entitled to a refund will have to file a tax return (within three years from the end of the year for which a refund is due) to obtain a refund.

Computation of Individual Income Tax Illustrated

LO 4: Determine the tax liability of an individual

The computation of the 1997 federal and provincial income tax for Sam Lee is illustrated on the next page. The illustration highlights some of the main features of the income tax law and is based on the following assumed data:

1. Mr. Sam Lee is married and has a sixteen-year-old son who has $860 net income from various part-time jobs. Also, Mrs. Lee has a net income of $500.
2. Mr. Lee's income, withholdings, and disbursements include:

Income:
Salary from employment (before tax withholding)	$60,000
Dividends from taxable Canadian corporations	8,000
Interest from Canada Savings Bonds	1,800
Gain on sale of shares of Canadian Ltd.	1,200

Withholdings:
Income taxes	16,000
Canada Pension Plan contributions	945
Employment insurance premiums	1,131
Contribution to a registered pension plan*	4,869
Union membership dues	530

Disbursements:
Medical expenses	900
Charitable donations	1,600
Professional membership dues	690

*Assumed amount for the year. The determination of the maximum amount can be very complex, depending on the types of pension plan and such elements as pensionable earnings, years of services, etc.

3. Mr. Lee has a net capital loss carryover of $1,000.
4. Provincial tax rate is 55%.

SAM LEE
Illustrative Federal and Provincial Income Tax Computation
For the Year 1997

Total income:		
Salary		$60,000
Dividends ($8,000 plus 25% gross-up)		10,000
Interest		1,800
Taxable capital gain (¾ of the $1,200 gain)		900
		$72,700
Deductions		
Registered pension plan contributions	$4,869	
Union and professional dues	1,220	6,089
Net income		$66,611
Other deductions		
Net capital loss carryover*		900
Taxable income		$65,711
Federal income tax calculation:		
$29,590 at 17%		$ 5,030
29,590 at 26%		7,693
6,531 at 29%		1,894
$65,711		$14,617
Tax credits:		
Canada Pension Plan contributions credit (17% × $945)	$ 161	
Employment insurance premiums credit (17% × $1,131)	192	
Basic personal credit (17% × $6,456)	1,098	
Spousal (married) credit (17% × $5,380)	915	
Charitable donations credits ($200 at 17% and $1,400 at 29%)	440	
Dividend credit (13⅓ % of the grossed-up amount of $10,000)	1,333	4,139
Basic federal tax		10,478
3% federal surtax (3% × $10,478)		314
Federal tax payable		$10,792
Add:		
Provincial tax—55% of "basic federal tax"		5,763
Total tax payable		$16,555
Less: income taxes withheld		16,000
Amount to be paid		$ 555

*Cannot exceed taxable capital gain for the year.

Note: Since the amount of medical expenses of $900 is less than 3% of net income, there is no tax credit for medical expenses.

INCOME TAXES: CORPORATIONS

Taxation and Tax Rates

A corporation is a separate taxable entity. Every corporation, unless specifically exempt from taxation, must file an income tax return (Form T2) within six months from the end of its taxation year, whether or not it has taxable income or owes any tax. Also, corporations are required to pay their income taxes on a monthly instalment basis. Our discussion is focused on the ordinary business public corporations, with only brief references to certain other types of corporations for which special tax treatment applies.

As with individuals, the federal income tax rate applies to the corporation's taxable income. The tax rates for 1997 are as shown below:

Type of Business	Tax Rate
General business	*28%*
Manufacturing business	*21%*
Small business (excluding public corporations and on the first $200,000 income each year)	*12%*[7]

Also, there is a 4% surtax on federal corporate income tax that increases all the above rates by 1.12%.

In addition to federal tax, all provinces levy income tax on corporations. The provincial tax rate for 1997 for general business public corporations ranges from 8.9% to 17%. Also, provincial rates are lower for certain businesses, such as manufacturing and processing and small businesses.

Computation of Taxable Income of Corporations

The taxable income of corporations is computed in much the same way as for individuals. For example, corporations, like individuals, report three-quarters of capital gains as income and may deduct the **allowable** capital losses **only** to the extent of **taxable** capital gains. Also, corporations may carry back and forward the remaining net capital losses against taxable capital gains in the same manner as for individuals, as discussed earlier. However, there are a number of differences. The major ones include:

1. **Donations** Donations are deducted from income in corporations. They are deducted as tax credits for individuals.
2. **Dividends received** The dividends received by a corporation from other taxable Canadian corporations are **not** included in the corporation's taxable income. Since these dividends are not taxable, the dividend tax credit for individuals does not apply to corporations. However, certain private corporations pay a special refundable tax on certain dividends received, which will be refunded when the corporation subsequently pays a taxable dividend to its shareholders.
3. **Interest income** Corporations must use the accrual basis for interest income while individuals can use either the cash or modified accrual basis.

---

[7] This low tax rate is no longer available to those corporations with taxable capital employed in Canada of $15 million or more. Also, for corporations with taxable capital between $10 and $15 million, the amount subject to this low rate is reduced on a straight-line basis.

Computation of Taxable Income and Federal Income Tax for Corporation Illustrated

LO 5: Determine the taxable income and income tax of a corporation

To highlight some of the main features of income tax law as it applies to corporations, the computation of federal tax for Stone Corporation, a public corporation that is not a manufacturer, for the 1997 taxation year follows. Remember this illustration is not an income statement and does not show items in the sequence of an income statement.

STONE CORPORATION
Illustrative Federal Tax Computation
(In thousands of dollars)

Revenue:		
Sales		$780,000
Dividends received from taxable Canadian corporations		10,000
Total revenue		$790,000
Expenses:		
Cost of goods sold	$510,000	
Other expenses (includes capital loss of $2,000)	96,000	606,000
Income for accounting purposes		$184,000
Add back:		
Capital loss deducted as part of operating expenses		2,000
Net income for tax purposes		$186,000
Deduct (item not subject to tax)		
Dividends received from taxable Canadian corporations		10,000
Taxable income		$176,000
Federal tax computation:		
28% on $176,000	$ 49,280	
4% surtax (4% × $49,280)	1,971	$ 51,251
Deduct: Monthly instalment payments		50,600
Balance of federal tax payable		$651

Notice the difference between accounting income ($184,000) and taxable income ($176,000)

Accounting Income versus Taxable Income

In the determination of **accounting income**, the objective is to measure business operating results as accurately as possible in accordance with generally accepted accounting principles. **Taxable income**, on the other hand, is a legal concept governed by statute and subject to frequent change by Parliament. In setting the rules for determining taxable income, Parliament is interested not only in meeting the revenue needs of government but also in achieving certain public policy objectives. Since accounting income and taxable income are determined with different purposes in mind, it is not surprising that they often differ by material amounts.

The following are some of the major areas of difference between accounting income and taxable income:

1. Certain income and expense items included in computing accounting income are either excluded or partly excluded from computing taxable income. For example, dividends received by a taxable Canadian corporation from other taxable Canadian corporations are

included in accounting income but are excluded from taxable income; goodwill and organization costs may be amortized for accounting purposes, but only three-quarters of them can be amortized for tax purposes; entertainment expenses such as meals are deducted from accounting income but only 50% can be deducted for tax purposes.
2. Capital gains and losses are fully included in computing accounting income, but only a portion (3/4) of these gains and losses is included in computing taxable income.
3. Methods used for computing accounting income may differ from those used for computing taxable income. For example, lifo method of inventory may be used for accounting purposes, but is not allowed for tax purposes; straight-line method of depreciation may be used for computing accounting income, but a declining balance method based on tax regulations is used to compute depreciation, called "capital cost allowance," for tax purposes.

Capital Cost Allowance

LO 6: Determine the amount of capital cost allowance.

There are special tax regulations for recognizing a portion of a depreciable asset as an expense each year. This expense is called **capital cost allowance** rather than depreciation. The recognition of capital cost allowance for tax purposes differs significantly from depreciation for accounting purposes. The main features of capital cost allowance are:

1. Depreciable assets of a similar nature are grouped into a particular class or pool.
2. Costs of additions are added to, and proceeds of disposals (up to the original cost of the asset) and capital cost allowances are deducted from, the balance of the class or pool.
3. When a class or pool has a negative balance at the end of a taxation year, the negative balance, known as "recapture," is to be included in income for tax purposes. When a pool has a positive balance but without any assets, this balance, known as "terminal loss," is deducted from income.
4. A stipulated rate is applied to the balance of each class or pool to obtain the amount of capital cost allowance for the year. However, in the year where there is a net addition of assets (i.e., total addition exceeds total disposal), only one-half of such net addition is eligible for capital cost allowance for that year.
5. Capital cost allowances may be claimed to the maximum or may be deferred to a future year.

Some of the more common classes of depreciable assets and their stipulated rates are:

Class		Maximum Rate
1	Buildings (other than those in Classes 6, 31, or 32)	4%
8	Machinery, equipment, and furniture*	20%
10	Automobiles, trucks, and tractors	30%

If the machinery and equipment are for manufacturing, they are included in class 43.

Taxpayers may claim an amount of capital cost allowance in each taxation year up to the maximum amount allowed for each class. The following example illustrates the application of the main features of capital cost allowance.

X Ltd. has a number of trucks (Class 10) used in its business operations. The beginning balance is $100,000. During the year, two trucks costing $48,000 were purchased and one old truck, with an original cost of $12,000, was sold for $8,000.

The capital cost allowance for the year is computed as follows:

Beginning balance	$ 100,000
Add: purchase of two trucks	48,000
	$ 148,000
Deduct: proceeds of disposal of one truck	8,000
Ending balance	$ 140,000
Capital cost allowance: 30% on beginning balance of $100,000	$ 30,000
30% on ½ of net asset addition of $40,000 (($48,000 − $8,000) × ½ × 30%))	6,000
	$ 36,000

X Ltd. may claim a capital cost allowance for class 10 of up to a maximum of $36,000 for the year.

Future (Deferred) Income Taxes[8]

LO 7: Describe the circumstances that create a liability for future (deferred) income taxes.

We have seen that differences between generally accepted accounting principles and income tax rules can be material. Some businesses might consider it more convenient to maintain their accounting records in conformity with the tax rules, but the result would be to distort financial statements. It is clearly preferable to maintain accounting records by the principles that produce relevant information about business operations. The data in the records can then be adjusted by the use of work sheets to arrive at taxable income.

When a corporation follows one method in its accounting records and financial statements but uses a different method for its income tax return, a financial reporting problem arises. The difference in method will usually have the effect of postponing the recognition of income on the tax return. The items causing this difference fall into two broad categories: permanent differences and timing (temporary) differences.

Permanent differences are revenue or expenses that enter into the computation of one type of income, but never are considered in determining the other. Most permanent differences are the result of special tax law provisions unrelated to accounting principles. For example, dividends received by a corporation from other taxable Canadian corporations are included in the determination of accounting income but are excluded from the computation of taxable income. Also, certain expenses such as politi-

---

[8] Section 3465 of the *CICA Handbook* recommends that the term "future income taxes" replace "deferred income taxes" for financial statements after January 1, 2000 and it encourages early adoption of this term.

cal contributions are deducted from accounting income but are not deducted from the computation of taxable income.

Timing differences arise when the **same dollar amount** of revenue or expense is recognized for tax purposes and for accounting purposes, but the ***timing*** of the recognition under tax rules differs from that under accounting principles. For example, a company may use an accelerated method of depreciation in its income tax return but use the straight-line method in its income statement. Over the life of the depreciable asset, however, the total amount of depreciation claimed in the tax returns will be the same as that reported in the company's income statements.

Most businesses have a policy of using in their income tax returns those accounting methods that will ***accelerate as much as possible the recognition of expenses, and delay as long as possible the recognition of revenue***. As a result of using these methods, many businesses are able to defer the recognition of significant portions of their pretax accounting income into the tax returns of future years. Hence, they are able to defer payment of the related income taxes.

Accounting for Future (Deferred) Taxes: An Illustration

When differences between pretax accounting income and taxable income are caused by timing differences, a business bases its income tax expense for the period upon its pretax accounting income. This practice achieves a proper ***matching*** of income taxes expense with the related earnings. However, some of this income taxes expense will not be paid until later years, when the income is included in future tax returns. Through timing differences, payment of part of a company's income taxes expense may be deferred on a long-term basis.

To illustrate, let us consider a very simple case involving only one timing difference. Assume that Pryor Corporation has before-tax accounting income of $600,000 in both 2000 and 2001. However, the company takes as a tax deduction in 2000 an expense of $200,000, which is not deducted as expense in the income statement until 2001. The company's accounting income, taxable income, and the actual income taxes due (assuming an average federal and provincial tax rate of 45%) are shown below.

	2001	2000
Accounting income (before income taxes)	$600,000	$600,000
Taxable income	800,000	400,000
Actual income taxes due each year at 45% rate:		
2000: $600,000 − $200,000 = $400,000 taxable income × 45%		$180,000
2001: $600,000 + $200,000 = $800,000 taxable income × 45%	$360,000	

Let us assume the Pryor Corporation reports as an expense in its income statement each year the amount of income taxes due for that year. The effect on reported net income as shown in the company's financial statements would be as follows:

Company reports actual taxes

	2001	2000
Accounting income (before income taxes)	$600,000	$600,000
Income taxes expense (amount actually due)	360,000	180,000
Net income	$240,000	$420,000
Income taxes expense as a percentage of pretax accounting income	60%	30%

The readers of Pryor Corporation's income statement might well wonder why the same $600,000 accounting income before income taxes in the two years produced such widely varying amounts of tax expense and net income.

To deal with this distortion between pretax income and after-tax income, an accounting policy known as **interperiod income tax allocation** is required for financial reporting purposes.[9] Briefly, the objective of income tax allocation is to *accrue income taxes expense in relation to accounting income*, even if the items comprising accounting income will be taxable or deductible in a different period.

In the Pryor Corporation example, this means we would report in the 2000 income statement a tax expense based on $600,000 of accounting income even though a portion of this income ($200,000) will not be subject to income tax until the second year. The effect of this accounting procedure is demonstrated by the following journal entries to record the income tax expense in each of the two years:

Entries to record income tax allocations

```
2000  Income Taxes Expense .................... 270,000
          Income Taxes Payable ................          180,000
          Future Income Taxes .................           90,000
      To record current and future income taxes at 45%
      of accounting income of $600,000.
```

As explained in Chapter 16, classification of future income taxes as current or long-term depends upon the nature of the items causing the tax deferral.

In 2001, the timing difference will "reverse," and Pryor will report taxable income of $200,000 in excess of its pretax accounting income. Thus, the income taxes deferred in 2000 are coming due. The entry to record income taxes expense in 2001 is:

```
2001  Income Taxes Expense .................... 270,000
      Future Income Taxes ......................  90,000
          Income Taxes Payable ................          360,000
      To record income taxes at 45% of accounting
      income of $600,000 and to record actual income
      taxes due.
```

Notice that as in 2000, income tax expense is based upon the pretax accounting income shown in the company's income statement.

---

[9] For a more complete discussion of tax allocation procedures, see *CICA Handbook*, section 3465, on "Income taxes."

Using these interperiod tax allocation procedures, Pryor Corporation's financial statements would report net income during the two-year period as follows:

	2001	2000
Accounting income (before income taxes)	$600,000	$600,000
Income taxes expense (tax allocation basis)	270,000	270,000
Net income	$330,000	$330,000
Income taxes expense as a percentage of pretax accounting income	45%	45%

Future (Deferred) Taxes: An Evaluation In 2001, Pryor Corporation faces the unpleasant prospect of paying an amount of income taxes that is *greater* than its income taxes expense for the current year. Although this situation can arise, it does not usually happen as long as a company continues to grow.

A growing company usually defers more taxes each year than the previous deferrals that are coming due. Thus, a growing company may pay less in taxes each year than the amount of its current tax expense, and its liability for future (deferred) income taxes continues to grow. The liability for future (deferred) taxes is, in essence, an *interest-free loan*— capital made available to the business by selecting advantageous tax methods for use in the company's income tax returns. Hence, deferring income taxes generally is viewed as a desirable business strategy.

CASE IN POINT The balance sheets of many companies showed large amounts of deferred or future income taxes. As of a recent year, the deferred or future income taxes for Shell Canada were $799 million; BCE Inc., $454 million; Dofasco, $317 million; and Domtar, $212 million.

TAX PLANNING OPPORTUNITIES

Income tax laws have become so complex that careful tax planning has become a way of life for most business firms. Almost all companies today engage professional tax specialists to review the tax aspects of major business decisions and to develop plans for legally minimizing income taxes. We will now consider some areas in which tax planning may offer substantial benefits.

Form of Business Organization

LO 8: Explain how tax planning is used in choosing the form of business organization, timing and nature of transactions, and the capital structure.

Tax factors should be carefully considered at the time a business is organized. As a sole proprietor or partner, a business owner will pay taxes at individual rates on the business income earned in any year *whether or not it is withdrawn from the business*. On the other hand, corporations deduct salaries paid to owners for services but cannot deduct dividends paid to shareholders. Both *salaries and dividends* are taxable income to the persons receiving them. However, the tax on dividends is reduced by a dividend tax credit.

These and other factors must be weighed in deciding in any given situation whether the corporate or noncorporate form of business organization is preferable. There is no simple answer, even considering only these basic differences. To illustrate, suppose that Able, a married man, starts a small business that he expects will produce, before any compensation to himself and before income taxes, an average annual income of $80,000. Able plans to recognize a salary of $20,000 and to withdraw all income from the business. The combined corporate and individual taxes (based on 1997 tax rates) under the corporate and sole proprietorship form of business organization are summarized below (***surtax is excluded*** to simplify the computations).

Which form of business organization produces a lower tax?

	Corporation	Sole Proprietorship
Business income	$80,000	$80,000
Salary to Able	20,000	
	$60,000	$80,000
Corporate taxes (on the $60,000 taxable income of a small business)		
Federal 12% ... $7,200		
Provincial 10%* ... 6,000	13,200	
Amount to Able (the $46,800 as dividends)	$46,800	$80,000
Combined corporate and individual tax:		
Corporate tax on $60,000 taxable income	$13,200	
Individual tax (assume a total deduction of $8,500, tax credits of $2,123, dividend tax credit of $7,800 and 55% provincial tax rate)		
On Able's $20,000 salary and $46,800 dividends	9,204	
On Able's $80,000 share of business income		$21,968
Total income taxes on business income	$22,404	$21,968

*The more common rate for 1997.

Under these assumptions, the formation of a corporation is not favourable from an income tax viewpoint. However, the tax difference between the corporation and sole proprietorship of $436 is very small. Another factor to be considered is that, with the corporation, Able can postpone the amount of tax payable by retaining the income in the corporation rather than paying it out as dividends. Of course, factors other than income tax (such as limited liability) must be considered in deciding whether to incorporate the business.

Planning Business Transactions to Minimize or Postpone Income Taxes

Business transactions may often be arranged in such a way as to produce favourable tax treatment. For example, timing of disposal of investments (usually at or near the year-end date) in securities can postpone income taxes because capital losses from securities can be offset against capital gains. However, the sale of an investment in securities to generate a capital loss must not be accompanied by the purchase of the same securities within 30 days or the capital loss would be disallowed as it would be considered a superficial loss.

Sometimes sellers try to arrange a transaction one way to their tax benefit and buyers try to shape it another way to produce tax savings for them. Income tax effects thus become a part of price negotiation. For example, in buying business property, the purchasers will try to allocate as much of the cost of the property for the building and as little to the land as possible, since building costs can be depreciated for tax purposes. Similarly, in buying a business, the buyers will want as much as possible of the total purchase price to be attributed to inventories or to depreciable assets rather than goodwill. The cost of goods sold and depreciation are deductible against income, whereas only three-quarters of goodwill can be amortized for tax purposes. Thus, the main point is: ***any failure to consider tax effects on major business transactions can be costly***.

Tax Planning in the Choice of Financial Structure

In deciding upon the best means of raising capital to start or expand a business, consideration should be given to income taxes. Different forms of business financing produce different amounts of tax expense. Interest on debt, for example, is ***fully deductible***, but dividends on preferred or common stock are not. This factor operates as a strong incentive to finance expansion by borrowing.

Let us suppose that a company subject to a 45% marginal tax rate needs $100,000 to invest in productive assets on which it can earn a 16% annual return. If the company obtains the needed money by issuing $100,000 in 9% preferred stock, it will earn **after taxes** only $8,800, which is not even enough to cover the $9,000 preferred dividend. (This after-tax amount is computed as $16,000 income less taxes at 45% of $16,000.)

Now let us assume, on the other hand, that the company borrowed $100,000 at 12% interest. (Interest rate is usually higher than dividend rate because interest is tax deductible and dividend provides a dividend tax credit.) The additional gross income would be $16,000 but interest expense of $12,000 would be deducted, leaving taxable income of $4,000. The tax on the $4,000 at 45% would be $1,800, leaving after-tax income of $2,200. Analysis along these lines is also needed in choosing between debt financing and financing by issuing common stock.

End-of-Chapter Review

Key Terms Introduced or Emphasized in Chapter 18

Basic federal tax *(p.909)* The gross amount of federal tax minus tax credits. The basic federal tax is the basis for computing provincial tax.

Capital cost allowance *(p.915)* The amount of expense for depreciable assets for tax purposes.

Capital gain or loss *(p.907)* The difference between the cost or adjusted-cost base of a capital asset and the amount received from its sale.

Dividend tax credit *(p.909)* This credit is intended to minimize the impact of "double taxation" on corporate income. It is computed by applying $13^{1}/_{3}\%$ to the taxable (grossed-up) amount of dividends and is deducted from federal income tax.

Gross federal tax *(p.908)* Taxable income times federal tax rate equals gross federal tax.

Interperiod tax allocation *(p.918)* Allocation of income tax expense among accounting periods because of timing differences between accounting income and taxable income. Causes income tax expense reported in financial statements to be in logical relation to accounting income.

Marginal tax rate *(p.905)* The tax rate to which a taxpayer is subject on an additional dollar of income received.

Tax credit *(p.908)* An amount to be subtracted from gross federal income tax to arrive at basic federal tax, including credits for Canada Pension Plan contributions, employment insurance premiums, basic personal, married, equivalent to married, age, disability, tuition fees, and charitable donations.

Tax planning *(p.902)* A systematic process of legally minimizing income taxes by considering in advance the tax consequences of alternative business or investment actions.

Taxable income *(p.908)* The computed amount to which the appropriate tax rate is to be applied to arrive at the gross amount of federal tax.

Total income *(p.906)* An individual's world income from all sources, including income from office, employment, business, property and pension, and capital gain.

Self-Test Questions

Answers to these questions appear on page 934.

1. Which of the following is applicable to the income tax system?
   a. The only objective of income tax laws is to raise as much revenue as possible to finance government spending.
   b. A taxpayer is required to pay instalment tax if tax withheld at source is greater than $2,000.
   c. It is a self-assessment system.
   d. The three classes of taxpayers are: individuals, partnerships, and corporations.

2. In preparing the income tax return for an individual taxpayer:
   a. Income taxes withheld from an individual's salary are deducted from total income.
   b. Income from sources outside Canada must be included in the determination of total income.
   c. Income from illegal sources is excluded from the computation of total income.
   d. Receipt of a large refund each year indicates better tax planning than receipt of a small refund.

3. Which of the following are eligible for tax credits? (More than one answer may be correct.)

    a. Registered pension plan contributions and employment insurance premiums.
    b. Tuition fees, charitable donations, and education amount.
    c. Basic personal amount for the taxpayer, Canada Pension Plan contributions, and employment insurance premium.
    d. Medical expenses, union dues, and allowable capital losses.

4. When a business is organized as a corporation (more than one answer may be correct):
    a. Income taxes expense recorded in the accounting records is based upon accounting income and may differ from the income taxes liability shown in the corporate income tax return.
    b. The treatment of capital gains and losses is the same as for individuals.
    c. Taxable income is the same as net income before income taxes in the income statement.
    d. Dividends received from other taxable Canadian corporations must be included in the corporation's taxable income.

5. Which of the following are valid statements regarding tax planning and the choice of business organization? (More than one answer may be correct.)
    a. When a business is organized as a corporation, no income tax is paid on earnings that remain invested in the business.
    b. In computing a corporation's taxable income, the corporation may deduct salaries paid to owners, but may not deduct dividends.
    c. When a business is organized as a sole proprietorship, the owner must pay taxes at individual rates on the entire amount of business income, regardless of amounts withdrawn by the owner.
    d. An individual who organizes a business as a corporation must pay individual income taxes on any salary and dividends received from the corporation after deducting the appropriate amount of dividend tax credit.

Assignment Material

Discussion Questions

1. What are some broad objectives of the federal income tax legislation other than providing revenue for the government?
2. List the five most striking characteristics of the 1988 tax reform legislation.
3. List three examples of tax credits other than dividend tax credit.
4. Explain the differences between *tax planning* and *tax evasion*, and give an example of each.
5. What are the major classes of taxpayers under the federal income tax law?
6. It has been claimed that corporate income is subject to "double taxation." Explain the meaning of this expression, and indicate whether there is provision in the tax law to minimize or neutralize it.
7. Why is the income tax system described as one of *self-assessment*? What means do tax authorities have of enforcing this system?

8. Taxes are characterized as either ***progressive***, ***proportional***, or ***regressive*** with respect to any given base. Describe an income tax rate structure that would fit each of these characterizations.

9. State whether you agree with the following statement and explain your reasoning: A person in a very high tax bracket who makes a cash contribution to a charitable organization will reduce his or her federal income tax liability by more than the amount of the donation.

10. State the federal income tax formula for individuals, beginning with total income and ending with basic federal tax.

11. From an individual taxpayer's viewpoint, it is better to have a $10,000 capital gain than $10,000 of ordinary income. Explain.

12. Cite two examples to illustrate the broadening of the tax base originated from the tax reform legislation.

13. Even when a corporation uses the accrual method of accounting, taxable income may differ from accounting income. Give four ***examples*** of differences between the tax treatment and accounting treatment of items that are included in the determination of income.

14. Under what circumstances is the accounting procedure known as ***interperiod income tax allocation*** appropriate? Explain the objective of this procedure.

15. The depreciation expense computed by Zane Corporation as the capital cost allowance (permitted by the income tax law) appeared in the tax return as $150,000. In the accounting records and financial statements, Zane's depreciation was computed on the straight-line basis and amounted to $100,000. Under interperiod tax allocation procedures, would Zane's balance sheet show future (deferred) income taxes as an asset or a liability? Explain.

16. List some tax factors to be considered in deciding whether to organize a new business as a corporation or as a partnership.

17. Explain the principal factors that should be considered by a taxpayer in determining ***when*** it would be most advantageous to sell an investment that will result in the recognition of a capital loss.

18. Explain how the corporate income tax makes debt financing in general more attractive than financing through the issuance of preferred stock.

19. Some of the decisions that business owners must make in the organization and operation of a business will affect the amount of income taxes to be paid. List some of these decisions that affect the amount of income taxes legally payable.

Exercises

EXERCISE 18-1
Accounting and Tax Terminology
(LO 1, 2, 6, 7)

Listed below are nine technical accounting and tax terms introduced in this chapter:

Capital gain   *Taxable income*   *Interperiod tax allocation*
Tax credit   *Gross federal tax*   *Cash basis of accounting*
Basic federal tax   *Tax planning*   *Capital cost allowance*

Each of the following statements may (or may not) describe one of these technical terms. For each statement, indicate the term described, or answer "None" if the statement does not correctly describe any of the terms.

a. Net income minus other deductions, which serves as a basis to compute gross federal tax.
b. Taxable income multiplied by an appropriate federal tax rate.
c. Gross federal tax minus tax credits.
d. Income tax recognized each period as a constant percentage of net sales.
e. Causes income tax expense reported in financial statements to be in logical relationship to accounting income.
f. Profit from disposal of such assets as stock and bonds acquired as long-term investments.
g. Revenue recorded when received in cash and expenses recorded in period payment is made.
h. An amount to be subtracted from gross federal tax.
i. Depreciation calculated according to tax law and regulations.

EXERCISE 18-2
Inclusion or Exclusion?
(LO 2, 3)

Some of the following items should be included in income; others on the list should be excluded. For each item listed, write the identifying letter and the word *included* or *excluded* to show whether the item belongs in income on the income tax return of an individual.

a. Kickbacks received by automobile salespeople from insurance brokers to whom they referred customers.
b. Dividends from investment in a taxable Canadian corporation.
c. Compensation received for damages suffered in automobile accident.
d. Gain on sale of shares of Canadian Ltd. common stock.
e. Gift from an uncle.
f. Money received from lottery winnings.
g. Tips received by waiter.
h. Interest received on investment bonds.

EXERCISE 18-3
Deductible or Nondeductible?
(LO 2)

Susan Rooney has a total income of $68,000 and a net income of $54,000. For each item listed, write the identifying letter and the word *deductible* or *nondeductible* (as a deduction from income or as a tax credit).

a. Interest paid on instalment contract on automobile	$ 180
b. Gift to an unemployed relative	300
c. Professional dues	660
d. Contribution to Red Cross	575
e. Cost of commuting between home and work	800
f. Canada Pension Plan contributions	945
g. Employment insurance premiums	1,131
h. Registered pension plan contributions	4,800
i. Medical expenses (not covered by insurance)	500
j. Cash stolen while on business trip	80
k. Interest paid on a bank loan for investment purposes	450
l. Safety deposit box fee (to keep investment certificates)	35

EXERCISE 18-4
Determine Total, Net, and Taxable Income, and Federal Tax for an Individual
(LO 2)

Angela Lambert has the following information for her first tax return, one year after graduation from a top university.

Salary	$88,000
Interest from a bank account	388
Canada Pension Plan contributions	945
Employment insurance premiums	1,131
Professional dues	800
Registered pension plan contributions	3,500
Basic personal tax credits	1,098
Dental expenses	2,980
Charitable donations	2,600

Compute (a) total income, (b) net income, (c) taxable income, (d) gross federal tax, and (e) basic federal tax for Angela Lambert. The federal tax rates are assumed to be: 17% the first $29,590, 26% on the second $29,590, and 29% on the remaining taxable income.

EXERCISE 18-5
Determine Taxable Income for an Individual
(LO 2, 3)

Pier Fiorino has the following sources of income for 1997:

Interest from Canada Savings Bonds	$ 1,000
Dividends from taxable Canadian corporations	12,000
Gains on sales of shares in Canadian National Ltd.	3,000

Compute the **net** amount that should be included as taxable income, assuming a net capital loss carryover of $4,000.

EXERCISE 18-6
Determine Taxable Income and Federal Tax Liability for a Corporation
(LO 5, 6)

Sunset Limited reports the following income during Year 1:

Operating income (after deducting depreciation of $100,000)	$600,000
Capital gains	180,000
Dividends received from taxable Canadian corporations	60,000
Capital cost allowances	116,000

Compute the taxable income and **federal** income tax liability for Sunset Limited for Year 1. Assume a 28% federal tax rate and ignore any surtax.

EXERCISE 18-7
Interperiod Tax Allocation
(LO 7)

Sea King Corporation deducted on its tax return for Year 1 an expense of $50,000 that was not recognized as an expense for accounting purposes until Year 2. The corporation's accounting income before income taxes in each of the two years was $485,000. The company uses tax allocation procedures.

a. Prepare the journal entries required at the end of Year 1 and Year 2 to record income tax expense, assuming a combined federal and provincial tax rate of 45%.

b. Prepare a two-column schedule showing the net income to appear on the financial statements for Year 1 and Year 2, assuming tax allocation procedures are used. Also prepare a similar schedule on the assumption that tax allocation procedures are not used.

Problems

PROBLEM 18-1
Inclusion in or Exclusion from Income?
(LO 2, 3)

State whether each item listed below should be included in or excluded from an individual's income for federal income tax purposes. Add explanatory comments if they are necessary.
1. Share of income from partnership.
2. An honorarium of $100 for a speech to charitable organizations.
3. Interest received on Canada Savings Bonds.
4. Salary received from a corporation by a shareholder who owns directly or indirectly all the shares of the corporation's outstanding stock.
5. Amount received as damages in a libel lawsuit.
6. Trip to Hawaii given by employer as reward for outstanding service.
7. Taxpayer owed $1,500 on a note payable. During the current year the taxpayer painted a building owned by the creditor, and in turn the creditor cancelled the note.
8. Gain on sale of taxable Canadian Ltd. capital stock.
9. Value of a colour TV set won as a prize in a quiz contest.
10. Inheritance received on death of a rich uncle.
11. Cash dividends received from Canadian Oil Ltd.
12. Employment insurance benefits.

PROBLEM 18-2
Inclusion in or Exclusion from Income?
(LO 2, 3)

State whether each item listed below should be included in or excluded from an individual's income for federal income tax purposes. Add explanatory comments if needed.
1. Lottery winnings.
2. Cash dividends received on stock of Canadian Ltd.
3. Premium on group term life insurance paid by employer.
4. Tips received by a door attendant at a luxury hotel.
5. Income from a business of an illegal nature.
6. Employment insurance benefits.
7. Drawing received from a proprietorship.
8. Income from personal injury awards.
9. Interest received on a savings account in Scotia Bank.
10. Gain on sale of Loris Ltd. shares of common stock.
11. Painted a building owned by the creditor in return for the cancellation of a note payable of $1,000.
12. Las Vegas vacation paid by employer as reward for outstanding services.

PROBLEM 18-3
Deductible or Not Deductible?
(LO 2)

State whether each item listed below is deductible or not deductible by an individual for federal income tax purposes, and if deductible, whether it is from total income or net income, or as a tax credit.
1. Fees for preparation of personal income tax return.
2. Lawyer's fee for appealing an assessment by Revenue Canada, Taxation.
3. Registered pension plan contributions.
4. Professional membership fee.
5. Interest on a loan that was used to invest in a taxable Canadian corporation.
6. Interest paid on mortgage covering personal residence.
7. Capital loss on the sale of securities.
8. Life insurance premium paid by a taxpayer.
9. Lottery losses.
10. Expenses incurred in moving from Calgary to Vancouver to accept a new position with a different company, not reimbursed by employer.
11. Spousal support payments.
12. Education amount.

PROBLEM 18-4
Deductible or Not Deductible?
(LO 2)

State whether each of the following items is deductible or not deductible by an individual for federal income tax purposes, and if deductible, whether it is from total income or net income, or as a tax credit.
1. Tuition fees.
2. Fee paid to chartered accountant for services in contesting assessment of additional income taxes by Revenue Canada, Taxation.
3. Expenses incurred in moving across country to accept a position with different employer. Not reimbursed.
4. Charitable donations.
5. Loss on sale of investment in securities.
6. Cost of commuting between home and place of employment.
7. Registered retirement savings plan contributions for spouse.
8. Employment insurance premiums.
9. Registered pension plan contributions.
10. Interest paid on mortgage on personal residence.
11. Union dues.
12. Interest expense for a loan to finance investment in securities.

PROBLEM 18-5
Determine Income Tax for an Individual
(LO 2, 3 4)

Stew Dius quit his job during the current year to go back to school. He has asked you for help with his tax return. He gives you the following information:

Income
Salary (for eight months)	$25,000
Dividends received from taxable Canadian Corporation	600

Withholdings
Income taxes	4,000
Canada Pension Plan contributions	663
Employment insurance premiums	725

Disbursements
Tuition (for four months, full-time university program)	1,500
Medical expenses	1,200

INSTRUCTIONS

Complete Dius's federal and provincial (tax rate of 55%) income taxes for the current year (including surtax).

PROBLEM 18-6
Determine Income Tax for an Individual
(LO 2, 3, 4)

Lisa Ovalsan, a resident of a province with a 55% tax rate, asks you to prepare her tax return for the current year. She provides you with the following information:

Income
Salary from employment	$68,000
Dividends from taxable Canadian corporations	3,000
Interest from Canada Savings Bonds	1,200
Gains on sale of shares of B.C. Ltd.'s common stock	2,000
Rental income (net)	8,000

Withholdings:
Income taxes	20,000
Canada Pension Plan contributions	945
Employment insurance premiums	1,131
Registered pension plan contributions	4,680

Disbursements:
Dental expenses	2,200
Charitable donations	2,500
Professional membership fees	800

Others:
Loss on sale of shares in Victoria Mines Ltd.	5,000
Lottery winnings	9,600
Basic personal tax credit	1,098

INSTRUCTIONS

Compute Ovalsan's federal and provincial income taxes for the year by using the following federal tax rates: 17% on the first $29,590, 26% on the second $29,590 and 29% on the balance. There is also a 3% federal surtax on basic federal tax and a 5% surtax on basic federal tax in excess of $12,500.

PROBLEM 18-7
Determine Income Tax for an Individual
(LO 2, 3, 4)

The following information is related to Gloria Hoysum, resident of a province with a tax rate of 55%.

Income:
Salary from employment	$70,000
Director's fee (on the board of directors of Toysun Ltd.)	8,000
Dividends from taxable Canadian corporations	6,000
Interest from savings account with Bank of Nova Scotia	600
Gain on sale of shares of Halifax Ltd.	1,800

Withholdings:
Income taxes	22,000
Canada Pension Plan contributions	945
Employment insurance premiums	1,131
Contribution to a registered pension plan	4,980

Disbursements:
Charitable donations	3,200
Professional membership fees	1,200

Others:
Loss on sale of shares of Sydney Mines Ltd.	600
Lottery losses	890
Tax credits relating to the taxpayer	1,098

INSTRUCTIONS

Compute Hoysum's federal and provincial income tax for the year by using the following federal tax rates: 17% on the first $29,590, 26% on the second $29,590, and 29% on the remaining amount. Assume that there is a 3% federal surtax on basic federal tax and a 5% surtax on basic federal tax in excess of $12,500.

PROBLEM 18-8
Determine Taxable Income, Capital Cost Allowance, and Income Tax for a Corporation
(LO 5, 6, 7)

The financial statements for BLW Corporation show a net income before taxes of $300,000 for the current year. Included in the calculation of net income was an expense for depreciation in the amount of $5,000 and dividends received from a taxable Canadian corporation totalling $10,000. The company also has equipment (class 8) with a balance of $35,000 at the beginning of the year and additions of $8,000 during the year.

INSTRUCTIONS

For the current year:
a. Compute the amount of capital cost allowance on the equipment.
b. Compute taxable income for the corporation.
c. Compute federal taxes payable, excluding surtax. BLW Corporation is a manufacturer.
d. Prepare the entry to record current and future income taxes, assuming combined tax rate is 37%.

PROBLEM 18-9
Determine Capital Cost Allowance, Federal Tax, and Future (Deferred) Tax for a Corporation
(LO 5, 6 7)

Macor Corporation has the following operation results for the current year:

Operating income (after depreciation of $138,000 and before capital gains and losses and dividends)	$800,000
Net capital gains from sale of securities (capital gains of $30,000 less capital losses of $18,000)	12,000
Dividends received from taxable Canadian corporations	45,000

The company's only depreciable assets are machinery, equipment, and furniture. The ending balance from last year's tax return was $600,000. During the current year, the company added equipment and furniture at a cost of $450,000 and sold a machine (original cost $66,000) for $50,000. The capital cost allowance rate for tax purposes is 20%.

INSTRUCTIONS

a. Compute the amount of capital cost allowance for the current year.
b. Compute the federal income tax for the current year, based on 28% tax rate.
c. Compute the amount of federal income tax deferred by claiming the maximum capital cost allowance rather than the amount of depreciation for accounting purposes.

PROBLEM 18-10
Determine Capital Cost Allowance, Federal Tax, and Future (Deferred) Tax
(LO 5, 6, 7)

The following information is related to Warner Limited for the current year:

Operating income (before depreciation, dividends, capital gains, and capital losses)	$980,000
Depreciation (automobiles and trucks, straight-line basis)	150,000
Dividends received from taxable Canadian corporations	80,000
Capital gains from sale of securities	30,000
Capital losses from sale of securities	50,000
Automobiles and trucks (class 10, maximum rate 30%):	
Beginning balance	700,000
Additions during the last month of the year	350,000
Proceeds from disposal of trucks (original cost $460,000) during the year	250,000

INSTRUCTIONS

a. Compute the amount of capital cost allowance for the current year.
b. Compute the federal income tax for the current year, based on a 28% tax rate.
c. Compute the amount of federal income tax deferred by claiming the maximum capital cost allowance rather than the amount of depreciation for accounting purposes.

CHAPTER 18 INCOME TAXES AND BUSINESS DECISIONS 931

PROBLEM 18-11
Determine Accounting and Taxable Income, Income Tax and Future (Deferred) Tax, and Tax Advantage of Financing Method
(LO 5, 6, 7, 8)

The accounting records of Garden Corporation included the following information for the current year:

Net sales	$8,600,000
Cost of goods sold	6,000,000
Dividends received from a taxable Canadian corporation	53,000
Operating expenses (including depreciation of $250,000)	1,700,000
Capital gains from sales of securities	28,000
Capital losses from sales of securities	12,000
Capital cost allowance	360,000

Garden is considering expanding its facilities as a result of increased sales, financed either by issuing $500,000, 12% bonds or 9% cumulative preferred stock.

INSTRUCTIONS

a. Compute the accounting income for the current year.
b. Compute the taxable income for the current year.
c. Compute the federal and provincial income taxes for the current year. Assume that the federal rate is 28% and provincial rate is 14%.
d. Prepare the journal entry to record the current and future (deferred) income taxes for the year.
e. Explain which method of financing the $500,000 expansion is more beneficial to the company from an income tax viewpoint.

PROBLEM 18-12
Determine Accounting and Taxable Income, Income Tax and Future (Deferred) Tax, and Tax Advantage of Financing Method
(LO 5, 6, 7, 8)

The following information appears in the records of LM Corporation for the current year:

Net sales	$988,000
Cost of goods sold	707,000
Operating expenses (including depreciation of $90,000)	151,000
Dividends received from taxable Canadian corporations	38,000
Net capital losses from sale of securities (capital losses of $37,000 less capital gains of $19,000)	18,000
Capital cost allowance	190,000

The company is considering whether it should issue bonds or cumulative preferred stock to finance its expanded operations. The amount needed would be $600,000. The interest rate would be 11% and the dividend rate would be at 8%.

INSTRUCTIONS

a. Compute the accounting income for the current year.
b. Compute the taxable income for the current year.
c. Compute the federal and provincial income taxes for the current year, based on the respective rates of 28% and 14%.
d. Prepare the journal entry to record the current and future (deferred) income taxes for the year.
e. Explain which method of financing the $600,000 expansion is more beneficial to the company from an income tax viewpoint.

Analytical and Decision Problems and Cases

A&D 18-1
Determine Income Tax for Two Couples and Evaluate Fairness of Tax
(LO 2, 3, 4)

The Smiths and the Whites are neighbours in Ontario. Neither couple have any children. Both couples earn $55,000 annually. Mr. and Mrs. Smith each earn $27,500. Mr. White earns $55,000 and Mrs. White spends her time volunteering for various charities. Neither couple has any tax credits except personal credits.

INSTRUCTIONS

a. Compute the income taxes payable for each couple.
b. Explain the difference in income taxes payable between the two couples and comment on its fairness under the current income tax legislation.

A&D 18-2
Determine Income Tax for an Individual and Capital Cost Allowance
(LO 2, 3, 4, 6)

Ms. Molly has a rental property. Net income before capital cost allowance in Year 1 was $8,000 for the rental property. Her other income (net of deductions) totalled $18,000. The building had a beginning balance in Year 1 of $100,000 (Class 1—4%). The original cost of the building was $110,000. Early in January, Year 2, Ms. Molly sold the rental property, resulting in a capital gain of $30,000. Her other incomes (net of deductions) in Year 2 is expected to be $18,000 also.

INSTRUCTIONS

a. Assuming Ms. Molly claims capital cost allowance in Year 1, what would her income taxes payable be in Year 1 and Year 2 (use 48% as a provincial tax rate)?
b. Can Ms. Molly do anything to reduce the total amount of income taxes for the two years? Explain and show supporting computation.

A&D 18-3
What's Wrong with My Tax Return?
(LO 2, 3, 4)

After one look at his tax return, Tim Pearl is stunned by the income tax he has to pay. "After I inherited $500,000 from Uncle Tom and won a $30,000 lottery this year, I thought I was O.K. for life. Now, this year's tax is more than double last year's and I have to pay thousands of dollars on April 30. I just don't have this much cash every April 30 to pay the taxes," Tim complains to his wife. The tax return that Tim is complaining about shows the following information:

Total income:

Salary		$ 46,000
Dividends received		22,000
Interest		25,500
Capital gains		6,000
Lottery winnings		30,000
		$129,500
Deduct: union dues		500
Net income and taxable income		$129,000

Federal income tax calculation:

$ 29,590 at 17%		$ 5,030
29,590 at 26%		7,693
69,820 at 29%		20,248
$129,000		$ 32,971

Tax credits

Registered pension plan contributions (17% × $3,820)	$ 649	
Canada Pension Plan contributions (17% × 945)	161	
Employment insurance premium (17% × 1.131)	192	
Basic personal amount (17% × $6,456)	1,098	
Married amount (17% × $5,380)	915	
Medical (17% × $2,188)	372	3,387
Basic federal tax		$ 29,584
Provincial tax: 55% of basic federal tax		16,271
Total tax payable		$ 45,855
Deduct: amount withheld (on salary)		10,966
Tax payable		$ 34,889

INSTRUCTIONS	Explain how each of the errors in Tim's return should be corrected. (Do *not* prepare a corrected return.) Assume that Tim is subject to a 55% provincial tax and federal tax of: 17% on the first $29,590, 26% on the second $29,590, and 29% on the remaining taxable income. (Ignore surtax.) Also, comment on Tim's concern regarding the cash need on April 30 in future years.
A&D 18-4 Investors Choose between Debt and Equity (LO 8)	Bill and Hannah Bailey own a successful small company, Bailey Corporation. The outstanding capital stock consists of 1,000 shares, of which 400 shares are owned by Bill and 600 by Hannah. In order to finance a new branch operation, the corporation needs an additional $100,000 in cash. Bill and Hannah have this amount on deposit with a bank and intend to put these personal funds into the corporation in order to establish the new branch. They will either arrange for the corporation to issue to them an additional 1,000 shares of stock, or they will make a loan to the corporation at an interest rate of 12%. ***Income before taxes*** of the corporation has been consistently averaging $150,000 a year, and annual dividends of $64,000 have been paid regularly on the $100,000 of capital stock. It is expected that the new branch will cause income before taxes to increase by $30,000. If new common stock is issued to finance the expansion, the total annual dividend of $64,000 will be continued unchanged. If a loan of $100,000 is arranged, the dividend will be reduced by $12,000, the amount of annual interest on the loan.
INSTRUCTIONS	**a.** From the income tax standpoint of Bill and Hannah Bailey (with a federal marginal tax rate of 29%), would there be any savings as between the stock issuance and the loan? Explain. **b.** From the standpoint of getting their money out of the corporation (assuming that the new branch is profitable), should Bill and Hannah choose capital stock or a loan for the infusion of new funds to the corporation? **c.** Prepare a two-column schedule, with one column headed If New Stock Is Used and the other headed If Loan Is Used. For each of these proposed methods of financing, show (1) the present corporate income ***before taxes***; (2) the corporate income ***before taxes*** after the expansion; (3) the corporate income taxes (12% federal tax rate) after the expansion; and (4) the corporate net income after the expansion. (Disregard provincial tax.) **d.** Compare total taxes paid by the corporation and its shareholders under the two alternatives.
A&D 18-5 Tax Advantage: Sole Proprietorship versus Corporation (LO 8)	Stephen Glenn is in the process of organizing a business that is expected to produce, before any compensation to him and before income taxes, an income of $98,000 per year. In deciding whether to operate as a sole proprietorship or as a corporation, he is willing to make the choice on the basis of the relative income tax advantage under either form of organization. If the business is organized as a corporation, Glenn will own all the shares and will pay himself a salary of $32,000. He will distribute the remaining after-tax income as dividends. It may be assumed that the accounting income and taxable income for the corporation would be the same and that the corporation would be qualified as a small business for income tax purposes. Glenn is a resident of a province where the tax rate for individuals is 58% and has a total deduction of $8,000, and a total tax credit (not including any dividend tax credit) of $1,800.

INSTRUCTIONS

Determine the relative income tax advantage to Stephen Glenn of operating the business as a sole proprietorship or as a corporation, and make a recommendation as to the form of organization he should adopt. Would it be beneficial to Glenn, from an income tax viewpoint, to keep the remaining after-tax income in the corporation rather than distribute it as dividend? Assume a combined federal and provincial tax rate of 20% for a corporation qualified as a small business and that the federal income tax rates for individuals are: 17% for the first $29,590, 26% for the second $29,590, and 29% on the balance. (Ignore surtax.)

Answers to Self-Test Questions

1. c   2. b   3. b and c   4. a and b   5. b, c, and d

CHAPTER 19

Measuring Cash Flows

Every business measures its cash flows. Why? Management needs this information to keep the business solvent, maintain internal control, evaluate departmental performance, plan future business activities, and meet financial reporting requirements. Investors and creditors, too, look closely at a company's cash flows. A business that does not generate enough cash to meet its obligations just isn't going to "make it."

CHAPTER LEARNING OBJECTIVES

1. Explain the purpose and usefulness of a cash flow statement.
2. Describe how cash transactions are classified within a cash flow statement.
3. Compute the major cash flows relating to operating activities.
4. Explain why net income differs from net cash flow from operating activities.
5. Distinguish between the direct and indirect methods of reporting operating cash flow.
6. Compute the cash flows relating to investing and financing activities and explain why and how noncash investing and financing activities are disclosed in a cash flow statement.
*7. Compute net cash flow from operating activities using the *indirect* method.
**8. Explain the role of a work sheet in preparing a cash flow statement.

In Chapter 1, we introduced two key financial objectives of every business organization: ***operating profitably*** and ***staying solvent***. Operating profitably means increasing the amount of the owners' equity through the activities of the business; in short, providing the owners with a satisfactory return on their investment. Staying solvent means being able to pay the debts and obligations of the business as they come due.

An income statement is designed to measure the success or failure of the business in achieving its objective of profitable operations. To some extent, a balance sheet shows whether or not the business is solvent. It shows, for example, the nature and amounts of current assets and current liabilities. From this information, users of the financial statements may compute such measures of solvency as the current ratio and the amount of working capital.

However, assessing the ability of a business to remain solvent involves more than just evaluating the liquid resources on hand at the balance sheet date. How much cash does the company receive during a year? What are the sources of these cash receipts? What expenditures are made each year for operating activities and for investing and financing activities? To answer these questions, companies prepare a third major financial statement called the ***cash flow statement*** or ***statement of cash flows***.[1]

CASH FLOW STATEMENT

Purpose of the Statement

LO 1: Explain the purpose and usefulness of a cash flow statement.

The basic purpose of a cash flow statement is to provide information about the **cash receipts** and **cash payments** of a business entity during the accounting period. (The term **cash flows** includes both cash receipts and cash payments.) In addition, the statement is intended to provide information about all the ***investing*** and ***financing*** activities of the company during the period. Thus a cash flow statement should assist investors, creditors, and others in assessing such factors as:

- The company's ability to generate positive cash flows in future periods
- The company's ability to meet its obligations and to pay dividends

---
* *Supplemental Topic A*, "The Indirect Method."
** *Supplemental Topic B*, "A Work Sheet for Preparing a Cash Flow Statement."
[1] These two titles are used interchangeably.

- The company's need for external financing
- Reasons for differences between the amount of net income and the related net cash flow from operating activities
- Both the cash and noncash aspects of the company's investing and financing transactions for the period
- Causes of the change in the amount of cash and cash equivalents between the beginning and the end of the accounting period.

In summary, a cash flow statement helps users of financial statements evaluate a company's ability to "come up with the cash"—both in the short-run and on a long-run basis. For this reason, the cash flow statement is useful to virtually everyone interested in the company's financial health: short- and long-term creditors, investors, management—and both current and prospective competitors.

Example of a Cash Flow Statement

The following is an example of a cash flow statement together with a schedule of cash and cash equivalents, using the ***direct method*** for net cash flow from operating activities. (The alternative ***indirect method*** is illustrated later in this chapter.) Cash outflows are shown in parentheses.

ALLISON CORPORATION
Cash Flow Statement
For the Year Ended December 31, 20__

Cash flows from operating activities:		
Cash received from customers	$ 870,000	
Interest and dividends received	10,000	
Cash provided by operating activities		$880,000
Cash paid to suppliers and employees	$(764,000)	
Interest paid	(28,000)	
Income taxes paid	(38,000)	
Cash used in operating activities		(830,000)
Net cash provided by operating activities		$ 50,000
Cash flows from investing activities:		
Purchases of marketable securities	$ (65,000)	
Proceeds from sales of marketable securities	40,000	
Loans made to borrowers	(17,000)	
Collections on loans	12,000	
Purchases of plant assets	(160,000)	
Proceeds from sales of plant assets	75,000	
Net cash used in investing activities		(115,000)
Cash flows from financing activities:		
Proceeds from short-term borrowing	$ 45,000	
Payments to settle short-term debts	(55,000)	
Proceeds from issuing bonds payable	100,000	
Proceeds from issuing capital stock	50,000	
Dividends paid	(40,000)	
Net cash provided by financing activities		100,000
Net increase (decrease) in cash		$ 35,000
Cash and cash equivalents, beginning of year		20,000
Cash and cash equivalents, end of year		$ 55,000

Schedule of Cash and Cash Equivalents	Dec. 31	Jan. 1
Cash	$40,000	$12,000
Short-term investments	15,000	8,000
	$55,000	$20,000

Classification of Cash Flows

LO 2: Describe how cash transactions are classified within a cash flow statement.

The cash flows shown in the statement are grouped into three major categories: (1) **operating activities**, (2) **investing activities**, and (3) **financing activities**.[2] We will now look briefly at the way cash flows are classified among these three categories.

Operating Activities The operating activities section shows the *cash effects* of revenue and expense transactions. To illustrate this concept, consider the effects of credit sales. Credit sales are reported in the income statement in the period when the sales occur. But the "cash effects" occur later—when the receivables are collected in cash. Similar differences may exist between the recognition of an expense and the related cash payment. Consider, for example, the expense of postretirement benefits earned by employees during the current period. If this expense is not funded with a trustee, the cash payments may not occur for many years—after today's employees have retired.

In summary, cash flows from operating activities include:

Cash Receipts	Cash Payments
Collections from customers for sales of goods and services	Payments to suppliers of merchandise and services, including payments to employees
Interest and dividends received	Payments of interest
Other receipts from operations, as, for example, proceeds from settlement of litigation.	Payments of income taxes
	Other expenditures relating to operations, as, for example, payments in settlement of litigation

Notice that receipts and payments of *interest* are classified as operating activities, not as investing or financing activities.

Investing Activities Cash flows relating to investing activities include:

Cash Receipts	Cash Payments
Cash proceeds from selling investments or plant assets	Payments to acquire investments or plant assets
Cash proceeds from collecting principal amounts on loans	Amounts advanced to borrowers

---

[2] A fourth classification, "Effects of changes in exchange rates on cash," is used in the cash flow statements of companies with holdings of foreign currency. This fourth classification will be discussed in the intermediate accounting course.

Financing Activities Cash flows classified as financing activities include the following:

Cash Receipts	Cash Payments
Proceeds from both short-term and long-term borrowing	Repayments of amounts borrowed (excluding interest payments)
Cash received from owners as, for example, from issuing capital stock	Payments to owners, such as cash dividends, or redemption of capital stock

Repayment of amounts borrowed refers to repayment of **loans**, not to payments made on accounts payable or accrued liabilities. Payments of accounts payable and of accrued liabilities are considered "payments to suppliers of merchandise and services..." and are classified as a cash outflow from operating activities. Also, remember that all interest payments are classified as operating activities.

Why Are Receipts and Payments of Interest "Operating Activities"? One might argue that interest receipts result from investing activities, and that interest payments are related to financing activities. The CICA's Accounting Standards Board considered this point of view but decided instead to classify interest receipts and payments as operating activities. It wanted net cash flow from operating activities to reflect the cash effects of the revenue and expense transactions entering into the determination of net income. As interest revenue and interest expense enter into the determination of net income, the Accounting Standards Board decided to classify the related cash flows as operating activities. Payments of dividends, however, ***do not*** enter into the determination of net income. Therefore, dividend payments are viewed as financing activities.

Cash and "Cash Equivalents" For purposes of preparing a cash flow statement, the Accounting Standards Board has defined "cash" as including ***both cash and cash equivalents***. **Cash equivalents** are short-term, highly liquid investments that are (1) readily convertible to known amounts of cash and (2) subject to an insignificant risk of changes in value. Thus, cash equivalents are limited to such investments as money market funds, commercial paper, Treasury bills, and bonds that mature in a few months or less. Transfers of money between a company's bank accounts and these cash equivalents are ***not viewed as cash receipts or cash payments***. Money is considered "cash" regardless of whether it is held in currency, in a bank account, or in the form of cash equivalents. However, any interest received from owning cash equivalents is included in cash receipts from operating activities.

Marketable securities, such as investments in the stocks and bonds (whose maturity date is longer than a few months) of other companies, ***do not qualify as cash equivalents***. Therefore, purchases and sales of marketable securities ***do*** result in cash flows to be reported in the cash flow statement. The CICA's Accounting Standards Board requires that the components of cash and cash equivalents should be disclosed.

Critical Importance of Cash Flow from Operating Activities

In the long run, a business must generate a positive net cash flow from its operating activities if the business is to survive. A business with negative cash flows from operations will not be able to raise cash from other sources indefinitely. In fact, the ability of a business to raise cash through financing activities is highly dependent upon its ability to generate cash from its normal business operations. Creditors and shareholders are reluctant to invest in a company that does not generate enough cash from operating activities to assure prompt payment of maturing liabilities, interest, and dividends.

The Approach to Preparing a Cash Flow Statement

The items listed in an income statement or a balance sheet represent the balances of specific general ledger accounts. Notice, however, the captions used in the cash flow statement *do not* correspond to specific ledger accounts. A cash flow statement summarizes ***cash transactions*** during the accounting period. The general ledger, however, is maintained on the ***accrual basis*** of accounting, not the cash basis. Thus, an amount such as "Cash received from customers...$870,000" does not appear as the balance in a specific ledger account.

In a very small business, it may be practical to prepare a cash flow statement directly from the special journals for cash receipts and cash payments. For most businesses, however, it is easier to prepare the cash flow statement by examining the income statement and the ***changes*** during the period in all of the balance sheet accounts ***except for*** Cash (that is, Cash and Cash Equivalents). This approach is based upon the double-entry system of accounting; any transaction affecting cash must also affect some other asset, liability, or owners' equity account.[3] The change in these ***other accounts*** makes clear the nature of the cash transaction.

To illustrate this approach, assume that the Marketable Securities controlling account of Allison Corporation shows the following activities during the year:

Balance, January 1, 20__	**$70,000**
Debit entries during the year	**65,000**
Credit entries during the year	**(44,000)**
Balance, December 31, 20__	**$91,000**

Also assume that the company's income statement for the year includes a ***$4,000 loss*** on sales of marketable securities.

The ***debit entries*** in the Marketable Securities account represent the cost of securities ***purchased*** during the year. These debit entries provide the basis for the item ***"Purchases of marketable securities...$(65,000)"*** appearing in the investing activities section of the cash flow statement (page 938). Thus, increases in the asset Marketable Securities correspond to an outflow of cash.

---

[3] Revenue, expenses, and dividends represent changes in owners' equity and, therefore, may be regarded as "owners' equity accounts."

The credit entries of $44,000 represent the **cost** of securities sold during the year. Remember, however, that the income statement shows that these securities were sold at a **loss of $4,000**. The cash proceeds from these sales, which also appear in the cash flow statement, may be computed as follows:

Cost of marketable securities sold	$44,000
Less: Loss on sales of marketable securities	4,000
Proceeds from sales of marketable securities	$40,000

By looking at the changes occurring in the Marketable Securities account and the related income statement account, we were able to determine quickly two items appearing in the company's cash flow statement. We could have assembled the same information from the company's cash journals, but we would have had to review the journals for the entire year and then added together the cash flows of numerous individual transactions. In summary, it usually is more efficient to prepare a cash flow statement by analyzing the **changes in noncash accounts** (that is, noncash and noncash equivalent accounts) than by locating and combining numerous entries in the company's journals.

PREPARING A CASH FLOW STATEMENT: AN ILLUSTRATION

Earlier in this chapter we illustrated the cash flow statement of Allison Corporation. We will now show how this statement was developed from the company's accrual-basis accounting records.

Basically, a cash flow statement can be prepared from the data contained in an income statement and **comparative** balance sheets at the beginning and end of the period. It is also necessary, however, to have some detailed information about the **changes** occurring during the period in certain balance sheet accounts. Shown below and on the following pages are Allison's income statement and comparative balance sheets for the current year, and also the necessary information about the changes in balance in accounts.

ALLISON CORPORATION
Income Statement
For the Year Ended December 31, 20__

Revenue and gains:		
Net sales		$900,000
Dividends revenue		3,000
Interest revenue		6,000
Gain on sales of plant assets		31,000
Total revenue and gains		$940,000
Costs, expenses, and losses:		
Cost of goods sold	$500,000	
Operating expenses (including depreciation of $40,000)	300,000	
Interest expense	35,000	
Income taxes expense	36,000	
Loss on sales of marketable securities	4,000	
Total costs, expenses, and losses		875,000
Net income		$ 65,000

ALLISON CORPORATION
Comparative Balance Sheets
Current Year

Assets	End of the Year (Dec. 31)	Beginning of the Year (January 1)
Current assets:		
Cash and cash equivalents, (short-term investments: beginning, $8,000; end, $15,000)	$ 55,000	$ 20,000
Marketable securities	85,000	64,000
Notes receivable	17,000	12,000
Accounts receivable	110,000	80,000
Interest receivable	2,000	3,000
Inventory	100,000	90,000
Prepaid expenses	4,000	1,000
Total current assets	$373,000	$270,000
Plant and equipment (net of accumulated depreciation)	616,000	500,000
Total assets	$989,000	$770,000

Liabilities & Shareholders' Equity		
Current liabilities:		
Notes payable (short-term)	$ 45,000	$ 55,000
Accounts payable	76,000	61,000
Interest payable	22,000	15,000
Income taxes payable	8,000	10,000
Other accrued expenses payable	3,000	9,000
Total current liabilities	$154,000	$150,000
Long-term liabilities:		
Notes payable (long-term)	40,000	-0-
Bonds payable	400,000	300,000
Total liabilities	$594,000	$450,000
Shareholders' equity:		
Capital stock	$200,000	$150,000
Retained earnings	195,000	170,000
Total shareholders' equity	$395,000	$320,000
Total liabilities & shareholders' equity	$989,000	$770,000

Additional Information An analysis of changes in the balance sheet accounts of Allison Corporation provides the following information about the company's activities in the current year. To assist in the preparation of a cash flow statement, we have classified this information into the categories of operating activities, investing activities, and financing activities.

Operating Activities

1. Accounts receivable increased by $30,000 during the year.
2. Dividend revenue is recognized on the cash basis, but interest revenue is recognized on the accrual basis. Interest receivable decreased by $1,000 during the year.
3. Inventory increased by $10,000 and accounts payable increased by $15,000 during the year.
4. During the year, short-term prepaid expenses increased by $3,000 and accrued expenses payable (other than for interest or income taxes) decreased by $6,000. Depreciation for the year amounted to $40,000.

5. The accrued liability for interest payable increased by $7,000 during the year.
6. The accrued liability for income taxes payable decreased by $2,000 during the year.

Investing Activities

7. Analysis of the Marketable Securities account show debit entries of $65,000 representing the cost of securities purchased, and credit entries of $44,000, representing the cost of securities sold. (None of the marketable securities is viewed as a cash equivalent.)
8. Analysis of the Notes Receivable account shows $17,000 in debit entries, representing cash lent to borrowers by Allison Corporation during the year, and $12,000 in credit entries, representing collections of notes receivable. (Collections of interest were recorded in the Interest Revenue account and are considered cash flows from operating activities.)
9. Allison's plant asset accounts increased by $116,000 during the year. An analysis of the underlying transactions indicates the following:

	Effect Upon Plant Asset Accounts
Purchased $200,000 in plant assets, paying $160,000 cash and issuing a long-term note payable for the $40,000 balance	$200,000
Sold for $75,000 cash plant assets with a book value of $44,000	(44,000)
Recorded depreciation expense for the period	(40,000)
Net change in plant asset controlling accounts	$116,000

Financing Activities

10. During the year, Allison Corporation borrowed $45,000 cash by issuing short-term notes payable to banks. Also, the company repaid $55,000 in principal amounts due on these loans and other notes payable. (Interest payments are classified as operating activities.)
11. The company issued bonds payable for $100,000 cash.
12. The company issued for cash 1,000 shares of no-par value capital stock at a price of $50 per share.
13. Cash dividends declared and paid to shareholders amounted to $40,000 during the year.

Cash and Cash Equivalents

14. Cash and cash equivalents as shown in Allison Corporation's balance sheets amounted to $20,000 at the beginning of the year and $55,000 at year-end—a net increase of $35,000.

Using this information, we will now illustrate the steps in preparing Allison Corporation's cash flow statement and also a supporting schedule disclosing the "noncash" investing and financing activities. (These activities also may be disclosed in the form of a note to the financial statements.) In our discussion, we will often refer to these items of "Additional Information" by citing the paragraph numbers shown in the above list.

The distinction between **accrual-basis** measurements and cash flows is of fundamental importance in understanding financial statements and other accounting reports. To assist in making this distinction, we use two colours in our illustrated computations. We show in **blue** the accrual-based data from Allison Corporation's income statement and the preceding numbered paragraphs. The cash flows that we compute from this data are shown in **black**.

Cash Flows from Operating Activities

LO 3: Compute the major cash flows relating to operating activities.

As shown in our cash flow statement on page 938, the net cash flow from operating activities is determined by combining certain cash inflows and subtracting certain cash outflows. The inflows are cash received from customers, and interest and dividends received; the outflows are cash paid to suppliers and employees, interest paid, and income taxes paid.

In computing each of these cash flows, our starting point is an income statement amount, such as net sales, the cost of goods sold, or interest expense. As you study each computation, be sure that you ***understand why*** the income statement amount must be increased or decreased to determine the related cash flow. You will find that an understanding of these computations will do more than show you how to compute cash flows: it will also strengthen your understanding of the income statement and the balance sheet.

Cash Received from Customers To the extent that sales are made for cash, there is no difference between the amount of cash received from customers and the amount recorded as sales revenue. Differences do arise, however, when sales are made on account. If accounts receivable have increased during the year, credit sales have exceeded collections of accounts receivable. Therefore, we must ***deduct the increase*** in accounts receivable over the year from net sales in order to determine the amount of cash received. If accounts receivable have decreased over the year, collections of these accounts must have exceeded credit sales. Therefore, we must ***add the decrease*** in accounts receivable to net sales to determine the amount of cash received. The relationship between cash received from customers and net sales is summarized below:

$$\text{Cash received from customers} = \text{Net Sales} \begin{cases} + \text{Decrease in Accounts Receivable} \\ \text{or} \\ - \text{Increase in Accounts Receivable} \end{cases}$$

The increase or decrease in accounts receivable is determined simply by comparing the year-end balance in the account to its balance at the beginning of the year.

In our Allison Corporation example, paragraph **1** of the Additional Information tells us that accounts receivable have ***increased*** by $30,000 during the year. The income statement shows net sales for the year of $900,000. Therefore, the amount of cash received from customers may be computed as follows:

Net sales (accrual basis)	$900,000
Less: Increase in accounts receivable	30,000
Cash received from customers	$870,000

Interest and Dividends Received Our next objective is to determine the amounts of cash received during the year as dividends and interest. As explained in paragraph **2** of the Additional Information, dividend revenue is recorded on the cash basis. Therefore, the $3,000 shown in the income statement also represents the amount of cash received as dividends.

Interest revenue, on the other hand, is recognized on the accrual basis. We have already shown how to convert one type of revenue, net sales, from the accrual basis to the cash basis. We may use the same approach in converting interest revenue from the accrual basis to the **cash basis**. Our formula for converting net sales to the cash basis may be modified to convert interest revenue to the cash basis as follows:

$$\text{Interest received} = \text{Interest Revenue} \begin{Bmatrix} + \text{ Decrease in Interest Receivable} \\ \text{or} \\ - \text{ Increase in Interest Receivable} \end{Bmatrix}$$

The income statement for Allison Corporation shows interest revenue of $6,000, and paragraph **2** states that the amount of interest receivable has *decreased* by $1,000 during the year. Thus, the amount of cash received as interest may be computed as follows:

Interest revenue (accrual basis)	$6,000
Add: Decrease in interest receivable	1,000
Interest received (cash basis)	$7,000

The amounts of interest and dividends received in cash are combined for presentation in the cash flow statement:

Interest received (cash basis)	$ 7,000
Dividends received (cash basis)	3,000
Interest and dividends received	$10,000

Cash Payments for Merchandise and for Operating Expenses

The next item in the cash flow statement, "Cash paid to suppliers and employees," includes all cash payments for purchases of merchandise and for operating expenses (all expenses other than interest and income taxes). Payments of interest and income taxes are listed as a separate item in the statement. The amounts of cash paid for purchases of merchandise and for operating expenses are computed separately.

Cash Paid for Purchases of Merchandise An accrual basis income statement reflects the *cost of goods sold* during the year, regardless of whether the merchandise was acquired or paid for in that period. The cash flow statement, on the other hand, reports the *cash paid* for merchandise during the year, even if the merchandise was acquired in a previous period or remains unsold at year-end. The relationship between cash payments for merchandise and the cost of goods sold depends upon the changes during the period in *two* related balance sheet accounts: inventory and accounts payable to suppliers of merchandise. This relationship may be stated as follows:

$$\text{Cash payments for purchases} = \text{Cost of Goods Sold} + \begin{Bmatrix} +\text{Increase in Inventory} \\ \text{or} \\ -\text{Decrease in Inventory} \end{Bmatrix} \text{ and } \begin{Bmatrix} +\text{Decrease in Accounts Payable} \\ \text{or} \\ -\text{Increase in Accounts Payable} \end{Bmatrix}$$

Using information from the Allison Corporation income statement and paragraph **3**, the cash payments for purchases may be computed as follows:

Cost of goods sold	$500,000
Add: Increase in inventory	10,000
Net purchases (accrual basis)	$510,000
Less: Increase in accounts payable to suppliers	15,000
Cash payments for purchases of merchandise	$495,000

Let us review the logic behind this computation. If a company is increasing its inventory, it is **buying more merchandise than it sells** during the period. However, if the company is increasing its account payable to merchandise creditors, it is **not paying cash** for all of these purchases.

Cash Payments for Operating Expenses Operating expenses, as shown in the income statement, represent the cost of goods and services used up during the period. However, the amounts shown as expenses may differ significantly from the cash payments made during the period. Consider, for example, depreciation expense. Recording depreciation expense *requires no cash payment*, but it does increase total expenses measured on the accrual basis. Thus, in converting accrual-basis expenses to the cash basis, we must deduct depreciation expense and any other "noncash" expenses from our accrual-basis operating expenses. The other "noncash" expenses—expenses not requiring cash outlays—include amortization of intangible assets, any unfunded portion of postretirement benefits expense, and amortization of bond discount.

A second area of difference arises from short-term *timing differences* between the recognition of expenses and the actual cash payments. Expenses are recorded in accounting records when the related goods or services are *used*. However, the cash payments for these expenses might occur (1) in an earlier period, (2) in the same period, or (3) in a later period. Let us briefly consider each case.

1. If payment is made in advance, the payment creates an asset, termed a prepaid expense, or, in our formula, a "prepayment." Thus, to the extent that prepaid expenses increase over the year, cash payments *exceed* the amount recognized as expense.
2. If payment is made in the same period, no problem arises because the cash payment is equal to the amount of expense.
3. If payment is made in a later period, the payment reduces a liability for an accrued expense payable. Thus, to the extent that

accrued expenses payable decrease over the year, cash payments exceed the amount recognized as expense.

The relationship between cash payments and accrual-basis expenses are summarized below:

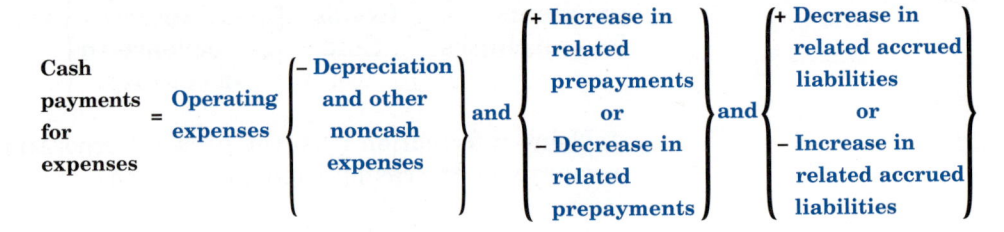

$$\text{Cash payments for expenses} = \text{Operating expenses} \begin{Bmatrix} -\text{Depreciation and other noncash expenses} \end{Bmatrix} \text{and} \begin{Bmatrix} +\text{Increase in related prepayments} \\ \text{or} \\ -\text{Decrease in related prepayments} \end{Bmatrix} \text{and} \begin{Bmatrix} +\text{Decrease in related accrued liabilities} \\ \text{or} \\ -\text{Increase in related accrued liabilities} \end{Bmatrix}$$

In a cash flow statement, cash payments for interest and for income taxes are shown separately from cash payments for operating expenses. Using data from Allison Corporation's income statement and from paragraph **4**, we may compute the company's cash payments for operating expenses as follows:

Operating expenses (including depreciation)		$300,000
Less: Noncash expenses (depreciation)		40,000
Subtotal		$260,000
Add: Increase in short-term prepayments	$3,000	
Decrease in accrued liabilities	6,000	9,000
Cash payments for operating expenses		$269,000

Cash Paid to Suppliers and Employees The caption used in our cash flow statement, "Cash paid to suppliers and employees," includes both cash payments for purchases of merchandise and for operating expenses. This cash outflow may now be computed as follows:

Cash payments for purchases of merchandise	$495,000
Cash payments for operating expenses	269,000
Cash payments to suppliers and employees	$764,000

Cash Payments for Interest and Taxes Interest expense and income taxes expense may be converted to cash payments with the same formula we used to convert operating expenses. Allison Corporation's income statement shows interest expense of $35,000, and paragraph **5** states that the liability for interest payable increased by $7,000 during the year. The fact that the liability for unpaid interest *increased* over the year means that ***not all of the interest expense shown in the income statement was paid in cash***. To determine the amount of interest actually paid, we must ***subtract*** from total interest expense the portion that has been financed through an increase in the liability for interest payable. This computation is shown below:

Interest expense	$35,000
Less: Increase in related accrued liability	7,000
Interest paid	$28,000

Similar reasoning is used in determining the amount of income taxes paid by Allison Corporation during the year. The accrual-based income taxes expense, reported in the income statement, amounts to $36,000. However, paragraph **6** states that the company has reduced its liability for income taxes payable by $2,000 over the year. Incurring income taxes expense increases the tax liability; making cash payments to tax authorities reduces it. Thus, if the liability *decreases* over the year, cash payments to tax authorities *must have been greater* than the income taxes expense for the current year. The amount of the cash payments is determined as follows:

Income taxes expense	$36,000
Add: Decrease in related accrued liability	2,000
Income taxes paid	$38,000

A Quick Review We have now shown the computation of each cash flow relating to Allison Corporation's operating activities. Previously we illustrated a complete cash flow statement for the company. For your convenience, we will again show the operating activities section of that statement, illustrating the information developed in the preceding paragraphs.

Cash flows from operating activities:		
Cash received from customers	$ 870,000	
Interest and dividends received	10,000	
Cash provided by operating activities		$880,000
Cash paid to suppliers and employees	$(764,000)	
Interest paid	(28,000)	
Income taxes paid	(38,000)	
Cash used in operating activities		(830,000)
Net cash provided by operating activities		$ 50,000

Differences Between Net Income and Net Cash Flow from Operating Activities

LO 4: Explain why net income differs from net cash flow from operating activities.

Allison Corporation reported net income of **$65,000**, but net cash provided by operating activities of only **$50,000**. What caused this $15,000 difference?

The answer, in short, is many things. First, ***depreciation expense*** reduces net income but does not affect net cash flow. Next, all the adjustments that we made to net sales, cost of goods sold, and expenses represented short-term ***timing differences*** between net income and the underlying net cash flow from operating activities. Finally, ***nonoperating gains and losses*** may cause substantial differences between net income and net cash flow from operations.

Nonoperating gains and losses may result from sales of plant assets, marketable securities, and other investments; and from the retirement of long-term debt. These gains and losses affect the cash flows relating to investing or financing activities, not the cash flows from operating activities. Similarly, extraordinary gains and losses relating to investing or financing activities should be shown ***separately*** under investing or financing activities.

Reporting Operating Cash Flow: The Direct and Indirect Methods

LO 5: Distinguish between the direct and indirect methods of reporting operating cash flow.

In our illustration, we use the **direct method** of computing and reporting the net cash flow from **operating activities**. The direct method shows the ***specific cash inflows and outflows*** comprising the operating activities of the business. The CICA's Accounting Standards Board has expressed its preference for the direct method, but it also allows companies to use an alternative, called the **indirect method**.

Computation of net cash flow from operating activities by the indirect method looks quite different from the direct method computation. However, both methods result in the ***same net cash flow*** from operating activities. Under the indirect method, the computation begins with accrual-based net income (as shown in the income statement) and then shows the various adjustments necessary to ***reconcile net income with net cash flow from operating activities***. The general format of this computation is summarized below:

Net income
Add: • *Expenses that do not require cash outlays in the period (such as depreciation expense)*
• *Operating cash inflows not recorded as revenue in the period*
• *"Nonoperating" losses deducted in the determination of net income*
Less: • *Revenue that does not result in cash inflows in the period*
• *Operating cash outflows not recorded as expense in the period*
• *"Nonoperating" gains included in the determination of net income*
Net cash flow from operating activities

The preceding summary describes the differences between net income and net cash flow from operating activities in broad, general terms. In an actual cash flow statement a dozen or more specific items may appear in this reconciliation. (*Supplemental Topic A* illustrates the application of the indirect method to the operating activities of Allison Corporation.)

In this chapter we emphasize the ***direct*** method, as we consider it to be the more informative approach, and it is the method recommended by the Accounting Standards Board. Most of our assignment material is based upon the direct method. Further coverage of the indirect method is provided in *Supplemental Topic A* at the end of the chapter.

Cash Flows from Investing Activities

LO 6: Compute the cash flows relating to investing and financing activities...

Paragraphs **7** through **9** in the Additional Information for our Allison Corporation example provide most of the information necessary to determine the cash flows from investing activities. In the following discussion, we will illustrate the presentation of these cash flows and also explain the sources of the information contained in the numbered paragraphs.

Much information about investing activities can be obtained simply by looking at the changes in the related asset accounts during the year. Debit entries in these accounts represent purchases of the assets, or cash outlays. Credit entries represent sales of the assets, or cash receipts. However, credit entries in asset accounts represent only the ***cost (or book value)*** of the assets sold. To determine the cash proceeds from these sales transactions, we must adjust the amount of the credit entries for any gains or losses recognized on the sales.

Purchases and Sales of Securities To illustrate, consider paragraph **7**, which summarizes the debit and credit entries to the Marketable Securities account. As explained earlier in this chapter, the $65,000 in debit entries represent purchases of marketable securities. The $44,000 in credit entries represent the ***cost*** of marketable securities sold during the period. However, the income statement shows that these securities were sold at a ***$4,000 loss***.

Thus, the cash proceeds from these sales amounted to only ***$40,000*** ($44,000 cost, minus $4,000 loss on sale). In the cash flow statement, these investing activities are summarized as follows:

Purchases of marketable securities	$(65,000)
Proceeds from sales of marketable securities	$ 40,000

Loans Made and Collected Paragraph **8** provides all the information necessary to summarize the cash flows from making and collecting loans:

Loans made to borrowers	$(17,000)
Collections on loans	$ 12,000

This information comes directly from the Notes Receivable account. Debit entries in the account represent new loans made during the year; credit entries indicate collections of the ***principal*** amount on outstanding notes (loans). (Interest received is credited to the Interest Revenue account and is included among the cash receipts from operating activities.)

... and explain why and how noncash investing and financing activities are disclosed in a cash flow statement.

Cash Paid to Acquire Plant Assets Paragraph **9** states that Allison Corporation purchased plant assets during the year for $200,000, paying $160,000 in cash and issuing a long-term note payable for the $40,000 balance. Notice that ***only the $160,000 cash payment*** appears in the cash flow statement. However, one objective of this financial statement is to show all of the company's ***investing and financing activities*** during the year. Therefore, the ***noncash aspects*** of these transactions are shown in a supplementary schedule (or note) as follows:

Supplementary Schedule of Noncash Investing and Financing Activities

Purchases of plant assets	$200,000
Less: Portion financed through issuance of long-term debt	40,000
Cash paid to acquire plant assets	$160,000

This supplementary schedule accompanies the cash flow statement.

Proceeds from Sales of Plant Assets An analysis of the plant asset accounts shows net credit entries totalling $44,000 in the year. ("Net credit entries" means all credit entries, net of related debits to accumulated depreciation when assets were sold.) These "net credit entries" represent the ***book value***

of plant assets sold during the year. However, the income statement shows that these assets were sold at a **gain of $31,000**. Therefore, the **cash proceeds** from sales of plant assets amounted to $75,000, as shown below:

Book value of plant assets sold	$44,000
Add: Gain on sales of plant assets	31,000
Proceeds from sales of plant assets	$75,000

The depreciation expense credited to the Accumulated Depreciation account is not a cash flow and is ignored.

Cash Flows from Financing Activities

Cash flows from financing activities are determined by analyzing the debit and credit changes recorded during the period in the related liability and shareholders' equity accounts. In a sense, cash flows from financing activities are more easily determined than those relating to investing activities, because financing activities seldom involve gains or losses.[4] Thus, the debit or credit changes in the balance sheet accounts usually are equal to the amounts of the related cash flows.

Credit changes in such accounts as Notes Payable and the accounts for long-term debt and capital stock usually indicate cash receipts; debit changes indicate cash payments.

Short-Term Borrowing Transactions To illustrate, consider paragraph **10**, which provides the information supporting the following cash flows:

Proceeds from short-term borrowing	$ 45,000
Payments to settle short-term debts	$(55,000)

Is it possible to determine the proceeds of short-term borrowing transactions throughout the year without carefully reviewing each cash receipt? The answer is **yes**—easily. The proceeds from short-term borrowing are equal to the **sum of the credit entries** in the short-term **Notes Payable** account. Payments to settle short-term debts are equal to the **sum of the debit entries** in this account.

Proceeds from Issuing Bonds Payable and Capital Stock Paragraph **11** states that Allison Corporation received cash of $100,000 by issuing bonds payable. This amount was determined by summing the credit entries in the Bonds Payable account. The Bonds Payable account included no debit entries during the year; thus, no bonds were retired.

Paragraph **12** states that during the year Allison Corporation issued capital stock for $50,000. The proceeds from issuing stock are equal to the sum of the credit entries made in the Capital Stock account.

Cash Dividends Paid to Shareholders Paragraph **13** states that Allison Corporation declared and paid cash dividends of $40,000 during the year.

---

[4] An early retirement of debt is an example of a financing transaction that may result in a gain or a loss.

In practice, most corporations pay cash dividends in the same year in which these dividends are declared. In these situations, the cash payments are equal to the related debit entries in the Retained Earnings account.

If the balance sheet includes a liability for dividends payable, the amounts debited to Retained Earnings represent dividends *declared* during the period, which may differ from the amount of dividends *paid*. To determine cash dividends paid, we must adjust the amount of dividends declared by **adding any decrease** (or **subtracting any increase**) in the Dividends Payable account over the period.

Relationship Between the Cash Flow Statement and the Balance Sheet

The first asset appearing in the balance sheet is **Cash and cash equivalents**. The cash flow statement explains in some detail the change in this asset from one balance sheet date to the next. The last three lines in the cash flow statement illustrate this relationship, as shown in our Allison Corporation example:

Net increase (decrease) in cash	$35,000
Cash and cash equivalents, beginning of year	20,000
Cash and cash equivalents, end of year	$55,000

Using the Cash Flow Statement

The users of a cash flow statement usually are most interested in the **net cash flow from operating activities**. Is the amount large enough to provide for necessary replacements of plant assets and maturing liabilities? And if so, is there enough left for the current dividend to look secure—or even be increased?

Even more important than the net cash flow from operating activities in any one year is the **trend** in this cash flow over a period of years—and the **consistency** of that trend from year to year. From everyone's perspective, the "best" results are a net cash flow from operating activities that increases each year by a substantial—but also predictable—percentage.[5]

By studying the cash flow statements for a series of years, users gain insight into such questions as:

- Is the company becoming more or less solvent?
- Do operating activities consistently generate enough cash to assure prompt payment of operating expenses, maturing liabilities, interest obligations, and dividends?
- Do operating activities also generate enough cash to finance growth and/or create a likelihood of increases in the dividends paid to shareholders?
- Is the company's ability to generate cash from operating activities improving or deteriorating?

---

[5] Percentage change is the dollar amount of change from one year to the next, expressed as a percentage of (divided by) the amount from the *earlier* of the two years.

In the short run, solvency and profitability may be *independent* of one another. That is, even a profitable business may run out of cash and become insolvent. On the other hand, an unprofitable business may remain solvent for years if it has vast resources or borrowing ability. In assessing the future prospects of any business organization, equity investors should evaluate both the company's profitability *and* its solvency. Creditors—especially short-term creditors—often attach greater importance to solvency than to profitability.

"Free Cash Flow" Many analysts put a company's cash flows into perspective by computing a subtotal called **free cash flow**. Free cash flow is intended to represent the cash flow available to management for discretionary purposes, *after* the company has met all of its basic obligations relating to business operations.

The term "free cash flow" is widely cited within the business community. Unfortunately, different analysts compute this measure in different ways, because there is no widespread agreement as to the "basic obligations relating to business operations." For example, are all expenditures for plant assets "basic obligations," or only those expenditures made to maintain the current level of productive capacity?

One common method of computing free cash flow is to deduct from the net cash provided by operating activities any net cash used for investing activities and any dividends paid. This computation is shown below, using data from the Allison Corporation cash flow statement shown earlier:

What's left for discretionary purposes?

Net cash provided by operating activities		$ 50,000
Less: Net cash used for acquiring plant assets		
($160,000 − $75,000 proceeds)	$85,000	
Dividends paid	40,000	125,000
Free cash flow		$(75,000)

This computation suggests that Allison Corporation *did not* generate enough cash from operations to meet its basic obligations. Thus, management had to raise cash from other sources. But, of course, an analyst always should "look behind" the numbers. For example, was Allison's purchase of plant assets during the year a "basic obligation," or did it represent a discretionary expansion of the business?

As we have stated throughout this text, no single ratio or financial measurement ever tells the "whole story."

*Supplemental Topic A

THE INDIRECT METHOD

LO 7: Compute net cash flow from operating activities using the indirect method.

In a cash flow statement, the net cash flow from operating activities may be determined either by the **direct method** or the **indirect method**. We now illustrate both methods below, using the data in our Allison Corporation example. (Accrual-based data appears in blue; cash flows are shown in black.

Direct Method

Cash flows from operating activities:		
Cash received from customers	$ 870,000	
Interest and dividends received	10,000	
Cash provided by operating activities		$880,000
Cash paid to suppliers and employees	$(764,000)	
Interest paid	(28,000)	
Income taxes paid	(38,000)	
Cash used in operating activities		(830,000)
Net cash provided by operating activities		$ 50,000

Indirect Method

Net income		$ 65,000
Add: Depreciation expense		40,000
Decrease in interest receivable		1,000
Increase in accounts payable		15,000
Increase in interest payable		7,000
Nonoperating loss on sales of marketable securities		4,000
Subtotal		$132,000
Less: Increase in accounts receivable	$ 30,000	
Increase in inventory	10,000	
Increase in prepaid expenses	3,000	
Decrease in income taxes payable	2,000	
Decrease in accrued operating expenses payable	6,000	
Nonoperating gain on sales of plant assets	31,000	82,000
Net cash provided by operating activities		$ 50,000

Comparison of the Direct and Indirect Methods

The two methods of computing net cash flow from operating activities are more similar than they appear at first glance. Both methods are based upon the same accounting data and both result in the **same net cash flow**. Also, the computations underlying both methods are quite similar. Both methods convert accrual-based income statement amounts into cash flows by adjusting for changes in related balance sheet accounts.

To illustrate the similarity in the computations, look briefly at the formulas for computing the cash inflows and outflows shown under the direct method (pages 945–948). Each formula begins with an income statement amount and then adds or subtracts the change during the period in related balance sheet accounts. Now look at our illustration of the indirect method. Notice that this computation also focuses upon the net changes during the period in balance sheet accounts.

The differences between the two methods lie only in format. However, the two formats provide readers of the cash flow statement with different types of information. The direct method informs these readers of the nature and dollar amounts of the **specific cash inflows and outflows** comprising the operating activities of the business. The indirect method, in contrast, **explains why** the net cash flow from operating activities differs from another measurement of performance—net income.

Differences Between Net Income and Net Cash Flow from Operating Activities

As previously stated, net cash flow from operating activities differs from net income for three major reasons. (**Note:** In the following discussions, we will assume that both net income and net cash flow are positive amounts.)

1. **"Noncash" expenses.** Some expenses, such as depreciation expense, reduce net income but do not require any cash outlay during the current period.
2. **Timing differences.** Revenue and expenses are measured using the concepts of accrual accounting. Net cash flow, on the other hand, reflects the effects of cash transactions. Thus, revenue and expenses may be recognized in a different accounting period from the related cash flows.
3. **"Nonoperating" gains and losses.** By definition, net cash flow from operating activities shows only the effects of those cash transactions classified as "operating activities." Net income, on the other hand, may include gains and losses relating to investing and financing activities.

Reconciling Net Income with Net Cash Flow

To acquaint you with the indirect method, we will now discuss some common types of adjustments needed in reconciling net income with net cash flow from operating activities. The nature and dollar amounts of these adjustments are determined by an accountant using a work sheet or a computer program; they are **not** entered in the company's accounting records.

1. Adjustments for "Noncash" Expenses

Depreciation is an example of a "noncash" expense—that is, depreciation expense reduces net income but does not require any cash outlay during the period. Thus, expenses on the accrual basis exceed cash payments, and net income for the period is less than the net cash flow. To reconcile net income with net cash flow, we must add back to net income the amount of depreciation and any other "noncash" expenses. (Other "noncash" expenses include unfunded pension expense, amortization of intangible assets, depletion of natural resources, and amortization of bond discount.)

2. Adjusting for Timing Differences

Timing differences between net income and net cash flow arise whenever revenue or expense is recognized by debiting or crediting an account *other than* cash. Changes over the period in the balances of these asset and liability accounts represent differences between the amount of revenue or expense recognized in the income statement and the net cash flow from operating activities. The balance sheet accounts that give rise to these timing differences include accounts receivable, inventories, prepaid expenses, accounts payable, and accrued expenses payable. Let us look separately at the effects of changes in each type of account.

Changes in Accounts Receivable Receivables increase as revenue is earned and decrease as cash is collected from customers. A net increase in accounts receivable over the period indicates that the revenue from credit sales exceeds collections from customers. Thus, net income measured on the accrual basis is *greater than* net cash flow; in our reconciliation of these two amounts, the net increase in accounts receivable is *deducted* from net income.

On the other hand, a net decrease in accounts receivable indicates cash receipts in excess of revenue from credit sales and is added to the amount of net income.

Changes in Inventory The balance in the Inventory account increases as merchandise is purchased and decreases as goods are sold. A net increase in the Inventory account during the period indicates that purchases during the period exceed the cost of goods sold. Thus, to reconcile net income with net cash flow, we deduct from net income the amount of these additional purchases (the net increase in the balance of the Inventory account).

A net decrease in the balance of the Inventory account over the period indicates that the cost of goods sold (reported in the income statement) exceeds purchases made during the period. To the extent that the cost of goods sold consists of a decrease in inventory, no cash payment is required in the current period. Therefore, we add to net income the amount of a net decrease in inventory.

Changes in Prepaid Expenses Prepaid expenses appear in the financial statements as assets. Increases in these assets result from cash payments, and decreases result from expiring amounts being recognized as expenses of the period. A net *increase* over the period in the amount of prepaid expenses indicates that cash payments made for these items must exceed the amounts recognized as expense. Thus, in determining net cash flow from operating activities, we deduct from net income the net increase in a company's prepaid expenses.

A net *decrease* in prepaid expenses indicates that cash outlays during the period were less than the amounts deducted as expense in the computation of net income. Thus, a net decrease in prepaid expenses is added back to net Income.

Changes in Accounts Payable Accounts payable are increased by purchases on account and are reduced by cash payments to suppliers. A net increase in accounts payable indicates that the accrual-based figure for purchases, which is included in the cost of goods sold, is greater than the cash payments made to suppliers. Therefore, in converting net income to cash flow, we add back the amount of merchandise purchases financed by a net increase in accounts payable.

A net decrease in accounts payable indicates that cash payments to suppliers exceed the purchases made during the period. Thus, a net decrease in accounts payable is subtracted from net income in the computation of net cash flow.

Changes in Accrued Expenses Payable The liability for accrued expenses payable increases with the recognition of expenses that will be paid in the future and decreases as cash payments are made. A net increase in accrued expenses payable indicates that expenses in the period exceed the related cash payments. Thus, net income is less than net cash flow, and the increase in the accrued expenses payable accounts should be added to net income.

A net decrease in accrued expenses payable indicates that cash payments exceed the related amounts of expense. This decrease, therefore, is subtracted from net income.

The liability for future (deferred) income taxes may be viewed as a long-term accrued expense payable. However, in the reconciliation of net income with net cash flow from operating activities, the change in the liability for future (deferred) income taxes is shown separately from the net change in other accrued expenses payable. A net increase in this liability is added to net income; a net decrease is subtracted.

A Helpful Hint Based on Debits and Credits In our preceding discussion, we explain **why** increases and decreases in a number of asset and liability accounts represent differences between the net income and net cash flow for the period. We do not expect you to memorize the effects of all of these changes. Rather, we hope that you will identify the types of transactions that cause a given account balance to increase or decrease and will then **evaluate the effects** of these transactions upon net income and net cash flow. This type of analysis will enhance your understanding of the relationships between accrual accounting and cash transactions.

However, let us offer you a quick hint. Double-entry accounting provides a simple rule that will let you check your analysis. For those asset and liability accounts that explain timing differences between net income and net cash flow, *a net credit change in the account's balance is always added to net income; a net debit change is always subtracted*. (For practice, test this rule on the adjustments in the illustration of the indirect method on page 957 and above. It applies to every adjustment that describes an increase or a decrease in a balance sheet account.)

3. Adjusting for "Nonoperating" Gains and Losses

In a cash flow statement, cash flows are classified as operating activities, investing activities, or financing activities. "Nonoperating" gains and losses, by definition, do not affect **operating activities**. However, these gains and losses do enter into the determination of net income. Therefore, in converting net income to net cash flow from operating activities, we **add back any nonoperating losses** and **deduct any nonoperating gains** included in net income.

Nonoperating gains and losses include gains and losses from sales of investments, plant assets, and discontinued operations (that relate to investing activities); and gains and losses on early retirement of debt (that relate to financing activities).

The Indirect Method: A Summary

The adjustments to net income explained in our preceding discussion are summarized in the following diagram:

Net income
Add: *Depreciation*
         Decrease in accounts receivable
         Decrease in inventories
         Decrease in prepaid expenses
         Increase in accounts payable
         Increase in accrued expenses payable
         Increase in future (deferred) income taxes payable
         "Nonoperating" losses deducted in computing net income
Deduct: *Increase in accounts receivable*
         Increase in inventories
         Increase in prepaid expenses
         Decrease in accounts payable
         Decrease in accrued expenses payable
         "Nonoperating" gains included in net income
Net cash provided by (used in) operating activities

**Supplemental Topic B

A Work Sheet for Preparing a Cash Flow Statement

LO 8: Explain the role of a work sheet in preparing a cash flow statement

A cash flow statement is developed by **systematically analyzing changes in the noncash balance sheet accounts**. This process can be formalized and documented through the preparation of a specially designed work sheet. The work sheet also provides the accountant with visual assurance that the changes in balance sheet accounts have been fully explained.

Data for an Illustration

We will illustrate the "work sheet approach" using the 2001 financial data of Auto Supply Limited.[1]

Shown below are the balances in Auto's balance sheet accounts at the beginning and end of 2001.

Changes in the noncash accounts are the key to identifying cash flows

AUTO SUPPLY LIMITED
Comparative Balance Sheets

Assets	December 31, 2001	2000
Cash	$ 45,000	$ 50,000
Marketable securities	25,000	40,000
Accounts receivable	330,000	320,000
Inventory	235,000	240,000
Plant and equipment (net of accumulated depreciation)	640,000	600,000
Totals	$1,275,000	$1,250,000

Liabilities & Shareholders' Equity		
Accounts payable	$ 160,000	$ 150,000
Accrued expenses payable	45,000	60,000
Mortgage note payable (long-term)	70,000	-0-
Bonds payable (due in 2015)	350,000	500,000
Capital stock (no par value)	160,000	160,000
Retained earnings	490,000	380,000
Totals	$1,275,000	$1,250,000

Additional Information The following information also will be used in the preparation of the work sheet. (Accrual-based measurements appear in **blue**; cash flows, in **black**.

1. Net income for the year amounted to **$250,000**. Cash dividends of **$140,000** were declared and paid.

---

[1] Our example involving Allison Corporation was quite comprehensive. Therefore, a work sheet for Allison Corporation would be too long and detailed to use as an introductory illustration. Also, Auto Supply does not have any cash equivalents.

2. Auto's only "noncash expense" was depreciation, which totalled **$60,000**.
3. Marketable securities costing **$15,000** were sold for **$35,000** cash, resulting in a **$20,000** nonoperating gain.
4. The company purchased plant assets for **$100,000**, making a **$30,000** cash down payment and issuing a **$70,000** mortgage note payable for the balance of the purchase price.
5. The company retired **$150,000** of its bonds payable.

The Work Sheet

Auto Supply Limited reports cash flow from operating activities by the ***indirect method***.[2] A work sheet for preparing a cash flow statement appears on the following page.

Let us briefly explain how this work sheet "works." The company's balance sheet accounts are listed in the top portion of the work sheet, with the beginning balances in the first column, and the year-end balances in the last (right-hand) column. (For purposes of illustration, we have shown these accounts and account balances in **grey**.)

The two middle columns are used to (1) explain the changes in each balance sheet account over the year, and (2) indicate how each change affected cash.

Entries in the Two Middle Columns The entries in the ***top portion of the work sheet*** summarize the transactions recorded in the account over the year. (Because these entries summarize transactions recorded on the **accrual basis**, they are shown in **blue**.)

For each summary entry in the top portion of the work sheet, we make an "off-setting entry" (in the opposite column) in the ***bottom portion*** of the work sheet indicating the **cash effects** of the transactions. These cash effects are classified as operating, investing, or financing activities, and are explained with a descriptive caption. (Entries representing the **cash effects** of transactions, and the related descriptive captions, appear in **black**.)

Entries in the two middle columns may be made in any sequence, but we recommend the following approach:

1. Explain the changes in the Retained Earnings account.
2. Account for depreciation expense (and any other "noncash" expenses).
3. Account for "timing differences" between net income and cash flow from operating activities.
4. Explain any remaining changes in balance sheet accounts **other than Cash**. (Hint: Changes in asset accounts will represent investing activities; changes in liability and equity accounts will represent financing activities.)
5. Compute and record the net increase or decrease in cash.

---

[2] If the work sheet utilizes the direct method, numerous subclassifications are required within the operating activities section. Such work sheets are illustrated in the intermediate accounting course.

AUTO SUPPLY LIMITED
Work Sheet for a Cash Flow Statement
For the Year Ended December 31, 2001

		Effects of Transactions		
Balance sheet effects:	Beginning Balance	Debit Changes	Credit Changes	Ending Balance
Assets				
Cash	50,000		(x) 5,000	45,000
Marketable securities	40,000		(8) 15,000	25,000
Accounts receivable	320,000	(4) 10,000		330,000
Inventory	240,000		(5) 5,000	235,000
Plant and equipment, (net of accumulated depreciation)	600,000	(9) 100,000	(3) 60,000	640,000
Totals	1,250,000			1,275,000
Liabilities & Shareholders' Equity				
Accounts payable	150,000		(6) 10,000	160,000
Accrued expenses payable	60,000	(7) 15,000		45,000
Mortgage note payable	-0-		(9) 70,000	70,000
Bonds payable	500,000	(10) 150,000		350,000
Capital stock	160,000			160,000
Retained earnings	380,000	(2) 140,000	(1) 250,000	490,000
Totals	1,250,000	415,000	415,000	1,275,000

Cash effects:	Sources	Uses
Operating activities:		
Net income	(1) 250,000	
Depreciation expense	(3) 60,000	
Increase in accounts receivable		(4) 10,000
Decrease in inventory	(5) 5,000	
Increase in accounts payable	(6) 10,000	
Decrease in accrued expenses payable		(7) 15,000
Gain on sales of marketable securities		(8) 20,000
Investing activities:		
Proceeds from sales of marketable securities	(8) 35,000	
Cash paid to acquire plant assets		(9) 30,000
Financing activities:		
Dividends paid		(2) 140,000
Payments to retire bonds payable		(10) 150,000
Subtotals	360,000	365,000
Net decrease in cash	(x) 5,000	
Totals	365,000	365,000

Up here we explain the changes in each noncash account

Down here we identify and classify the related cash effects of these changes

Cash provided by operations— $280,000

Cash provided by investing activities— $5,000

Cash used in financing activities— $290,000

Using this approach, the entries in our illustrated work sheet are explained below:

Entry

Step 1: Explain the changes in Retained Earnings

(1) Auto's net income explains a $250,000 **credit change** in the Retained Earnings account. In the bottom portion of the working paper, an offsetting entry is made in the **Sources** column and is classified as an operating activity.[3]

(2) Cash dividends of $140,000 caused a **debit change** in the Retained Earnings account during 2001. The offsetting entry falls into the **Uses** column; payments of dividends are classified as a financing activity.

With these first two entries, we have explained how Auto's Retained Earnings account increased during 2001 from $380,000 to $490,000.

Step 2: Account for noncash expenses

(3) Auto's only noncash expense was depreciation. In the top portion of the work sheet, depreciation explains a $60,000 credit change (decrease) in Plant and Equipment (which includes the Accumulated Depreciation accounts). The offsetting entry in the bottom of the work sheet falls into the Sources column. We have explained that depreciation is not really a "source" of cash, but that it **is** added back to net income as a step in computing the cash flow from operating activity.

Step 3: Account for timing differences

(4–7) Fluctuations in noncash current assets and current liabilities create **timing differences** between net income and the net cash flow from operating activities. In the top portion of the work sheet, entries (4) through (7) summarize the changes in these current asset and current liability accounts. In the bottom portion, they show how these changes affect the computation of cash flow from operating activities.

Step 4: Explain any remaining changes in noncash accounts

(8) In 2001, Auto sold marketable securities with a cost of $15,000 for $35,000 cash, resulting in a $20,000 nonoperating gain. In the top portion of the work sheet, the entry explains the $15,000 credit change in the Marketable Securities account. In the bottom portion, it reports cash proceeds of $35,000. The difference? The $20,000 nonoperating gain, which is **removed from the Operating Activities section** of the work sheet and included instead within the amount reported as "Proceeds from sales of marketable securities."

(9) Auto purchased $100,000 in plant assets, paying $30,000 cash and issuing a $70,000 note payable. These events explain a $100,000 debit change in Plant and Equipment, the $70,000 credit change in Mortgage Note Payable, and involved a cash outlay of $30,000, which is classified as an investing activity. (The $70,000 financed by issuance of a note payable is a **noncash** investing and financing activity, to be disclosed in a schedule or note.)

(10) The $150,000 credit change in Auto's Bonds Payable account indicates that this amount of the liability has been repaid—that is, $150,000 in bonds has been retired.

---

[3] When the **indirect method** is in use, net income serves as the **starting point** for computing net cash flow from operating activities.

Step 5: Compute and record the net change in cash

At this point, we should check to determine that our entries in the two middle columns *fully explain* the differences between the beginning and ending balance of each noncash balance sheet account. If the top portion of the work sheet explains the changes in every noncash account, the bottom section should include all of the cash flows for the year.

(x) We now total the Sources and Uses columns in the bottom portion of the work sheet. The difference between these column subtotals represents the *net increase or decrease* in cash. In our example, the Sources column totals $360,000 while the Uses column totals $365,000, indicating a **$5,000 decrease** in cash over the period. Our last entry, labelled **(x)**, explains the credit change in the Cash account at the top of the work sheet, and brings the bottom of the work sheet "into balance."

A formal cash flow statement, reporting the cash flow from operating activities by the indirect method, can be prepared directly from the bottom portion of this work sheet. (Amounts appearing in accrual-based accounting records are shown in **blue**; cash flows appear in **black**.)

Compare the content of this statement with the work sheet on page 962.

AUTO SUPPLY LIMITED
Cash Flow Statement
For the Year Ended December 31, 2001

Cash flows from operating activities:		
Net income		$ 250,000
Add: Depreciation expense		60,000
Decrease in inventory		5,000
Increase in accounts payable		10,000
Subtotal		$ 325,000
Less: Increase in accounts receivable	$ 10,000	
Decrease in accrued expenses payable	15,000	
Gain on sales of marketable securities	20,000	45,000
Net cash provided by operating activities		$ 280,000
Cash flows from investing activities:		
Proceeds from sales of marketable securities	$ 35,000	
Cash paid to acquire plant assets (see supplementary schedule below)	(30,000)	
Net cash provided by investing activities		5,000
Cash flows from financing activities:		
Dividends paid	$(140,000)	
Payments to retire bonds payable	(150,000)	
Net cash used in financing activities		(290,000)
Net decrease in cash		$ (5,000)
Cash, Dec. 31, 2000		50,000
Cash, Dec. 31, 2001		$ 45,000
Supplementary Schedule: Noncash Investing and Financing Activities		
Purchases of plant assets		$ 100,000
Less: Portion financed through issuance of long-term debt		70,000
Cash paid to acquire plant assets		$ 30,000

End-of-Chapter Review

Key Terms Introduced or Emphasized in Chapter 19

Accrual basis *(p.945)* A method of summarizing operating results in terms of revenue earned and expenses incurred, rather than cash receipts or cash payments.

Cash basis *(p.946)* The practice of summarizing operating results in terms of cash receipts and cash payments, rather than revenue earned or expenses incurred.

Cash equivalents *(p.940)* Highly liquid short-term investments, such as Treasury bills, money market funds, commercial paper, and bonds maturing in a few months or less. For purposes of preparing a cash flow statement, money held in cash equivalents is still viewed as "cash." Thus, transfers between a bank account and cash equivalents are not considered receipts or disbursements of cash.

Cash flows *(p.937)* A term describing both cash receipts (inflows) and cash payments (outflows).

Direct method *(p.950)* A method of reporting net cash flow from operating activities by listing specific types of cash inflows and outflows. This is the method recommended by the CICA, but the **indirect method** is an acceptable alternative.

Financing activities *(p.939)* Transactions such as borrowing, repaying borrowed amounts, raising equity capital, or making distribution to owners. The cash effects of these transactions are reported in the financing activities section of a cash flow statement. Noncash aspects of these transactions are disclosed in a supplementary schedule or note.

Free cash flow *(p.954)* The portion of the annual net cash flow from operating activities that remains available for discretionary purposes, after the basic obligations of the business have been met. Can be computed in several different ways.

Indirect method *(p.950)* A format of reporting net cash flow from operating activities that reconciles this figure with the amount of net income shown in the income statement. An alternative to the **direct method**.

Investing activities *(p.939)* Transactions involving acquisitions or sales of investments or plant assets. The cash aspects of these transactions are shown in the investing activities section of a cash flow statement. Noncash aspects of these transactions are disclosed in a supplementary schedule or note to this financial statement.

Operating activities *(p.939)* Transactions entering into the determination of net income, with the exception of gains and losses relating to financing or investing activities. The category includes such transactions as selling goods or services, earning investment income, and incurring costs and expenses. The cash effects of these transactions are reflected in the operating activities section of a cash flow statement.

DEMONSTRATION PROBLEM

You are the chief accountant for Universal Modem. Your assistant has prepared an income statement for the current year and has also developed the following "Additional Information" by analyzing changes in the company's balance sheet accounts.

UNIVERSAL MODEM
Income Statement
For the Year Ended December 31, 20__

Revenue and gains
Net sales		$9,500,000
Interest income		320,000
Gain on sales of marketable securities		70,000
Total revenue and gains		$9,890,000

Costs, expenses, and losses:
Cost of goods sold	$4,860,000	
Operating expenses (including depreciation of $700,000)	3,740,000	
Interest expense	270,000	
Income taxes	300,000	
Loss on sales of plant assets	90,000	
Total costs, expenses, and losses		9,260,000
Net income		$ 630,000

Information about changes in the company's balance sheet accounts over the year is summarized below:

1. Accounts receivable decreased by $85,000.
2. Interest receivable increased by $15,000.
3. Inventory decreased by $280,000, and accounts payable to suppliers of merchandise decreased by $240,000.
4. Short-term prepayments of operating expenses decreased by $18,000, and accrued liabilities for operating expenses increased by $35,000.
5. The liability for interest payable decreased by $16,000 during the year.
6. The liability for income taxes payable increased by $25,000 during the year.
7. The following schedule summarizes the total debit and credit entries during the year in other balance sheet accounts:

	Debit Entries	Credit Entries
Marketable securities	$ 120,000	$ 210,000
Notes receivable (cash loans made to others)	250,000	190,000
Plant assets (see paragraph 8)	3,800,000	360,000
Notes payable (short-term borrowing)	620,000	740,000
Bonds payable		1,100,000
Capital stock		890,000
Retained earnings (see paragraph 9 below)	320,000	630,000

8. The $360,000 in credit entries to the plant asset accounts are net of any debits to accumulated depreciation when plant assets were retired. Thus, the $360,000 in credit entries represents the **book value** of all plant assets sold or retired during the year.
9. The $320,000 debit to retained earnings represents dividends declared and paid during the year. The $630,000 credit entry represents the net income shown in the income statement.
10. All investing and financing activities were cash transactions.
11. Cash and cash equivalents (consisting of short-term investments of $80,000 at the beginning of the year and $60,000 at the end) amounted to $448,000 at the beginning of the year, and to $330,000 at year-end.

CHAPTER 19 MEASURING CASH FLOWS

INSTRUCTIONS

You are to prepare a cash flow statement for the current year and a schedule of cash and cash equivalents, following the format illustrated in this chapter. Cash flow from operating activities is to be determined by the ***direct method***. Place brackets around dollar amounts representing cash outlays. Show separately your computations of the following amounts:

1. Cash received from customers
2. Interest received
3. Cash paid to suppliers and employees
4. Interest paid
5. Income taxes paid
6. Proceeds from sales of marketable securities
7. Proceeds from sales of plant assets
8. Proceeds from issuing capital stock

SOLUTION TO DEMONSTRATION PROBLEM

UNIVERSAL MODEM
Cash Flow Statement
For the Year Ended December 31, 20__

Cash flows from operating activities:		
Cash received from customers (1)	$ 9,585,000	
Interest received (2)	305,000	
Cash provided by operating activities		$ 9,890,000
Cash paid to suppliers and employees (3)	$(7,807,000)	
Interest paid (4)	(286,000)	
Income taxes paid (5)	(275,000)	
Cash used in operating activities		(8,368,000)
Net cash provided by operating activities		$ 1,522,000
Cash flows from investing activities:		
Purchases of marketable securities	$ (120,000)	
Proceeds from sales of marketable securities (6)	280,000	
Loans made to borrowers	(250,000)	
Collections on loans	190,000	
Cash paid to acquire plant assets	(3,800,000)	
Proceeds from sales of plant assets (7)	270,000	
Net cash used in investing activities		(3,430,000)
Cash flows from financing activities:		
Proceeds from short-term borrowing	$ 740,000	
Payments to settle short-term debts	(620,000)	
Proceeds from issuing bonds payable	1,100,000	
Proceeds from issuing capital stock	890,000	
Dividends paid	(320,000)	
Net cash provided by financing activities		1,790,000
Net increase (decrease) in cash		$ (118,000)
Cash and cash equivalents, beginning of year		448,000
Cash and cash equivalents, end of year		$ 330,000

Schedule of Cash and Cash Equivalents	Dec. 31	Jan. 1
Cash	$270,000	$368,000
Short-term investments	60,000	80,000
	$330,000	$448,000

Supporting computations:

(1) Cash received from customers:

Net sales		$9,500,000
Add: Decrease in accounts receivable		85,000
Cash received from customers		$9,585,000

(2) Interest received:

Interest income		$ 320,000
Less: Increase in interest receivable		15,000
Interest received		$ 305,000

(3) Cash paid to suppliers and employees:

Cash paid for purchases of merchandise:

Cost of goods sold		$4,860,000
Less: Decrease in inventory		280,000
Net purchases		$4,580,000
Add: Decrease in accounts payable to suppliers		240,000
Cash paid for purchases of merchandise		$4,820,000

Cash paid for operating expenses:

Operating expenses		$3,740,000
Less: Depreciation (a "noncash" expense)	$700,000	
Decrease in prepayments	18,000	
Increase in accrued liabilities for operating expenses	35,000	753,000
Cash paid for operating expenses		$2,987,000
Cash paid to suppliers and employees ($4,820,000 + $2,987,000)		$7,807,000

(4) Interest paid:

Interest expense		$ 270,000
Add: Decrease in interest payable		16,000
Interest paid		$ 286,000

(5) Income taxes paid:

Income taxes expense		$ 300,000
Less: Increase in income taxes payable		25,000
Income taxes paid		$ 275,000

(6) Proceeds from sales of marketable securities:

Cost of marketable securities sold (credit entries to the Marketable Securities account)		$ 210,000
Add: Gain reported on sales of marketable securities		70,000
Proceeds from sales of marketable securities		$ 280,000

(7) Proceeds from sales of plant assets:

Book value of plant assets sold (paragraph 8)		$ 360,000
Less: Loss reported on sales of plant assets		90,000
Proceeds from sales of plant assets		$ 270,000

Self-Test Questions

Answers to these questions appear on page 991.

1. The cash flow statement is designed to assist users in assessing each of the following, **except**:
   a. The ability of a company to remain solvent.
   b. The company's profitability.
   c. The major sources of cash receipts during the period.
   d. The reasons why net cash flow from operating activities differs from net income.

2. Which of the following is **not** included in the cash flow statement, or in a supplementary schedule accompanying the cash flow statement?
   a. Disclosure of the amount of cash invested in money market funds during the accounting period
   b. The changes in the marketable securities account
   c. Disclosure of investing or financing activities that did not involve cash
   d. The amount of cash and cash equivalents owned by the business at the end of the accounting period

3. The cash flows shown in the cash flow statement are grouped into the following major categories:
   a. Operating activities, investing activities, and financing activities
   b. Cash receipts, cash disbursements, and noncash activities
   c. Direct cash flows and indirect cash flows
   d. Operating activities, investing activities, and collecting activities

4. Shown below is a list of various cash payments and cash receipts:

Cash paid to suppliers and employees	$400,000
Dividends paid	18,000
Interest paid	12,000
Purchases of plant assets	45,000
Interest and dividends received	17,000
Payments to settle short-term debt	29,000
Income taxes paid	23,000
Cash received from customers	601,000

   Based only upon the above items, net cash flow from operating activities is:
   a. $138,000   b. $91,000   c. $183,000   d. $120,000

5. During the current year, two transactions were recorded in the Land account of Nolan Industries. One involved a debit of $320,000 to the Land account; the second was a $210,000 credit to the Land account. Nolan Industries' income statement for the year reported a loss on sale of land in the amount of $25,000. All transactions involving the Land account were cash transactions. These transactions would be shown in the cash flow statement as:
   a. $320,000 cash provided by investing activities, and $210,000 cash used in investing activities.
   b. $210,000 cash provided by investing activities, and $320,000 cash used in investing activities.
   c. $235,000 cash provided by investing activities, and $320,000 cash used in investing activities.
   d. $185,000 cash provided by investing activities, and $320,000 cash used in investing activities.

Assignment Material

Discussion Questions

1. Briefly state the purposes of a cash flow statement.
2. Does a cash flow statement or an income statement best measure the profitability of a financially sound business? Explain.
3. Give two examples of cash receipts and two examples of cash payments that fall into each of the following classifications:
   a. Operating activities
   b. Investing activities
   c. Financing activities
4. Why are payments and receipts of interest classified as operating activities rather than as financing or investing activities?
5. Describe the two criteria for cash equivalents.
6. Define *cash equivalents* and list three examples.
7. During the current year, Delta Corporation transferred $300,000 from its bank account into a money market fund. Will this transaction appear in a cash flow statement? If so, in which section? Explain.
8. In the long run, is it more important for a business to have positive cash flows from its operating activities, investing activities, or financing activities? Why?
9. Of the three types of business activities summarized in a cash flow statement, which type is *least* likely to show a positive net cash flow in a successful growing business? Explain your reasoning.
10. The items and amounts listed in a balance sheet and an income statement correspond to specific accounts in a company's ledger. Is the same true about the items and amounts in a cash flow statement? Explain.
11. Sommersby Corporation had net sales for the year of $840,000. Accounts receivable increased from $90,000 at the beginning of the year to $162,000 at year-end. Compute the amount of cash collected during the year from customers and explain the logic behind your computations.
12. Describe the types of cash payments summarized by the caption "Cash paid to suppliers and employees."
13. Identify three factors that may cause net income to differ from net cash flow from operating activities.
14. Briefly explain the difference between the *direct* and *indirect methods* of computing net cash flow from operating activities. Which method results in the higher net cash flow?
15. Are cash payments of accounts payable viewed as operating activities or financing activities? Referring to the cash flow statement illustrated on page 938, state the caption that includes amounts paid on accounts payable.
16. Discount Club acquired land by issuing $500,000 worth of capital stock. No cash changed hands in this transaction. Will the transaction be disclosed in the company's cash flow statement? Explain.

17. The only transaction recorded in the plant asset accounts of Rogers Corporation in the current year was a $150,000 credit to the Land account. Assuming that this credit resulted from a cash transaction, does this entry indicate a cash receipt or a cash payment? Should this $150,000 amount appear in the cash flow statement, or is some adjustment necessary?

18. During the current year, the following credit entry was posted to the capital stock accounts of Moser Shipyards:

Capital Stock $108,500,000

Explain the type of cash transaction that probably caused this credit change, and illustrate the presentation of this transaction in a cash flow statement.

19. At the beginning of the current year, Burnside Corporation had dividends payable of $1,200,000. During the current year, the company declared cash dividends of $3,600,000, of which $900,000 appeared as a liability at year-end. Determine the amount of cash dividends *paid* during this year.

20. Define the term *free cash flow*. Explain the significance of this measurement to (1) short-term creditors, (2) long-term creditors, (3) shareholders, and (4) management.

Exercises

EXERCISE 19-1
Using a Cash Flow Statement
(LO 1, 2)

The cash flow statement for Auto Supply Limited appears on page 964. Assume that with respect to routine business operations, this was a typical year. Use this cash flow statement to evaluate the company's ability to maintain the current level of dividend payments over the foreseeable future. Explain your reasoning.

EXERCISE 19-2
Accounting Terminology
(LO 2, 5)

Listed below are nine technical accounting terms introduced or emphasized in this chapter.

Free cash flow	*Income statement*	*Operating activities*
Direct method	*Cash flow statement*	*Investing activities*
Indirect method	*Cash equivalents*	*Financing activities*

Each of the following statements may (or may not) describe one of these technical terms. For each statement, indicate the term described, or answer "None" if the statement does not correctly describe any of the terms.

a. Transactions involving investments by owners, issuance and repayment of debt, and the payment of dividends.

b. The financial statement showing the financial position of the business at one particular date.

c. The portion of the net cash flow from operating activities that is available to management for discretionary purposes.

d. The process of recognizing revenue as it is earned and expenses as they are incurred, regardless of when cash is received or paid.

e. The method of reporting net cash flow from operating activities that is favoured by the CICA's Accounting Standards Board.

f. An asset consisting of readily marketable investments in the stocks and bonds of large corporations.

g. The section of a cash flow statement that includes purchases of plant assets.

h. The financial statement that best describes the profitability of a business receiving most of its revenue in cash.

EXERCISE 19-3
Computing Cash Flows
(LO 6)

An analysis of the Marketable Securities controlling account of Cliffhanger Mills Inc. shows the following entries during the year:

Balance, January	$390,000
Debit entries	125,000
Credit entries	(140,000)
Balance, December 31	$375,000

In addition, the company's income statement includes a $27,000 loss on sales of marketable securities. None of the company's marketable securities is considered a cash equivalent.

Compute the amounts that should appear in the cash flow statement as:
a. Purchases of marketable securities.
b. Proceeds from sales of marketable securities.

EXERCISE 19-4
Comparing Net Sales and Cash Receipts
(LO 3, 4)

During the current year, Grafton Labs made cash sales of $250,000 and credit sales of $490,000. During the year, accounts receivable decreased by $32,000.
a. Compute for the current year the amounts of:
   1. Net sales reported as revenue in the income statement
   2. Cash received from collecting accounts receivable
   3. Cash received from customers
b. Write a brief statement explaining *why* cash received from customers differs from the amount of net sales.

EXERCISE 19-5
Computing Cash Paid for Purchases of Merchandise
(LO 3)

The general ledger of H-G Tech provides the following information relating to purchases of merchandise:

	End of Year	Beginning of Year
Inventory	$820,000	$780,000
Accounts payable to merchandise suppliers	430,000	500,000

The company's cost of goods sold during the year was $2,875,000. Compute the amount of cash payments made during the year to suppliers of merchandise.

EXERCISE 19-6
Reporting Lending Activities and Interest Revenue
(LO 3, 6)

During the current year, P and L Corporation made new loans of $12 million. In addition, the company collected $36 million from borrowers, of which $31 million was interest revenue. Explain how these cash flows will appear in the company's cash flow statement, indicating the classification and the dollar amount of each cash flow.

EXERCISE 19-7
Disclosing "Noncash" Investing and Financing Activities
(LO 6)

During the current year, Nordic Incorporated purchased a factory from Fisher Industries. The journal entry made to record this transaction is shown below:

Land	500,000	
Buildings	750,000	
Equipment	1,800,000	
Mortgage Payable		2,100,000
Cash		950,000

This was Nordic's only purchase of plant assets during the year. Nordic prepares a supplementary schedule to its cash flow statement for the purpose of disclosing any "noncash" aspects of investing and financing activities.

a. Prepare the supplementary schedule to disclose the "noncash" aspects of this transaction. (Follow the general format illustrated in this chapter.)

b. Illustrate the presentation of this transaction in Nordic's cash flow statement. Begin your illustration by indicating the section of the statement (operating, investing, or financing activities) in which this transaction will appear.

EXERCISE 19-8
Format of a Cash Flow Statement
(LO 2)

The accounting staff of Scarborough Crafts Inc. has assembled the following information for the year ended December 31, 2000:

Cash and cash equivalents, beginning of year	*$ 45,200*
Cash and cash equivalents, end of year	*64,200*
Cash paid to acquire plant assets	*21,000*
Proceeds from short-term borrowing	*10,000*
Loans made to borrowers	*5,000*
Collections on loans (excluding interest)	*4,000*
Interest and dividends received	*17,000*
Cash received from customers	*795,000*
Proceeds from sales of plant assets	*9,000*
Dividends paid	*65,000*
Cash paid to suppliers and employees	*635,000*
Interest paid	*19,000*
Income taxes paid	*71,000*

Using this information, prepare a formal cash flow statement (disregard the schedule of cash and cash equivalents). Include a proper heading for the financial statement, and classify the given information into the categories of operating activities, investing activities, and financing activities. Net cash flows from operating activities are determined by the direct method. Place brackets around the dollar amounts of all cash disbursements.

*EXERCISE 19-9
An Analysis of Possible Reconciling Items
(LO 4, 7)

An analysis of the annual financial statements of Waste Disposal Corporation reveals the following:

a. The company had a $4 million loss from the early retirement of bonds payable.
b. Depreciation for the year amounted to $9 million.
c. During the year, $2 million in cash was transferred from the company's chequing account into a money market fund.
d. Accounts receivable from customers increased by $5 million over the year.
e. Cash received from customers during the year amounted to $165 million.
f. Prepaid expenses decreased by $1 million over the year.
g. Dividends declared during the year, $7 million; dividends paid during the year, $6 million.
h. Accounts payable (to suppliers of merchandise) increased by $3 million during the year.
i. The liability for income taxes payable amounted to $5 million at the beginning of the year and $3 million at year-end.

In the computation of net cash flow from operating activities by the **indirect method**, explain whether each of the above items should be **added to net income, deducted from net income**, or **omitted from the computation**. Briefly explain your reasons for each answer.

---

* *Supplemental Topic A,* "The Indirect Method."

*EXERCISE 19-10
Computation of Net Cash Flow from Operating Activities—Indirect Method
(LO 7)

The data below are taken from the income statement and balance sheets of All Night Pharmacies Inc.:

	Dec. 31 2001	Jan. 1 2001
Income statement:		
Net income	$400,000	
Depreciation expense	120,000	
Amortization of intangible assets	40,000	
Gain on sale of plant assets	80,000	
Loss on sale of investments	35,000	
Balance sheets:		
Accounts receivable	$335,000	$380,000
Inventory	503,000	575,000
Prepaid expenses	22,000	10,000
Accounts payable (to merchandise suppliers)	379,000	410,000
Accrued expenses payable	180,000	155,000

Using this information, prepare a partial cash flow statement for the year ended December 31, 2001, showing the computation of net cash flow from operating activities by the *indirect* method.

Problems

PROBLEM 19-1
Classifying Cash Flows
(LO 2, 6)

Among the transactions of Titanic Communications were the following:
a. Made payments on accounts payable to merchandise suppliers.
b. Paid the principal amount of a note payable to Bank of Montreal.
c. Paid interest charges relating to a note payable to Bank of Montreal.
d. Issued bonds payable for cash; management plans to use this cash in the near future to expand manufacturing and warehouse capabilities.
e. Paid salaries to employees in the finance department.
f. Collected an account receivable from a customer.
g. Transferred cash from the general bank account into a money market fund.
h. Used the cash received in **d**, above, to purchase land and building suitable for a manufacturing facility.
i. Made a year-end adjusting entry to recognize depreciation expense.
j. At year-end, purchased for cash an insurance policy covering the next 12 months.
k. Paid the quarterly dividend on preferred stock.
l. Paid the semiannual interest on bonds payable.
m. Received a quarterly dividend from an investment in the preferred stock of another corporation.
n. Sold for cash an investment in the preferred stock of another corporation.
o. Received cash upon the maturity of an investment in cash equivalents. (Ignore interest.)

INSTRUCTIONS

Most of the preceding transactions should be included among the activities summarized in a cash flow statement. For each transaction that should be included in this statement, indicate whether the transaction should be classified as an operating activity, an investing activity, or a financing activity. If the transaction *should not be included* in the current year's cash flow statement, briefly explain why not. (Assume that the net cash flow from operating activities is determined by the *direct method*.)

---

* Supplemental Topic A, "The Indirect Method."

PROBLEM 19-2
Format of a Cash Flow Statement
(LO 2, 3, 6)

The accounting staff of Educators' Outlet Inc. has assembled the following information for the year ended December 31, 19__.

Cash sales	$ 800,000
Credit sales	2,500,000
Collections on accounts receivable	2,200,000
Cash transferred from the money market fund to the general bank account	250,000
Interest and dividends received	100,000
Purchases (all on account)	1,800,000
Payments on accounts payable to merchandise suppliers	1,500,000
Cash payments for operating expenses	1,050,000
Interest paid	180,000
Income taxes paid	95,000
Loans made to borrowers	500,000
Collections on loans (excluding receipts of interest)	260,000
Cash paid to acquire plant assets	3,100,000
Book value of plant assets sold	660,000
Loss on sales of plant assets	80,000
Proceeds from issuing bonds payable	2,500,000
Dividends paid	120,000
Cash and cash equivalents (short-term investments of $130,000), beginning of year	446,000
Cash and cash equivalents (short-term investments of $160,000), end of year	-?-

INSTRUCTIONS

Prepare a cash flow statement, including a schedule of cash and cash equivalents, in the format illustrated in this chapter. Place brackets around amounts representing cash outflows. Use the ***direct method*** of reporting cash flows from operating activities.

PROBLEM 19-3
Cash Flow Statement
(LO 1, 2)

For the last five years, ShowTime Video has successfully operated two video rental stores in Toronto. The company's cash flows for 2001 appear below:

Interest paid	$ (20,000)
Dividends paid	(50,000)
Cash receipts from customers	550,000
Payments to suppliers and employees	(370,000)
Purchases of plant assets	(420,000)
Proceeds from long-term borrowing	300,000
Repayment of short-term debt	(25,000)
Interest received from investments	10,000
Income taxes paid	(45,000)

INSTRUCTIONS

At December 31, **2000**, the company's balance sheet showed cash of $96,000.
a. Arrange this information into the format of a cash flow statement.
b. Is the company more or less solvent at the end of 2001, than it was at the beginning of the year? Explain.
c. ShowTime Video has a policy of paying dividends equal to approximately 40% of its net cash flow from operating activities. As operating cash flows have been very stable over the past five years, the company has paid divi-

dends of approximately $50,000 per year. In coming years, would you expect the amount of ShowTime's dividend payments to increase, decrease, or remain about the same? Explain your reasoning.

PROBLEM 19-4
Reporting Investing Activities
(LO 6)

An analysis of the income statement and the balance sheet accounts of Franklin Optical at December 31 provides the following information:

Income statement items:
Gain on sale of marketable securities	$ 42,000
Loss on sales of plant assets	33,000

Analysis of balance sheet accounts:
Marketable Securities account:
Debit entries	$ 81,000
Credit entries	90,000

Notes Receivable account:
Debit entries	210,000
Credit entries	162,000

Plant and equipment accounts:
Debit entries to plant asset accounts	186,000
Credit entries to plant asset accounts	120,000
Debit entries to accumulated depreciation accounts	75,000

ADDITIONAL INFORMATION

1. Except as noted in **4**, below, payments and proceeds relating to investing transactions were made in cash.
2. The marketable securities are not cash equivalents.
3. All notes receivable relate to cash loans made to borrowers, not to receivables from customers.
4. Purchases of new equipment during the year ($186,000) were financed by paying $60,000 in cash and issuing a long-term note payable for $126,000.
5. Debits to the accumulated depreciation account are made whenever depreciable plant assets are retired.

INSTRUCTIONS

a. Prepare the ***Investing activities*** section of a cash flow statement. Show supporting computations for the amounts of (1) proceeds from sales of marketable securities and (2) proceeds from sales of plant assets. Place brackets around numbers representing cash outflows.
b. Prepare the supporting schedule that should accompany the cash flow statement in order to disclose the "noncash" aspects of the company's investing and financing activities.
c. Assume that Franklin Optical's management expects approximately the same amount of cash to be used for investing activities next year. In general terms, explain how the company might generate cash for this purpose.

PROBLEM 19-5
Reporting Investing Activities
(LO 6)

An analysis of the income statement and the balance sheet accounts of Caravan Imports at December 31 provides the following information:

Income statement items:
　　Gain on sales of plant assets .... $ 8,000
　　Loss on sales of marketable securities 16,000

Analysis of balance sheet accounts:
　　Marketable Securities account:
　　　　Debit entries .... $ 74,000
　　　　Credit entries 62,000
　　Notes Receivable account:
　　　　Debit entries 52,000
　　　　Credit entries 60,000
　　Plant and equipment accounts:
　　　　Debit entries to plant asset accounts 130,000
　　　　Credit entries to plant asset accounts 140,000
　　　　Debit entries to accumulated depreciation accounts 100,000

ADDITIONAL INFORMATION

1. Except as noted in **4**, below, payments and proceeds relating to investing transactions were made in cash.
2. The marketable securities are not cash equivalents.
3. All notes receivable relate to cash loans made to borrowers, not to receivables from customers.
4. Purchases of new equipment during the year ($130,000) were financed by paying $50,000 in cash and issuing a long-term note payable for $80,000.
5. Debits to the accumulated depreciation account are made whenever depreciable plant assets are sold or retired.

INSTRUCTIONS

a. Prepare the ***Investing activities*** section of a cash flow statement. Show supporting computations for the amounts of (1) proceeds from sales of marketable securities and (2) proceeds from sales of plant assets. Place brackets around amounts representing cash outflows.
b. Prepare the supplementary schedule that should accompany the cash flow statement in order to disclose the "noncash" aspects of the company's investing and financing activities.

PROBLEM 19-6
Reporting Operating Cash Flow by the Direct Method
(LO 3)

The following income statement and selected balance sheet account data are available for Satellite Transmissions Inc. at December 31:

SATELLITE TRANSMISSIONS INC.
Income Statement
For the Year Ended December 31, 20__

Revenue and Gains:
　　Net sales $2,850,000
　　Dividend income 104,000
　　Interest income 70,000
　　Gain on sales of marketable securities 4,000
　　　Total revenue and gains $3,028,000
Costs and expenses:
　　Cost of goods sold $1,550,000
　　Operating expenses 980,000
　　Interest expense 185,000
　　Income taxes 110,000
　　　Total costs and expenses 2,825,000
Net income .... $ 203,000

(continued)	End of Year	Beginning of Year
Selected account balances:		
Accounts receivable	$ 650,000	$ 720,000
Interest receivable	9,000	6,000
Inventories	800,000	765,000
Short-term prepayments	20,000	15,000
Accounts payable (merchandise suppliers)	570,000	562,000
Accrued operating expenses payable	65,000	94,000
Interest payable	21,000	12,000
Income taxes payable	22,000	35,000

ADDITIONAL INFORMATION

1. Dividend revenue is recognized on the cash basis. All other income statement amounts are recognized on the accrual basis.
2. Operating expenses include depreciation expense of $115,000.

INSTRUCTIONS

a. Prepare a partial cash flow statement, including only the operating activities section of the statement. Use the **direct method**. Place brackets around numbers representing cash payments. Show supporting computations for the amounts of:
   1. Cash received from customers
   2. Interest and dividends received
   3. Cash paid to suppliers and employees
   4. Interest paid
   5. Income taxes paid

b. Management of Satellite Transmissions Inc. is exploring ways to increase the cash flows from operations. One way that cash flows could be increased is through more aggressive collection of receivables. Assuming that management has already taken all the steps possible to increase revenues and reduce expenses, describe two other ways that cash flows from operations could be increased.

*PROBLEM 19-7
Reporting Operating Cash Flow—Indirect Method
(LO 4, 7)

Using the information presented in Problem 19-6, prepare a partial cash flow statement for the current year, showing the computation of net cash flow from operating activities by the **indirect method**. Use the format and captions illustrated in this chapter.

---

* *Supplemental Topic* A, "The Indirect Method."

PROBLEM 19-8
Reporting Operating Cash Flow by the Direct Method
(LO 3)

The following income statement and selected balance sheet account data are available for Child's Play Inc. at December 31, of the current year:

CHILD'S PLAY INC.
Income Statement
For the Year Ended December 31, 20__

Revenue:		
Net sales		$3,100,000
Interest income		50,000
Dividend income		47,000
Total revenue		$3,197,000
Costs, expenses, and losses:		
Cost of goods sold	$1,850,000	
Operating expenses	920,000	
Interest expense	140,000	
Income taxes	90,000	
Loss on sales of plant assets	7,000	
Total costs, expenses, and losses		3,007,000
Net income		$ 190,000

	End of Year	Beginning of Year
Selected account balances:		
Accounts receivable	$780,000	$700,000
Interest receivable	6,000	8,000
Inventories	670,000	690,000
Short-term prepayments	18,000	22,000
Accounts payable (merchandise suppliers)	577,000	590,000
Accrued operating expenses payable	38,000	21,000
Interest payable	13,000	19,000
Income taxes payable	36,000	28,000

ADDITIONAL INFORMATION

1. Dividend revenue is recognized on the cash basis. All other income statement amounts are recognized on the accrual basis.
2. Operating expenses include depreciation expense of $105,000.

INSTRUCTIONS

Prepare a partial cash flow statement, including only the operating activities section of the statement. Net cash flow from operating activities is to be presented using the ***direct method***. Place brackets around amounts representing cash payments. Show supporting computations for the amounts of:
1. Cash received from customers
2. Interest and dividends received
3. Cash paid to suppliers and employees
4. Interest paid
5. Income taxes paid

*PROBLEM 19-9
Reporting Operating Cash Flow—Indirect Method
(LO 4, 7)

Using the information that is presented in Problem 19-8, prepare a partial cash flow statement for the current year, showing the computation of net cash flow from operating activities by the ***indirect method***. Use the format and captions illustrated in this chapter.

---

* *Supplemental Topic A*, "The Indirect Method."

PROBLEM 19-10
Preparing a Cash Flow Statement: A Comprehensive Problem
(LO 1, 2, 3, 4, 6)

The accounting department of Inland Waste Management Inc. has prepared an income statement for the current year and also has developed the "Additional Information" listed below by analyzing changes in the company's balance sheet accounts.

INLAND WASTE MANAGEMENT INC.
Income Statement
For the Year Ended December 31, 20__

Revenue and gains:
Net sales		$2,450,000
Interest revenue		130,000
Gain on sales of plant assets		10,000
Total revenue and gains		$2,590,000

Costs, expenses, and losses:
Cost of goods sold	$1,300,000	
Operating expenses (including depreciation of $200,000)	825,000	
Interest expense	100,000	
Income taxes	95,000	
Loss on sales of marketable securities	30,000	
Total costs, expenses, and losses		2,350,000
Net income		$ 240,000

ADDITIONAL INFORMATION

Information about changes in the company's balance sheet accounts over the year is summarized below:

1. Accounts receivable decreased by $50,000.
2. Interest receivable increased by $15,000.
3. Inventory increased by $100,000, and accounts payable to suppliers of merchandise increased by $80,000.
4. Short-term prepayments of operating expenses decreased by $8,000, and accrued liabilities for operating expenses increased by $40,000.
5. The liability for interest payable decreased by $4,000 during the year.
6. The liability for income taxes payable increased by $9,000 during the year.
7. The following schedule summarizes the total debit and credit entries during the year in other balance sheet accounts:

	Debit Entries	Credit Entries
Marketable securities	$185,000	$170,000
Notes receivable (cash loans made to borrowers)	210,000	250,000
Plant assets (see paragraph 8)	625,000	50,000
Notes payable (short-term borrowing)	340,000	225,000
Capital stock		400,000
Retained earnings (see paragraph 9 below)	150,000	240,000

8. The $50,000 in credit entries to the plant assets account are net of any debits to accumulated depreciation when plant assets were retired.
9. The $150,000 debit to retained earnings represents dividends declared and paid during the year. The $240,000 credit entry represents the net income shown in the income statement.
10. All investing and financing activities were cash transactions.
11. Cash and cash equivalents amounted to $210,000 at the beginning of the year, and to $303,000 at year-end. Cash equivalent consisted of short-term investments of $90,000 at the beginning of the year and $100,000 at year-end.

INSTRUCTIONS

a. You are to prepare a cash flow statement for the current year, including a schedule of cash and cash equivalents, following the format illustrated in this chapter. Cash flows from operating activities are to be presented using the direct method. Place brackets around dollar amounts representing cash outlays. Show separately your computations of the following amounts:
  1. Cash received from customers
  2. Interest received
  3. Cash paid to suppliers and employees
  4. Interest paid
  5. Income taxes paid
  6. Proceeds from sales of marketable securities
  7. Proceeds from sales of plant assets

b. Inland's management has argued that issuance of a cash flow statement to creditors and investors is not necessary because the company clearly maintains an adequate cash balance. Explain why a cash flow statement is useful to creditors and investors even when the amount of cash on hand appears quite adequate.

PROBLEM 19-11
Preparing a Cash Flow Statement: A Second Comprehensive Problem
(LO 1,2,3,4 6)

You are the controller for Barraza Industries Inc. Your staff has prepared an income statement for the current year, and has also developed the following "Additional Information" by analyzing changes in the company's balance sheet accounts.

BARRAZA INDUSTRIES INC.
Income Statement
For the Year Ended December 31, 20__

Revenue and gains:		
Net sales		$3,200,000
Interest revenue		40,000
Gain on sales of marketable securities		34,000
Total revenue and gains		$3,274,000
Costs, expenses, and losses:		
Cost of goods sold	$1,620,000	
Operating expenses (including depreciation of $150,000)	1,240,000	
Interest expense	42,000	
Income taxes	100,000	
Loss on sales of plant assets	12,000	
Total costs, expenses, and losses		3,014,000
Net income		$ 260,000

ADDITIONAL INFORMATION

Information about changes in the company's balance sheet accounts over the year is summarized below:
1. Accounts receivable increased by $60,000.
2. Interest receivable decreased by $2,000.
3. Inventory decreased by $60,000, and accounts payable to suppliers of merchandise decreased by $16,000.
4. Short-term prepayments of operating expenses increased by $6,000, and accrued liabilities for operating expenses decreased by $8,000.
5. The liability for interest payable increased by $4,000 during the year.
6. The liability for income taxes payable decreased by $14,000 during the year.

7. The following schedule summarizes the total debit and credit entries during the year in other balance sheet accounts:

	Debit Entries	Credit Entries
Marketable securities	$ 60,000	$ 38,000
Notes receivable (cash loans made to borrowers)	44,000	28,000
Plant assets (see paragraph 8 below)	500,000	36,000
Notes payable (short-term borrowing)	92,000	82,000
Capital stock		180,000
Retained earnings (see paragraph 9 below)	120,000	260,000

8. The $36,000 in credit entries to the plant assets account are net of any debits to accumulated depreciation when plant assets were retired.
9. The $120,000 debit to retained earnings represents dividends declared and paid during the year. The $260,000 credit entry represents the net income shown in the income statement.
10. All investing and financing activities were cash transactions.
11. Cash and cash equivalents amounted to $244,000 at the beginning of the year, and to $164,000 at year-end. Cash equivalents consisted of short-term investments of $62,000 at the beginning of the year and $32,000 at the year-end.

INSTRUCTIONS

a. You are to prepare a cash flow statement for the current year, including a schedule of cash and cash equivalents, following the format illustrated in this chapter. Use the ***direct method*** of reporting cash flows from operating activities. Place brackets around dollar amounts representing cash outflows. Show separately your computations of the following amounts:
  1. Cash received from customers
  2. Interest received
  3. Cash paid to suppliers and employees
  4. Interest paid
  5. Income taxes paid
  6. Proceeds from sales of marketable securities
  7. Proceeds from sales of plant assets
b. Explain the ***primary reason*** why:
  1. The amount of cash provided by operating activities was substantially greater than the company's net income.
  2. There was a net decrease in cash over the year, despite the substantial amount of cash provided by operating activities.
c. The company's controller thinks that through more efficient "cash management," the company could have held the increase in accounts receivable for the year to $10,000, without affecting net income. Explain how holding down the growth in receivables affects cash. Also, compute the effect that limiting the growth in receivables to $10,000 would have had upon the company's net increase or decrease in cash (and cash equivalents) for the year.

PROBLEM 19-12
Prepare a Cash Flow Statement and Comment on Issues
(LO 1, 2, 3, 4, 6)

When the controller of Southern King Corporation presented the following condensed comparative financial statements to the board of directors, the reaction of the board members was favourable.

SOUTHERN KING CORPORATION
Comparative Financial Position
As of December 31
(in thousands of dollars)

	2002	2001
Current assets	$ 410	$ 395
Less: Current liabilities	200	225
Working capital	$ 210	$ 170
Plant and equipment (net)	962	660
Patents (net of amortization)	8	10
Other—assets of a business segment	-0-	150
Total assets minus current liabilities	$1,180	$ 990
Long-term liabilities	$ 250	$ -0-
Preferred stock (non-cumulative)	-0-	170
Common stock (10,000 shares)	600	600
Retained earnings	330	220
Total long-term debt and capital	$1,180	$ 990

SOUTHERN KING CORPORATION
Comparative Income Statements
(in thousands of dollars)

	2002	2001
Net sales	$1,000	$ 680
Cost of goods sold	590	480
Gross profit	$ 410	$ 200
Operating expenses, including depreciation of $80 in 2002 and $60 in 2001	(180)	(140)
Loss on sale of a business segment	(30)	-0-
Income taxes expense	(90)	(25)
Net income	$ 110	$ 35

Noting that net income rose from $3.50 per share of common stock to $11 per share, one member of the board proposed that a substantial cash dividend be paid. "Our working capital is up by $40,000; we should be able to make a distribution to shareholders," he commented. The controller replied that the company's cash position was precarious and pointed out that at the end of 2002 a cash balance of only $15,000 was on hand, a decline from $145,000 at the end of 2001. The controller also reminded the board that the company bought some new equipment during 2002. When another board member asked for an explanation of the increase of $40,000 in working capital, the controller presented the following schedule (in thousands of dollars):

	EFFECT ON WORKING CAPITAL
Increase in working capital:	
Accounts receivable increased by	$ 83
Inventories increased by	72
Accounts payable reduced by	62
Accrued operating expenses payable reduced by	28
Total increases in working capital	$245
Decreases in working capital:	
Cash decreased by	$130
Prepaid expenses reduced by	10
Income taxes payable increased by	65 205
Increase in working capital during 2002	$ 40

After examining this schedule, the board member shook his head and said, "I still don't understand how our cash position can be so tight in the face of a tripling of net income and a substantial increase in working capital!

INSTRUCTIONS

a. Prepare a cash flow statement for the year ended December 31, 2002.
b. Comment on the issues raised by the board members.

*PROBLEM 19-13
Prepare and Analyze a Cash Flow Statement; Requires a Work Sheet
(LO 1–8)

SPACENET 2000 was founded in 2000 to apply a new technology for efficiently transmitting closed-circuit (cable) television signals without the need for an inground cable. The company earned a profit of $115,000 in 2000, its first year of operations, even though it was serving only a small test market. In 2001, the company began dramatically expanding its customer base. Management expects both sales and net income to more than triple in each of the next five years.

Comparative balance sheets at the ends of 2000 and 2001, the company's first two years of operations, appear below.

**SPACENET 2000
Comparative Balance Sheets**

	December 31	
Assets	**2001**	**2000**
Cash and cash equivalents (short-term investment: $20,000 in Year 2000 and $10,000 in Year 2001)	$ 37,000	$ 80,000
Accounts receivable	850,000	100,000
Plant and equipment (net of accumulated depreciation)	2,653,000	600,000
Totals	$3,540,000	$780,000
Liabilities & Shareholders' Equity		
Note payable (short-term)	$1,450,000	$ -0-
Accounts payable	63,000	30,000
Accrued expenses payable	32,000	45,000
Notes payable (long-term)	740,000	390,000
Capital stock (no par value)	700,000	200,000
Retained earnings	555,000	115,000
Totals	$3,540,000	$780,000

---

* *Supplemental Topics A and B*, "The Indirect Method," "A Work Sheet for Preparing a Cash Flow Statement."

ADDITIONAL INFORMATION

The following information regarding the company's operations in 2001 is available in either the company's income statements or its accounting records:

1. Net income for the year was $440,000. The company has never paid a dividend.
2. Depreciation for the year amounted to $147,000.
3. During the year, the company purchased plant assets costing $2,200,000, for which it paid $1,850,000 in cash and financed $350,000 by issuing a long-term note payable. (Much of the cash used in these purchases was provided by short-term borrowing, as described below.)
4. In 2001, SPACENET 2000 borrowed $1,450,000 against a $5 million line of credit with a bank. In its balance sheet, the resulting obligations are reported as notes payable (short-term).
5. Additional shares of capital stock (no par value) were issued to investors for $500,000 cash.

INSTRUCTIONS

a. Prepare a working paper for a cash flow statement, following the general format illustrated in this chapter. (*Note:* If this problem is completed as a group assignment, each member of the group should be prepared to explain in class all entries in the work sheet, as well as the group's conclusions in parts **c** and **d**.)
b. Prepare a formal cash flow statement for 2001, including supplementary schedules of cash and cash equivalents and noncash investing and financing activities. (Cash provided by operating activities is to be presented by the ***indirect method***.)
c. Briefly explain how operating activities can be a net *use* of cash when the company is operating so profitably.
d. Because of the expected rapid growth, management forecasts that operating activities will be an even greater use of cash in 2002 than in 2001. If this forecast is correct, does SPACENET 2000 appear to be heading toward insolvency? Explain.

*PROBLEM 19-14
Prepare and Analyze a Cash Flow Statement; Involves Preparation of a Work Sheet
(LO 1–8)

TV Wonder Tool sells a single product (a combination screwdriver, pliers, hammer, and crescent wrench) exclusively through television advertising. Shown below are comparative income statements and balance sheets for the last two years:

TV WONDER TOOL
Comparative Income Statements
For the Year Ended December 31

	December 31 2001	December 31 2000
Sales	$350,000	$500,000
Less: Cost of goods sold	140,000	200,000
Gross profit	$210,000	$300,000
Less: Operating expenses (including depreciation of $34,000 in 2000 and $35,000 in 2001)	243,000	260,000
Loss on sale of marketable securities	1,000	-0-
Net income (loss)	$ (34,000)	$ 40,000

---

*Supplemental Topics A and B, "The Indirect Method," "A Work Sheet for Preparing a Cash Flow Statement."

TV WONDER TOOL
Comparative Balance Sheets

Assets	December 31, 2001	December 31, 2000
Cash and cash equivalents (short-term investments; none for 2000, $15,000 for 2001)	$ 60,000	$ 10,000
Marketable securities	5,000	20,000
Accounts receivable	23,000	40,000
Inventory	122,000	120,000
Plant and equipment (net of accumulated depreciation)	285,000	300,000
Totals	$495,000	$490,000

Liabilities & Shareholders' Equity		
Accounts payable	$ 73,000	$ 50,000
Accrued expenses payable	14,000	17,000
Note payable	253,000	245,000
Capital stock (no par value)	135,000	120,000
Retained earnings	20,000	58,000
Totals	$495,000	$490,000

ADDITIONAL INFORMATION

The following information regarding the company's operations in 2001 is available from the company's accounting records:

1. Early in the year, the company declared and paid a $4,000 cash dividend.
2. During the year, marketable securities costing $15,000 were sold for $14,000 cash, resulting in a $1,000 nonoperating loss.
3. The company purchased plant assets for $20,000, paying $2,000 in cash and issuing a note payable for the $18,000 balance.
4. During the year, the company repaid a $10,000 note payable, but incurred an additional $18,000 in long-term debt as described in **3**, above.
5. The owners invested $15,000 cash in the business as a condition of the new loans described in paragraph **4** above.

INSTRUCTIONS

a. Prepare a working paper for a cash flow statement, following the general format illustrated in this chapter. (*Note:* If this problem is completed as a group assignment, each member of the group should be prepared to explain in class all entries in the work sheet, as well as the group's conclusions in parts **c**, **d**, and **e**.)
b. Prepare a formal cash flow statement for 2001, including a schedule of cash and cash equivalents and a supplementary schedule of noncash investing and financing activities. (Cash provided by operating activities is to be presented by the *indirect method*.)
c. Explain how Wonder Tool achieved a positive cash flow from operating activities, despite incurring a net loss for the year.
d. Does the company's financial position appear to be improving or deteriorating? Explain.
e. Does TV Wonder Tool appear to be a company whose operations are growing or contracting? Explain.

Analytical and Decision Problems and Cases

A&D 19-1
Another Look at Allison Corporation
(LO 1)

This case is based upon the cash flow statement for Allison Corporation, illustrated on page 938. You are to use this statement to evaluate the company's ability to continue paying the current level of dividends—$40,000 per year. The following information also is available:

1. The net cash flow from operating activities shown in the statement is relatively "normal" for Allison Corporation. In fact, net cash flows from operating activities have not varied by more than a few thousand dollars in any of the last three years.
2. The net outflow for investing activities was unusually high, because the company modernized its production facilities during the year. The "normal" investing cash outflow is about $45,000 per year, the amount required to replace existing plant assets as they are retired. Over the long run, marketable securities transactions and lending transactions have a very small impact upon Allison's net cash flow from investing activities.
3. The net cash flow from financing activities was unusually large in the current year, because of the issuance of bonds payable and capital stock. These securities were issued to finance the modernization of the production facilities. In a typical year, financing activities include only short-term borrowing transactions and payments of dividends.

INSTRUCTIONS

a. Based solely upon the company's past performance, do you believe that the $40,000 annual dividend payments are secure? That is, does the company appear able to pay this amount in dividends every year without putting any strain on its cash position? Do you think it is more likely that Allison Corporation will increase or decrease the amount of dividends that it pays? Explain fully.

b. Should any of the "unusual" events appearing in the cash flow statement for the current year affect your analysis of the company's ability to pay future dividends? Explain.

A&D 19-2
Lookin' Good?
(LO 1, 4, 6)

It is late summer and National Motors, an auto manufacturer, is facing a financial crisis. A large issue of bonds payable will mature next March, and the company must issue stock or new bonds to raise the money to retire this debt. Unfortunately, profits and cash flows have been declining over recent years. Management fears that if cash flows and profits do not improve in the current year, the company will not be able to raise the capital needed to pay off the maturing bonds. Therefore, members of management have made the following proposals to improve the cash flows and profitability that will be reported in the financial statements dated this coming December 31.

1. Switch from the LIFO method to the FIFO method of valuing inventories. Management estimates that the FIFO method will result in a lower cost of goods sold but in higher income taxes for the current year. However, the additional income taxes will not actually be paid until early next year. (Assume both inventory methods are allowed for tax purposes.)
2. Switch from the 150%-declining-balance method of depreciation to the straight-line method and also lengthen the useful lives over which assets are depreciated. (These changes would be made only for financial reporting purposes, not for income tax purposes.)
3. Pressure dealers to increase their inventories—in short, to buy more cars. (The dealerships are independently owned; thus, dealers are the "customers" to whom National Motors sells automobiles.) It is estimated that this strategy could increase sales for the current year by 5%. However, any additional sales in the current year would be almost entirely offset by fewer sales in the following year.

4. Require dealers to pay for purchases more quickly. Currently, dealers must pay for purchases of autos within 60 days. Management is considering reducing this period to 30 days.
5. Pass up cash discounts offered for prompt payment (i.e., 2/10, n/30) and do not pay any bills until the final due date.
6. Borrow at current short-term interest rates (about 10%) and use the proceeds to pay off long-term debt bearing an interest rate of 13%.
7. Substitute stock dividends for the cash dividends currently paid on capital stock.

INSTRUCTIONS

a. Prepare a schedule with four columns. The first column is to be headed "Proposals," and is to contain the paragraph numbers of the seven proposals listed above. The next three columns are to be headed with the following financial statement captions: (1) "Net income," (2) "Net cash flow from operating activities," and (3) "Cash."

For each of the seven proposals in the left column, indicate whether you expect the proposal to "Increase," "Decrease," or have "No Effect" in the current year upon each of the financial statement captions listed in the next three columns. (*Note:* Only a few months remain in the current year. Therefore, you are to determine the **short-term** effects of these proposals.)

b. For each of the seven proposals, write a short paragraph explaining the reasoning behind your answers to part **a**.

A&D 19-3
Cash Flow Statement
(LO 1, 2)

The Emerald City and Humpty's are retail stores that sell computer software. A summary of each store's net cash flows for the last three years appears below. (Dollar amounts are stated in thousands.)

	2001	2000	1999
The Emerald City			
Net cash provided by (used in) operating activities	$ (10)	$ 40	$ 85
Net cash provided by (used in) investing activities	50	20	(10)
Net cash provided by (used in) financing activities	80	50	20
Increase (decrease) in cash during the year	$ 120	$ 110	$ 95
Cash balance at year-end (per balance sheet)	$ 335	$ 215	$105
Humpty's			
Net cash provided by operating activities	$320	$ 260	$210
Net cash provided by (used in) investing activities	(200)	(100)	(50)
Net cash provided by (used in) financing activities	(150)	(100)	(70)
Increase (decrease) in cash during the year	$ (30)	$ 60	$ 90
Cash balance at year-end (per balance sheet)	$ 260	$ 290	$230

INSTRUCTIONS

a. Explain briefly the nature of (1) *operating activities*, (2) *investing activities*, and (3) *financing activities* as these terms are used in a cash flow statement.
b. Explain the meaning of the phrase, "Net cash provided by (used in) ... activities." As part of your answer, explain the use of brackets ( ) as indicated by this caption.
c. For each of the three cash flow classifications discussed in part **a**, describe two types of transactions that involve (1) cash receipts, and (2) cash payments.
d. Which of these stores appears "healthier" in terms of its cash flows? Explain your reasoning and include a brief discussion of any *trends* relevant to your conclusion.

A&D 19-4
Effects of Business Strategies
(LO 1, 2)

Computer World is a retail computer store that sells both to business organizations and individuals. Credit-worthy businesses are allowed to purchase merchandise on 30-day credit terms; individuals normally are required to pay cash. Merchandise on the sales floor is displayed on racks and counter tops, but is not hooked up for actual operation. There are two demonstration rooms in the back of the store where salespeople can demonstrate the operation of various products.

Computer World's management is considering the probable future effects of the following three business strategies:

1. Allow credit-worthy individuals to purchase merchandise on 6- and 12-month instalment plans.
2. Change to a new supplier for purchases of certain high-cost merchandise. The new supplier charges slightly higher prices than the current supplier, but will allow Computer World 90 days to pay for credit purchases, instead of only 30 days.
3. Remodel the interior of the store around six functional "workstations" that will permit immediate demonstration of various products. (The remodelling would involve some construction work. This work would be inconvenient but would not require any suspension of business operations.)

INSTRUCTIONS

a. Indicate the effects that you would expect implementation of each strategy to have upon net income and upon net cash flow from operating activities in (1) the immediate future—say, the next two months—and (2) the "long run"—say, after the strategy has been in effect for one year. Organize your answer in the columnar format illustrated below; use the code letters *I* for increase, *D* for decrease, and *NE* for no effect.

	Short-term Effects		Long-term Effects	
Strategy	Net Income	Operating Cash Flow	Net Income	Operating Cash Flow
1				

b. Explain the reasoning behind your answers.

A&D 19-5
Prepare a Cash Flow Statement from Accrual and Cash Basis Income Statement and Other Information, Comment on Policies and Relevancy of Information
(LO 1, 2, 3, 4, 6)

In an attempt to provide the most relevant information on cash flows to the members of the board of directors, the controller of Ancaster Corporation presented the following:

Ancaster Corporation
Income Statement on an Accrual and Cash Basis
For the Year Ended December 31, 2000
(in thousands of dollars)

	Accrual Basis	Add (or Deduct)	Cash Basis
Net Sales	$800	$28	$828
Add: Decrease in accounts receivable			
Cost of goods sold	510	46	
Add: Increase in inventories		(93)	463
Less: Increase in accounts payable			
Gross profit	$290		$365
Operating expenses	$180	(35)	
Less: Depreciation expenses		(16)	$129
Increase in accrued liabilities			
Income taxes	36	(12)	24
Less: Increase in income tax liability			
Nonoperating gain	(22)		
Total expenses less nonoperating gain	$194		$153
Net income	$ 96		
Cash provided by operating activities			$212

In his presentation to the board, the controller also mentioned:
1. Disposal of an old plant asset for $30,000 cash, resulting in a nonoperating gain of $22,000.
2. Purchase of a tract of land for a new plant for $325,000 cash.
3. Issuance of common stock for $500,000 cash.
4. Issuance of 10-year bonds payable, $1,000,000, for cash.
5. Net income before nonoperating gain and cash from operating activities have been stable over the past two-year period and cash from operating activities in 2001 would be similar to that of 2000.
6. Cash dividends of $150,000 were declared and paid.
7. Cash balance at December 31, 2000, was $1,500,000. There were no cash equivalents.

"Ladies and gentlemen," concluded the controller, "you can see that our cash position is improving and our profitability is stable. Our future looks good, as we will substantially increase our production capacity when our new plant is completed next year. The cost of construction and equipment will be $2 million and we have agreed to pay it off during next year."

However, some board members were not quite sure whether the company would have sufficient cash to finance its operations, the $150,000 annual dividends, and immediate plant expansion in 2001, since the board had decided not to incur more short- or long-term debt or issue more capital stock.

INSTRUCTIONS

a. From the information provided by the controller, prepare a cash flow statement for 2000.
b. Comment on the issue raised by the board members.

*A&D 19-6
Analysis of Data from an Annual Report
(LO 7)

Shown below is an excerpt from a recent annual report of **Bombardier Inc.** (Dollar amounts are in millions.)

Operating activities		
Net income		$420.2
Non-cash items		
Depreciation and amortization		180.1
Net change in non-cash balances relating to operations:		
Accounts receivable	$(158.0)	
Inventories	(323.2)	
Accounts payable and accrued liabilities	119.5	
Income taxes payable	(9.2)	
		(336.3)
Cash provided by operating activities		$416.8

The company did not state whether the changes in the balance sheet accounts listed were increases or decreases, apparently assuming that the reader of the financial statements could determine this from the effect of each adjustment upon net income. (Of course, this information also may be determined by comparing the company's balance sheets at the beginning and end of the year.)

INSTRUCTIONS

By analyzing the effects of the adjustments upon net income in the above schedule, indicate whether the balance in each of the four accounts listed below *increased* or *decreased* over the year. Explain the reasoning behind your answer.
a. Accounts receivable
b. Inventories
c. Accounts payable
d. Income taxes payable

Answers to Self-Test Questions
1. b **2.** a **3.** a **4.** c **5.** d

---

*Supplemental Topic A, "The Indirect Method."

CHAPTER 20

Analysis and Interpretation of Financial Statements

In today's global economy, investment capital is always "on the move." Through organized capital markets such as the *Toronto Stock Exchange*, investors each day shift billions of investment dollars among different companies, industries, and nations. Capital flows to those areas in which investors expect to earn the greatest returns with the least risk. How do investors forecast risk and potential returns? Primarily by analyzing accounting information.

CHAPTER LEARNING OBJECTIVES

1. Explain the elements essential to the analysis and interpretation of financial statements.
2. Explain the uses of dollar and percentage changes, trend percentages, component percentages, and ratios.
3. Discuss the "quality" of a company's earnings, assets, and working capital.
4. Analyze financial statements from the viewpoints of common shareholders, creditors, and others.
5. Compute the ratios widely used in financial statement analysis and explain the significance of each.

Essential Elements for Financial Statement Analysis and Interpretation

LO 1 Explain the elements essential to the analysis and interpretation of financial statements.

The goal of accounting is to provide useful information to economic decision making groups such as management, investors, creditors, investment advisors, union officials, politicians, and government agencies. The information need of each of these groups is somewhat different because each tends to concentrate on particular aspects of the financial picture of the company. Most of such information is contained in the financial statements. In addition, the **annual report** (which includes the financial statements) of a large public company such as Loblaw Companies Limited, which appears at the end of this text, is an important source of information.

CASE IN POINT

A recent annual report of Hudson's Bay Company contains such information as: highlights of the year, reviews and visions of the CEO, acquisition of Kmart Canada Co., profile/results of the year for the Bay and Zellers, management's statement on financial reporting and its discussion and analysis of the current year's operations, financial statements, auditors' report to shareholders, and a ten-year financial summary.

It also contains an interesting and informative profile of the company: "Hudson's Bay Company, established in 1670, is Canada's oldest corporation and its largest department store retailer. Through its major divisions, the Bay with 100 stores, and Zellers with 298, Hudson's Bay Company covers the Canadian retail market across all price zones and from coast to coast. It accounts for approximately 37% of Canadian department store sales and almost 8% of all retail sales, other than food and automobiles."

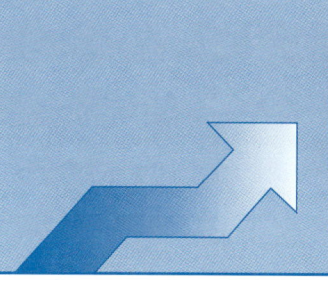

Another source of information about a large public company are the publications issued by various investment advisory groups. These groups study the financial position, operating results, and future prospects of public companies and sell their analyses, conclusions, and investment recommendations for a fee. For example, detailed financial analyses of most large corporations are published by *The Financial Post* (now the *National Post*), Dun & Bradstreet of Canada, Canada Business Services (*The Investment Reporter*), Moody's Investor Services, Standard & Poor's, and the Value Line Investment Survey. Anyone may subscribe to these investment advisory services.

To properly analyze and interpret the information in the financial statements, decision makers must have an understanding of the significance and limitations of the information in the financial statements and other information in the annual report and of the accounting principles upon which financial statements are based. They must understand the uses and limitations of the tools or techniques for the analysis. Equally important, they must be knowledgeable of the nature and scope of the company's operations, its management, its position in the industry and the industry itself, and its future plans.

In this chapter, our discussion will be limited mostly to the kind of analysis that can be made by "outsiders" who do not have access to internal accounting records and reports. These investors must rely to a considerable extent on financial statements in published annual and quarterly reports as well as other information in such reports.

Bankers and major creditors usually are able to obtain detailed financial information from borrowers simply by requesting it as a condition for granting a loan. Suppliers and other trade creditors may obtain some financial information about almost any business from credit-rating companies, such as Dun & Bradstreet of Canada.

Comparative Financial Statement

Significant changes in financial data are easy to see when financial statement amounts for two or more years are placed side by side in adjacent columns. Such a statement is called a **comparative financial statement**. The amounts for the most recent year are usually placed in the left-hand money column. All financial statements are usually prepared in the form of comparative statements. A highly condensed comparative income statement covering three years is shown below.

Condensed three-year income statement

BENSON CORPORATION
Comparative Income Statement
For the Years Ended December 31, 2001, 2000, 1999
(in thousands of dollars)

	2001	2000	1999
Net sales	$600	$500	$400
Cost of goods sold	370	300	235
Gross profit	$230	$200	$165
Expenses	194	160	115
Net income	$ 36	$ 40	$ 50

Tools of Analysis

Few figures in a financial statement are highly significant in and of themselves. It is their relationship to other quantities or the amount and direction of change that is important. Analysis is largely a matter of establishing significant relationships and identifying changes and trends. Four widely used analytical techniques are (1) dollar and percentage changes, (2) trend percentages, (3) component percentages, and (4) ratios.

Dollar and Percentage Changes

LO 2: Explain the uses of dollar and percentage changes, trend percentages, component percentages, and ratios.

The dollar amount of change from year to year is significant, but expressing the change in percentage terms adds perspective. For example, if sales this year have increased by $100,000, the fact that this is an increase of 10% over last year's sales of $1 million puts it in a different perspective than if it represented a 1% increase over sales of $10 million for the prior year.

The dollar amount of any change is the difference between the amount for a **comparison** year and for a **base** year. The percentage change is computed by dividing the amount of the change between years by the amount for the base year. This is illustrated in the tabulation below, using data from the comparative income statement on the preceding page.

Dollar and percentage changes

	In Thousands			Increase or (Decrease)			
				2001 over 2000		2000 over 1999	
	Year 2001	Year 2000	Year 1999	Amount	%	Amount	%
Net sales	$600	$500	$400	$100	20%	$100	25%
Net income	36	40	50	(4)	(10%)	(10)	(20%)

Although net sales increased $100,000 in both 2000 and 2001, the percentage of change differs because of the shift in the base from 1999 to 2000. These calculations present no problems when the figures for the base year are positive amounts. If a negative amount or a zero amount appears in the base year, however, a percentage change cannot be computed. Thus if Benson Corporation had incurred a net loss in 2000, the percentage change in net income from 2000 to 2001 could not have been calculated.

Evaluating Percentage Changes in Sales and Earnings Computing the percentage changes in sales, gross profit, and net income from one year to the next gives insight into a company's rate of growth. If a company is experiencing growth in its economic activities, sales and earnings should increase at **more than the rate of inflation**. Assume, for example, that a company's sales increase by 6% while the general price level rises by 10%. It is probable that the entire increase in the dollar amount of sales may be explained by inflation, rather than by an increase in sales volume (the number of units sold). In fact, the company may well have sold **fewer** goods than in the preceding year.

In measuring the dollar or percentage change in **quarterly** sales or earnings, it is customary to compare the results of the current quarter with those of the **same quarter in the preceding year**. Use of the same quarter of the preceding year as the base period prevents our analysis from being distorted by seasonal fluctuations in business activity.

Percentages Become Misleading When the Base is Small Percentage changes may create a misleading impression when the dollar amount used as a base is unusually small. Occasionally we hear a television newscaster say that a company's net income has increased by a very large percentage, such as 900%. The initial impression created by such a statement is that the company's net income must now be excessively large. But assume, for example, that a company had net income of $100,000 in its first year; that in the second year net income drops to $10,000; and that in the third year net income returns to the $100,000 level. In this third year, net income has increased by $90,000, representing a 900% increase over the net income of the second year. What needs to be added is that this 900% increase in net income in the third year *exactly offsets* the 90% decline in net income in the second year. Few people realize that a 90% decline in earnings must be followed by a 900% increase just to get back to the starting point.

> **CASE IN POINT**
>
> In 1997, Domtar Inc. had a net income of $25 million, as compared to 1996's net income of $97 million. This represented a 74% decline in net income ($97 million minus $25 million divided by $97 million). How much of an increase in net income would be required in 1998 in order for the net income to return to the 1996 level? The answer is 288%, as computed as follows:
>
> | | |
> |---|---:|
> | *Required increase to reach the 1996 net income level (from $25 million to $97 million)* .... | $72 million |
> | *Base period earnings (1997)* .... | $25 million |
> | *Required percentage increase ($72 million ÷ $25 million)* ...... | 288% |

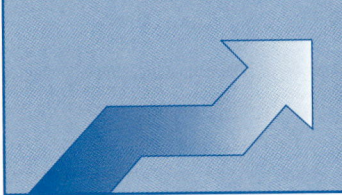

Trend Percentages

The changes in financial statement items from a base year to following years are often expressed as **trend percentages** to show the extent and direction of change. Two steps are necessary to compute trend percentages. First, a base year is selected and each item in the financial statements for the base year is given a weight of 100%. The second step is to express each item in the financial statements for following years as a percentage of its base-year amount. This computation consists of dividing an item such as Sales in the years after the base year by the amount of Sales in the base year.

For example, assume that 1996 is selected as the base year and that Sales in the base year amounted to $300,000 as shown below. The trend percentages for Sales are computed by dividing the Sales amount of each following year by $300,000. Also shown in the illustration are the yearly amounts of net income. The trend percentages for net income are computed by dividing the Net Income amount for each following year by the base-year amount of $15,000.

	2001	2000	1999	1998	1997	1996
Sales	$450,000	$360,000	$330,000	$320,000	$312,000	$300,000
Net income	22,950	14,550	21,450	19,200	15,600	15,000

When the computations described above have been made, the trend percentages will appear as shown below.

	2001	2000	1999	1998	1997	1996
Sales	150%	120%	110%	107%	104%	100%
Net income	153%	97%	143%	128%	104%	100%

The above trend percentages indicate a very modest growth in sales in the early years and accelerated growth in 2000 and 2001. Net income also shows an increasing growth trend with the exception of the year 2000, when net income declined despite a solid increase in sales. This variation could have resulted from an unfavourable change in the gross profit margin or from unusual expenses. However, the problem was overcome in 2001 with a sharp rise in net income. Overall the trend percentages give a picture of a profitable growing enterprise.

As another example, assume that sales are increasing each year but that the cost of goods sold is increasing at a faster rate. This means that the gross profit margin is shrinking. Perhaps the increases in sales are being achieved through excessive price cutting. The company's net income may be declining even though sales are rising.

Component Percentages

Component percentages indicate the ***relative size*** of each item included in a total. For example, each item on a balance sheet could be expressed as a percentage of total assets. This shows quickly the relative importance of current and noncurrent assets as well as the relative amount of financing obtained from current creditors, long-term creditors, and shareholders. By computing component percentages for several successive balance sheets, we can see which items are increasing in importance and which are becoming less significant.

Common Size Income Statement Another application of component percentages is to express all items in an income statement as a percentage of net sales. Such a statement is called a common size income statement. A condensed income statement in dollars and in common size form is illustrated below.

Income Statement

Are the year-to-year changes favourable?

	Dollars 2001	Dollars 2000	Component Percentages 2001	Component Percentages 2000
Net sales	$1,000,000	$600,000	100.0%	100.0%
Cost of goods sold	700,000	360,000	70.0	60.0
Gross profit	$ 300,000	$240,000	30.0%	40.0%
Expenses (including income taxes)	250,000	180,000	25.0	30.0
Net income	$ 50,000	$ 60,000	5.0%	10.0%

Looking only at the component percentages, we see that the decline in the gross profit rate from 40% to 30% was only partially offset by the decrease in expenses as a percentage of net sales, causing net income to decrease from 10% to 5% of net sales.

Ratios

A ratio is a simple mathematical expression of the relationship of one item to another. Every percentage may be viewed as a ratio—that is, one number expressed as a percentage of another.

Ratios may be stated in several ways. To illustrate, let us consider the current ratio, which expresses the relationship between current assets and current liabilities. If current assets are $100,000 and current liabilities are $50,000, we may say either that the current ratio is 2 to 1 (which is written as 2:1) or that current assets are 200% of current liabilities. Either statement correctly summarizes the relationship—that is, that current assets are twice as large as current liabilities.

If a ratio is to be useful, the two amounts being compared must be logically related. Our interpretation of a ratio often requires investigation of the underlying data.

Comparative Data in Annual Reports of Major Corporations

The annual reports of major corporations usually contain comparative balance sheets covering two years and comparative income statements for two or three years. Supplementary schedules showing sales, net income, and other key amounts are often presented for periods of five to 11 years. Shown below are selected items from an annual report of Bombardier Inc. showing some interesting trends for a five-year period ending January 31.

BOMBARDIER INC.
(Dollars in millions, except per share data)

	1998	1997	1996	1995	1994
Revenue	$8,509	$7,976	$7,123	$5,943	$4,769
Net income	420	406	158	247	177
Net earnings per common share	1.18	1.18	0.45	0.73	0.56
Dividends per share (class A)	0.30	0.20	0.20	0.15	0.10
Market price per share (year-end), class A	28.25	26.10	20.38	11.44	10.50
Book value per common share	7.14	6.01	4.92	4.85	4.05

Standards of Comparison

In using dollar and percentage changes, trend percentages, component percentages, and ratios, financial analysts constantly search for some standard of comparison against which to judge whether the relationships that they have found are favourable or unfavourable. Two such standards are (1) the past performance of the company and (2) the performance of other companies in the same industry.

Past Performance of the Company Comparing analytical data for a current period with similar computations for prior years affords some basis for judging whether the condition of the business is improving or worsening. The comparison of data over time is sometimes called **horizontal** or ***trend analysis***, to express the idea of reviewing data for a number of consecutive periods. It is distinguished from **vertical** or ***static* analysis**, which refers to the review of the financial information for only one accounting period.

In addition to determining whether the situation is improving or becoming worse, horizontal analysis may aid in making estimates of future prospects. Because changes may reverse their direction at any time, however, projecting past trends into the future always involves risk.

A weakness of horizontal analysis is that comparison with the past does not afford any basis for evaluation in absolute terms. The fact that net income was 2% of sales last year and is 3% of sales this year indicates improvement, but if there is evidence that net income ***should be*** 7% of sales, the record for both years is unfavourable.

Industry Standard The limitations of horizontal analysis may be overcome to some extent by finding an appropriate "yardstick" against which to measure a particular company's performance. The yardsticks most widely used by most analysts are the performance of comparable companies and the average performance of several companies in the same industry.

Assume, for example, that the revenue of Alpha Airlines drops by 5% during the current year. If the revenue for the airlines industry had dropped an average of 15% during this year, Alpha's 5% decline might be viewed as a ***favourable*** performance. As another example, assume that Omega Limited earns a net income equal to 2% of net sales. This would be substandard if Omega were a manufacturer of commercial aircraft, but it would be satisfactory performance if it were a grocery chain.

When we compare a given company with its competitors or with industry averages, our conclusions will be valid only if the companies in question are reasonably comparable. Because of the large number of diversified companies formed in recent years, the term ***industry*** is difficult to define, and companies that fall roughly within the same industry may not be comparable in many respects. For example, one company may engage only in the marketing of oil products; another may be a fully integrated producer from the well to the gas pump, yet both are said to be in the "oil industry."

Quality of Earnings

LO 3: Discuss the "quality" of a company's earnings, assets, and working capital.

Earnings are the lifeblood of a business entity. No entity can survive for long and accomplish its other goals unless it is profitable. On the other hand, continuous losses will drain assets from the business, consume owners' equity, and leave the company at the mercy of creditors. In assessing the prospects of a company, we are interested not only in the total ***amount*** of earnings but also in the ***rate*** of earnings on sales, on total assets, and on owner's equity. In addition, we must look at the ***stability*** and ***source*** of earnings. An erratic earnings performance over a period of years, for example, is less desirable than a steady level of earnings. A history of increasing earnings is preferable to a "flat" earnings record.

A breakdown of sales and earnings by ***major product lines*** is useful in evaluating the future performance of a company. Publicly owned companies include with their financial statements supplementary schedules showing sales and earnings by product line and by geographical area. These schedules assist financial analysts in forecasting the effect upon the company of changes in consumer demand for particular types of products.

Financial analysts often express the opinion that the earnings of one company are of higher quality than earnings of other similar companies. This concept of **quality of earnings** arises because each company management can choose from a variety of accounting principles and methods, all of which are considered generally acceptable. A company's management often is under heavy pressure to report rising earnings, and accounting policies may be tailored toward this objective. We have already pointed out the impact on current reported earnings of the choice between the LIFO and FIFO methods of inventory valuation and the choice of depreciation policies. In judging the quality of earnings, the financial analyst should consider whether the accounting principles and methods selected by management lead to a conservative measurement of earnings or tend to inflate reported earnings.

Quality of Assets and the Relative Amount of Debt

Although a satisfactory level of earnings may be a good indication of the company's long-run ability to pay its debts and dividends, we must also look at the composition of assets, their condition and liquidity, the relationship between current assets and current liabilities, the cash flows, and the total amount of debt outstanding. A company may be profitable and yet be unable to pay its liabilities on time; sales and earnings may appear satisfactory, but plant and equipment may be deteriorating because of poor maintenance policies; valuable patents may be expiring; substantial losses may be imminent due to slow-moving inventories and past-due receivables. Companies with large amounts of debt often are vulnerable to increases in interest rates and to even temporary reductions in cash inflows.

Impact of Inflation

During a period of significant inflation, financial statements prepared in terms of historical costs do not reflect fully the economic resources or the real income (in terms of purchasing power) of a business enterprise. It is desirable that companies include in their annual reports supplementary schedules showing the effects of inflation upon their financial statements. Most companies, however, do ***not*** include these supplementary schedules because of the high cost of developing this information.

Illustrative Analysis for Seacliff Corporation

Keep in mind the preceding discussion of analytical principles as you study the illustrative financial analysis that follows. The basic information for our analysis is contained in a set of condensed two-year comparative financial statements for Seacliff Corporation shown on the following pages. Summarized statement data, together with computations of dollar increases and decreases, and component percentages where applicable, have been compiled. For convenience in this illustration, relatively small dollar amounts have been used in the Seacliff financial statements.

CHAPTER 20 ANALYSIS AND INTERPRETATION OF FINANCIAL STATEMENTS

Using the information in these statements, let us consider the kind of analysis that might be of particular interest to (1) common shareholders, (2) long-term creditors, (3) preferred shareholders, and (4) short-term creditors.

SEACLIFF CORPORATION
Comparative Income Statement
For the Years Ended December 31, 2000 and December 31, 1999

	2000	1999	Increase or (Decrease) Dollars	%	Percentage of Net Sales 2000	1999
Net sales	$900,000	$750,000	$150,000	20.0	100.0	100.0
Cost of goods sold	530,000	420,000	110,000	26.2	58.9	56.0
Gross profit	$370,000	$330,000	$ 40,000	12.1	41.1	44.0
Operating expenses:						
Selling expenses	$117,000	$ 75,000	$ 42,000	56.0	13.0	10.0
General and administrative expenses	126,000	95,000	31,000	32.6	14.0	12.7
Total operating expenses	$243,000	$170,000	$ 73,000	42.9	27.0	22.7
Operating income	$127,000	$160,000	$(33,000)	(20.6)	14.1	21.3
Interest expense	24,000	30,000	(6,000)	(20.0)	2.7	4.0
Income before income taxes	$103,000	$130,000	$(27,000)	(20.8)	11.4	17.3
Income taxes	28,000	40,000	(12,000)	(30.0)	3.1	5.3
Net income	$ 75,000	$ 90,000	$(15,000)	(16.7)	8.3	12.0
Earnings per share of common stock	$ 13.20	$ 20.25	$ (7.05)	(34.8)		

SEACLIFF CORPORATION
Statement of Retained Earnings
For the Years Ended December 31, 2000 and December 31, 1999

	2000	1999	Increase or (Decrease) Dollars	%
Retained earnings, beginning of year	$176,000	$115,000	$61,000	53.0
Net income	75,000	90,000	(15,000)	(16.7)
	$251,000	$205,000	$46,000	22.4
Less: Dividends on common stock ($5.00 per share in 1999, $4.80 per share in 2000)	$ 24,000	$ 20,000	$ 4,000	20.0
Dividends on preferred stock ($9 per share)	9,000	9,000		
	$ 33,000	$ 29,000	$ 4,000	13.8
Retained earnings, end of year	$218,000	$176,000	$42,000	23.9

SEACLIFF CORPORATION
Condensed Comparative Balance Sheet*
December 31, 2000 and December 31, 1999

Assets	2000	1999	Increase or (Decrease) Dollars	%	Percentage of Total Assets 2000	1999
Current assets	$390,000	$288,000	$102,000	35.4	41.1	33.5
Plant and equipment (net)	500,000	467,000	33,000	7.1	52.6	54.3
Other assets (loans to officers)	60,000	105,000	(45,000)	(42.9)	6.3	12.2
Total assets	$950,000	$860,000	$ 90,000	10.5	100.0	100.0

Liabilities & Shareholders' Equity

Liabilities:

Current liabilities	$112,000	$ 94,000	$ 18,000	19.1	11.8	10.9
12% bonds payable	200,000	250,000	(50,000)	(20.0)	21.1	29.1
Total liabilities	$312,000	$344,000	$(32,000)	(9.3)	32.9	40.0

Shareholders' equity:

$9 preferred stock, no-par, callable at 105, 1,000 shares	$100,000	$100,000			10.5	11.6
Common stock (2000, 5,000 shares; 1999, 4,000 shares)	320,000	240,000	$ 80,000	33.3	33.7	27.9
Retained earnings	218,000	176,000	42,000	23.9	22.9	20.5
Total shareholders' equity	$638,000	$516,000	$122,000	23.6	67.1	60.0
Total liabilities & shareholders' equity	$950,000	$860,000	$ 90,000	10.5	100.0	100.0

*In order to focus attention on important subtotals, this statement is highly condensed and does not show individual asset and liability items. These details will be introduced as needed in the next discussion. For example, a list of Seacliff Corporation's current assets and current liabilities appears on page 1014.

SEACLIFF CORPORATION
Condensed Comparative Cash Flow Statements
For the Years Ended December 31, 2000 and December 31, 1999

	2000	1999	Increase or (Decrease) Dollars	%
Cash flows from operating activities:				
Net cash flow from operating activities	$ 19,000	$ 95,000	$(76,000)	(80.0)
Cash flows from investing activities:				
Purchases of plant assets	(63,000)	(28,000)	(35,000)	125.0
Collections of loans from officers	45,000	(35,000)	80,000	N/A*
Net cash used by investing activities	$(18,000)	$(63,000)	$ 45,000	(71.4)
Cash flows from financing activities:				
Dividends paid	$(33,000)	$(29,000)	$ (4,000)	13.7
Repayment of long-term debt	(50,000)	-0-	(50,000)	N/A*
Proceeds from issuing capital stock	80,000	-0-	80,000	N/A*
Net cash used by financing activities	$ (3,000)	$(29,000)	$ 26,000	(89.7)
Net increase (decrease) in cash and cash equivalents	$ (2,000)	$ 3,000	$ (5,000)	N/A*
Cash and cash equivalents, beginning of the year	40,000	37,000	3,000	8.1
Cash and cash equivalents, end of the year	$ 38,000	$ 40,000	$ (2,000)	(5.0)

*N/A indicates that computation of the percentage change is not appropriate. Percentage changes cannot be determined if the base year is zero, or if a negative amount (cash outflow) changes to a positive amount (cash inflow).

CHAPTER 20 ANALYSIS AND INTERPRETATION OF FINANCIAL STATEMENTS 1003

> **SEACLIFF CORPORATION**
> **Note to Financial Statements**
> **For the Years Ended December 31, 2000 and December 31, 1999**
>
> **Note 1—Accounting Policies**
> *Inventories* Inventories are valued at the lower of FIFO and net realizable value.
> *Depreciation* Depreciation is computed by the straight-line method. Buildings are depreciated over 40 years, and equipment and fixtures over periods of 5 or 10 years.
>
> **Note 2—Unused Lines of Credit**
> The company has a confirmed line of credit in the amount of $35,000. None was in use at December 31, 2000.
>
> **Note 3—Contingencies and Commitments**
> As of December 31, 2000, the company has no material commitments or non-cancellable obligations. There currently are no contingent losses known to management.
>
> **Note 4—Current Values of Financial Instruments**
> All financial instruments appear in the financial statements at dollar amounts that closely approximate their current values.
>
> **Note 5—Concentrations of Credit Risk**
> The company engages in retail sales to the general public from a single location in Toronto, Ontario. No individual customer accounts for more than 2% of the company's total sales or accounts receivable. Accounts receivable are unsecured.

ANALYSIS BY COMMON SHAREHOLDERS

LO 4: Analyze financial statements from the viewpoints of common shareholders, creditors, and others.

Common shareholders and potential investors in common stock look first at a company's earnings record. Their investment is in shares of stock, so ***earnings per share and dividends per share*** are of particular interest.

Earnings per Share of Common Stock As indicated in Chapter 15, earnings per share of common stock are computed by dividing the income applicable to the common stock by the weighted-average number of shares of common stock outstanding during the year. Any preferred dividend requirements must be subtracted from net income to determine income applicable to common stock, as shown in the following computations for Seacliff Corporation:

Earnings per Share of Common Stock

Earnings related to number of common shares outstanding

	2000	1999
Net income	$75,000	$90,000
Less: Preferred dividend requirements	9,000	9,000
Income applicable to common stock	(a) $66,000	$81,000
Shares of common stock outstanding, during the year	(b) 5,000	4,000
Earnings per share of common stock (a ÷ b)	$ 13.20	$ 20.25

Notice that earnings per share have decreased by ***$7.05*** in 2000, representing a decline of nearly ***35%*** from their level in 1999 ($7.05 ÷ $20.25

= 34.8%). Common shareholders consider a decline in earnings per share to be an extremely unfavourable development. A decline in earnings per share generally represents a decline in the profitability of the company, and creates doubt as to the company's prospects for future growth.

With such a significant decline in earnings per share, we should expect to see a **substantial** decline in the market value of Seacliff's common stock during 2000. [For purposes of our illustration, we will assume the common stock had a market value of **$160** at December 31, 1999 and of **$132** at the end of 2000. This drop of $28 per share represents a **17½%** decline in the market value of every common shareholder's investment ($28 decline ÷ $160 = 17.5%)].

Price-Earnings Ratio The relationship between the market price of common stock and earnings per share is so widely recognized that it is expressed as a ratio, called the price-earnings ratio (or **p/e** ratio). The p/e ratio is determined by dividing the market price per share by the annual earnings per share.

The p/e ratio of the 300 stocks included in the TSE 300 Composite (Toronto Stock Exchange) has varied widely in recent years. Its recent weighted average is 30. The outlook for future earnings is the major factor influencing a company's p/e ratio. Companies with track records of rapid growth may sell at p/e ratios of perhaps 40 to 1, or even higher. Companies with "flat" earnings or earnings expected to decline in future years often sell at price-earnings ratios below, say, 10 to 1.

At the end of 1999, Seacliff's p/e ratio was approximately **8 to 1** ($160 ÷ $20.25 = 7.9), suggesting that investors **were expecting** earnings to decline in 2000. At December 31, 2000, the price-earnings ratio was **10 to 1** ($132 ÷ $13.20 = 10.0). A p/e ratio in this range suggests that investors expect future earnings to stabilize around the current level.

Dividend Yield Dividends are of prime importance to some shareholders but a secondary factor to others. In other words, some shareholders invest primarily to receive regular cash income, while others invest in stocks principally with the hope of securing capital gains through rising market prices. If a corporation is profitable and retains its earnings for expansion of the business, the expanded operations should produce an increase in the net income of the company and thus tend to make each share of stock more valuable.

In comparing the merits of alternative investment opportunities, we should relate earnings and dividends per share to the **market value** of the stock. Dividends per share divided by market price per share determine the **yield** rate of a company's stock. Dividend yield is especially important to those investors whose objective is to maximize the dividend revenue from their investments.

Summary of Earnings and Dividend Data for Seacliff The relationships of Seacliff's per-share earnings and dividends to its year-end stock prices are summarized below:

Earnings and Dividends per Share of Common Stock

Earnings and dividends related to market price of common stock

Date	Assumed Market Value per Share	Earnings per Share	Price-Earnings Ratio	Dividends per Share	Dividend Yield, %
Dec. 31, 1999	$160	$20.25	8	$5.00	3.1
Dec. 31, 2000	132	13.20	10	4.80	3.6

The decline in market value during 2000 presumably reflects the decreases in both earnings and dividends per share. Investors appraising this stock at December 31, 2000, should consider whether a price-earnings ratio of **10** and a dividend yield of **3.6%** represent a satisfactory situation in the light of *alternative* investment opportunities in the same or other industries. These investors will also place considerable weight on estimates of the company's prospective future earnings and the probable effect of such estimated earnings on the market price of the stock and on dividend payments.

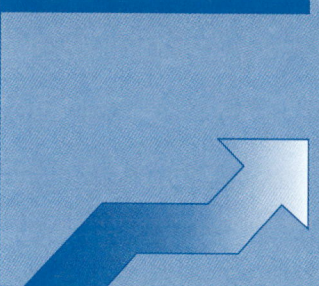

> **CASE IN POINT**
>
> The price-earnings (p/e) ratio varies from industry to industry. At the high range of the p/e ratios are the industries such as technology software (85), oil and gas producers (79), technology hardware (69), and biotechnology pharmaceuticals (69); at the low range are steels (10), oil and gas services (11), and transportation and environmental (12).
>
> Similarly, the dividend yield varies among industries. The high yield ones are: pipelines (4.43%), gas and electrical utilities (3.38%); the low ones are: biotechnology pharmaceuticals (0.05%), cable and entertainment (0.14%), and oil and gas producers (0.27%).

Book Value per Share of Common Stock The procedures for computing book value per share were fully described in Chapter 14 and will not be repeated here. We will, however, determine the book value per share of common stock for Seacliff:

Book Value per Share of Common Stock

Why did book value per share increase?

		2000	1999
Total shareholders' equity		$638,000	$516,000
Less: Equity of preferred shareholders (1,000 shares at call price of $105)		105,000	105,000
Equity of common shareholders	(a)	$533,000	$411,000
Shares of common stock outstanding	(b)	5,000	4,000
Book value per share of common stock (a ÷ b)		$106.60	$102.75

Book value indicates the net assets represented by each share of stock. This statistic is often helpful in estimating a reasonable price for a company's stock, especially for small corporations whose shares are not publicly traded.[1] However, if a company's future earnings prospects are unusually good or unusually poor, or the market value of the company's assets is different from their carrying (book) value, the market price of its shares may differ significantly from their book value.

Return on Investment (ROI)

The **rate of return on investment** (often called **ROI**) is a measure of management's efficiency in using available resources. Regardless of the size of the organization, capital is a scarce resource and must be used efficiently. In judging the performance of branch managers or of companywide management, it is reasonable to raise the question: What rate of return have you earned on the resources under your control? The concept of return on investment can be applied to a number of situations: for example, evaluating the profitability of a branch, a product line, an individual investment, or a business as a whole. A number of different ratios have been developed for the ROI concept, each well suited to a particular situation. We shall consider the **return on assets** and the **return on common shareholders' equity** as examples of the return on investment concept.

Return on Assets An important test of management's ability to earn a reasonable return on resources supplied from all sources is the rate of return on total assets.

The income figure used in computing this ratio should be ***operating income***, since interest expense and income taxes are determined by factors other than the efficient use of resources. Operating income is earned throughout the year and therefore should be related to the ***average*** investment in assets during the year. The computation of this ratio of Seacliff is as follows (assuming the 1999 beginning balance of total assets is $820,000):

Percentage Return on Assets

Earnings related to investment in assets

	2000	1999
Operating income	(a) $127,000	$160,000
Total assets, beginning of year	(b) $860,000	$820,000
Total assets, end of year	(c) $950,000	$860,000
Average investment in assets ((b + c) ÷ 2)	(d) $905,000	$840,000
Return on assets (a ÷ d)	14%	19%

This ratio shows that the rate of return earned on the company's assets has fallen off in 2000. Before drawing conclusions as to the effectiveness of Seacliff's management, however, we should consider the trend in the return on assets earned by other companies of similar kind and size.

---

[1] As pointed out in Chapter 14, book value per share is regularly reported in such financial news media as *The Financial Post* (now the *National Post*) and also in the annual reports of large corporations such as Dofasco Inc., Royal Bank of Canada, and Moore Corporation Limited.

CASE IN POINT

The rate of return on assets varies from industry to industry, as well as among companies in the same industry. Also, the rate for a company may change from year to year. The recent rates for companies in such industries as department store retailing, food distributing, airline, steel, and petroleum are:

Company	Rate of Return on Assets
Hudson's Bay Company	5.2%
Loblaw Companies Limited	11.3%
Provigo Inc.	12.4%
Air Canada	6.4%
Canadian Airlines Corporation	5.1%
Dofasco Inc.	8.1%
Shell Canada Limited	13.5%

It is important to make sure the companies that you are comparing are in the same industry and are of similar size.

Return on Common Shareholders' Equity Because interest and dividends paid to creditors and preferred shareholders are fixed in amount, a company may earn a greater or smaller return on the common shareholders' equity than of its total assets. This return reflects management's ability to earn a reasonable return for common shareholders. The computation of return on shareholders' equity for Seacliff is shown below:

Return on Common Shareholders' Equity

Does the use of leverage benefit common shareholders?

	2000	1999
Net income	$ 75,000	$ 90,000
Less: Preferred dividend requirements	9,000	9,000
Net income applicable to common stock	(a) $ 66,000	$ 81,000
Common shareholders' equity, beginning of year	(b) $416,000	$355,000*
Common shareholders' equity, end of year	(c) $538,000	$416,000
Average common shareholders' equity ((b + c) ÷ 2)	(d) $477,000	$385,500
Return on common shareholders' equity (a ÷ d)	13.8%	21.0%

*Assumed

In both years, the rate of return on common shareholders' equity was higher than the 12% rate of interest paid to long-term creditors or the 9% dividend rate paid to preferred shareholders. This result was achieved through the favourable use of leverage by management. However, the rate of return should be compared against those earned by other similar companies in the industry.

> **CASE IN POINT**
>
> The return on common shareholders' equity, like the return on assets, varies from year to year, company to company, and industry to industry. The following are the recent returns for a few well-known companies in the furniture retailing, retail and wholesale food distributing, steel, and petroleum industries:
>
> | Company | Return on Common Equity |
> |---|---|
> | Leon's Furniture Limited | 15.1% |
> | Loblaw Companies Limited | 15.2% |
> | Provigo Inc. | 27.0% |
> | Algoma Steel Inc. | 15.2% |
> | Dofasco Inc. | 10.7% |
> | Shell Canada Limited | 14.8% |

Measures of Profitability

Measures of a company's profitability are of great interest to common shareholders. These measures help common shareholders evaluate which company is more profitable. Measures of profitability include earnings per share, return on assets, return on common shareholders' equity, sales, gross profit, operating income, and net income. Since the first three measures have been covered in the preceding sections, we will focus on the last four measures here.

Sales Common shareholders are vitally interested in the trend of net sales. As one means of evaluating this trend, they often compute the percentage change in net sales from year to year. If a company's sales grow faster than the industry average, the company increases its *market share*—that is, its share of total industry sales (the total market).

> **CASE IN POINT**
>
> A recent annual report of Loblaw Companies Limited indicates that while the total market is growing at about 3% per year, the company's sales have been growing at about 10% each year for the past two years. It also expects the same growth rate for the next two years. Similarly, Air Canada's recent annual report shows that its domestic passenger market share has increased by 1%, from 57% to 58%. This 1% translates into millions of dollars in revenue.

The trend of net sales for Seacliff, as computed earlier, shows a 20% growth from 1999 to 2000. Viewing this increasing trend by itself, it is a good sign. However, unless this increase brings higher earnings (profitability), it produces little benefit for the company. Let's assume that further investigation reveals that Seacliff decided in 2000 to reduce its sales prices in an effort to generate greater sales volume. To determine whether this strategy is beneficial to the company, we have to look at its impact on gross profit, operating income, and net income.

Gross Profit The significance of gross profit and gross profit rate was discussed in Chapter 5. For example, a rising gross profit rate usually indicates that demand for a company's products is strong enough that it has been able to increase its sales prices. The trend of gross profit and of gross profit rates for Seacliff, as computed earlier, is as follows:

	Amount	Percentage
Increase in gross profit from 1999 to 2000	$40,000	12.1
Decrease in gross profit rate from 1999 to 2000 (44% − 41.1%)		2.9

Even though the gross profit rate has decreased by 2.9% from 1999 to 2000, gross profit has increased 12.1% or $40,000. Thus, the strategy of reducing sales prices to increase sales volume apparently has been successful.

Operating Income As pointed out in Chapter 5, operating income measures the profitability of a company's basic business operations. Seacliff's trend of operating income, computed earlier, is as follows:

	Amount	Percentage
Decrease in operating income from 1999 to 2000	$33,000	20.6
Decrease in operating income rate (% of net sales) from 1999 to 2000 (21.3% − 14.1%)		7.2

In spite of an increase of 20% in net sales and 12.1% in gross profit, operating income declined 20.6% in 2000. This indicates that operating expenses increase at a greater rate than net sales and gross profit, as shown below.

Does a higher operating expense ratio indicate higher net income?

Operating Expense Ratio

	2000	1999
Operating expenses	(a) $243,000	$170,000
Net sales	(b) $900,000	$750,000
Operating expense ratio (a ÷ b)	27.0%	22.7%

The 4.3% (27% − 22.7%) increase in operating expenses points to the need for a more detailed analysis of the expenses. As shown in Seacliff's comparative income statement, both selling expenses and general and administrative expenses have increased substantially from 1999 to 2000. The substantial increase in selling expenses presumably reflects greater selling effort during 2000 in an attempt to improve sales volume. However, the fact that selling expenses increased $42,000 while gross profit increased only $40,000 indicates that the cost of this increased sales effort was not justified in terms of results. Even more disturbing is the increase in general and administrative expenses. Some growth in administrative expenses might be expected to accompany increased sales volume, but

because some of the expenses are fixed, the growth generally should be *less than proportional* to any increase in sales. The increase in general and administrative expenses from 12.7% to 14% of sales would be of serious concern to informed common shareholders.

Management generally has greater control over operating expenses (and therefore over operating income) than over net sales. The **operating expense ratio** is often used as a measure of management's ability to control its operating expenses.

Net Income Net income measures a company's ultimate profitability and determines a company's long-term survival. The trends of net income and of **net income rate** (as a percent of net sales) of Seacliff, as computed earlier in the comparative income statement, are as follows:

	Amount	Percentage
Decrease in net income from 1999 to 2000	$15,000	16.7
Decrease in net income rate from 1999 to 2000 (12.0% – 8.3%)		3.7

The substantial decline in net income and net income rate was due primarily to the large increase in operating expenses, especially selling expenses, as explained in the preceding section.

If management were able to increase the sales volume while at the same time increasing the gross profit rate and decreasing the operating expense ratio, the effect on net income could be quite dramatic. For example, if in 2001 Seacliff can increase its sales by 11% to $1,000,000, increase its gross profit rate from 41.1 back to 44% (1999 level), and reduce the operating expense ratio from 27 to 24%, its operating income will increase from $127,000 to $200,000 ($1,000,000 - $560,000 - $240,000), an increase of over 57%.

Leverage

The term **leverage** means operating a business with borrowed money. If the borrowed capital can be used in the business to earn a return *greater* than the cost of borrowing, then the net income and the return on common shareholders' equity will *increase*. In other words, if you can borrow money at 8% and use it to earn 12%, you will benefit by doing so. However, leverage can act as a "double-edged sword"; the effects may be favourable or unfavourable to the holders of common stock.

If the rate of return on total assets should fall *below* the average rate of interest on borrowed capital, leverage will *reduce* net income and the return on common shareholders' equity. In this situation, paying off the loans that carry high interest rates would appear to be a logical move. However, most companies do not have enough cash to retire long-term debt on short notice. Therefore, the common shareholders may become "locked in" to the unfavourable effects of leverage.

In deciding how much leverage is appropriate, the common shareholders should consider the **stability** of the company's return on assets as well as the relationship of this return to the average cost of borrowed capital. If a business incurs so much debt that it becomes unable to meet the required interest and principal payments, the creditors may force liquidation or reorganization of the business.

> **CASE IN POINT**
>
> After two mega acquisitions in the United States for a total price tag of over $13 billion, most of which was financed by debt, Campeau Corporation was highly leveraged. With more than $11 billion in debt and only slightly over $110 million in equity, Campeau's equity ratio was exceedingly low. The rising interest rate, coupled with poor operating results, led to serious financial trouble for Campeau. In a span of six months, Campeau's stock plummeted from a high of $22 per share to less than $2. Consequently, the company had to be restructured, reorganized, and drastically "downsized."

Equity Ratio One indicator of the amount of leverage used by a business is the equity ratio. This ratio measures the proportion of the total assets financed by shareholders, as distinguished from creditors. It is computed by dividing total shareholders' equity by total assets. A *low* equity ratio indicates an extensive use of leverage, that is, a large proportion of financing provided by creditors. A high equity ratio, on the other hand, indicates that the business is making little use of leverage.

The equity ratio at year-end for Seacliff is determined as follows:

Equity Ratio

Proportion of assets financed by shareholders

	2000	1999
Total shareholders' equity	(a) $638,000	$516,000
Total assets (or total liabilities & shareholders' equity)	(b) $950,000	$860,000
Equity ratio (a ÷ b)	67.2%	60.0%

Seacliff has a higher equity ratio in 2000 than in 1999. Is this favourable or unfavourable?

From the viewpoint of the common shareholder, a low equity ratio will produce maximum benefits if management is able to earn a rate of return on assets greater than the rate of interest paid to creditors. However, a low equity ratio can be very ***unfavourable*** if the return on assets falls ***below*** the rate of interest paid to creditors. Since the return on total assets earned by Seacliff has declined from 19% in 1999 to a relatively low 14% in 2000, the common shareholders probably would ***not*** want to risk a low equity ratio. The action by management in 2000 of retiring $50,000 in long-term liabilities will help to protect the common shareholders from the unfavourable effects of leverage if the rate of return on assets continues to decline.

ANALYSIS BY LONG-TERM CREDITORS

Bondholders and other long-term creditors are primarily interested in three factors: (1) the rate of return on their investment, (2) the firm's ability to meet its interest requirements, and (3) the firm's ability to repay the principal of the debt when it falls due.

Yield Rate on Bonds The yield rate on bonds or other long-term indebtedness cannot be computed in the same manner as the yield rate on shares of stock, because bonds, unlike stocks, have a definite maturity date and amount. The ownership of a 12%, 10-year, $1,000 bond represents the right to receive $120 each year for 10 years plus the right to receive $1,000 at the end of 10 years. If the market price of this bond is $950, the yield rate on an investment in the bond is the rate of interest that will make the present value of these two contractual rights equal to $950. When bonds sell at maturity value, the yield rate is equal to the bond interest rate. ***The yield rate varies inversely with changes in the market price of the bond.*** If interest rates rise, the market price of existing bonds will fall; if interest rates decline, the price of bonds will rise. If the price of a bond is above maturity value, the yield rate is less than the bond interest rate; if the price of a bond is below maturity value, the yield rate is higher than the bond interest rate.

Interest Coverage Ratio Bondholders feel that their investments are relatively safe if the issuing company earns enough income to cover its annual interest obligations by a wide margin.

A common measure of creditors' safety is the ratio of operating income available to cover the annual interest expense, called the ***interest coverage ratio***. This computation for Seacliff would be:

Interest Coverage Ratio

		2000	1999
Operating income (before interest and income taxes)	(a)	$127,000	$160,000
Annual interest expense	(b)	$ 24,000	$ 30,000
Interest coverage (a ÷ b)		5.3 times	5.3 times

Long-term creditors watch this ratio

The ratio remained unchanged at a satisfactory level during 2000. A ratio of 5.3 times interest earned would be considered strong in many industries. In the electric utilities industry, for example, the interest coverage ratio for the leading companies generally averaged about 3, with the ratios of individual companies varying from 2 to 6.

Debt Ratio Long-term creditors are interested in the percentage of total assets financed by debt, as distinguished from the percentage financed by shareholders. The percentage of total assets financed by debt is measured by the debt ratio. This ratio is computed by dividing total liabilities by total assets, shown below for Seacliff.

Debt Ratio

		2000	1999
Total liabilities	(a)	$312,000	$344,000
Total assets (or total liabilities & shareholders' equity)	(b)	$950,000	$860,000
Debt ratio (a ÷ b)		32.8%	40.0%

What portion of total assets is financed by creditors?

From a creditor's viewpoint, the lower the debt ratio (or the higher the equity ratio) the better, since this means that shareholders have contributed the bulk of the resources to the business, and therefore the margin of protection to creditors against a shrinkage of the assets is high.

Secured Claims Sometimes the claims of long-term creditors are secured with specific collateral, such as the land and buildings owned by the borrower. In these situations, the secured creditors may look primarily to the ***value of the collateral*** in assessing the safety of their claims.

Assets pledged as collateral to secure specific liabilities are disclosed in notes to the financial statements. As Seacliff makes no such disclosures, we may assume that none of its assets have been pledged as collateral to secure specific liabilities.

ANALYSIS BY PREFERRED SHAREHOLDERS

Some preferred stocks are convertible into common stock at the option of the holder. However, many preferred stocks do not have the conversion privilege. If a preferred stock is convertible, the interests of the preferred shareholders are similar to those of common shareholders. If a preferred stock is not convertible, the interests of the preferred shareholders are more like those of long-term creditors.

Preferred shareholders are interested in the yield on their investment. The yield is computed by dividing the dividend per share by the market value per share. The dividend per share of Seacliff preferred stock is $9. If we assume that the market value at December 31, 2000, is $75 per share, the yield rate at that time would be 12% ($9 ÷ $75).

The primary measurement of the safety of an investment in preferred stock is the ability of the firm to meet its preferred dividend requirements. The best test of this ability is the ratio of the net income to the amount of the annual preferred dividends, as follows:

Preferred Dividends Coverage Ratio

	2000	1999
Net income	(a) $75,000	$90,000
Annual preferred dividend requirements	(b) $ 9,000	$ 9,000
Preferred dividend coverage (a ÷ b)	8.3 times	10 times

Is the preferred dividend safe?

Although the margin of protection declined in 2000, the annual preferred dividend requirement still appears well protected.

As previously discussed in Chapter 14 the market price of a preferred stock tends to ***vary inversely*** with interest rates. When interest rates are moving up, preferred stock prices tend to decline; when interest rates are dropping, preferred stock prices rise.

ANALYSIS BY SHORT-TERM CREDITORS

Bankers and other short-term creditors share the interest of shareholders and bondholders in the profitability and long-run stability of a business. Their primary interest, however, is in the current position of the firm—its ability to generate sufficient funds (working capital) to meet current operating needs and to pay current debts promptly. Thus the analysis of financial statements by a banker considering a short-term loan, or by a trade creditor investigating the credit status of a customer, is likely to centre on the working capital position of the prospective debtor.

Amount of Working Capital The details of the working capital of Seacliff are as follows:

SEACLIFF CORPORATION
Comparative Schedule of Working Capital
As of December 31, 2000 and December 31, 1999

	2000	1999	Increase or (Decrease) Dollars	%	Percentage of Total Current Items 2000	1999
Current assets:						
Cash	$ 38,000	$ 40,000	$ (2,000)	(5.0)	9.7	13.9
Accounts receivable (net)	117,000	86,000	31,000	36.0	30.0	29.9
Inventories	180,000	120,000	60,000	50.0	46.2	41.6
Prepaid expenses	55,000	42,000	13,000	31.0	14.1	14.6
Total current assets	$390,000	$288,000	$102,000	35.4	100.0	100.0
Current liabilities:						
Notes payable to creditors	$ 14,600	$ 10,000	$ 4,600	46.0	13.1	10.7
Accounts payable	66,000	30,000	36,000	120.0	58.9	31.9
Accrued liabilities	31,400	54,000	(22,600)	(41.9)	28.0	57.4
Total current liabilities	$112,000	$ 94,000	$ 18,000	19.1	100.0	100.0
Working capital	$278,000	$194,000	$ 84,000	43.3		

The amount of working capital is measured by the *excess of current assets over current liabilities*. Thus, working capital represents the amount of cash, near-cash items, and cash substitutes (prepayments) on hand after providing for payment of all current liabilities.

This schedule shows that current assets increased $102,000, while current liabilities rose by only $18,000, with the result that working capital increased $84,000.

Quality of Working Capital In evaluating the debt-paying ability of a business, short-term creditors should consider the quality of working capital as well as the total dollar amount. The principal factors affecting the quality of working capital are (1) the nature of the current assets and (2) the length of time required to convert these assets into cash.

The preceding schedule shows an unfavourable shift in the composition of Seacliff's working capital during 2000; cash decreased from 13.9% to 9.7% of current assets, while inventory rose from 41.6% to 46.2%. Inventory is a less liquid resource than cash. Therefore, the quality of working capital is not as liquid as in 1999. *Turnover rates* (or *ratios*) may be used to assist short-term creditors in estimating the time required to turn assets such as accounts receivable and inventory into cash.

Accounts Receivable Turnover Rate As explained in Chapter 8, the accounts receivable turnover rate indicates how quickly a company converts its accounts receivable into cash. The accounts receivable turnover *rate* is determined by dividing net sales by the average balance of accounts receivable.[2] The number of *days* required (on average) to collect accounts receivable then

---
[2] Ideally, the accounts receivable turnover is computed by dividing net *credit* sales by the *monthly* average of receivables. Such detailed information, however, generally is not provided in annual financial statements.

Are customers paying promptly?

may be determined by dividing the number of days in a year (365) by the turnover rate. These computations are shown below using the data in our Seacliff example:

Accounts Receivable Turnover

	2000	1999
Net sales	(a) $900,000	$750,000
Accounts receivable, beginning of year	$ 86,000	$ 80,000*
Accounts receivable, end of year	$117,000	$ 86,000
Average accounts receivable	(b) $101,500	$ 83,000
Accounts receivable turnover per year (a ÷ b)	8.9 times	9.0 times
Average number of days to collect accounts receivable (divide 365 days by accounts receivable turnover)	41 days	41 days

*Assumed

There has been no significant change in the average time required to collect accounts receivable. The interpretation of the average age of accounts receivable depends upon the company's credit terms and the seasonal activity immediately before year-end. For example, if the company grants 30-day credit terms to its customers, the above analysis indicates that accounts receivable collections are lagging. If the terms are for 60 days, however, collections are being made ahead of schedule.

Inventory Turnover Rate The inventory turnover rate indicates how many times during the year the company is able to sell a quantity of goods equal to its average inventory. Mechanically, this rate is determined by dividing the cost of goods sold for the year by the average amount of inventory on hand during the year. The number of days required to sell this amount of inventory may be determined by dividing 365 days by the turnover rate. These computations were explained in Chapter 9, and are demonstrated below using the data of Seacliff:

Inventory Turnover

	2000	1999
Cost of goods sold	(a) $530,000	$420,000
Inventory, beginning of year	$120,000	$100,000*
Inventory, end of year	$180,000	$120,000
Average inventory	(b) $150,000	$110,000
Average inventory turnover per year (a ÷ b)	3.5 times	3.8 times
Average number of days to sell inventory (divide 365 days by inventory turnover)	104 days	96 days

*Assumed

The trend indicated by this analysis is unfavourable, since the length of time required for Seacliff to turn over (sell) its inventory is increasing.

Companies that have low gross profit rates often need high inventory turnover rates in order to operate profitably. This is merely another way of saying that if the gross profit rate is low, a high volume of transactions is necessary to produce a satisfactory amount of profits. Companies that sell "high markup" items, such as jewellery stores and art galleries, can operate successfully with much lower inventory turnover rates.

Operating Cycle In Chapter 5 we defined the term *operating cycle* as the average time period between the purchase of merchandise and the conversion of this merchandise back into cash. In other words, the merchandise acquired for inventory is gradually converted into accounts receivable by selling goods to customers on credit, and these receivables are converted into cash through the process of collection. The work *cycle* refers to the circular flow of assets from cash to inventory to receivables and back into cash.

Seacliff's operating cycle in 2000 was approximately 145 days, computed by adding the 104 days required to turn over inventory and the average 41 days required to collect receivables. This compares to an operating cycle of only 137 days in 1999, computed as 96 days to dispose of the inventory plus 41 days to collect the resulting receivables. From the viewpoint of short-term creditors, the shorter the operating cycle, the better the quality of the borrower's working capital. Therefore, these creditors would regard the lengthening of Seacliff's operating cycle as an unfavourable trend.

Current Ratio The current ratio (current assets divided by current liabilities) expresses the relationship between current assets and current liabilities. As debts come due, they must be paid out of current assets. Therefore, short-term creditors frequently compare the amount of current assets with the amount of current liabilities. The current ratio indicates a company's short-run, debt-paying ability. It is a measure of liquidity and of solvency. A strong current ratio provides considerable assurance that a company will be able to meet its obligations coming due in the near future. The current ratio for Seacliff is computed as follows:

Does this indicate satisfactory debt-paying ability?

Current Ratio

		2000	1999
Total current assets	(a)	$390,000	$288,000
Total current liabilities	(b)	$112,000	$ 94,000
Current ratio (a ÷ b)		3.5	3.1

A general rule is that a current ratio of 2 to 1 is satisfactory. By this standard, Seacliff's current ratio appears quite strong. Creditors tend to feel that the higher the current ratio the better. From a managerial point of view, however, there is an upper limit. Too high a current ratio may indicate that capital is not being used productively in the business as the amount of cash, accounts receivable, and inventories may be excessive.

Use of both the current ratio and the amount of working capital helps to place debt-paying ability in its proper perspective. For example, if Company X has current assets of $200,000 and current liabilities of $100,000 and Company Y has current assets of $2,000,000 and current liabilities of $1,900,000, each company has $100,000 of working capital, but the current position of Company X is clearly superior to that of Company Y. The current ratio for Company X is quite satisfactory at 2 to 1, but Company Y's current ratio is very low—only slightly above 1 to 1.

As another example, assume that Company A and Company B both have current ratios of 3 to 1. However, Company A has working capital of

$50,000 and Company B has working capital of $500,000. Although both companies appear to be good credit risks, Company B would no doubt be able to qualify for a much *larger* bank loan than would Company A.

Quick Ratio Because inventories and prepaid expenses are further removed from conversion into cash than other current assets, a statistic known as the quick ratio is sometimes computed as a supplement to the current ratio. The *quick ratio* compares the highly liquid current assets (cash, marketable securities, and receivables) with current liabilities. Seacliff has no marketable securities; its quick ratio is computed as follows:

Quick Ratio

A measure of liquidity

	2000	1999
Quick assets (cash and accounts receivable)	(a) $155,000	$126,000
Current liabilities	(b) $112,000	$ 94,000
Quick ratio (a ÷ b)	1.4	1.3

Here again the analysis reveals a favourable trend and a strong position. If the credit periods extended to customers and granted by creditors are roughly equal, a general rule is that a quick ratio of 1.0 is considered satisfactory.

Unused Lines of Credit From the viewpoint of a short-term creditor, a company's unused lines of credit represent a "resource" almost as liquid as cash. An unused line of credit means that a bank has agreed in advance to lend the company any amount, up to the specified limit. As long as this line of credit remains available, creditors know that the business can borrow cash quickly and easily for any purpose, including payments of creditors' claims.

Existing unused lines of credit are *disclosed* in notes accompanying the financial statements and in the management's discussion and analysis section of the annual report.

CASE IN POINT The unused lines of credit can be substantial in amount. The recent annual reports of the following corporations provide a glimpse of such a picture: Bell Canada, unused lines of credit of $920 million; Canadian Pacific Limited, unused lines of credit for short-term and long-term financing of $1,064.8 million; Domtar Inc., $400 million bank credit facility undrawn; Dofasco Inc., $200 million revolving bank credit; and Shell Canada Limited, unused lines of credit of $100 million. Of course, there is a cost for such unused lines of credit. The annual commitment fees on the unused long-term credit lines may range from 1/10 to 1/8 of one percent of the unused amount.

Cash Flow Analysis

We often have stressed the importance of a company being able to generate sufficient cash flow from its operations. In 1999, Seacliff generated a net cash flow of $95,000 from its operating activities—a relatively "normal" amount, considering that net income for the year was $90,000. This $95,000 net cash flow remained **after** payment of interest to creditors and amounted to more than three times the dividends paid to shareholders. Thus, in 1999 the net cash flow from operating activities appeared quite sufficient to ensure that Seacliff could pay its interest obligations and also pay dividends.

In 2000, however, net cash flow from operating activities declined to only $19,000, an amount far below the company's $75,000 net income and slightly more than one-half of the amount of dividends paid. Shareholders and creditors alike would view this dramatic decline in cash flow as a negative and potentially dangerous development.

A reconciliation of Seacliff's net income in 2000 with its net cash flow from operating activities is shown below:

Why was the cash flow from operations so low?

Net income		$ 75,000
Add:		
Depreciation expense	$30,000	
Increase in notes payable to suppliers	4,600	
Increase in accounts payable	36,000	70,600
		$145,600
Less:		
Increase in accounts receivable	$31,000	
Increase in inventories	60,000	
Increase in prepaid expenses	13,000	
Decrease in accrued liabilities	22,600	126,600
Net cash flow from operating activities		$ 19,000

(As explained in Chapter 19, this is the indirect method of showing the cash flows from operating activities.)

The primary reasons for Seacliff's low net operating cash flow appear to be the growth in uncollected accounts receivable and inventories, and the substantial reduction in accrued liabilities. Given the significant increase in sales during 2000, the increase in accounts receivable is to be expected. The large reduction in accrued liabilities probably is a one-time event, not likely to recur next year. The large increase in inventory, however, may have reduced Seacliff's liquidity unnecessarily. Also, the substantial increase (31%) in prepaid expenses may be hard to justify.

Seacliff's financial position would appear considerably stronger if its increased sales volume were supplied by a higher **inventory turnover rate**, instead of a larger inventory.

Usefulness of Notes to Financial Statements

A set of financial statements normally is accompanied by several pages of **notes**, disclosing information useful in **interpreting** the statements. Users should view these notes as an **integral part** of the financial statements.

In preceding chapters, we have identified many items that are disclosed in notes accompanying the financial statements. Among the most useful disclosures are:

- Accounting policies and methods.
- Subsequent events.
- Unused lines of credit.
- Significant commitments and contingencies.
- Current values of financial instruments (if different from the carrying values shown in the statements).
- Dividends in arrears.
- Concentrations of credit risk.
- Assets pledged to secure specific liabilities.

The notes accompanying Seacliff's financial statements are quite "clean"—that is, they contain no surprises or cause for concern. Of course, the unused line of credit disclosed in Note 2 would be of interest to anyone evaluating the company's short-term debt-paying ability.

SUMMARY OF ANALYTICAL MEASUREMENTS

LO 5: Compute the ratios widely used in financial statement analysis and explain the significance of each.

Presented below is a summary of the financial statement **ratios** and measurements discussed in this chapter. Included is a brief description of each ratio or measurement's significance.

Bear in mind that the significance of any financial ratio or measurement depends both upon its (1) trend over time, and (2) relationship to some logical "benchmark," such as industry averages or measurements within similar companies.

Ratio or Other Measurement	Method of Computation	Significance
Measures of short-term solvency:		
Current ratio	$\dfrac{\text{Current assets}}{\text{Current liabilities}}$	A measure of short-term debt paying ability.
Quick ratio	$\dfrac{\text{Quick assets}}{\text{Current liabilities}}$	A measure of short-term debt paying ability.
Working capital	Current assets less Current liabilities	A measure of short-term debt paying ability.
Net cash provided by operating activities	Appears in the cash flow statement	Indicates the cash generated by operations after allowing for cash payment of expenses and operating liabilities.
Accounts receivable turnover	$\dfrac{\text{Net sales}}{\text{Average accounts receivable}}$	Indicates how quickly receivables are collected.
Days to collect average accounts receivable	$\dfrac{365 \text{ days}}{\text{Accounts receivable turnover rate}}$	Indicates in days how quickly receivables are collected.
Inventory turnover rate	$\dfrac{\text{Cost of goods sold}}{\text{Average inventory}}$	Indicates how quickly inventory sells.
Days to sell the average inventory	$\dfrac{365 \text{ days}}{\text{Inventory turnover rate}}$	Indicates in days how quickly inventory sells.

Ratio or Other Measurement	Method of Computation	Significance
Operating cycle	Days to sell inventory plus Days to collect accounts receivable	Indicates in days how quickly inventory converts into cash.
Measures of long-term credit risk:		
Debt ratio	$\dfrac{\text{Total liabilities}}{\text{Total assets}}$	Percentage of assets financed by creditors; indicates relative size of the debt position or leverage.
Equity ratio	$\dfrac{\text{Total shareholders' equity}}{\text{Total assets}}$	Percentage of assets financed by shareholders; indicates relative size of the equity position.
Trend in net cash provided by operating activities	Appears in comparative cash flow statement	Indicator of a company's ability to generate the cash necessary to meet its obligations.
Interest coverage ratio	$\dfrac{\text{Operating income}}{\text{Annual interest expense}}$	Indicator of a company's ability to meet its interest payment obligations.
Measures of profitability:		
Percentage changes (e.g., in net sales and net income)	$\dfrac{\text{Dollar amount of change}}{\text{Financial statement amount in the earlier year}}$	The rate at which a key measure is increasing or decreasing; the "growth rate."
Gross profit rate	$\dfrac{\text{Gross profit}}{\text{Net sales}}$	A measure of the profitability of the company's products.
Operating expense ratio	$\dfrac{\text{Operating expenses}}{\text{Net sales}}$	A measure of management's ability to control operating expenses.
Operating income	Gross profit, less Operating expenses	The profitability of a company's basic business operations.
Operating income rate (operating income as a percentage of net sales)	$\dfrac{\text{Operating income}}{\text{Net sales}}$	The rate of profitability of a company's basic business operations.
Net income as a percentage of net sales (net income rate)	$\dfrac{\text{Net income}}{\text{Net sales}}$	An indicator of management's ability to control all costs and expenses.
Earnings per share	$\dfrac{\text{Net income, less Preferred dividends}}{\text{Average number of common shares outstanding}}$	Net income applicable to each share of common stock.
Return on assets	$\dfrac{\text{Operating income}}{\text{Average total assets}}$	A measure of the productivity of assets, regardless of how the assets are financed.
Return on common shareholders' equity	$\dfrac{\text{Net income less Preferred dividends}}{\text{Average common shareholders' equity}}$	The rate of return earned upon the common shareholders' equity (Appropriate when company has both common and preferred stock).

Ratio or Other Measurement	Method of Computation	Significance
Measures for evaluating the current market price of common stock:		
Price-earnings ratio	$\dfrac{\text{Market price per share}}{\text{Earnings per share}}$	A measure of investors' enthusiasm about the company's future prospects.
Dividend yield	$\dfrac{\text{Annual dividend per share}}{\text{Market price per share}}$	Dividends expressed as a rate of return on the market price of the stock.
Book value per share	$\dfrac{\text{Common shareholders' equity}}{\text{Shares of common stock outstanding}}$	The recorded value of net assets underlying each share of common stock.
Measures for preferred shareholders:		
Dividend yield	$\dfrac{\text{Annual dividend per share}}{\text{Market price per share}}$	Dividends expressed as a rate of return on the market price of the stock.
Dividend coverage ratio	$\dfrac{\text{Net income}}{\text{Annual preferred dividend}}$	Indicator of a company's ability to meet its preferred dividend obligations.

End-of-Chapter Review

Key Terms Introduced or Emphasized in Chapter 20

Annual report *(p.993)* A document issued annually by publicly owned companies to their shareholders. Includes audited comparative financial statements, management's discussion and analysis of performance and liquidity, and other information about the company.

Comparative financial statement *(p.994)* Financial statement data for two or more successive years placed side by side in adjacent columns to facilitate study of changes.

Component percentage *(p.997)* The percentage relationship of any financial statement item to a total including that item. For example, each type of asset as a percentage of total assets.

Horizontal analysis *(p.998)* Comparison of the change in a financial statement item such as inventories during two or more accounting periods.

Leverage *(p.1010)* Refers to the practice of financing assets with borrowed capital. Extensive leverage creates the possibility for the rate of return on common shareholders' equity to be substantially above or below the rate of return on total assets. When the rate of return on total assets exceeds the average cost of borrowed capital, leverage increases net income and the return on common shareholders' equity. However, when the return on total assets is less than the average cost of borrowed capital, leverage reduces net income and the return on common shareholders' equity.

Quality of assets *(p.1000)* The concept that some companies have assets of better quality than others, such as well-balanced composition of assets, well-maintained plant and equipment, and receivables that are all current. A lower quality of assets might be indicated by poor maintenance of plant and equipment, slow-moving inventories with higher danger of obsolescence, past-due receivables, and patents approaching an expiration date.

Quality of earnings *(p.1000)* Earnings are said to be of high quality if they are stable, the source seems assured, and the methods used in measuring income are conservative. The existence of this concept suggests that the range of alternative but acceptable accounting principles may still be too wide to produce financial statements that are comparable.

Rate of return on investment (ROI) *(p.1006)* A measure of management's ability to earn a satisfactory return on the assets under its control. Numerous variations of the ROI concept are used, such as return on total assets, return on total shareholders' equity, and return on common shareholders' equity.

Ratios *(p.1019)* See pages 1019–1021 for list of ratios, methods of computation, and significance.

Trend percentages *(p.996)* The purpose of computing trend percentages is to measure the increase or decrease in financial items (such as sales, net income, cash, etc.) from a selected base year to a series of following years. For example, the dollar amount of net income each year is divided by the base year net income to determine the trend percentage.

Vertical analysis *(p.999)* Comparison of a particular financial statement item to a total including that item, such as inventories as a percentage of current assets, or operating expenses in relation to net sales.

DEMONSTRATION PROBLEM

The accounting records of Southgate Corporation showed the following balances at the end of 1999 and 2000:

	2000	1999
Cash	$ 35,000	$ 25,000
Accounts receivable (net)	91,000	90,000
Inventory	160,000	140,000
Short-term prepayments	4,000	5,000
Investment in land	90,000	100,000
Equipment	880,000	640,000
Less: Accumulated depreciation	(260,000)	(200,000)
Total assets	$1,000,000	$ 800,000
Accounts payable	$ 105,000	$ 46,000
Income taxes payable and other accrued liabilities	40,000	25,000
Bonds payable—8%	280,000	280,000
Premium on bonds payable	3,600	4,000
Capital stock (33,000 shares in 2000; 22,000 shares in 1999)	165,000	110,000
Retained earnings	406,400	335,000
Total liabilities and shareholders' equity	$1,000,000	$800,000
Sales (net of discounts and allowances)	$2,200,000	$1,600,000
Cost of goods sold	1,606,000	1,120,000
Gross profit	$ 594,000	$ 480,000
Expenses (including $22,400 interest expense)	(336,600)	(352,000)
Income taxes	(91,000)	(48,000)
Net income	$ 166,400	$ 80,000

Cash dividends of $40,000 were paid and a 50% stock dividend was distributed early in 2000. All sales were made on credit at a relatively uniform rate during the year. Inventory and accounts receivable did not fluctuate materially. The market price of the company's stock on December 31, 2000, was $86 per share; on December 31, 1999, it was $43.50 (before the 50% stock dividend distributed in 2000).

INSTRUCTIONS

Compute the following for 2000 and 1999:
1. Quick ratio.
2. Current ratio.
3. Equity ratio.
4. Debt ratio.
5. Book value per share of capital stock (based on shares outstanding after 50% stock dividend in 2000).
6. Earnings per share of capital stock.
7. Price-earnings ratio.
8. Gross profit percentage.
9. Operating expense ratio.
10. Net income as a percentage of net sales.
11. Inventory turnover. (Assume an average inventory of $150,000 for both years.)
12. Accounts receivable turnover. (Assume average accounts receivable for $90,000 for 1999.)
13. Interest coverage ratio.

Solution to Demonstration Problem

	2000	1999
(1) Quick ratio:		
$126,000 ÷ $145,000	.9 to 1	
$115,000 ÷ $71,000		1.6 to 1
(2) Current ratio:		
$290,000 ÷ $145,000	2 to 1	
$260,000 ÷ $71,000		3.7 to 1
(3) Equity ratio:		
$571,400 ÷ $1,000,000	57%	
$445,000 ÷ $800,000		56%
(4) Debt ratio:		
$428,600 ÷ $1,000,000	43%	
$355,000 ÷ $800,000		44%
(5) Book value per share of capital stock:		
$571,400 ÷ 33,000 shares	$17.32	
$445,000 ÷ 33,000* shares		$13.48
(6) Earnings per share of capital stock:		
$166,400 ÷ 33,000 shares	$5.04	
$80,000 ÷ 33,000* shares		$2.42
(7) Price-earnings ratio:		
$86 ÷ $5.04	17 times	
$43.50 ÷ 1.5* = $29, adjusted market price; $29 ÷ $2.42		12 times
(8) Gross profit percentage:		
$594,000 ÷ $2,200,000	27%	
$480,000 ÷ $1,600,000		30%
(9) Operating expense ratio:		
($336,600 − $22,400) ÷ $2,200,000	14%	
($352,000 − $22,400) ÷ $1,600,000		20.6%
(10) Net income as a percentage of net sales:		
$166,400 ÷ $2,200,000	7.6%	
$80,000 ÷ $1,600,000		5%
(11) Inventory turnover:		
$1,606,000 ÷ $150,000	10.7 times	
$1,120,000 ÷ $150,000		7.5 times
(12) Accounts receivable turnover:		
$2,200,000 ÷ $90,500	24.3 times	
$1,600,000 ÷ $90,000		17.8 times
(13) Interest coverage ratio:		
($166,400 + $22,400 + $91,000) ÷ $22,400	12.5 times	
($80,000 + $22,400 + $48,000) ÷ $22,400		6.7 times

*Adjusted retroactively for 50% stock dividend.

CHAPTER 20 ANALYSIS AND INTERPRETATION OF FINANCIAL STATEMENTS

Self-Test Questions

Answers to these questions appear on page 1047.

1. Which of the following is *not* an accurate statement?
   a. Expressing the various items in the income statement as a percentage of net sales illustrates the use of component percentages.
   b. An increase in the market price of bonds causes the yield rate to decline.
   c. A high debt ratio is viewed favourably by long-term creditors as long as the number of times interest earned is at least 1.
   d. In measuring the dollar or percentage change in quarterly sales or earnings, it is appropriate to compare the results of the current quarter with those of the same quarter in the preceding year.

2. Which of the following actions will improve the "quality" of earnings, even though the total dollar amount of earnings may not increase?
   a. Increasing the uncollectible accounts expense from 1% to 2% of net credit sales to reflect current conditions.
   b. Switching from an accelerated method to the straight-line method for depreciating assets.
   c. Changing from LIFO to the FIFO method of inventory valuation during a period of rising prices.
   d. Lengthening the estimated useful lives of depreciable assets.

3. Hunter Corporation's net income was $400,000 in 2000 and $160,000 in 2001. What percentage increase in net income must Hunter achieve in 2002 to offset the decline in profits in 2001?
   a. 60%   b. 150%   c. 600%   d. 67%

4. Of the following situations, which would be considered the most favourable for the common shareholders?
   a. The company stops paying dividends on its cumulative preferred stock; the price-earnings ratio of common stock is low.
   b. Equity ratio is high; return on assets exceeds the cost of borrowing.
   c. Book value per share of common stock is substantially higher than market value per share; return on common shareholders' equity is less than the rate of interest paid to creditors.
   d. Equity ratio is low; return on assets exceeds the cost of borrowing.

5. In each of the last five years, the net sales of Tunnel Ltd. have increased at about half the rate of inflation, but net income has increased at approximately *twice* the rate of inflation. During this period, the company's total assets, liabilities, and equity have remained almost unchanged; dividends are approximately equal to net income. These relationships suggest (indicate all correct answers):
   a. Management is successfully controlling costs and expenses.
   b. The company is selling more merchandise every year.
   c. The annual return on assets has been increasing.
   d. Financing activities are likely to result in a net use of cash.

6. From the viewpoint of a common shareholder, which of the following relationships do you consider of the *least* significance?
   a. The return on assets consistently is higher than the industry average.
   b. The return on equity has increased in each of the last five years.
   c. Net income is greater than the amount of working capital.
   d. The return on assets is greater than the rate of interest being paid to creditors.

7. Which of the following usually is **least** important as a measure of short-term liquidity?
   a. Quick ratio.
   b. Current ratio.
   c. Debt ratio.
   d. Cash flow from operating activities.

8. During 2001, Ganey Corporation had sales of $4,000,000, all on credit. Accounts receivable averaged $400,000 and inventory levels averaged $250,000 throughout the year. If Ganey's gross profit rate during 2001 was 25% of net sales, which of the following statements are correct? (More than one statement may be correct.)
   a. Ganey "turns over" its accounts receivable more times per year than it turns over its average inventory.
   b. Ganey collects the amount of its average accounts receivable in about 36 to 37 days.
   c. Ganey's operating cycle is about 66 days.
   d. The quality of Ganey's working capital would improve if the company could reduce its inventory and receivables turnover rates.

9. In financial statement analysis, the most difficult of the following items to predict is whether:
   a. The company's market share is increasing or declining.
   b. The company will be solvent in six months.
   c. Profits will increase in the coming year.
   d. The market price of capital stock will rise or fall over the next two months.

Assignment Material

Discussion Questions

1. What elements are essential to the proper analysis and interpretation of financial statements?
2. What kind of information, other than the financial statements, is usually included in an annual report of a publicly owned corporation?
3. a. What groups are interested in the financial affairs of publicly owned corporations?
   b. List some of the more important sources of financial information for investors.
4. In financial statement analysis, what is the basic objective of observing trends in data and ratios? Suggest some other standards of comparison.
5. Distinguish between **trend percentages** and **component percentages**. Which would be better suited to analyzing the change in sales over a term of several years?
6. In financial statement analysis, what information is produced by computing a ratio that is not available in a simple observation of the underlying data?
7. "Although net income declined this year as compared with last year, it increased from 3% to 5% of net sales." Are sales increasing or decreasing?
8. Differentiate between **horizontal** and **vertical** analysis.

9. Assume that Chemco Corporation is engaged in the manufacture and distribution of a variety of chemicals. In analyzing the financial statements of this corporation, why would you want to refer to the ratios and other measurements of companies in the chemical industry? In comparing the financial results of Chemco Corporation with another chemical company, why would you be interested in the accounting practices used by the two companies?

10. Explain how the following accounting practices will tend to raise or lower the quality of a company's earnings. (Assume the continuance of inflation.)
    a. Adoption of an accelerated depreciation method rather than straight-line depreciation.
    b. Adoption of FIFO rather than LIFO for the valuation of inventories.
    c. Adoption of a 7-year life rather than a 10-year life for the depreciation of equipment.

11. A number of ratios and measures often are computed by users of financial statements. In general terms, with what standards are the results of these computations compared? Explain the purpose of these comparisons.

12. What single ratio do you think should be of greatest interest to:
    a. A banker considering a short-term loan?
    b. A common shareholder?
    c. An insurance company considering a long-term mortgage loan?

13. Modern Corporation earned a 16% return on its total assets. Current liabilities are 10% of total assets. Long-term bonds carrying a 13% interest rate are equal to 30% of total assets. There is no preferred stock. Is this application of leverage favourable or unfavourable from the viewpoint of Modern's shareholders?

14. Identify four ratios or measures used to evaluate profitability. Explain briefly how each is computed.

15. Assume that the net sales of a large department store have grown annually at a rate of 5% over each of the last several years. Do you think that the store is selling 5% more merchandise each year? Explain.

16. Net sales of the Springfield General Store have been increasing at a reasonable rate, but net income has been declining steadily as a percentage of these sales. What appears to be the problem?

17. Why might earnings per share be more significant to a shareholder in a large corporation than the total amount of net income?

18. In deciding whether a company's equity ratio is favourable or unfavourable, creditors and shareholders may have different views. Why?

19. How is the debt ratio computed? Is this ratio a measure of short-term solvency, or something else?

20. Ahi Ltd. has a current ratio of 3 to 1. Ono Corp. has a current ratio of 2 to 1. Does this mean that Ahi's operating cycle is longer than Ono's? Why?

21. What is the *quick ratio*? Under what circumstances are short-term creditors most likely to regard a company's quick ratio as more meaningful than its current ratio?

22. An investor states, "I bought this stock for $50 several years ago and it now sells for $100. It paid $5 per share in dividends last year so I'm earning 10% on my investment." Criticize this statement.

23. Alpine Products experiences a considerable seasonal variation in its business. The high point in the year's activity comes in November, the low point in July. During which month would you expect the company's current ratio to be higher? If the company were choosing a fiscal year for accounting purposes, how would you advise them? Explain.

24. Auto Parts' inventory turnover and accounts receivable turnover both increased from 2000 to 2001, but net income decreased. Can you offer some possible reasons for this?

25. Is the rate of return on investment (ROI) intended primarily to measure liquidity, solvency, or some other aspect of business operations? Explain.

26. Mention three financial amounts to which corporate earnings can logically be compared in judging their adequacy or reasonableness.

27. Under what circumstances would you consider a corporate net income of $1 million for the year as being unreasonably low? Under what circumstances would you consider a corporate net income of $1 million as being unreasonably high?

28. If all profitability measures for a particular company show positive trends, is the company's stock price sure to rise? Explain.

Exercises

EXERCISE 20-1
Accounting Terminology
(LO 2, 4)

Listed below are eleven technical accounting terms introduced or emphasized in this chapter.

Inventory turnover   *Trend percentages*   *Leverage*   *Market share*
Operating cycle   *Vertical analysis*   *Dividend yield*   *Operating income*
Price-earning ratio   *Return on assets*   *Quick ratio*

Each of the following statements may (or may not) describe one of these technical terms. For each statement, indicate the accounting term described, or answer "None" if the statement does not correctly describe any of the terms.

a. The proportion of total assets financed by shareholders, as distinguished from creditors.
b. Market price per common share divided by earnings per common share.
c. Changes in financial statement items from a base year to following years expressed as a percentage of the base year amount and designed to show the extent and direction of change.
d. Dividends per share divided by market price per share.
e. Average time period between the purchase of merchandise and the conversion of this merchandise back into cash.
f. Study of relationships among the data of a single accounting period.
g. Net sales divided by average inventory.
h. Comparison of highly liquid current assets (cash, marketable securities, and receivables) with current liabilities.
i. Buying assets with money raised by borrowing.
j. A measure of the profitability of a company's basic business operations.

EXERCISE 20-2
Intuition versus Calculation
(LO 2)

Tait Corporation had net income of $4 million in its first year. In the second year, net income decreased by 75%. In the third year, due to an improved business environment, net income increased by 250%.

CHAPTER 20 ANALYSIS AND INTERPRETATION OF FINANCIAL STATEMENTS

INSTRUCTIONS

a. Prior to making any computations, do you think Tait's net income was higher or lower in the third year than in the first year?

b. Compute Tait's net income for the second year and for the third year. Do your computations support your initial response in part **a**?

EXERCISE 20-3
Percentage Changes
(LO 2, 4)

Selected information taken from financial statements of Kowloon Corporation for two successive years follows. You are to compute the percentage change from 1999 to 2000 whenever possible.

	2000	1999
a. Accounts receivable	$126,000	$150,000
b. Marketable securities	-0-	250,000
c. Retained earnings	80,000	(80,000)
d. Notes receivable	120,000	-0-
e. Notes payable	860,000	800,000
f. Cash	82,400	80,000
g. Sales	990,000	900,000

EXERCISE 20-4
Trend Percentages
(LO 2, 4)

Compute **trend percentages** for the following items taken from the annual report of **Dofasco Inc.** over a five-year period. Treat 1993 as the base year. State whether the trends are favourable or unfavourable. (Dollar amounts are stated in millions.)

	1997	1996	1995	1994	1993
Sales	$3,070.4	$2,942.0	$2,635.9	$2,424.8	$2,102.9
Cost of sale	$2,439.9	$2,317.0	$2,047.1	$1,936.2	$1,778.2

EXERCISE 20-5
Common Size Income Statements
(LO 4)

Prepare **common size** income statements for Redot Company, a sole proprietorship, for the two years shown below by converting the dollar amounts into percentages. For each year, sales will appear as 100% and other items will be expressed as a percentage of sales. (Income taxes are not involved as the business is not incorporated.) Comment on whether the changes from 2000 to 2001 are favourable or unfavourable.

	2001	2000
Sales	$500,000	$400,000
Cost of goods sold	330,000	268,000
Gross profit	$170,000	$132,000
Operating expenses	140,000	116,000
Net income	$ 30,000	$ 16,000

EXERCISE 20-6
Measures of Profitability
(LO 4)

Shown below is an income statement for **The Gap**, a specialty retailer. (Dollar amounts in thousands, except per share amounts.)

Net sales	$2,960,409
Costs and expenses:	
Cost of goods sold and occupancy expenses	(1,955,553)
Operating expenses	(661,252)
Interest expense	(3,763)
Earnings before income taxes	$ 339,841
Income taxes	(129,140)
Net earnings	$ 210,701

Comparative balance sheets indicate average total assets for the year of **$1,263,331**, and average total equity of **$782,814** (dollar amounts in thousands).

INSTRUCTIONS Compute the (1) gross profit rate, (2) the operating income rate, (3) net income as a percentage of net sales, (4) return on assets, and (5) return on equity for the year. (Round computations to the nearest one-tenth of one percent.)

EXERCISE 20-7
Computing and Interpreting Rate of Change in Profitability
(LO 4, 5)

Selected information from the financial statements of Golden Harvest appears below:

	2001	2000
Net sales	$2,200,000	$2,000,000
Total operating expenses	1,798,200	1,620,000

INSTRUCTIONS
a. Compute the percentage change in 2001 for the amounts of (**1**) net sales and (**2**) total operating expenses.
b. Using the information developed in part **a**, express your opinion as to whether the company's **operating income** for 2001:
  1. Increased at a greater or lower percentage rate than did net sales.
  2. Represented a larger or smaller percentage of net sales than in 2000.
  For each answer, explain your reasoning *without* making any computations or references to dollar amounts.

EXERCISE 20-8
Measuring and Interpreting Profitability
(LO 4, 5)

The following information is from the recent financial statements of **Algoma Steel Inc.** (Dollars are in millions.)

	Current Year	Last Year
Operating profit	$ 202	$ 213
Operating income	104	121
Net income	52	68
Total assets	1,538	1,347
Total shareholders' equity (common)	394	288

INSTRUCTIONS
a. Compute, both in amount and in percentage, the change in
  1. Gross profit
  2. Operating income
  3. Net income
  4. Return on assets (percentage only, use the amount at the end of the year, rather than the average)
  5. Return on shareholders' equity (percentage only, use the amount at the end of the year rather than the average)
b. Comment on the analysis in **a** above.

EXERCISE 20-9
Ratios for a Retail Store
(LO 4, 5)

Selected financial data for Vashon's, a retail store, appear below. Since monthly figures are not available, the average amounts for inventories and for accounts receivable should be based on the amounts shown for the beginning and end of 2001.

	2001	2000
Sales (terms 2/10, n/30)	$750,000	$600,000
Cost of goods sold	495,000	408,000
Inventory at end of year	85,500	94,500
Accounts receivable at end of year	87,500	100,000

INSTRUCTIONS

Compute the following for 2001:
a. Gross profit percentage
b. Inventory turnover
c. Accounts receivable turnover

EXERCISE 20-10
Computing Ratios
(LO 4, 5)

A condensed balance sheet for Durham Corporation prepared at the end of the year appears below.

Assets		Liabilities & Shareholders' Equity	
Cash	$ 55,000	Notes payable	
Accounts receivable	155,000	(due in 6 months)	$ 40,000
Inventory	270,000	Accounts payable	110,000
Prepaid expenses	60,000	Long-term liabilities	330,000
Plant & equipment (net)	570,000	Capital stock (60,000 shares)	300,000
Other assets	90,000	Retained earnings	420,000
Total	$1,200,000	Total	$1,200,000

During the year the company earned a gross profit of $1,116,000 on sales of $2,790,000. Accounts receivable, inventory, and plant assets remained almost constant in amount throughout the year.

INSTRUCTIONS

Compute the following:
a. Current ratio
b. Quick ratio
c. Working capital
d. Equity ratio
e. Accounts receivable turnover (all sales were on credit)
f. Inventory turnover
g. Book value per share of capital stock

EXERCISE 20-11
Current Ratio, Debt Ratio, and Earnings per Share
(LO 4, 5)

Selected items from successive annual reports of Hastings Inc. appear below.

	2002	2001
Total assets (40% of which are current)	$400,000	$325,000
Current liabilities	$ 80,000	$100,000
Bonds payable, 12%	100,000	50,000
Capital stock (20,000 shares)	100,000	100,000
Retained earnings	120,000	75,000
Total liabilities & shareholders' equity	$400,000	$325,000

Dividends of $26,000 were declared and paid in 2002.

INSTRUCTIONS

Compute the following:
a. Current ratio for 2002 and 2001.
b. Debt ratio for 2002 and 2001
c. Earnings per share for 2002.

EXERCISE 20-12
Ratio Analysis for Two Similar Companies
(LO 4, 5)

Selected data from the financial statements of Italian Marble Ltd. and Yukon Stone Products for the year just ended follow. Assume that for both companies dividends declared were equal in amount to net earnings during the year and therefore shareholders' equity did not change. The two companies are in the same line of business.

	Italian Marble Ltd.	Yukon Stone Products
Total liabilities	$ 200,000	$ 100,000
Total assets	800,000	400,000
Sales (all on credit)	1,800,000	1,200,000
Average inventory	240,000	140,000
Average receivables	200,000	100,000
Gross profit as a percentage of sales	40%	30%
Operating and other expenses as a percentage of sales	36%	25%
Net income as a percentage of sales	4%	5%

INSTRUCTIONS

Compute the following for each company:
a. Net income
b. Net income as a percentage of shareholders' equity
c. Accounts receivable turnover
d. Inventory turnover

Problems

PROBLEM 20-1
Analysis to Identify Favourable and Unfavourable Trends
(LO 2, 4, 5)

The following information was developed from the December 31, year-end financial statements of Custom Logos Inc. At the beginning of 2000, the company's former supplier went bankrupt, and the company began buying merchandise from another supplier.

	2000	1999
Gross profit	$1,008,000	$1,134,000
Operating income	230,400	252,000
Net income	172,800	189,000
Net income as a percentage of net sales	6.0%	7.5%

INSTRUCTIONS

a. Compute the net sales for each year.
b. Compute the cost of goods sold in dollars and as a percentage of net sales for each year.
c. Compute operating expenses in dollars and as a percentage of net sales for each year.
d. Prepare a condensed comparative income statement for 1999 and 2000. Include the following items: net sales, cost of goods sold, gross profit, operating expenses, operating income, income taxes expense, and net income. Omit earnings per share statistics.
e. Identify the significant favourable trends and unfavourable trends in the performance of Custom Logos Inc. Comment on any unusual changes.

PROBLEM 20-2
Comparing Operating Results with Average Performance in the Industry
(LO 2, 4)

Sub Zero Inc. manufactures camping equipment. Shown below for the current year are the income statement for the company and a common size summary for the industry in which the company operates. (Notice that the percentages in the right-hand column are *not* for Sub Zero Inc., but are average percentages for the industry.)

CHAPTER 20 ANALYSIS AND INTERPRETATION OF FINANCIAL STATEMENTS

	Sub Zero Inc.	Industry Average
Sales (net)	$20,000,000	100%
Cost of goods sold	9,800,000	57
Gross profit	$10,200,000	43%
Operating expenses:		
Selling	$ 4,200,000	16%
General and administrative	3,400,000	20
Total operating expenses	$ 7,600,000	36%
Operating income	$ 2,600,000	7%
Income taxes	1,200,000	3
Net income	$ 1,400,000	4%
Return on assets	18%	9%

INSTRUCTIONS

a. Prepare a two-column common size income statement. The first column should show for Sub Zero Inc., all items expressed as a percentage of net sales. The second column should show as an industry average the percentage data given in the problem. The purpose of this common size statement is to compare the operating results of Sub Zero Inc. with the average for the industry.

b. Comment specifically on differences between Sub Zero Inc. and the industry average with respect to gross profit, selling expenses, general and administrative expenses, operating income, net income, and return on assets. Suggest possible reasons for the more important disparities.

PROBLEM 20-3
Ratios Based on Balance Sheet and Income Statement Data
(LO 4, 5)

Barnum Corporation has issued common stock only. The company has been successful and has a gross profit rate of 25%. The information shown below was derived from the company's financial statements.

Beginning inventory	$ 700,000
Ending inventory	800,000
Average accounts receivable	250,000
Average common shareholders' equity	1,800,000
Sales (80% on credit)	4,000,000
Net income	225,000

INSTRUCTIONS

On the basis of the above information, compute the following:
a. Accounts receivable turnover and the average number of days required to collect the accounts receivable
b. The inventory turnover and the average number of days required to turn over the inventory
c. Length of Barnum Corporation's operating cycle
d. Return on common shareholders' equity

PROBLEM 20-4
Ratios; Consider Advisability of Incurring Long-Term Debt
(LO 4, 5)

At the end of the year, the following information was obtained from the accounting records of Carleton Office Products:

Sales (all on credit)	$2,700,000
Cost of goods sold	1,755,000
Average inventory	351,000
Average accounts receivable	300,000
Interest expense	45,000
Income taxes	84,000
Net income	159,000
Average investment in assets	1,800,000
Average shareholders' equity	795,000

INSTRUCTIONS

a. From the information given, compute the following:
 1. Inventory turnover
 2. Accounts receivable turnover
 3. Total operating expenses
 4. Gross profit percentage
 5. Return on average shareholders' equity
 6. Return on average assets
b. Carleton has an opportunity to obtain a long-term loan at an annual interest rate of 12% and could use this additional capital at the same rate of profitability as indicated above. Would obtaining the loan be desirable from the viewpoint of the shareholders? Explain.

PROBLEM 20-5
Ratios: Consider Advisability of Incurring Long-Term Debt—A Second Problem
(LO 4, 5)

At the end of the year, the following information was obtained from the accounting records of Santa Fe Boot Limited.

Sales (all on credit)	$800,000
Cost of goods sold	480,000
Average inventory	120,000
Average accounts receivable	80,000
Interest expense	6,000
Income taxes	8,000
Net income for the year	36,000
Average investment in assets	500,000
Average shareholders' equity	400,000

The company declared no dividends of any kind during the year and did not issue or retire any capital stock.

INSTRUCTIONS

a. From the information given, compute the following for the year:
 1. Inventory turnover
 2. Accounts receivable turnover
 3. Total operating expenses
 4. Gross profit percentage
 5. Return on average shareholders' equity
 6. Return on average assets
b. Santa Fe Boot Limited has an opportunity to obtain a long-term loan at an annual interest rate of 12% and could use this additional capital at the same rate of profitability as indicated in *a*. Would obtaining the loan be desirable from the viewpoint of the shareholders? Explain.

PROBLEM 20-6
Analysis and Interpretation from Viewpoint of Short-Term Creditor
(LO 3,4)

Shown below are selected financial data for Mondo Corporation and Global Inc., at the end of the current year.

	Mondo Corporation	Global Inc.
Net sales (all on credit)	$2,160,000	$1,785,000
Cost of goods sold	1,890,000	1,237,500
Cash	54,000	105,000
Accounts receivable (net)	270,000	210,000
Inventory	756,000	247,500
Current liabilities	360,000	225,000

Assume that the year-end balances shown for accounts receivable and for inventory also represent the average balances of these accounts throughout the year.

INSTRUCTIONS	**a.** For each company, compute the following: 1. Working capital 2. Current ratio 3. Quick ratio 4. Number of times inventory turned over during the year and the average number of days required to turn over inventory 5. Number of times accounts receivable turned over during the year and the average number of days required to collect accounts receivable. (Round to the nearest day.) 6. Operating cycle **b.** From the viewpoint of a short-term creditor, comment upon the *quality* of each company's working capital. To which company would you prefer to sell $75,000 in merchandise on a 30-day open account?
PROBLEM 20-7 Ratios: Evaluation of Two Companies for Short-Term Credit (LO 3, 4)	Shown below are selected financial data for Another World and Imports Inc., at the end of the current year:

	Another World	Imports Inc.
Net credit sales	$1,350,000	$1,120,000
Cost of goods sold	1,008,000	960,000
Cash	102,000	40,000
Accounts receivable (net)	150,000	140,000
Inventory	168,000	320,000
Current liabilities	210,000	200,000

Assume that the year-end balances shown for accounts receivable and for inventory also represent the average balances of these items throughout the year.

INSTRUCTIONS	**a.** For each of the two companies, compute the following: 1. Working capital. 2. Current ratio. 3. Quick ratio. 4. Number of times inventory turned over during the year and the average number of days required to turn over inventory. (Round computation to the nearest day.) 5. Number of times accounts receivable turned over during the year and the average number of days required to collect accounts receivable. (Round computation to the nearest day.) 6. Operating cycle. **b.** From the viewpoint of a short-term creditor, comment upon the *quality* of each company's working capital. To which company would you prefer to sell $60,000 in merchandise on a 30-day open account?
PROBLEM 20-8 Evaluating Short-Term Debt-Paying Ability (LO 4, 5)	Listed below is the working capital information for Imperial Products Limited at the beginning of the year.

Cash	$405,000
Short-term investments in marketable securities	216,000
Notes receivable—current	324,000
Accounts receivable	540,000
Allowance for doubtful accounts	27,000
Inventory	432,000
Prepaid expenses	54,000
Notes payable within one year	162,000
Accounts payable	445,500
Accrued liabilities	40,500

The following transactions are completed during the year:

0 Sold on account inventory costing $72,000 for $65,000.
1 Issued additional shares of capital stock for cash, $800,000.
2 Sold short-term investments (not cash equivalents) costing $60,000 for $54,000 cash.
3 Acquired short-term investments, (not cash equivalents) $105,000. Paid cash.
4 Wrote off uncollectible accounts, $18,000.
5 Sold on account inventory costing $75,000 for $90,000.
6 Acquired plant and equipment for cash, $480,000.
7 Declared a cash dividend, $240,000.
8 Declared a 10% stock dividend.
9 Paid accounts payable, $120,000.
10 Purchased goods on account, $90,000.
11 Collected cash on accounts receivable, $180,000.
12 Borrowed cash from a bank by issuing a short-term note, $250,000.

INSTRUCTIONS

a. Compute the amount of quick assets, current assets, and current liabilities at the beginning of the year as shown by the above account balances.

b. Use the data compiled in part **a** to compute: (1) current ratio; (2) quick ratio; and (3) working capital.

c. Indicate the effect (Increase, Decrease, and No Effect) of each independent transaction listed above on the current ratio, quick ratio, working capital, and net cash flow from operating activities. Use the following four-column format (item **0** is given as an example):

Effect on

Item	Current Ratio	Quick Ratio	Working Capital	Net Cash Flow from Operating Activities
0	Decrease	Increase	Decrease	No Effect

PROBLEM 20-9
Effects of Transactions on Various Ratios
(LO 4, 5)

Listed in the left-hand column below is a series of 12 business transactions and events relating to the activities of Wabash Industries. Opposite each transaction is listed a particular ratio used in financial analysis.

Transaction	Ratio
(1) Purchased inventory on open account.	Quick ratio
(2) A larger physical volume of goods was sold at smaller unit prices.	Gross profit percentage
(3) Corporation declared a cash dividend.	Current ratio
(4) An uncollectible account receivable was written off against the allowance account.	Current ratio
(5) Issued additional shares of common stock and used proceeds to retire long-term debt.	Debt ratio
(6) Paid stock dividend on common stock, in common stock.	Earnings per share
(7) Conversion of a portion of bonds payable into common stock. (Ignore income taxes.)	Interest coverage ratio

Transaction	Ratio
(8) Appropriated retained earnings.	Rate of return on shareholders' equity
(9) During period of rising prices, company changed from FIFO to LIFO method of inventory pricing.	Inventory turnover
(10) Paid a previously declared cash dividend.	Debt ratio
(11) Purchased office supplies on open account.	Current ratio (assume that ratio is greater than 1:1)
(12) Issued shares of capital stock in exchange for patents.	Equity ratio (assume that there are liabilities)

INSTRUCTIONS

What effect would each transaction or event have on the ratio listed opposite to it; that is, as a result of this event would the ratio increase, decrease, or remain unchanged? Your answer for each of the 12 transactions should include a brief explanation.

PROBLEM 20-10
Financial Statement Analysis
(LO 4, 5)

Shown below is selected data from the financial statements of Carriage Trade, a retail furniture store.

From the balance sheet:

Cash	$ 30,000
Accounts receivable	150,000
Inventory	200,000
Plant assets (net of accumulated depreciation)	500,000
Current liabilities	150,000
Total shareholders' equity	300,000
Total assets	1,000,000

From the income statement:

Net sales	$1,500,000
Cost of goods sold	1,080,000
Operating expenses	315,000
Interest expense	84,000
Income taxes expense	6,000
Net income	15,000

From the cash flow statement:

Net cash provided by operating activities (including interest paid of $79,000)		$ 40,000
Net cash used in investing activities		(46,000)
Financing activities:		
Amounts borrowed	$50,000	
Repayment of amounts borrowed	(14,000)	
Dividends paid	(20,000)	
Net cash provided by financing activities		16,000
Net increase in cash during the year		$ 10,000

INSTRUCTIONS

a. Explain how the interest expense shown in the income statement could be $84,000, when the interest payment appearing in the cash flow statement is only $79,000.

b. Compute the following (round to one decimal place):
  1. Current ratio.
  2. Quick ratio.
  3. Working capital.
  4. Debt ratio.

c. Comment upon these measurements and evaluate Carriage Trade's short-term debt-paying ability.
d. Complete the following ratios (assume that the year-end amounts of total assets and total shareholders' equity also represent the average amounts throughout the year):
   1. Return on assets.
   2. Return on equity.
e. Comment upon the company's performance under these measurements. Explain *why* the return on assets and return on equity are so different.
f. Discuss (1) the apparent safety of long-term creditors' claims, and (2) the prospects for Carriage Trade continuing its dividend payments at the present level.

PROBLEM 20-11
Analysis and Interpretation from Viewpoint of Common Shareholders and of Bondholders
(LO 4, 5)

The following financial information for Continental Transfer and Canadian Van Lines (except market price per share of stock) is stated in ***thousands of dollars***. The figures are as of the end of the current year. The two companies are in the same industry and are quite similar as to operations, facilities, and accounting methods. Assume that both companies pay income taxes equal to 50% of income before income taxes.

Assets	Continental Transfer	Canadian Van Lines
Current assets	$ 97,500	$132,320
Plant and equipment	397,500	495,680
Less: Accumulated depreciation	(55,000)	(78,000)
Total assets	$440,000	$550,000

Liabilities & Shareholders' Equity		
Current liabilities	$ 34,000	$ 65,000
Bonds payable, 12%, due in 15 years	120,000	100,000
Capital stock, no par	150,000	200,000
Retained earnings	136,000	185,000
Total liabilities & shareholders' equity	$440,000	$550,000
Analysis of retained earnings:		
Balance, beginning of year	$125,200	$167,200
Net income for the year	19,800	37,400
Dividends	(9,000)	(19,600)
Balance, end of year	$136,000	$185,000
Market price of capital stock, per share	$30	$61
Number of shares of capital stock outstanding	6 million	8 million

INSTRUCTIONS

a. Compute for each company:
   1. The interest coverage ratio (number of times bond interest was earned during the current year).
   2. The debt ratio.
b. In light of the information developed in **a** above, write a paragraph indicating which company's bonds you think would trade in the market at the higher price. Which would probably provide the higher yield? Explain how the ratios developed influence your answer. (It may be assumed that the bonds were issued several years ago.)
c. For each company compute the dividend yield, earnings per share, the price-earnings ratio, and the book value per share. (Show supporting com-

putations. Remember that dollar amounts in the problem are in thousands of dollars, that is, three zeros omitted.)

d. Assume that you expect both companies to grow at the same rate. Express an opinion, based solely on the data developed in **c** above, as to which company's stock is a better investment at the present market price.

Real World Problems and Cases (RW)

RW 20-1
Is Safeway Solvent?
(LO 1, 4, 5)

Safeway, Inc., is one of the world's largest supermarket chains. Shown below are selected items from a Safeway balance sheet. (Amounts are in millions.)

Cash	$ 96.5
Receivables	135.7
Merchandise inventories	1,201.7
Prepaid expenses	95.1
Fixtures and equipment	1,668.7
Retained earnings (deficit)	(404.9)
Total current liabilities	1,501.8

INSTRUCTIONS

a. Using the information above, compute the amounts of Safeway's total current assets and total quick assets.
b. Compute the company's (1) current ratio, (2) quick ratio, and (3) working capital. (Round to one decimal place.)
c. From these computations, are you able to conclude whether Safeway is a good credit risk for short-term creditors, or on the brink of bankruptcy? Explain.
d. Is there anything unusual about the operating cycle of supermarkets that would make you think that they normally would have lower current ratios than, say, large department stores?
e. What *other types of information* could you utilize in performing a more complete analysis of Safeway's solvency?

RW 20-2
Balance Sheet Measures of Liquidity and Credit Risk
(LO 4, 5)

A recent balance sheet of **Tootsie Roll Industries** included the following items, among others. (Dollar amounts are stated in thousands.)

Cash and cash equivalents	$ 995
Investments (in marketable securities)	87,947
Accounts receivable	12,889
Inventories	24,845
Prepaid expenses	2,989
Retained earnings	90,285
Notes payable to banks (due within one year)	253
Accounts payable	4,674
Dividends payable	791
Accrued liabilities (short-term)	13,661
Income taxes payable	3,119
Postretirement health care and life insurance benefits (a long-term liability)	3,976

The company also reported total assets of $222,478, total liabilities of $40,774, and a return on assets of **23.6%**.

INSTRUCTIONS

a. Compute Tootsie Roll's (1) quick assets, (2) current assets, and (3) current liabilities.

b. Compute Tootsie Roll's (1) quick ratio, (2) current ratio, (3) working capital, and (4) debt ratio. (Round to one decimal place.)
c. Discuss the company's liquidity from the viewpoints of (1) short-term creditors, (2) long-term creditors, and (3) shareholders.

RW 20-3
Basic Ratio Analysis
(LO 1, 2, 4, 5)

Blockbuster Entertainment Corporation operates under the name **Blockbuster Video** and is engaged primarily in the business of renting video tapes and discs. Shown below are selected data from its annual report. (Dollar amounts are stated in thousands.)

	Beginning of the Year	End of the Year
Total current assets	$ 54,130	$ 92,592
Total current liabilities	63,481	83,357
Total assets	234,698	417,413
Total shareholders' equity	124,058	208,189
Operating income		76,141
Net income		44,152

The company has long-term liabilities that bear interest at annual rates ranging from 11% to 16%.

INSTRUCTIONS

a. Compute the company's current ratio at (1) the **beginning** of the year and (2) the **end** of the year. (Carry to two decimal places.)
b. Compute the company's working capital at (1) the beginning of the year, and (2) the end of the year. (Express dollar amounts in thousands.)
c. Is the company's short-term debt paying ability improving or deteriorating? As a short-term creditor, would you consider the company to be as good a credit risk as, say, **Maritime Telegraph and Telephone Company Limited**—a regional telephone company with a current ratio of **0.5 to 1**? Explain.
d. Compute the company's (1) return on average total assets, and (2) return on average shareholders' equity. (Round final computations to the nearest 1 percent.)
e. As an equity investor, do you think that Blockbuster's management is utilizing the company's resources in a reasonably efficient manner? Explain.

RW 20-4
Ratios; Comparison of Two Companies
(LO 2, 4, 5)

Gibson Greetings, Inc. and **American Greetings** are two of the world's largest publicly owned manufacturers of greeting cards and gift wrap products. Shown below are data from the companies' annual reports. Dollar amounts are stated in thousands.

	Gibson Greetings, Inc.	American Greetings
Total current assets	$310,957	$ 680,945
Total current liabilities	164,281	200,756
Average total assets	382,628	1,114,318
Average total shareholders' equity	206,074	584,796
Operating income[a]	67,191	144,106
Net income	42,369	72,177

[a]Neither company includes the subtotal operating income in its income statement. The authors have computed this subtotal from the companies' published data in a manner consistent with the discussion in this chapter.

INSTRUCTIONS

a. Compute the following for each company (round computations to one decimal place.)
   1. Current ratio.
   2. Working capital.
   3. Return on average total assets.
   4. Return on average total shareholders' equity.
b. From the viewpoint of a short-term creditor, which of these companies appears to have the greater short-term debt-paying ability? Explain.
c. In which company does management appear to be using the resources under its control most efficiently? Explain the reasons for your answer.

RW 20-5
Solvency, Profitability, and Objective Standards
(LO 1, 2, 4, 5)

Canadian Airlines Corporation is one of the two major airline companies in Canada (the other one is Air Canada). Certain information is adapted from its recent annual report.

	(Dollars in millions)	
	Current Year	Last Year
Current assets	$ 593.7	$ 456.5
Current liabilities	878.1*	898.4
Average total assets	1,889.5	2,050.0
Average total common shareholders' equity (deficiency)	(25.9)	52.7
Common shareholders' deficiency	(23.2)	(28.6)
Operating revenues	3,075.5	3,096.4
Operating income	97.1	(100.5)
Net income (loss)	5.4	(187.1)
Net cash provided by operating activities	103.2	2.3
Unused line of credit	119.0	113.1

*$129 million of the current liabilities were current portion of long-term debt, bearing interest at between 4.5% to 11%.

INSTRUCTIONS

a. Compute, for the current year and last year, the following:
   1. Current ratio
   2. Working capital
   3. Return on assets
   4. Return on common shareholders' equity
   5. Operating income rate
   6. Net income as a percentage of operating revenues
b. Explain whether the company's short-term debt-paying ability is improving or deteriorating.
c. Explain whether you consider the company to be solvent at the end of the current year and at the end of last year.
d. Comment on the profitability trend of the company.
e. What objective measures may you use to evaluate the company's trend on liquidity and profitability?

RW 20-6
Evaluate Liquidity, Profitability, Leverage, and Management Efficiency
(LO 2, 4, 5)

Air Canada is Canada's largest air carrier. The following information is adapted from its recent annual report (dollars in millions):

	Current Year	Last Year
Operating revenues	$5,572	$4,880
Operating income	368	215
Net income *	427	149
Cash provided by operating activities	366	64

	Current Year End	Current Year Beginning
Current assets	$1,394	$1,059
Current liabilities	1,139**	1,111
Total assets (beginning of last year $5,397)	5,991	5,441
Total shareholders' equity (beginning of last year $833)	1,435	985
Unused lines of credit	550	0

*including gain on sale of investments and other assets: current year—$236 million, last year—$133 million; and recovery of prior years income tax benefits: current year $168 million, last year $52 million

** $71 million of current liabilities and $3,199 million of long-term debts are bearing interest at 4.625% to 12.8%

INSTRUCTIONS

Evaluate the company's
a. Liquidity
b. Profitability
c. Leverage
d. Management in the efficiency of utilizing the resources.

RW 20-7
Evaluation of Liquidity and Profitability
(LO 2, 4, 5)

The following data is adapted from an annual report of **Toys "R" Us** (dollar amounts in millions):

	Current Year	Last Year
Balance sheet data:		
Quick assets	$ 486	$ 890
Current assets	2,531	2,708
Current liabilities	2,137	2,075
Average shareholders' equity	3,289	3,019
Average total assets	6,360	5,736
Income statement data:		
Net sales	$8,746	$7,946
Gross profit	2,738	2,451
Operating income	912	821
Net income	532	483
Cash flow data:		
Net cash provided by operating activities	$ 589	$ 657

INSTRUCTIONS

a. Compute the following for the current year and last year (round to one decimal place):
  1. Quick ratio.
  2. Current ratio.
  3. Working capital.
b. Comment upon the trends in the liquidity measures and state whether the company appears solvent at the end of the current year.
c. Compute the percentage changes for the current year in the amounts of net sales and net income.

d. Compute the following for the current year and last year (round to one-tenth of one percent):
   1. Gross profit rate.
   2. Net income as a percentage of net sales.
   3. Return on average assets.
   4. Return on average shareholders' equity.
e. Comment upon the trends in the profitability measures computed in parts **c** and **d**.

RW 20-8
Evaluation of Liquidity, Profitability and Leverage—a Mini but Different Version of Comprehensive Problem 6 (LO 2, 4, 5)

The following information is adapted from a recent annual report of **Loblaw Companies Limited**, Canada's largest retail and wholesale food distributor (dollars in millions, except for per share data):

	Current Year	Last Year
Quick assets	$ 926	$ 878
Current assets	1,681	1,553
Current liabilities	1,479*	1,399
Average total assets (total for current year $4,013)	3,772	3,364
Average total common shareholders' equity (total for current year $1,495)	1,383	1,215
Sales	11,008	9,848
Operating income	426	359
Net income	213	174
Net cash provided by operating activities	426	262
Dividends per common share	15 cents	12 cents
Market price per common share	26	14.25

* $12 million of the current liabilities and $911 million of the long-term debts are interest bearing, ranging from 5.39% to 11.4% (of which, $56 million with a weighted average of 12.1%)

INSTRUCTIONS

a. Compute the following for the current year and last year (round to one decimal place or one-tenth of one percent)
   1. Quick ratio
   2. Current ratio
   3. Working capital
   4. Operating income rate
   5. Net income as a percentage of sales
   6. Return on assets
   7. Return on common shareholders' equity
   8. Dividend yield rate
b. Compute the percentage changes of sales, operating income, and net income from last year.
c. Comment on the trend in the liquidity measures and explain whether the company appears solvent at the end of the current year.
d. Comment on the trend of profitability measures.
e. Comment on leverage.

RW 20-9
Which One Flies Higher? (LO 1, 2, 4, 5)

Selected information from the annual reports of **Canadian Airlines Corporation** and **Air Canada** is presented in RW 20-5 and RW 20-6. Use the "current year" information of the two airlines to evaluate the relative performance of these two companies.

1044 INCOME TAXES, CASH FLOWS, FINANCIAL STATEMENT ANALYSIS, AND MANAGERIAL ACCOUNTING   PART 5

INSTRUCTIONS

a. Compare the performance of the companies for
   1. Liquidity
   2. Profitability, and
   3. Leverage
b. Comment on the Canadian airline industry regarding liquidity, profitability, and leverage.

RW 20-10
Performance Evaluation for Long-term Creditors and Common Shareholders
(LO 2, 4, 5)

Canadian Pacific Limited is one of the largest companies in Canada. Its operations cover energy, transportation, and hotels. The following is adapted from its recent annual report:

	(Dollars in Millions)	
	Current Year	Last Year
Revenues	$ 9,560.0	$ 8,471.3
Operating income	1,765.7	1,467.0
Net income (including income and gain from discontinued operations: current year $309.1; last year $29.1)	1,255.8	869.1
Average number of common shares outstanding	345.4	344.4
Dividends for common shares	165.3	165.5
Cash flow from operating activities	1,745.8	1,610.0

	Current Year	
	End	Beginning
Total assets (last year's beginning, $16,555.7)	$17,331.9	$15,805.9
Total common shareholders' equity (last year's beginning, $6,129.9)	7,573.4	6,727.8

OTHER INFORMATION

The market price per share has fluctuated from last year's $36.05 to current year's $38.50. The current year's interest expense on the long-term debts amounts to $265.2 million, at an average interest rate of about 9.3%. For the current year, total liabilities amounted to $9,407.9 million and non-controlling interest (minority shareholders' interest in subsidiary companies) amounts to $350.6 million.

INSTRUCTIONS

Evaluate Canadian Pacific's performance from the viewpoint of
a. Long-term creditors
b. Common shareholders.

RW 20-11
Comprehensive Evaluation
(LO 2, 4, 5)

Leon's Furniture Limited is "one of the most well-known retailers in Canada." It sells "a vast array of quality furniture, major home appliances, and consumers electronics, ..." The following information is adapted from its recent annual report:

	(Dollars in Thousands)	
	Current Year	Last Year
Current assets:		
Cash and short-term investments	$ 49,187	$ 54,030
Marketable securities	34,787	9,642
Accounts receivable (last year's beginning balance $7,256)	8,314	8,303
Inventory (last year's beginning balance $42,253)	43,746	41,834
Total current assets	136,034	113,809
Current liabilities	65,139	58,990
Total assets (last year's beginning balance $177,774)	217,641	193,089
Total common shareholders' equity (last year's beginning balance $129,690)	152,315	133,804
Cash provided by operating activities	30,591	32,360
Sales	315,817	289,241
Cost of sales	187,680	173,271
Gross profit	128,137	115,970
Operating income (computed from statement of income)	29,303	22,010
Interest expense	33	48
Net income	21,635	17,654
Dividends	4,471	13,952
Weighted average number of common shares (in thousands)	19,987	19,861
Market price per share (not in thousands of dollars)—High	22.00	13.45

OTHER INFORMATION Interest-bearing (9.25%) long-term debt is secured by certain land and buildings.

INSTRUCTIONS Evaluate Leon's Furniture Limited's financial position and operating results.

Analytical and Decision Problems and Cases

A&D 20-1
Season's Greetings
(LO 1, 2)

Holiday Greeting Cards is a local company organized late in July of 2000. The company's net income for each of its first six calendar quarters of operations is summarized below. The amounts are stated in thousands of dollars.

	2001	2000
First quarter (January through March)	$ 253	—
Second quarter (April through June)	308	—
Third quarter (July through September)	100	$ 50
Fourth quarter (October through December)	450	500
Total for the calendar year	$1,111	$550

Glen Wallace reports the business and economic news for a local radio station. On the day that Holiday Greeting Cards released the above financial information, you heard Wallace make the following statement during his broadcast: "Holiday Greeting Cards enjoyed a 350% increase in its net income for the fourth quarter, and net income for the entire year was up by over 100%."

INSTRUCTIONS

a. Show the computations that Wallace probably made in arriving at his statistics.
b. Do you believe that Wallace's percentage changes present a realistic impression of Holiday Greeting Cards' rate of growth in 2000? Explain.

c. What figure would you use to express the percentage change in Holiday's fourth quarter net income in 2000? Explain why you would compute the change in this manner.

**A&D 20-2
Limit on Dividends
(LO 4)**

During each of the last 10 years, Reese Corporation has increased the common stock dividend per share by about 10%. Total dividends now amount to $9 million per year, consisting of $2 million paid to preferred shareholders and $7 million paid to common shareholders. The preferred stock is cumulative but not convertible. Annual net income had been rising steadily until two years ago, when it peaked at $44 million. Last year, increased competition caused net income to decline to $37 million. Management expects net income to stabilize around this level for several years. This year, Reese Corporation issued bonds payable. The contract with bondholders requires Reese Corporation to limit total dividends to not more than 25% of net income.

INSTRUCTIONS

Evaluate this situation from the perspective of:
a. Common shareholders
b. Preferred shareholders

**A&D 20-3
Improving Cash Flow
(LO 4)**

Reynolds Labs develops and manufactures pharmaceutical products. The company has been growing rapidly during the past 10 years, due primarily to having discovered, patented, and successfully marketed dozens of new products. Net income has increased annually by 30% or more. The company pays no dividend but has a very high price-earnings ratio. Due to its rapid growth and large expenditures for research and development, the company has experienced occasional cash shortages. To solve this problem, Reynolds has decided to improve its cash position by (1) requiring customers to pay for products purchased on account from the company in 30 days instead of 60 days and (2) reducing expenditures for research and development by 20%.

INSTRUCTIONS

Evaluate this situation from the perspective of:
a. Short-term creditors.
b. Common shareholders.

**A&D 20-4
Declining Interest Rate
(LO 4)**

Metro Utilities has outstanding 16 issues of bonds payable, with interest rates ranging from $5\frac{1}{2}$% to 14%. The company's rate of return on assets consistently averages 12%. Almost every year, the company issues additional bonds to finance growth, to pay maturing bonds, or to call (redeem) outstanding bonds when advantageous. During the current year, long-term interest rates have fallen dramatically. At the beginning of the year, these rates were between 12% and 13%; now, however, they are down to between 8% and 9%. Management currently is planning a large 8% bond issue.

INSTRUCTIONS

Evaluate this situation from the perspective of:
a. Holders of $5\frac{1}{2}$% bonds, maturing in 11 years but redeemable now at 103.
b. Holders of 14% bonds, maturing in 23 years but redeemable now at 103.
c. Common shareholders.

**A&D 20-5
Which One is Better?
(LO 3, 4, 5)**

The following presents certain financial information relating to two companies, London Toyland and Nathan Toymart as of the end of the current year. All figures (except market price per share of stock) are in ***thousands of dollars***.

Assets	London Toyland	Nathan Toymart
Cash	$ 252	$ 360
Marketable securities, at lower of cost and market	258	906
Accounts receivable, net	290	334
Inventories, at lower of cost and market	1,510	770
Prepaid expenses	50	30
Plant and equipment, net	3,360	3,140
Intangibles and other assets	280	60
Total assets	$6,000	$5,600

Liabilities & Shareholders' Equity		
Accounts payable	$ 690	$ 608
Accrued liabilities, including income taxes	310	192
Bonds payable, 8%, due in 10 years	400	1,000
Capital stock (London, 150,000 shares; Nathan, 120,000 shares)	2,780	2,700
Retained earnings	1,820	1,100
Total liabilities & shareholders' equity	$6,000	$5,600
Analysis of retained earnings:		
Balance, beginning of year	$1,424	$ 860
Add: Net income	690	480
Less: Dividends	(294)	(240)
Balance, end of year	$1,820	$1,100
Market price per share of stock, end of year	$ 46	$ 40
Net sales	$6,900	$6,000
Income taxes	$ 460	$ 320

INSTRUCTIONS

London Toyland and Nathan Toymart are generally comparable in the nature of their operations, products, and accounting procedures used. Use whatever analytical computations you feel will best support each of the following evaluations.

a. Evaluate these two companies from the perspective of short-term creditors and explain which company you feel is more credit worthy.

b. Evaluate these two companies from the perspective of common shareholders and explain which company you feel is a better investment.

Answers to Self-Test Questions

1. c **2.** a **3.** b **4.** d **5.** a, c, d **6.** c **7.** c **8.** b, c **9.** d

COMPREHENSIVE PROBLEM 6

LOBLAW COMPANIES LIMITED

Analysis of the Financial Statements of a Publicly Owned Corporation

The purpose of this Comprehensive Problem is to acquaint you with the content of an annual report and to provide you with the opportunity to analyze and to evaluate a real world situation. It is based upon the 1997 annual report of Loblaw Companies Limited, most of which is reproduced at the end of this textbook. The problem contains three major parts, which are independent of one another. *Part I* is designed to familiarize you with the content of an annual report; *Part II* involves analysis of the company's liquidity; and *Part III* focuses on the trend in its profitability.

If you work this problem as a group assignment, each group member should be prepared to discuss the group's findings and conclusions in class.

Note that Loblaw ends *its fiscal years on unusual dates*. This is because the company, under an accounting convention common in the food distribution industry, follows a 52-week reporting cycle that periodically necessitates a fiscal year of 53 weeks, such as the 1997 fiscal year.

Part I

Loblaw's annual report includes not only comparative financial statements, but also, among others, the following sources of information:

- Nature and scope of operation—such as corporate objectives and fundamental operating principles and geographic divisions.
- Report to shareholders—on current operations and future growth.
- Management discussion and analysis—explaining in detail the company's operating results and financial position of the current year and planned action for the next year.
- Notes to financial statements—such as on the accounting policies used and additional details regarding key items in the financial statements.
- Report by management on its responsibility for financial reporting.
- Auditors' report—in which the independent auditors express their opinion on the financial statements.
- Key operating results by quarter for a three-year period.
- An eleven-year summary of financial statistics.
- A corporate directory—showing the company's directors and officers.

- Shareholder information—such as the corporate address, stock listings, average trading volume, transfer agent and registrar, general counsel, and majority shareholder.

Answer each of the following questions and state **where** in the statements, notes, auditors' report, or other information in the annual report (presented at the end of this textbook) you located the information used in your answer.

a. What is the nature and scope of Loblaw's operations?
b. What is Loblaw's objective for its shareholders and what are its fundamental operating principles?
c. What is Loblaw's plan for Montreal in 1998 and beyond, and what is Loblaw's expected growth rate in sales for 1998 and 1999? Is this growth rate higher or lower than the rate for the total market?
d. What are the rates of return on common equity for 1995, 1996, and 1997? Are these rates increasing or decreasing?
e. Who is responsible for the content of the financial statements and other information in the annual report—the independent auditors, management, or the company's board of directors? In general terms, what measures have been undertaken by **management** to ensure reliability of the statements?
f. How many years are covered by the comparative financial statements? Were all of these statements audited? Name the auditors. What was the auditors' conclusion concerning these statements?
g. Over the past three years, have the company's annual cash flows been positive or negative from (1) operating activities, (2) investing activities, and (3) financing activities? Has the company's cash balance increased or decreased during each of these three years?
h. What were included in the 1997 sales of $11,008 million?
i. What depreciation method is used for the fixed assets and what are the estimated useful lives for buildings and for equipment and fixtures?
j. What is the percentage increase in sales for 1997 over 1996 and how much of this increase is attributed to the one extra week in the 1997 fiscal year?
k. What are the estimated capital expenditures for 1998? Are they more than 1997?
l. What was the amount of sales during the **fourth quarter** of the fiscal year ended January 3, 1998? What was the percentage change in this fourth quarter's sales relative to sales in the fourth quarter of the prior year?
m. Who is Loblaw's largest shareholder and what percentage of common shares does it own?

Part II

Assume that in early 1998 you are the credit manager of a potential supplier of Loblaw Companies Limited. Loblaw wants to make credit purchases from your company of between $20 million and $25 million per month, with payment due in 60 days.

INSTRUCTIONS

a. As part of your credit investigation, compute the following for the years ended January 3, 1998 and December 28, 1996. (Follow the company's policy of stating dollar amounts in millions.)
   1. Current ratio.
   2. Quick ratio
   3. Working capital.
   4. Percentage of current assets comprised of cash and cash equivalents.
   5. The increase (or decrease) in cash and cash equivalents in 1996 and 1997. (As defined by the new section 1540 of the *CICA Handbook*, which is different from the one used in the 1997 Loblaw's statements.)
   6. Accounts receivable turnover rate and the average number of days required to collect accounts receivable.

b. Does the company have lines of credit that could assist it in meeting its short-term obligations for cash payments?

c. Based upon your above analyses, has this company's liquidity *increased* or *decreased* during 1997? Explain. If you indicated that liquidity has decreased, explain whether you consider this a serious problem.

d. Comment on the company's current ratio, quick ratio, and accounts receivable turnover rate in relation to the general rules mentioned in Chapter 20 and the nature of the company's operations.

e. Your company assigns each customer one of the four credit ratings listed below. Assign a credit rating to Loblaw and write a memorandum explaining your decision. (In your memorandum, you may use any of your computations in **a** or **b**, and may refer to other information in the financial statements and in the annual report.)

Possible Credit Ratings

A **Outstanding.** Little or no risk of inability to pay. For customers in this category, we fill any reasonable order, without imposing a credit limit. The customer's credit is reevaluated annually.

B **Good.** Customer has good debt-paying ability, but is assigned a credit limit that is reviewed every four months. Orders above the established credit limit are accepted only on a cash basis.

C **Marginal.** Customer appears sound, but credit should be extended only on a 30-day basis with a relatively low credit limit. Credit status and credit limit are reevaluated every 90 days.

D **Unacceptable.** Customer does not qualify for credit.

Part III

Based on the information in Loblaw's annual report presented at the end of this text, answer the following:

INSTRUCTIONS

a. Compute the following for the fiscal years ending January 3, 1998 and December 28, 1996 (round percentages to the nearest tenth of one percent):

1. Percentage change in net sales (relative to the prior year).
2. Percentage change in net income.
3. Operating income as a percentage of sales.
4. Net income as a percentage of sales.
5. Return on average total assets.
6. Return on average common shareholders' equity.

b. Explain the significance of sales increase in the 1997 fiscal year.
c. Assume no dramatic changes in the retail and wholesale food distribution business. Prepare *your* estimate of Loblaw's sales for the 1998 fiscal year. Express your estimate as a **reasonable range** that you think will include the actual amount of sales, not as a single dollar amount. In developing your estimate, you may use any of the computations in **a**, as well as any other information included in the annual report. Explain fully *the reasoning* behind your estimate.

   Note: We are interested in your **reasoning processes**, not in the accuracy of your estimate. You are *not* to look up the actual sales for fiscal 1998.

d. Starting with your estimate of sales for fiscal 1998, estimate the range of **operating income** and **net income** that you expect the company to earn. Again, explain fully the reasoning behind your estimate.

e. At the end of 1997, the market price of the company's common shares was approximately $26 per share. Assume that sales, operating income, and net income increase to amounts right in the middle of your estimated ranges. Does this mean that the market price of the company's common shares also will increase during 1998? Explain.

CHAPTER 21

Introduction to Managerial Accounting; Accounting for Manufacturing Operations

Think of a business as a building under construction. Creditors and investors use financial reports in evaluating the success of the project. But managers act as the architects and engineers who oversee construction. They too use financial reports—but they also work daily with plans, schedules, building permits, and unforeseen problems. Thus, managers need much more information about the business than do "outsiders."

CHAPTER LEARNING OBJECTIVES

1. Distinguish between the fields of managerial accounting and financial accounting.
2. Describe the three basic types of manufacturing costs.
3. Distinguish between product costs and period costs.
4. Describe how manufacturing costs "flow" through perpetual inventory accounts.
5. Distinguish between direct and indirect manufacturing costs.
6. Explain the purpose of overhead application rates and the importance of basing these rates upon significant "cost drivers."
7. Prepare a schedule of the cost of finished goods manufactured.

INTRODUCTION TO MANAGERIAL ACCOUNTING

LO 1: Distinguish between the fields of managerial accounting and financial accounting.

In preceding chapters we emphasized the study of **financial accounting**. In doing so, we learned how economic events are analyzed, recorded, and reported in accordance with **generally accepted accounting principles**. More importantly, we discovered how outsiders, primarily investors and creditors, **use** financial information to analyze a company's profitability, solvency, and liquidity.

Beginning with this chapter, we shift our emphasis toward the study of managerial accounting. **Managerial accounting** (or management accounting) involves the preparation and use of accounting information for planning and controlling the operations of a business. In short, managerial accounting applies to the decision needs of **managers**, as opposed to the decision needs of investors and creditors.

Since managerial information is used exclusively by company insiders, report contents and formats are **not** governed by generally accepted accounting principles or by income tax rules. Instead, managerial reports are designed to **best suit the needs of those who use them**. In this regard, perhaps the greatest challenge to managerial accountants is determining what information is most relevant to a particular business decision.

The diagram on the following page compares the basic characteristics of financial and managerial accounting. Notice that both types of information are developed within the same accounting information **system**. Thus, the system must be designed to provide customized reports used by management as well as general purpose financial statements used primarily by investors and creditors.

Managerial Accounting

Managerial accounting may be divided into two broad categories: (1) **cost accounting**, emphasizing the determination of what it costs to perform specific business activities and to manufacture products, and (2) **managerial planning and decision making**. These closely related topics provide an overview of the nature and use of managerial accounting information.

Cost Accounting Before deciding upon a course of action, managers usually ask, "What will it cost?" The accounting concepts and procedures for measuring the cost of performing different business activities and of manufacturing various products are termed **cost accounting**.

THE ACCOUNTING SYSTEM

Financial Accounting

Purpose
To provide a wide variety of decision makers with useful information about the financial position and operating results of a business entity.

Types of Reports
Financial statements, income tax returns, and special reports, such as loan applications and reports to regulatory agencies or authorities.

Standards for Presentation
In financial statements, generally accepted accounting principles. In income tax returns, tax regulations.

Reporting Entity
Usually the company viewed as a whole.

Time Periods Covered
Usually a year, quarter, or month. Most reports focus upon completed periods. Emphasis is placed on the current (latest) period, with prior periods often shown for comparison.

Users of the Information
Outsiders as well as managers. For financial statements, these outsiders include shareholders, creditors, prospective investors, tax and regulatory authorities, and the general public. Income tax returns normally go only to tax authorities.

Managerial Accounting

Purpose
To provide managers with information useful in planning and controlling business operations, and in making managerial decisions.

Types of Reports
Many different types of reports, depending upon the nature of the business and the specific information needs of management.

Standards for Presentation
No specific rules; whatever information is most relevant to the needs of management.

Reporting Entity
Usually a subdivision of the business, such as a department, a product line, or a type of activity.

Time Periods Covered
Any period: year, quarter, month, week, day, even a work shift. Some reports are historical in nature; others focus on estimates of results expected in future periods.

Users of the Information
Management (different reports to different managers). Managerial accounting reports usually are not distributed to outsiders.

Cost information is critical in setting prices, determining whether resources are being used efficiently, and evaluating which product lines are most profitable. Cost figures are also essential in monitoring support functions within the business, including the operations of personnel, marketing, and accounting departments.

Managerial Planning and Decision Making The term *planning* refers to the setting of objectives and goals for future performance. Managers must constantly make decisions regarding plans for production, for growth, and for achieving performance goals. The effectiveness of their planning and decision making often depends on the relevance and reliability of the accounting information they receive, and upon their ability to interpret this information correctly.

Due to rapidly evolving information needs of business managers, the study of managerial accounting may be continued throughout one's professional career. To encourage a professional level of training and competence for managerial accountants, the provincial societies of Certified Management Accountants offer a program leading to the CMA designation. To become a *CMA*, an individual must (1) complete a university degree with prerequisite studies, (2) pass an entrance examination (8-hour over 2 days), and (3) complete a two-year professional program that focuses on leading edge management accounting practices and advanced management concepts.

The Interdisciplinary Nature of Managerial Accounting

We hope that preceding chapters have convinced you that an understanding of financial accounting is important to *anyone* confronting an investment or credit decision. Similarly, managerial accounting serves an interdisciplinary audience as well. In fact, anyone functioning in a managerial capacity—market researchers, health care professionals, school administrators, or concert hall managers—will benefit from a basic understanding of managerial accounting principles.

The Overlap of Managerial and Financial Accounting

It is useful to recognize that financial and managerial accounting are *not* entirely separate disciplines. In fact, certain financial information is widely used in managerial decisions. For example, it is common for managers to use information about revenues, expenses, and income taxes in their daily decisions. However, they typically require that revenues and expenses be broken down by department or by product line. In short, much managerial information is financial information, rearranged to suit a particular managerial purpose.

ACCOUNTING FOR MANUFACTURING OPERATIONS

A merchandising company buys its inventory in a ready-to-sell condition. Therefore, its cost of goods sold is simply the purchase price of the products it sells. A *manufacturing* company, however, *produces* the goods that it sells. As a consequence, its cost of goods sold consists of various **manufacturing costs**, including the cost of materials, wages earned by production workers, and a variety of other costs relating to the operation of a production facility.[1]

---

[1] Manufacturing costs are the cost of producing inventory, which is an asset. Therefore, these expenditures are termed *costs* rather than *expenses*. Unexpired costs are assets; expired costs are expenses.

Manufacturing operations are an excellent example of how managerial and financial accounting overlap because manufacturing costs are of vital importance to both financial and managerial accountants. Financial accountants use manufacturing costs to determine the cost of goods sold and inventory values reported in financial statements. Managerial accountants also rely upon prompt and reliable information about manufacturing costs to help answer such questions as:

- What sales price must we charge for our products to earn a reasonable profit?
- Is it possible to lower the cost of producing a particular product line in order to be more price competitive?
- Is it less expensive to buy certain parts used in our products than to manufacture these parts ourselves?
- Should we automate our production process with a robotic assembly line?

Classifications of Manufacturing Costs

A typical manufacturing company purchases raw materials and converts these materials into finished goods through the process of production. The conversion from raw materials to finished goods results from utilizing a combination of labour and machinery. Thus, manufacturing costs are often divided into three broad categories:

LO 2: Describe the three basic types of manufacturing costs.

1. **Direct materials**—the raw materials and component parts used in production whose costs are directly traceable to the products manufactured.
2. **Direct labour**—wages and other payroll costs of employees whose efforts are directly traceable to the products they manufacture, either by hand or with machinery.
3. **Manufacturing overhead**—a "catch-all" classification, which includes all manufacturing costs *other than* the costs of direct materials and direct labour. Examples include factory utilities, supervisor salaries, equipment repairs, and depreciation on machinery.

It is important to note that manufacturing costs are *not* immediately recorded as current period expenses. Rather, they are costs of *creating inventory*, and they remain on the balance sheet until the inventory is sold. For this reason, manufacturing costs are often called ***product costs*** (or inventoriable costs).

Product Costs Versus Period Costs

LO 3: Distinguish between product costs and period costs.

The terms ***product costs*** and ***period costs*** are helpful in explaining the difference between manufacturing costs and operating expenses. In a manufacturing environment, ***product costs*** are those costs incurred to manufacture inventory. Thus, until the related goods are sold, product costs ***represent inventory***. As such, they are reported on the balance sheet as an asset. When the goods are ultimately sold, product costs are transferred from the balance sheet to the income statement, where they are deducted from revenue as the cost of goods sold.

Operating expenses that are associated with *time periods*, rather than with the production of inventory, are referred to as **period costs**. Period costs are charged directly to expense accounts on the assumption that their benefit is recognized entirely in the period when the cost is incurred. Period costs include all selling expenses, general and administrative expenses, interest expense, and income tax expenses. In short, period costs are classified on the income statement separately from cost of goods sold, as deductions from a company's gross profit.

The following diagram shows the flow of product costs and period costs through the financial statements.

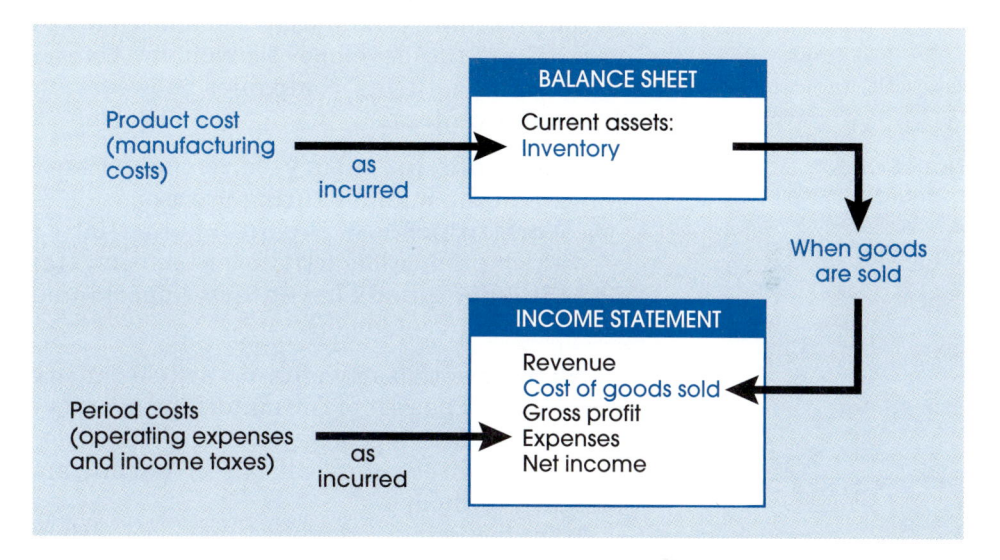

To further illustrate the distinction between product and period costs, consider two costs that, on the surface, appear quite similar: the depreciation of a warehouse used to store raw materials versus depreciation of a warehouse used to store finished goods. Depreciation of the raw materials warehouse is considered a ***product cost*** (a component of manufacturing overhead) because the building is part of the manufacturing process. Once the manufacturing process is complete and the finished goods are available for sale, all costs associated with their storage are considered selling expenses. Thus, the depreciation of the finished goods warehouse is a ***period cost***.

Product Costs and the Matching Principle

Underlying the distinction between product costs and period costs is a familiar financial accounting concept—the ***matching principle***. In short, product costs should be reported on the income statement only when they can be matched against product revenue. To illustrate, consider a real estate developer who starts a tract of ten homes in May of the current year. During the year, the developer incurs material, labour, and overhead costs amounting to $1 million dollars (assume $100,000 per house). By the end of December, all the houses have been completed but none has been sold. How much of the $1 million in construction costs should appear on the developer's income statement for the current year?

The answer is **none**. These costs are not related to any revenue earned by the developer during the current year. Instead, they are related to future revenues the developer will earn when the houses are eventually sold. Therefore, at the end of the current year, the $1 million of product costs should appear in the developer's balance sheet as **inventory**. As each house is sold, $100,000 will be deducted from sales revenue as cost of goods sold. This way, the developer's income statements in future periods will properly match sales revenue with the cost of each sale.

Inventories of a Manufacturing Business

In the preceding example, all ten houses were completed by the end of the year. Thus, the developer's inventory consisted only of finished goods. Most manufacturing companies, however, typically account for *three types* of inventory:

> Not all of a manufacturer's inventory is in a "ready to sell" condition

1. **Materials inventory**—direct materials on hand and available for use in the manufacturing process.
2. **Work in process inventory**—partially completed goods upon which production activities have been started but not yet completed.
3. **Finished goods inventory**—unsold finished products available for sale to customers.

All three of these inventories are classified on the balance sheet as current assets. The cost of the materials inventory is based upon its purchase price. The work in process and finished goods inventories are based upon the cost of direct material, direct labour, and manufacturing overhead assigned to them.

Manufacturing companies may use either a perpetual or a periodic inventory system. Perpetual systems have many advantages, however, such as providing managers with up-to-date information about the amounts of inventory on hand and the per-unit costs of manufacturing products. For these reasons, virtually all large manufacturing companies use *perpetual inventory systems*. Also, the flow of manufacturing costs through the inventory accounts and into the cost of goods sold is most easily illustrated in a perpetual inventory system. Therefore, we will assume the use of a perpetual inventory system in our discussion of manufacturing activities.

The Flow of Costs Parallels the Flow of Physical Goods

> LO 4: Describe how manufacturing costs "flow" through perpetual inventory accounts.

When a perpetual inventory system is in use, the flow of manufacturing costs through the company's general ledger accounts closely parallels the physical flow of goods through the production process. This relationship is illustrated on the next page. The grey shaded boxes in the bottom portion of the diagram represent six **general ledger accounts** used by manufacturing companies to account for their production activities: (1) Materials Inventory, (2) Direct Labour, (3) Manufacturing Overhead, (4) Work in Process Inventory, (5) Finished Goods Inventory, and (6) Cost of Goods Sold.

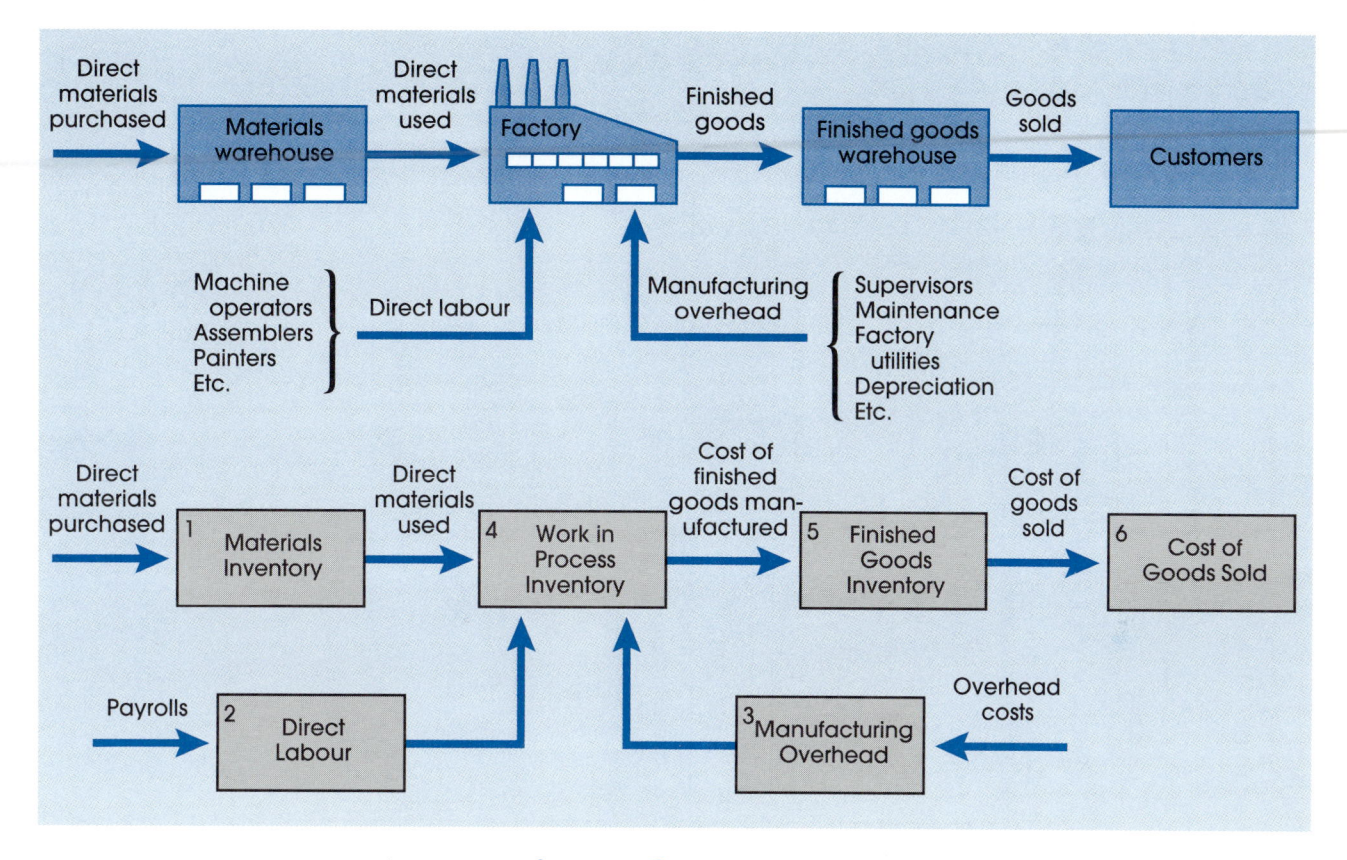

Accounting for Manufacturing Costs: An Illustration

To illustrate accounting for manufacturing costs, we will assume that Conquest Inc. manufactures high-quality mountain bikes in Calgary, Alberta. The company relies upon cost information to monitor its production efficiency, set prices, and maintain control over its inventories.

Conquest carefully tracks the flow of manufacturing costs through its general ledger accounts as illustrated on the following page. The figures shown represent all of Conquest's manufacturing costs for 2001. The debit and credit entries summarize the numerous transactions recorded by the company throughout the year.

Our use of several colours in this illustration will help you follow the flow of manufacturing costs through these accounts. The beginning balances in the three inventory accounts are shown in black. Manufacturing costs, and the arrows showing the transfer of these costs from one account to another, are shown in dark blue. Account balances at year-end, which will appear in the company's financial statements, are shown in light blue.

Let us now look more closely at exactly how the company's manufacturing costs flow through these general ledger accounts.

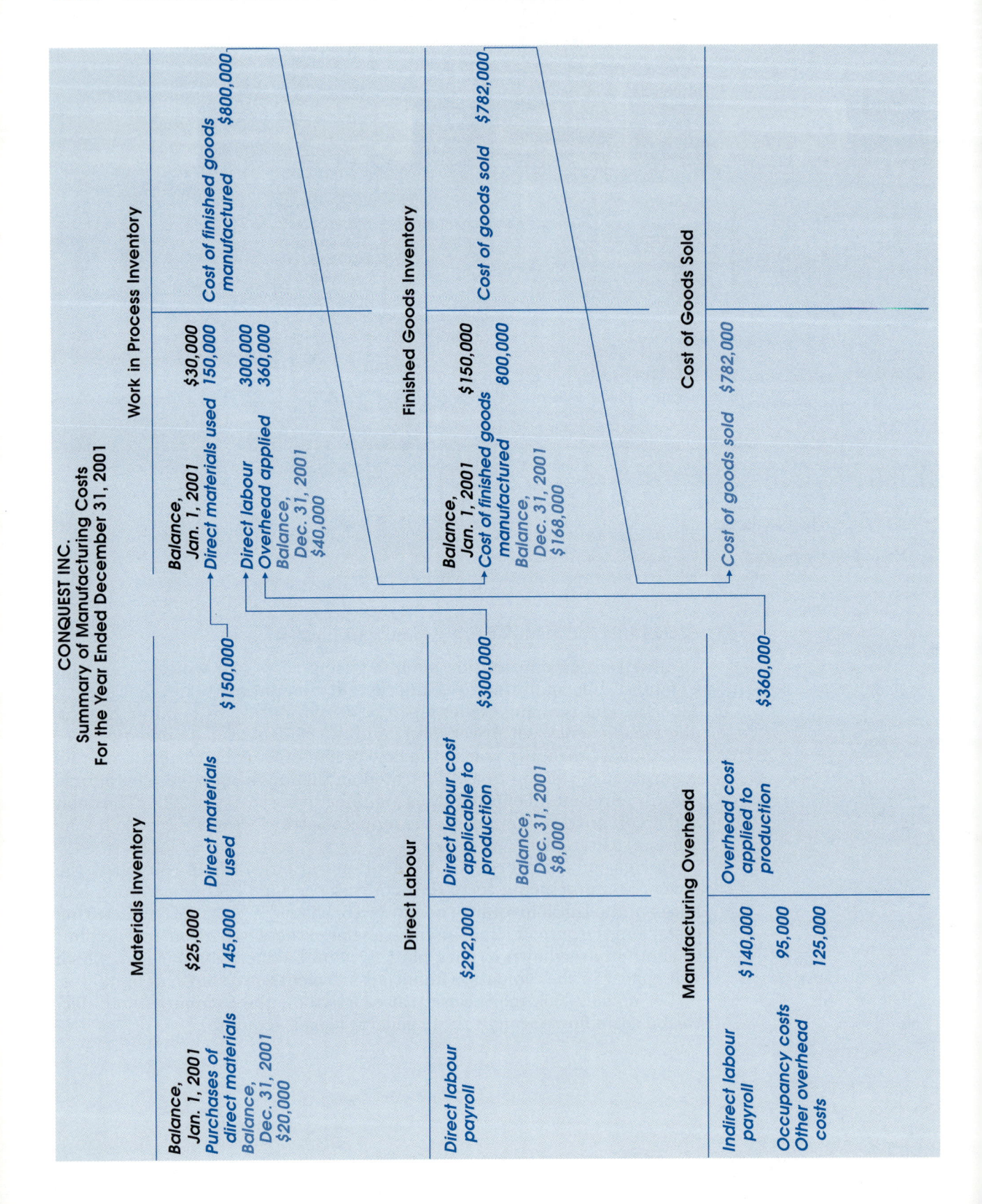

CONQUEST INC.
Summary of Manufacturing Costs
For the Year Ended December 31, 2001

Materials Inventory

Balance, Jan. 1, 2001	$25,000	Direct materials used	145,000
Purchases of direct materials			
Balance, Dec. 31, 2001	$20,000		

Direct materials used → $150,000

Work in Process Inventory

Balance, Jan. 1, 2001	$30,000	Cost of finished goods manufactured	$800,000
Direct materials used	150,000		
Direct labour	300,000		
Overhead applied	360,000		
Balance, Dec. 31, 2001	$40,000		

Direct Labour

Direct labour payroll	$292,000	Direct labour cost applicable to production	$300,000
Balance, Dec. 31, 2001	$8,000		

Direct labour cost applicable to production → $300,000

Finished Goods Inventory

Balance, Jan. 1, 2001	$150,000	Cost of goods sold	$782,000
Cost of finished goods manufactured	800,000		
Balance, Dec. 31, 2001	$168,000		

Manufacturing Overhead

Indirect labour payroll	$140,000	Overhead cost applied to production	$360,000
Occupancy costs	95,000		
Other overhead costs	125,000		

Overhead cost applied to production → $360,000

Cost of Goods Sold

Cost of goods sold $782,000

Direct Materials

Direct materials are the raw materials and component parts that become an integral part of finished products and can be traced directly and conveniently to products manufactured. Conquest's direct materials include light-weight alloy tubing for cycle frames, brakes, shifting levers, peddles, sprockets, tires, etc. The mountain bikes assembled from these components are Conquest's ***finished goods***.

The terms ***direct materials*** and ***finished goods*** are defined from the viewpoint of individual manufacturing companies. For example, Conquest views brake components as a direct material. However, Quinset Point Limited (a brake manufacturer) views the brake components it sells to Conquest as finished goods.

Conquest uses a perpetual inventory system. Accordingly, the costs of direct materials purchased are debited directly to the Materials Inventory account. As these materials are placed into production, their costs are transferred from the Materials Inventory account to the Work in Process Inventory account by debiting Work in Process Inventory and crediting Materials Inventory. The balance remaining in the Materials Inventory account at year-end represents the cost of direct materials on hand and ready for use.

Some materials used in the production process cannot be traced conveniently or directly to the finished goods manufactured. For Conquest, examples include bearing grease, welding materials, and material used in factory maintenance such as cleaning compounds. These items are referred to as **indirect materials** and are classified as part of manufacturing overhead.

Direct Labour

The Direct Labour account is used to record the payroll cost of direct workers and assign this cost to the goods they help manufacture.[2] Direct workers are those employees who work directly on the goods being manufactured, either by hand or with machines.

Conquest employs five classifications of direct labourers. Each classification and its corresponding job description is shown below:

Classification	Job Description
Cutters	*Cut alloy tubing into appropriate lengths.*
Welders	*Transform the cut pieces of alloy tubing into bicycle frames.*
Painters	*Prime and paint each frame.*
Assemblers	*Partially assemble each bicycle in preparation for packing.*
Packers	*Pack the partially assembled bicycles in boxes.*

---

[2] As explained in Chapter 11, payroll costs include such factors as payroll taxes and "fringe benefits" as well as the wages earned by employees.

There are two separate and distinct aspects of accounting for direct labour costs. The first involves the **payment** of cash made to the direct workers at the end of each pay period. At each payroll date, the Direct Labour account is debited for the total direct labour payroll, and an offsetting credit is made to Cash. The second aspect involves the **application** of direct labour costs to the goods being produced. As direct labour employees contribute to the production process during the period, the cost of their labour is **applied** to production by debiting the Work in Process Inventory account and crediting the Direct Labour account.

In our T accounts on page 1060, the flow of direct labour costs looks similar to the flow of direct materials costs. There is, however, one significant difference. Materials are purchased **before** they are used; therefore, the Materials Inventory account has a **debit** balance equal to the cost of unused materials on hand. The services of employees, however, are used before the employees are paid. Thus, the credits to the Direct Labour account are recorded **throughout** the payroll period, but the debits are not recorded until the **end** of the payroll period. If the balance sheet date falls between payroll dates, the Direct Labour account will have a **credit** balance representing the amount owed to employees for work already performed. This credit balance should be listed in the balance sheet as **wages payable**, a current liability.

Many employees in a manufacturing plant do not work directly on the goods being manufactured. Examples at Conquest include factory supervisors, maintenance personnel, forklift drivers, and security guards. These **indirect labour** costs, which are handled in a fashion similar to that used for indirect materials costs, are considered part of Conquest's manufacturing overhead.

Manufacturing Overhead

All manufacturing costs **other than** direct materials and direct labour are classified as **manufacturing overhead**. The Manufacturing Overhead account is used to record all costs classified as "overhead" and assign these costs to products being manufactured.

There are many types of overhead costs. Consequently, Manufacturing Overhead is treated as a **controlling account** for which subsidiary records are typically maintained to keep track of various overhead classifications.

Because of the diverse nature of manufacturing companies, it simply isn't possible to prepare a complete list of all overhead cost types. However, specific examples at Conquest include:

1. *Indirect materials costs*
    a. Factory supplies that do not become an integral part of finished goods, such as oil used to lubricate the cutting machines and solvents used to clean the painting machines
    b. Materials that become an integral part of finished goods but whose cost would require great effort to actually trace to finished goods. These items include grease used in each bike's bearing assembly and the nuts and bolts used to attach shift levers and other component parts

2. *Indirect labour costs*
    a. Supervisors' salaries
    b. Salaries of factory maintenance workers, forklift drivers, receiving clerks in the materials warehouse, and factory security personnel
3. *Plant occupancy costs*
    a. Depreciation of the factory and the materials warehouse
    b. Insurance and property taxes on land and buildings
    c. Maintenance and repairs on buildings
    d. Utilities and telephone costs
4. *Machinery and equipment costs*
    a. Depreciation of machinery
    b. Maintenance of machinery
5. *Cost of regulatory compliance*
    a. Meeting factory safety requirements
    b. Disposal of waste materials such as empty paint canisters
    c. Control over factory emissions (meeting clean air standards)

Selling expenses and general and administrative expenses do **not** relate to the manufacturing process and are **not** included in manufacturing overhead. Certain costs, such as insurance, property taxes, and utilities, sometimes apply in part to manufacturing operations and in part to administrative and selling functions. In such cases, these costs are *apportioned* among manufacturing overhead, general and administrative expenses, and selling expenses.

Recording Overhead Costs The Manufacturing Overhead account is debited to record any cost classified as "overhead." Examples of costs debited to this account include the payment of indirect labour payrolls, the payment of factory utilities, the recording of depreciation on factory assets, and the purchase of indirect materials.[3] The account credited will vary depending on the nature of the overhead cost. For example, in recording the purchase of indirect materials, the account credited is usually Accounts Payable. In recording depreciation on machinery, however, the account credited is Accumulated Depreciation.

As the items included in total overhead costs are "consumed" by production activities, the related costs are transferred from the Manufacturing Overhead account into the Work in Process Inventory account (debit Work in Process Inventory, credit Manufacturing Overhead). In the course of the year, all the overhead costs incurred should be assigned to units of product manufactured. Thus, at year-end, the Manufacturing Overhead account should have a zero balance.

---

[3] Some companies record the purchase of indirect materials in the Materials Inventory account or in a separate inventory account. Our approach is commonly used when the quantity of indirect materials purchased does not differ significantly from the quantity of indirect materials used during each period.

Direct and Indirect Manufacturing Costs

LO 5: Distinguish between direct and indirect manufacturing costs.

The costs of direct materials and direct labour may be traced conveniently and directly into specific units of product. At Conquest, for example, it is relatively easy to determine the cost of the metal tubing and the cost of the direct labour that go into making a particular bicycle. For this reason, accountants call these items **direct manufacturing costs.**

Overhead, however, is an **indirect manufacturing cost**. Consider, for example, the types of costs that Conquest classifies as overhead. These costs include property taxes on the factory, depreciation on tools and equipment, supervisors' salaries, and repairs to equipment. How much of these indirect costs should be assigned to each bicycle?

There is no easy answer to this question. By definition, indirect costs ***cannot*** be traced easily and directly to specific units of production. While these costs are often easier to view ***as a whole*** than on a per-unit basis, we will see that both financial and managerial accountants require unit cost information. Therefore, manufacturing companies must develop methods of allocating an appropriate portion of total manufacturing overhead to each product manufactured. The allocation of overhead costs to production is accomplished through the use of **overhead application rates**.

Overhead Application Rates

LO 6: Explain the purpose of overhead application rates and the importance of basing these rates upon significant "cost drivers."

There are two reasons why manufacturing overhead isn't applied to products by simply dividing the company's annual overhead cost by the number of units produced during the year. First, total overhead costs and total units produced are not known until the end of the period. Second, not all products "consume" an equal amount of overhead cost.

Thus, overhead application rates are used to assign manufacturing overhead costs to specific units of production as those units are being produced throughout the accounting period. The rate expresses an expected relationship between manufacturing overhead costs and some ***activity base*** related to the production process (direct labour hours, machine hours, etc.) Overhead is then assigned to products ***in proportion*** to this activity base. For example, a company using direct labour hours as an activity base would allocate the greatest proportion of its overhead costs to those products requiring the most direct labour hours.

The overhead application rate is determined at the ***beginning*** of the period and is based on ***estimated*** amounts. The rate is typically computed as follows:

$$\text{Overhead application rate} = \frac{\text{Estimated manufacturing overhead costs}}{\text{Estimated units in the activity base}}$$

The mechanics of computing and using an overhead application rate are quite simple. The challenging problems for accountants are: (1) selecting an appropriate activity base, and (2) making reliable estimates at the beginning of the accounting period regarding the total of the overhead costs to be incurred, and the total units in the activity base that will be required.[4] We will examine the easy topics first—the mechanics underlying the computation and use of overhead application rates.

Computation and Use of Overhead Application Rates Assume that at the beginning of 2001, Conquest's management makes the following estimates relating to bicycle manufacturing activity for the upcoming year:

Estimated total manufacturing overhead costs for the year	*$360,000*
Estimated total direct labour hours for the year	*30,000 hours*
Estimated total machine hours for the year	*10,000 hours*

Using the above estimations, we will illustrate the use of an overhead application rate under two independent assumptions:

Assumption 1: Conquest Uses Direct Labour Hours as Its "Activity Base" If Conquest uses direct labour hours to apply overhead costs, the application rate will be ***$12 per direct labour hour*** ($360,000 of estimated overhead costs, divided by 30,000 estimated direct labour hours). Throughout the year, manufacturing overhead costs will be assigned in direct proportion to the *actual* direct labour hours required to manufacture the bicycles produced. For example, if a production run of a particular bicycle model uses 200 direct labour hours, $2,400 of manufacturing overhead will be assigned to those units (200 direct labour hours used, multiplied by the $12 application rate). The assignment will be made by debiting the Work in Process Inventory account and crediting the Manufacturing Overhead account for $2,400.

Assumption 2: Conquest Uses Machine Hours as Its "Activity Base" If Conquest chooses to use machine hours to apply overhead costs, its application rate will be ***$36 per machine hour*** ($360,000 of estimated overhead costs, divided by 10,000 estimated machine hours). Using this approach, manufacturing overhead costs will be assigned to bicycles based on the number of machine hours required to produce them. If 10 machine hours are required for a particular production run, the bicycles in that run will be assigned $360 of overhead costs (10 hours times $36 per hour). Again, the assignment will be made by debiting the Work in Process Inventory account and crediting the Manufacturing Overhead account for $360.

What "Drives" Overhead Costs?

For overhead application rates to provide reliable results, an activity base must be a significant "driver" of overhead costs. To be a **cost driver**, an

---

[4] Errors in estimating the amount of total overhead costs for the coming period or the number of units in the activity base will cause differences between the actual overhead incurred and the amounts assigned to units manufactured. These differences usually are small and are eliminated by an adjusting entry at the end of the accounting period.

activity base must be a ***causal factor*** in the incurrence of overhead costs. In other words, an increase in the number of activity base units (e.g., direct labour hours worked) must cause a proportional increase in the actual overhead costs incurred.

Historically, direct labour hours (or direct labour costs) were viewed as the primary driver of overhead costs—and for good reason. Products that required more direct labour often required more indirect labour (supervision), resulted in more wear and tear on machinery (maintenance costs), and consumed a greater amount of factory supplies. Therefore, many manufacturing companies followed the practice of applying all manufacturing overhead costs in proportion to direct labour hours or direct labour costs.

As factories became more highly automated, direct labour became much less of a causal factor in driving many overhead costs. Today, many manufacturing companies find that activity bases such as machine hours, computer time, or the time required to set up a production run result in a more realistic allocation of overhead costs.

CASE IN POINT Historically, the automobile industry was primarily labour intensive. But today, due to the increased use of robotics, it takes only 15 to 20 hours of direct labour to assemble a car. For instance, Toyota's labour costs are about 20% of total revenue, Chrysler's constitute 19%, and Volvo's only 18%.

The Use of Multiple Overhead Application Rates In an attempt to gain a more realistic picture of what it costs to manufacture different types of products, many companies have begun to implement overhead allocation techniques that rely upon the use of ***multiple*** allocation bases. One such approach, **activity-based costing** is illustrated in the appendix following this chapter.

In essence, activity-based costing uses multiple allocation bases that represent different types of manufacturing overhead costs. For instance, machine maintenance costs may be allocated using machine hours as an activity base, whereas supervision costs may be allocated using direct labour hours. Different application rates may also be used in each production department and in applying overhead costs to different types of products.

The key point is that each manufactured product should be charged with the overhead costs ***generated by*** the manufacture of that product. If the activity base used to apply overhead costs is ***not*** a primary overhead cost driver, the relative production cost of different products may become ***significantly distorted***.

Consider, for example, a company that makes one product that is highly labour intensive and another product on a highly automated assembly line. Due to the extremely high maintenance and electricity costs associated with the automation process, the automated assembly line is responsible for 80% of the company's total overhead cost. If manufacturing overhead is allocated in proportion to direct labour hours, the labour intensive products will be assigned too much of the total cost. The product responsible for most of these high overhead costs will be charged with a relatively small share of the total allocation. This, in turn, may lead to many faulty decisions on the part of management.

> **CASE IN POINT** A large dairy products company allocated its overhead costs to production in proportion to the amount of butterfat used in each product. The quantity of butterfat used in producing a product had been a major driver of overhead costs until the dairy began producing dehydrated milk.
>
> The manufacture of dehydrated milk required the use of expensive machinery and greatly increased overhead costs. However, the dehydrated milk contained almost no butterfat. Based on the "butterfat method" of allocating overhead costs, the increased overhead stemming from the manufacture of dehydrated milk was allocated primarily to ice cream and other products high in butterfat. The cost of manufacturing dehydrated milk appeared to be quite low, because almost no overhead costs were allocated to this product.
>
> As a result of the distorted cost figures, management cut back on the production of ice cream and increased production of dehydrated milk. This strategy, however, resulted in a substantial decline in the company's profitability. Only after a business consultant pointed out the improper allocation of overhead costs did management learn that ice cream was the company's most profitable product, and that dehydrated milk was being sold to customers at a price below its actual production cost.

The Increasing Importance of Proper Overhead Allocation In today's global economy, competition among manufacturing companies is greater than ever before. If a company is to determine whether it can compete effectively in the marketplace, it must first know with some degree of precision its manufacturing costs on a per-unit basis. In highly automated factories, overhead is often the largest of the three basic categories of manufacturing costs. Therefore, the proper allocation of overhead costs is one of the major challenges facing managerial accountants.

Work in Process Inventory, Finished Goods Inventory, and the Cost of Goods Sold

We have devoted much of this chapter to discussing the three types of manufacturing costs—direct materials, direct labour, and manufacturing overhead. We will now shift our attention to the three accounts that provide the structure for the flow of these costs—the Work in Process Inventory account, the Finished Goods Inventory account, and the Cost of Goods Sold account.

The Work in Process Inventory account is used (1) to record the accumulation of manufacturing costs associated with the units of product worked on during the period, and (2) to allocate these costs between those units completed during the period and those that are only partially completed.

As direct materials, direct labour, and manufacturing overhead are applied to production, their related costs are debited to the Work in

Process Inventory account. The flow of costs into this inventory account (rather than into a corresponding expense account) is consistent with the idea that manufacturing costs are **product costs**, not period costs.

As specific units are completed, the cost of manufacturing them is transferred from the Work in Process Inventory account to the Finished Goods Inventory account. Thus, the balance in the Work in Process account represents only the manufacturing costs associated with units still "in process."

It is important to realize that once products are classified as finished goods, *no additional costs are allocated to them*. Therefore, the costs of storing, marketing, or delivering finished goods are regarded as **selling expenses**, not manufacturing costs. When units of finished goods are sold, their related costs must "flow" from the balance sheet through the income statement in compliance with the matching principle. Accordingly, as products are sold, their costs are transferred from the Finished Goods Inventory account to the Cost of Goods Sold account.

The Need for Per-Unit Cost Data

Transferring the cost of specific units from one account to another requires knowledge of each unit's **per-unit cost**—that is, the total manufacturing costs assigned to specific units. The determination of unit cost is one of the primary goals of every cost accounting system.

Unit costs are of importance to both financial and managerial accountants. Financial accountants use unit costs in recording the transfer of completed goods from Work in Process to Finished Goods and from Finished Goods to Cost of Goods Sold. Managerial accountants use the same information to make pricing decisions, evaluate the efficiency of current operations, and plan for future operations.

Determining the Cost of Finished Goods Manufactured

LO 7: Prepare a schedule of the cost of finished goods manufactured.

Most manufacturing companies prepare a **schedule of the cost of finished goods manufactured** to provide managers with an overview of manufacturing activities during the period. Using the information from our illustration on page 1060, a schedule of Conquest's cost of finished goods manufactured is as follows.

CHAPTER 21 INTRODUCTION TO MANAGERIAL ACCOUNTING; ACCOUNTING FOR MANUFACTURING OPERATIONS 1069

CONQUEST INC.
Schedule of the Cost of Finished Goods Manufactured
For the Year Ended December 31, 2001.

Work in process inventory, beginning of the year		$ 30,000
Manufacturing cost assigned to production:		
Direct materials used	$150,000	
Direct labour	300,000	
Manufacturing overhead	360,000	
Total manufacturing costs		810,000
Total cost of all work in process during the year		$840,000
Less: Work in process inventory, end of the year		(40,000)
Cost of finished goods manufactured		$800,000

Notice that all of the figures in this schedule were obtained from Conquest's Work in Process Inventory account illustrated on page 1060. In short, this schedule summarizes the flow of manufacturing costs into and out of the Work in Process Inventory account.

Purpose of the Schedule A schedule of the cost of finished goods manufactured is *not* a formal financial statement and generally does not appear in the company's annual report. Rather, it is intended primarily to *assist managers* in understanding and evaluating the overall cost of manufacturing products. By comparing these schedules for successive periods, for example, managers can determine whether direct labour or manufacturing overhead is rising or falling as a percentage of total manufacturing costs. In addition, the schedule is helpful in developing information about unit costs.

If a company manufactures only a single product line, its *cost per unit* simply equals its *cost of finished goods manufactured* divided by the *number of units produced*. For example, if Conquest produces only one line of mountain bike, its average cost per unit would be *$80* had it produced *10,000* finished units during 2001 ($800,000 divided by 10,000 units). If Conquest produced multiple lines of mountain bikes, it would prepare a separate schedule of the cost of finished goods manufactured for *each product line*.

Financial Statements of a Manufacturing Company

Let us now illustrate how the information used in our example will be reported in the 2001 income statement and balance sheet of Conquest Inc.

The company's 2001 income statement is presented as follows:

CONQUEST INC.
Income Statement
For the Year Ended December 31, 2001

Sales		$1,300,000
Cost of goods sold		782,000
Gross profit		$ 518,000
Operating expenses:		
Selling expenses	$135,000	
General and administrative expenses	265,000	
Total operating expenses		400,000
Income from operations		$ 118,000
Less: Interest expense		18,000
Income before income taxes		$ 100,000
Income taxes expenses		30,000
Net income		$ 70,000

Notice that no manufacturing costs appear among the company's operating expenses. In fact, manufacturing costs appear in only two places in a manufacturer's financial statements. Costs associated with units **sold** during the period appear in the income statement as the **cost of goods sold**. The $782,000 cost of goods sold figure reported in Conquest's income statement was taken directly from the company's perpetual inventory records. However, this amount may be verified as follows:

Beginning finished goods inventory, Jan. 1, 2001	$150,000
Add: Cost of finished goods manufactured during the year	800,000
Cost of finished goods available for sale	$950,000
Less: Ending finished goods inventory, Dec. 31, 2001	168,000
Cost of Goods Sold	$782,000

All manufacturing costs associated with goods **still on hand** are classified as **inventory** and appear in the balance sheet. The balance sheet presentation of Conquest's three types of inventory is illustrated below:

CONQUEST INC.
Partial Balance Sheet
December 31, 2001

Notice the three types of inventory

Current assets:		
Cash and cash equivalents		$ 60,000
Accounts receivable (net of allowance for doubtful accounts)		190,000
Inventories:		
Materials	$ 20,000	
Work in process	40,000	
Finished goods	168,000	228,000
Total current assets		$478,000

As previously mentioned, Conquest's balance sheet includes a current liability for wages payable equal to the $8,000 credit balance in the Direct Labour account.

End-of-Chapter Review

Key Terms Introduced or Emphasized in Chapter 21

Activity-based costing *(p.1066)* A method of allocating manufacturing overhead to products using multiple application rates and a wide variety of cost drivers.

Cost accounting *(p.1053)* The accounting concepts and practices used in determining the costs of manufacturing various products or of performing different business activities.

Cost driver *(p.1065)* An activity base that can be traced directly to units produced and that serves as a causal factor in the incurrence of overhead costs. Serves as an activity base in an **overhead application rate**.

Direct labour *(p.1056)* Payroll costs for employees who work directly on the products being manufactured, either by hand or with tools or machine.

Direct manufacturing cost *(p.1064)* A manufacturing cost that can be traced conveniently and directly into the quantity of finished goods manufactured. Examples include **direct materials** and **direct labour**.

Direct materials *(p.1056)* Materials and component parts that become an integral part of the manufactured goods and can be traced directly to the finished products.

Finished goods inventory *(p.1058)* The completed units that have emerged from the manufacturing process and are on hand available for sale.

Indirect labour *(p.1062)* Payroll costs relating to factory employees who do not work directly upon the goods being manufactured. Examples are wages of security guards and maintenance personnel. Indirect labour costs are classified as **manufacturing overhead**.

Indirect manufacturing cost *(p.1064)* A manufacturing cost that cannot be conveniently traced into the specific products being manufactured. Examples include property taxes, depreciation on machinery, and other types of **manufacturing overhead**.

Indirect materials *(p.1061)* Materials used in the manufacturing process that cannot be traced conveniently to specific units of production. Examples include lubricating oil, maintenance supplies, and glue. Indirect materials are accounted for as part of **manufacturing overhead**.

Managerial accounting *(p.1053)* Developing and interpreting accounting information specifically suited to the needs of a company's management.

Manufacturing costs *(p.1055)* The cost of manufacturing goods that will be sold to customers. The basic types of manufacturing costs are **direct materials**, **direct labour**, and **manufacturing overhead**.

Manufacturing overhead *(p.1056)* A "catch-all" category including all manufacturing costs other than the costs of **direct materials used** and **direct labour**.

Materials inventory *(p.1058)* The cost of direct materials on hand and available for use in the manufacturing process.

Overhead application rate *(p.1064)* A device used to assign overhead costs to the units being manufactured. Expresses the relationship between estimated overhead costs and some activity base that can be traced directly to manufactured units.

Period costs *(p.1057)* Costs that are charged to expense accounts in the period that the costs are incurred. Includes all items classified as "expense."

Product costs *(p.1056)* The costs of purchasing or manufacturing inventory. Until the related goods are sold, these product costs represent an asset—inventory. Once the goods are sold, these costs are deducted from revenue as the cost of goods sold.

Schedule of the cost of finished goods manufactured *(p.1068)* A schedule summarizing the flow of manufacturing costs into and out of the Work in Process Inventory account. Intended to assist managers in evaluating manufacturing costs.

Work in process inventory *(p.1058)* Goods at any stage of the manufacturing process short of completion. As these units are completed, they become finished goods.

DEMONSTRATION PROBLEM

The following T accounts summarize the flow of manufacturing costs during the current year through the ledger accounts of Marston Manufacturing Limited:

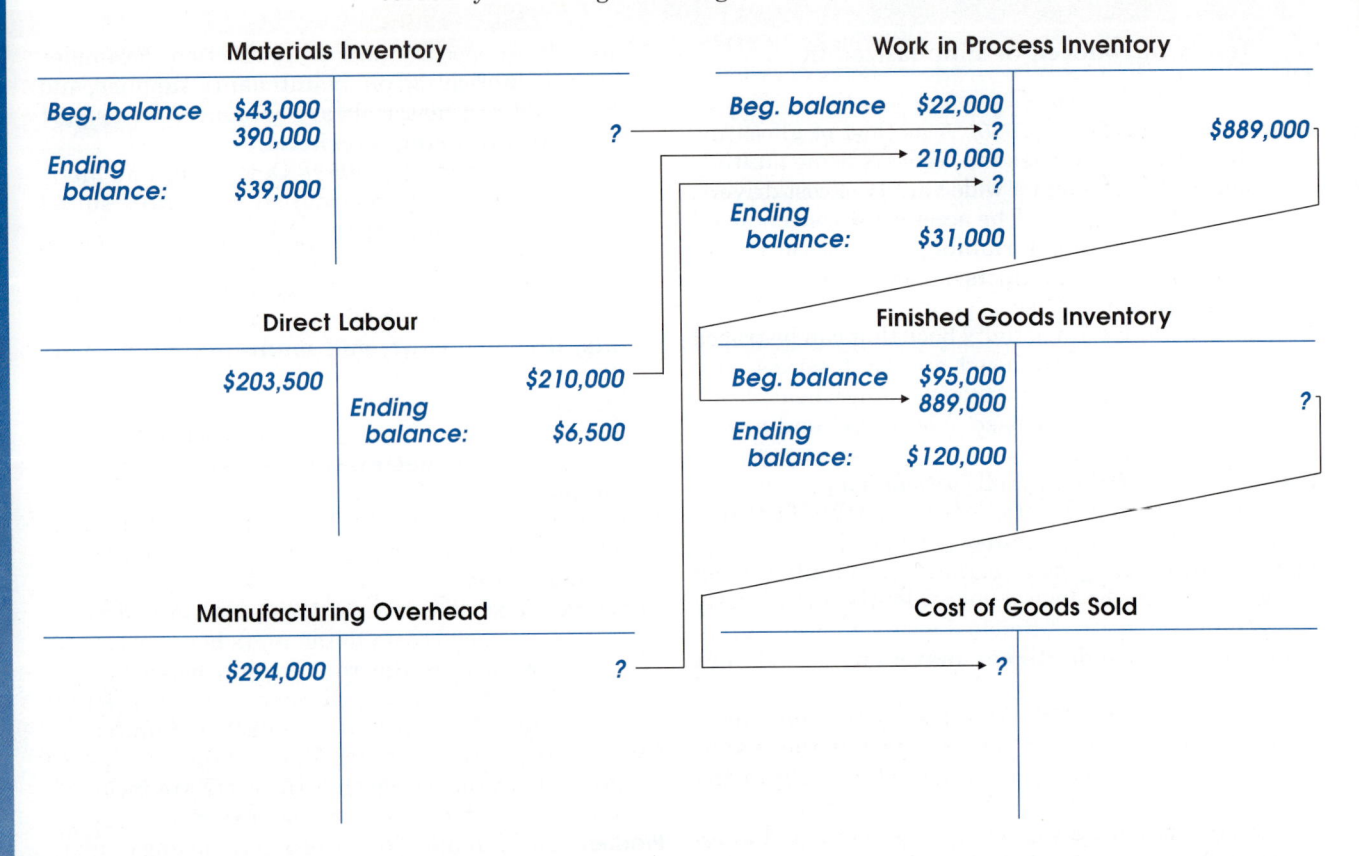

Materials Inventory		Work in Process Inventory	
Beg. balance $43,000	?	Beg. balance $22,000	$889,000
390,000		→ ?	
		210,000	
Ending balance: $39,000		→ ?	
		Ending balance: $31,000	

Direct Labour		Finished Goods Inventory	
$203,500	$210,000	Beg. balance $95,000	?
Ending balance: $6,500		889,000	
		Ending balance: $120,000	

Manufacturing Overhead		Cost of Goods Sold	
$294,000	?	?	

INSTRUCTIONS

From the data supplied above, indicate the following amounts. Some amounts already appear in the T accounts; others require short computations.

a. Purchases of direct materials
b. Direct materials used during the year
c. Direct labour costs assigned to production
d. The year-end liability to direct workers for wages payable
e. The overhead costs applied to production during the year, assuming that overhead was applied at a rate equal to 140% of direct labour costs
f. Total manufacturing costs charged to production during the year
g. The cost of finished goods manufactured
h. The cost of goods sold
i. The total costs classified as "inventory" in the year-end balance sheet.

SOLUTION TO DEMONSTRATION PROBLEM

a. Purchases of direct materials $390,000

b. Computation of direct materials used:
Materials inventory, beginning of year	$ 43,000
Purchases of direct materials	390,000
Direct materials available for use	$433,000
Less: Materials inventory, end of year	39,000
Direct materials used	$394,000

c. Direct labour costs assigned to production $210,000

d. Year-end liability for direct wages payable .... $ 6,500

e. Overhead costs applied during the year
($210,000 direct labour costs x 140%) $294,000

f. Total manufacturing costs charged to production:
Direct materials used (part b)	$394,000
Direct labour costs assigned to production	210,000
Manufacturing overhead applied (part e)	294,000
Total manufacturing costs charged to production	$898,000

g. Cost of finished goods manufactured $889,000

h. Computation of cost of goods sold:
Beginning inventory of finished goods	$ 95,000
Cost of finished goods manufactured	889,000
Cost of goods available for sale	$984,000
Less: Ending inventory of finished goods	120,000
Cost of goods sold	$864,000

i. Total year-end inventory:
Materials	$ 39,000
Work in process	31,000
Finished goods	120,000
Total inventory	$190,000

Self-Test Questions

Answers to these questions appear on page 1087.

1. Indicate which of the following statements are more descriptive of managerial accounting than of financial accounting. (More than one answer may be appropriate.)
   a. Recognized standards are used for presentation.
   b. Information is tailored to the needs of individual decision makers.
   c. Information is more widely distributed.
   d. Emphasis is on expected future results.

2. In a manufacturing company, the costs debited to the Work in Process Inventory account represent:
   a. Direct materials used, direct labour, and manufacturing overhead.
   b. Cost of finished goods manufactured.

c. Period costs and product costs.
d. None of the above; the types of costs debited to this account will depend upon the type of products being manufactured.

3. The Work in Process Inventory account had a beginning balance of $4,200 on February 1. During February, the cost of direct materials used was $29,000 and direct labour cost applied to production was $3,000. Overhead is applied at the rate of $20 per direct labour hour. During February, 180 direct labour hours were used in the production process. If the cost of finished goods manufactured was $34,100, compute the balance in the Work in Process Inventory account at the *end* of February.
   a. $9,900   b. $1,500   c. $2,100   d. $5,700

4. The purpose of an overhead application rate is to:
   a. Assign an appropriate portion of indirect manufacturing costs to each product manufactured.
   b. Determine the type and amount of costs to be debited to the Manufacturing Overhead account.
   c. Charge the Work in Process Inventory account with the appropriate amount of direct manufacturing costs.
   d. Allocate manufacturing overhead to expense in proportion to the number of units manufactured during the period.

5. The accounting records of Newport Mfg. Co. include the following information for 2000:

	Dec. 31	Jan. 1
Inventory of work in process	$ 20,000	$10,000
Inventory of finished goods	80,000	60,000
Direct materials used	200,000	
Direct labour	120,000	
Manufacturing overhead (150% of direct labour)	180,000	
Selling expenses	150,000	

Indicate which of the following are correct. (More than one answer may be correct.)
   a. Amount debited to the Work in Process Inventory account during 2000, $500,000
   b. Cost of finished goods manufactured, $490,000
   c. Cost of goods sold, $470,000
   d. Total manufacturing costs for the year, $650,000

ASSIGNMENT MATERIAL

Discussion Questions

1. Briefly distinguish between managerial and financial accounting information in terms of (a) the intended users of the information and (b) the purpose of the information.

2. Briefly explain what is meant by the terms *managerial accounting* and *cost accounting*. Are the two terms related to one another? Explain.

3. Are financial accounting and managerial accounting two entirely separate disciplines? Explain.

4. Is managerial accounting information developed in conformity with generally accepted accounting principles or some other set of prescribed standards? Explain.

5. What are the three basic types of manufacturing costs?

6. A manufacturing firm has three inventory controlling accounts. Name each of the accounts, and describe briefly what the balance in each at the end of any accounting period represents.

7. Explain the distinction between **product costs** and **period costs**. Why is this distinction important?

8. Is the cost of disposing of hazardous waste materials resulting from factory operations a product cost or a period cost? Explain.

9. During the current year, Coronado Boat Yard has incurred manufacturing costs of $420,000 in building three large sailboats. At year-end, each boat is about 70% complete. How much of these manufacturing costs should be recognized as expense in Coronado Boat Yard's income statement for the current year? Explain.

10. What amounts are **debited** to the Materials Inventory account? What amounts are **credited** to this account? What type of balance (debit or credit) is this account likely to have at year-end? Explain.

11. During the current year the net cost of direct materials purchased by a manufacturing firm was $340,000, and the direct material inventory increased by $20,000. What was the cost of direct materials **used** during the year?

12. What amounts are debited to the Direct Labour account during the year? What amounts are credited to this account? What type of balance (debit or credit) is this account likely to have at year-end? Explain.

13. The illustration on page 1060 includes six ledger accounts. Which of these six accounts often have balances at year-end that appear in the company's formal financial statements? Briefly explain how these balances will be classified in the financial statements.

14. Explain the distinction between a **direct** manufacturing cost and an **indirect** manufacturing cost. Provide two examples of each type of cost.

15. East Greenwich Mfg. Co. uses approximately $1,200 in janitorial supplies to clean the work area and factory equipment each month. Should this $1,200 be included in the cost of direct materials used? Explain.

16. What is meant by the term **overhead application rate**?

17. What is meant by the term **overhead cost driver**? How does the cost driver enter into the computation of an overhead application rate?

18. Identify two possible overhead cost drivers for a company that:
    a. Manufactures handmade furniture using skilled craftspersons and small hand tools.
    b. Manufactures microchips for computers using an assembly line of computer-driven robots.

19. What amounts are **debited** to the Work in Process Inventory account during the year? What amount is **credited** to this account? What does the year-end balance in this account represent?

20. What amount is **debited** to the Finished Goods Inventory account during the year? What amount is **credited** to this account? What type of balance (debit or credit) is this account likely to have at year-end?

21. Briefly describe the computation of the cost of finished goods manufactured as it appears in a schedule of the cost of finished goods manufactured.
22. A schedule of the cost of finished goods manufactured is a helpful tool in determining the per-unit cost of manufactured products. Explain several ways in which information about per-unit manufacturing costs is used by (a) managerial accountants and (b) financial accountants.
23. Briefly discuss the potential shortcoming of using direct labour hours or direct labour dollars as a primary cost driver in a highly automated company.

Exercises

EXERCISE 21-1
Accounting Terminology
(LO 1–6)

Listed below are nine technical accounting terms introduced or emphasized in this chapter:

Work in Process Inventory   *Cost of finished goods manufactured*
Overhead application rate   *Cost of Goods Sold*
Period costs   *Managerial accounting*
Product costs   *Manufacturing overhead*
Cost accounting

Each of the following statements may (or may not) describe one of these technical terms. For each statement, indicate the accounting term described, or answer "None" if the statement does not correctly describe any of the terms.

a. The preparation and use of accounting information designed to assist managers in planning and controlling the operations of a business.
b. All manufacturing costs other than direct materials used and direct labour.
c. A means of assigning indirect manufacturing costs to work in process during the period.
d. A manufacturing cost that can be traced conveniently and directly to manufactured units of product.
e. The concepts and procedures used in determining the cost of manufacturing a specific product or performing a particular type of business activity.
f. The account debited at the time that the Manufacturing Overhead account is credited.
g. The amount transferred from the Work in Process Inventory account to the Finished Goods Inventory account.
h. Costs that are debited directly to expense accounts when the costs are incurred.

EXERCISE 21-2
Basic Types of Manufacturing Costs
(LO 2)

Into which of the three elements of manufacturing cost would each of the following be classified?

a. Tubing used in manufacturing bicycles
b. Wages paid by an automobile manufacturer to employees who test-drive completed automobiles
c. Property taxes on machinery
d. Gold bullion used by a jewellery manufacturer
e. Wages of assembly-line workers who package frozen food
f. Salary of plant superintendent
g. Electricity used in factory operations
h. Salary of a nurse in a factory first-aid station

EXERCISE 21-3
Product Costs and Period Costs
(LO 3, 5)

Indicate whether each of the following should be considered a **product cost** or a **period cost**. If you identify the item as a product cost, also indicate whether it is a ***direct*** or an ***indirect*** cost. For example, the answer to item **0** is "indirect product cost." Begin with item **a**.

0. Property taxes on factory building
a. Cost of disposal of hazardous waste materials to a chemical plant
b. Amounts paid by a mobile home manufacturer to a subcontractor who installs plumbing in each mobile home
c. Depreciation on sales showroom fixtures
d. Salaries of security guards in administrative office building
e. Salaries of factory security guards
f. Salaries of office workers in the credit department
g. Depreciation on raw materials warehouse
h. Income taxes on a profitable manufacturing company

EXERCISE 21-4
Flow of Costs through Manufacturing Accounts
(LO 4)

The following information was taken from the accounting records of Reliable Tool Corporation:

Work in process inventory, beginning of the year	$ 35,000
Cost of direct materials used	245,000
Direct labour cost applied to production	120,000
Cost of finished goods manufactured	675,000

Overhead is applied to production at a rate of $30 per machine hour. During the current year, 10,000 machine hours were used in the production process.

Compute the amount of the work in process inventory on hand at year-end.

EXERCISE 21-5
Computation and Use of an Overhead Application Rate
(LO 6)

The production manager of Del Mar Manufacturing Limited has made the following estimates for the coming year:

Estimated manufacturing overhead	$1,200,000
Estimated direct labour cost	$ 500,000
Estimated machine hours	80,000 hours

a. Compute the overhead application rate based on:
  1. Direct labour cost.
  2. Machine hours.
b. Assume that the manufacture of a particular product requires $2,000 in direct materials, $400 in direct labour, and 62 machine hours. Determine the total cost of manufacturing this product assuming that the overhead application rate is based upon:
  1. Direct labour cost.
  2. Machine hours.

EXERCISE 21-6
Preparing a Schedule of the Cost of Finished Goods Manufactured
(LO 7)

The accounting records of NuTronics Inc. include the following information for the year ended December 31, 2001.

	Dec. 31	Jan. 1
Inventory of materials	$ 24,000	$20,000
Inventory of work in process	8,000	12,000
Inventory of finished goods	90,000	80,000
Direct materials used	210,000	
Direct labour	120,000	
Selling expenses	170,000	
General and administrative expenses	140,000	

Overhead is applied to production at a rate of $24 per direct labour hour. Direct labour workers logged 8,000 hours during the period.

a. Prepare a schedule of the cost of finished goods manufactured.
b. Assume that the company manufactures a single product and that 20,000 units were completed during the year. What is the average per-unit cost of manufacturing this product?

EXERCISE 21-7
Overhead Cost Drivers; Determination and Use of Unit Cost
(LO 6)

During June, Assembly Department no. 4 of Riverview Electronics produced 12,000 model 201 computer keyboards. Assembly of these units required 1,476 hours of direct labour at a cost of $26,400, direct materials costing $318,960, and 2,880 hours of machine time. Based upon an analysis of overhead costs at the beginning of the year, overhead is applied to keyboards using the following formula:

$$\text{Overhead} = 75\% \text{ of Direct Labour Cost} + \$32 \text{ per Machine Hour}$$

a. Compute the total amount of overhead cost applied to the 12,000 keyboards.
b. Compute the *per-unit cost* of manufacturing these keyboards.
c. Briefly explain *why* the department might use *two separate activity bases* in applying overhead costs to one type of product.
d. Identify at least two types of overhead costs that might be "driven" by each of the two cost drivers indicated in this situation.
e. What appears to be the *primary* driver of overhead costs in the manufacture of keyboards?
f. Compute the gross profit that will result from the sale of 2,000 of these keyboards at a sales price of $75 each.

EXERCISE 21-8
Manipulating Accounting Figures
(LO 1)

Joe Felan is the production manager at Utex Corporation. He was recently quoted as saying, "Since managerial reports aren't subject to generally accepted accounting principles, and they aren't directly used by outside investors and creditors, it's really okay for managers to manipulate the reports as they see fit." Do you agree with Felan's statement? Defend your answer.

Problems

PROBLEM 21-1
An Introduction to Product Costs
(LO 3, 4, 7)

Aqua-Marine manufactures fibreglass fishing boats. The manufacturing costs incurred during its first year of operations are shown below:

Direct materials purchased	$225,000
Direct materials used	216,000
Direct labour assigned to production	200,000
Manufacturing overhead	350,000
Cost of finished goods manufactured (112 boats)	728,000

During the year, 112 completed boats were manufactured, of which 100 were sold. (Assume that the amount of the ending inventory of finished goods and the cost of goods sold are determined using the average per-unit cost of manufacturing a completed boat.)

INSTRUCTIONS

a. Compute each of the following and show all computations:
   1. The average per-unit cost of manufacturing a completed boat during the current year
   2. The year-end balances of the inventories of materials, work in process, and finished goods

CHAPTER 21 INTRODUCTION TO MANAGERIAL ACCOUNTING; ACCOUNTING FOR MANUFACTURING OPERATIONS   **1079**

3. The cost of goods sold during the year

b. For the current year, the costs of direct materials purchased, direct labour assigned to production, and actual manufacturing overhead total $775,000. Is this the amount of manufacturing costs deducted from revenue in the current year? Explain fully.

PROBLEM 21-2
An Introduction to Product Costs
(LO 2–4)

Road Ranger Corporation began operations early in the current year, building luxury motor homes. During the year, the company started and completed 50 motor homes at a cost of $60,000 per unit. Of these, 48 were sold for $95,000 each and 2 remain in finished goods inventory. In addition, the company had 9 partially completed units in its factory at year-end. Total costs for the year (summarized alphabetically) were as follows:

Direct materials used	$ 750,000
Direct labour applied to production	900,000
Income taxes expense	100,000
General and administrative expenses	500,000
Manufacturing overhead	1,800,000
Selling expenses	500,000

INSTRUCTIONS

Compute for the current year:
a. Total manufacturing costs assigned to work in process during the period
b. Cost of finished goods manufactured
c. Cost of goods sold
d. Gross profit
e. Ending inventories of (1) work in process and (2) finished goods

PROBLEM 21-3
The Flow of Manufacturing Costs Through Ledger Accounts
(LO 4)

The "flow" of manufacturing costs through the ledger accounts of Superior Locks Inc. in the current year is illustrated below in summarized form:

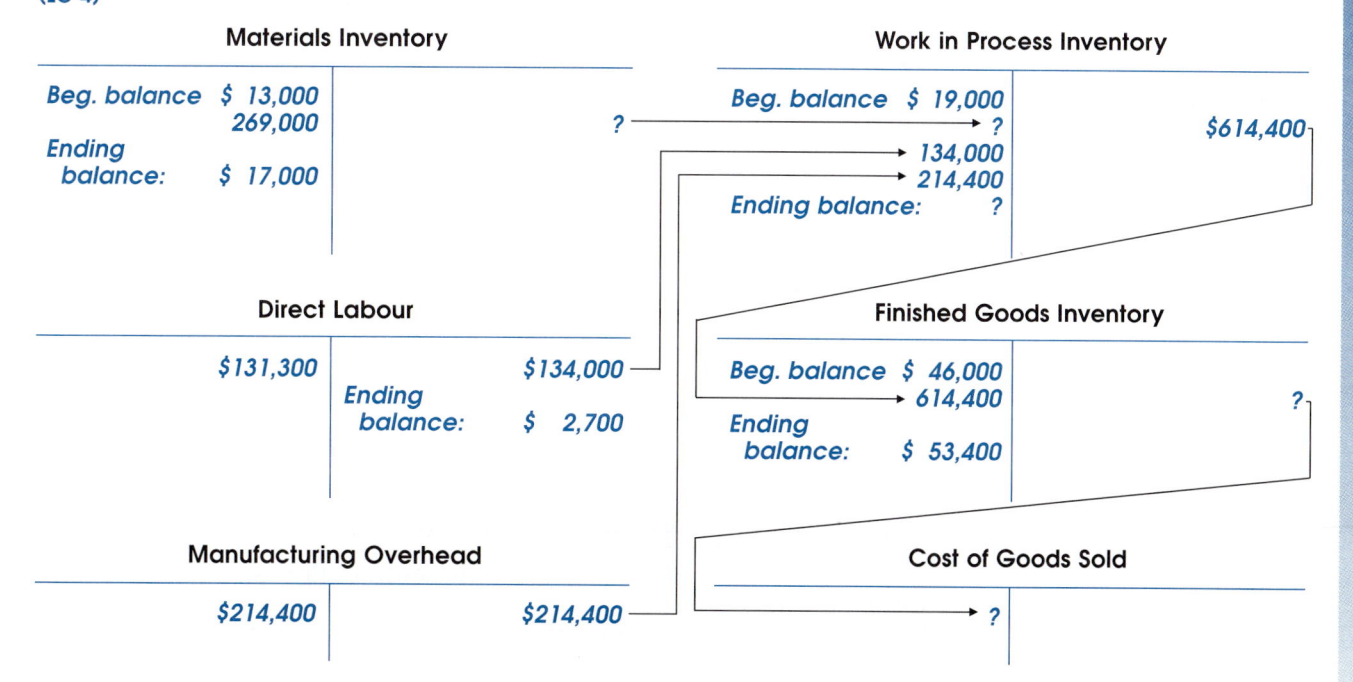

Materials Inventory

Beg. balance $ 13,000
              269,000
Ending balance: $ 17,000

Work in Process Inventory

Beg. balance $ 19,000
              ?
              134,000
              214,400
Ending balance: ?

$614,400

Direct Labour

$131,300 $134,000
Ending balance: $ 2,700

Finished Goods Inventory

Beg. balance $ 46,000
              614,400
Ending balance: $ 53,400

?

Manufacturing Overhead

$214,400 $214,400

Cost of Goods Sold

?

INSTRUCTIONS

Indicate the amounts requested below; show supporting computations, if any.
a. Purchases of direct materials
b. The cost of direct materials used
c. Direct labour costs assigned to production
d. The year-end liability for direct wages payable
e. The overhead application rate in use throughout the year, assuming that overhead is applied as a percentage of direct labour costs
f. Total manufacturing costs assigned to the Work in Process Inventory account during the current year
g. The cost of finished goods manufactured
h. The year-end balance in the Work in Process Inventory account
i. The cost of goods sold
j. The total amount of "inventory" listed in the year-end balance sheet

PROBLEM 21-4
The Flow of Manufacturing Costs Through Perpetual Inventory Records
(LO 4)

The following T accounts summarize the flow of manufacturing costs during the current year through the ledger accounts of Gronback Corporation:

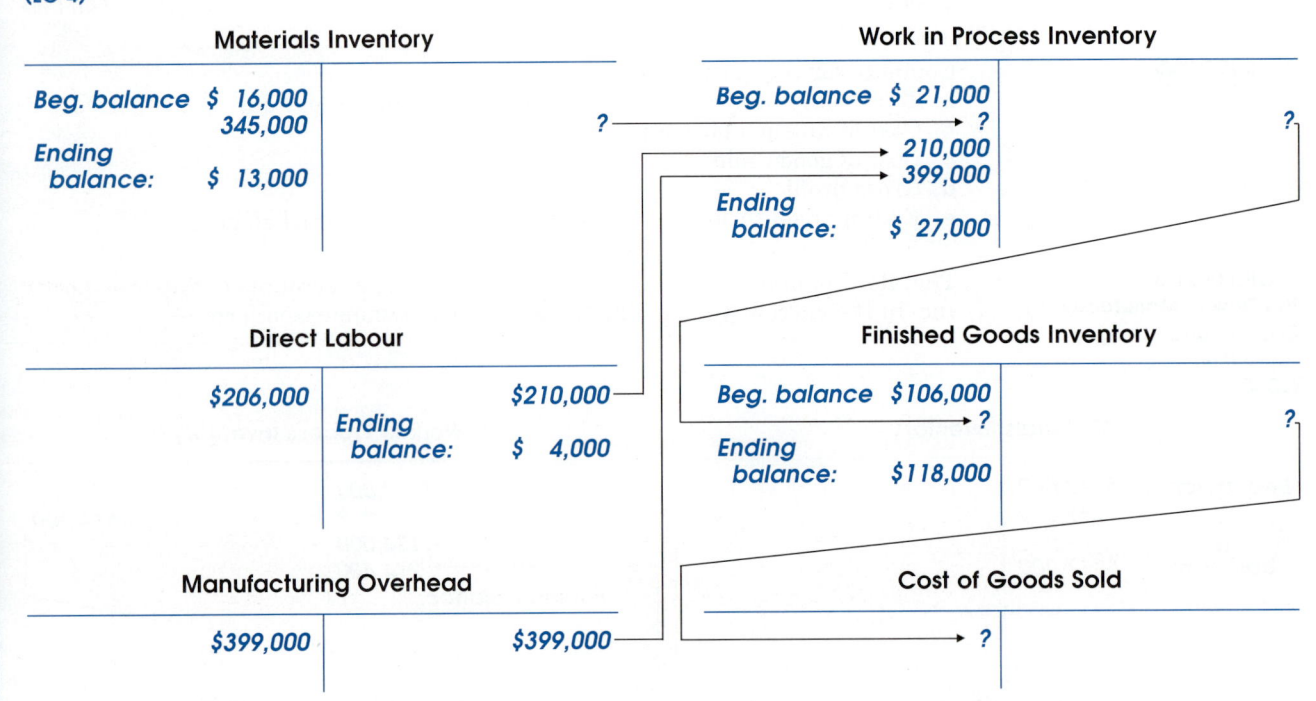

Materials Inventory

Beg. balance $ 16,000	
345,000	?
Ending balance: $ 13,000	

Work in Process Inventory

Beg. balance $ 21,000	?
210,000	
399,000	
Ending balance: $ 27,000	

Direct Labour

$206,000	$210,000
Ending balance: $ 4,000	

Finished Goods Inventory

Beg. balance $106,000	?
Ending balance: $118,000	

Manufacturing Overhead

$399,000	$399,000

Cost of Goods Sold

?	

INSTRUCTIONS

From the data supplied above, indicate the following amounts. (Show all supporting computations.)
a. Purchases during the year of direct materials
b. The cost of direct materials used
c. Direct labour payrolls paid during the year
d. Direct labour costs assigned to production
e. The overhead application rate in use during the year, assuming that overhead is applied as a percentage of direct labour costs
f. Total manufacturing costs assigned to the Work in Process Inventory account during the year
g. The cost of finished goods manufactured

h. The cost of goods sold
i. The total costs to be classified as "inventory" in the year-end balance sheet

PROBLEM 21-5
The Flow of Manufacturing Costs: A Comprehensive Problem
(LO 3, 4, 7)

The balances in the perpetual inventory accounts of Hillsdale Manufacturing Corporation at the beginning and end of the current year are as follows:

	End of Year	Beginning of Year
Inventory accounts:		
Materials	$26,000	$22,000
Work in process	9,000	5,000
Finished goods inventory	25,000	38,000

The total dollar amounts debited and credited during the year to the accounts used in recording manufacturing activities are summarized below:

Account:	Debit Entries	Credit Entries
Materials Inventory	$410,000	$?
Direct Labour	189,000	192,000
Manufacturing Overhead	393,600	393,600
Work in Process Inventory	?	?
Finished Goods Inventory	?	?

INSTRUCTIONS

a. Using this data, state or compute for the year the amounts of:
 1. Direct materials purchased
 2. Direct materials used
 3. Payments of direct labour payrolls
 4. Direct labour cost assigned to production
 5. The overhead application rate used during the year, assuming that overhead was applied as a percentage of direct labour costs
 6. Total manufacturing costs assigned to the Work in Process Inventory account during the year
 7. The cost of finished goods manufactured
 8. Cost of goods sold
 9. The total amount to be classified as "inventory" in the year-end balance sheet

b. Prepare a schedule of the cost of finished goods manufactured.

PROBLEM 21-6
Determining and Reporting Product Cost Information
(LO 3, 4, 7)

Shown below are 2001 data regarding Baby Buddy, one of the major products manufactured by Toledo Toy Ltd.:

Purchases of direct materials	$332,000
Direct materials used	333,600
Direct labour payrolls (paid during the year)	176,700
Direct labour costs assigned to production	180,000
Manufacturing overhead (incurred and applied)	288,000

During the year 60,000 units of this product were manufactured and 62,100 units were sold. Selected information concerning inventories during the year is shown as follows:

1082 INCOME TAXES, CASH FLOWS, FINANCIAL STATEMENT ANALYSIS, AND MANAGERIAL ACCOUNTING PART 5

	Dec. 31	Jan. 1
Materials	$?	$12,800
Work in process	4,700	4,100
Finished goods, Jan. 1 (3,000 units @ $13)	?	39,000

INSTRUCTIONS

a. Prepare a schedule of the cost of finished goods manufactured for the Baby Buddy product in 2001.
b. Compute the average cost of Baby Buddy completed in 2001.
c. Compute the cost of goods sold associated with the sale of Baby Buddy in 2001. Assume that there is a first-in, first-out (FIFO) flow through the Finished Goods Inventory account and that all units completed in 2001 are assigned the per-unit costs determined in part **b**.
d. Compute the amount of "inventory" relating to Baby Buddy that will be listed in the company's balance sheet at December 31, 2001. Show supporting computations for the year-end amounts of materials inventory and finished goods inventory.
e. Explain how the $180,000 in direct labour costs assigned to production in 2001 affect the company's 2001 income statement and balance sheet.

PROBLEM 21-7
Determining and Reporting Product Cost Information
(LO 3, 4, 7)

Shown below are the beginning and ending balances in the inventory accounts of Nevis Tools for 2002:

	End of Year	Beginning of Year
Inventory accounts:		
Materials	$62,400	$ 56,400
Work in process	28,800	31,200
Finished goods inventory	?	117,600

The amounts debited and credited during the year to the accounts used in recording manufacturing costs are summarized below:

	Debit Entries	Credit Entries
Account:		
Materials Inventory	$ 828,000	$?
Direct Labour	474,000	480,000
Manufacturing Overhead	1,056,000	1,056,000
Cost of Goods Sold	2,370,000	-0-
Work in Process Inventory	?	?
Finished Goods Inventory	?	?

INSTRUCTIONS

a. Using the above information, state (or compute) for 2002 the following amounts:
  1. Direct materials purchased
  2. Direct materials used
  3. Direct labour payrolls paid during the year
  4. Direct labour costs assigned to units being manufactured
  5. The year-end liability for direct wages payable
  6. The overhead application rate, assuming that overhead costs are applied to units being manufactured using 24,000 direct labour hours as an estimated activity base.
  7. Total manufacturing costs debited to the Work in Process Inventory account
  8. Cost of finished goods manufactured

9. Ending inventory of finished goods
b. Prepare a schedule of the cost of finished goods manufactured for the year.

PROBLEM 21-8
Determining Unit Costs Using the Cost of Finished Goods Manufactured
(LO 4, 7)

The accounting records of the Idaho Paper Company include the following information relating to the current year:

	Dec. 31	Jan. 1
Materials inventory	$ 20,000	$ 25,000
Work in process inventory	37,500	40,000
Finished goods inventory, Jan. 1 (10,000 units @ $21 per unit)	?	210,000
Purchases of direct materials during year	330,000	
Direct labour costs assigned to production	375,000	
Manufacturing overhead applied to production	637,500	

The company manufactures a single product; during the current year, **45,000** units were manufactured and **40,000** units were sold.

INSTRUCTIONS

a. Prepare a schedule of the cost of finished goods manufactured for the current year. (Show a supporting computation of the cost of direct materials *used* during the year.)
b. Compute the average per-unit cost of production during the current year.
c. Compute the cost of goods sold during the year, assuming that the FIFO (first-in, first-out) method of inventory costing is used.
d. Compute the cost of the inventory of finished goods at December 31 of the current year, assuming that the FIFO (first-in, first-out) method of inventory costing is used.

PROBLEM 21-9
Preparing an Income Statement Using the Cost of Finished Goods Manufactured
(LO 4, 7)

Mayville Company, a sole proprietorship, reports the following information pertaining to its 2001 operating activities:

	Dec. 31, 2001 Balance	Jan. 1, 2001 Balance
Materials Inventory	$20,000	$40,000
Work in Process Inventory	29,000	60,000
Finished Goods Inventory	52,000	42,000

During the year, the company purchased $30,000 of direct materials and incurred $21,000 of direct labour costs. Total manufacturing overhead costs for the year amounted to $18,000. Selling and administrative expenses amounted to $60,000, and the company's annual sales amounted to $200,000.

INSTRUCTIONS

a. Prepare Mayville's schedule of the cost of finished goods manufactured for 2001.
b. Prepare Mayville's 2001 income statement.

PROBLEM 21-10
Preparing an Income Statement Using the Cost of Finished Goods Manufactured
(LO 4, 7)

Ridgeway Company reports the following information pertaining to its 2001 operations:

	Dec. 31, 2001 Balance	Jan. 1, 2001 Balance
Materials Inventory	$70,000	$60,000
Work in Process Inventory	41,000	29,000
Finished Goods Inventory	16,000	21,000

During the year, the company purchased $35,000 of direct materials and incurred $22,000 of direct labour costs. Total manufacturing overhead costs for the year amounted to $19,000. Selling and administrative expenses amounted to $30,000, and the company's annual sales amounted to $80,000.

INSTRUCTIONS

a. Prepare Ridgeway's schedule of the cost of finished goods manufactured for 2001.
b. Prepare Ridgeway's 2001 income statement (ignore income taxes).

PROBLEM 21-11
Measuring Unit Cost
(LO 3, 4, 7)

Early in the year, John Raymond founded Raymond Engineering Ltd. for the purpose of manufacturing a special flow control valve that he had designed. Shortly after year-end, the company's accountant was injured in a skiing accident, and no year-end financial statements have been prepared. However, the accountant had correctly determined the year-end inventories at the following amounts:

Materials	$46,000
Work in process	31,500
Finished goods (3,000 units)	88,500

As this was the first year of operations, there were no beginning inventories.

While the accountant was in the hospital, Raymond improperly prepared the following income statement from the company's accounting records:

Net sales		$610,600
Cost of goods sold:		
Purchases of direct materials	$181,000	
Direct labour costs assigned to production	110,000	
Manufacturing overhead applied to production	170,000	
Selling expenses	70,600	
Administrative expenses	132,000	
Total costs		663,600
Net loss for year		$ (53,000)

Raymond was very disappointed in these operating results. He states, "Not only did we lose more than $50,000 this year, but look at our unit production costs. We sold 10,000 units this year at a cost of $663,600; that amounts to a cost of $66.36 per unit. I know some of our competitors are able to manufacture similar valves for about $35 per unit. I don't need an accountant to know that this business is a failure."

INSTRUCTIONS

a. Prepare a schedule of the cost of finished goods manufactured for the year. Show a supporting computation for the cost of direct materials used during the year.
b. Compute the average cost per unit manufactured.
c. Prepare a corrected income statement for the year, using the multiple-step format. If the company has earned any operating income, assume an income tax rate of 30%. (Omit earnings per share figures.)
d. Explain whether you agree or disagree with Raymond's remarks that the business is unprofitable and that its unit cost of production ($66.36, according to Raymond) is much higher than that of competitors (around $35). If you disagree with Raymond, explain any errors or shortcomings in his analysis.

PROBLEM 21-12
Effect on Income Statement of Errors in Handling Manufacturing Costs
(LO 3, 4, 7)

William Nelson, the chief accountant of Canton Guitar Limited was injured in an automobile accident shortly before the end of the company's first year of operations. At year-end, a clerk with a very limited understanding of accounting prepared the following income statement, which is unsatisfactory in several respects:

CANTON GUITAR LIMITED
Income Statement
For the Year Ended December 31, 20__

Net sales		$1,300,000
Cost of goods sold:		
Purchases of direct materials	$460,000	
Direct labour	225,000	
Indirect labour	90,000	
Depreciation on machinery—factory	50,000	
Rent	144,000	
Insurance	16,000	
Utilities	28,000	
Miscellaneous manufacturing overhead	34,600	
Other operating expenses	273,800	
Dividends declared on common stock	46,000	
Cost of goods sold		(1,367,400)
Loss for year		(67,400)

You are asked to help management prepare a corrected income statement for the first year of operations. Management informs you that 60% of the rent, insurance, and utilities apply to factory operations, and that the remaining 40% should be classified as operating expense. Also, the correct ending inventories are as follows:

Material	$ 38,000
Work in process	10,000
Finished goods	110,400

As this is the first year of operations, there were no beginning inventories.

INSTRUCTIONS

a. Identify the shortcomings and errors in the above income statement. Based upon the shortcomings you have identified, explain whether you would expect the company's actual net income for the first year of operations to be higher or lower than the amount shown.
b. Prepare schedules to determine:
   1. The cost of direct materials used.
   2. Total manufacturing overhead.
c. Prepare a schedule of cost of finished goods manufactured during the year.
d. Prepare a corrected income statement for the year, using a multiple-step format. Assume that income taxes expense amounts to 30% of income before income taxes.

Analytical and Decision Problems and Cases

A&D 21-1
Poor Drivers Are Cost Drivers
(LO 6)

Ye Olde Bump & Grind Inc. is an automobile body and fender repair shop. Repair work is done by hand and with the use of small tools. Customers are billed based on time (direct labour hours) and materials used in each repair job.

The shop's overhead costs consist primarily of indirect materials (welding materials, metal putty, and sandpaper), rent, indirect labour, and utilities. Rent is equal to a percentage of the shop's gross revenue for each month. The indirect labour relates primarily to ordering parts and processing insurance claims. The amount of indirect labour, therefore, tends to vary with the size of each job.

Harold Beazley, manager of the business, is considering using either direct labour hours or number of repair jobs as the basis for allocating overhead costs. He has estimated the following amounts for the coming year:

Estimated total overhead	$123,000
Estimated direct labour hours	10,000
Estimated number of repair jobs	300

INSTRUCTIONS

a. Compute the overhead application rate based on (1) direct labour hours, and (2) number of repair jobs.
b. Shown below is information for two repair jobs:
   Job 1 Repair a dented fender. Direct material used, $25; direct labour hours, 5; direct labour cost, $150.
   Job 2 Repair an automobile involved in a serious collision. Direct materials used, $3,800; direct labour hours, 200; direct labour cost, $6,000.
   Determine the *total cost* of each repair job, assuming that overhead costs are applied to each job based upon:
   1. Direct labour hours.
   2. Number of repair jobs.
c. Discuss the results obtained in part **b**. Which overhead application method appears to provide the more realistic results? Explain the reasoning behind your answer, addressing the issue of what "drives" overhead costs in this business.

A&D 21-2
The Meadowbrooke Miracle
(LO 2, 3, 4, 7)

Prescott Manufacturing operates several plants, each of which produces a different product. Early in the current year, John Walker was hired as the new manager of the Meadowbrooke Plant. At year-end, all the plant managers are asked to summarize the operations of their plants at a meeting of the company's board of directors. John Walker displayed the following information on a chart as he made his presentation.

	Current Year	Last Year
Inventories of finished goods:		
Beginning of the year (30,000 units in the current year and 10,000 units last year)	$255,000	$ 85,000
End of the year (20,000 units in the current year and 30,000 units last year)	202,000	255,000
Cost of finished goods manufactured	909,000	1,020,000

Walker made the following statements to the board: "As you know, sales volume has remained constant for the Meadowbrooke Plant. Both this year and last, our sales amounted to 100,000 units. We have made real gains, however, in controlling our manufacturing costs. Through efficient plant operations, we have reduced our cost of finished goods manufactured by over $100,000. These economies are reflected in a reduction of the manufacturing cost per unit sold from $10.20 last year ($1,020,000 ÷ 100,000 units) to $9.09 in the current year ($909,000 ÷ 100,000 units)."

Father William Stewart is president of St. Mary's University and is a member of Prescott Manufacturing's board of directors. However, Father Stewart has little background in the accounting practices of manufacturing companies, and he asks you for assistance in evaluating Walker's statements.

INSTRUCTIONS

a. As a preliminary step to your analysis, compute the following for the Meadowbrooke Plant in each of the two years:
   1. Cost of goods sold
   2. Number of finished units manufactured
   3. Average cost per unit manufactured
   4. Average cost per unit sold
b. Evaluate the statements made by Walker. Comment specifically upon Walker's computation of the manufacturing cost of units sold and upon whether it appears that the reduction in the cost of finished goods sold was achieved through more efficient operations.

Answers to Self-Test Questions

1. b, d **2.** a **3.** d **4.** a **5.** a, b, c

APPENDIX D

THE NEW MANUFACTURING ENVIRONMENT; ACTIVITY-BASED COSTING

Intended for Use for Chapter 21

In this appendix, we illustrate and explain *activity-based costing*—a technique that uses many different activity bases in applying overhead costs to the products manufactured.

LEARNING OBJECTIVES

1. Discuss characteristics of the "new manufacturing environment."
2. Describe the operation of an ABC system and explain the potential benefits to management.
3. Define *activity cost pools* and provide several examples.
4. Suggest cost drivers for applying a particular cost pool to units produced.

THE NEW MANUFACTURING ENVIRONMENT

LO 1: Discuss characteristics of the "new manufacturing environment."

Increased global competition, scarce resources, and the public's demand for high quality goods and services have resulted in a movement to revolutionize manufacturing throughout the world. In what is commonly called "the new manufacturing environment," creative efforts to increase efficiency and improve information have become essential elements of survival.

Examples of new manufacturing technologies and techniques are numerous and well publicized. For instance, computer-aided manufacturing and robotics are widely used to improve product design, testing, and quality. Computerized cost control systems that rapidly detect production problems caused by faulty machinery or defective materials are commonplace. Along with computer technology, creative inventory management, flexible production scheduling, and employee work teams all help to reduce costs without sacrificing customer satisfaction, product quality, or delivery schedules.

One major goal in the new manufacturing environment is to **more accurately measure per-unit costs**—not only the costs of producing finished units, but also the costs of performing **each activity** within the manufacturing process. As a step toward this goal, many companies have adopted a technique called **activity-based costing**.

CHAPTER 21 INTRODUCTION TO MANAGERIAL ACCOUNTING; ACCOUNTING FOR MANUFACTURING OPERATIONS 1089

> **CASE IN POINT**
>
> When the production line at American Paper Products comes to a screeching halt, management is delighted. Why? Because the company's automated quality control system has detected a problem. Using computer and laser technologies, the texture, thickness, and consistency of paper products are constantly monitored throughout the production process. If the quality control system detects any variance from the company's strictly set standards, the manufacturing process is automatically shut down and a team of production specialists immediately goes to work to correct the problem. In the new manufacturing environment, systems such as these help companies to reduce waste, improve efficiency, and maintain strict quality standards.

ACTIVITY-BASED COSTING (ABC)

In Chapter 21, we illustrated how manufacturing overhead costs may be applied to production using an overhead application rate based upon a single cost driver (such as direct labour hours). This approach works well for many companies, especially if all products are manufactured in a similar manner.

But now consider a company that uses ***very different processes*** in manufacturing different products. The factors that drive overhead costs may vary greatly among different product lines. Such companies may benefit from an ***activity-based costing system*** (called ABC).

LO 2: Describe the operation of an ABC system and explain the potential benefits to management.

In an ABC system, ***many different*** activity bases (or cost drivers) are used in applying overhead costs to products. Thus, ABC recognizes the "special overhead considerations" of each product line. Overhead costs tend to be allocated more accurately, resulting in a more precise measurement of each product's "true" unit cost. In addition, an ABC system provides management with information about the per-unit cost of performing various overhead activities.

LO 3: Define activity cost pools and provide several examples.

How ABC Works The first step in an ABC system is to subdivide overhead costs into a number of ***activity cost pools***. Each cost pool represents a type of overhead ***activity***, such as building maintenance, purchasing materials, heating the factory, machinery repairs, etc. The overhead costs in each pool then are applied to production ***separately***, using the most appropriate cost driver.

In short, ABC separately identifies and makes use of the ***most appropriate cost driver*** for applying each category of overhead costs.

The Benefits of ABC A more accurate measurement of unit costs may assist managers in several ways. For example, it helps them in setting sales prices and in evaluating the profitability of each product line. ABC also helps managers to better understand what "drives" overhead costs. This understanding may inspire them to develop new operating procedures that may reduce overhead costs.

CASE IN POINT

As explained in Chapter 9, just-in-time inventory systems almost eliminate the costs of storing direct materials. But what inspired the "just-in-time" concept? Probably an activity-based costing system in which "Storing direct materials" appeared as a large cost pool.

ABC Versus a Single Application Rate: A Comparison

Assume that Master File Inc. makes two lines of file cabinets: (1) metal file cabinets, sold through office supply outlets for commercial use, and (2) wooden file cabinets, sold through fine furniture stores for home use.

In a typical year, the company produces and sells approximately 42,000 metal cabinets and 9,000 wooden cabinets. Total manufacturing overhead at this level of production averages **$249,600 per year**, and is currently allocated to products at a rate of **$1.60 per direct labour hour (DLH)**, as computed below.

Step 1: Compute total direct labour hours at "normal" levels of production

Overhead applied using Direct Labour Hours

Metal cabinets (42,000 units per year × 2 DLH per unit)	84,000 DLH
Wooden cabinets (9,000 units per year × 8 DLH per unit)	72,000 DLH
Total DLH at normal production levels	156,000 DLH

Step 2: Compute the overhead application rate per DLH

Overhead application rate ($249,600 ÷ 156,000 DLH)	$1.60 per DLH

Using direct labour hours as a single activity base, the company's total manufacturing costs per unit average **$38.20** for metal cabinets, and **$117.80** for wooden cabinets, as shown below.

Total unit cost

	Metal Cabinets	Wooden Cabinets
Direct materials	$15.00	$ 25.00
Direct labour (at $10.00 per hour)	20.00	80.00
Manufacturing overhead (at $1.60 per DLH)	3.20	12.80
Total manufacturing costs per unit	$38.20	$117.80

Master File sets its selling prices at **160%** of total manufacturing costs. Thus, the company sells its metal cabinets for **$61.12** (total unit cost of $38.20 × 160%), and its wooden cabinets for **$188.48** (total unit cost of $117.80 × 160%). At these prices, the metal cabinets sell for about **$3 less** per unit than comparable cabinets sold by Master File's competitors. However, the price of wooden cabinets averages **$10 more** per unit than comparable products available on the market.

Glen Brown, Master File's Marketing Director, believes that sales of the wooden cabinets have suffered as a result of the company's pricing policy. He recently hired a consultant, Lisa Scott, to evaluate how prices are set. Scott drafted the following memo summarizing her findings:

> **MEMO**
>
> **DATE:** January 16
>
> **TO:** Glen Brown, Marketing Director, Master File Inc.
>
> **FROM:** Lisa Scott, Consultant, Scott & Associates
>
> Having carefully examined Master File's pricing policy, I find it consistent with pricing policies used throughout the office furniture industry. Therefore, I recommend that you continue setting prices at 160% of total manufacturing costs.
>
> I do, however, strongly encourage management to change the method currently used to allocate manufacturing overhead to products. The use of direct labour hours as an activity base is causing an excessive share of total overhead costs to be allocated to the wooden cabinet line. Let me explain what is happening.
>
> The wooden product line is very labour intensive in comparison to the metal cabinet line (i.e., it takes an average of eight direct labour hours to manufacture a wooden cabinet, compared to an average of two direct labour hours to manufacture a metal cabinet). Because manufacturing overhead is allocated on the basis of direct labour hours, each wooden cabinet receives a far greater cost allocation than each metal cabinet. This would be appropriate if direct labour hours were the primary overhead **cost driver**. The fact is, however, that direct labour hours are not a significant driver of your overhead costs.
>
> My analysis of manufacturing overhead at Master File Inc. reveals that the most **significant cost drivers** are activities most closely associated with the **metal cabinet line**. Thus, it would make sense if your company selected activity bases that allocate more overhead costs to the metal cabinets. This would indicate a lower cost for the wooden cabinets and provide justification for lowering their selling prices, making them more in line with the competition.
>
> I suggest that we make an appointment to discuss using an **activity-based costing** system at Master File Inc.

Assume that Master File decides to implement an ABC system as suggested by the consultant. Remember that the company's **total overhead costs** at normal levels of production average **$249,600 per year**. Let us assume that these overhead costs fall into two broad categories: (1) maintenance department costs, and (2) utilities costs. The following diagram illustrates how these costs may be allocated to Master File's product lines using an ABC system.

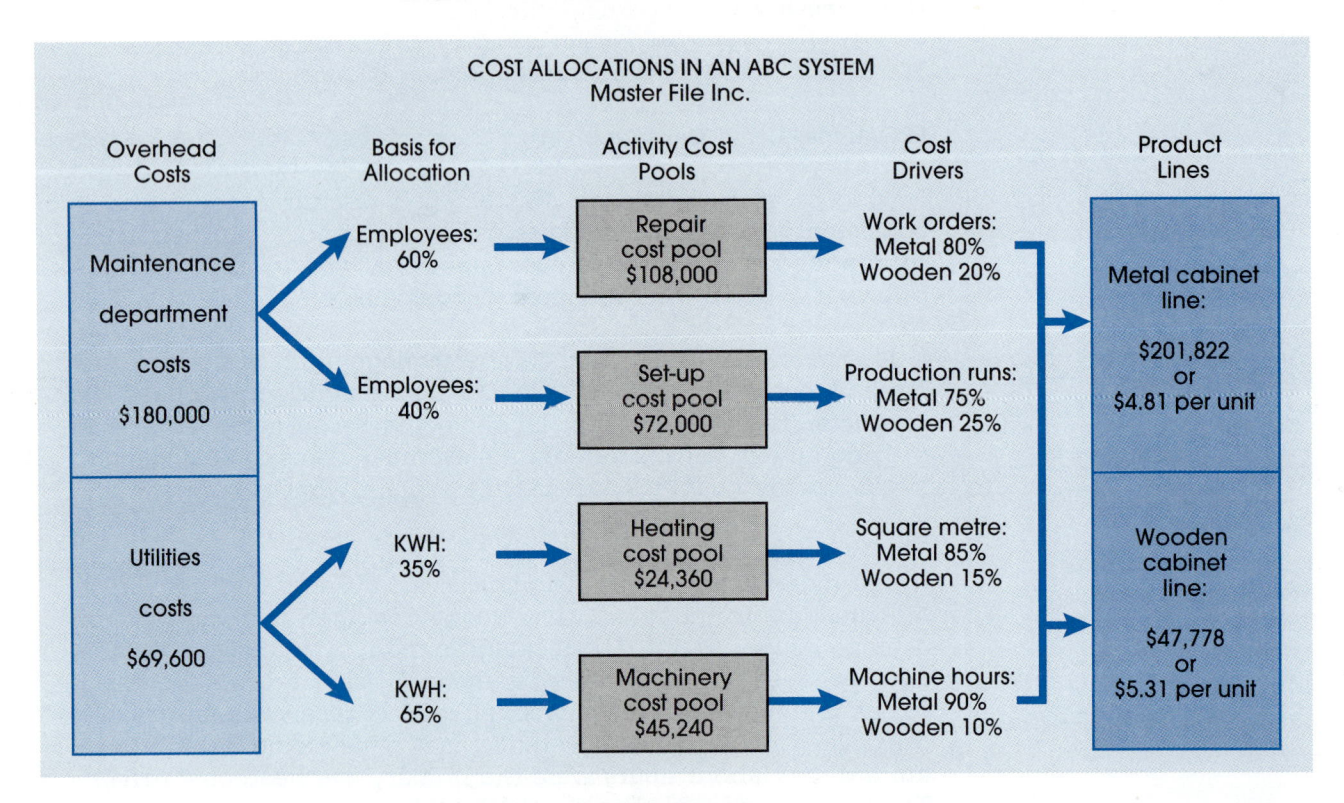

COST ALLOCATIONS IN AN ABC SYSTEM
Master File Inc.

Overhead Costs	Basis for Allocation	Activity Cost Pools	Cost Drivers	Product Lines
Maintenance department costs $180,000	Employees: 60%	Repair cost pool $108,000	Work orders: Metal 80% Wooden 20%	Metal cabinet line: $201,822 or $4.81 per unit
	Employees: 40%	Set-up cost pool $72,000	Production runs: Metal 75% Wooden 25%	
Utilities costs $69,600	KWH: 35%	Heating cost pool $24,360	Square metre: Metal 85% Wooden 15%	Wooden cabinet line: $47,778 or $5.31 per unit
	KWH: 65%	Machinery cost pool $45,240	Machine hours: Metal 90% Wooden 10%	

Maintenance Department Costs The maintenance department incurs approximately **$180,000** of Master File's total overhead costs. The department has five full-time employees. Three employees are responsible for repair work, such as fixing the large cutting and bending machines used to manufacture metal file cabinets. The other two employees are responsible for set-up activities, such as adjusting machinery prior to each production run.

In its ABC system, Master File identifies repair activities and set-up activities as separate **activity cost pools**. Thus, each pool is assigned a portion of the department's $180,000 in total costs. Management believes that the **number of employees** engaged in each activity is the most significant **cost driver** of the maintenance department's total costs. Using the number of employees as an **activity base, $108,000** is assigned to the **repair cost pool**, and **$72,000** is assigned to the **set-up cost pool**, computed as follows.

CHAPTER 21 INTRODUCTION TO MANAGERIAL ACCOUNTING; ACCOUNTING FOR MANUFACTURING OPERATIONS 1093

Assigning Maintenance Department Costs to Activity Pools

Step 1: Establish the percent of total maintenance department costs to be assigned to each activity cost pool using the number of employees as an activity base

		% of total
Employees engaged in repair activities	3	60%
Employees engaged in set-up activities	2	40%
Employees in the maintenance department	5	100%

Step 2: Assign total maintenance department costs of $180,000 to each activity cost pool based on the percentages computed in step 1

Maintenance costs assigned to cost pools

Costs assigned to the repair cost pool ($180,000 × 60%)	$108,000
Costs assigned to the set-up cost pool ($180,000 × 40%)	72,000
Total maintenance department costs assigned	$180,000

LO 4: Suggest cost drivers for applying a particular cost pool to units produced.

The costs assigned to each cost pool must now be allocated to Master File's two product lines. Management has determined that the **number of work orders** is the most appropriate activity base for allocating the **repair cost pool** to each product line. The maintenance department receives approximately **250** repair work orders each year. Of these, about **200** are related to the metal cabinet line, and **50** are related to the wooden cabinet line. In a typical year, the metal cabinets are allocated approximately **$86,400** from the repair costs pool, whereas wooden cabinets are allocated approximately **$21,600**, as computed below.

Allocation of Repair Cost Pool to Each Product Line

Step 1: Establish the percent of repair cost pool to be allocated to each product line using the number of work orders as an activity base

		% of total
Work orders related to metal cabinet line per year	200	80%
Work orders related to wooden cabinet line per year	50	20%
Total work orders per year	250	100%

Step 2: Allocate $108,000 from the repair cost pool to each product line based on the percentages computed in step 1

Repair cost pool allocated to each product line

Costs allocated to the metal cabinet line ($108,000 × 80%)	$ 86,400
Costs allocated to the wooden cabinet line ($108,000 × 20%)	21,600
Total repair costs allocated to both product lines	$108,000

The **number of production runs** is determined to be the most significant cost driver of set-up costs. Thus, production runs will serve as the activity base for allocating the **set-up cost pool** to each product line. Master File schedules approximately **200** production runs each year. Of these, about **150** are for metal cabinets, and **50** are for wooden cabinets. Thus, in a typical year, the metal cabinets are allocated approximately **$54,000** from the set-up cost pool, whereas wooden cabinets are allocated about **$18,000**, computed as follows.

Allocation of Set-up Cost Pool to Each Product Line

Step 1: Establish the percent of set-up cost pool to be allocated to each product line using the number of production runs as an activity base

		% of total
Production runs of metal cabinets per year	150	75%
Production runs of wooden cabinets per year	50	25%
Total Production runs per year	200	100%

Step 2: Allocate $72,000 from the set-up cost pool to each product line based on the percentages computed in step 1

Set-up cost pool allocated to each product line

Costs allocated to the metal cabinet line ($72,000 x 75%)	$54,000
Costs allocated to the wooden cabinet line ($72,000 x 25%)	18,000
Total set-up costs allocated to both product lines	$72,000

In summary, the maintenance department averages $108,000 in repair-related costs, and $72,000 in set-up costs each year (or total costs of $180,000). Thus, at normal levels of production, an ABC system allocates $86,400 in repair costs to the metal cabinet line, and $21,600 in repair costs to the wooden cabinet line. In addition, the ABC system allocated $54,000 in set-up costs to the metal cabinet line, and $18,000 in set-up costs to the wooden cabinet line.

Utilities Costs Utilities costs account for nearly **$69,600** of Master File's total manufacturing overhead costs. A large portion of this amount is incurred to heat the factory and supply power to the large machines used in manufacturing the metal cabinet line.

Thus, in its ABC system, Master File identifies heating demands and machinery power demands as separate **activity cost pools**. As such, each of these pools is assigned a portion of the $69,600 utility costs. Management believes that the **number of kilowatt hours (KWH)** required for each activity is the most significant cost driver of utilities costs. Using KWH as an **activity base, $24,360** is assigned to the **heating cost pool,** whereas **$45,240** is assigned to the **machinery cost pool**, as computed below.

Assigning Utilities Costs to Activity Pools

Step 1: Establish the percent of total utilities costs to be assigned to each activity cost pool using the number of KWH as an activity base

		% of total
KWH per year for heating requirements	175,000	35%
KWH per year for machinery requirements	325,000	65%
KWH required per year	500,000	100%

CHAPTER 21 INTRODUCTION TO MANAGERIAL ACCOUNTING; ACCOUNTING FOR MANUFACTURING OPERATIONS   1095

Step 2: Assign total utilities costs of $69,600 to each activity cost pool based on the percentages computed in step 1

Utility costs assigned to cost pools

Costs assigned to the heating cost pool ($69,600 × 35%)	$24,360
Costs assigned to the machinery cost pool ($69,600 × 65%)	45,240
Total utilities costs assigned	$69,600

The costs assigned to each of these cost pools must now be allocated to the metal and wooden product lines. Management believes that **square metres** of production space occupied by each product line is the most appropriate activity base for allocating the **heating cost pool**. Of the company's 10,000 square metres of production space, about **8,500** is dedicated to the metal cabinet line, and **1,500** is dedicated to the wooden cabinet line. Thus, in a typical year, the metal cabinets are allocated **$20,706** of heating pool costs, whereas wooden cabinets are allocated only **$3,654**, computed below.

Allocation of Heating Cost Pool to Each Product Line

Step 1: Establish the percent of heating cost pool to be allocated to each product line using square metres of production space as an activity base

		% of total
Square metres occupied by the metal cabinet line	8,500	85%
Square metres occupied by the wooden cabinet line	1,500	15%
Square metres of total production space occupied	10,000	100%

Step 2: Allocate $24,360 in heating cost pool to each product line based on the percentages computed in step 1

Heating cost pool allocated to each product line

Costs allocated to the metal cabinet line ($24,360 × 85%)	$20,706
Costs allocated to the wooden cabinet line ($24,360 × 15%)	3,654
Total heating cost allocated to both product lines	$24,360

The **number of machine hours** is determined to be the most significant cost driver of machinery power costs. Thus, machine hours will serve as the activity base for allocating the **machinery cost pool** to each product line. The company utilizes approximately **50,000** machine hours each year. Of these, about **45,000** pertain to machinery used to manufacture metal cabinets, and **5,000** pertain to machines used for making wooden cabinets. Thus, in a typical year, the metal cabinets are allocated approximately **$40,716** of machinery pool costs, whereas wooden cabinets are allocated approximately **$4,524**, as shown below.

Allocation of Machinery Cost Pool to Each Product Line

Step 1: Establish the percent of machinery cost pool to be allocated to each product line using the number of machine hours as an activity base

		% of total
Machine hours used for metal cabinets per year	45,000	90%
Machine hours used for wooden cabinets per year	5,000	10%
Total machine hours per year	50,000	100%

Step 2: Allocate $45,240 in machinery cost pool to each product line based on the percentages computed in step 1

Machinery costs allocated to each product line

Costs allocated to the metal cabinet line ($45,240 × 90%)	$40,716
Costs allocated to the wooden cabinet line ($45,240 × 10%)	4,524
Total machinery cost allocated to both product lines	$45,240

In summary, annual utilities costs average $24,360 for heating and $45,240 for powering machinery (for a total of $69,600). At normal levels of production, an ABC system allocated approximately $20,706 of heating costs to the metal cabinet line and $3,654 of heating costs to the wooden cabinet line. In addition, it allocates $40,716 of machinery power costs to the metal cabinet line, and $4,524 to the wooden cabinet line.

Determining Unit Costs in an ABC System

We may now compute Master File's overhead costs on a ***per unit*** basis. At normal levels of activity, the company produces and sells 42,000 metal file cabinets and 9,000 wooden file cabinets per year. Thus, the unit manufacturing overhead cost of each metal cabinet is ***$4.81***, compared to ***$5.31*** for each wooden cabinet. These unit costs are computed below.

Unit costs using ABC

	Metal Cabinets	Wooden Cabinets
Maintenance Department Costs:		
Allocated from the repair cost pool	$ 86,400	$21,600
Allocated from the set-up cost pool	54,000	18,000
Utilities Costs:		
Allocated from the heating cost pool	20,706	3,654
Allocated from the machinery cost pool	40,716	4,524
Total manufacturing costs allocated to each line	$201,822	$47,778
Total units produced and sold per year	42,000	9,000
Manufacturing overhead costs per unit	$ 4.81	$ 5.31

Two observations should be made regarding these figures. First, at normal levels of activity, Master File's ABC system allocates the entire $249,600 in annual overhead costs to each product line ($201,822 to the metal cabinet line and $47,778 to the wooden cabinet line). Second, the amount of manufacturing overhead allocated to each product is significantly ***different*** than what was allocated using a single activity base.

Comparing methods

	Metal Cabinets	Wooden Cabinets
Manufacturing overhead allocated using ABC	$4.81	$ 5.31
Manufacturing overhead applied using direct labour hours (DLH):		
Metal cabinets (2 DLH × $1.60 per DLH)	3.20	
Wooden cabinets (8 DLH × $1.60 per DLH)		12.80
Differences in overhead application per unit	$1.61	$(7.49)

As indicated, manufacturing overhead applied to the metal file cabinets using the ABC system is **$1.61** more than it was when a single activity base of direct labour hours was used. However, the amount applied to the wooden cabinets using the ABC system is **$7.49 less** than it was previously. As a consequence, Master File is likely to **raise** the selling price of its metal file cabinets, and **lower** the selling price of its wooden file cabinets, as shown below.

Change in selling price using ABC

	Metal Cabinets	Wooden Cabinets
Direct materials	$15.00	$25.00
Direct labour (at $10.00 per hour)	20.00	80.00
Manufacturing overhead (using the ABC system)	4.81	5.31
Total manufacturing costs per unit	$39.81	$110.31
Sales price as a percentage of total manufacturing cost	160%	160%
Selling prices indicated by the ABC system	$63.70	$176.50
Selling prices indicated by the single activity base system	61.12	188.48
Price increase (reduction) indicated by the ABC system	$2.58	$ (11.98)

If Master File maintains its current pricing policy, it will raise the price of metal file cabinets by **$2.58** per unit, and lower the price of its wooden file cabinets by **$11.98** per unit.[1]

You will recall that Master File currently is selling its metal filing cabinets for about **$3 less** than competitive products. Therefore, the metal cabinet prices will remain competitive even if their sales price is raised by $2.58 per unit. However, the company's wooden file cabinets have been priced at **$10.00 more** than competitive products. Thus, by lowering unit selling price by $11.98, Master File's wooden cabinets can now be priced competitively **without sacrificing product quality**.

Summary

For many companies, the use of a single activity base remains an appropriate method of allocating manufacturing overhead costs to products. However, we have illustrated that using a single cost driver may result in serious costing distortions in some situations. Companies that manufacture a diverse line of products are especially prone to these distortions. In short, the special characteristics of each product line may require the use of several different cost drivers.

In an ABC system, the allocation of manufacturing overhead is based upon the specific activities that drive overhead costs. Thus, ABC should provide a more accurate measure of each product's "true" cost.

---

[1] To keep our illustration short, we assumed that maintenance and utilities costs were Master File's **only** manufacturing overhead costs. Consequently, overhead costs are relatively low in comparison to the cost of direct materials and direct labour. In many companies, overhead represents a much larger component of total manufacturing costs. Thus, cost distortions often are significantly greater than those shown here.

Assignment Material

Discussion Questions

1. What is meant by the term **new manufacturing environment**? What are some examples of innovative manufacturing approaches characteristic of the new environment?
2. Define the term **activity base**.
3. Define the term **cost driver**.
4. Why is the use of a single activity base inappropriate for some companies?
5. Describe how an activity-based costing system can improve overhead cost allocations in companies that produce a diverse line of products.
6. What is an **activity cost pool**?
7. Why is the use of direct labour hours as an activity base likely to be inappropriate in a highly mechanized production facility?
8. Describe the steps in implementing an activity-based costing system.
9. Discuss the potential benefits associated with using an activity-based costing system.

Problems

PROBLEM D-1
Selecting Activity Bases
(LO 4)

Listed below are the eight activity-cost pools used by the Charvez Corporation

Production set-up costs   *Maintenance costs*
Heating costs   *Design and engineering costs*
Machinery power costs   *Materials warehouse costs*
Purchasing department costs   *Product inspection costs*

Suggest an appropriate activity base for allocating each of the above activity cost pools to products. (Consider each cost pool independently.)

PROBLEM D-2
Implementing an ABC System
(ETHICS)

Dave Miller is the controller of the Mica Corporation. Mica produces five different industrial cleaning products. Miller recently decided to implement an activity-based costing system at Mica. In designing the system, he decided to identify heating costs as a separate cost pool. These costs will be allocated to products using the square metres of production space as a cost driver. Thus, the more square metres a particular product line requires, the greater its allocation of heating costs will be.

Miller has asked each production manager to submit an estimate of the production space occupied by their respective product lines. The figures he receives will be used to allocate the heating cost pool. The five production managers at Mica are paid an annual bonus based on their ability to control production costs traceable to their respective product lines.

What ethical concern do you have regarding the method used to gather information about space utilization at Mica? What suggestions do you have regarding how this information should be gathered?

PROBLEM D-3
Allocating Activity Cost Pools
(LO 3, 4)

Costume Kings has two product lines: machine-made costumes and hand-made costumes. The company assigns $80,000 in manufacturing overhead costs to two cost pools: power costs and inspection costs. Of this amount, the power cost pool has been assigned $32,000 and the inspection cost pool has been assigned $48,000. Additional information about each product line is shown below:

	Machine-Made	Hand-Made
Sales revenue	$240,000	$160,000
Direct labour and materials costs	$120,000	$ 96,000
Units produced and sold	48,000	16,000
Machine hours	96,000	4,000
Square metres of production space	1,560	1,040
Material orders received	150	100
Quality control inspection hours	2,000	500

INSTRUCTIONS

a. Allocate the manufacturing overhead from the activity cost pools to each product line. Use what you believe are the most significant cost drivers from the information provided.
b. Compute the cost per unit of machine-made costumes and hand-made costumes.
c. On a per-unit basis, which product line appears to be the most profitable? Explain.

PROBLEM D-4
Applying Overhead Costs Using ABC
(LO 2, 3, 4)

Norton Chemical Company produces two products: Amithol and Bitrite. The company uses an activity-based costing (ABC) system to allocate manufacturing overhead to these products. The costs incurred by Norton's purchasing department average $80,000 per year and constitute a major portion of the company's total manufacturing overhead.

Purchasing department costs are assigned to two activity cost pools: (1) the order cost pool, and (2) the inspection cost pool. Costs are assigned to the pools based on the number of employees engaged in each activity. Of the department's five full-time employees, one is responsible for ordering raw materials, and four are responsible for inspecting incoming shipments of materials.

Costs assigned to the order pool are allocated to products based on the total number of purchase orders generated by each product line. Costs assigned to the inspection pool are allocated to products based on the number of inspections related to each product line.

For the upcoming year, Norton estimates the following activity levels:

	Total	Amithol	Bitrite
Purchase orders generated	10,000	2,000	8,000
Inspections conducted	2,400	1,800	600

In a normal year, the company conducts 2,400 inspections to sample the quality of raw materials. The large number of Amithol-related inspections is due to quality problems experienced in the past. The quality of Bitrite materials has been consistently good.

INSTRUCTIONS

a. Assign the purchasing department's costs to the individual cost pools.
b. Allocate the order cost pool to the individual product lines.
c. Allocate the inspection cost pool to the individual product lines.
d. Suggest how Norton might reduce manufacturing costs incurred by the purchasing department.

PROBLEM D-5
ABC vs. Use of a Single Activity Base
(LO 2, 3, 4)

Dixon Robotics manufactures three robot models: the A3B4, the BC11, and the C3PO. Dixon allocates manufacturing overhead to each model based on machine hours. A large portion of the company's manufacturing overhead costs is incurred by the maintenance department. This year, the department anticipates that it will incur $100,000 in total costs. The following estimates pertain to the upcoming year:

Model	Estimated Machine Hours	Estimated Units or Production
A3B4	20,000	6,250
BC11	15,000	5,000
C3PO	5,000	2,500

Ed Smith, Dixon's cost accountant, suspects that unit costs are being distorted by using a single activity base to allocate maintenance department costs to products.

Thus, he is considering the implementation of an activity-based costing (ABC) system.

Under the proposed ABC system, the costs of the maintenance department would be allocated to the following activity cost pools using the number of work orders as an activity base: (1) the repairs pool, and (2) the janitorial pool. Of the 2,000 work orders filed with the maintenance department each year, approximately 400 relate to repair activities, and 1,600 relate to janitorial activities.

Machinery repairs correlate with the number of production runs of each robot model. Thus, the repairs pool would be allocated to robots based on each model's corresponding number of production runs. Janitorial services correlate with square metres of production space. Thus, the janitorial pool would be allocated to products based on the square metres of production space devoted to each robot model. The following table provides a summary of annual production run activity and square metres requirements:

Model	Estimated Number of Production Runs	Estimated Square Metres of Production Space Used
A3B4	50	5,000
BC11	150	10,000
C3PO	200	25,000

INSTRUCTIONS

a. Calculate the amount of maintenance department costs that would be allocated to each robot model (on a per-unit basis) using machine hours as an activity base.
b. Calculate the amount of maintenance department costs that would be allocated to each robot model (on a per-unit basis) using the proposed ABC system.
c. Are cost allocations distorted using machine hours as a single activity base? Explain your answer.

ANNUAL REPORT OF LOBLAW COMPANIES LIMITED

On the following pages we present the 1997 annual report of Loblaw Companies Limited, a publicly held corporation. This report was selected to illustrate many of the financial reporting concepts discussed in this textbook. But not all of the terminology and accounting policies appearing in this report are consistent with our text discussions. This illustrates some of the diversity that exists in financial reporting.

AR-2

Loblaw Companies Limited
Annual Report 1997

Loblaw Companies Limited is Canada's largest retail and wholesale food distributor with operations across the country.

Loblaw Companies strives to provide superior returns to its shareholders through a combination of share price appreciation and dividends. To this end, it follows certain fundamental operating principles. It concentrates on food retailing, with the objective of providing consumers with the best in one-stop shopping for everyday household needs. It maintains a significant program of reinvestment in and expansion of its existing markets. It is highly selective in acquisitions and continues to invest in products and technology. Loblaw seeks long term, stable growth, taking managed operating risks from a strong balance sheet position.

Loblaw Companies is one of the largest private employers in Canada with over 70,000 employees throughout the business and has a responsibility to provide fair wages and secure employment. Loblaw believes this responsibility can best be met in a stable, low cost operating environment where all associated with the Company accept the need to continuously improve its ability to serve our customers.

Contents

Geographic Divisions	
Financial Highlights	1
Retail Operations	2
Wholesale Operations	3
Report to Shareholders	4
Review of Operations	9
Operating Segments	17
Financial Report	18

AR-4

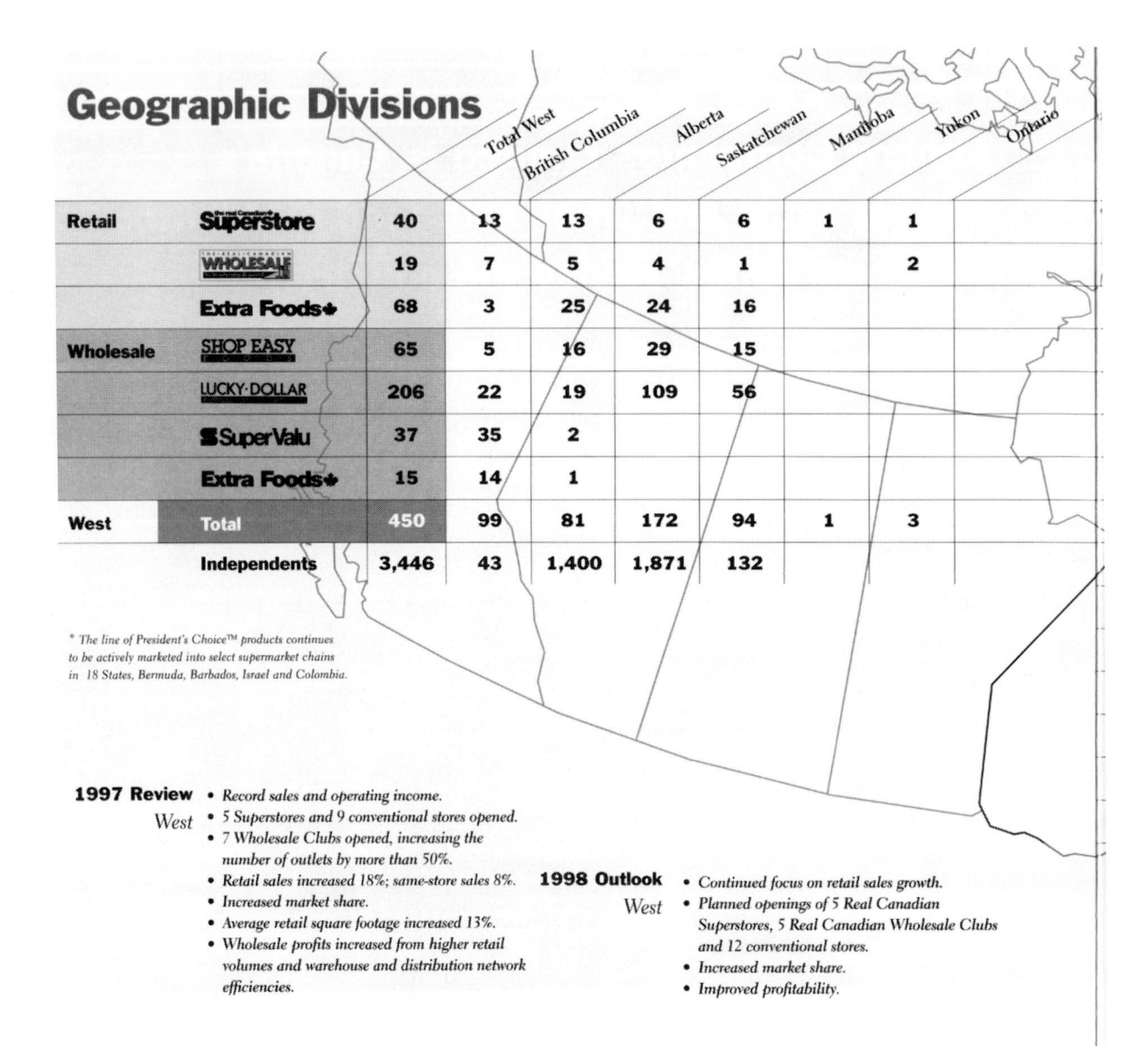

Geographic Divisions

			Total West	British Columbia	Alberta	Saskatchewan	Manitoba	Yukon	Ontario
Retail	Superstore	40	13	13	6	6	1	1	
	WHOLESALE	19	7	5	4	1	2		
	Extra Foods*	68	3	25	24	16			
Wholesale	SHOP EASY	65	5	16	29	15			
	LUCKY·DOLLAR	206	22	19	109	56			
	SuperValu	37	35	2					
	Extra Foods*	15	14	1					
West	Total	450	99	81	172	94	1	3	
	Independents	3,446	43	1,400	1,871	132			

*The line of President's Choice™ products continues to be actively marketed into select supermarket chains in 18 States, Bermuda, Barbados, Israel and Colombia.

1997 Review
West
- Record sales and operating income.
- 5 Superstores and 9 conventional stores opened.
- 7 Wholesale Clubs opened, increasing the number of outlets by more than 50%.
- Retail sales increased 18%; same-store sales 8%.
- Increased market share.
- Average retail square footage increased 13%.
- Wholesale profits increased from higher retail volumes and warehouse and distribution network efficiencies.

1998 Outlook
West
- Continued focus on retail sales growth.
- Planned openings of 5 Real Canadian Superstores, 5 Real Canadian Wholesale Clubs and 12 conventional stores.
- Increased market share.
- Improved profitability.

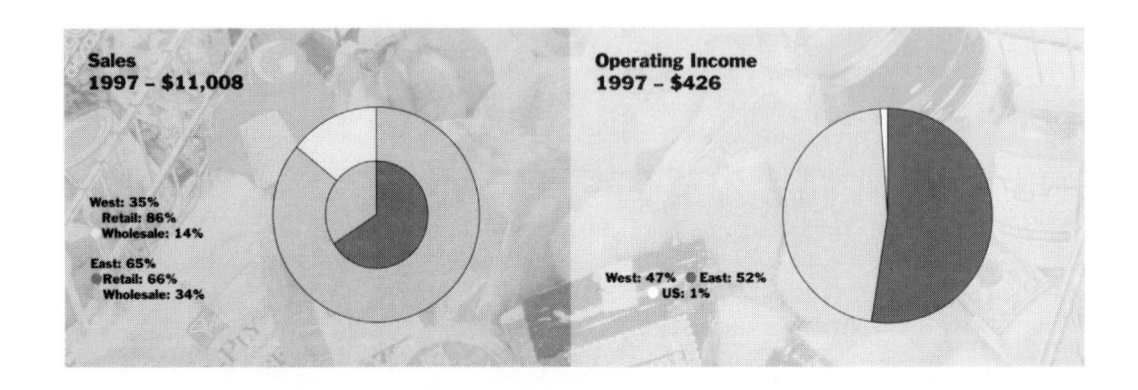

Sales
1997 – $11,008

West: 35%
  Retail: 86%
  Wholesale: 14%
East: 65%
  Retail: 66%
  Wholesale: 34%

Operating Income
1997 – $426

West: 47% East: 52%
  US: 1%

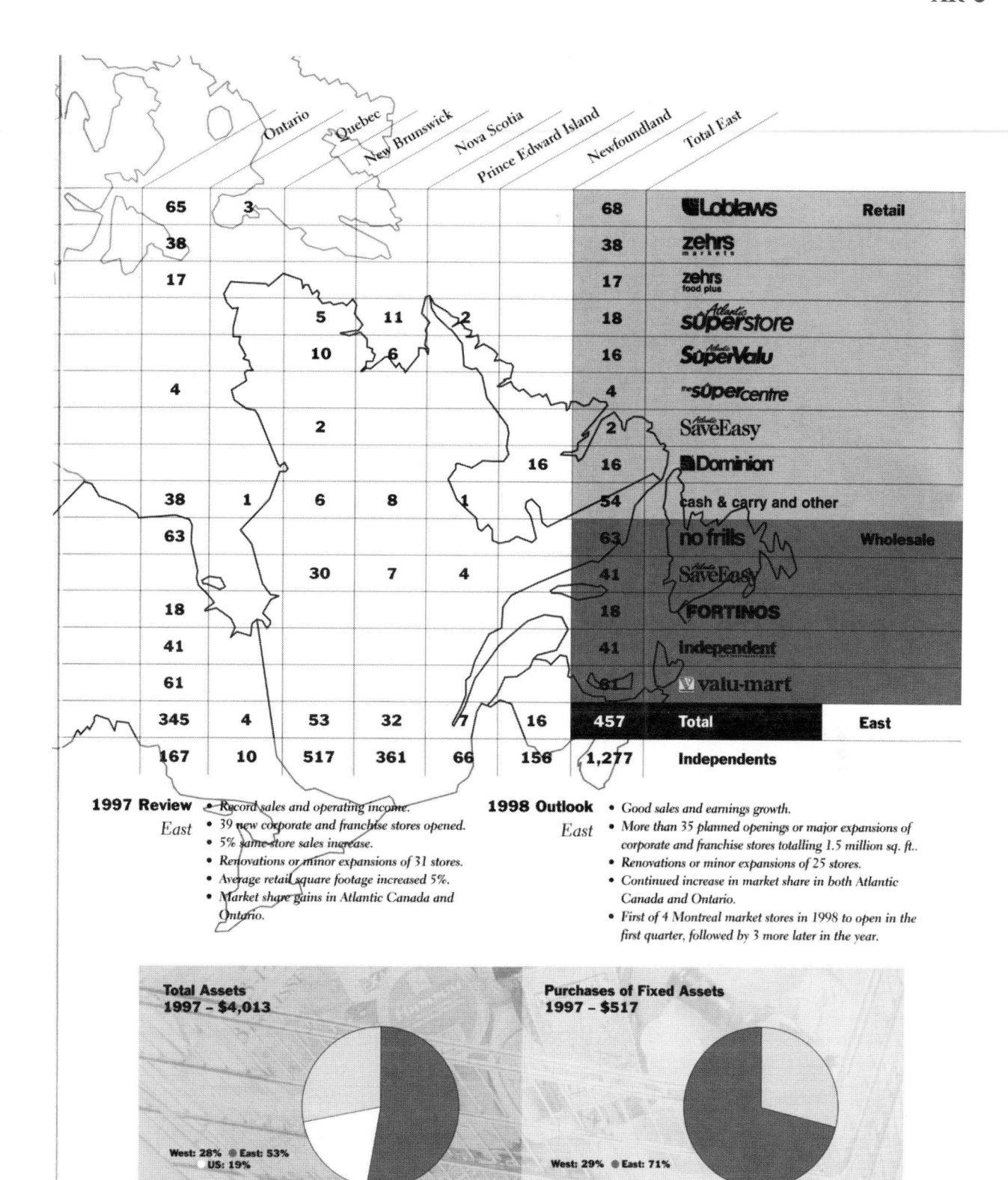

Ontario	Quebec	New Brunswick	Nova Scotia	Prince Edward Island	Newfoundland	Total East		
65	3					68	Loblaws	Retail
38						38	zehrs	
17						17	zehrs food plus	
		5	11	2		18	Atlantic superstore	
		10	6			16	Atlantic SuperValu	
4						4	the supercentre	
		2				2	Atlantic SaveEasy	
					16	16	Dominion	
38	1	6	8	1		54	cash & carry and other	
63						63	no frills	Wholesale
		30	7	4		41	Atlantic SaveEasy	
18						18	FORTINOS	
41						41	independent	
61						61	valu-mart	
345	4	53	32	7	16	457	**Total**	East
167	10	517	361	66	156	1,277	**Independents**	

1997 Review
East
- Record sales and operating income.
- 39 new corporate and franchise stores opened.
- 5% same-store sales increase.
- Renovations or minor expansions of 31 stores.
- Average retail square footage increased 5%.
- Market share gains in Atlantic Canada and Ontario.

1998 Outlook
East
- Good sales and earnings growth.
- More than 35 planned openings or major expansions of corporate and franchise stores totalling 1.5 million sq. ft..
- Renovations or minor expansions of 25 stores.
- Continued increase in market share in both Atlantic Canada and Ontario.
- First of 4 Montreal market stores in 1998 to open in the first quarter, followed by 3 more later in the year.

Total Assets
1997 – $4,013

West: 28% East: 53%
US: 19%

Purchases of Fixed Assets
1997 – $517

West: 29% East: 71%

Financial Highlights

(in millions of dollars)		**1997**	1996	1995
Operating Results	Sales	**11,008**	9,848	9,854
	Trading profit (EBITDA) [1]	**573**	481	449
	Operating income (EBIT)	**426**	359	320
	Earnings before income taxes	**382**	313	271
	Net earnings	**213**	174	147
Financial Position	Total debt and debt equivalents	**1,289**	1,155	980
	Total shareholders' equity	**1,495**	1,311	1,160
	Total assets	**4,013**	3,531	3,197
Cash Flow	Cash flow from operations	**426**	262	270
	Purchases of fixed assets	**517**	389	302
Per Common Share (dollars)	Net earnings	**.88**	.72	.60
	Cash flow from operations	**1.76**	1.08	1.12
	Dividends declared	**.15**	.12	.11
	Year end dividend rate	**.16**	.12	.12
	Book value	**6.08**	5.35	4.74
	Market price – year end	**26.00**	14.25	10.29
	– high	**26.85**	14.50	10.50
	– low	**14.15**	10.33	7.75
Financial Ratios [2]	Return on common equity	**15.3 %**	14.2 %	13.4 %
	Return on total assets	**14.1 %**	13.5 %	12.2 %
	Return on sales			
	Trading profit (EBITDA) [1]	**5.2 %**	4.9 %	4.6 %
	Earnings before income taxes	**3.5 %**	3.2 %	2.8 %
	Net earnings	**1.9 %**	1.8 %	1.5 %
	Cash flow from operations	**3.9 %**	2.7 %	2.7 %
	Interest coverage on total debt and debt equivalents	**9.7:1**	7.9:1	6.0:1
	Total debt and debt equivalents to equity	**.34:1**	.33:1	.25:1

1. Trading profit is defined as operating income before depreciation and amortization (EBITDA).
2. For purposes of calculating financial ratios, debt is reduced by cash and short term investments net of bank advances and notes payable.

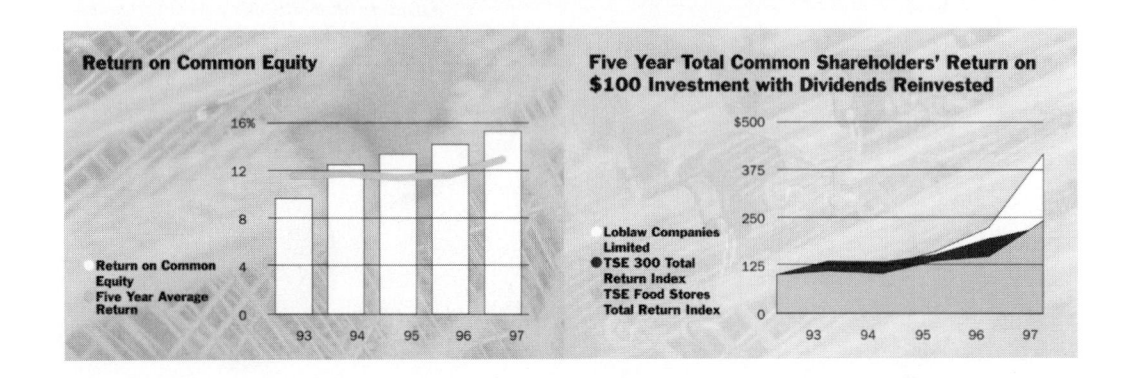

Report to Shareholders

W. Galen Weston
Chairman

Richard J. Currie
President

The year 1997 was an outstanding one for Loblaw Companies by any measure. Sales were up 12 percent from 1996, at $11.01 billion, with operating income of $426 million, net earnings of $213 million and earnings per share of $.88 all setting new highs.

Earnings per share have tripled ($.88 from $.29) in the last five years.

Sales throughout the Canadian business are now increasing rapidly, at the rate of about $1 billion in 1997, following a $.7 billion growth in 1996, as stores in existing markets are enlarged and modernized and as we enter new markets. This growth follows a six year period (1990 - 1995) of flat sales in the West of approximately $2.9 billion per year, during which time, store and customer rationalizations in wholesale operations were completed.

In fact, sales is the "big story" in Loblaw Companies today. In a total market (food sold through stores of any type) that is growing about 3 percent a year, our Canadian sales have grown by 20 percent in the last 2 years (26 percent in the West and 17 percent in the East). We expect sales to at least match these growth rates in 1998 and 1999.

Report to Shareholders   *page 5*

The rapidly improving sales and operating performance has been driven over the last five years, by average corporate store size increasing 36 percent (from 32.0 thousand square feet in 1992 to 43.6 thousand square feet in 1997), while sales per average square foot also improved ($519 in 1992 vs. $534 in 1997). The larger store size has enabled us to provide consumers with a greater variety of everyday household needs, thereby increasing our gross margin dollars, without increasing our expenses at the same rate. One example of more fully meeting customer needs is that we now operate 167 full line pharmacies within corporate stores across Canada and an additional 29 pharmacies in franchised stores.

The financial implication of this change in store size and product mix is that Loblaw can increase sales and profitability rates at the same time. To illustrate, in 1995 operating income was 3.2% of sales, in 1996 it improved to 3.6% of sales and in 1997 a further improvement to 3.9% took place.

The present capital investment program and sales expectations are based on our belief that there is still much room for Loblaw Companies to grow across all of Canada. In March of 1998 we will open our first store in the Montreal area, the second-largest city in the country and one in which we currently have no presence. Plans are to open 3 to 5 stores per year in that market over the next several years. Growth opportunities in the West are also significant as current market shares in Alberta and British Columbia could triple before matching those already achieved in Ontario.

Growth is not only driven by asset investments but also by marketing initiatives emanating from our controlled label program, which continues to represent a unique and growing part of our product offering to consumers. In 1997, of the $11.01 billion total sales, $1.6 billion or 15 percent was controlled label, including the famous President's Choice™ and no name™ products. An important part of this program has been the establishment of our Club Pack™, or large-size and multipack packages in response to

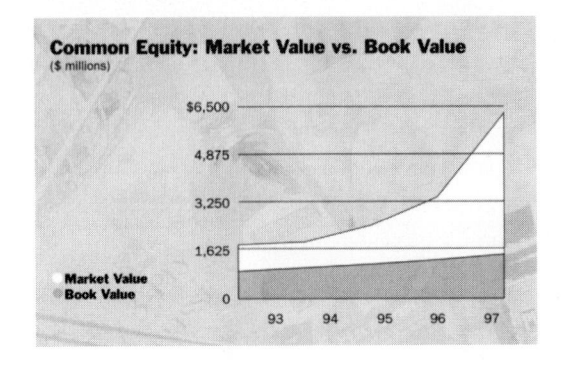

Report to Shareholders

consumer demand. Their sales in 1997 approached $470 million, from a virtual standing start five years ago as we responded to the warehouse membership club incursion into Canada.

Again in 1997, Loblaw Companies increased its number of unionized employees, now at 55,700, compared with 50,200 at year end 1996 and 33,000 at the beginning of the decade. We continue to employ one of the largest number of unionized Canadians of any company in Canada and we are growing that number faster than any other business. Our union relations have been solid, based on straight talk and the ensuing respect on both sides. At present, we are working towards convincing union leadership that 100 percent unionization of stores or warehouses leads in many cases to less total union members than does a partial unionization. All our new food competitors, be they mass merchandisers (Wal-Mart, Zellers, etc.), warehouse clubs (Price-Costco) or promotional drug stores are not unionized. They are non-union for a reason and it is that non-union is a lower cost operation. Lower cost means lower prices. But no customer can be expected to pay higher prices to us because we pay higher wages to our workers. Just as we have adapted and reduced our costs in a creative fashion to grow despite these new, non-union non-traditional formats, so must unions now use their creative energies to increase and even maintain their membership in a changing retail world.

Loblaw Companies has no intention of pausing or resting on its laurels and it is operating from a clear strategic direction.

The massive capital investment program now well under way is increasing our total store square footage by about 10 percent a year. Large, modern stores will improve our market share and market share per store in every region.

Within that program, we are committed to making total perishables (from meat and produce to home meal solutions, i.e., in-store prepared meals) comparable in quality and value to the controlled label program that forms the base or core of our marketing activities. We intend that our perishables be superior to any other chain. To that end we have established and enhanced our own produce procurement operations in California, Florida and Texas to distinguish our quality from the products generally available to the Canadian market. We have also recently established a relationship with Mövenpick™, to expand into the best mix of in-store prepared home meal solutions.

With stores, controlled labels and perishables of the highest order, we are strongly building and positioning towards our objective of providing Canadian consumers with the best in "one-stop shopping for everyday household needs". Those

Report to Shareholders

needs have increased dramatically over the years, from food to pharmacy, health and beauty care, to general merchandise, to photo finishing, dry cleaning, flowers and books. Those needs now even include banking, an industry to which we are bringing "fresh financial thinking" with President's Choice Financial™ in trials presently under way in Ottawa and St. Thomas, Ontario and Calgary, Alberta.

For some years we have noted in the Annual Report that "the success or failure of retailers depends on the attitude of the employees". The business is now investing over half a billion dollars a year in its future, over twice its net earnings and is also paying out well over $1 billion each year in wages and benefits to its employees. Such figures demonstrate more than words ever can the depth of our commitment to the business and its future. We believe that food retailing is about the seemingly conflicting elements of innovation and detail, growth and low cost, people and technology, and finally, fear and courage. Over the past 20+ years, this Company has faced and overcome risks of all types, both internally and in the marketplace. While the market value of Loblaw Companies has increased by over 150 times in that period, we think its best days are still ahead of it and we look forward to what is yet to come.

W. Galen Weston
Chairman

Richard J. Currie
President

Responsibility for Financial Reporting

Management is responsible for the preparation and presentation of the consolidated financial statements and all other information in the Annual Report. This responsibility includes the selection of appropriate accounting principles and methods in addition to making the judgements and estimates necessary to prepare financial statements in accordance with generally accepted accounting principles. It also includes ensuring that the other financial information presented elsewhere in the Annual Report is consistent with the financial statements.

To provide reasonable assurance that assets are safeguarded and that relevant and reliable financial information is being produced, management maintains a system of internal controls. Internal auditors who are employees of the Company, review and evaluate internal controls on management's behalf, coordinating this work with the independent shareholders' auditors. The financial statements have been audited by the independent shareholders' auditors, KPMG, whose report follows.

The Board of Directors, acting through an Audit Committee which is comprised solely of directors who are not employees of the Company, is responsible for determining that management fulfills its responsibilities in the preparation of financial statements and the financial control of operations. The Audit Committee recommends the independent auditors for appointment by the shareholders. It meets regularly with financial management, internal auditors and independent auditors to discuss internal controls, auditing matters and financial reporting issues. The independent shareholders' auditors have unrestricted access to the Audit Committee. The Committee reviews the Consolidated Financial Statements and the Management Discussion and Analysis prior to the Board approving them for inclusion in the Annual Report.

Richard J. Currie
President

Donald G. Reid
Executive Vice President

Stephen A. Smith
Senior Vice President, Controller

Toronto, Canada March 9, 1998

Auditors' Report

To the Shareholders of Loblaw Companies Limited:

We have audited the consolidated balance sheets of Loblaw Companies Limited as at January 3, 1998, December 28, 1996 and December 30, 1995 and the consolidated statements of earnings, retained earnings and cash flow for the 53, 52 and 52 week periods then ended. These consolidated financial statements are the responsibility of the Company's management. Our responsibility is to express an opinion on these consolidated financial statements based on our audits.

We conducted our audits in accordance with generally accepted auditing standards. Those standards require that we plan and perform an audit to obtain reasonable assurance whether the consolidated financial statements are free of material misstatement. An audit includes examining, on a test basis, evidence supporting the amounts and disclosures in the consolidated financial statements. An audit also includes assessing the accounting principles used and significant estimates made by management, as well as evaluating the overall consolidated financial statement presentation.

In our opinion, these consolidated financial statements present fairly, in all material respects, the financial position of the Company as at January 3, 1998, December 28, 1996 and December 30, 1995 and the results of its operations and the changes in its financial position for the periods then ended in accordance with generally accepted accounting principles.

KPMG
Chartered Accountants Toronto, Canada March 9, 1998

Consolidated Statement of Earnings

page 20

53 Weeks Ended January 3, 1998 (in millions of dollars)		**1997** **(53 Weeks)**	1996 (52 Weeks)	1995 (52 Weeks)
Sales		**$11,008**	$9,848	$9,854
Operating Expenses	Cost of sales, selling and administrative expenses	**10,435**	9,367	9,405
	Depreciation and amortization	**147**	122	129
		10,582	9,489	9,534
Operating Income		**426**	359	320
Interest Expense (Income)	Long term	**78**	67	66
	Short term	**(34)**	(21)	(12)
		44	46	54
Net Gain on Sale of United States Retail Business (note 2)				5
Earnings Before Income Taxes		**382**	313	271
Income Taxes (note 3)		**169**	139	124
Net Earnings for the Period		**$ 213**	$ 174	$ 147
Net Earnings per Common Share (in dollars)		**$ .88**	$ .72	$ .60

Consolidated Statement of Retained Earnings

53 Weeks Ended January 3, 1998 (in millions of dollars)		**1997** **(53 Weeks)**	1996 (52 Weeks)	1995 (52 Weeks)
Retained Earnings, Beginning of Period		**$ 1,046**	$ 902	$ 783
	Net earnings for the period	**213**	174	147
		1,259	1,076	930
	Dividends declared			
	Preferred shares	**1**	1	2
	Common shares, per share – 15¢ (1996 – 12¢, 1995 – 11¢)	**37**	29	26
		38	30	28
Retained Earnings, End of Period		**$ 1,221**	$1,046	$ 902

Consolidated Balance Sheet

page 21

As at January 3, 1998
(in millions of dollars)

		1997	1996	1995
Assets				
Current Assets	Cash and short term investments (note 4)	**$ 776**	$ 720	$ 692
	Accounts receivable	**150**	158	164
	Inventories	**707**	659	610
	Prepaid expenses and other assets	**48**	16	25
		1,681	1,553	1,491
Franchise Investments and Receivables		**113**	113	94
Fixed Assets (note 5)		**2,093**	1,738	1,491
Goodwill		**38**	40	42
Other Assets		**88**	87	79
		$4,013	$3,531	$3,197
Liabilities				
Current Liabilities	Bank advances and notes payable	**$ 362**	$ 413	$ 311
	Accounts payable and accrued liabilities	**1,084**	938	937
	Taxes payable	**21**	40	42
	Long term debt and debt equivalents due within one year (note 7)	**12**	8	22
		1,479	1,399	1,312
Long Term Debt and Debt Equivalents (note 7)		**915**	734	647
Other Liabilities		**47**	30	41
Deferred Income Taxes		**77**	57	37
		2,518	2,220	2,037
Shareholders' Equity				
Share Capital (note 8)		**274**	265	258
Retained Earnings		**1,221**	1,046	902
		1,495	1,311	1,160
		$4,013	$3,531	$3,197

Approved by the Board

W. Galen Weston
Director

Richard J. Currie
Director

Consolidated Cash Flow Statement

53 Weeks Ended January 3, 1998
(in millions of dollars)

		1997 (53 Weeks)	1996 (52 Weeks)	1995 (52 Weeks)
Operations	Net earnings	$ 213	$ 174	$ 147
	Depreciation and amortization	147	122	129
	Gain on sale of fixed assets	(8)	(5)	(6)
	Deferred income taxes	15	12	19
		367	303	289
Provided from (used for) Working Capital		59	(41)	(19)
Cash Flow from Operations		**426**	**262**	**270**
Investment	Purchases of fixed assets	(517)	(389)	(302)
	Sale of United States retail business (note 2)			368
	Proceeds from sale of fixed assets	25	25	19
	(Increase) in franchise investments and receivables		(19)	(8)
	Net decrease (increase) in other items	24	(11)	(25)
		(468)	(394)	52
Net Cash (Out) In Before Financing and Dividends		(42)	(132)	322
Financing	Long term debt and debt equivalents			
	– Issued	200	100	6
	– Retired	(15)	(27)	(78)
	Share Capital			
	– Issued	9	8	3
	– Retired		(1)	(60)
		194	80	(129)
Dividends		(45)	(22)	(28)
Increase (Decrease) in Cash		107	(74)	165
Cash at Beginning of Period		307	381	216
Cash at End of Period		$ 414	$ 307	$ 381

Cash is defined as cash and short term investments net of bank advances and notes payable.

Notes to Consolidated Financial Statements 53 Weeks Ended January 3, 1998
(In millions of dollars except Share Capital)

1. Summary of Significant Accounting Policies

Basis of Consolidation The consolidated financial statements include the accounts of the Company and all subsidiaries. The effective interest of Loblaw Companies Limited in the equity share capital of all principal subsidiaries is 100%.

Revenue Recognition Sales include retail sales revenues to consumers through corporate stores operated by the Company and wholesale sales to and service fees from franchised independent stores and independent accounts but exclude sales to corporate stores and other inter-company sales.

Cash Offsetting Cash balances, for which the Company has a right and intent of offset, are used to reduce reported short term borrowings.

Inventories Retail store inventories are stated at the lower of cost and net realizable value less normal profit margin. Wholesale inventories are stated at the lower of cost and net realizable value.

Fixed Assets Fixed assets are stated at cost, including capitalized interest. Depreciation is recorded principally on a straight line basis to amortize the cost of these assets over their estimated useful lives.

Estimated useful lives range from 25 to 40 years for buildings and 3 to 8 years for equipment and fixtures. Leasehold improvements are depreciated over the lesser of the applicable useful life and term of the lease.

Translation of Foreign Currencies Foreign currency balances are translated at the current exchange rate at each period end. Exchange gains or losses arising from the translation of foreign currency balances are included in the current period's earnings. Revenues and expenses are translated at the average exchange rate for the period.

Goodwill Goodwill arises on the acquisition of subsidiaries. It is the excess of the cost of the acquisition over the fair value of the underlying net tangible assets acquired. Goodwill is being amortized on a straight line basis determined for each acquisition over the estimated life of the benefit. The weighted average remaining amortization period is 23 years. Any permanent impairment in value, based on projected future earnings, is written off against earnings.

Derivative Financial Instruments The Company uses interest rate derivatives and cross-currency swaps to manage risks arising from fluctuations in exchange and interest rates. The income or expense arising from these instruments is included in interest expense. Unrealized gains or losses on cross-currency swaps are offset by unrealized gains or losses on the United States dollar net assets. The net exchange difference is recorded in the income statement.

Post Retirement Benefits The cost of post retirement health, insurance and other benefits, other than pensions, is expensed when paid. The cost of pension benefits is accrued as earned.

2. Sale of United States Retail Business

Substantially all of the assets of the United States retail business were sold at the end of the second quarter of 1995 for proceeds of $368. The net pre-tax gain of $5 included proceeds in excess of net book value, net of costs associated with the disposal. Operating income for the period to date of sale was not significant. Income taxes of $5 applicable to the disposal transaction were included in income taxes.

Notes to Consolidated Financial Statements 53 Weeks Ended January 3, 1998

3. Income Taxes The Company's effective income tax rate is made up as follows:

	1997	1996	1995
Combined basic Canadian federal and provincial income tax rate	**44.5 %**	44.2 %	43.5 %
Net impact of operating in foreign countries with lower effective tax rates	**(.6)**	(.3)	(1.5)
Other	**.3**	.6	3.9
	44.2 %	44.5 %	45.9 %

4. Cash and Short Term Investments The Company has $773 (1996 – $717, 1995 – $685) in cash and short term investments held by its non-Canadian subsidiaries. The $41 (1996 – $37, 1995 – $31) income from these investments is included as a reduction of interest expense.

At year end, the Company has included in cash and short term investments an interest bearing demand note receivable of $214 ($150 U.S.) from George Weston Limited, the Company's majority shareholder. Interest has been set at market rates based on LIBOR plus .25%.

5. Fixed Assets

	1997			1996		1996	1995
	Cost	**Accumulated Depreciation**	**Net Book Value**	Cost	Accumulated Depreciation	Net Book Value	Net Book Value
Properties held for development	**$ 93**		**$ 93**	$ 126		$ 126	$ 90
Land	**486**		**486**	380		380	332
Buildings	**1,148**	**$ 267**	**881**	996	$235	761	695
Equipment and fixtures	**1,057**	**637**	**420**	898	574	324	242
Leasehold improvements	**315**	**117**	**198**	225	98	127	108
	3,099	**1,021**	**2,078**	2,625	907	1,718	1,467
Capital leases – buildings and equipment	**56**	**41**	**15**	56	36	20	24
	$3,155	**$1,062**	**$2,093**	$2,681	$943	$1,738	$1,491

Interest capitalized as part of fixed assets during the period is $11 (1996 – $6, 1995 – $6).

6. Pensions The Company maintains defined benefit pension plans. Current actuarial estimates indicate that the Company's registered pension plans have a present value of accrued pension benefits of $472 (1996 – $449, 1995 – $446) and a market related value of pension fund assets of $547 (1996 – $498, 1995 – $460). As at January 3, 1998, prepaid pension costs of $79 (1996 – $78, 1995 – $67) relating to these plans are included in other assets.

Notes to Consolidated Financial Statements 53 Weeks Ended January 3, 1998

7. Long Term Debt and Debt Equivalents

	1997	1996	1995
Debentures			
Series 5, 10%, due 2006, retractable annually commencing 1996, redeemable in 2001	$ 50	$ 50	$ 50
Series 6, 9.75%, due 2001, retractable annually commencing 1993, redeemable in 1998	75	75	75
Series 7, 9%, redeemed 1996			14
Series 8, 10%, due 2007, redeemable in 2002	61	61	61
Notes			
11.4%, due 2031	169	172	175
8.75%, due 2033	200	200	200
Medium Term Notes			
7.34%, due 2001	100	100	
5.39% to 2000 and 7.91% thereafter, due 2007, redeemable in 2000	100		
6.65%, due 2027, redeemable on demand	100		
Other at a weighted average interest rate of 12.1%, due 1998 to 2009	56	67	77
Total long term debt	911	725	652
Total debt equivalents	16	17	17
	927	742	669
Less due within one year	12	8	22
Total long term debt and debt equivalents	**$915**	$734	$647

The five year schedule of repayments of long term debt and debt equivalents, at the earlier of maturity or first retraction date, excluding the Series 5 and Series 6 debentures which may be renewed dependent on market conditions at the time of renewal, is as follows: 1998 – $12; 1999 – $11; 2000 – $12; 2001 – $178; 2002 – $1.

Debentures The interest rates on the Series 5 and Series 6 debentures were reset in 1997 at 10% and 9.75% respectively. Current intentions are to reset the interest rate on the Series 5 debentures in 1998 to encourage renewal. The renewal of the Series 6 debentures in 1998 will depend on market conditions. Both Series 5 and Series 6 debentures are excluded from the amount due within one year.

Debt Equivalents First preferred shares, second series (authorized – 1,000,000) – $3.70 cumulative dividend redeemable at $70 each. In 1997, 253,782 shares were issued and outstanding (1996 – 260,006, 1995 – 266,429) in the amount of $16 (1996 – $17, 1995 – $17). Subject to certain exceptions, in each fiscal year, the Company is obligated to apply $.4 to the retirement of these shares.

Subsequent to year end, the Company filed a shelf prospectus to issue up to $500 of Medium Term Notes. During the first quarter of 1998, the Company issued $100 of these notes at 6.45%, due 2028, redeemable on demand.

Notes to Consolidated Financial Statements 53 Weeks Ended January 3, 1998

8. Share Capital

	Number of shares issued			Capital stock (in millions of dollars)		
	1997	1996	1995	**1997**	1996	1995
First preferred shares, first series	**410,852**	410,852	432,752	**$ 20**	$ 20	$ 21
Common shares	**242,780,858**	241,341,158	240,119,838	**254**	245	237
Total capital stock				**$274**	$265	$258
Weighted average common shares	**242,033,135**	240,630,561	239,840,013			

Share Description (in dollars)

First preferred shares, first series (authorized – 1,000,000) – $2.40 cumulative dividend redeemable at $50 each.
Second preferred shares, fourth series - redeemed according to their terms at $500,000 each on March 1, 1995.
Common shares (authorized – unlimited) In 1997, the Company issued 1,439,700 (1996 – 1,221,320, 1995 – 655,800) common shares for cash consideration of $8,822,871 (1996 – $8,332,508, 1995 – $3,782,084) on exercise of employee stock options.

At year end, there were outstanding stock options, which were granted at the market price on the day preceding the grant, to purchase 6,656,965 (1996 – 7,216,450, 1995 – 8,522,920) common shares at prices ranging from $6.125 to $14.25 with a weighted average price of $8.491 (1996 – $7.029, 1995 – $7.01). All options expire on dates ranging from January 6, 1999 to January 3, 2004. The exercise of the stock options would not materially dilute net earnings per common share.

On March 9, 1998, the Company announced its intention to purchase on the Toronto Stock Exchange up to 12,218,040 of its common shares, representing 5% of the common shares outstanding pursuant to a Normal Course Issuer Bid effective March 18, 1998 to March 17, 1999. Purchases will be made by the Company in accordance with the rules and by-laws of the Toronto Stock Exchange and the price which the Company will pay for any such common shares will be the market price of such shares at the time of acquisition.

9. Financial Instruments

Derivatives The Company has entered into cross-currency swaps to exchange $704 Canadian dollar debt for United States dollar debt. The swaps provide a hedge against exchange rate fluctuations on United States dollar net assets, principally cash. The swaps mature as follows: 1999 – $7; 2000 – $119; 2001 – $85; 2002 – $77 and thereafter to 2007 – $416. Currency adjustments receivable or payable arising from the swaps may be settled in cash on maturity or the swap term can be extended. As at January 3, 1998, a currency adjustment of $38 (1996 – $8, 1995 – $8) has been included in other liabilities.

In addition, the Company has entered into interest rate derivatives, converting a net notional $314 of 7.8% fixed rate debt into floating rate debt. The net maturities are as follows: 1998 – $82; 1999 – $46; 2000 – $152; 2001 – $6 and thereafter to 2004 – $28.

An event of default by the counterparties to these derivatives does not create a significant risk because the principal amounts on cross-currency swaps are netted by agreement and there is no exposure to loss of the notional principal amounts on interest rate derivatives.

Notes to Consolidated Financial Statements 53 Weeks Ended January 3, 1998

Fair Value of Financial Instruments The fair value of financial instruments is determined by reference to various market data and other valuation techniques as appropriate. With the exception of the following, the fair value of financial instruments including cash, short term investments, accounts receivable, bank advances, notes payable, accounts payable, accrued liabilities and taxes payable approximates their recorded values.

	1997		1996		1995	
	Carrying Amount	**Estimated Fair Value**	Carrying Amount	Estimated Fair Value	Carrying Amount	Estimated Fair Value
Long term debt and debt equivalents	**$927**	**$1,098**	$742	$898	$669	$760
Interest rate derivatives net asset		**$ 7**		$ 18		$ 2

The following methods and assumptions were used to estimate the fair value of each class of financial instrument for which it is practical to estimate that value.

Long Term Debt and Debt Equivalents The fair value of the Company's long term debt is estimated based on discounted cash flows of the debt using the estimated incremental borrowing rate of the Company for debt of the same remaining maturities. The fair value of the Company's debt equivalents is estimated based on market quotes or the last trade closest to the valuation date.

Interest Rate Derivatives The fair value of the net notional principal of the interest rate derivatives is estimated by discounting cash flows of the derivatives based on the market derivative rates for derivatives of the same remaining maturities.

10. Other Information

Segmented Information The Company's only significant industry segment is food distribution. Geographically segmented information is as follows:

		1997	1996	1995
Sales	Eastern Canada	**$7,182**	$6,514	$6,155
	Western Canada	**3,826**	3,334	3,034
	United States			665
Operating income	Eastern Canada	**$ 220**	$ 173	$ 165
	Western Canada	**200**	168	139
	United States	**6**	18	16
Total assets	Eastern Canada	**$2,122**	$1,875	$1,604
	Western Canada	**1,111**	936	870
	United States	**780**	720	723

United States Operating Income Operating income earned in 1997 is primarily net service fee revenue. The 1996 operating income earned includes $16 received for certain rights related to the cessation of an agreement with Wal-Mart, net service fee revenue and costs related to the disposition of some of the remaining net assets of the former United States businesses. In 1995, operating income is primarily net service fee revenue.

Notes to Consolidated Financial Statements 53 Weeks Ended January 3, 1998

Contingent Liabilities and Commitments Commitments for net operating lease payments total $767 ($901 gross, net of $134 of expected sub-lease income). Net payments for each of the next five years and thereafter are as follows: 1998 – $121; 1999 – $103; 2000 – $79; 2001 – $62; 2002 – $56 and thereafter to 2056 – $346. Gross rentals under leases assigned at the time of sale of United States divisions for which the Company is contingently liable amount to $117.

Related Party Transactions The Company's majority shareholder, George Weston Limited and its subsidiaries are related parties. It is the Company's policy to conduct all transactions and settle balances with related parties on normal trade terms. Total purchases from related companies represent about 4% of cost of sales, selling and administrative expenses.

Pursuant to an investment management agreement, the Company, through a wholly owned subsidiary, manages certain United States cash and short term investments on behalf of a wholly owned subsidiary of George Weston Limited. Management fees are based on market rates and have been included in interest income.

Subsequent to year end, the Company sold its investment in an inactive subsidiary to George Weston Limited resulting in inter-company investment holdings. A legal right of offset exists to ensure no financial statement impact to either company.

Management Discussion and Analysis

page 29

Earnings per share improved to $.88 in 1997, a 22% increase from the $.72 earned in 1996. Sales for the year, which included an extra week in 1997, increased by 12% and exceeded $11 billion for the first time.

Operating income improved to $426 million, a 19% increase over the $359 million earned in 1996. After adjusting for the inclusion in 1996 operating income of a $20 million special provision for labour restructuring and a $16 million one time cessation payment received from Wal-Mart, operating income increased by 17% over 1996. The operating margin, defined as operating income (EBIT) divided by sales, improved to 3.9% from 3.6% in 1996 while trading margin, defined as operating income before depreciation and amortization (EBITDA) divided by sales, strengthened to 5.2% from 4.9% in 1996.

Interest expense declined by 4% to $44 million from $46 million in 1996. The effect of the increase in average borrowing levels was offset by lower effective borrowing rates and higher capitalized interest as a result of the increased capital expenditures.

The effective income tax rate declined marginally to 44.2% in 1997 from 44.5% in 1996.

Results of Operations

Sales Loblaw Companies, under an accounting convention common in the food distribution industry, follows a 52 week reporting cycle which periodically necessitates a fiscal year of 53 weeks. The current fiscal year is a 53 week year. The additional week in 1997 added approximately 2% to the year-over-year sales increase. The remaining 10% increase in sales is attributable to an increase in same-store sales and to additional square footage. Excluding the impact of the extra week, same-store sales increased by 4% in 1997 and 1996. Price inflation was not significant in either year. Volume increases were also driven by the addition during the last two years of approximately 3 million net square feet to the network of corporate and franchise stores, representing an increase of 15% in total square footage. As was the case in 1996, retail sales represent approximately 73% of total sales and the remaining 27% are wholesale sales.

Sales (in millions of dollars)	**1997**	**Change**	1996	Change	1995
Eastern Canada	$ 7,182	10 %	$6,514	6 %	$6,155
Western Canada	3,826	15 %	3,334	10 %	3,034
United States					665
	$11,008	12 %	$9,848		$9,854

Note: For an understanding of the geographic areas covered by these operating segments, please refer to the map at the beginning of the book.

Eastern Canadian sales represent 65% (1996 - 66%) of total Company sales and include sales from retail operations which generate 43% of total Company sales (1996 - 44%) and wholesale sales which account for 22% of total Company sales (1996 - 22%).

Retail sales increased by 9% in 1997. Substantial capital investment continued to expand the retail store network and strengthen the existing store base by renovating, expanding or replacing existing stores. Within the retail business, 24 new stores (1996 - 24) were opened and 24 stores (1996 - 10) underwent major renovation or minor expansion. New stores include major expansions to existing locations. When weighted for openings throughout the year and considering the impact of the closure of older, smaller stores, the net effect on average square footage in 1997 was an increase of approximately 5% as compared to an increase of 8% in 1996. Excluding the impact of the extra week, 1997 same-store sales grew 4% (1996 - 2%).

The 13% (1996 - 3%) increase in wholesale sales in Eastern Canada came from increased sales through franchised stores. Franchise retail sales growth of 15% surpassed the 1996 increase of 6%. During 1997, 15 new stores (1996 - 14) were opened and 7 underwent minor expansion (1996 - 12). Partially offsetting this franchised business growth was the decline in wholesale sales to independents.

Management Discussion and Analysis

In 1998, the Company plans to open, expand or remodel approximately 60 corporate and franchised independent stores in Eastern Canada with an expected net increase of 1.5 million square feet or a 10% average net increase which is expected to result in additional sales growth.

Western Canadian sales represent 35% (1996 - 34%) of total Company sales and include sales from retail operations which generate 30% of total Company sales (1996 - 29%) and wholesale sales which account for 5% of total Company sales (1996 - 5%).

Retail sales increased by 18% (1996 - 14%) driven once again by strong superstore sales growth. A total of 5 new superstores were opened in 1997 in addition to the 2 opened in 1996. These 5 new stores represented an increase in average net superstore square footage of 11%. An additional 7 Real Canadian Wholesale Clubs were added during 1997, increasing by more than 50% the number of wholesale club locations. Growth in retail sales during 1997 was further increased by the opening of 9 conventional stores (1996 - 10). All of this activity, when weighted for openings throughout the year, had the effect of increasing the average net square footage in Western Canada by 13% (1996 - 10%). Both in 1996 and 1997, sales increases were aided by competitors' work stoppages. The 1996 competitors' strike in British Columbia had a positive impact on 1996 sales in that region and a corresponding negative impact on 1997 comparative sales in that market. The 1997 competitor's strike in Alberta had less of a positive impact on total 1997 sales. Excluding the impact of the extra week, 1997 same-store sales grew 6% (1996 - 8%).

Wholesale sales decreased 3% following a decline of 6% in 1996. This decrease was due to a rationalization in the number of independent accounts and in the number of affiliated franchise stores. A partial offset to this decline was the sales growth in food services achieved through aggressive sales efforts and pricing.

In 1998, Western Canada's capital program includes the opening of 5 superstores, 5 Real Canadian Wholesale Clubs and 12 conventional stores resulting in an expected net increase of 1.1 million square feet or 19% average net increase which is expected to result in additional sales growth.

Operating Income Operating income has increased by 19% over 1996 to $426 million. In 1997, approximately 52% of operating income was generated in Eastern Canada, 47% in Western Canada and 1% in the United States. The operating margin improved to 3.9% in 1997 from 3.6% in 1996. This improvement was predominantly from continued focus on cost control, including the rationalization of administrative and buying functions, and from higher volumes leveraging off of fixed costs.

Operating Income (in millions of dollars)		1997	Change	1996	Change	1995
Eastern Canada	Operations	$220	14 %	$193	17 %	$165
	Store labour restructuring			$ (20)		
	Operating margin [1]	3.1 %		3.0 %		2.7 %
Western Canada	Operations	$200	19 %	$168	21 %	$139
	Operating margin	5.2 %		5.0 %		4.6 %
United States	Operations	$ 6	(67)%	$ 18	13 %	$ 16
Combined		$426	19 %	$359	12 %	$320
	Operating margin	3.9 %		3.6 %		3.2 %

1. 1996 operating margin is before store labour restructuring charge.

Management Discussion and Analysis   *page 31*

Eastern Canadian operating income improved to $220 million from $193 million excluding the one time charge of $20 million for store labour restructuring in 1996. This resulted in an increase in operating margin to 3.1% from 3.0% (excluding the one time labour charge) in 1996. Operations in both Ontario and in the Atlantic provinces have contributed to strengthening the margin.

Retail operating income increased by approximately 14% (1996 - 17% excluding the one time labour charge). Gross margins improved in 1997 but were still hampered by competitive pressures. Cost control contributed to the increased operating income which included reduced labour costs as the benefits from the store labour restructuring began to be realized.

Wholesale operating income increased by approximately 14% (1996 - 16%). Similar to retail, increased sales and containment of costs and a slight increase in gross margin provided the increase in operating income.

The results for 1998 are expected to maintain the trend of increasing sales and operating income.

Western Canadian operating income improved to $200 million from $168 million in 1996. These operations continue to generate a strong operating margin of 5.2% (1996 - 5.0%). In 1997, Western Canadian operations provided 47% of total Company operating income.

Retail operating income increased by approximately 15% (1996 - 27%), principally from the Real Canadian Superstores which continued to generate good sales increases while maintaining steady gross margins and containing costs.

Wholesale operating income increased by approximately 32% (1996 - 3%), buoyed by the increase of Western Canadian retail sales and the associated product flow through the distribution centres. In addition, 1996 results included costs associated with the closing of the Foremost Dairy milk processing operation.

Earnings growth in 1998 is expected to be consistent with 1997 as stores opened during the past couple of years continue to mature.

United States operating income is composed primarily of the net service fee revenue generated through the sale of selected President's Choice™ and no name™ products to non-affiliated retailers in the United States. The decrease in 1997 was attributable to the 1996 inclusion of the one time $16 million cessation payment from Wal-Mart, net of costs related to the disposition of some of the remaining net assets of the former United States businesses. As expected, service fee revenue declined in 1997 upon the expiration of the Wal-Mart agreement. Service fee revenue for 1998 is expected to increase marginally.

Interest Expense decreased $2 million in 1997 and $8 million in 1996. The 1997 decrease was due to a combination of declining Canadian interest rates and an increase in capitalized interest offset by an increase in the average net borrowing levels of approximately $170 million. Borrowing levels increased in 1997 due to the significant capital investment program offset by higher net earnings. In 1996, average net borrowing levels were $50 million lower than 1995, reflecting the impact of investing the proceeds from the sale of the United States business for a full year in 1996 versus a partial year in 1995. The positive impact of

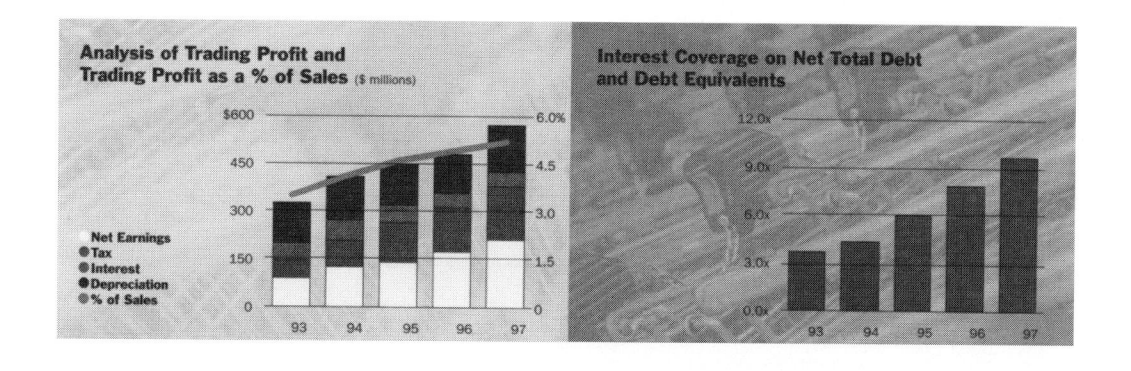

Management Discussion and Analysis

interest rate derivatives, as discussed in Note 9 to the financial statements, was partially offset in 1997 by the negative impact of cross-currency swaps. Total interest expense in 1998 is expected to be higher than the 1997 expense due to an anticipated increase in average net borrowing levels required to finance additional planned capital expenditures.

The **effective income tax rate** decreased in 1997 to 44.2% which was slightly lower than the 1996 level of 44.5%, and is expected to increase marginally in 1998.

Capital Resources and Liquidity The sound financial position of the Company did not change significantly in 1997 nor is it expected to in 1998. The Company maintains treasury centres which operate under Company approved policies and guidelines covering funding, investing, foreign exchange and interest rate management. The 1997 **total debt and debt equivalents to equity** ratio, net of cash, increased slightly to .34:1 from .33:1 in 1996. The ratio continued to be relatively low, as the proceeds from the sale of the United States assets continue to be invested short term. The 1998 ratio is expected to remain consistent with 1997 and therefore, will be well within the Company's internal guideline of a ratio of less than 1:1. **Interest coverage** improved to 9.7 times in 1997 from 7.9 times in 1996 mainly from higher earnings. The 1998 interest coverage is expected to remain at the 1997 level.

The 1997 **capital expenditure** program reached a record high of $517 million and may be analyzed as follows:

Capital Expenditures (in millions of dollars)	**1998 Estimate**	1997	1996
Eastern Canada	**$355**	$367	$294
% of Total	**69 %**	71 %	75 %
Western Canada	**$160**	$150	$ 95
% of Total	**31 %**	29 %	25 %
	$515	$517	$389
% for Retail Stores	**86 %**	85 %	87 %

Note: Projects-in-progress which the Company has effectively committed to complete total approximately $130 million of the $515 million in 1998.

Capital expenditures increased significantly over 1996 reflecting the Company's commitment to invest for growth across Canada, including new stores and significant remodeling and refurbishing and an initial capital investment supporting the planned entry into the Montreal market.

Cash flow from operations increased to $426 million from $262 million in 1996 mainly reflecting improved net earnings and improved working capital management.

Short term liquidity is provided by a combination of internally generated cash flow, net cash and short term investments and access to the commercial paper market. The Company maintains a $500 million commercial paper program which is rated A-1 and R-1 (low) by the Canadian Bond Rating Service (CBRS) and the Dominion Bond Rating Service (DBRS) respectively. The Company's commercial paper program is supported by lines of credit, extended by several banks, totaling $600 million. This program serves to finance fluctuations in working capital. Financial instruments are used to manage the effective interest rate on total debt including underlying commercial paper and short term investments.

During the second quarter of 1996, the Company filed a shelf prospectus to issue up to $300 million of Medium Term Notes (MTN) with maturities of not less than one year. The Company issued $100 million during the third quarter of 1996 and two subsequent $100 million issues during each of the first quarter and fourth quarter of 1997.

Management Discussion and Analysis *page 33*

In the first quarter of 1998, the Company filed another shelf prospectus to issue up to $500 million of MTN. This program enables the Company to issue, until January 7, 2000, unsecured debt obligations with maturities of not less than one year. This debt will be rated the same as other unsecured long term debt obligations of the Company. The Company expects to meet its 1998 cash requirements through internally generated funds and, when necessary, drawing on the $500 million MTN facility. During the first quarter of 1998, the Company issued $100 million of the new MTN at 6.45%, due 2028, redeemable on demand.

Longer term capital resources are provided by direct access to capital markets. The Company has a debt rating of A+ (low) from CBRS and A (high) from DBRS. In the fourth quarter of 1996, $14 million Series 7, 9% Debentures were redeemed. The 1997 year end weighted average interest rate on fixed rate long term debt (excluding capital lease obligations included in other long term debt, and debt equivalents) was 8.8%, down from 9.6% last year. The weighted average term to maturity, measured both on the basis of maturity date and on the earlier of maturity or first retraction date, was 21 and 20 years respectively at year end 1997 compared to 23 and 21 years at the end of 1996. The MTN issues in both 1996 and 1997, reduced the weighted average interest rate and marginally decreased the term to maturity.

Common shareholders' equity reached $1.5 billion in 1997, an increase of $184 million primarily from current earnings retained in the business. The Company's dividend policy is to declare dividends equal to approximately 20 to 25% of the prior year's earnings per common share giving consideration to year end cash flow position and future cash flow requirements and investment opportunities.

On March 9, 1998, the Company announced its intention to purchase on the Toronto Stock Exchange up to 5% or 12,218,040 of its common shares outstanding pursuant to a Normal Course Issuer Bid effective March 18, 1998 to March 17, 1999. Purchases will be made by the Company in accordance with the rules and by-laws of the Toronto Stock Exchange and the price which the Company will pay for any such common shares will be the market price of such shares at the time of acquisition.

Risk and Risk Management The Company successfully competes in the Canadian food distribution industry. Its operating philosophy is indicative of its long term objectives of security and growth. The Company employs various strategies, which may carry some short term risk, in order to achieve these objectives and to minimize the impact of perceived threats related to competitive erosion and loss of cost advantage.

Strategies employed by the Company include utilization and refinement of a variety of store formats, store banners and store sizes in order to appeal to the changing demographics of various markets. Developing and operating new departments and services which complement the traditional supermarket, allows the Company to compete effectively and efficiently in an evolving market. The

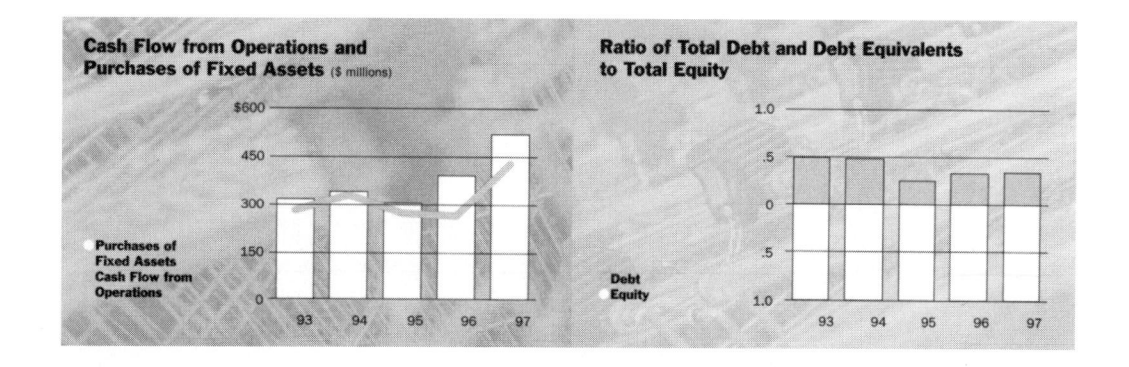

Management Discussion and Analysis

Company follows a policy of enhancing profitability on a 'market-by-market' basis by selecting a store format, store size and store banner that is the best fit for each market. By successfully competing across Canada in both retail and wholesale operations, the Company has strategically minimized and balanced its exposure to regional and industry economic risk.

The Company maintains a significant portfolio of owned sites and, whenever practical, follows the strategy of purchasing sites. This enhances the Company's operating flexibility and also allows the Company to benefit from any long term property appreciation. A significant competitive advantage the Company has developed is its powerful controlled label products such as President's Choice™, no name™, Club Pack™, G•R•E•E•N™, "TOO GOOD TO BE TRUE!"™ and EXACT™ which enhance customer loyalty by providing superior overall value and some protection against national brand price cutting.

During the first quarter of 1998, the Company will enter the Montreal market and will also enter other new smaller markets and will review acquisitions when the opportunities arise. The Company will also exit a particular market and reallocate assets elsewhere when there is a strategic advantage to do so.

The success of these strategies depends to a large extent on the financial strength of the Company and the strategic deployment of the Company's financial resources. The Company maintains a strong balance sheet in order to minimize its vulnerability to short term earnings pressure and to provide a stable base for long term growth.

Low cost, non-union competitors are a threat to the Company's cost structure. The Company is willing to accept the short term costs of labour disruption in order to achieve competitive labour costs for the longer term which helps to ensure long term sustainable sales and earnings growth. In 1998, 27 labour agreements affecting approximately 5,200 employees will be negotiated with the single largest agreement covering 3,500 employees. Management's objective is to continue to negotiate longer term contracts to provide a more stable labour environment. The Company has good relations with its employees and unions and, although possible, no labour disruption is anticipated.

The Company self-insures its own risks to an appropriate level and limits its exposure through the purchase of excess insurance from financially stable insurance companies. The Company has comprehensive loss prevention programs in place and actively manages its claims handling and litigation processes to reduce the risk it retains.

Loblaw Companies Limited is aware of the year 2000 date change issues and is actively working to resolve the potential impact on the technology assets and processing of date-sensitive information by the Company's computerized information systems. A coordinated program is in place to ensure all vital business and technical issues are managed and appropriately dealt with, including consideration of electronic data interchange (EDI) with suppliers. During 1997, a number of critical systems within the various operations were successfully converted or modified to ensure year 2000 compliance. Throughout 1998, all remaining critical business systems will be converted or modified and compliance testing will be completed during 1998 and 1999. Loblaw is expensing all systems modification costs and these costs are not currently expected to have a material adverse impact on the Company's financial position or results of operations.

Loblaw endeavours to be a socially and environmentally responsible company and recognizes that the competitive pressures for economic growth and cost efficiency must be integrated with environmental stewardship and ecological considerations. Environmental committees throughout the Company meet regularly to monitor and enforce the maintenance of responsible business operations. This includes conducting environmental audits of warehouses, stores, equipment and gas stations and implementing packaging, waste reduction and recycling programs.

The Company is confident that it is well positioned to provide continued 1998 earnings growth and continued superior food industry returns.

Results by Quarter

(in millions of dollars)		1997	1996	1995
Sales	1st Quarter	$ 2,287	$2,096	$2,303
	2nd Quarter	2,497	2,298	2,460
	3rd Quarter	3,386	3,070	2,867
	4th Quarter	2,838	2,384	2,224
		$11,008	$9,848	$9,854
Operating Income	1st Quarter	$ 74	$ 61	$ 58
	2nd Quarter	92	82	76
	3rd Quarter	113	99	84
	4th Quarter	147	117	102
		$ 426	$ 359	$ 320
Interest Expense	1st Quarter	$ 10	$ 11	$ 17
	2nd Quarter	8	8	13
	3rd Quarter	13	16	13
	4th Quarter	13	11	11
		$ 44	$ 46	$ 54
Net Earnings	1st Quarter	$ 36	$ 28	$ 24
	2nd Quarter	46	40	35
	3rd Quarter	56	45	38
	4th Quarter	75	61	50
		$ 213	$ 174	$ 147
Net Earnings Per Common Share (in dollars)	1st Quarter	$ .15	$ .12	$ .10
	2nd Quarter	.19	.16	.14
	3rd Quarter	.23	.19	.16
	4th Quarter	.31	.25	.20
		$ .88	$ .72	$ .60

Eleven Year Summary

page 36

Earnings Statement

(in millions of dollars)	1997	1996	1995	1994	1993	1992	1991	1990	1989	1988	1987
Sales	11,008	9,848	9,854	10,000	9,356	9,262	8,533	8,417	7,934	8,308	8,631
Trading profit[1]	573	481	449	410	326	313	328	324	295	260	290
Depreciation and amortization	147	122	129	138	126	120	109	109	104	100	100
Operating income	426	359	320	272	200	193	219	215	191	160	190
Interest expense	44	46	54	63	54	62	63	71	91	84	74
Income taxes	169	139	124	83	56	45	57	55	39	19	48
Minority interest									2	4	4
Earnings before extraordinary items	213	174	147	126	90	76	99	89	59	31	64
Extraordinary items										(15)	
Net earnings	213	174	147	126	90	76	99	89	59	16	64

Return on Sales (%)

Operating income	3.9	3.6	3.2	2.7	2.1	2.1	2.6	2.5	2.4	1.9	2.2
Trading profit[1]	5.2	4.9	4.6	4.1	3.5	3.4	3.8	3.8	3.7	3.1	3.4
Earnings before income taxes	3.5	3.2	2.8	2.1	1.6	1.3	1.8	1.7	1.3	.7	1.3
Net earnings	1.9	1.8	1.5	1.3	1.0	.8	1.2	1.1	.7	.2	.7
Cash flow from operations	3.9	2.7	2.7	3.2	2.9	2.8	2.4	2.8	2.8	1.6	1.7

Cash Flow

(in millions of dollars)	1997	1996	1995	1994	1993	1992	1991	1990	1989	1988	1987
Cash flow from operations	426	262	270	328	279	269	215	242	220	135	145
Purchases of fixed assets	517	389	302	339	315	198	159	171	166	192	248
Net cash (out) in before financing and dividends	(42)	(132)	322	3	(61)	55	61	103	21	44	(161)
Increase (decrease) in cash	107	(74)	165	(56)	64	(45)	222	15	56	29	(94)

1. Trading profit is defined as operating income before depreciation and amortization (EBITDA).

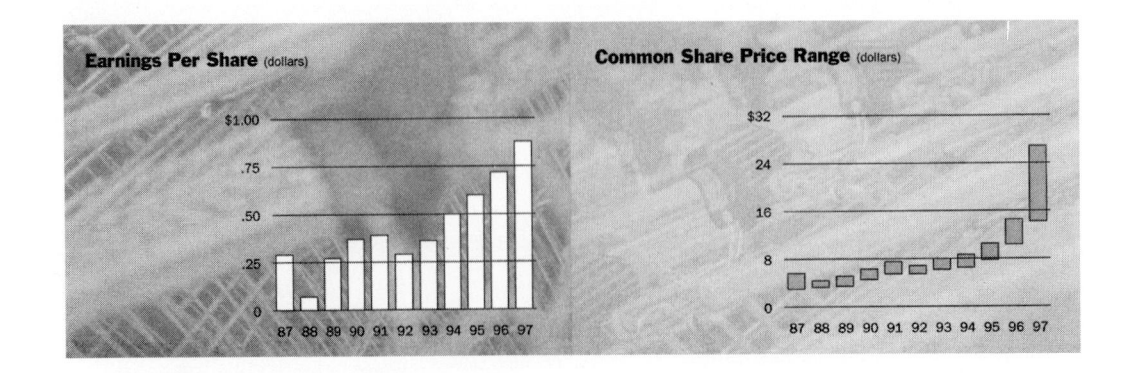

Eleven Year Summary *page 37*

Financial Position

(in millions of dollars)	**1997**	1996	1995	1994	1993	1992	1991	1990	1989	1988	1987
Current assets	**1,681**	1,553	1,491	1,214	1,117	1,082	1,050	987	761	765	983
Current liabilities	**1,479**	1,399	1,312	1,185	969	937	788	937	727	685	843
Working capital	**202**	154	179	29	148	145	262	50	34	80	140
Fixed assets (net)	**2,093**	1,738	1,491	1,603	1,414	1,231	1,115	1,078	1,044	1,052	1,057
Total assets	**4,013**	3,531	3,197	3,042	2,743	2,504	2,362	2,282	2,040	2,004	2,214
Long term debt[1]	**927**	742	669	741	778	634	650	567	636	709	737
Total debt[1]	**1,289**	1,155	980	836	778	664	650	747	644	773	836
Retained earnings	**1,221**	1,046	902	783	684	618	568	499	434	390	396
Shareholders' equity	**1,495**	1,311	1,160	1,105	985	916	884	718	652	501	541
Average capital employed	**2,730**	2,385	2,114	1,911	1,726	1,624	1,479	1,360	1,379	1,433	1,393

Ratios[2]

	1997	1996	1995	1994	1993	1992	1991	1990	1989	1988	1987
Earnings Ratios[3] (percent)											
Return on common equity	**15.3**	14.2	13.4	12.5	9.7	8.8	13.4	14.6	11.7	5.9	12.5
Return on total assets	**14.1**	13.5	12.2	10.5	8.4	8.8	10.5	10.5	9.6	7.7	9.3
Financial Ratios (xx:1)											
Total debt to equity	**.34**	.33	.25	.48	.49	.46	.45	.75	.95	1.49	1.49
Cash flow from operations to long term debt	**.83**	.60	.94	.62	.58	.63	.54	.45	.35	.19	.20
Interest coverage on total debt[1]	**9.68**	7.88	5.97	4.32	3.68	3.11	3.50	3.03	2.11	1.90	2.56

Per Common Share

(dollars)	**1997**	1996	1995	1994	1993	1992	1991	1990	1989	1988	1987
Net earnings	**.88**	.72	.60	.50	.36	.29	.39	.37	.27	.07	.29
Dividends – declared	**.15**	.12	.11	.09	.08	.08	.08	.07	.07	.07	.07
– year end rate	**.16**	.12	.12	.09	.08	.08	.08	.07	.07	.07	.07
Book value	**6.08**	5.35	4.74	4.27	3.79	3.52	3.17	2.66	2.37	2.21	2.37
Price range – high	**26.85**	14.50	10.50	8.67	8.00	6.83	7.50	6.29	5.08	4.38	5.63
– low	**14.15**	10.33	7.75	6.50	6.17	5.46	5.46	4.54	3.42	3.29	3.00
Cash flow from operations[4]	**1.76**	1.08	1.12	1.35	1.15	1.11	.90	1.07	1.01	.62	.67

1. Debt includes debt equivalents.
2. For purposes of calculating financial ratios, debt is reduced by cash and short term investments net of bank advances and notes payable.
3. Earnings ratios have been computed as follows:
   Return on common equity – Earnings before extraordinary items less preferred dividends divided by average common share capital, retained earnings, foreign currency translation adjustment and the applicable portion of contributed surplus.
   Return on total assets – Operating income divided by average total assets (less cash and short term investments).
4. Cash flow from operations per common share is after preferred dividends.

Corporate Directory

Directors

W. Galen Weston, O.C., B.A., LL.D. [2]
Chairman, Loblaw Companies Limited
Chairman, George Weston Limited
Chairman, Wittington Investments, Limited
Chairman, Holt, Renfrew & Co., Limited
Chairman, Brown Thomas Group Limited
Chairman, The Windsor Club
President, The W. Garfield Weston Foundation
Director, Associated British Foods plc
Director, CIBC
Director, Fortnum & Mason plc
Director, United World Colleges

Richard J. Currie, C.M., MBA, LL.D., P.Eng. [2]
President, Loblaw Companies Limited
President, George Weston Limited
Director, Imperial Oil Limited
Director, BCE Inc.

Camilla H. Dalglish [4,5]
Corporate Director
Director, The W. Garfield Weston Foundation
Former Member of The Board of Directors, Royal Botanical Gardens

Robert J. Dart, FCA [1,3]
President, Wittington Investments, Limited
Former Senior Tax Partner, Price Waterhouse Canada
Director, Holt, Renfrew & Co., Limited
Director, Brown Thomas Group Limited

Sheldon V. Durtsche [1,4]
Corporate Director
Former Chairman, National Tea Co.

G. Joseph Reddington [2,3]
Chief Executive Officer, Breuners Home Furnishings Corp.
Former Chairman and CEO, The Signature Group
Former President and CEO, Sears Canada
Director, Trans World Airlines

T. Iain Ronald, FCA [1,5]
Corporate Director
Former Vice Chairman, CIBC Group of Companies
Director, Toronto Symphony Orchestra
Director, Northwest Company Inc.

Joseph H. Wright [3,5]
Corporate Director
Managing Partner, Crosbie & Co.
Former President and CEO, Swiss Bank Corporation (Canada)
Director, St. Laurent Paperboard Inc.
Director, Wolf Group Integrated Communications
Director, Brooke Capital Corporation
Director, Clarke Institute of Psychiatry Foundation

---

1 member – Audit Committee
2 member – Executive Committee
3 member – Governance and Compensation Committee
4 member – Environmental, Health and Safety Committee
5 member – Pension Committee

Corporate Officers Includes age and years of service:

W. Galen Weston, O.C., 57 and 26 years
Chairman of the Board

Richard J. Currie, C.M., 60 and 26 years
President

David K. Bragg, 49 and 14 years
Executive Vice President

Serge K. Darkazanli, 55 and 23 years
Executive Vice President

John A. Lederer, 42 and 16 years
Executive Vice President

Donald G. Reid, 48 and 18 years
Executive Vice President

Harold A. Seitz, 59 and 22 years
Executive Vice President

John W. Thompson, 49 and 19 years
Executive Vice President

David M. Williams, 55 and 21 years
Executive Vice President

Robert G. Chenaux, 54 and 22 years
Senior Vice President, Corporate Brand Development

Roy R. Conliffe, 47 and 16 years
Senior Vice President, Labour Relations

Stewart E. Green, 53 and 21 years
Senior Vice President and Secretary

David R. Jeffs, 40 and 19 years
Senior Vice President, Sourcing and Procurement

Richard P. Mavrinac, 45 and 15 years
Senior Vice President, Finance

David F. Poirier, 40 and 16 years
Senior Vice President, Logistics, Planning and Systems

Stephen A. Smith, 40 and 12 years
Senior Vice President, Controller

Robert A. Balcom, 36 and 4 years
Vice President, General Counsel

Manny Di Filippo, 38 and 5 years
Vice President, Corporate Development

J. Bradley Holland, 34 and 4 years
Vice President, Taxation

Michael Kimber, 42 and 13 years
Vice President, Legal Counsel

Louise M. Lacchin, 40 and 14 years
Vice President, Treasurer

Kevin P. Lengyell, 39 and 2 years
Vice President, Internal Audit Services

Glenn D. Leroux, 43 and 11 years
Vice President, Risk Management

Kenneth Mulhall, 35 and 14 years
Vice President, Environmental Affairs

George D. Seslija, 42 and 18 years
Vice President, Real Estate Development

Franca Smith, 34 and 9 years
Vice President, Financial Control

Ann Marie Yamamoto, 37 and 11 years
Vice President, Information Technology and Systems Audit

Janice A. Hollett, 28 and 1 year
Corporate Controller, Financial Reporting

Barbara T. Cook, 44 and 14 years
Assistant Controller

Marian M. Burrows, 43 and 19 years
Assistant Secretary

Shareholder Information

Executive Offices
22 St. Clair Avenue East
Toronto, Canada
M4T 2S8
Tel: (416) 922-8500
Fax: (416) 922-7791
Internet: www.loblaw.com

Stock Listings
Toronto, Montreal and Vancouver Stock Exchanges

Share Symbol — "L"

Common Shares Outstanding
71 percent of the common shares are owned beneficially by George Weston Limited.
Total outstanding   242,780,858
Shares available for public trading   71,577,288

Average Daily Trading Volume   26,422

Dividend Policy
It is the Company's policy to maintain a stable dividend payment of 20 to 25% of the prior year's earnings per common share.

Common Dividend Payment Dates
April 1
July 1
October 1
December 30

Normal Course Issuer Bid
The Company has a Normal Course Issuer Bid on the Toronto Stock Exchange effective from March 18, 1998 to March 17, 1999.

Value of Common Shares
December 22, 1971 (Valuation Day) $ .958
February 22, 1994 $7.670

Investor Relations
Copies of the Company's Annual Information Form filed with regulatory authorities and additional copies of this Annual Report may be obtained from the Secretary upon specific request.

Other information requests should be directed to Mr. Donald G. Reid, Executive Vice President.

Transfer Agent and Registrar
Montreal Trust Company of Canada
151 Front Street West
Toronto, Canada
M5J 2N1

General Counsel
Borden & Elliot
Toronto, Canada

Auditors
KPMG
Toronto, Canada

Annual and General Meeting
April 28, 1998 at 11:00 a.m.
Toronto, Canada

Materials in this report are environmentally friendly. The cover and operating section papers are acid-free and recyclable. The financial section paper is acid-free and contains 20 percent post-consumer de-inked fibre.

INDEX

A

Access codes, **315**
Accommodation endorsement, **809**
Account. *see* Ledger account
Account form for the balance sheet, **130**
Accountant(s)
   Certified General (CGA), **31**
   Certified Management (CMA), **31, 34**
   controller as, **35**
   ethical responsibilities of, **631–636**
   income taxes, **34**
   public, **319**
   self-regulating, **631**
Accounting
   accrual basis of, **138**
   careers, **34–36**
   cash basis of, **138, 904**
   defined, **3**
   financial, **4–5**
   focusing management's attention, **189**
   general purpose, **4–5**
   managerial (or management), **5, 35, 632, 633, 635, 1053–1055**
   partnership, **658–660**
   profession, as, **34, 631**
   public, **9, 34–35, 319, 632, 633, 635**
   purpose of, **4**
   as a "stepping stone" to senior management, **36**
Accounting changes, **747–749**
Accounting controls. *see* Internal control
Accounting cycle
   a comparison, **75–78**
   complete (without work sheet), **137–138**
   introduction to, **75–78**
   in perspective, **139**
Accounting education
   careers in, **36**
   focus of this course, **6**
Accounting entity, **14, 617–618**

Accounting equation
   defined, **19**
   effects of business transactions, **23–24**
   resources, **18**
Accounting income and taxable income, **914–915**
Accounting periods, **109, 189–190**
   fiscal year. *see* Fiscal year
Accounting policies, small business example, **20**
Accounting principles. *see* Generally accepted accounting principles
Accounting records, role of, **57**
Accounting standards. *see* Generally accepted accounting principles
Accounting Standards Board, **13**
   Canadian Institute of Chartered Accountants (CICA), **615–616**
Accounting systems
   basic functions of, **7–8, 298**
   chapter coverage of, **296–352**
   computer-based. *see* Computer-based accounting systems
   cost effectiveness of, **298**
   design of, **35, 298–299**
   determining information needs, **297–298**
   manual. *see* Manual accounting systems
Accounts payable
   balance sheet, **14, 251, 846**
   defined, **17**
   subsidiary ledgers, **230**
Accounts receivable
   aging of, **429–30, 431**
   balance sheet, **14, 251, 425, 846**
   chapter coverage of, **422–447**
   collection, **22**
   conservatism, **425–426**
   direct write-off, **431**
   factoring, **432–433**
   income statement approach, **430–431**
   instalment receivables, **446–447**

Accounts receivable, *(Cont.)*
   internal control over, **432**
   management of, **432**
   present value concept, **443, 445**
   quality of, **438–440**
   recoveries of uncollectible accounts (bad debts), **428**
   subsidiary ledgers, **230, 426–428**
   turnover rate, **438–440, 1014–1015**
   uncollectible accounts, **424–425**
Accrual basis accounting, **138, 168**
Accrual of interest, **834–835**
Accrual of wages expense, **176–77**
Accrual-basis measurements, distinguished from cash flows, **945, 947**
Accrued expenses, **176–179**
   cash flow statement, **958**
Accrued liabilities, **570–572**
   matching principle, **570**
Accrued revenue, **179**
Accumulated depletion, contra-asset account, **540**
Accumulated depreciation
   balance sheet, **125**
   contra-asset account, **125**
Acid test ratio, **581**
Acquisitions, **873**
Activity base. *see* Cost driver
Adequate disclosure. *see* Generally accepted accounting principles
Adjusted trial balance, **126–127, 193**
   preparation of statements from, **183–184**
Adjusting entries
   accounting cycle, **121–127**
   bond interest expense, **751**
   characteristics of, **169**
   concept of materiality, **180**
   defined, **122**
   effects of, **182–183**
   and goals of accrual accounting, **168**
   illustrations of, **171–174, 179**
   link between accounting periods, **170**

I-1

Index

Adjusting entries, *(Cont.)*
  perpetual inventory systems, 244–245
  reasons for, **168**
  types of, **168–169**
    apportioning recorded costs, 172–174
    recording unearned revenue, 174–176
    recording unrecorded expenses, 176–179
    recording unrecorded revenue, 179–180
  used assets into expense, 122–23
  in work sheet, **193–194**
Administrative controls. *see* Internal control
Advance, **175**
After-closing trial balance, 136–137, 187–188
Aging of accounts receivable, 429–30, 431
Air Canada, **175**, **720**, **1007**, **1008**
Algoma Steel Inc., **720**, **1008**
Allied Crude Vegetable Oil Corporation, **317**
Allocation
  of cost to expense over useful life, **624**
  of a lump-sum purchase, **520**
  of purchase costs, 540–541
Allowance, **241**
  for doubtful accounts, **425–426**, 427–431, 437
Amortization
  bond discount, **813–814**, 865
  bond premium, **814**, 865
  discount on notes receivable, **442**
  discount on short-term notes, 567–568
  intangible assets, **534**
  straight-line method, **748**, 752
  tables, **752–753**
  unearned interest revenue, **442**
Amortization table
  first illustration, **574–575**
  preparing, **574–575**
  purpose of, **573–574**
  using, **575–576**, 847–848
Analysis of accounting information
  basic tools of, **994**
  chapter coverage of, **992–1021**
  classified financial statements, 249–253
  debt ratio, **1012**
  department managers, **139**

Analysis of accounting information, *(Cont.)*
  earnings per share, **749–753**, 1003–1004
  evaluating
    adequacy of net income, 258–259
    cash flows, **878–881**, 937–941, 1017–1018
    liquidity of inventory, 492–493
    solvency, **378**
  examples of analytical aspects, **139**
  financial ratios, **251–252**, 492–493, 998
  and other measurements, 1019–1021
  see also Financial ratios and subtotals
  financial statements. *see* Classified financial statements; Comparative financial statements
  impact of inflation, **1000**
  interest coverage ratio, **1012**
  interpreting financial ratios, **252–253**, 492–493, 998
  leverage, **1010–1011**
  liquidity of inventory, **1015**
  net income (profitability), **257**, 258–259
  perspective of
    common shareholders, **27–28**, 1003–1011
    long-term creditors, **28**, 581–582, 809–810, 1011–1013
    management *see* Management's interest in
    preferred shareholders, **1013**
    short-term creditors, **28**, 378, 439–440, 494, 580–581, 1013–1019
  profitability, **1008**
  quality of earnings, **999–1000**
  quality of receivables, **438–440**, 1014–1015
  quality of working capital, **1014**
  return on investment, **1006**
  safety of creditors' claims, **580–583**, 809–810, 1011–1013
  solvency, **580–583**, 809–810
  sources of financial information, **6–7**, 10, 253, 993–994
  standards for comparison, **253**, 998–999

Analysis of accounting information, *(Cont.)*
  trends, **1008–1010**
  yield rate on bonds, **1012**
Annual reports, **167**, **1048–1051**
  comparative data, **998**
  content of, **10**, **993**
  Loblaw Companies Ltd., comprehensive problem, 1048–1051
Annuity
  future amount of, **839–840**
  present value, **843–845**
  table, **839–840**, **844–845**
Appropriations, **760**
Articles of incorporation, **700**
Assets
  allocation of a lump-sum purchase, **520**
  current. *see* Current assets
  defined, **15**
  intangible. *see* Intangible assets
  liquid, **14**
  marketable securities, **722**
  permanent, **14**
  plant. *see* Plant and equipment
  pledged as collateral, **1013**
  purchase on account, **21**
  purchase for cash, **20**
  purchase and financing cost, **21**
  quality and relative debt, **1000**
  return on, **810**
  sale of, **22**
  used assets become expense, **122**
  valuation of, **15–17**, **426**, 518–519
Atlantic Acceptance Corporation Limited, **317**
Audit
  ethics, **322**, 632–633
  financial statements, **9**, **32**, **167**, 319, 323, 630, 632–633
  income taxes, **904**
  materiality, **322**
  negligence, **322**
Audit committee of board of directors, **318**
Auditing
  compliance, **310**, **324**
  internal, **310**, **318**
  operational, **310**
Auditors
  ethical responsibilities, **632–633**
  independence, **9**, **319**
  liability to users of financial statements, **322**

Auditors, *(Cont.)*
   report, **9, 319, 632–633**
   responsibility for detection of fraud, **321–322**
   work of, **319–324**

B

Bad debts. *see* Uncollectible accounts
Balance sheet
   account form, **130**
   analyzing accounts receivable, **429–430, 431**
   classified, **249–250**
      evaluating solvency with, **250–253**
   comparative, **1002**
      and cash flow statement, **942, 943–944, 953**
   consolidated, **876–882**
   date, **14**
   described, **6, 129**
   effects of business transactions, **19–23**
   equation. *see* Accounting equation
   first illustration (account form), **14**
   marketable securities in. *see* Marketable securities
   report form, **130**
   use by outsiders, **27–28**
Bank credit cards, sales recorded as cash sales, **433**
Bank of Montreal, **714, 763**
Bank of Nova Scotia, **714**
Bank reconciliation, **389–394**
Bank service charges, **389, 391**
Bank statement, **388, 390**
Bankruptcy, **27**
   effects, **810**
Basic earnings per share, **753**
Bay, (The), **109**
BCE Inc., **919**
Bell Canada, **252, 626, 712, 1017**
Board of directors, **380, 698, 700–701**
   functions and power, **702–703**
   internal control of top management, **318**
Bombardier Inc., **712, 720, 807–808, 998**
Bond certificate, **788**
Bond discount, accounting for, **812–814**

Bond discount and premium
   amortization of, **812–814**
   cost of borrowing, **812, 814**
Bond premium, accounting for, **814**
Bond prices and interest rate, **795–796**
Bonds
   accounting for, **812–815, 864–865**
   authorization for issue, **788**
   call price, **790**
   callable (redeemable), **790**
   convertible, **790–791**
   debenture, **790**
   discount, **790, 795**
   liquidity, **788**
   market rate, **794–795**
   mortgage, **790**
   premium, **790, 795**
   present value, **794–795**
   redemption price, **790**
   sinking fund, **790**
   transferability, **787, 788**
   yield rate, **1012**
Bonds payable
   accounting for, **792–794**
   characteristics of, **788**
   classified as long-term liabilities, **797**
   contract rate, **787–788**
   convertible into common stock, **816–817**
   creditors, **788**
   early retirement of, **796–797**
   fair value of, **806**
   interest payments and accrual, **788–789, 792–794**
   interest rate, **789**
   market prices, **795–796**
   maturity date, **788**
   sinking fund for, **797**
   tax advantage, **791–792**
Bonus in partnership
   former partners, **670–671**
   new partners, **671–672**
Book of original entry, **67**
Book value, **174**
   common stock, **718–720, 724, 1005–1006**
   plant assets, **522**
Bookkeeping, **36**
British Columbia Telephone, **252**
Budgeting, capital. *see* Capital budgeting
Budgets, **167, 302**
   cash budgets, **381, 383, 395**

Buildings, **519**
Business combinations, **873**
Business documents, **311–314**
Business entity, **15, 617–618, 871–872**
Business organization, forms compared, **26**
Bylaws of corporation, **700**

C

Cambridge Shopping Centres Ltd., **873**
Campeau Corporation, **873, 1011**
Canada Pension Plan and payroll accounting, **588–589**
Canadian Airlines Corporation, **580, 1007**
Canadian Institute of Chartered Accountants (CICA)
   Accounting Standards Board, **13, 615–616**
   Code of Professional Conduct, **32**
Canadian Pacific Ltd., **378, 1017**
Canadian Utilities Ltd., **788**
Canutilities Holdings, **711**
Capital account, **27**
   partnership, **676–678**
Capital assets
   chapter coverage of, **516–541**
   defined, **517**
Capital budgeting
   nature of, **35**
   present value concept, **851–852**
Capital cost allowance
   depreciation, **915**
   income taxes, corporations, **915–916**
Capital expenditures, **520–521**
Capital gains and losses, **907**
   income taxes, corporations, **915**
   individual income tax, **907**
Capital lease, present value concept in accounting for, **848–850**
Capital stock, **26–27, 697, 698, 704, 707–710**
   authorization of, **707–708**
   book value, **718–721**
      and market price, **724**
   common stock. *see* Common stock
   defined, **26–27**
   issuance of, **709–710, 721**
   issued in exchange, **716**

I-4 INDEX

Capital stock, *(Cont.)*
   market value, **721–724**
   no-par value, **708–709**
   par value, **708, 709–710**
   preferred stock. *see* Preferred stock
   subscriptions to, **716**
Capital structure, defined, **563**
Capone, Al, **903**
Carrying value, **174**
   see also Book value
CASES IN POINT (by topic)
   accounting periods, J. Paul Getty, **109**
   accounts receivable
      Shell Canada, **439**
      large companies, **423**
   accrual basis accounting, airline industry, **138**
   allocating overhead costs, unidentified dairy, **1067**
   annual reports
      Hudson's Bay Company, **993**
      McDonald's, **10**
   bond prices and interest rates, **795**
      Ontario Hydro, **796**
   book value per share, **720**
   cash as corporate asset, **378**
   closely held corporations, **699**
   commitments
      Canadian Airlines Corporation, **580**
      Quebecor Inc., **580**
   computer-based fraud, **314**
   computer-based internal control, **315**
   contingent losses, Dow Corning Corp., **579**
   depreciation, Empire State Building, **124**
   disclosing lines of credit, Canadian Pacific Ltd., **378**
   disclosure (subsequent events)
      Bank of Montreal, **29**
      Hudson's Bay Company, **29**
   disclosure of contingencies
      Bombardier, Inc., **578**
      IPL Energy Inc., **578**
   disclosure of events occurring after end of accounting period, *see also* subsequent events
      Bell Canada, **626**
      Hudson's Bay Company, **626**
   disclosures of depreciation, Toromont, Maple Leaf Foods, and Quebecor, **530**

CASES IN POINT, *(Cont.)*
   discontinued operations
      George Weston Ltd, **746**
      Placer Dome, **746**
      Shell Canada, **746**
   dividend preference, Bell Canada, **712**
   dividends on preferred stock
      floating rates, **712**
      non-cumulative, **714**
   doubtful accounts, Canadian banks, **437**
   ethical issues, **634, 635, 636**
   fair value of financial instruments, Bombardier, Inc., **807–808**
   financial reporting media, business publications, **10**
   fiscal year, Walt Disney Company, **109**
   fraudulent statement of ending inventory, **489**
   future (deferred) income taxes
      BCE Inc., **919**
      Dofasco Inc., **919**
      Domtar Inc., **919**
      Shell Canada, **919**
   internal control over cash, **388**
   interpreting ratios, telephone companies, **252**
   inventory, Loblaw and Quebecor, **469**
   inventory management, **492**
   inventory valuation, survey of Canadian companies, **476**
   inventory write-downs, Johnson & Johnson, **483**
   just-in-time inventory systems, Toyota, **481**
   LCM rule for inventory valuation, Canadian companies, **484**
   leverage, Campeau Corporation, **1011**
   loan guarantees by shareholders, **254**
   management fraud
      Allied Crude Vegetable Oil Corporation, **317**
      Atlantic Acceptance Corporation Ltd., **317**
      savings and loan crisis in U.S., **318**
   market price of stock
      Ford Motor Company, **723**
      IBM, **721**
   market share
      Air Canada, **1008**

CASES IN POINT, *(Cont.)*
      Loblaw Companies Ltd., **1008**
   market value and book value of common stock, Microsoft Corp., **725**
   matching principle, pharmaceutical companies, **625**
   materiality, Corel Corp., **181, 627**
   mergers
      Cambridge Shopping Centres Ltd., **873**
      Campeau Corp., **873**
      Daimler-Benz-Chrysler, **873**
      Great West Life, **873**
      Imasco Ltd., **873**
      Interprovincial Pipe Line, **873**
      Molson and Carling O'Keefe, **873**
      Noranda Inc., **873**
      Nova Corporation, **873**
      Stone Container Corp (U.S.), **873**
   par value shares, Maritime Telegraph and Telephone, **708**
   parent and subsidiaries, BCE Inc., **872**
   partnership accounting, **659**
   partnership formation, PricewaterhouseCoopers, **655**
   percentage changes, Domtar Inc., **996**
   perpetual inventory systems, Bay, The, **248**
   preferred stock, **711**
   price of convertible bonds, Norcen, **817**
   price-earnings ratio, dividend yield, **1005**
   public accountants, Price Waterhouse, **25**
   recording transactions in perpetual inventory system, point-of-sale terminals, **248**
   research and development, pharmaceutical companies, **625**
   return on equity, **1008**
   segments of business
      Imasco, **745**
      Shoppers Drug Mart, **745**
   shareholders in large corporations, **699**
   tax evasion, Al Capone, **903**

INDEX I-5

CASES IN POINT, *(Cont.)*
  treasury stock
    Bank of Montreal, **763**
    Northern Telecom, **763**
    Shell Canada, **763**
    various companies, **763**
  unearned revenue, Air Canada, **175**
  unused lines of credit, **1017**
Cash
  in balance sheet, **377–379, 846**
  budgets, **381, 383, 395**
  chapter coverage of, **376–395**
  controlling account, **377**
  credit memos, **383**
  defined, **377, 940**
  discounts, **237**
  equivalents, **940**
  fraud, **380–381**
  internal control over, **380–388**
    disbursements, **383–388**
    receipts, **381–383**
  management, **379–380**
  petty, **381, 394–395**
  point-of-sale terminals, **382**
  receipts, **381–383**
  responsibility accounting systems, **381, 395**
  restricted, **378–379**
  sales returns, **383**
Cash balances, **379–380**
Cash basis accounting, **138**
Cash disbursements, **379**
Cash discounts, **237, 242**
Cash dividends, **380, 753–754**
Cash equivalents, **377, 940**
  commercial paper, **798**
Cash flow statement, **7, 379, 937–964**
  accounts payable, **946–949**
  accounts receivable, **945–946**
  adjustments needed in indirect method, **956–959**
  cash payments for operating expenses, **947–948**
  classification of cash flows, **939–940**
  comparative, **1002**
  depreciation, **947, 949**
  described, **7, 379**
  direct and indirect methods, **938**
  example, **938–939**
  financing activities, **940, 952–953**
  and income statement, **945–949**
  income taxes, **949**
  investing activities, **939, 950–952**
  operating activities, **945–949**

Cash flow statement, *(Cont.)*
  postretirement payments as operating activities, **804**
  preparation, **941–953**
    changes in noncash accounts, **941–942**
  purpose, **937–938**
  relationship with comparative balance sheets, **953**
  use, **953–954**
  work sheet for, **960–964**
Cash flows
  analysis of, **1017–1018**
  classifications of, **939–940**
  computation of, **945–949**
  defined, **937**
  determination of, **942**
  distinguished from accrual-basis measurements, **945, 947**
  financing activities, **940, 950–953**
  free cash flow, **954**
  from operating activities, **945–949**
  investing activities, **939, 950–952**
  net cash flow distinguished from net income, **949, 950, 956**
  operating activities, **939, 940, 941**
    see also Net cash flow from operating activities
  statement of. *see* Cash flow statement
Cash management, **379–380**
Cash Over and Short, **382**
Cash payments journal, **346–349**
  posting, **347–349**
Cash receipts, **379, 381–383**
Cash receipts journal, **343–346**
Cash register, as special journal, **299–300**
Cash sales, bank credit cards, **433**
Certificate of incorporation, **700**
Certified General Accountant (CGA)
  professional certification of, **34**
  work of, **34**
Certified Management Accountant (CMA), **1055**
  ethical responsibilities, **31–32**
  professional certification, **34**
  work, **35**
Changes in accounting policy, **747–748, 749**
Changes in estimates, **748**
Chart of accounts, **66, 303**

Cheque register, **302, 337–338, 386**
Cheques
  control listing, **381**
  reconciliation, **389–394**
  restrictive endorsement, **381**
Chequing accounts, **388**
Chrysler, **873**
CICA Handbook, **13**
  accounting changes, **747–749**
  correction of errors, **748–749**
  estimates, **748**
  leases, **800**
  restatement, **748**
Classified financial statements
  classified balance sheet, **249–253**
  multiple-step income statement, **254–257**
  single-step income statement, **257–258**
Closing the accounts, **186–188**
Closing entries
  accounting cycle, in, **137–138**
  corporation, **707**
  definition and purpose of, **131**
  drawing accounts, **135, 661–662**
  expense accounts, **132–133**
  Income Summary account, **134–135**
  partnership, **661–662**
  in perpetual inventory system, **245**
  revenue accounts, **131–132**
  summary of process, **136**
CMA. *see* Certified Management Accountant
Coding transactions. *see* Data base systems
Collection of account receivable, **22**
Collusion, **315**
Commercial paper, **797–798**
Commitments, **579–580**
Common stock
  book value, **718–720, 1005–1006**
  contrasted with preferred, **710–711**
  earnings per share, **749–753**
  market price, **722–724**
  net assets, **718**
  outstanding shares, **720**
Comparative data in annual reports, example, **998**
Comparative financial statements, **994**
  annual reports, **10**
  comprehensive illustration, **1000–1003**

Competence, **31**
Compliance auditing, **310, 324**
Component percentages, **997–998**
Compound journal entry, **132**
Compounding the interest, **836**
Comprehensive Problems
    Alpine Village and Nordic Sports, **559–560**
    Friend with a Truck, **222–224**
    Little Bear Railroad, Inc., **103–104**
    Loblaw Companies Ltd., **1048–1051**
    Shadow Mountain Hotel, **856–861**
    The Next Dimension, **359–374**
Computer-based accounting systems
    access codes, **315**
    amortization tables in, **575**
    basic functions of, **298**
    classifying data in, **303–305**
    compared to manual systems, **75–78, 305–306**
    data base, **76, 303–305**
    design of, **298–299**
    illustrated, **77**
    internal control in, **314–315**
    inventory, **300, 487**
    on-line, real-time, **300–302**
    passwords, **315**
    payroll processing in, **592–593**
    point-of-sale terminals, **300**
    recording transactions, **76, 233–234**
    subsidiary ledgers, **233–234**
    work sheets, **194**
Computers, allow focus on analytical aspects, **139**
Concentrations of credit risk, **440**
Concept of adequate disclosure, **12**
Conceptual flow of costs, **173**
Conservatism, **483**
    defined, **112, 425–426**
    goodwill, **536**
    lower-of-cost-and-market rule, **628, 867**
    valuation of accounts receivable, **425–426**
    valuation of inventory, **479**
    valuation of plant assets, **529**
Consistency principle, **472, 479, 530, 625**
Consolidated entity, **873–874**
Consolidated financial statements
    concept, **874–875**
    interpretation, **874**

Consolidated financial statements methods, *(Cont.)*
    pooling of interest, **874–875**
    purchase, **874**
    preparation, **875–883**
Consumers Gas, **711**
Contingent liability. *see* Contingent losses
Contingent losses, **577–579**
    generally accepted accounting principles (GAAP), **626**
    impairment of assets, **577**
    uncertainty, **577**
Continuing operations, **744–745**
    income from, **745**
Contra-asset accounts, **125, 425**
    accumulated depletion, **540**
    accumulated depreciation, **522**
Contra-liability account, **567**
Contra-revenue accounts, **241–242, 242–243, 243**
    periodic inventory systems, **286–287**
Contributed capital, **704**
Control account, **230**
Control environment, **307**
Control listing, **381**
    cheques, **381**
Control systems, **307**
Controller, **35, 703**
Controlling account, **230, 303, 349**
    cash, **377**
    manufacturing overhead, **1062**
    reconciliation, **350–351**
Conversion ratio, **816**
Convertible bonds, **790–791, 816–817**
Copyrights, **538**
Corel Corp., **627**
Corporate charter, **700**
Corporate dividends, **380**
Corporate securities. *see* Bonds; Capital stock; Common stock; Investments in corporate securities; Preferred stock
Corporate securities
    accounting for, **864**
    stocks, **865–866**
Corporations
    advantages and disadvantages, **698**
    balance sheet, **718, 719–720**
    board of directors, **698, 700, 701, 702–703**
    bylaws, **700**

Corporations, *(Cont.)*
    characteristics, **25–26, 697, 698**
    closely held, **699**
    closing entries, **707**
    continuous existence, **698**
    control, **698**
    defined, **25, 697**
    dividend payments, **705, 706–707**
    formation, **700–703**
    income taxes, **698, 903**
    as legal entity, **25–26**
    limited liability, **697, 698**
    loan "guarantees," **254**
    privately owned, **697**
    professional management, **698**
    publicly owned, **6, 698**
    reasons for incorporation, **697**
    regulation, **698**
    shareholders' equity. *see* Shareholders' equity
    shareholders' liability for debts, **26, 254, 259, 698**
    taxation, **698**
Cost, **108**
    per unit, **1068**
Cost accounting, defined, **35, 1053**
Cost drivers, **1066–1067**
Cost of finished goods manufactured, **1061, 1068–1069**
Cost flow assumptions, **472–477**
Cost of goods sold, **1070**
    cost flow assumptions, **472–477**
    defined, **228**
    estimating techniques, **490–491**
    income statement, **228, 229, 256**
    periodic inventory systems, **246**
    perpetual inventory system, **234**
Cost principle, **12, 15–16, 235, 620**
Cost ratio, **490**
Cost-effective information, **180, 298**
Costs, conceptual flow of, **173**
Credit, **237**
    ledger account(s), **58, 59**
Credit balance, **59, 60**
Credit card draft, **433**
Credit card sales, **433–434**
Credit losses. *see* Uncollectible accounts receivable
Credit memos as cash, **383**
Credit rating, **580**
Credit report, **424**
Credit risk, **440**
Credit terms, **237–239, 242**

Creditors, 5
  defined, 27
  interest in solvency, 27, 378
  liabilities, 17
  long-term interest in accounting information, 1011–1013
  secured claims, 1013
  users of financial statements, 27, 28
Cross-footing, 193, 346
Current assets, 67, 250–251
Current liabilities
  accounts payable, 565
  accrued expenses, 570–572
  current portion of long-term debt, 568, 570, 573–576
  defined, 251
  notes payable, 566–568, 569
  payroll tax liabilities, 571–572, 587
  unearned revenue, 572
Current ratio, 251–252, 253, 565, 582, 1016–1017
Current replacement cost of inventory, 483
Customer ledger, 230

D

Data base, 76
Data base systems, 303–305
  code, 303, 304
  compared to ledger accounts, 305
  compared to ledgers, 305
  data field, 304
  reports, 305
  sort, 303, 304
  using, 304
Debenture bonds, 790
Debit balance, 59–60
Debit and credit entries, 58–59
  equality of, 61
  rules, 61, 112
Debit and credit memoranda, 314
Debit and ledger account(s), 58
Debt
  and assets, 1000
  financing a business with, 810–811
Debt ratio, 581, 809, 810, 811, 1012, 1012–1013
Default (of a note receivable), 436–437
Deferred charges, 538
Deferred (future) income taxes, 28–30, 185–186, 804–806, 916–919

Deferred Interest Income, 446
Deficit, 706
Delivery expenses (a selling expense), 243
Depletion of natural resources, 539–540
Deposits in transit, 389
Depreciation
  basic purpose, 521
  capital cost allowance, 915
  causes, 522–523
  concept, 123
  conservatism, 529
  contra-asset account, 522
  cost allocation process, as, 522
  defined, 123, 521
  disclosure of method, 529
  fractional periods, for, 525–526, 531
  management's responsibility for estimates, 529
  matching principle, 521
  methods
    accelerated, 523, 524
    declining balance, 526–528
    double-declining balance, 527
    effects of different methods, 529
    fixed percentage-of-declining balance, 526–527
    straight-line, 523, 524–526
    units-of-production (output), 527–528
  a "noncash" expense, 126
  revision of estimated useful life, 530–531
  selecting a method, 528–529
Depreciation rate, 525, 526–527
Direct costs, 1062
Direct labour, 1061–1062
  see also Manufacturing costs
Direct materials, 1061
  see also Manufacturing costs
Direct write-off of uncollectible accounts, 431
Disclosure, 185–186
  accounting methods, 477, 494, 529
  cash flows. see Cash flow statement
  commitments, 580
  concentrations of credit risk, 440
  contingent losses, 577–579
  dividends in arrears, 713
  extraordinary items, 746–747

Disclosure, (Cont.)
  fair (market) values of financial instruments, 580, 850–851, 869
  financial instruments, 806–809
  impairment of assets, 541
  lines of credit, 378, 1017
  long-term debt, 581
  off-balance-sheet risk, 433, 809
  postretirement benefits for employees, 804
  principle, 28, 78, 625–626
  restrictions of retained earnings, 760
  subsequent events, 28, 29
Discontinued operations, 745–746
Discount, 237
  bonds, 753–754, 790, 794–795
  period, 237
  sales, 237
  voucher, 386
Discount on bonds payable, 813–814
  amortization, 748–751
  concept, 794–795
  presentation, 747
Discount on notes payable, 567
  amortization, 567–568
Discount on notes receivable
  amortization, 442
  short-term, 442
Discount period, 237, 845
Discount rate, 841
  present value, 841–845
Discounting the future amount, 841–845
Discounting future cash flows, see also Present value
Discounting notes receivable, 438
Disposals of plant and equipment, gains and losses on, 532
Dividend, 380, 702
  arrears, 713
  corporate income taxes, 913
  date of payment, 754
  date of record, 754
  declaration date, 754
  declaration and payment, 706–707
  defined, 380, 705, 706
  ex-dividend date, 754, 755
  liquidating, 756
  preferred stock, 712–713
    and earnings per share, 751
  reinvestment, 755
  yield, 722

I-8 INDEX

Dividend yield, **722, 1004, 1013**
Dividends
   in arrears, **713**
   preferred stock, **712–713**
   stock. *see* Stock dividends
Dofasco Inc., **919, 1007, 1008, 1017**
Dollar signs, not used in journals or ledgers, **81**
Domtar Inc., **712, 720, 723, 724, 919, 996, 1017**
Donated capital, **717**
Donations, **913**
Double rule for final totals, **81**
Double taxation of corporate earnings, **698**
Double-entry system of accounting, **56, 57**
   equality of debits and credits, **61**
Drawing accounts
   closing entries, **135, 661–662**
   owner's equity, **113–114**
   partner's, **661**

E

Earnings and owner's equity, **18**
Earnings per share, **1003–1004**
   of common stock, **749–753**
   income statement, **751–752**
   preferred dividends and, **751**
Economic entity, **871–872**
Economic substance, **573**
Effective interest rate, **794**
Electronic funds transfer, **394**
Embezzlement, **316**
Employee compensation. *see* Payroll accounting
Employee fraud, **316, 395**
Employees
   bonded, **316**
   competence, and internal control, **310**
   rotation, and internal control, **310–311**
Employment insurance in payroll accounting, **587–588**
Entity principle, **12**
Equipment, **520**
Equity, **6**
   ratio, **1011**
   return on, **1007–1008**
Equity method, **867**
Equity ratio, **1011**
Errors and irregularities, **316**
   locating, **80–81**

Ethics. *see* Professional ethics
Ex-dividend date, **754, 755**
Exchanges of plant assets, **532–533**
Expense account, **238**
Expenses, **108**
   closing entries, **132–133**
   debit and credit rules, **112**
   defined, **111**
   ledger account(s), **112–113**
   recognition, **114–118**
   used assets become expense, **122**
Extraordinary items, **746–747**
   disclosure, **746–747**
   income statement, **746–747**

F

Factoring receivables, **432–433**
Fair market value of goodwill, **535–536**
Fair presentation, **9, 31, 319, 632, 633–634**
Fair value
   of financial instruments, **806, 807–808**
   unfunded liability for postretirement costs, **804**
Fair value of financial instruments, **850–851, 869**
Fidelity bonds, **316**
FIFO inventory valuation method. *see* Inventory flow assumptions
Final totals indicated by double rule, **81**
Finance charge, **238**
Financial accounting
   contrasted with managerial accounting, **1054**
   defined, **4–5**
   general purpose, **4–5**
   Financial Accounting Standards Board (FASB), **13**
   role, **13**
   statements of Financial Accounting Standards, **13**
Financial forecasts, **35, 310**
   see also Budgets; Capital budgeting
Financial instruments
   creating off-balance-sheet risk, **433, 809**
   defined, **845**
   disclosures about, **806–809**

Financial instruments, *(Cont.)*
   fair value, **807–808, 869**
   liability and equity, **808**
   valuation, **845–851**
Financial position, **6**
   defined, **6**
   evaluation, **28, 250–253, 377–379, 438–440, 580–583**
   statement. *see* Balance sheet
Financial ratios and subtotals
   accounts receivable turnover rate, **438–440, 493, 1014–1015**
   book value per share, **718–721, 1005–1006**
   component percentages, **997–998**
   current ratio, **251–252, 253, 565, 1016–1017**
   debt ratio, **581, 809, 810, 811, 1012–1013**
   dividend yield, **1004, 1013**
   earnings per share, **749–753, 1003–1004**
   effects of accounting methods, **493–494**
   equity ratio, **1011**
   gross profit, **256**
   interest coverage ratio, **581–582, 809, 810, 1012**
   interpreting financial ratios, **252–253, 998**
   inventory turnover rate, **492–493, 1015**
   net sales, **247–248, 255–256**
   operating cycle, **493, 1016**
   operating expense ratio, **1009–1010**
   operating income, **257**
   percentage changes, **995–996**
   preferred dividend coverage ratio, **1013**
   price-earnings ratio, **749, 1004**
   quick ratio, **581, 1017**
   return on assets, **1006–1007**
   return on equity, **1007–1008**
   summary, **1019–1021**
   trend percentages, **996–997**
   working capital, **252, 565**
   working capital turnover rate, **1014**
   yield rate on bonds, **747, 795–796, 1012**
Financial reporting, **35**
   defined, **6**
   flow chart of process, **11**

Financial reporting, *(Cont.)*
  multimedia process, **10**
  professional judgment, **628–629**
Financial statements
  accounting periods, **189–190**
  analysis of. *see* Analysis of accounting information
  audit, **319–322**
  balance sheet. *see* Balance sheet
  classified. *see* Classified financial statements
  comparative. *see* Comparative financial statements
  compared with income tax returns, **7**
  consolidated. *see* Consolidated financial statements
  defined, **6–7**
  end product of accounting process, **13**
  future (deferred) income taxes in, **805–806**
  income statement. *see* Income statement
  manufacturing company, **1069–1070**
  not affected by change in price of shares, **723**
  notes to. *see* Notes to financial statements
  partnership, **668**
  preparation, **183–190**
  preparing, **127–130**
  relationships among, **130**
  reliability, **30, 633–634**
  review of, **323**
  statement of retained earnings. *see* Statement of retained earnings
  users, **6**
Financing activities
  cash flow statement, **952–953**
  from comparative balance sheets, **944**
  leverage, **810–811**
Financing activities (in cash flow statement), **940**
Finished goods, **1058, 1061, 1068**
  inventory, **470**
First-in, first-out (FIFO) inventory valuation method. *see* Inventory flow assumptions
Fiscal year, **109**
  year-end, **166, 167–168**
  see also Accounting periods

Fixed assets, defined, **517**
Ford Motor Company, **723**
Forecasts, **302**
Franchises, **538**
Fraud
  auditors' responsibilities for detection, **321–322**
  cash, **380–381**
  employee, **316**
  internal control, **9**
  management, **317–319**
  payroll, **584**
  petty cash, **395**
  prevention, **316**
Free cash flow, **954**
Fringe benefits, **593**
Fully diluted earnings per share, **753**
Future amounts, **836–841**
  of annuity, **839–840**
  discounting, **841–845**
  and interest period, **840–841**
  relationship with present value, **834–835**
  table, **837–838**
Future income taxes. *see* Deferred (future) income taxes
Future prospects, **7**

G

Gains and losses
  on bonds, **796–797**
  capital, **907**
  commitments, **580**
  extraordinary, **746–747**
  from sales of investments, **866**
  owner's equity, **18**
General journal, **67–73, 349–350**
  unique characteristics, **299**
General ledger, **57–67, 230**
Generally accepted accounting principles (GAAP), **7**
  accounting entity, concept, **15, 617–618**
  adequate disclosure, **12, 28–30, 378, 479, 494, 529, 541, 577, 625–626, 713, 760**
  comparability, **12**
  concepts, **12**
  conservatism, **112, 425–426, 479, 529, 628**
  consistency, **479, 530, 625**
  consistency principle, **472**
  cost principle, **12, 15–16, 235, 620**

Generally accepted accounting principles (GAAP), *(Cont.)*
  entity, **12, 15**
  going-concern assumption, **12, 16, 618**
  matching principle, **111, 138, 168, 180, 235, 424–425, 521, 541, 570, 577, 623–625**
  materiality, **180, 431, 482, 483, 565, 626–627, 700**
  nature, **12, 616**
  objectivity principle, **12, 16, 112, 619–620**
  realization (recognition) principle, **110, 168, 180, 235, 620–623**
  relevance, **620, 626**
  reliability, **12, 620**
  sources, **13, 616–617, 628–629**
  stable-dollar assumption, **12, 16–17, 619**
  time-period principle, **109, 618–619**
George Weston Ltd., **746**
Getty, J. Paul, **109**
Going-concern assumption, **12, 16, 618**
Goods, **227**
Goods and Services Tax, **243–244**
Goodwill, **534–537, 878–879**
  fair market value, **535–536**
  partnership, **673**
  recording in accounts, **536–537**
Governmental accounting, **35–36**
Great-West Life, **873**
Gross margin, **229**
Gross pay, **586–587**
Gross price method, **239**
Gross profit, **228, 229, 255, 256**
  method of estimating inventory, **490–491**
  rate, **256**

H

Half-year convention, **525–526**
Historical cost. *see* Cost principle
Horizontal analysis, **998–999**
Hudson's Bay Company, **29, 626, 720, 993, 1007**

I

IBM, **721**
Imasco Ltd., **745, 873**
Impairment of assets, **541**
  contingent losses, **577**

Income
- continuing operations, from, **745**
- deferred recognition for tax purposes, **804–805**
- evaluating business income, **140**
- extraordinary items, before, **747**
- net, **106, 107–108, 257, 258–259, 1010**
- operating, **257**
- taxable, **7, 908, 913–914**
- trend of earnings over time, **140**

Income statement
- alternative titles for, **129**
- and cash flow statement, **945–949**
- classified, **254–255**
- common size, **997–998**
- comparative, **1001**
- consolidated, **882**
- described, **7, 108, 127, 129**
- earnings per share, **751–752**
- extraordinary items, **746–747**
- first illustration, **108**
- illustrated, **128**
- limitations, **127, 129**
- matching principle, **256**
- multiple-step, **254–257**
- partnership, **662**
- periodic inventory system, **287, 288, 289, 290–291**
- predictive information, **743–744**
- single-step, **257–258**
- unusual events, **743**

Income statement approach to accounts receivable, **430–431**

Income Summary account, **131**
- closing, **134–135**

Income tax accounting, as a field of specialization, **5, 919**

Income taxes
- accrual vs. cash basis, **904**
- audit, **904**
- bonds, **791–792**
- cash flow statement, **949**
- chapter coverage, **900–921**
- classes of taxpayer, **903**
- corporation, **25–26, 698, 903**
- deferred (future), **804–806**
- depreciation methods, **528–529**
- enforcement, **903–904**
- evasion, **903**
- expense, **571, 700**
- future (deferred), **804–806, 851**
- history and objectives, **901**

Income taxes, (Cont.)
- importance, **902**
- income tax returns, **5, 7**
- inventory, **478**
- liability for, **903**
- partnership, **663, 919**
- partnerships, **25**
- payroll accounting, **587**
- planning, **902**
- provincial income tax, **901**
- self-assessment, **903**
- sole proprietorship, **25, 919, 920**

Income taxes, corporations, **912–921**
- capital cost allowance, **915–916**
- capital gains and losses, **915**
- computation, **914**
- dividends, **913**
- future (deferred), **916–919**
  - accounting for, **917–919**
  - evaluation, **919**
  - permanent or timing differences, **916–917**
- planning, **919–921**
- tax shelters, **920–921**

Income taxes, individuals, **904–912**
- basic federal tax, **909**
- capital gains, **907**
- capital gains and losses, **907**
- capital losses, **907**
- computation illustrated, **911–912**
- deductions, **907**
- dividends received, **903**
- federal dividend tax credit, **909–910**
- income, **907**
- income from business, **907**
- income from office or employment, **907**
- income from property, **907**
- income tax returns, **910–911**
- instalment payment, **910**
- net income, **908**
- other deductions, **908**
- other income, **907**
- progressive, **905**
- proportional, **905**
- provincial, **909**
- refunds, **911**
- regressive, **905**
- tax credits, **908–909, 909–910**
- tax rate, **905**
- tax rate schedules, **905**
- taxable income, **908**
  - capital gains and losses, **907**
- total income, **906**

Incorporation and materiality, **700**

Independence (auditors'), **319**
Independent contractor, **594**
Indirect costs, **1062**
Indirect labour, **1062**
Indirect materials, **1061**
Individual earnings register, **590, 592**
Industry standard, **999**
Inflation, **16–17, 479, 1000**
- revenue, **256**
Information fields, **304**
Insolvency, **27**
Instalment method, **621–622**
Instalment notes payable, **573–576**
Instalment receivables, **446–447**
Institutes of Chartered Accountants, **34**
Intangible assets, **518, 533–539**
- versus operating expenses, **534**
Integrity, **31–32**
Intercompany eliminations, **876–877**
Intercompany transactions, **875, 882**

Interest
- accrual, **834–835**
  - on bonds but not stocks, **864**
- compound, **836**
Interest coverage ratio, **809, 810, 1012**
- operating income, **581–582**
Interest expense
- accrual of, **177–179, 570–571**
- bonds payable, **787–798**
- capital lease agreements, **799–800**
- coverage ratio, **581–582, 1012**
- instalment notes payable, **573–576**
- payments classified as operating activities, **940**
Interest income, **913**
Interest payable, **570–571**
Interest period and future amounts, **840–841**
Interest rate
- bond prices, **795–796**
- effect on difference between present value and future amount, **834–835**
- effect on future value, **839**
- effect on present values, **850–851**
- effective, **794**
- and market price of preferred stocks, **722**

Interest revenue, **842**
   receipts classified as operating activities, **940**
Interest-free loan, **919**
Interim financial statements, **191**
Internal auditors
   work, **35, 310**
Internal control
   accounts receivable, **432**
   components, **307**
   computer-based systems, **314–315**
   defined, **9, 307**
   fraud, **9**
   guidelines to achieving, **307–314**
   limitations and costs, **315**
   over cash, **380–388**
   payrolls, **584–586**
   prevention of fraud, **315–316**
Internal control procedure, subsidiary ledgers, **233**
International Accounting Standards Committee, **13, 628–629**
Interperiod income tax allocation, **918**
Interprovincial Pipe Line, **873**
Inventoriable costs. *see* Product costs
Inventory, **1056, 1058**
   balance sheet listing, **469, 470**
   chapter coverage, **468–495**
   cost flow assumptions. *see* Inventory flow assumptions
   current asset, as, **469**
   current replacement cost, **483**
   defined, **227, 469**
   effects of errors in inventory valuation, **488–489**
   finished goods, **470, 1058–1060, 1061, 1068**
   flow assumptions. *see* Inventory flow assumptions
   flow of costs in, **470–481, 1058–1059**
   goods in transit, **485**
   income taxes, **478**
   just-in-time inventory systems, **481**
   levels, **494–495**
   lower-of-cost-and-market rule, **483–484, 628**
   management of, **494–495**
   manufacturing concern, **470, 1058–1061, 1068**
   market value, **483**

Inventory, *(Cont.)*
   materiality, **482, 483**
   materials, **470, 1058, 1061**
   net realizable value, **483**
   no subsidiary ledger in periodic system, **246**
   operating cycle, **469**
   periodic inventory systems. *see* Periodic inventory systems
   perpetual inventory systems. *see* Perpetual inventory systems
   physical counts, **237, 244–245, 481–482**
   selecting a system, **248–249**
   shrinkage losses, **237, 244, 245, 481, 482**
   subsidiary ledgers, **230, 234, 236–237, 471–472, 474–476**
   turnover rate, **492–493, 1015**
   valuation, **470–480**
   work in process, **470, 1058, 1059, 1060, 1068**
   write-downs, **482–483**
Inventory flow assumptions
   average-cost (moving average) method, **473–474, 477, 486, 487–488**
   estimating techniques
     gross profit method, **490–491**
     retail method, **491**
   evaluation of methods, **476–479, 480**
   first-in, first-out (FIFO), **474–475, 478, 486–487**
   homogeneity requirement, **476**
   last-in, first-out (LIFO), **475–476, 478–479, 487, 488**
   specific identification, **472, 477, 486, 487**
   summary of methods, **480**
Investee, **867**
Investing activities (in cash flow statement), **939, 950–952**
   from comparative balance sheets, **944**
Investment
   of owner's equity, **18**
   two factors determining profit, **841**
Investments in corporate securities
   chapter coverage, **862–883**
   marketable securities, **722, 863–869**

Investments in corporate securities, *(Cont.)*
   for significant influence, **869–871**
     equity method, **870–871**
   for significant influence or control, **869–883**
   summary of accounting methods, **883**
Investor(s), **5**
   defined, **27**
   users of financial statements, **27–28**
Invoice, **237, 311, 312–313**
Invoice approval form (voucher), **311, 314, 383–387**
Irregularities, **316**
Issue price of stock, **721**

J

Johnson & Johnson, **483**
Journal, record of transactions (illustration), **119**
Journal entries
   compound, **68–69**
   educational devices, as, **78–79**
   illustrated, **68–70**
   posting, **67, 70–73**
   usefulness to management, **79**
Journalizing, **68**
Journals
   cross-reference, **69, 70**
   general, **67–73, 299**
   special, **78, 299, 300, 302**
Judgment. *see* Professional judgment
Junk bonds, **791, 809**
Just-in-time inventory systems, **481, 494**

K

Kmart, **109**

L

Labour costs, **1056**
Land and land improvements, **519**
Last-in, first-out (LIFO) inventory valuation method. *see* Inventory flow assumptions
Leases, **798–800**
   capital, **799–800**
   CICA Handbook, **800**
   operating, **799, 800**

Ledger account(s), **58**
  balance column, **66**
  chart of accounts, **303**
  chart of, **66**
  comparisons with data base, **305**
  credit, **58**
  cross-reference, **69, 70**
  date column, **65**
  debit, **58**
  defined, **58**
  expenses, **112–113**
  explanation column, **65**
  financial statement order, **66, 121**
  illustrated, **58, 59, 119–121**
  manufacturing costs, **1058–1060**
  recording transactions in, **61–65**
  reference column, **65–66**
  responsibility accounting systems, **303**
  revenue, **112–113**
  running balance form, **65–66**
  sequence and numbering, **66**
  T format, **65**
  usefulness to management, **79**
Ledger, general, **57–67, 230**
  subsidiary, **230–234, 236–237**
Legal capital, **709**
Legal entity, corporation as, **25–26**
Leon's Furniture Ltd., **1008**
Lessee, **798, 799**
Lessor, **798, 799**
Leverage, **810–811**
  use of, **1010–1011**
Liabilities
  accrued, **570–572**
  bonds payable. *see* Bonds payable
  chapter coverage, **562–583, 786–852**
  contingent. *see* Contingent losses
  contrasted with equity, **563–564**
  creditor, **17**
  current, **565–572**
    see also Current liabilities
  defined, **17, 563**
  estimated, **564, 576**
  evaluating safety of creditors' claims, **580–583**
  general credit obligations, **564**
  indenture contract, **564**
  interest, **564**
  long-term, **572–576**
    see also Long-term liabilities

Liabilities, *(Cont.)*
  matching principle, **570**
  nature, **563–564**
  payment by sole proprietor, **23**
  postretirement benefits as unfunded liabilities, **802–804**
  priority, **17, 564**
  small corporations and loan "guarantees," **254**
Liability, limited, **26**
LIFO inventory valuation method. *see* Inventory flow assumptions
Limited liability, **26, 697, 698**
Limited partnership, **25, 658**
Lines of credit, **378, 1017**
Liquid assets, **377**
  see also Current assets; Solvency
Liquidity, **698**
  bonds, **788**
Loan guarantees, **254, 809**
Loblaw Companies Ltd., **7, 1007, 1008, 1048–1051**
Long-term investments, **379**
Long-term liabilities
  bonds payable. *see* Bonds payable
  bonds payable, **787–798**
  concept of present value, **794–795**
  future (deferred) income taxes, **804–806, 916–919**
  instalment notes payable, **573–576**
  lease payment obligations. *see* Leases
  maturing obligations intended to be refinanced, **573**
  pensions and other post-retirement benefits, **800–804**
Losses. *see* Gains and losses
Lower-of-cost-and-market (LCM) rule
  conservatism, **628, 867**
  inventory, **483–484**
  marketable equity securities, **867–868**

M

McDonald's Corporation, **10**
Maker of notes receivable, **434**

Management accountant. *see* Certified Management Accountant
Management accounting
  defined, **5**
  general purpose, **5**
  nonfinancial factors, **5**
Management advisory services, **34–35**
Management fraud, **317–319**
Management information systems. *see* Accounting systems
Management's interest in
  accounts receivable, **428, 429, 432, 439**
  budgeted amounts, **302, 383, 395**
  cash, **379–380**
  depreciation estimates, **529**
  financial forecasts, **310**
  financial statements, **30**
  inventory levels, **481, 494–495**
  journals and ledgers, **79**
  revenue and expense data, **138–39**
  subsidiary ledgers, **231, 233, 237**
Managerial accounting
  contrasted with financial accounting, **1054**
  defined, **1053**
  interdisciplinary nature, **1055**
  introduction, **1053–1055**
  overlaps with financial accounting, **1055**
Managerial planning and decision making, **1055**
Managerial responsibility, **302**
Manual accounting systems
  compared with computer-based systems, **75–78, 305**
  general journal in, **67–73**
  general ledger in, **58–67**
  illustrated, **77**
Manufacturing companies, **227, 1055–1070**
Manufacturing costs, **1055**
  accounting for, **1055–1070**
  basic types, **1056**
  direct, **1064**
  flow, **1057**
  indirect, **1064**
  ledger account(s), **1058–1060**

INDEX I-13

Manufacturing overhead, **1056, 1059-1060, 1062–1063**
  application rate, **1064–1067**
Maple Leaf Foods, **720**
Maritime Telegraph and Telephone, **252, 708**
Market price of stock
  following market prices, **723–724**
  no effect on financial statements, **723**
Market prices
  bonds, **788–790, 795–796**
  common stock, **722, 723, 724**
  preferred stock, **722**
  securities, **869**
Market share, **1008**
Market value
  capital stock, **721–724**
  inventory, **483**
Marketable securities, **722, 863–869**
  accounting for, **864**
  balance sheet disclosure, **846, 866–867**
    long-term (cost or equity method), **867**
    portfolio investments, **867**
    short-term (LCM rule), **867–868**
  bonds, **864–865**
  not cash equivalents, **940**
  stocks, **865–866**
Matching principle
  accrual accounting, **138, 168**
  accrued liabilities, **570**
  adjusting entries, **168**
  cost of goods sold, **235, 484**
  credit losses, **427**
  depreciation, **521, 541**
  estimated liabilities, **577**
  expense recognition, **623–624**
  income statement, **256**
  interest expense, and, **570**
  liabilities, **570**
  materiality, **180**
  plant assets, and, **521**
  postretirement benefits, **804**
  product costs, and, **1057–1058**
  rationale for depreciation, **123**
  relationship between revenue and expenses, **111**
  transportation costs, **240**
  uncollectible accounts, and, **424–425**
  year-end cutoff of sales transactions, **484**

Materiality
  accounting for
    capital expenditures and revenue expenditures, **521**
    cutoff of transactions, **485**
    transportation-in, **240**
  amortization
    bond discount, **865**
    bond premium, **865**
  audit, **322**
  combined effect, **181**
  concept, **180, 626–627**
  credit losses, **431**
  cumulative effect, **181**
  GAAP. *see* Generally accepted accounting principles (GAAP)
  incorporation, **700**
  inventory losses, **482, 483**
  matching principle, **180**
  organization costs for corporation, **700**
  recording of financial instruments, **846**
  residual value, **525**
  salvage value, **525**
  simplifies process of adjusting entries, **180–181**
Materials costs, **1056**
Materials inventory, **470, 1058, 1061, 1068**
Maturity date
  of liability, **564**
  note receivable, **435**
Memorandum entry, **865–866**
Merchandising companies
  adjusted trial balance, **288**
  closing entries, **291–292**
  cost of goods sold, **228, 288**
  defined, **227**
  general discussion, **227–245**
  income statement, **228–229, 287, 288, 289, 290–291**
  information needs, **229–230**
  inventory account, **290**
  operating cycles, **227, 228**
  purchase transactions, **237–240**
  retailers and wholesalers, **228**
  sales transactions, **240–244**
  trial balances, **288**
  work sheet, **288–290**
Mergers, **873**
Microsoft Corp., **725**
Minority (non-controlling) interest, **880, 881–882**
Misrepresentation and professional ethics, **634, 635**

Molson Breweries, **873**
Mortgage bonds, **790**
Mutual agency, **657**

N

Natural resources, **518, 539–541**
Negative assurance, **323**
Negligence in audit, **322**
Net assets
  common stock, **718**
  partnership, **659**
Net cash flow from operating activities
  computation
    direct and indirect methods compared, **955–956**
    indirect method, **950, 955–959**
  contrasted with net income, **949, 950, 956**
  "noncash" expenses, adjusting for, **956**
  nonoperating gains and losses, **958–959**
  timing differences, adjusting for, **957–958**
  trends in, **953–954**
  see also Cash flow statement
Net cost, **238**
Net earnings per share, **752**
Net income (and net loss)
  contrasted with cash flow, **949, 950, 956**
  defined, **107**
  evaluation, **258–259**
  income statement. *see* Income statement
  owner's equity, **107**
  partnership, **663–667**
  sole proprietorship, **140**
Net income rate, **1010**
Net present value
  defined, **852**
  see also Present value
Net realizable value of accounts receivable, **425**
Net realizable value of inventory, **483**
Net sales, **240–241, 255**
Net worth. *see* Owner's equity
New Brunswick Telephone, **252**
No-par value capital stock, **708–709**
Nominal accounts, **130**
Non-controlling (minority) interest, **880, 881–882**

Noncash expenses
  adjusting for, **956**
  unfunded postretirement costs, **803**
Nonfinancial information, **8**
Nonoperating gains and losses, **958–959**
Nonoperating items, defined, **257**
Noranda Inc., **873**
Norcen, **817**
Normal return on net identifiable assets, **535**
Northern Telecom, **763**
Not-for-profit institutions, **36**
Notes payable, **177, 566–568, 569**
  defined, **17**
  form of notes
    interest included in face amount, **567**
    interest stated separately, **566**
    two forms compared, **568, 569**
  instalment notes payable, **573–576**
  principal, **566**
  recording "non-interest bearing," **846–848**
Notes receivable, **434–438**
  face amount, **436**
  form of notes
    interest included in face amount, **441–442**
    interest stated separately, **441**
    two forms compared, **443, 444**
  grace period, **435**
  interest, **435**
  maker, **434**
  maturity value, **435**
  payee, **434**
  recording "non-interest bearing," **846–848**
  renewal of, **437–438**
  uncollectible, **437**
Notes to financial statements
  accounting methods, **477, 494, 529**
  commitments, **580**
  contingent losses, **577–579**
  dividends in arrears, **713**
  drafting, **185**
  events occurring after the balance sheet date, **28, 29**
  example, **1003**
  restrictions on retained earnings, **760**

Notes to financial statements, *(Cont.)*
  unused lines of credit, **379, 1017**
  usefulness of, **7, 28, 1018–1021**
Nova Corporation, **873**
NSF cheques, **389–390**

O

Objectivity principle, **8, 12, 16, 112, 619–620**
  losses on marketable securities, **867**
Obsolescence, **523**
Off-balance-sheet financing, **799**
Off-balance-sheet risk, **809**
  disclosure of, **433**
On-line, real-time (OLRT) systems, **300–302**
Ontario Hydro, **796**
Operating activities, from comparative balance sheets, **943–944**
Operating activities (in cash flow statement), **939, 940**
  importance, **941**
Operating cycle, **227, 228, 469, 493, 1016**
  inventory, **469**
Operating expense ratio, **1009–1010**
Operating expenses
  classification, **256–57**
  versus intangible assets, **534**
Operating income, **255, 257, 1009–1010**
  interest coverage ratio, **581–582**
Operational auditing, **310, 323–324**
  effectiveness, **323**
  efficiency, **323**
Organization chart, **308, 309**
Organization costs, **700**
Outside directors, **703**
Outstanding cheques, **389**
Overhead, **1062–1067**
  accounting for, **1064–1067**
  activity-based costing, **1066–1067**
  cost drivers, **1066–1067**
  defined, **1056**
  examples, **1063**
  see also Manufacturing overhead

Overhead application rates, **1064–1065**
  multiple rates, **1066–1067**
Owner's capital account, **130, 131**
  closing to, **134**
Owner's drawing account, **113–114**
Owner's equity
  balance sheet, **27**
  credit balances in accounts, **60**
  defined, **18**
  earnings, **18**
  investment, **18**
  losses, **18**
  net income, **107**
  residual amount, **18**
  withdrawal, **18**
  see also Partners' equity; Shareholders' equity
Ownership equity for forms of business organization, **26–27**

P

Pacioli, Luca, **56, 61**
Par value capital stock, **709–710**
Parent and subsidiary companies, **871–872**
Partners' equity
  balance sheet, **27**
  defined, **26**
  partnership, **662**
Partnership
  accounting, **658–660**
  accounting and legal viewpoints, **25**
  additional investment, **660**
  admission of new partner, **668–672**
  advantages and disadvantages, **657**
  bonus to former partners, **670–671**
  bonus to new partner, **671–672**
  capital account, **676–678**
  chapter coverage, **654–678**
  characteristics, **26, 655–657**
  closing entries, **661–662**
  death of partner, **674**
  definition, **25, 655**
  dissolution, **674–678**
  drawing accounts, **661**
  evaluating financial statements, **668**
  excess investment, **670**
  formation, **656, 658–660**
  general, **658**

Partnership, *(Cont.)*
   goodwill, **673**
   income, **657**
   income statement, **662**
   income taxes, **25, 663**
   interest allowances on
       partners' capital, **665–666**
   liability, **657**
   life insurance, **674**
   limited, **25, 658**
   limited life, **656**
   liquidation, **674–678**
   loans from partners, **661**
   market value, **673**
   net assets, **659**
   net income, **663–667**
   ownership of property, **657**
   partner's equity, **662**
   partnership agreement
       (contract), **658**
   personal liability, **657**
   purchase of interest, **672–674**
   relative income-sharing ratio,
       673
   salary allowance, **664–665**
   sale of business, **675**
   sale of interest, **672**
   unlimited liability, **657**
   unlimited liability of partners,
       25, 657
   withdrawal of partner, **672–674**
Partnership net income
   allocation among partners,
       663–667
   income tax treatment, **663**
Passwords, **315**
   computer-based accounting
       systems, **315**
Patents, **537**
Payee on notes receivable, **434**
Payroll accounting, **584–594**
   Canada Pension Plan, **588–589**
   employment insurance, **587–588**
   fringe benefits, **593**
   income taxes, **587**
   total payroll cost, **593–594**
   union dues, **589**
   voluntary deductions, **589**
Payroll fraud, **584**
Payroll register, **589, 590, 591**
Payroll taxes, **571–572, 592**
Pensions and postretirement
       benefits, **800–804**
Per-unit cost, **1068**
Percentage-of-completion method
       of revenue recognition,
       622–623

Period costs, **1057**
Periodic inventory systems, **338, 341**
   advantages and disadvantages, **249, 284**
   characteristics, **283**
   closing entries, **291–292**
   closing procedures, **246**
   comparison with perpetual
       inventory system,
       247–248, 487–488
   determining cost of goods sold
       and ending inventory, **246, 485–487**
   operation, **245–246, 284–286**
   physical inventory, **245**
   purchase discounts, **285–286**
   purchases, **246, 284–285**
      returns and allowances, **285**
   record-keeping requirements, **292**
   sales transactions, **286–287**
   short-cut method, **246–247**
   transportation-in, **285**
   see also Inventory
Periodic payments, computing, **840**
Perpetual inventory systems
   adjusting entries, **244–245**
   closing entries, **245**
   comparison with periodic
       inventory system,
       247–248, 487–488
   defined, **234**
   inventory subsidiary ledger, **236–237, 471–472**
   manufacturing concern, **1058, 1061**
   merchandising companies, **234–237**
   need for annual physical
       inventory, **237, 244–245, 481–482**
   point-of-sale terminals, **248**
   recording transactions in
       alternative costing methods, **472–473**
      basic, **234–237**
      other purchase transactions, **237–240**
      other sales transactions, **240–244**
   returns of unsatisfactory
       merchandise, **239–240**
   shrinkage, **237, 244, 245**
   special journals, **351–352**
   see also Inventory
Petty cash fund, **381, 394–395**

Physical inventory, **237, 244–245**
Placer Dome, **746**
Planning, managerial, **1055**
Plant assets, **67**
Plant and equipment
   book value, **522**
   capital and revenue
       expenditures, **520–521**
   categories, **518**
   cost, **518–520**
   defined, **517–518**
   disposals, **531–533**
   impairment, **541**
   trade-ins, **532–533**
Point-of-sale terminals, **296**
   cash, **382**
   perpetual inventory system, **248**
   as special journals, **300**
Posting, **70–73**
   cash payments journal, **347–349**
   cash receipts journal, **345, 346**
   computer-based systems, **76**
   cross-reference, **69, 70**
   illustrations, **70–73**
   process described, **70**
   purchases journal, **342–343**
   sales journal, **340–341**
   subsidiary ledgers, **231–233**
Postretirement benefits, **800–804**
   present value, **850**
   unfunded liabilities, **802–804**
Preferred shareholders, analysis
       of accounting information, **1013**
Preferred stock
   call price (redemption value), **720**
   callable (redeemable), **714**
   characteristics, **711–712**
   convertible, **712, 714–715**
   cumulative, **713**
   dividends, **712–713**
   floating rate, **712**
   market price, **722**
   noncumulative, **713, 714**
   par value, **712**
   participating, **715**
   as to assets, **714**
Premium on bonds payable, **790, 795**
   amortization, **750–751**
   concept, **750–751**
   presentation, **750**
Premium on Capital Stock, **709–710**
Prepaid expenses, **172**

Present value
  accounting application, bonds, 848
  annual net cash flow, 843–845
  of annuity, 843–845
  applications
    accounting for leases, 799
    accounting for postretirement benefits, 800–804
    concept, 443, 445
    estimating goodwill, 535–536
    valuation of notes payable, 567, 581
    valuation of receivables, 445, 446
  capital budgeting, 851–852
    notes payable or receivable, 846–848
  capital lease, 848–850
  concept, 794–795, 834
  determining, 841–845
  discount period, 845
  discount rate, 841
  effects on bond prices, 747
  fair value, as, 581
  relationship with future amounts, 834–835
  "tables approach," 837–838
  valuation of financial instruments, 845–851
President, 703
Price-earnings (p/e) ratio, 749, 752, 1004
Principal on notes payable, 566
Principles of accounting. *see* Generally accepted accounting principles
Product code, 304
Product costs, 1056, 1057, 1068
Profession, accounting as a, 34, 631
Professional accountants
  ethical responsibility, 31–32
Professional ethics, 629–636
  codes, 32, 631–632
  concept of a profession, 631
  confidentiality, 634
  disclosure, 634
  discussion of ethical concepts, 629–630
  independence or objectivity, 632–633
  integrity, 633–634
  misrepresentation, 634, 635
  need for, 31–32
  price of ethical behaviour, 635

Professional judgment
  accounting cycle, 78
  accounting for contingent losses, 577–579
  ethical conduct, 636
  evaluating financial information, 258–259
  financial reporting, 628–629
  general discussion, 9, 31–32
  making appropriate disclosure, 28–30
  making estimates, 438, 529–530, 576, 577–579
  selecting accounting methods, 472, 528–529
Profit, gross, 228, 229, 1009
Profit and loss statement. *See* Income statement
Profit-oriented business organizations, 6
Profitability, 7, 27–28
  evaluating, 188
  and solvency, 954
  see also Net income
Promissory note, 434
Provigo Inc., 1007, 1008
Proxy statement, 702
Public accounting. *see* Accounting
Public information, 6
Publicly owned corporations, 6
Purchase on account, 21
Purchase for cash, 20–21
Purchase discounts, 237
Purchase and financing part of cost, 21
Purchase invoice, 313
Purchase of merchandise on account, 341
Purchase orders, 311, 312
Purchase requisition, 311–312
Purchases journal, 341–343, 342–343
Purchases and returns of merchandise. *see* Periodic inventory system; Perpetual inventory system

Q

Quality of
  assets, 1000
  earnings, 999–1000
  receivables, 438–440, 1014–1015
  working capital, 1014
Quebecor Inc., 580

Quick assets, 581
Quick ratio, 581, 582, 1017

R

Raw materials. *see* Manufacturing costs; Materials inventory
Ready-to-sell, 227
Realization (recognition) principle
  adjusting entries, 168, 180
  concept, 110
  instalment method, 621–622
  percentage-of-completion, 622–623
  sales of merchandise, 235
Receiving reports, 311, 313–314
Reconciliation
  bank, 389–394
  cheques, 389–394
  controlling account, 350–351
  subsidiary ledgers, 350–351
Record-keeping procedures, tips on, 80–81
Relevance, 305, 306
  generally accepted accounting principles (GAAP), 620, 626
Reliability, 8, 305
  generally accepted accounting principles (GAAP), 620
Replacement cost of inventory, 483, 484
Report form for the balance sheet, 130
Research and development (R&D) costs, 538–539
Reserves, 760
Residual value, 524
  defined, 524
  materiality, 525
  revision of estimate, 530–531
  useful life, 529–530
Responsibility accounting
  systems, 303, 395
  cash, 381, 395
Restrictive endorsement on cheques, 381
Results of operations, 5
Retail method of inventory valuation, 491
Retained earnings (or deficit)
  balance sheet, 27, 706
  capitalizing (small stock dividends), 757
  defined, 26, 27, 704, 705
  statement. *see* Statement of retained earnings

Index I-17

Return on assets, **810, 1006–1007**
Return on common shareholders' equity, **1007–1008**
Return on equity, **811**
Return on investment (ROI), **1006**
Returns of unsatisfactory merchandise, **239–240**
Revenue, **108**
  closing entries, **131–132**
  commissions, **110**
  commissions earned, **110**
  debit and credit rules, **112**
  defined, **110**
  fees earned, **110**
  income statement, **108**
  inflation, **256**
  interest earned, **110**
  ledger account(s), **112–113**
  realization principle. *see* Realization (recognition) principle
  recognition, **114–118**
  sales, **110**
  unearned, **169**
  unrecorded, **169**
Revenue Canada, **7**
Revenue expenditures, **520–521**
Reviews of financial statements, **323**
Risk, and present value, **843**
Rotation of employees, **310–311**
Royal Bank, **714**
Royal Trustco, **714**

S

St. Jude Medical, Inc., **416**
Sale of an asset, **22**
Sale of merchandise on account, **339**
Sales, change in net sales, **1008**
Sales discounts, **237, 242, 242–243**
Sales invoice, **313, 339**
Sales journal, **339–341**
  posting, **340–341**
Sales price, **108**
Sales returns and allowances, **241–242**
Sales returns as cash, **383**
Sales taxes, **243–244**
Salvage value, **524**
  defined, **524**
  materiality, **525**
Schedule of the Cost of Finished Goods Manufactured, **1068–1069**

Secretary, **703**
Securities and Exchange Commission (SEC), **13**
Segments of a business, reporting discontinuance, **745**
Selling expenses, **1068**
Serially numbered documents, **311**
Share certificate, **701**
Shareholders, **25**
  defined, **697**
  limited liability, **26**
  records for, **717**
  rights, **700–702**
Shareholders' equity, **704–706**
  balance sheet, **27**
  defined, **26**
Shareholders subsidiary ledger, **717**
Shares, **697, 698**
Shell Canada, **746, 763, 919, 1007, 1008, 1017**
Shoppers Drug Mart, **745**
Short-term investments, **377**
Shrinkage
  perpetual inventory systems, **237, 244, 245**
  physical count, **481, 482**
Sinking fund for bonds, **790**
Slide, **80**
Society of Management Accountants, **34**
Sole proprietorship
  characteristics, **26**
  income taxes, **25**
  net income, **140**
  owner's equity in balance sheet, **24, 27**
  owner's liability for debts, **24, 254, 258**
Solvency
  defined, **27, 937**
  evaluating, **28, 188–189, 250–253, 378, 438–440, 580–582, 668**
  and profitability, **954**
  trends in net cash flow, **953**
Sources of financial information, **6–7, 10, 253, 580–582, 993–994**
Special journals
  cash registers as, **299–300**
  manual, **302, 337–352**
  nature, **78, 299**
  other automated types, **302**
  perpetual inventory systems, **351–352**
  point-of-sale terminals, **300**
Specific identification, **472, 477**

Stable-dollar assumption, **12, 16–17, 619**
  Accounting Standards Board, **17**
Standards. *see* Generally accepted accounting principles
Standards of comparison, **998–999**
Stated capital, **709**
Statement of cash flows. *see* Cash flow statement
Statement of earnings. *See* Income statement
Statement of Financial Accounting Standards, **13**
Statement of financial position. *see* Balance sheet
Statement of operations. *See* Income statement
Statement of owner's equity, **7, 129**
Statement of partners' equity, **662**
Statement of retained earnings, **7, 759–760, 1001**
Statement of shareholders' equity, **763–764**
Static analysis, **999**
Stock. *see* Capital stock; Common stock; Preferred stock; Treasury stock
Stock "buyback" programs, **762–763**
Stock certificate, **701**
Stock dividends, **756–758**
  retained earnings, **757**
Stock exchanges, **697**
Stock registrar and transfer agent, **718**
Stock splits, **758–759**
Stock value of bonds, **809**
Stone Container Corp. (U.S.), **873**
Subscriptions to capital stock, **716**
Subsequent events, **28, 29**
Subsidiary companies, **871–872**
Subsidiary ledgers, **303, 349**
  accounts payable, **230**
  accounts receivable, **230, 426–428**
  computer-based, **233–234**
  computer-based systems, **303**
  internal control procedure, **233**
  inventory, **230, 234, 236–237, 471–472, 474–476**
  investments in stocks and bonds, **864**
  need for, **230–231, 237**
  posting, **231–233**
  reconciliation, **233, 350–351**
  shareholders, **717**
  types, **230, 231, 232**
Substance over form, **573**

I-18 INDEX

T

T accounts, 58
  determining balance, 59
Table of future amounts, 837–838
Tables
  amortization table, 847–848
  present value, 842–843
  present value annuity table, 844–845
Tangible plant assets, 518
Tax accounting, 5
  see also Income tax accounting
Tax credits, 908–909
Tax evasion, 903
Tax planning, 5, 902, 919–921
Tax shelters, 920–921
Taxable income, 7, 908
  and accounting income, 914–915
Taxes. see Income taxes; Payroll taxes; Sales taxes
Temporary debit balance, 428
Temporary (owner's equity) accounts, 130, 291
Time period principle, 618–619
Time-value of money, 834–845
  capital budgeting, 851–852
  concept, 834–836
  future amounts, 836–841
  present values, 841–845
  valuation of financial instruments, 845–851
Timeliness, 305, 306
Timing differences, adjusting for, 957–958
Toronto Dominion Bank, 714
Toyota Motor Corp., 481
Trade names, 538
Trade-ins, 532–533
Trademarks, 537–538
Transactions, 67
  effect on accounting equation, 23–24
  effects upon financial statements
    balance sheet, 19–23
    income statement, 121
Transactions approach, 8
Transportation-in, 240

Transposition errors, 80
Treasurer, 703
Treasury stock, 760–762
  contributed capital, 761, 762
  purchases, 761
  reissuance, 761
  restriction of retained earnings, 762
Trend analysis, 582, 953, 998–99, 1008–1010
Trend percentages, 996–997
Trial balance
  adjusted, 126–127
  after-closing, 136–137, 187–188
  defined, 73
  illustration, 121
  unadjusted, 171
  uses and limitations, 74–75
  work sheet, 193
Turnover rates
  accounts receivable, 1014–1015
  defined, 582
  inventory, 1015
  working capital, 1014

U

Uncertainty and contingent losses, 577
Uncollectible accounts receivable, 424–425
Underwriters, 715, 788
Unearned Finance Charges, 446
Unearned interest revenue, 442
  amortization, 442
Unearned revenue, 169, 174–176, 572
  adjusting entries, 169
Unit costs (per unit cost), 1069
Unlimited liability of business owners, 25–26
Unlimited liability of partnership, 657
Unrealized gains and losses (on marketable securities), 868
Unrecorded expenses, 169, 176–179
  adjusting entries, 169

Unrecorded revenue, 169, 179
  adjusting entries, 169
Useful life. see Residual value

V

Vertical analysis, 999
Voucher, 314
  discount, 386
  petty cash, 394–395
Voucher register, 384
Voucher system, 383–387

W

Wages payable, 1062
Walt Disney Company, 109
Window dressing, 30
Withdrawal of owner's equity, 18
Work in process, 1058, 1059, 1060, 1067–1068
  inventory, 470
Work sheet, 191–194
  for cash flow statement, 960–964
  example, 192
  preparation, 193–194
  purposes, 191
  steps in preparation, 193–194
Working capital, 252, 565, 582, 1014
  turnover rate, 1014
Write-off of uncollectible accounts, 426–428
  direct write-off, 431

Y

Year-end
  "busy season," 166, 167–68
  cutoff of transactions, 484
Yield on dividends, 722
Yield rate
  bonds, 747, 795–796, 1012
  stocks, 1004, 1013

Z

Zellers, 109
Zero-coupon bonds, 815

PHOTOGRAPH CREDITS

Volume 1
p. 1: James Balog/Tony Stone Images; p. 2: J.L. Pelaez/First Light; p. 56: Hulton Getty/Liaison Agency; p. 106: Carl Lavigne/Ottawa Senators; p. 166: Steven Weinberg/Tony Stone Images; p. 225: J. Feingersh/First Light; p. 226: J. Héguy/First Light; p. 375: "Coca-Cola" trademark appears courtesy of Coca-Cola Ltd. and the Coca-Cola Company; p. 376: J. Cochrane/First Light; p. 422: C. Gupton/First Light; p. 468: R. Watts/First Light; p. 516: T. Kitchin/First Light; p. 562: Steiner/First Light; p. 614: T. Bonderud/First Light.

Volume 2
p. 653: Hudson's Bay logo courtesy of Hudson's Bay Company, KPMG logo courtesy of KPMG Chartered Accountants, McGraw-Hill Ryerson logo courtesy of McGraw-Hill Ryerson Limited; p. 654: Logos courtesy of Arthur Andersen, Deloitte & Touche, Ernst & Young, KPMG Chartered Accountants, and PricewaterhouseCoopers; p. 696: David Madison/Tony Stone Images; p. 742: Steven Peters/Tony Stone Images; p. 786: D.C. Lowe/First Light; p. 862: Stock Certificate/PhotoDisc, Inc.; p. 936: Chris Windsor/Tony Stone Images; p. 992: Courtesy of the Toronto Stock Exchange; p. 1052: Jon Riley/Tony Stone Images.

(continued from inside front cover)

13-5	(a) (4) Pascal's share, $28,000	16-10	(a) (1) Interest expense recognized Mar. 1, $1,010,000
13-6	(a) (2) Martin's share, $51,500		
13-7	(a) Conrad's share, $102,600	16-11	(c) (1) $29,750,000
13-8	(c) Stein's share, $26,100		
13-9	(c) Bonus to Lee, $70,000	C-1	(d) $87,120
13-10	(c) Bonus to Ritter, $30,000	C-2	(b) $281,478
13-11	(d) Debit to Spence, Capital, $22,500	C-3	(d) $85,665
13-12	(c) Bonus to Kim, $60,000	C-4	(a) $46,889,500
13-13	(a) Cash to Nix, $23,200	C-5	(c) Current liability, $23,197
13-14	(b) Cash payment to Merit, $18,000	C-6	(d) $40,184
		C-7	(a) 10-year lease, $8,032,300
14-1	(b) Retained earnings, Dec. 31, 2000, $1,490,000	C-8	(a) $640,080
14-2	(a) Total shareholders' equity, $3,405,000		
14-3	(a) Total shareholders' equity, $8,360,000	CP-5	(b) Adjusted trial balance totals, $35,295,400; net income, $384,000
14-4	(a) Total shareholders' equity, $2,112,000		
14-5	(a) (2) Total shareholders' equity, (Parker), $6,320,000	17-1	(b) (2) Loss on sale, $6,200
14-6	(d) Total shareholders' equity, $887,600	17-2	(5) Gain on sale, $3,700
14-7	(b) Total shareholders' equity, $843,500	17-3	No key figure
14-8	(b) Total assets, $1,509,200	17-4	(b) Market value, $224,000
14-9	(c) $20.50 average issue price	17-5	(b) Market value, $305,000
14-10	(f) Total contributed capital, $9,660,000	17-6	(b) (3) Carrying value, Dec. 31, 2000, $5,460,000
14-11	(d) Equity of common shareholders, $151,342	17-7	(b) (3) Carrying value, Dec. 31, 2001, $1,710,000
		17-8	No key figure
15-1	(a) Income before extraordinary items, $13,620,000	17-9	(c) Consolidated total assets, $10,670,000
15-2	(a) Cumulative effect, $91,000	17-10	(c) Consolidated total assets, $7,525,000
15-3	(a) Dec. 31, 2001, retained earnings, $606,800	17-11	Consolidated total assets, $7,760,000
15-4	(a) Income before extraordinary items, $2,500,000	17-12	Consolidated total assets, $3,928,000
15-5	(a) Income before extraordinary items, $384,000	17-13	Consolidated total assets, $1,326,000
15-6	Book value per share, Dec. 31, $16.90	18-1	No key figure
15-7	(b) Total shareholders' equity, $8,792,800	18-2	No key figure
15-8	(b) Total shareholders' equity, Dec. 31, $9,318,000	18-3	No key figure
15-9	No key figure	18-4	No key figure
15-10	(b) Total shareholders' equity, $5,914,000	18-5	Taxable income, $25,750
15-11	(a) Income from continuing operations, $326 (in millions); net income, $595 (in millions)	18-6	Taxable income, $75,470
		18-7	Taxable income, $80,820
		18-8	(b) Taxable income, $287,200
16-1	(d) Interest expense recognized May 1, $3,000,000	18-9	(a) Capital cost allowance, $160,000
		18-10	(a) Capital cost allowance, $225,000
16-2	(c) Debit to Bond Interest Expense, $450,000	18-11	(b) Taxable income, $802,000
16-3	No key figure	18-12	(b) Taxable income, $30,000
16-4	No key figure		
16-5	(d) $173,500	19-1	No key figure
16-6	(d) $23,870	19-2	Cash and cash equivalents, $341,000
16-7	(a) (2) Debit to Nonpension Postretirement Benefits Expense, $700,000	19-3	(a) Cash, Dec. 31, 2001, $26,000
		19-4	(a) Net cash used in investing activities, $(45,000)
16-8	(a) Total current liabilities, $234,201	19-5	(a) Net cash used in investing activities, $(22,000)
16-9	(b) Long-term net liability, $58,880,000	19-6	(a) Net cash flow from operating activities, $316,000